About the Author

Satyajit Das is currently the Treasurer of TNT Limited, a position he has held since September 1988.

Prior to this, between 1977 and 1987, he worked in banking with the Commonwealth Bank of Australia, Citicorp Investment Bank and Merrill Lynch Capital Markets specialising in fund raising for Australian and New Zealand borrowers in domestic and international capital markets and corporate risk management involving the use of derivative products, including swaps, futures and options.

In 1987, Mr Das took an extended break from banking to become Visiting Fellow at the Centre for studies in Money Banking and Finance, Macquarie University. During his time at the Centre, he was involved in teaching in the post-graduate Master of Applied Finance program and in consulting to various Australian corporations and international banks.

Mr Das was born in Calcutta, India. He emigrated at the age of 12 with his parents to Sydney, Australia, where he now lives and works.

SWAP FINANCING

Interest Rate and Currency Swaps, LTFX, FRAs, Caps, Floors and Collars: Structures, Pricing, Applications and Markets

Swap Financing

Interest rate and currency swaps
LTFX, FRAs, caps, floors and collars:
structures, pricing, applications and markets

Satyajit Das

B Com, LLB, MBA (NSW)

With Chapters by

Coudert Brothers

and

KPMG Peat Marwick
Sydney London New York

IFR Publishing Ltd

IFR Publishing Ltd, South Quay Plaza II, 183 Marsh Wall, London E14 9FU

British Library
Cataloguing-in-Publication Data

Das, Satyajit

Swap Financing
1. Swap markets
I. Title
332

ISBN 0-946559-62-7

Typeset by Midland Typesetters, Maryborough, Victoria
Printed by Hogbin Poole (Printers) Pty Ltd, Redfern, N.S.W.

For
my parents
Sukumar and Aparna Das
and
my friend
Jade Novakovic

Preface

Origins of the book

The late 1970s and the 1980s have seen significant changes in the way the global capital market operates. During this period, a variety of innovations in financial instruments and techniques have been introduced. It may well be that when the economic history of this period comes to be written swaps will be recognised as *the* major innovation in financial markets of the period.

My own interest in swaps dates from early 1983 when I first became aware of the possibility of transacting US$ interest rate swaps. During the latter half of 1983, I was fortunate enough to be at the periphery of the first two A$ swaps to be undertaken. Over the next few years swaps occupied a central role in my professional life as I became involved in originating, structuring and executing a variety of swaps or swap related transactions.

The concept of the book dates back to early 1987. At that time I took up a position at the Centre for Studies in Money, Banking and Finance at Macquarie University. As part of my teaching duties, I designed and taught a course called "Swap Financing" to post-graduate students in the Master of Applied Finance course offered by the university. The introduction of the course reflected my belief that swap financing was an integral part of corporate finance and students in any course on applied finance should have exposure to this type of financing technique.

In designing the course, I discovered that the literature on swaps which was readily available was not totally satisfactory. This led me to write an extensive set of notes for my students. These notes proved highly successful with not only students but also a number of practitioners who acquired copies of these notes as reference materials or for the purposes of training junior staff. The success of these notes encouraged me to take on the task of converting them into a book.

Objectives and organisation of the book

Swap Financing is unashamedly ambitious in its objectives. The book seeks to bring together all aspects of the *global* swap market within a comprehensive conceptual framework to allow the structure, economics and pricing, applications and institutional aspects of these transactions to be understood.

A number of aspects of the book should be especially noted:

- The book does not confine itself to interest rate and currency swaps but uses the phrase "swaps" generically to describe a variety of interest and currency rate exchange contracts. This means that derivatives of basic swap structures, such as forward rate agreements, long-term forward exchange contracts and caps, floors and collars, are examined as an integral part of the swap market.

- The book is written from a practical point of view. It seeks fundamentally to give the reader a reasonably sophisticated understanding of swap financing techniques and their applications. However, every attempt is made to analyse the structure and practice of the market in terms of basic corporate finance theory to enhance the reader's understanding. This mix of practical and theoretical perspectives is designed to allow the reader to apply the basic swap concept as a problem solving instrument within his or her area of interest.

- The book is global in focus. The integrating nature of swaps dictates that a discussion of swaps denominated in a particular currency is restrictive. Consequently, the book draws on examples from almost every major swap market around the world. While the A$ and US$ are used as the base currencies of some generic examples, the basic concepts being discussed apply to *every* swap market, irrespective of currency.

The book is primarily intended as a practical reference work for finance professionals, including commercial and investment bankers, either directly involved in swap transactions or with more general corporate finance responsibilities entailing advice to clients regarding funding and/or risk management, finance directors, corporate treasurers, and corporate treasury staff, responsible for the financial management of organisations in both the public and private sector.

The book should have relevance to both experienced swap professionals and to less experienced practitioners. For the experienced professional, the book offers:

- a useful reference work listing a wide variety of transactions and structures from different markets, including historical information on several aspects of the swap market (such as spread data) in a number of currencies;
- an analytical perspective on the functioning of various aspects of the swap market which seeks to identify the economic logic and value characteristics of a variety of transactions.

In contrast, the novice will find the book useful in improving his or her knowledge of swaps. The detailed descriptions of structures, economics and pricing, various applications and the accounting, taxation and legal or documentary requirements will allow individuals to improve their knowledge base and their consequential capacity to undertake actual transactions.

This latter aspect of the book, which is reflected in its organisation, should allow the book to provide the basis for practical "in house" training courses such as banking executive development seminars. In addition, the book should find a place in post-graduate programmes, such as MBA courses in financial management, or in advanced undergraduate courses in corporate finance and capital markets, if not as a primary text then as supplementary or recommended reading. I hope that the availability of this book will encourage universities and other institutions to introduce either courses or modules within existing courses dealing with this most important topic.

The overall structure of the book merits some comment. As noted above, the book does not differentiate between swaps in any particular currency or different swap structures seeking rather to develop a number of fundamental principles relating to the whole area prior to analysing the actual products or markets themselves. Consistent with this objective and strategy, the book is structured as follows:

- *Part 1* provides a historical background to the function of swaps and the development of the markets.

- *Part 2* describes the basic structures and key characteristics of the different types of swap instruments such as interest rate and currency swaps, long-term forward exchange contracts, forward rate agreements, and caps, floors and collars.

- *Part 3* analyses the economics and pricing of each of these instruments. As in Part 2, the various inter-relationships between the different types of instruments are explored in considerable detail.

- *Part 4* discusses the evolution of the swap market. This part prepares the reader for the rest of the book as it outlines the key areas of development of the swap market and the factors underlying these developments.

- *Part 5* focuses on the utilisation of swaps, primarily its use as a means for accessing funding on a more cost effective basis as well as utilisation of these instruments to manage asset liability portfolios.

- *Part 6* examines structural variations to the basic instruments themselves. The various innovative swap structures available are considered together with variations such as option swaps and swaps involving assets.

- *Part 7* analyses the various global swap markets, focusing, in particular, on the institutional structure and practice in different market segments, classified by currency.

- *Part 8* focuses on the activity of financial institutions making markets in, or warehousing, swap transactions. The rationale for this type of activity, the risks, as well as portfolio risk management techniques, are analysed in detail.

- *Part 9* deals with the issue of credit exposure in swap transactions including a discussion of recent regulatory pronouncements on the calculation of swap credit exposure.

- *Part 10* focuses on the accounting, taxation and legal and documentary aspects of swap transactions.

- *Part 11* concludes the book with a discussion of the current state of the swap market and its likely future.

Each chapter includes numerous exhibits which provide either diagrammatic expositions of particular structures or statistical and graphical data on various aspects of swap markets. All major mathematical and structural concepts discussed in the text are illustrated by detailed exhibits which predominantly feature actual examples and transaction "walk-throughs". These examples should allow both experienced and inexperienced professionals to follow the structuring and pricing or economics of particular types of transactions. The book also includes an extensive bibliography and a detailed index. These features should contribute to the book's value as a resource volume for professionals active in swaps.

The book was written in the period late 1987 to early 1988 and extensively revised in early 1989. The material covered is, to the best of my knowledge, current as at April 1989.

Acknowledgements

An undertaking such as this cannot be a solo effort. In this regard, I would like to acknowledge the assistance of a wide variety of people who contributed in various ways to this work. I have tried to include all relevant parties but any acknowledgement of assistance can never be complete and I fear this endeavour is no different.

My debt to others in compiling this book is both at a general and specific level. I am grateful to the various colleagues of mine, over many years, who have provided the intellectual basis for this work. In particular, I am grateful to Ron Fryer, Ray Freebody and Neville Cleary, for providing me with the opportunities at the beginning of my banking career to develop my interests in these areas of corporate finance. I am also grateful for the various students and professionals whom I have had the opportunity to teach at various times over the last three to four years. Their continued questioning of my various assumptions and their capacity to provide insights to the subject matter have not been insignificant. I suspect that they taught me more than I taught them!

I am grateful to Macquarie University for making available a position at the Centre which allowed me to develop both my teaching and research interests in this area. I would like to thank my colleague at the Centre, Richard Allan and also my friend David Ferris for their suggestions and various stimulating discussions which assisted me in clarifying my own thoughts on a variety of subjects relevant to the book.

I am particularly very grateful to Doug Jukes, Norman Craig, Malcolm Thompson, Matt Hayes, Mark Donnellan and Nicholas Stojan of Peat Marwick Hungerfords in Sydney and Charles Wolfson of Coudert Brothers who contributed the chapters on accounting, taxation and legal and documentary aspects of swap transactions.

I would like also to thank a number of individuals who made material available without which the book would be a lot less satisfactory. These include the International Swap Dealers Association, Paribas (Robert Elstone, Greg Nottle, Henrik Wallenberg and Louis LeGuyader), Salomon Brothers (especially Steve Roberts, Ross Clark, Bruce LaFranchi and Arjun Krishnamachari), the Australian Industries Development Corporation (Stephen Sloan), the Commonwealth Bank of Australia (Geoff Kelly), Nomura Securities (Blaine Tomlinson and Nick Burge), Union Bank of Switzerland (Lynne New, Adrian Ryser and J. Gasser), State Bank of New South Wales (Phil Gray), Shearson Lehman Hutton (Greg Godsell), Hambros (Graham Jones and Renee Standing), SEK, Security Pacific (Stephanie Warren and Ron Erdos) and Drexel Burnham and Lambert (Joseph Cole). I am also grateful to Citibank (Stephen Partridge-Hicks, John Thom, Steve Anthony, David Croft and Martin Dorf), Bill Jones (Reserve Bank of Australia) and Kenny Koh, a former student, who assisted with the preparation of material for a number of exhibits.

I am particularly grateful to a variety of secretarial assistants who typed the manuscript for this book at various times. They include Ann Hatch, Madelaine Undercliff, Joan Judge, Karrin Van Houstenden and Dianne Johnston. In particular, I would like to thank Alison Thomas for her effort, in co-ordinating and producing the manuscript in a highly efficient manner.

I am grateful to the publishers, The Law Book Company, in particular, Victor Kline who as Managing Editor was extremely helpful in preparing the book for publication. I would also like to thank Ruth Sheard who edited the book magnificently and put up patiently with a demanding, first time author. Grateful thanks are also due to Gillian Armitage (The Law Book Company) and Vicki Proudfoot (who designed the cover).

Last but by no means least, my thanks go to my family and to my friends for their support and encouragement during the writing of the book. In particular, my parents, Sukumar and Aparna Das, who provided enormous support and encouragement. Last, but by no means least, I would like to thank my friend Jade Novokovic, who cheerfully lived with my obsession with the book and endured its often tortuous path to publication. Without their support, the book would never have been finished.

It remains only to say that any errors remain my sole responsibility.

SATYAJIT DAS

1 June 1989
Sydney Australia

Table of Contents

Part 5

Utilising Swaps

Part 6

Non-generic Swap Structures

Part 7

Global Swap Markets

Part 8

Swap Marketmaking and Warehousing

Part 9

Credit Exposure in Swap Transactions

List of Exhibits

Exhibit

Exhibit

Exhibit

Exhibit

Exhibit

Exhibit

Abbreviations

For reasons of clarity, the following abbreviations have been used throughout the text.

Currencies

US$	United States dollars
A$	Australian dollars
NZ$	New Zealand dollars
C$	Canadian dollars
HK$	Hong Kong dollars
£	Pound sterling
Dm	Deutschmarks
Ff	French francs
SFR	Swiss francs
Dfl	Dutch guilders
¥	Japanese yen
ECU	European Currency Unit

Instruments

CD	Certificate of Deposit
CP	Commercial Paper
FRN	Floating Rate Note

Rates

BBR	Bank Bill Rate
LIBID	London Interbank Bid Rate
LIBOR	London Interbank Offered Rate

Miscellaneous

bps	Basis points (1bps = 0.01% pa)
% pa	Percentage per annum
% pa (S/A)	Interest rate expressed as percentage per annum compounding semi-annually
% pa (A)	Interest rate expressed as percentage per annum compounding annually
IRR	Internal Rate of Return
NPV	Net Present Value

Swap terminology

FRA	Forward Rate Agreement
FSA	Forward Spread Agreement
LTFX	Long-Term Foreign Exchange Contract

Organisations

AIDC	Australian Investment Development Corporation
BIS	Bank for International Settlements
ISDA	International Swap Dealers Association
SEK	AB Svensk Exportkredit (Swedish Export Credit Corporation)

Select Bibliography

"Aetna Takes On Swap Insurance" (1986) (May) *Euromoney* 12-13.

Antl, Boris, "Pricing The Hedge To Cut The Cost" (1983) (May) *Euromoney* 230-233.

Antl, Boris, "Quantifying Risk in Swap Transactions" (1984) (December) *Corporate Finance, Euromoney Publications* 19-21.

Antl, Boris (ed.) (1986), *Swap Finance*, London: Euromoney Publications Limited, Volumes 1 and 2.

Antl, Boris (ed.) (1987), *Swap Finance Update Service*, London: Euromoney Publications Limited.

Antl, Boris (ed.) (1983), *Swap Financing Techniques*, London: Euromoney Publications Limited.

Arak, Marcell, Estrella, Arturo, Goodman, Lawrie and Silver, Andrew, "Interest Rate Swaps: An Alternative Explanation" (1988) (No. 2) *Financial Management* 12.

Arnold, Tanya S., "How to Do Interest Rate Swaps" (1984) (September-October) *Harvard Business Review* 96-101.

Asay, Michael and Edelsburg, Charles, "Can a Dynamic Strategy Replicate the Return of an Option" (1986) 6 (No. 1) *Journal of Futures Markets* 63-70.

"Asset Swap—How Denmark Dog Won Its Stars and Stripes" (1987) (December) *Corporate Finance, Euromoney Publications* 57.

"Asset Swap—The New Global Synthesis" (1986) (No. 647, 8 November) *International Financing Review* 3314-3317.

"Australian Swap—The Light Through the Window" (1986) (December) *Corporate Finance, Euromoney Publications* 18-19.

"A Back Door to Fixed-Rate Loan", *Business Week*, 13 December 1982, p. 63.

Bankers Trust Company, "The International Swap Market" (1985) (September) *Euromoney*, Specially Sponsored Supplement.

Bardwell, Tim and Ireland, Louise, "Swaps Checklist" (1988) (May) *Euromoney* 21.

Basle Supervisors Committee, "Proposals for International Convergence of Capital Measurement and Capital Standards".

Bates, "Documenting the Withholding Tax Risk in Swaps" (1988) *Journal of International Banking and Financial Law* 453.

Beenstock, Michael, "The Robustness of the Black-Scholes Option Pricing Model" (1981) 61 (July) *The Investment Analyst* 12-19.

Beidelman, Carl R. (1985), *Financial Swaps: New Strategies in Currency and Coupon Risk Management*, Homewood, Illinois: Dow Jones-Irwin.

Beidleman, C. R., Hilley, J. L. and Greenleaf, J. A., "Alternatives in Hedging Long-Date Contractual Foreign Exchange Exposure" (1983) (Summer) *Sloan Management Review* 45-54.

"Beware of LIBOR in Arrears" (1988) 1 (No. 5) *Risk* 2.

Bicksler, James and Chen, Andrew H., "An Economic Analysis of Interest Rate Swaps" (1986) (3 July) *Journal of Finance* 645-655.

Bierwag, Gerald O. (1987), *Duration Analysis—Managing Interest Rate Risk*, USA: Ballinger Publishing Company.

Bierwag, G. O., Kaufman, George G. and Toers, Alder, "Duration: Its Development and Use in Bond Portfolio Management" (1983) (July-August) *Financial Analysis Journal* 15-34.

"Big Leap in Canadian Dollar Market" (1986) (July) *Corporate Finance, Euromoney Publications* 44-45.

Binks, Tom, "Caps and Collars" (1984) (December) *Corporate Finance, Euromoney Publications* 29.

Black, Fischer, "How to Use the Holes in Black—Scholes" (1989) 1 (No. 4) *The Continental Bank Journal of Applied Corporate Finance* 59.

Black, Fischer and Scholes, Myron, "The Pricing of Options and Corporate Liabilities" (1973) 81 *Journal of Political Economy* 637.

Blake, Victoria, "Swap Deal Closeouts" (1984) (December) *Corporate Finance, Euromoney Publications* 29.

"The Booker Prize to Warburg for Some Fairly Novel Work" (1987) (June) *Corporate Finance, Euromoney Publications* 20-21.

Brodeur, Brian J., "Rate Swaps or Caps" (1985) (May) *Intermarket* 19-23.

Brown, J., Dickson and Linegar, C., "Interest Rate and Currency Swaps in Company Financing" (1983) (January) *Rydge's* 100-102.

Brown, Robert L. (1986), *Some Simple Condition For Determining Swap Feasibility*, Working Paper No. 27, Department of Accounting and Finance, Monash University.

Burkett, Shannon, "Tightening up on Swap Credit Risk" (1989) (March) *Corporate Finance, Euromoney Publications* 35.

"Calls Coming Through Loud and Clear for Kleinwort" (1987) (May) *Corporate Finance, Euromoney Publications* 22-24.

Cohen, Edi, "No Overnight Solutions" (1988) (March) *The Banker* 21-29.

Cooper, Dale F. and Watson, Ian R., "How to Assess Credit Risks in Swaps" (1987) (February) *The Banker* 28-31.

Cooper, Ron, "Still Plenty of Room to Grow" (1988) (October) *Euromoney* 35.

Cooper, Ron, "Swap Houses Switch to New Values" (1987) (January) *Euromoney* 32-33.

Cooper, Ron, "They're Teaching the Old Swap New Tricks" (1989) (April) *Euromoney* 43-52.

Copeland, Thomas E. and Weston, Fred J. (1983), *Financial Theory and Corporate Policy* (2nd ed.), Reading Massachusetts: Addison-Wesley Publishing Company.

"Corporate Speculators' Loophole—or Noose?" (1987) (November) *Corporate Finance, Euromoney Publications* 17-18.

"Council Swaps Grab the Headlines (1989) (April) *Corporate Finance, Euromoney Publications* 14-16.

Cox, John C. and Rubinstein, Mark (1984), *Option Markets*; Englewood Cliffs, New Jersey: Prentice-Hall Inc.

Crable, Matthew, "Clearing House for Swaps" (1986) (September) *Euromoney* 345-351.

Cunningham and Rogers, "The Status of Swap Agreements in Bankruptcy" in *Interest Rate and Currency Swaps 1987* (Practicing Law Institute, Corporate Practice Handbook No. 564. 1987), p. 417.

(1986), *Currency and Interest Rate Swaps*, New York: Merrill Lynch Capital Markets.

(1987), *Currency and Interest Rate Swaps: Accounting, Tax and Control Considerations*, Sydney, Australia: Peat, Marwick, Mitchell & Co.

Das, Satyajit, "The Evolution of Swap Financing as an Instrument of International Finance" (1985-1986) (No. 2) *Bulletin of Money, Banking and Finance* 1-68.

Das, Satyajit, "Granting Options: The Risk Management Process" (1987) 4 *Bulletin of Money, Banking and Finance* 1-77.

Das Satyajit, "Interest Rate Swaps" (1983) (No. 1) *JASSA* 10-13.

Das, Satyajit, "Interest Rate Swaps" (1983-1984) (No. 1) *Bulletin of Money, Banking and Finance* 1-40.

Das, Satyajit, "Options on Debt Instruments for Australian Investment Managers" (1985) (No. 1) *Journal of the Securities Institute of Australia* 3-12.

Das, Satyajit, "Options on Debt Instruments for Australian Corporate Treasurers Parts 1 and 2" (1985) 99 *The Australian Banker* 147-155 and 194-201.

Das, Satyajit, "Option Swaps: Securitising Options Embedded in Securities Issues" (1988) (Summer) *Journal of International Securities Market* 117-138.

Das, Satyajit, "Swap Arbitrages: An Analysis of theEconomic Gains in Interest Rate and Currency Swaps" (1988) 1 *Bulletin of Money Banking and Finance* 1-55.

Das, Satyajit, "Swaps as an Instrument for Asset/Liability Management" (1986) *The Australian Corporate Treasurer* 8-11 and 8-12 October.

Das, Satyajit, "Utilising Swaps as an Instrument for Dynamic Asset-Liability Management" (1987) 101 *The Australian Banker* 63-68 and 108-114.

Das, Satyajit and Ferris, David, "Innovations in Bond Portfolio Management" (1983-1984) 164 *Bulletin of Money, Banking and Finance* 17-74.

"Denmark TOPS Libor . . ." (1987) (March) *Corporate Finance, Euromoney Publications* 16-20.

Dickens, Paul, "Fast Forward with FRAs" (1988) (April) *Corporate Finance* 27.

Discepolo, Alfred J. and Burchett, Shannon B. "The Long Hedge is Here to Stay" (1984) (March) *Euromoney* 195-196.

"Dollar Seekers Forsake Aussie for the Kiwi Route" (1987) (October) *Corporate Finance, Euromoney Publications* 22-25.

"Engineering Swaps" (1986) (April) *Corporate Finance, Euromoney Publications* 25-34.

Euro-Financing and Capital Markets, Conference organised by IIR Pty Ltd, 13 and 14 August 1986, Sheraton-Wentworth Hotel, Sydney.

Evans, Ellen and Parente, Gloria M. (1987), *What Drives Interest Rate Swap Spreads*, New York: Salomon Brothers Inc. Bond Market Research.

(1986), *The Explosive Growth of the Yen/Dollar Swap Market*, London: Nomura International Limited.

Fall, William, "Caps versus Swaps versus Hybrids" (1988) 1 (No. 5) *Risk* 21.

Fall, William, "Taking Off-Balance Sheet Products into Account" (1989) (April) *Institutional Investor* 96-97.

Falloon, William, "The Corporate Problem Solver" (1987) (March) *Intermarket* 23-58.

Falloon, William, "Will New Requirements Strangle Swaps?" (1987) (July) *Intermarket* 10-14.

"The Fast-Moving World of the Asset Swap" (1986) (No. 630, 12 July) *International Financial Review* 2043-2044.

"FDIC Tells Swap Dealers Failed Banks' Swaps Would Likely Be Honored" (1989) 52 *Banking Report (BNA)* 320.

Ferron, Mark and Handjinicolaou, George, "Understanding Swap Credit Risk: The Simulation Approach" (1987) (Winter) *Journal of International Security Markets* 135-148.

Fetzer, Rodney and Janney, Den, "Zero Coupon Bond Swaps" (1984) (December) *Corporate Finance, Euromoney Publications* 24.

Firth, Denys C., "Swaps with Warrants" (1984) (December) *Corporate Finance, Euromoney Publications* 24-25.

Fisher, Lawrence and Weil, Roman L., "Coping with the Risk of Interest Rate Fluctuations: Returns to Bondholders from Naive and Optional Strategies" (1971) 44 *Journal of Business* 418.

Fitzgerald, Desmond M. (1987), *Financial Options*, London: Euromoney Publications Limited.

(1986), *Forward Rate Agreements: Accounting, Tax and Control Considerations*, Sydney: Peat, Marwick, Mitchell and Co., Banking and Financial Services Group Briefing Notes.

(1986), *Forward Spread Agreements*, London: Fulton Prebon Capital Markets.

Gerlardin, Jacques P. and Swenson, David, "The Changing World of Swaps" (1983) (June) *Euromoney* 33-35.

"The Global Swaps Market" (1986) (June) *Corporate Finance, Euromoney Publications*, Supplement.

Gooch, Antony C. and Klein, Linda B., "Damages provisions in Swap Agreements" (1984) (October) *International Financial Law Review* 36.

Gooch, Anthony C. and Klein, Linda B. (1986), *Swap Agreement Documentation*, London: Euromoney Publications Limited.

Grant, Charles, "Why Treasurers are Swapping Swaps" (1985) (April) *Euromoney* 19-30.

Grant, Charles, "Can Caps Beat Swaps" (1985) (July) *Euromoney* 12-14.

Haghani, Victor J. and Stavis, Robert M. (1986), *Interest Rate Caps and Floors: Tools for Asset/Liability Management*, New York: Salomon Brothers Inc., Bond Portfolio Analysis Group.

Hanna, J., Britain, R. and Parente, G. M. (1983), *The Case for Currency-Hedged Bonds*, New York: Salomon Brothers Inc., Bond Market Research.

Hecht, Liz, "Dual Currency Dual Swaps in the Swiss Franc Market" (1985) (April) *Corporate Finance, Euromoney Publications* 13-14.

Henderson, "Swap Credit Risk: A Multi-Perspective Analysis" (1989) 44 *Business Law* 365.

Henderson, John, "How to Create an Interest Rate Cap" (1985) (May) *Euromoney* 63-64.

Henderson, Schuyler K., "Exposure of Swaps and Termination Provisions of Swap Agreements" in Antl, Boris (ed.) (1986), *Swap Finance*, London: Euromoney Publications Limited, Vol. 2, p. 125.

Hilley, J. L., Beidleman, C. R., and Greenleaf, J. A., "Does Covered Interest Arbitrage Dominate in Foreign Exchange Markets?" (1979) (Winter) *The Columbia Journal of World Business* 99-107.

Hilley, J. L., Beidleman, C. R., and Greenleaf, J. A., "Why there is 'No Long' Forward Market in Foreign Exchange" (1981) (January) *Euromoney* 94-103.

Houghton, "Regulatory Provision on Off-Balance Sheet Capital Requirements: Netting Off Agreements—The Legal Perspective (1987) 4 *Journal of International Banking Law* 241.

"How Big Swappers Can Offset Credit Risk" (1988) (No. 2) *Risk* 50-51.

"How to Manage Exposures with Swaptions" (1986) (January) *Corporate Finance, Euromoney Publications* 51-52.

"How to Use the Global Swap Market" (1987) (January) *Corporate Finance, Euromoney Publications*, Supplement.

Humphrey, Gary, "Discount Wars: A New Weapon Is Wheeled In" (1987) (February) *Euromoney* 17-18.

(1986), *Interest Rate Caps*, United Kingdom: Peat Marwick, Banking and Finance Briefing Notes.

Interest Rate Caps, Floors and Collars, Conference organised by Institute for International Research, 19 and 20 June 1986, 10 St James Square, London SW1.

Interest Rate Swaps, London: Credit Suisse First Boston Limited.

International Swap Dealer's Association Inc. (1987), *User's Guide to the Standard Form Agreements*.

"If It Doesn't Sell—Swap It" (1986) (April) *Euromoney* 11-13.

(1985), *Inside the Swap Market*, London: IFR Publishing Limited.

(1986), *Inside the Swap Market* (2nd ed.), London: IFR Publishing Limited.

(1988), *Inside the Swap Market* (3rd ed.), London: IFR Publishing Limited.

Ireland, Louise, "Counting on Your Counterparty (1989) (March) *Corporate Finance, Euromoney Publications* 31-34.

Ireland, Louise, "Dollar Caps Set to Top Swaps Market" (1988) (July) *Corporate Finance* 36.

Ireland, Louise, "Call of the Swaptions Market" (1988) (July) *Corporate Finance* 38.

Jaffe, Violet, "Swap Fever: The Changing Shape of the Debt Markets" (1985) (October) *Institutional Investor*, Special Advertising Section.

Jarratt, John (1987), *Simple Valuation Techniques* and *Advanced Valuation Techniques*, Notes Prepared for Securities Institute of Australia, Diploma Course, Options Markets and Trading.

Jarrow, Robert A. and Rudd, Andrew (1983), *Option Pricing*, Homewood, Illinois: Richard D. Irwin.

Jensen, Michael C. and Ruback, Richard S., "Theory of the Firm: Managerial Behaviour, Agency Costs and Ownership Structure" (1976) 3 (No. 4) *Journal of Financial Economics* 305-360.

Jonas, Stan, "Eurodollar Futures—How Swaps, Futures Markets Work in Parallel" (1987) (No. 661, 21 February) *International Financing Review* 642-643.

Jones, William R. (1987), "Swap Agreements and the Bank of England Federal Reserve Proposal", unpublished research paper, presented to course on Swap Financing, Centre for Studies in Money, Banking and Finance, Macquarie University.

Kalvaria, Leon,"Financial Management with Swaps" (1984) (December) *Corporate Finance, Euromoney Publications* 21-24.

Kalvaria, Leon, "You've Come a Long Way, Baby" (1985) (September) *Intermarket* 17-21.

Kemp, D. S., "Hedging a Long-Term Financing" (1981) (February) *Euromoney* 102-105.

Kerr, William D., "UK/US Proposal On Swap Capital Requirements" (1987) (May) *International Financial Law Review* 19-23.

Kirby, Richard and Davies, Helen, "How Treasurers Can Swap Pitfalls for Potential" (1987) (August) *Corporate Finance, Euromoney Publications* 36-37.

Klaffsky, Thomas E., (1982), *Coupon Stripping: The Theoretical Spot Rate Curve*, New York: Salomon Brothers Inc.

Klein, Linda, "Swap Agreement Terms Enforced" (1989) (April) *International Financial Law Review* 42.

Kleinbard, Duncan and Greenberg, "US Reduces Tax Risk for Swaps" (1987) (February) *International Financial Law Review* 26.

Kolman, Joe, "The Sultans of Swap" (1985) (October) *Institutional Investor* 76-84.

Kopprasch, Robert W. (1983), *Understanding Duration and Volatility*, New York: Salomon Brothers Inc.

Kopprasch, Robert W. and Haghani, Victor J. (1986), *Foreign Exchange Annuity Swap*, New York: Salomon Brothers Inc.

Kopprasch, Robert, Macfarlane, John, Ross, Daniel R. and Showers, Janet (1985), *The Interest Rate Swap Market: Yield Mathematics, Terminology and Conventions*, New York: Salomon Brothers Inc.

Kreca, Michael E., "Pricing Versus Credit: An Art or A Science" (1986) (May) *Intermarket* 38-43.

Kreca, Michael E., "The Currency Swap—Sleeping Giant or Second Fiddle" (1986) (July) *Intermarket* 38-41.

Lecky Jnr, Robert P. (1987), *Synthetic Asset Handbook*, New York: First Boston, Derivative Product Groups.

Lee, Peter, "Why Investors Are Missing Profits" (1989) (April) *Euromoney* 56-57.

Leggett, Desmond, "Interest Rate Swaps—A New Financing Technique" (1983) (June) *The Bankers' Magazine* 101-103.

Lipsky, John and Elhabaski, Sahar (1985), *Swap-Driven Primary Issuance In The International Bond Market*, New York: Salomon Brothers Inc.

"The London Code of Conduct—Part 2: The Swap Market" in Bank of England (1987), *The Regulation of the Wholesale Markets in Sterling, Foreign Exchange and Bullion*, London: Bank of England.

Lynn, Leslie and Hein, Michael, "Interest Rate Caps and Collars" (1985) (December) *Corporate Finance, Euromoney Publications*, Special Sponsored Section.

McGoldrick, Beth, "If you Feel Sure You Know Where LIBOR's Taking You, Lie Back and Float" (1989) (April) *Euromoney* 52.

McGoldrick, Beth, "The Interest Rate Swap Comes of Age" (1983) (August) *Institutional Investor* 83-86, 90.

McGoldrick, Beth, "New Life for Interest Swaps" (1983) (August) *Institutional Investor* 91-94.

McGoldrick, Beth, "Some Tax Driven Swaps Are Legal" (1989) (April) *Euromoney* 49.

McGoldrick, Beth, "Swaptions Have Charms for the Investors Too" (1989) (April) *Euromoney* 49.

McGoldrick, Beth, "The Wild, Wild World of Interest Rate Swaps" (1984) (November) *Institutional Investor* 89-94.

"Man Han Claims US$ 600m in One Year" (1989) (No. 769, 1 April) *International Financing Review* 75.

Marki, Frederick R. V. (1986), *Size and Structure of Worlds Bond Markets: Special Report No. 14—Domestic and International Bond Markets (As of December 1985)*, New York: Merrill Lynch Capital Market, International Fixed Income Research Department.

Massey, Les, "One Borrower's Experience of a Eurobond Issue Case Study of a Straight Issue and Swap", Paper presented at *Globalisation of Capital Markets*, Conference organised by IIR Pty Ltd, 12 and 13 March 1987, Hilton International Hotel, Sydney.

Meisner, James F., and Labuszewski, "Modifying the Black Scholes Option Pricing Model for Alternative Underlying Instruments" (1984) (November-December) *Financial Analysts Journal* 23-30.

Militello Jnr, Frederick C., "Swap Financing—A New Approach to International Transactions" (1984) (October) *Financial Executive* 34-39.

Miller, Gregory, "Making a Market in Slightly Used Swaps" (1984) (November) *Institutional Investor* 99-104.

Miller, Gregory, "When Swaps Unwind" (1986) (November) *Institutional Investor* 127-136.

Morris, John, "The Unsurest Insurance" (1984) (November) *Euromoney* 89-95.

Ollard, Will, "How SEK Borrows at 50 Below" (1985) (May) *Euromoney* 13-23.

Pitman, Joanna, "Swooping On Swaps" (1988) (January) *Euromoney* 68-82.

Pitts, Mark and Goldstone, Rebecca, "Trading Strategies—Playing the Eurodollar Strip/US Treasury Note Spread" (1987) (No. 662, 28 February) *International Financing Review* 746-747.

Platt, Gordon, "Swap: The Building Block" (1987) (October) *Intermarket* 39-41.

"Policing a Permanent Revolution" (1988) 1 (No. 5) *Risk* 14.

Pollard, "Treatment of Swaps in Bankruptcy" (1988) 3 *Butterworths Journal of International Banking and Finance Law* 514.

Price, John, "Modern Currency Exchange Financing Techniques" (1983) (October) *The Chartered Accountant in Australia* 30-34.

Price, John and Henderson, Schuyler K. (1984), *Currency and Interest Rate Swaps*, London: Butterworths.

Price, John and Henderson, Schuyler K. (1987), *Currency and Interest Rate Swaps* (2nd ed.), London: Butterworths.

Price, John A. M., Keller, Jules and Neilson, Max, "The Delicate Art of Swaps" (1983) (April) *Euromoney* 118-125.

Priestley, Sarah, "US and UK Companies Warm to DM Swap Market" (1985) (September) *Corporate Finance, Euromoney Publications* 40.

Pritchard, David, "Swap Financing Techniques: A Citicorp Guide" (1984) (May) *Euromoney*, Special Advertising Section.

Pritchard, David, "Swaps" in Perry, Simon (ed.) (1985), *Euromoney Year Book '85*, London: Euromoney Publications, pp. 187-191.

Rawls, Waite S. and Smithson, Charles, W., "The Evolution of Risk Management Products" (1989) 1 (No. 4) *The Continental Bank Journal of Applied Corporate Finance* 48.

Read, Pat, "Regulators Focus on Swap Dealers" (1987) (April) *Triple A* 75-79.

"Real Flavour of Synthetics" (1986) (July) *Corporate Finance, Euromoney Publications* 44-45.

"Recent Developments in the Swap Market" (1987) (February) *Bank of England Quarterly Bulletin* 66-79.

Recent Trends, Latest Developments, New Techniques and Advanced Strategies in Swaps, Conference organised by IIR Pty Ltd, 1 November 1985, Hotel Intercontinental Sydney.

"Redland's Coup: Coupon Saving in Dollars on a Convertible" (1987) (September) *Corporate Finance, Euromoney Publications* 18-19.

"Reducing Risk Through FXNET" (1986) (July) *International Financial Law Review* 24.

"Regulation: Capital Punishment for Some?" (1987) (April) *Corporate Finance, Euromoney Publications* 27-31.

"Repackaging: Flying in the Face of Misfortune" (1987) (April) *Corporate Finance, Euromoney Publications* 54-66.

Reier, S., "The Boon in Long-Dated Forwards" (1983) (October) *Institutional Investor* 353-354.

Reier, S., "The Rise of Interest Rate Swaps" (1982) (October) *Institutional Investor* 95-96.

Reier, S., "The Enduring Appeal of Currency Swaps" (1981) (April) *Institutional Investor* 261-262.

"The 'Revolving' Currency Swap" (1987) (June) *The Banker* 18.

Ricards, Trevor S., "Interest Rate Swaps Offer Flexible Financing, Lower Interest Costs" (1985) (March) *The Australian Corporate Treasurer* 2-3.

Robb, Richard G., "The Black-Scholes Model and Common Sense" (1985) (July) *Intermarket* 49-51.

Rogers, "Interest Rate Swaps: The Secondary Market" in *Interest Rate and Currency Swaps 1987* (Practising Law Institute, Corporate Law and Practice Handbook No. 564, 1987), p. 25.

Rowley, Ian, "Pricing Options Using the Black-Scholes Model" (1987) (May) *Corporate Finance, Euromoney Publications* 108-112.

Rowley, Ian, "Option Pricing Models: How Good is Black-Scholes?" (1987) (June) *Corporate Finance, Euromoney Publications* 30-34.

Rowley, Ian and Neuhaus, Henrik, "How Caps and Floors Can Influence Desired Cash Flow" (1986) (July) *Corporate Finance, Euromoney Publications* 37-42.

Rubinstein, Mark and Leland, Hayne E., "Replicating Options With Positions in Stock and Cash" (1981) (July-August) *Financial Analysts Journal* 63-72.

Schaefer, Stephen, "Immunisation and Duration: A Review of Theory, Performance and Applications" (1984) 2 (No. 3) *Midland Corporate Finance Journal* 41-58.

"Senate Judiciary Urged to Amend Bankruptcy Code to Honour Swap Contracts" (1989) 52 *Banking Reports (BNA)* 870.

Sender, Henry, "The Boom in Yen-Yen Swaps" (1988) (February) *Institutional Investor* 143.

"Set LIBOR in Arrears for Cheaper Funding" (1988) (April) *Corporate Finance* 27.

Shah, Ayesha, "Asset Swaps: The Repackaging Game" (1988) (Summer) *Journal of International Securities Markets* 83-88.

Sharpe, William F. (1985) *Investments* (3rd ed.), Englewood Cliffs, New Jersey: Prentice-Hall Inc.

Shegog, Andrew, "Who's Top in Swaps?" (1987) (January) *Euromoney* 25-29.

Shirreff, David, "The Dangerous New Protection Racket" (1986) (March) *Euromoney* 26-40.

Shirreff, David, "The Fearsome Growth of Swaps" (1985) (October) *Euromoney* 247.

Shirreff, David, "Turning Down the Gaz de France Swap Credit Exposure" (1987) 1 (No. 1) *Risk* 28-29.

"The Show Goes On . . ." (1987) (December) *Corporate Finance, Euromoney Publications*, Supplement.

Smith Jnr, Clifford, W. and Macdonald, Wakeman L., "The Evolving Market for Swaps" (1986) (Winter) *Midland Corporate Finance Journal* 20-32.

Smith, Clifford W., Smithson, Charles W. and Wilfor, Sykes, D., "Managing Financial Risk" (1989) 1 (No. 4) *The Continental Bank Journal of Applied Corporate Finance* 49.

Smith, Donald J., "The Arithmetic of Financial Engineering" (1989) 1 (No. 4) *The Continental Bank Journal of Applied Corporate Finance* 49.

Smith, Donald J., "Putting the Cap on Options" (1987) (January) *Corporate Finance, Euromoney Publications* 20-22.

Smithson, Charles W., "A LEGO^R Approach to Financial Engineering: An Introduction to Forwards, Futures, Swaps and Options" (1987) (Winter) *Midland Corporate Finance Journal* 16-28.

Sood, Arivinder, "Opportunities in Low Coupon Currency Swaps" (1987) (May) *Intermarket* 10-13.

Sood, Arivinder, "The Long and Short of Interest Rate Swap Spreads" (1988) 1 (No. 5) *Risk* 24.

Spender, Michael, "Interest Rate Swaps—The Great Futures Vs Treasury Yield Pricing Argument" (1986) (No. 638, 6 September) *International Financing Review* 2683-2684.

Spender, Michael, "Interest Rate Swaps—Further Thoughts on the Futures Pricing Model" (1986) (No. 641, 27 September) *International Financing Review* 2922-2923.

Stavis, Robert M. and Haghani, Victor J. (1987), *Puttable Swaps Tools for Managing Callable Assets*, New York: Salomon Brothers Inc.

Stillit, Daniel, "Switching on to Swaps" (1987) (May) *Corporate Finance, Euromoney Publications* 68-75.

Stillit, Daniel, "The Imperceptible Nod Opens Windows for Yen/Yen Market" (1987) (August) *Corporate Finance, Euromoney Publications* 18-21.

Stillit, Daniel and Ireland, Louise, "Equity Warrants: Why Japanese Want That Negative Feeling" (1987) (July) *Corporate Finance, Euromoney Publications* 20-23.

Stoakes, Christopher, "How to Terminate a Swap" (1985) (April) *Euromoney* 18.

Stoakes, Christopher, "Standardising Swaps Documentation" (1985) (March) *International Financial Law Review* 11.

Suhar, V. V. and Lyons, D. D., "Choosing Between a Parallel Loan and a Swap" (1979) (March) *Euromoney* 114-116.

"Survey Shows Losses are Low in Swap Market" (1988) (20 July) *American Banker* 2.

"Swap Credit Risk" (1989) (March) *Corporation Finance* 31.

"Swaps" (1985) (November) *Corporate Finance, Euromoney Publications* 69-86.

"Swaps: The Revolution in Debt Management Techniques" (1984) (December) *Corporate Finance, Euromoney Publications* 15-29.

(1986) Swaps, London: Orion Royal Bank Limited.

Swaps, Conference organised by IIR Pty Ltd, 4 and 5 May 1987, Sheraton-Wentworth Hotel, Sydney.

Swaps and Swap Derivatives, Conference organised by IIR Pty Ltd, 2 and 3 May 1989, Regent Hotel, Sydney.

Swaps, Derivatives and Synthetic Products, Conference organised by IIR Pty Ltd, 28 and 29 April 1988, Hotel Inter-Continental, Sydney.

"The Swaps that Unlock Credit", *Business Week*, 2 August 1982, p. 39.

"Swaps—New Moves" (1987) (July) *Euromoney* and (1987) (July) *Corporate Finance, Euromoney Publications*, Supplement.

Synthetic Securities, London: Citicorp Investment Bank.

Tait, Simon, "It Takes Two to Tango" (1983) (February) *Euromoney* 75-81.

Taylor, "The Magic Kingdom of Swaps: From Space Mountain to Dumbo—A Lawyer's Guide to Interest Rate and Exchange Rate Risk" in *Interest Rate and Currency Swaps 1987* (Practicing Law Institute, Corporate Law and Practice Handbook No. 564, 1987), p. 65.

Taylor, Barry W., "Swaps: A Creditor's Perspective on Rate Risk" (1987) (Autumn) *Journal of International Securities Markets* 33-39.

"Tender Panel Fits into Grand Met Scheme" (1987) (June) *Corporate Finance, Euromoney Publications* 21-22.

Tolhurst, A., Wallace, E. and Zipfinger, F. (1979), *Stamp Duties*, Sydney, Australia: Butterworths.

"Treasury Swap Goes Native" (1987) 1 (No. 1) *Risk* 6-7.

Turnbull, Stuart M., "Swaps: A Zero Sum Game?" (1987) (Spring) *Financial Management* 15-21.

"Two More Innovations in Eurobond Year", *Asian Finance*, 15 September 1982, p. 14.

"Unlocking Bonds from the Balance Sheet" (1988) 1 (No. 2) *Risk* 2-3.

"Unravelling the Asset Swap" (1987) (April) *Corporate Finance, Euromoney Publications* 24-27.

Uren, David, "Swaps Come to the Company Tax Party" (1986) (August) *Triple A* 15-19.

Uren, David, "Westfield Rides a Non-Recourse Winner" (1987) (May) *Triple A* 15-17.

Van Horne, James C. (1984), *Financial Market Rates and Flows* (2nd ed.), Englewood Cliffs, New Jersey: Prentice Hall Inc.

"The Way into Any Market" (1983) (November) *Euromoney* 60-75.

Walmsley, Julian, "Interest Rate Swaps: The Hinge Between Money and Capital Markets" (1985) (April) *The Banker* 37-40.

Walther, Arthur, "Commercial Paper Swaps" (1984) (December) *Corporate Finance, Euromoney Publications* 25-28.

(1987) *Warrants and Options, Euromoney Publications*, London: IFR Publishing Limited.

Yamada, H., "The Euroyen Swap Market—How Most Euroyen Issues Are Swapped" (1986) (No. 649, 22 November) *International Financing Review*, Special Survey by Daiwa Europe Limited, pp. ix-x.

Part 1
Introduction

Chapter 1

The Function of Swap Transactions

INTRODUCTION

The emergence of an increasingly large and liquid international swap market represents an important development in finance. Unlike many other techniques which have emerged as specific responses to particular market conditions, including regulatory and tax factors, the development of swaps represents a fundamental change in the way in which capital markets function. It is this unique aspect of swap transactions which is likely to ensure their survival irrespective of changes in market conditions, and to allow swaps to have a profound impact on the development of financing techniques and financial markets.

The prominence attained by swaps in the world capital markets is evident from several perspectives:

- the size of the swap market;
- the variety of participants utilising swaps;
- the variety of potential uses for swap transactions;
- the variety of swap instruments.

While no official figures exist on the size of the swap market today, the market is estimated to have grown from a negligible volume during 1980-1981 to some US$450 billion of outstanding swaps at the end of 1986. This total is comprised of an estimated aggregate notional principal of US$350 billion in outstanding interest rate swaps and US$80 billion to US$100 billion in currency swaps. *Exhibit 1.1* sets out estimated volumes of interest rate and currency swap activity as at the end of 1987.

The volume of swap transactions reflects their tremendous importance in capital market transactions. In sheer numerical terms, the volume of swap activity overwhelms other innovations in capital markets.

The importance of the swap market is also evidenced by the variety of participants. Participants in the swap market can be categorised in one of two groups: financial institutions and end users of swap transactions.

By the end of 1986, almost every financial institution of any size had made some commitment to the swap market by establishing their own swap group or department committed to the promotion of swap products and the market. Indeed, through 1985-1986 as swaps became popular, staffing requirements increased exponentially, leading to the movement of personnel between institutions in almost epidemic proportions.

The importance of swaps is also evident from the variety of end users of these types of transactions. Swaps are a technique widely used by the world's most prestigious financial institutions, corporations, supranational or official institutions and, indeed, anybody involved in the management of asset and liability portfolios. Swap transactions have now become an

Exhibit 1.1
Volume of Swap Transactions

Year	All swaps	Currency swaps	Interest rate swaps	US$ interest rate swaps	A$ swaps
1981	US$3	n/a	n/a	n/a	—
1982	US$10	n/a	n/a	n/a	—
1983	US$45	US$5	US$40	US$38	A$0.065
1984	US$70	US$10	US$60	US$55	A$2-4
1985	US$100	US$20	US$80	US$70	A$10-12
1986	US$200	US$40	US$160	US$140	A$16-20
1987	US$450	US$150	US$300	US$200	A$35-40

Notes:

1. Volumes are stated in US$ billion equivalent, calculated on notional value of contracts *entered into* except for A$ swaps which are in A$ billion equivalent.
2. The figures are author estimates based on data from various sources including International Swap Dealers' Association (ISDA) data.

accepted and respected technique in the funding strategy and risk management strategy of treasurers worldwide.

The importance of swap transactions is evident in the fact that swaps have become central to the World Bank's (perhaps the most prestigious borrowing institution) funding and liability management programme. Swaps have become an integral part of the funding strategy of the World Bank involving some 15.00-20.00% of the bank's annual medium and long-term borrowings. Swaps have represented the key vehicle through which the World Bank has broadened its funding base and yet has been able to achieve its desired mix of currency at the lowest possible cost (see *Exhibit 1.2*). In addition, the World Bank has utilised swaps to provide the bank with flexibility in acquiring and managing its portfolio of liabilities.

The importance of swaps also derives from their capacity to be utilised in a variety of functions. Swaps have been utilised to undertake at least three general types of functions:

- capital market arbitrage between various markets around the world to significantly lower borrowing costs or increase asset yields for investors;
- to manage the risk, both interest rate and currency, of asset or liability portfolios against sharp and unpredictable shifts in exchange and interest rates;
- to circumvent adverse market conditions or regulations which would otherwise make standard capital market transactions difficult or impossible.

The importance of the swap market is evident from the diversity in the types of swap techniques available. As the market has evolved, it has grown greatly in sophistication and has demonstrated the capacity to innovate and develop new financial instruments, within the basic swap framework and to align itself with evolving capital market opportunities. The development

Exhibit 1.2

World Bank Borrowings and Swaps—1987
(amounts in US$ m equivalent)

	Before swaps				After swaps		
	Amount	%	Maturity (years)	Swaps[a] (amount)	Amount	%	Cost (%)
Medium- and long-term fixed rate borrowings							
US $	2,535.6	27	11.9	−741.9	1,793.7	19	7.40
Deutsche mark	1,392.1	15	8.0	519.2	1,911.3	21	5.87
Swiss francs	1,494.7	16	8.2	791.4	2,286.1	24	5.02
Japanese yen[b]	1,853.9	20	12.3	248.3	2,102.2	23	5.29
Dutch guilders	552.1	6	11.1	76.1	628.2	7	6.41
Others[c]	950.1	10	8.6	−893.1	57.0	0	5.43
Subtotal	8,778.5	94	10.4		8,778.5	94	5.87
Short-term borrowings							
US $, central bank facility	325.6	4	1.0		325.6	4	6.38
US $, discount notes	216.7	2	0.1		216.7	2	6.14
Total	9,320.8	100	9.8		9,320.8	100	5.90

Note: Details may not add to totals because of rounding. Minus amounts after swaps may represent a swap out of the entire amount of a borrowing and/or a change in exchange rates between the date of the borrowing and the date of the swap transaction.
a. Swaps transactions totaled $1,635m.
b. Does not include $1.3 billion of refinancings of prepaid borrowings.
c. Represents borrowings before swaps in C$ ($180.2m), £ ($153.2m), Belgian francs ($165.4m), Austrian schilling ($28.5m), Swedish kronor ($43.1m), European currency units ($161.6m), A$ ($125.0m), Finnish markkaa ($66.1m), and Luxembourg francs ($26.8m).

Source: International Bank for Reconstruction and Development, Annual Report 1987.

of Forward Rate Agreements (FRAs) as well as markets in long-dated options (caps, ceilings, collars, floors etc.) is evidence of this growth in the types of swap techniques available.

These various dimensions of the swap market highlight the central role that this instrument has come to play in the development of capital markets. It is fair to say that swaps, more than any other instrument, represent *the* key development in the evolution of global capital markets.

HISTORY OF THE DEVELOPMENT OF THE SWAP MARKET

The history of the development of swap transactions is a much debated and disputed one. However, there appears to be agreement that the concept of swaps originated from the £ and US$ parallel loans arranged between British and American entities in the 1970s. It is important to note, however, that a type of currency swap transaction (involving foreign currencies and occasionally gold) has a long history. These transactions were usually undertaken between a number of key central banks and the Bank for International Settlements (BIS).

The central bank swap arrangements involved foreign currencies and, initially, monetary gold. They were and are similar to short-dated foreign exchange swaps combining a spot sale (purchase) of a currency with a simultaneous agreement to buy (sell) the currency at some time in the future. This swap network is designed to create additional international reserves through a cross-crediting system to facilitate central bank stabilisation of the international monetary system.

The genesis of modern swap structures is evident in the structure of these arrangements which sought to overcome structural regulatory barriers and which were predicated on the basis of risk free, mutually beneficial but offsetting transactions as between the parties involved.

However, it was in the 1970s with the introduction of exchange controls in the United Kingdom that parallel and back-to-back loans were arranged ultimately evolving into the first currency swap in 1976. In that transaction, Continental Illinois Ltd (now First Interstate Limited) and Goldman Sachs arranged a transaction between a Dutch (Bos Kalis Westminister) and British (ICI Finance) company involving the Dutch Guilder and £.

This transaction was followed by a transaction completed on behalf of Consolidated Goldfields in April 1977 and a transaction involving the government of Venezuala in connection with the construction of the Caracas Metro System involving a substantial US$ and French franc currency swap undertaken at about the same time.

The first currency swap transacted against a capital market issue was undertaken in 1979 by Roylease, the leasing subsidiary of the Royal Bank of Canada, involving a Deutschmark issue swapped into C$. In this transaction, Roylease undertook a five year Deutschmark 60m issue with a coupon of 6.75% pa which was swapped into fixed C$ at a coupon cost under the borrower's target cost of 11.00% pa. The transaction was apparently structured as a series of foreign exchange contracts which were used to hedge all the Deutschmark principal and interest payments first into US$ and then into the required C$.

However, it was not until August 1981 that currency swaps became an established feature of international capital markets when the World Bank swapped a US$290m bond issue into an equivalent amount of Deutschmarks and Swiss francs provided by IBM under an arrangement devised by Salomon Brothers. A brief summary of this historic transaction is set out in *Exhibit 1.3*.

The first interest rate swaps were also undertaken in 1981, initially by Citibank and Continental Illinois. The first interest rate swaps included a number of private transactions culminating in 1982 with a much publicised US$300m seven year bond issue by Deutsche Bank which was swapped into US$ LIBOR.

From that landmark transaction onwards, the interest rate swap market was to expand at a much more sustained pace than its foreign exchange counterpart, the currency swap market.

While initial developments were in the US$ market, the potential of swaps was quickly recognised and markets in other currencies developed rapidly.

Exhibit 1.3

1981 World Bank—IBM Swap

Some years ago IBM needed to raise substantial funds and as the amount required was greater than could be raised in any one capital market, IBM launched a worldwide borrowing programme which included raising large amounts in the Deutschmark and Swiss franc capital markets. The proceeds of these loans were sold for US$ and remitted back to head office where they were used for general corporate funding purposes. Coincidentally, the World Bank had (and still has) a declared policy of raising funds in currencies with low interest rates, such as the Deutschmark and the Japanese yen. It is faced with a problem in that its demand for fixed rate funds in these currencies is greater than the capacity of the respective capital markets to support. The third ingredient to this transaction was that the US$ had appreciated substantially against the Swiss franc and the Deutschmark from the time IBM borrowed these currencies to the time it entered into the swap transaction with the World Bank creating a significant unrealised foreign exchange gain.

IBM was approached to see if it would be interested in locking in the capital gain on its Swiss franc and Deutschmark borrowings, and effectively converting these liabilities into simulated US$ liabilities. At the same time, the World Bank was asked whether it would like to complement its Swiss franc and Deutschmark borrowing programme by raising US$s and converting the borrowing into Swiss francs and Deutschmarks via a cross-currency fixed-to-fixed debt swap with IBM. The result was that the World Bank issued a two-tranche US$ fixed rate Eurobond with maturities exactly matching IBM's Swiss franc and Deutschmark debt, and at the same time entered into a swap with IBM. Under the swap agreement, IBM agreed to pay all the future interest and principal payments on the World Bank's US$ Eurobonds in return for the World Bank agreeing to pay all future interest and principal payments on IBM's Swiss franc and Deutschmark debt. The transaction is depicted diagramatically below.

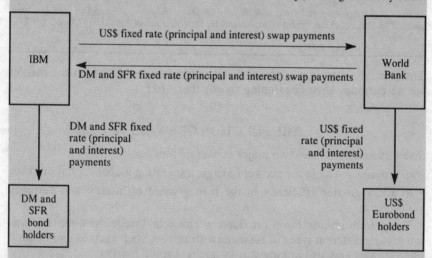

The detailed methodology can be illustrated utilising one of the key elements of the transaction—a 4.60 year (average life) US$210m issue by the World Bank to fund the swaps against the Swiss franc and Deutschmark cash flows provided by IBM.

The calculation procedure was:

• to discount the Swiss franc and Deutschmark cash flows at a negotiated interest rate;
• to convert the resulting present values into US$ at prevailing exchange rates;
• to construct matching US$ flows on the basis of prevailing dollar interest rates.

These three variables—the all-in cost in Swiss francs (or Deutschmarks), the spot exchange rate, and the all-in dollar cost accepted by the bank's counterparty—were the key points of negotiation in the swap transaction.

Exhibit 1.3—continued

Following is the schedule of flows being exchanged through the swap.

Exchange date	SFR amount	DM amount	US$ amount
30.3.82	12,375,000	30,000,000	20,066,667[1]
30.3.83	12,375,000	30,000,000	33,600,000
30.3.84	12,375,000	30,000,000	33,600,000
30.3.85	12,375,000	30,000,000	33,600,000
30.3.86	212,375,000	330,000,000	243,600,000
Compounding rate	8.00%	11.00%	16.80%[2]
Compounded value	191,367,478	301,315,273	205,485,000
Exchange rate	US$1.00: SFR2.18	US$1.00: DM2.56	US$1.00
Compounded value in US$	87,783,247	117,703,153	205,485,000

The compounded value of the US$ cash flows was then utilised to work back to the structure of the underlying World Bank issue. The coupon (16.00%) and the total discount from par to the bank on the issue (that is, the price of the issue less commissions and expenses) were given by the market. The percent proceeds (that is 97.85%) could then be used to gross up the absolute dollar proceeds in order to obtain the par amount of notes to be issued, as follows:

$$\frac{US\$205,485,000}{0.9785} = US\$210,000,000$$

Notes:
1. The first dollar amount is reduced to take account of the partial first period on the dollar bond issue.
2. The yield to maturity on a 16.00% bond, due on 30 March 1988 and purchased on 25 August is 16.61%.

Source: This discussion is based substantially on David R. Bock, "Fixed-to-Fixed Currency Swap: The Origins of the World Bank Borrowing Programme" in Antl (1985) Vol. 2 pp. 218–223.

The first A$ interest rate swaps were undertaken in 1983 with the market for A$ currency swaps beginning shortly thereafter.

THE FUNCTION OF SWAPS

Swap transactions have two major economic functions:
- to provide a vehicle for market linkage, integrating global capital markets;
- to allow greater efficiency in the management of interest and currency exposures.

Swap transactions have provided a classical bridge between markets integrating different types of financial instruments, such as fixed and floating interest rates and also linking various global capital markets.

This market linkage derives largely from the fact that swaps allow the extension of the theory of comparative advantage from the commodity and service markets to the world's capital markets. The theory of comparative advantage in trade states that each party should specialise in the production of those goods for which it has a relative comparative advantage. Having done so, the parties can exchange those goods through trade (if they desire) for a mix of commodities and hence increase their welfare beyond that which would have been possible had they attempted to provide for all their commodity needs directly.

Swap transactions fundamentally enable institutions to accomplish similar objectives in international capital markets allowing each institution to either borrow or invest where it has a relative comparative advantage and then obtain the desired interest rate or currency basis of the borrowing or investment through an accompanying interest rate or currency swap.

Swaps also enable institutions to take a much more flexible approach towards the management of assets and liabilities. Swaps enable institutions to manage these portfolios in the light of changed expectations as to interest rates and currencies in a flexible way, adjusting their portfolios to avoid potential losses or to lock in gains. In this regard, swaps are superior to alternative techniques for achieving similar objectives such as the early retirement of borrowings or the liquidation of asset portfolios.

The greater efficiency in managing asset liability portfolios possible through swap transactions derives from the unique characteristics of swaps which allow a fundamental unbundling of various aspects of borrowing or investment transactions. This unbundling element in swap transactions operates on two levels: first, swaps are separate from the underlying funding or investment transaction; and second, the swap transaction being separate is also independent from a timing perspective.

This separability of the swap transaction means that borrowers and investors can obtain liquidity or invest funds in a manner quite separate from the management of the interest rate and currency rate basis. A borrowing or investment transaction can be combined with an interest rate or currency swap to effectively generate the form of funding or investment desired by the borrower or investor.

The fact that the swap transaction is separate from the underlying funding or investment transaction in a timing sense allows existing liabilities or assets to be managed in the light of new information as to the future course of interest rates and currency values. By utilising a swap transaction, entered into sometime after the original funding or investment decision, the borrower or investor can transform the interest rate or currency basis of that liability or asset to better fit current expectations and performance objectives.

The development of currency swaps has led to the extension of the long-dated foreign exchange markets. Traditionally, foreign exchange markets have been limited to maturities of one and, at most, two years. However, the emergence and growth of swaps have added significant liquidity to the long-dated foreign exchange market whereby markets are routinely made in a wide variety of currencies for maturities of up to five years and in some cases for maturities of up to ten years. This growth in liquidity of the long-dated foreign exchange market allows greater flexibility in the management of future cash flows resulting from various contractual obligations enabling participants to hedge the currency risk of these future cash flows where they are denominated in a currency other than that of the borrower or investor.

THE IMPACT OF SWAPS ON PRIMARY DEBT MARKETS

The development of highly liquid markets in interest rate and currency swaps has had a fundamental impact on the operation of primary debt markets throughout the world. Increasingly, these primary debt markets have come to be *swap-driven*. A swap-driven transaction can be defined as a primary issue in a debt market, in the standard form of that market, where the borrower will have acquired an exposure in a currency or interest rate basis other than that of the issue through an interest rate or currency swap transaction undertaken in conjunction with the issuance of debt.

It is increasingly apparent that the bulk of primary issuance in debt markets is now swap-driven. Examples of typical swap-driven capital market transactions are set out in *Exhibit 1.4*.

The impact of swaps on primary debt markets is considered in detail in the context of new issue arbitrage in Chapter 13.

THE FUTURE OF SWAPS

The inherent nature of swap transactions which facilitate a more efficient global intermediation process and serve to foster more rapid growth in international trade and financial flows is likely to ensure their permanent place in global capital markets.

However, the future direction of the swap market may be significantly different from the current structure of the market in these types of transactions. The key factors impacting upon the future development of these markets will include:

- the evolution of more complex swap structures reflecting diverse user requirements;
- the development of increasingly liquid markets in interest rate and currency swaps;
- increasingly standardised documentation which facilitates liquidity;
- the potential development of a clearing system for swaps between acknowledged market makers in these transactions;
- the use of credit enhancement techniques to allow participants of lower credit quality to enter into swap transactions;
- the development of the swap market under a more active regulatory environment where the credit risk entailed in swap transactions will be incorporated in formal risk/asset ratios forcing greater attention to be directed towards the management of credit exposures entailed in swap transactions.

Exhibit 1.4
Swap-Driven Capital Market Issues

EXAMPLE OF EUROYEN BOND ISSUE SWAPPED INTO US$ LIBOR UTILISING CURRENCY SWAP

Swedish Export Credit (SEK)

Amount	¥20 billion
Maturity	five years (due 4 June, 1992)
Coupon	4.5%
Issue price	102
Yield	4.05% (gross); 4.33% (less selling concession)
Amortisation	bullet
Call option	none
Listing	Luxembourg
Denominations	¥1M
Commissions	1.875% (management and underwriting 5.8%, less 0.125% praecipuum; selling 1.25%)
Expenses	¥8M
Stabilisation	IPMA recommendations
Payment	4 June
Swap	*into sub-LIBOR floating rate dollars*
Governing law	English
Negative pledge	Yes
Cross default	Yes
Pari passu	Yes
Lead managers	Mitsubishi Finance Int. (books), CSFB, Nikko Securities (Europe), Nomura Int.
Co-managers	Bankers Trust Int., Bank of Tokyo Int., BBL, BNP, Banque Paribas Capital Markets, Citicorp Investment Bank, County Natwest, CCF, Credit Lyonnais, Daiwa Europe, Goldman Sachs, IBJ Int., LTCB Int., Merrill Lynch Capital Markets, Mitsui Trust Int., Morgan Guaranty, Morgan Stanley Int., Pru-Bache Securities, Salomon Brothers Int., Security Pacific Hoare Govett, Shearson Lehman Brothers Int., Societe Generale, Svenska Handelsbanken, Swedbank, SBCI, Toyo Securities (Europe), Yamaichi Int. (Europe).
Pre-market price	Less 1.875, less 1.625

Mitsubishi Finance Int. won this swap-driven mandate on a competitive bid. Market response was healthy and the lead manager reported strong global distribution. There were no complaints over the pricing and Mitsubishi Finance Int. claimed to have bought back only a small amount of the issue through the brokers. The grey market level was held within fees throughout the week, at one point ticking up to less 1.375 bid.

Scandinavian specialists in the market remarked that SEK normally hopes to achieve a level of at least LIBOR less 60bps on the swap and to achieve this figure a massaging of around 50bps on the swap would have had to be provided by Mitsubishi Finance Int. This would result in an opportunity loss of approximately $700,000.

Source (1987) (No. 673, May 16) *International Financing Review* 1640.

EXAMPLE OF US$ EUROBOND ISSUE SWAPPED INTO US$ COMMERCIAL PAPER UTILISING INTEREST RATE AND BASIS SWAPS

Toyota Motor Credit Corporation

Amount	$150m
Maturity	three years (due 17 September, 1990)
Coupon	8.625%
Issue price	101.3125
Yield	8.12% (gross); 8.45% (less selling concession)

Exhibit 1.4—continued

Amortisation	bullet
Call option	none
Listing	Luxembourg
Denominations	$5,000
Commissions	1.375% (management and underwriting 0.50%, less 0.10% praecipuum; selling 0.875%)
Expenses	$75,000
Stabilisation	IPMA recommendations
Payment	3 September, there is a long first coupon
Swap	*into sub-commercial paper rate floating US$*
Governing law	New York
Negative pledge	yes
Cross default	yes
Pari passu	yes
Lead managers	Morgan Stanley Int. (books), Sanwa Int., Bank of America Int., Nomura Int., Nikko Securities (Europe)
Co-managers	Bank of Tokyo Int., BNP Capital Markets, Chase Investment Bank, County Natwest, Credit Lyonnais, CSFB, Dresdner Bank, LTCB Int., Mitsui Finance Int., Morgan Guaranty, Salomon Brothers Int., Shearson Lehman Brothers Int., Tokai Int., UBS Securities.
Pre-market price	99.95, 100.05

Morgan Stanley, with the help of Sanwa Bank and Bank of America, emerged as the lead manager for this prestige deal following a protracted bidding contest. Recent Toyota deals have been dominated by Nomura Int. and Merrill Lynch, barring the previous issue from Nikko Securities (Europe).

The launch was delayed for a few days as Stanley waited for the right market conditions. In the event, 50 over treasuries was considered correct pricing for what is a solid name in the market. Even so, with the sector in its present stodgy state, underwriters were finding it hard going to make money on the deal. "It's all right if you're a co-lead, but there's very little in it for the co-managers," said a senior official at one house.

Morgan Stanley placed large amounts of bonds in the Far East and in Switzerland at levels around par, having made initial soundings in the Far East before launch. This left Stanley with a small technical short which was easily covered in the market. "We only bought back 15.00% or so of the issue through the brokers," said syndicate officials, adding that in total they had placed over twice their underwriting commitment with little difficulty.

The bonds traded in a narrow range throughout the week keeping fairly much in line with their launch spread. The outstanding three year bonds from Nikko Securities (Europe), launched in July, were reportedly trading at around 45 off.

Sanwa Bank and Bank of America provided the swap, which was said to be at super aggressive off-market levels, reportedly around 35bps under commercial paper. It is thought that BAIL arranged the swap into LIBOR based floating rate dollars, while Sanwa effected the LIBOR/CP swap. This level is, however, nowhere near what was reported for the last Toyota straight, said at the time to be an astonishing 70 through CP.

"All credit to Morgan Stanley. The main problem about getting the mandate for this deal was finding the Japanese bank to provide the swap," said one competing syndicate manager, citing the obvious strong domestic relationships as the reason why the US offshoot of Toyota attained such attractive funding.

Source: (1987) (No. 685, August 8) *International Financing Review* 2607, 2608.

EXAMPLE OF A$ EUROBOND AND DEUTSCHMARK ISSUE DIRECTLY SWAPPED

Bayerische Vereinsbank overseas

Security	a deposit with Bayerische Vereinsbank
Amount	A$80m
Maturity	nine years (due 1 June 1996)
Coupon	13.50%, payable annually on 1 June
Issue price	101.50
Yield	13.21% (gross)

Exhibit 1.4—continued

Amortisation	bullet
Call option	none
Listing	Luxembourg
Denominations	A$1,000, A$10,000
Commissions	2.125% (management, and underwriting 0.625%, praecipuum 0.125%; selling 1.50%)
Expenses	A$75,000
Payment	2 June
Swap	*yes*
Governing law	Federal Republic of Germany
Lead managers	Bayerische Vereinsbank (books), Hambros
Co-managers	ANZ Merchant Bank, ABC-Daus, Banque Paribas (Deutscheland), Bayerische Hypo, Bayerische Landesbank, Berliner Bank, County Natwest Capital Markets, CSFB, DKB Int., EBC AMRO, Fay Richwhite, IGJ (Germany), Landesbank Rheinland PFALZ, Landesbank Schleswig Holstein, Merck Fink, Merrill Lynch Capital Markets, Morgan Guaranty Ltd, Morgan Stanley Int., Norddeutsche Landesbank, Orion Royal Bank, Rabobank, Sanwa Int., Vereins-Und Westbank, Westlb, Westpac, Wood Gundy.
Pre-market price	Less 2.25, less 1.75

Some co-managers met with an initial unenthusiastic response as investors began to adapt themselves more permanently to the new lower coupon.

However, as said one German banker: "once the Bayerische machine moves, the deal will have power." The relatively rare nine year maturity will also help.

The Bayerische issue was said to have been directly swapped with the DM 100m 6.00% 1996 issue for Western Australian Treasury Corp. also issued last week. (See this week's DM session for details.)

Western Australian Treasury Corp

Guarantor	the Treasurer on behalf of the State of Western Australia
Amount	DM100m of unsecured and unsubordinated
Debt maturity	9 years (due 1 June 1996)
Coupon	6.00%, payable annually on 1 June
Issue price	100
Yield	6.22% (less selling concession)
Amortisation	bullet
Call option	none—except for tax reasons
Listing	Munich and Frankfurt
Denominations	DM1,000 and DM10,000
Commissions	2.50% (management and underwriting 1%, praecipuum 0.125%; selling 1.50%). In addition, there is a listing fee of 0.50%
Expenses	DM75,000
Stabilisation	IPMA
Payment	2 June
Swap	*yes*
Governing law	Federal Republic of Germany
Negative pledge	yes
Cross default	yes
Security number	480 900
Lead manager	Bayerische Vereinsbank (books)
Co-managers	Banque Paribas (Deutschland), Commerzbank, Deutsche Bank, Hambros, Schweizerische Bankgesellschaft (Deutschland), Schweizerischer Bankverein (Deutschland), Generale Bank, IBJ (Germany), Merrill Lynch Capital Markets, Morgan Stanley International, Pru-Bache, Societe Generale Elsaessische Bank, Trinkaus und Burkhardt, Vereins-und Westbank.
Pre-market price	Less 2.25, less 1.875

This relatively small transaction has been slow moving. But, even if it takes some time to disappear entirely into portfolios, there is no doubt about its placement. It is the borrower's first Euro transaction.

Exhibit 1.4—continued

The issue has been swapped for the A$ bond launched by Bayerische Vereinsbank overseas detailed elsewhere in this week's International Financial Review.

Source: (1987) (No. 671, May 2) *International Financing Review* 1459, 1468.

Note: All emphasis is that of the author.

Part 2

Swap Instruments

Chapter 2

Swap Transactions: Basic Structures and Key Characteristics

SWAP TRANSACTIONS: A CLASSIFICATION

The term swap is utilised to describe a variety of transactions. It can be used to refer to a specific type of transaction, such as an interest rate or currency swap. However, it can also be used generically to cover a range of specialised negotiated capital market transactions where two or more entities exchange or swap cash flows in the same or in two or several different currencies and/or interest rate bases for a pre-determined length of time.

It is useful to categorise swap transactions into four general categories:

- parallel or back-to-back loans
- swap transactions (which covers interest rate swaps, currency swaps and long-dated or long-term forward foreign exchange contracts (LTFX))
- FRAs;
- caps, collars and floors.

SWAPS: BASIC STRUCTURES, KEY CHARACTERISTICS, INTER-RELATIONSHIPS ETC.

Parallel or back-to-back loans (from which other types of swaps developed) represent a specialised technique which originally developed to avoid the investment premium on investments outside the United Kingdom imposed by foreign exchange regulations. The basic concept of a back-to-back loan has been adapted into a currency swap making the original structures largely redundant. However, while parallel and back-to-back loans are no longer commonly utilised, they remain a useful technique for mobilising otherwise potentially sterile cash balances in blocked funds situations.

Swap transactions, which evolved structurally from parallel and back-to-back loans, are the major type of swap financing transactions. They usually encompass three specific types of transactions: interest rate swaps, currency swaps and LTFX.

It is usual to classify LTFX transactions with swaps as they are functionally identical to a zero coupon currency swap. In essence, LTFX transactions can be used to replicate a fixed-to-fixed currency swap. LTFX transactions also represent an extension of the market in forward foreign exchange which operates in and between short-term money and foreign exchange markets across currencies.

The FRA market functions at a number of levels:

- a forward-forward deposit or borrowing market at rates nominated today;

17

- a short-term interest rate swap market, particularly in the two years and under maturity segment;
- an interest rate swap, dismembered into shorter time periods commencing some time in the future.

While the FRA market is largely a market in forward interest rates, in which respect it functions in a manner similar to a negotiated futures market in interest rates, it is closely linked with interest rate swap markets in the relevant currency.

This relationship arises from two separate sources. First, an interest rate swap and an FRA can be similar in that a series of FRAs locking in or fixing rates on future interest rate reset dates or "rolls"on a floating rate borrowing can be used as a substitute for a floating-to-fixed interest rate swap as both transactions effectively provide the party entering into the transaction with a known fixed cost of funding. Similarly, a reverse of this transaction can be utilised to generate a fixed-to-floating swap allowing a borrower to switch to a floating rate of interest on its borrowings.

The second type of linkage arises from the fact that an interest rate swap entered into can then be parcelled into known rates of interest for various periods within the term of the overall interest rate swap and sold into the market as FRAs. These two levels of linkage allow interest rate swaps and FRAs to coexist and complement each other within capital markets.

Interest rate caps, collars or floors are significantly different from swap transactions. They represent the purchase or sale of options on interest rates over extended time frames. It is usual in such transactions to buy not one but a series of options.

For example, an interest rate cap places an upper limit on the interest cost of the purchaser. Under the usual transaction structure, the purchaser of the cap, in return for the payment of an upfront fee or premium, is protected against rises in interest rates on its floating rate borrowings beyond a certain nominated upper limit. If rates breach this cap level, the writer of the cap agrees to make payments to the purchaser designed to effectively reduce the cost of funding to the level of the cap. Analytically, this represents the purchase of a series of put options on the relevant short-term rate index coinciding with rollover dates on the borrower's floating rate borrowings.

For a borrower, a collar places both a maximum and minimum rate on its borrowings and represents, analytically, the simultaneous purchase of a series of put options with the writing of a series of call options, representing the floor rate. In contrast, a floor agreement, usually utilised by investors, places a minimum yield constraint on the investor's portfolio of floating rate assets.

The market in caps, collars and floors is a subset of the market for debt options. However, these options markets are closely related to the market for interest rate swaps in the relevant currencies.

This linkage arises for a number of reasons. In particular, users of the swap market will usually view the cap or collar market as effectively a potential substitute for interest rate swaps and will constantly compare the price available in both markets to structure liability management transactions which best reflect their interest rate expectations.

In addition, the fact that analytically an interest rate swap can be characterised as the simultaneous purchase and sale of options provides a further basis for linkage between the two markets. For example, an interest rate swap where the entity in question pays the fixed rate in return for receiving the floating rate can be characterised as the purchase of a put option at the fixed rate with the simultaneous writing of a call option also at the fixed rate. This is effectively a collar with no difference between the floor and the cap rates. It is similarly possible to characterise a swap where the party in question is a receiver of the fixed rate as the simultaneous writing of a put option with the purchase of a call option.

An important aspect to note is that FRA, cap, collar and floor markets operate in a single currency. In this regard, FRAs and caps etc. are similar to interest rate swaps while currency swaps usually bear a greater relationship to parallel or back-to-back loans.

Exhibit 2.1 illustrates diagrammatically the basic structural relationships of the above types of transactions.

Exhibit 2.1
Swap Instruments—Structural Inter-relationships

		Currency	
		Single	Cross
Interest rate	Fixed	Interest rate swaps	LTFX and currency swaps
		FRAs	
	Floating	Caps, collars etc.	

SWAPS AND FINANCIAL ENGINEERING*

As is evident from the above discussion, the various instruments, usually referred to generically as swap transactions, have significant economic inter-relationships. However, it is in fact also possible to decompose these various instruments, that is, currency and interest rate swaps, LTFX, FRAs and caps, collars and floors, into two basic instruments: forward and option contracts.

---

* This discussion draws heavily on Smithson (1987).

The term "financial engineering" has increasingly come to be used as a general catch cry of financial markets. The wide variety of swap instruments available have, in particular, become synonymous with the use of the phrase *financial engineering*. While financial engineering in its purest form usually refers to the use of swap instruments to manage the cash flows of asset and liability transactions by borrowers and investors, the instruments themselves represent a form of financial engineering in that they are merely combinations and permutations of two relatively simple instruments, namely, forward and option contracts.

Decomposition of swap instruments into their basic elements and analysis of the inter-relationships is essential in understanding both the structural and economic aspects of such transactions. In this regard, it is essential to deal with currency and interest rate swaps, LTFX, FRAs, caps, floors and collars not as separate instruments but as a highly integrated set of financial transactions.

In decomposing and then re-engineering swap transactions from their basic elements, it is necessary to first define forward and option contracts.

A forward contract obligates the purchaser to buy a given asset on a specified date at a known price (known, usually, as the forward price). This forward price is specified at the time the contract is entered into. If at maturity the actual price is higher than the forward price, the contract owner will make a profit; if the price is lower, the owner suffers a loss.

A forward contract entailing the sale of a given asset on a specified date in the future at a known forward price is also feasible, representing the offsetting side of a forward purchase. In this case, the payoffs for the forward seller are clearly reversed.

In the case of forward contracts in capital markets, the underlying asset will usually be either a security or a specified amount of foreign currency. Where the asset is a security, its price will reflect interest rates. Consequently, a forward contract on such an asset would essentially operate functionally as a forward contract on interest rates. Similarly, where the underlying commodity is a specified amount of the foreign currency, the forward contract essentially represents a forward currency contract.

From a functional perspective, a futures contract is identical to a forward contract in that a futures contract also obligates its owner to purchase or sell a specified asset at a specified forward price on the contract maturity date.

The major difference between futures and forward contracts relates to the institutional structure of the two markets. In the case of futures contracts, the underlying asset to be traded is usually homogenised through a process of standardisation and the specification of nominated exercise dates (usually four per year). This is usually designed to enable the futures market to become relatively liquid. An additional difference of significance is the use of a futures exchange or clearing house which acts as a counterparty to each transaction. This is designed not only to facilitate liquidity but to reduce the likelihood of credit or default risk through a process of performance bonds, involving the posting of deposits and margins. Technically, a futures contract is a forward contract which is settled daily with a new forward contract being written simultaneously.

The relationship between interest rate swap contracts and forward contracts derives from the fact that, in effect, the swap contract is a series of forward contracts combined. As detailed in Chapter 3 an interest rate swap entails the exchange of specified cash flows determined by reference to two different interest rates. An interest rate swap can be represented by a series of cash inflows in return for a series of cash outflows. This contractual arrangement can be decomposed into a portfolio of simpler single payment contracts, which can in turn be decomposed into a series of forward contracts. Utilising this approach, it is possible to restate an interest rate swap as a series of implicit forward contracts on interest rates.

As noted above, an FRA contract is essentially a market in forward interest rates, in effect forward contracts on interest rates. Consequently, FRAs are logically linked to interest rate swaps in a manner identical to the linkage between forward contracts and interest rate swaps.

A forward contract, as specified above, entails an obligation to buy or sell the stated asset. In contrast, an option contract gives the purchaser the *right*, but not the *obligation*, to purchase or sell an asset. A call option gives the owner the right to purchase an asset while a put option gives the purchaser the right to sell the asset. In both cases, the purchase price or selling price is specified at the time the option contract is originated. This price is usually referred to as the exercise price. The financial price of the asset, as in the case of forward contracts, can be an interest rate or a currency exchange rate.

The purchaser of a call option contract has the right to purchase the asset at the exercise price. Consequently, if the price of the asset rises above the exercise price, then the value of the option also goes up. However, because the option contract does not obligate the purchaser to purchase the asset if the price falls, the value of the option does not fall by the same amount as the price decline. A similar but reverse logic applies in the case of put options.

The pay-off profile for the party who has sold (written or granted) the call or put option is different. In contrast to the purchaser of the option, the seller of the option has the obligation to perform. For example, if the holder of the option elects to exercise her or his option to purchase the asset, the seller of the option is obligated to sell the asset.

The relationship between option contracts and swap transactions operates at a number of levels:

• the relationship between option contracts and forward contracts;
• the relationship between option contracts and interest rate swaps.

As discussed in more detail in Chapter 11 it can be demonstrated that there are at least two inter-related linkages between options and forward contracts:

• A call option can be replicated by continuously adjusting or managing dynamically a portfolio of securities or forward contracts on the underlying asset (for example, securities or foreign exchange) and riskless securities or cash. As the price of the asset rises, the call option equivalent portfolio would contain an increasing proportion of the assets or forward contracts. As the financial price of the asset decreases, the call option equivalent portfolio would reduce its holding of the assets or forward contracts.

- Option contracts can be used to replicate forward contracts through a relationship known as put call parity (discussed in detail in Chapter 11). In terms of this relationship, the simultaneous purchase of a call option and the sale of a put option is equivalent to a forward purchase while the sale of a call option simultaneously combined with the purchase of a put option is equivalent to a forward sale.

These two levels of linkage between options and forward contracts imply a natural structural and economic relationship between the two instruments. In turn, option contracts impose a similar influence on interest rate swaps indirectly through their relationship with forward or futures contracts.

More directly, as noted above, options may have a direct relationship to interest rate swaps insofar as an interest rate swap can be characterised as a portfolio of purchased and sold options. This, of course, reflects the fact that an interest rate swap can be characterised as a series of forward contracts while forward contracts can be replicated through option contracts.

Swap instruments, such as caps, floors and collars are, in effect, a series of option contracts. This means that they are directly equivalent to underlying option contracts and consequently would enjoy a similar relationship to both forward and futures contracts or their customised equivalent FRAs as well as to interest rate swaps.

The discussion to date has confined itself to instruments in a single currency. However, the analysis is capable of extension to a multi-currency situation. A currency swap between two currencies is equivalent to a portfolio of currency forwards and futures or, alternatively, a portfolio of purchased and sold currency options. The currency forwards and currency options themselves are, first, linked to each other through option put call parity and replicating portfolio relationships, and, second, to the interest rate swap, forward and/ or futures and option markets in their respective currencies.

This complex inter-relationship between swap, forward and option markets is illustrated in *Exhibit 2.2* both in a single and multiple currency setting.

As illustrated, the capacity for swap transactions to be essentially dismembered into the basic constituent forward and option contracts is clearly evident. The ability to decompose swaps is not only elegant but highly useful for a number of reasons:

- the structural relationships allow the specific elements of individual transactions to be separated and recombined to create new instruments. This is particularly important in more complex liability and asset swap structures (see Part 6);
- the inter-relationships form the basis of pricing swap transactions. The established technology of pricing forward and option contracts provides the basis for the pricing and economic analysis of swaps;
- the decomposition process also facilitates the trading and hedging of swap transactions where financial institutions make markets in these instruments.

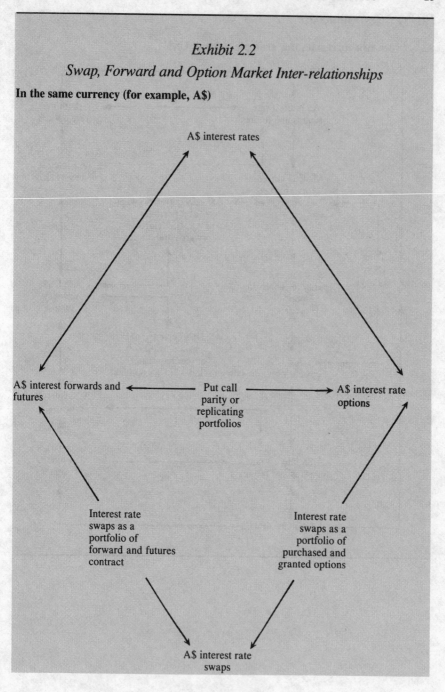

Exhibit 2.2
Swap, Forward and Option Market Inter-relationships

In the same currency (for example, A$)

Exhibit 2.2—continued

As between two currencies (for example, A$ and US$)

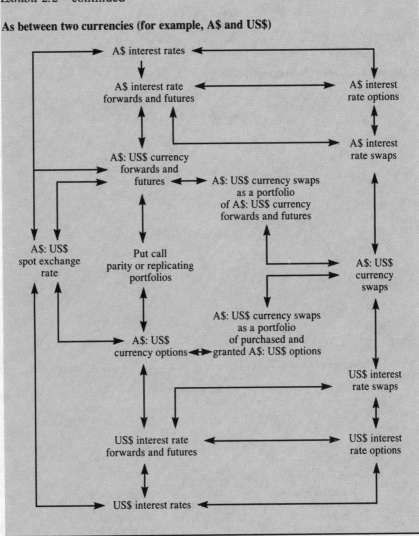

Chapter 3

Interest Rate and Currency Swap Structures

INTRODUCTION

Parallel or back-to-back loans and currency and interest rate swaps and LTFX represent two distinct categories of swap instruments. However, their historical relationship which is linked to the technical evolution of the various structures dictates that they are logically considered together.

PARALLEL OR BACK-TO-BACK LOANS

Parallel Loans

Parallel loans involve two entities, with headquarters in different countries, each having subsidiaries in the other's country, and each having mirror-image liquidity positions and financing requirements.

For example, a United States parent company with a subsidiary in Australia may have surplus US$ liquidity or ready access to new US$ borrowings in the United States while its Australian subsidiary needs additional A$ financing. Simultaneously, an Australian parent company (or institution) may have surplus A$ liquidity or access to new A$ borrowings in Australia and may be seeking US$ financing for its United States subsidiary (or to support a portfolio investment). A parallel loan transaction consists of a US$ loan from the United States parent company to the United States subsidiary of the Australian parent, and a simultaneous A$ loan of an equivalent amount from the Australian parent company to the Australian subsidiary of the United States company.

This structure (set out in *Exhibit 3.1*) satisfies the respective financing objectives of both parties, while avoiding any relevant exchange control inherent in direct investment by each parent, any higher costs of independent borrowing by each subsidiary, and currency exposure on the investment.

Interest rates on the two parallel loans are usually set at a fixed rate corresponding to commercial rates prevailing for each currency at the time of closing and may be subject to local government regulations. The spread between the two interest rates is subject to negotiation but would be a function of general interest rate levels in the two countries as well as the current equilibrium or disequilibrium in the market between providers and users of either currency.

In the above example, if A$ rates were 15.00% pa and US$ rates were 10.00% pa and the transaction was for a maturity of five years, then the transaction cash flows would be that set out in *Exhibit 3.2*.

25

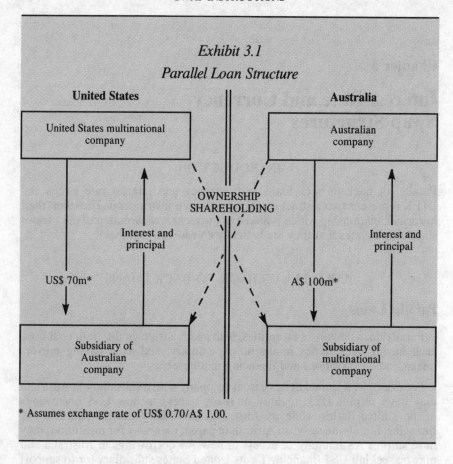

Exhibit 3.1
Parallel Loan Structure

United States   **Australia**

United States multinational company

Australian company

OWNERSHIP
SHAREHOLDING

Interest and principal

Interest and principal

US$ 70m*

A$ 100m*

Subsidiary of Australian company

Subsidiary of multinational company

* Assumes exchange rate of US$ 0.70/A$ 1.00.

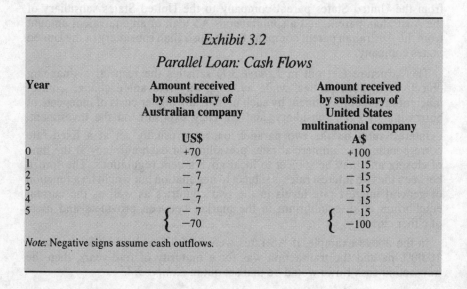

Exhibit 3.2
Parallel Loan: Cash Flows

Year	Amount received by subsidiary of Australian company US$	Amount received by subsidiary of United States multinational company A$
0	+70	+100
1	− 7	− 15
2	− 7	− 15
3	− 7	− 15
4	− 7	− 15
5	{ − 7 −70	{ − 15 −100

Note: Negative signs assume cash outflows.

The 5.00% annual differential would be paid by the United States multinational company. From an economic perspective, the Australian company, in receiving the 5.00% pa differential, is essentially compensated for any opportunity loss, that might otherwise be suffered, as a result of A$ interest rates being higher than US$ interest rates.

Mechanically, the interest differential is generally paid in the form of an annual fee. In the case of the earliest swaps, this was structured as a series of forward currency sales by the party with the higher interest rate funding. However, subsequently the Bank of England specified an alternative formula (set out in *Exhibit 3.3*) which in effect required payment of the two interest rates at a gross rate which was converted into one currency using prevailing spot exchange rates and then netted.

Exhibit 3.3

Bank of England Interest Differential Fee Calculation

$$\text{Annual fee} = \text{US\$ amount} \times \text{US\$ interest \%} - \frac{\text{DM amount} \times \text{DM interest \%}}{\text{future US\$/DM exchange rate}}$$

Where: future exchange rate = US$/DM exchange rate prevailing two days prior to fee payment date.

The following example illustrates the working of the formula and proves that it locks in local currency fixed rate financing costs.

Party A enters into a cross currency fixed-to-fixed three year debt swap with party B under which party A agrees to sell DM250 to party B in return for party B selling US$100 to party A. Both parties agree to the payment of an annual fee to be calculated in accordance with the Bank of England formula. Particulars of the swap are as follows:

Example

DM amount   = DM250
US$ amount   = US$100
DM interest rate = 10.50%
US$ interest rate = 15.00%

Future exchange rate

Year 1 US$1 = DM2.50
Year 2 US$1 = DM1.25
Year 3 US$1 = DM3.75

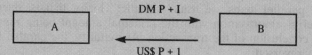

Calculation of fee

Year 1

$$\text{US\$100} \times 15.00\% - \frac{\text{DM250} \times 10.50\%}{\text{DM2.5}} = \text{fee}$$

$$\text{US\$15} - \text{US\$10.50} = \text{US\$4.50}$$

Therefore US$4.50 is payable by B to A.

Exhibit 3.3—continued

Year 2

$$US\$15 - US\$21 = -US\$6$$

Therefore US$6 is payable by A to B.

Year 3

$$US\$15 - US\$7 = US\$8$$

Therefore US$8 is payable by B to A.

Total amount in dollar terms payable by B

(That is, Deutschmark interest in dollar terms plus fee.)

(a) Deutschmark interest on bond at 10.50% payment	(b) Future exchange	(a) ÷ (b) = (c) Dollar equivalent	(d) Fee (see above)	(c) + (d) = (e) Total dollar
DM		US$	US$	US$
26.25	2.50	10.50	4.50	15.00
26.25	1.25	21.00	−6.00	15.00
26.25	3.75	7.00	8.00	15.00

As can be seen from the above calculations, the interest cost of servicing the simulated dollar loan, in dollar terms, is always US$15 (or 15.00%). Abolition of United Kingdom foreign exchange controls meant the Bank of England formula was no longer required. It is still used from time to time in order to simulate true borrowing cost. The same result is more customarily reached today by the parties agreeing to exchange defined amounts (determined implicitly by the parties agreeing to exchange defined amounts (determined implicitly by interest rates)) on the annual or semi-annual payment dates.

Source: Price and Henderson, *Currency and Interest Rate Swaps* (Butterworths 1984), pp. 13,14.

It is also feasible to structure parallel loan transactions where the relevant interest rates are variable or floating if the rate is set at a fixed margin over a recognised indicator rate.

Maturities generally range from five to ten years, depending on the currencies involved, although shorter maturities are not uncommon. Maturities over ten years are unusual.

Interest payments on the two loans are usually made at the same intervals and in most cases take place simultaneously on both loans. For administrative simplicity, parallel loans are usually "bullet" loans, that is, they provide for no interim amortisation with the principal amount being repayable in full at the conclusion of the transaction. At maturity, the parallel loans are thus simply reversed.

Transactions providing for interim amortisation are feasible where an appropriate counterparty can be located. Prepayment provisions, though unusual, may be included to enable one party to prepay its loan without accelerating the other's payment.

The creditworthiness of the participants to the transaction is an important element in the transaction, and the credit risk may be mitigated by the inclusion of offset rights which allow each party the right to offset payments not received against payments due. Parallel loans (as distinct from back-to-back loans) do not include a right of offset. If either counterparty considers the other's subsidiary less than creditworthy in its own right, specific security or a parent guarantee is usually negotiated.

A topping-up provision is often included to keep the principal amounts outstanding in balance where exchange rates move significantly during the life of the loans. A topping-up clause usually requires the lenders to make additional advances or repayments on one of the loans whenever the spot exchange rate moves past a trigger point, for example, in the A$ and US$ parallel loan example, additional A$ may have to be lent if the spot rate moves 10 cents lower, or paid back if the rate moves a corresponding amount higher.

Back-to-Back Loans

Parallel loans differ from back-to-back loans in that parallel loans do not include a right of offset or cross-collateralisation between loans, while back-to-back loans include a right of offset (see discussion below). As exchange control regulations of many countries prohibit rights of offset, parallel loans are more common than back-to-back loans.

The back-to-back loan differs from a parallel loan in structure as follows: under the back-to-back loan, the United States multinational company in the United States would lend to the Australian company in Australia whereas under a parallel loan structure the two parties would lend funds to their respective subsidiaries. This structure is set out in *Exhibit 3.4.*

The back-to-back loan entails the United States multinational company lending US$ to the Australian company in return for the Australian company lending the United States company A$. This is accompanied by an intercompany loan to their respective subsidiaries. Both loans are priced in line with market yields in the respective markets. Consequently, the transaction can be regarded as an initial exchange of currencies with an accompanying agreement to repay the respective loans in a form which could be regarded as a forward sale of US$ for A$ on the one hand and a forward sale of US$ for A$ on the other.

Significant structural differences between parallel and back-to-back loans include:

• a back-to-back loan entails cross-border funds flows which raise withholding tax issues;

• there is only one loan document in a back-to-back loan.

The general terms of a back-to-back loan are very similar to those for a parallel loan, although protection against withholding taxes may be included.

A comparison of parallel back-to-back loans and currency swaps

A parallel or back-to-back loan transaction and a currency swap (the structural successor to back-to-back loans) are similar techniques generally used to achieve similar objectives. In fact, currency swaps have, for most purposes, superseded parallel loans. However, a number of differences should be noted which might influence a company's choice between a parallel, back-to-back loan or a currency swap:

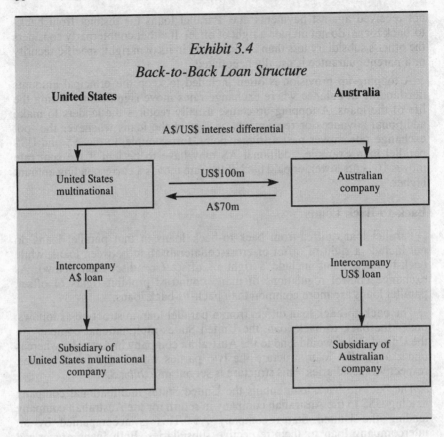

Exhibit 3.4

Back-to-Back Loan Structure

United States   **Australia**

A$/US$ interest differential

| United States multinational | US$100m → ← A$70m | Australian company |

Intercompany A$ loan   Intercompany US$ loan

| Subsidiary of United States multinational company | | Subsidiary of Australian company |

- Accountants differ on how parallel and back-to-back loans should be reported by the parent company on its balance sheet. Even if there exists a right of offset, some accountants feel that both loans should appear in the balance sheet rather than being treated as off-balance sheet items. Such treatment, which inflates the company's balance sheet, may produce adverse consequences under existing trust deeds or loan covenants and may therefore make a currency swap preferable. Where the currency swap does not entail new fund raising (that is, the party entering into the transaction has existing liquidity) the transaction entails the exchange of cash assets which effectively provides off-balance sheet financing as the future commitment to exchange currencies is analogous to a forward exchange contract which is not required to be reported on the balance sheet although it may require disclosure as a contingent liability or commitment.

- In a parallel loan transaction, each borrower has an unambiguous tax-deductible interest expense and each lender has taxable interest income. In a currency swap, the annual payments paid by one party to the other (representing in effect the differential between the interest rates in the respective currencies) may or may not be tax-deductible depending upon local law. Either a parallel loan transaction or a currency swap might be preferable depending upon the tax position of each counterparty.

- An implied right of offset often exists in the case of a currency swap, whereas no such right exists between parallel loans. If this right of offset is important as a credit matter, a currency swap or back-to-back loan might be preferable.

- The constituting documents of certain potential counterparties may permit entry into a parallel loan but not into a currency swap or vice versa.

- Two major structural differences between parallel, back-to-back loans and currency swaps are significant:

  —in a currency swap, no initial cash movements are necessary, since the swap is normally based on prevailing spot rates thereby allowing each party to obtain the relevant currency through the spot foreign exchange (FX) market (this is considered in detail later in this chapter);

  —swaps offer greater flexibility than parallel or back-to-back loans.

The modern role of parallel or back-to-back loan structures

Parallel and back-to-back loan structures are best regarded as earlier technical forms of swap transactions. The evolution of parallel loans into back-to-back structures, and the recognition that these transactions could be unbundled essentially into spot and forward currency contracts provided some of the important insights which underpin the modern swap market.

However, despite its structural obsolescence, parallel loans, in particular, continue to enjoy a secular role in the context of freeing blocked funds. Harking back to its original rationale of bypassing exchange controls, parallel loans continue to be used to circumvent exchange restrictions in countries which do not allow the free transfer of capital across its boundaries.

The modern parallel loan tends to be more custom-designed to the needs of the transaction, although the basic structure remains very close to the original transaction mechanics. The market operates primarily against US$ although transactions not involving the US$ are not uncommon.

SWAP TRANSACTIONS STRUCTURES

Interest rate swap

An interest rate swap is a transaction in which two parties agree to make to each other periodic payments calculated on the basis of specified interest rates and a hypothetical (or notional) principal amount.

An interest swap can be used to transform one type of interest obligation into another and thereby enable a swap participant to tailor its interest obligations to meet its needs in a given rate environment.

Typically, the payment to be made by one party is calculated using a floating rate of interest (such as LIBOR, the Bank Bill Rate (BBR) etc.) while the payment to be made by the other party is determined on the basis of a fixed rate of interest or a different floating rate.

In its most common form, an interest rate swap can be accomplished by two parties: the first, for example, may be a borrower which wants to pay interest at a fixed rate but which has already borrowed at a floating rate and the second may be a borrower which wants to pay interest at a floating rate but which has already borrowed at a fixed rate. The borrower wanting to pay a fixed rate borrows the principal amount that it needs, but on a floating rate basis. The borrower wanting to pay a floating rate borrows an identical amount at fixed rates. If a borrower was entering into the swap with respect to an existing debt, it would not undertake a new borrowing.

The two then enter into an agreement in which each undertakes to make periodic payments to the other in amounts equal to, or determined on the same basis as, the other's interest cost. Only payments calculated in the form of interest are made; payments corresponding to principal amounts are not made by either party. The net result of this exchange is that each party is able to obtain the type of interest rate, fixed or floating, which it wants and on acceptable terms.

Exhibit 3.5 sets out in diagrammatic form the basic structure of an interest rate swap.

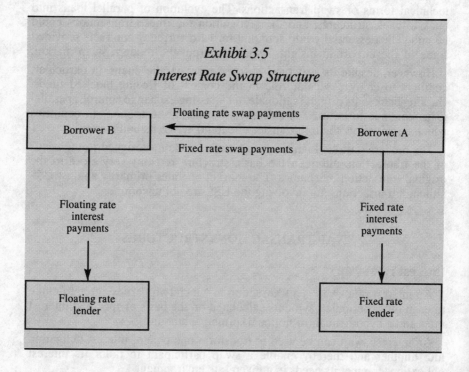

Exhibit 3.5

Interest Rate Swap Structure

Exhibit 3.6 sets out the cash flows for a three year A$ interest rate swap where company A borrows A$100m at a fixed rate of 14.00% pa (S/A) and enters into a swap with company B which borrows A$100m for three years on a floating rate basis at BBR plus 1.00% pa. The swap is undertaken on the following terms: company B pays 14.00% pa in return for receiving BBR flat.

Exhibit 3.6

Fixed-to-Floating Interest Rate Swap: Cash Flows and Costs (in A$m)

Year	Amount received from lender	Company A Swap Receipt	Company A Swap Payment	Net cash flow	Amount received from lender	Company B Swap Receipt	Company B Swap Payment	Net cash flow
0	+100	—	—	+100	+100	—	—	+100
0.5	− 7	+7	−BBR	−BBR	−BBR+0.5	+BBR	−7.0	−7.5
1.0	− 7	+7	−BBR	−BBR	−BBR+0.5	+BBR	−7.0	−7.5
1.5	− 7	+7	−BBR	−BBR	−BBR+0.5	+BBR	−7.0	−7.5
2.0	− 7	+7	−BBR	−BBR	−BBR+0.5	+BBR	−7.0	−7.5
2.5	− 7	+7	−BBR	−BBR	−BBR+0.5	+BBR	−7.0	−7.5
3.0	{ − 7	+7	−BBR	−BBR	−BBR+0.5	+BBR	−7.0	−7.5
	{ −100	—	—	−100	−100	—	—	−100

Notes:

1. Negative signs assume cash outflows.
2. BBR = six month BBR set each six months × 100 × (actual days ÷ 365). It is also assumed BBR on the loan and the swap are the same, that is, rates are (plus 1.00% in respect of the loan) set on the same day by the same rate setting or reference banks.

A number of essential features of the interest rate swap should be noted:

- The transaction amount is referred to as the notional principal or amount. It is notional in the sense that it is not usually exchanged as both participants do *not* obtain the underlying liquidity or funding through the swap. In any case, an exchange would be meaningless as each counterparty would provide the other with the same amount in the same currency. The notional amount is very important, nevertheless, as it provides the basis for interest calculations under the swap. For example, in the above example, the 14.00% and the BBR interest flows are calculated on $100 which is the notional principal amount.

- The swap transaction is totally independent from any underlying borrowing transactions for either party. The swap merely affects the coupon flows of a separately undertaken liability.

- Neither lender is a party to the swap; each borrower continues to be obligated to its own lender for the payment of both principal and interest. In fact, the lenders would not necessarily be aware that the swap had been undertaken. Each swap party takes the risk that the other may not make its swap payments, which would leave the non-defaulting party with the interest cost of its own borrowing uncovered by the swap. The swap does not relieve either borrower from the obligation to pay both principal and interest on its own borrowing.

This "decoupling" of the interest rate characteristics of a transaction is essentially one of the key features of swaps. It essentially allows a number of aspects of financing transactions to be separated or unbundled, including:

- Source of funding that is, which market or lender?
- Form of funding that is, fixed or floating rate?
- Timing of raising the required funding.

There are a number of common variations in interest rate swap structures, including:

- the incorporation of an intermediary;
- the use of structures not entailing entry by one party into the swap;
- the use of net as distinct from gross settlements under the swap.

In the basic structure (outlined above) both borrowers directly swap their obligations under their respective loans (refer *Exhibit 3.5*). Each borrower therefore takes the risk that the other may not make its swap payments.

However, under current market practice, most interest rate swaps do not utilise this direct structure. If either or both of the borrowers are unwilling to accept the risk of non-payment by the other, a third party, generally a bank or other financial institution, may be interposed between the borrowers to create an intermediated swap (refer *Exhibit 3.7*). Borrowers on both sides generally deal solely with the intermediary and have separate contracts with the intermediating bank. In this form the swap may be anonymous with the identity of both parties only being known to the intermediary.

The interposition of an intermediary in an interest rate swap insulates each borrower from the other and in so doing the intermediary, for a fee, guarantees that each borrower will receive the swap payment due from the other. The exact risk assumed by the intermediary varies between transactions. In general, in the type of transaction considered to date, the intermediating institution's guarantee is limited to the interest or coupon obligations swapped. If either party to the swap fails to make a swap payment

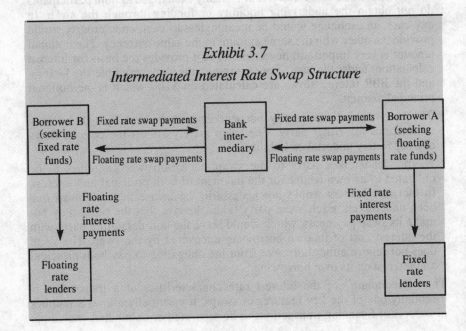

Exhibit 3.7
Intermediated Interest Rate Swap Structure

due to the intermediary, then the intermediary will not meet its corresponding payment under the swap. Consequently, the risk being assumed by the intermediary in respect of default is limited to any excess of the interest which the intermediary must pay to the other party over the interest payment to be received from the other party.

Where the swap encompasses exchanges of principal as well as interest or coupon obligations (see discussion of currency swap structures below), the intermediary may guarantee the principal amount in addition to the interest charges. The fee payable to the intermediary is based on the principal amount of the borrowing covered by the swap and/or the amount of the interest swap payments received by it and reflects the extent of credit risk assumed.

The presence of an intermediary also eliminates the need for exact matching of the two legs of the swaps. At its simplest, the separation of contractual obligations would generally enable transactions involving different amounts and a number of parties with slightly different needs to be matched. For example, some economies of scale and price advantages may be achieved by structuring a transaction using a very large bond offering by a particularly creditworthy borrower and swapping the proceeds with a number of floating rate borrowers. Additional flexibility in respect of early termination etc. may also be facilitated by the interposition of an intermediary. These advantages generally favour the intermediated form of interest rate swap and most transactions utilise this structure.

The credit exposure issues of swaps as well as the market making role of financial institutions in swap transactions are considered in detail in Parts 8 and 9.

In practice, certain transaction structures adopted make it unnecessary for borrowers to be parties to the interest swap itself. For example, if one borrower is unwilling or unable to enter into a swap, for example, for legal reasons, a special transaction structure may be adopted to enable the swap payments to be made between its lender and intermediary. Under this arrangement, the fixed rate borrower obtains fixed rate funds from the floating rate lender which converts its return to a floating rate basis through a swap with the intermediary which in turn enters into a complementary swap with the borrower (which seeks floating rate funds) which is willing to swap its fixed interest rate obligation for a floating rate obligation. Under this structure, the fixed rate borrower effectively achieves a conventional fixed rate loan although the payment flows and related risks and costs are determined to a large extent by the existence of the interest rate swap to which it is not a party. This type of transaction structure is depicted in *Exhibit 3.8*.

The third structural variation of importance is the use of net settlement terms under the swap. This is predicated on eliminating the flow of cash, representing the *full* interest payment to be made by each swap counterparty to the other. Instead, a *net* amount is either paid or received, representing the difference between the amount under the swap required to be paid to and the amount simultaneously due from the counterparty. *Exhibit 3.9* illustrates the use of the net settlement technique.

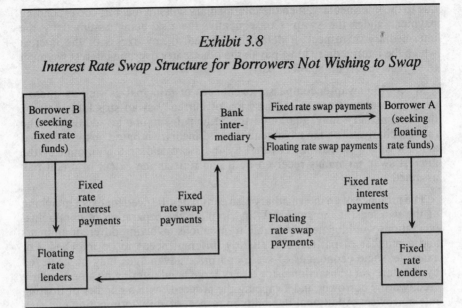

Exhibit 3.8

Interest Rate Swap Structure for Borrowers Not Wishing to Swap

Some other structural variations should also be noted. The examples, to date, have focused on transactions entailing new liabilities which are specifically undertaken as the basis for the swap. In practice, swaps can also be undertaken against existing liabilities and even, in the extreme, against no liabilities. In the later case, the swap is purely speculative in nature. Similarly, the swap need not be undertaken for the full term of the underlying borrowings. For example, the first two years of a three year obligation could be swapped based on interest rate expectations.

Exhibit 3.9

Calculation of Swap Net Settlement Amounts

Assume the same terms as for the swap described in *Exhibit 3.5*. Examining the transaction from the perspective of company A, the net settlement amounts under the swap (based on a notional principal amount of $100m) would be as follows:

Year	Assumed BBR	Swap flows Receipt (A$m)[1]	Payment (A$m)[2]	Net settlement amount (A$m)[3]
0.5	15.0%	7.00	7.50	−0.50
1.0	13.5%	7.00	6.75	+0.25
1.5	13.0%	7.00	6.50	+0.50

Notes:

1. The swap fixed rate is 14.00% pa (S/A).
2. The swap floating rate is calculated as BBR × Swap Notional Principal for the period of six months.
3. The (+) indicates a receipt, while a (−) indicates a payment.
   These settlement amounts achieve the following effective interest commitments for each party.

Exhibit 3.9—continued

Year	Interest paid (including margin if any) (A$m)	Net settlement amount from swap (A$m)	Effective interest payment (including margins if any) (A$m)	Effective interest rate (% pa)
Company A's position				
0.5	−7.00	−0.50	−7.50	15.00
1.0	−7.00	+0.25	−6.75	13.50
1.5	−7.00	+0.50	−6.50	13.00
Company B's position				
0.5	−8.00	+0.50	−7.50	15.00
1.0	−7.25	−0.25	−7.50	15.00
1.5	−7.00	−0.50	−7.50	15.00

As a result of the swap, company B ends up with an effective fixed interest rate of 15.00% pa and company A ends up with an effective floating rate of BBR.

Another structural variation of some importance is the use of discount instruments as part of the underlying funding for a swap. The difficulty relates to the fact that the proceeds of discount instruments, such as an A$ bank bill or promissory note or US$ commercial paper, are less than its face value or par. In order to allow exact cash flow matching under the swap, where a discount instrument is being used, it is necessary to structure the drawdown of, for example, bills such that the face value is varied to provide net proceed equal to the notional principal amount of the swap.

For example, in the example discussed in *Exhibit 3.5*, if BBR at commencement of the transaction was 16.00%, company B should have drawn down $104.24 face value of six month bank bills. These bills would provide B with proceeds of $100 (the notional principal amount of the swap) if discounted at 17.00% pa (BBR plus the margin of 1.00%). This procedure would be repeated every six months to maintain the underlying funding at the required level.

Currency swaps

A currency swap is similar to a parallel or back-to-back loan. In a currency swap, the counterparties do not lend currencies to each other but sell them to each other with a concomitant agreement to reverse the exchange of currencies at a fixed date in the future.

The amount to be swapped is established in one currency, and the prevailing spot exchange rate is used to establish the amount in the other currency. Currency swaps entail interest payments which take the form of a periodical (usually annual) payment by the counterparty in the lower interest rate country to the counterparty in the higher interest rate country. The interest cost is negotiable but generally approximates the interest rate differential between the countries. These rates can be either fixed or floating.

All currency swaps involve the buying and selling of different currency cash flows in the future, each respective sale being contingent upon the other. This is an important point as it distinguishes a currency swap from a loan and, by definition, being a forward conditional commitment makes it a contingent obligation therefore an off-balance sheet item.

Consider the following example: company A borrows A$100m for five years at 14.00% pa payable annually while company B borrows the US$ equivalent of A$100m, say US$65m for five years at LIBOR plus a margin (say 0.50%) payable semi-annually (assume A$1/US$0.65).

The currency swap would operate in three distinct phases: initial principal exchange, interest payments coverage and a re-exchange of principal at maturity.

At commencement of the transaction, company A would sell the proceeds of its A$ issue to company B in return for company B selling the proceeds of its US$ borrowing to company A. This exchange is effected at the prevailing spot exchange rate.

Each party agrees to service the other party's debt, that is, company A would pay the interest on company B's loan and company B the interest on company A's loan. In this example, it is assumed that company A does not pay the spread over LIBOR on company B's loan.

At maturity the parties would merely reverse the initial exchange. In other words, company A would sell US$65m to company B in return for company B selling A$100m to company A.

Exhibit 3.10 sets out in diagrammatic form the basic structure of a currency swap.

Exhibit 3.11 sets out the detailed cash flows and effective cost calculations of the transaction described.

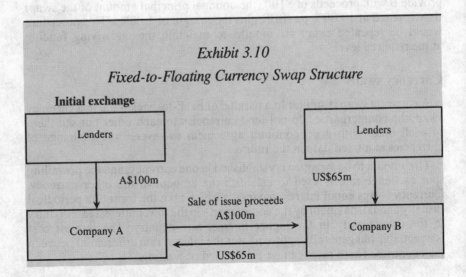

Exhibit 3.10
Fixed-to-Floating Currency Swap Structure

Initial exchange

Exhibit 3.10—continued

Periodic payments

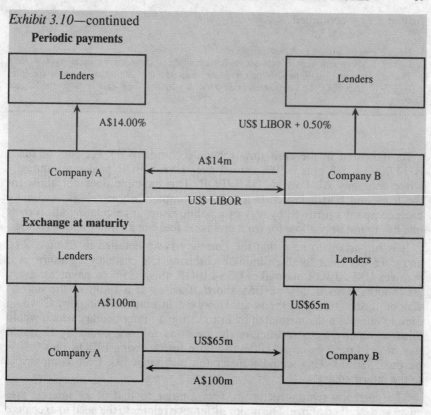

Exchange at maturity

Exhibit 3.11

Fixed-to-Floating Currency Swap: Cash Flows and Costs
(in millions)

		Company A				Company B		
	Amount received from	Swap		Net cash flow	Amount received from	Swap		Net cash flow
Year	lender A$	Receipt A$	Payment US$	US$	lender US$	Receipt US$	Payment A$	A$
0	+100	−100	+65	+65	+65	−65	+100	+100
0.5	—	—	−LIBOR	−LIBOR	−(LIBOR+0.25)	+LIBOR	—	−0.25
1.0	−14	+14	−LIBOR	−LIBOR	−(LIBOR+0.25)	+LIBOR	−14	−14.25
1.5	—	—	−LIBOR	−LIBOR	−(LIBOR+0.25)	+LIBOR	—	−0.25
2.0	−14	+14	−LIBOR	−LIBOR	−(LIBOR+0.25)	+LIBOR	−14	−14.25
2.5	—	—	−LIBOR	−LIBOR	−(LIBOR+0.25)	+LIBOR	—	−0.25
3.0	−14	+14	−LIBOR	−LIBOR	−(LIBOR+0.25)	+LIBOR	−14	−14.25
3.5	—	—	−LIBOR	−LIBOR	−(LIBOR+0.25)	+LIBOR	—	−0.25
4.0	−14	+14	−LIBOR	−LIBOR	−(LIBOR+0.25)	+LIBOR	−14	−14.25
4.5	—	—	−LIBOR	−LIBOR	−(LIBOR+0.25)	+LIBOR	—	−0.25
5.0	{ −14	+14	−LIBOR	−LIBOR	−(LIBOR+0.25)	+LIBOR	−14	−14.25
	−100	+100	−65	−65	−65	+65	−100	−100

Exhibit 3.11—continued

Notes:
1. Negative signs assume cash outflows.
2. LIBOR = six month LIBOR rate set each six months × US$65m × (actual days ÷ 365). It also assumes LIBOR on the loan and the swap are the same, that is, rates are (plus 0.50% in respect of the loan) set on the same day by the same rate setting or reference banks.

As indicated in the cash flow schedule company B's net cost of funds is 14.00% in A$ plus 0.50% spread over US$ LIBOR paid semi-annually while company A's cost is US$ LIBOR. This example does not allow for the front end borrowing costs for either company's borrowings. Assuming each company borrowed by way of a public issue, in calculating all-in costs one has to not only allow for front end issue fees but all other issue expenses.

It is important to note that the currency swap detailed in *Exhibits 3.10* and *3.11* does *not* totally eliminate company C's currency exposure as it receives US$ LIBOR but makes US$ LIBOR plus 0.25% pa payments every six months. This 0.25% pa US$ shortfall arises as a result of the normal economic structuring of the swap. However, in practice, company C would seek to eliminate the mismatch by introducing an intermediary which would allow company C to restructure the swap as follows: company C would pay, say, 14.65% pa on A$100m in return for receiving LIBOR plus 0.50% pa on US$65m. This would transfer the mismatch risk from company C to the intermediary.

The currency swap structure is very similar to that of an interest rate swap as described above. The major difference relates to the need to exchange principal amounts at the commencement and conclusion of a transaction. This exchange is designed to provide the parties to the swap with access to their desired currency for the life of the transaction while eliminating any foreign exchange exposure, other than in the nominated currency.

The exchanges in a currency swap can be eliminated. Instead of an initial exchange, a spot FX transaction can allow each party to generate its desired currency (refer *Exhibit 3.12*). However, the elimination of the initial exchange does not obviate the need *to set* a reference spot rate between the relevant currencies. This rate is, of course, the rate at which the re-exchange at maturity is to be effected.

Where an initial exchange is not undertaken the spot rate must be set using a defined market rate as quoted by a specified bank at a particular time. Care is necessary to ensure that the definition used is the same for all parties, particularly where a multi-legged swap is sought to be transacted. A major problem relates to the fact that the swap counterparties, respectively buyers and sellers of the currencies, will by definition be on the "wrong" side of the bid-offer spread. These slight mismatches in amount are problematic as they may open unintentional currency exposures or, alternatively, will affect the all-in cost achieved.

The most common reason for not using an initial exchange is that the swap is being undertaken against existing borrowings where there are no new cash flows which can be used to support the swap exchange.

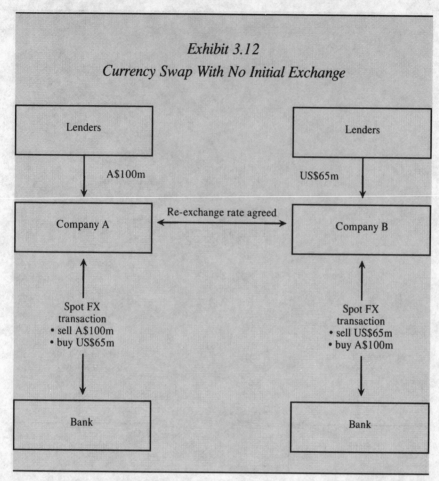

Exhibit 3.12
Currency Swap With No Initial Exchange

The final re-exchange can also be eliminated. This is achieved by the parties undertaking appropriate spot FX transactions and by a currency difference (reflecting the appreciation or depreciation of the currencies) being paid by one party to the other. The spot FX transaction, in conjunction with the settlement amount, will give the same result as if the re-exchange had been effected at the original nominated rate (refer *Exhibit 3.13*).

The analysis to date assumes that the initial exchange is undertaken at the prevailing swap rate. It is technically possible to structure currency swaps at off-market spot rates usually to accelerate or defer currency losses or gains. A variety of structures are feasible with the FX difference usually being incorporated in the interest rates under the swap.

The various structural differences discussed in the context of interest rate swaps are all also generally applicable to currency swap transactions. However, it is worth noting that net settlement procedures are less common in currency swaps and where utilised require the two swap flows to be translated into a common currency, usually US$.

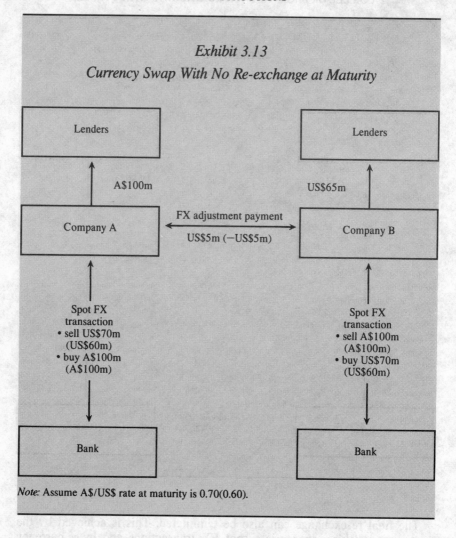

Exhibit 3.13
Currency Swap With No Re-exchange at Maturity

Note: Assume A$/US$ rate at maturity is 0.70(0.60).

LTFX agreements

Fixed-to-fixed currency swaps are similar conceptually to and can be used to effectively replicate LTFX transactions. In fact, technically a fixed-to-fixed currency swap is identical to a par forward FX contract (refer *Exhibit 3.14*).

LTFX agreements are outright forward transactions with no spot exchange taking place at time of closing. They are used primarily for hedging existing or anticipated exposures, such as long-term borrowings or future receivables. LTFX agreements normally call for a single specific exchange at a future date or a series of exchanges spread evenly over a number of years.

To illustrate, a United States company with A$ liability decides that its currency exposure is unacceptable and decides to buy A$ forward. At the same time, an Australian airline plans to purchase aircraft in the United

Exhibit 3.14

Par Forward Contract

Scenario 1

A purchase of US$1m every month for four months:

Spot A$1: US$0.6600

forward points:
- 7.07.X7 − 50
- 7.08.X7 − 100
- 7.09.X7 − 150
- 7.10.X7 − 200

NORMAL FORWARD COVER			PAR FORWARD COVER[1]		
Date	Rate (A$1/US$)	Cost	Date	Rate (A$1/US$)	Cost
7.07.X7	0.6550	A$1,526,717	7.07.X7	0.6476	A$1,544,163
7.08.X7	0.6500	A$1,538,461	7.08.X7	0.6476	A$1,544,163
7.09.X7	0.6450	A$1,550,387	7.09.X7	0.6476	A$1,544,163
7.10.X7	0.6400	A$1,562,500	7.10.X7	06.476	A$1,544,163

Note:

Par forward rate = nominal rate + funding cost

Nominal rate $= \dfrac{0.6550 + 0.6500 + 0.6450 + 0.6400}{4} = 0.6475$

Funding cost = Cost or benefit to the company due to different cash flows.

The cost to the company in the current example is A$785 which is compensated for in a benefit of one exchange point.

$0.6475 + 0.0001 = 0.6476$

Scenario 2

A purchase of US$1m one year forward can be transacted in one of the following ways:

- a forward purchase of US$1m for value in one years time at US$0.6200 reflecting a spot rate of A$1/US$0.6600 and the one year forward premium of 0.0400 (that is, 7.00% pa);
- a par forward with the forward being transacted at the spot rate of US$0.6200 with deferred settlement at an interest cost of 7.00%.

States and wants to guarantee the A$ price of its investment. To satisfy the respective hedging needs of the two companies, an LTFX contract could be structured. The United States company sells US$ to and buys A$ from the Australian company. The Australian company, on the other hand, will use the acquired US$ to pay for its US$ denominated investments. In brief, the currency risk of the two companies has been eliminated at the cost of the forward premium/discount between the two currencies.

Exhibit 3.15 sets out in diagrammatic form the structure of the LTFX transaction described.

The prices on forward contracts, that is, the premiums/discounts, are negotiable but generally reflect the prevailing market interest rates for the two currencies for the same maturity. The longer the maturity in general, the wider the bid/ask spread, reflecting the thinness of the market in the longer maturity ranges. In terms of credit and FX risk, the obligation to

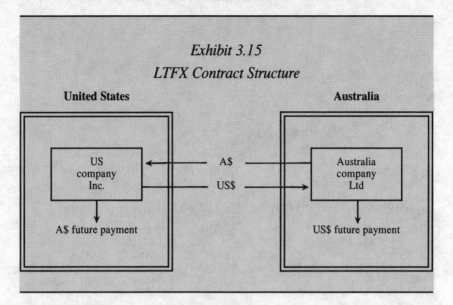

Exhibit 3.15
LTFX Contract Structure

The forward exchange commitment leg of a currency swap transaction which simply entails the purchase and sale of foreign currency is very similar to that of a normal currency forward contract. However, currency swaps provide a greater degree of structural flexibility relative to a long-dated forward contract. For example, in a swap, the normal par forward structure (the reversal of the currency exchange is at the initial rate of exchange) means that the premium or discount built into the forward rate is settled through periodic payment which enables the parties to cover the interest flows in the underlying borrowings, and also has the advantage that, for balance sheet purposes, the reported size of the borrowing before and after the swap is the same as the forward rate corresponding to the spot rate at inception of the transaction.

perform is implied in a forward FX agreement, and its terms and conditions are usually negotiated between the two parties.

Swaps are also probably easier to administer than a series of outright forwards, all at different rates and expressed as swap points deducted or added from the spot rate. Matching the cash flows in the foreign currency will mean uneven cash flows in the base currency.

Fixed rate currency swaps (both interest rates at fixed rates) also generally offer longer terms and better volume. Bid/offer spreads are, if anything, narrower in the swap market.

Exhibit 3.16 compares the actual cash flows for an identical currency swap and LTFX contract.

LTFX contracts are particularly useful for transactions which entail uneven cash flows, either in amount or, alternatively, in a certain timing or spacing irregularity over the full maturity. In contrast, currency swaps are more suitable where even cash flow streams such as those in a borrowing are required to be transferred into another currency. LTFX contracts are also

Exhibit 3.16

Currency Swap versus LTFX Cash Flows

Years	Currency swap cash flows		LTFX cash flows		
	A$	US$	Rate	A$	US$
	−150.00	+100	0.67	−150.00	+100
1	+22.50	−10	0.64	15.60	−10
2	+22.50	−10	0.61	16.40	−10
3	+22.50	−10	0.58	17.20	−10
3	+ 150.00	−100	0.58	172.40	−100
	67.50	−30		71.60	−30

Assumptions:

1. A$/US$ spot rate: 0.67
2. A$ interest rate: 15.00%
3. US$ interest rate: 10.00%
4. No bid or offer spread

Exhibit 3.17

Types of Swaps

Type	Interest rate		Currency	Example
	From	To		
Interest rate (coupon) swap	Floating	Fixed	Same	Swapping the interest cost of a floating rate Eurodollar loan into fixed rates
Cross-currency interest rate swap	Floating	Fixed	Different	Swapping fixed rate proceeds of a Swiss franc bond issue into floating rate US$
Fixed-to-fixed swap	Fixed	Fixed	Same	Swapping interest rate basis from a normal coupon fixed rate to a zero coupon fixed rate
Cross-currency fixed-to-fixed swap	Fixed	Fixed	Different	Swapping fixed rate proceeds of a Swiss franc bond issue into fixed rate US$
Floating-to-floating (basis) swap	Floating	Floating	Same	Swapping interest rate basis of floating rate US$ commercial paper funds into US$ LIBOR based funds
Cross-currency floating-to-floating (basis) swap	Floating	Floating	Different	Swapping interest rate basis of floating rate A$ bank bill funds into US$ LIBOR funds

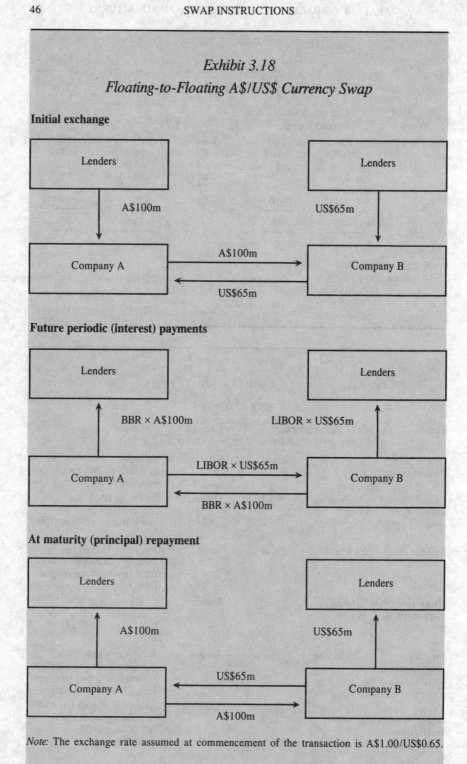

Exhibit 3.18
Floating-to-Floating A$/US$ Currency Swap

Initial exchange

Future periodic (interest) payments

At maturity (principal) repayment

Note: The exchange rate assumed at commencement of the transaction is A$1.00/US$0.65.

particularly useful where the transaction does not commence immediately but at some time in the future.

Types of swap transactions

The various types of swap transactions theoretically feasible are set out in *Exhibit 3.17.*

Two types of swaps require special comment: floating-to-floating currency swaps and cocktail swaps.

Theoretically cross-currency floating-to-floating swaps should not exist because a floating-to-floating swap is nothing more than a series of, for example, six month forward foreign exchange contracts rolled over every

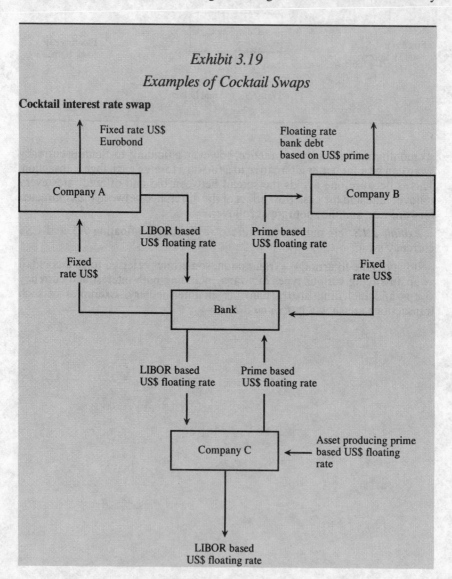

Exhibit 3.19

Examples of Cocktail Swaps

Cocktail interest rate swap

Exhibit 3.19—continued

Cocktail currency and interest rate swap

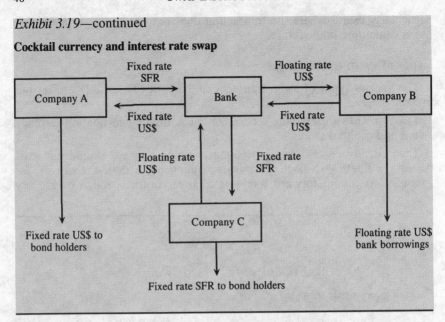

six months until maturity. In practice, however, a floating-to-floating currency swap can be a far better alternative to a forward foreign exchange transaction. This is because one avoids the spread between bid and offered rates every rollover date and the cash flow effect of the difference between the contracted forward rate and the spot rate at rollover.

Exhibit 3.18 sets out the structure of a floating-to-floating A$ and US$ currency swap.

It is possible to arrange a transaction, sometimes referred to as a cocktail swap, involving various types of swaps, including both interest and currency swaps and including also a bank as an intermediary. Examples of such transactions are shown in *Exhibit 3.19*.

Chapter 4

Forward Rate Agreements

FORWARD RATE AGREEMENTS

An FRA is an agreement between two parties who wish to protect themselves against a future movement in interest rates. The parties involved agree on an interest rate for a specific period of time from a specified future settlement date based on an agreed principal amount.

The *buyer* is the party to the FRA wishing to protect itself against a future rise in the relevant interest rate. The *seller* is the party to the FRA wishing to protect itself against a future fall in the relevant interest rate.

No commitment is made by either party to lend or borrow the principal amount. The exposure to both parties is only the interest difference between the agreed rate and actual settlement rate.

Cash settlement takes place on the settlement date. The settlement rate procedure will be agreed. For example, in the A$ FRA market, the settlement rate is based on market rates displayed on Reuters screen page BBSW.

If the settlement rate is higher than the agreed rate the borrower will receive the difference from the lender or vice versa:

$$\text{Settlement amount} = \frac{\left\{ \begin{array}{c} \text{The difference between} \\ \text{the settlement rate and} \\ \text{agreed rate} \end{array} \right\} \times \begin{array}{c} \text{contract} \times \text{principal} \\ \text{period} \quad \text{amount*} \end{array}}{36,500** + (\text{settlement rate} \times \text{contract period})}$$

*For A$ FRA this figure is the discounted amount of the face value at the agreed rate.

**36,000 for currencies where that is the basis for interest calculations.

Some key terms usually utilised in connection with FRAs are set out in *Exhibit 4.1*.

FORWARD RATE AGREEMENTS: TRANSACTION EXAMPLES

Future deposit

Assume a company will have A$1m to deposit in three months for a six month period. The company treasurer is concerned that interest rates will fall over the next few months and therefore wishes to secure today's implied interest rate.

Assume FRAs three month against nine month or 3×9 (that is, the six month interest rate in three months from the present) are quoted 17.75-18.00% pa and that the client agrees to the forward rate of 17.75% pa.

49

> ### Exhibit 4.1
> ### FRA Terminology
>
> | | |
> |---|---|
> | **FRA** | A forward (or future) rate agreement. |
> | **Forward rate** | A future rate of interest agreed between the parties at the outset. Sometimes called the agreed rate or the guaranteed rate. |
> | **Buyer (or borrower)** | The party wishing to protect itself from a rise in interest rates. |
> | **Seller (or lender)** | The party wishing to protect itself from a fall in interest rates. |
> | **Settlement date** | The start date of the loan or deposit upon which the FRA is based. |
> | **Contract period** | The period between the date the rate was agreed and the settlement date. |
> | **Maturity date** | The date on which the FRA contract period ends. |
> | **Fixing date** | For A$ FRA this will be on the settlement date. For other currencies two business days before the settlement date. |
> | **Settlement rate** | The mean rate quoted by specified reference banks for the relevant period and currency. For A$ FRAs the interest rate will be the BBR shown on Reuters Page BBSW. For other currencies LIBOR as shown on Telerate Page 3750 or Reuters Page 2180. |
> | **Run** | Period or term of underlying investment or borrowing—normally 90 or 180 days, that is, a three or six month run. |

Calculate the discount sum:

$$\frac{\text{face value} \times 36{,}500}{(\text{agreed rate} \times \text{days}) + 36{,}500} = \frac{1{,}000{,}000 \times 36{,}500}{(17.75 \times 182) + 36{,}500} = \text{A\$ }918{,}689.67$$

- If in three months' time the settlement rate is 15.00% then the FRA provider will settle the difference in favour of the company as follows:

$$\frac{(17.75 - 15.00) \times 182 \times 918{,}689.67}{36{,}500 + (15.00 \times 182)} = \text{A\$ }11{,}720.72$$

- If in three months' time the rate is 19.75% then the company will settle the difference in favour of the FRA provider as follows:

$$\frac{(19.75 - 17.75) \times 182 \times 918{,}689.67}{36{,}500 + (19.75 \times 182)} = \text{A\$ }8{,}340.37$$

Future borrowing

Assume a company will need to borrow US$1m in one month for a six month period. The company treasurer thinks that interest rates may rise by the time the company borrows the money and wishes to fix the borrowing cost today.

Assume the company and the FRA provider agree on a 1 × 7 FRA rate of 8.50%.

If in one month's time the settlement rate is 10.00% the FRA provider will settle the difference in favour of the company as follows:

$$\frac{(10.00 - 8.50) \times 182 \times 1,000,000}{36,000 + (10.00 \times 182)} = US\$ \ 7,218.40$$

If in one month's time the settlement rate is 7.00% the company will settle the difference in favour of the FRA provider as follows:

$$\frac{(8.50 - 7.00) \times 182 \times 1,000,000}{36,000 + (7.00 \times 182)} = US\$ \ 7,324.14$$

THE RATIONALE FOR FRAs

Some organisations use the futures market to protect themselves against interest rate fluctuations affecting their borrowings or investment . Assuming cancellation or reversal at the takedown date, the futures strategy to hedge a borrowing consists of selling financial futures, that is, contracting to sell a certain number of A$ bills or US$ LIBOR contracts for delivery at a future date simultaneously or as close as possible to when the company expects to borrow. At that time, if interest rates have increased, they will be offset by profits on the futures contract sale. If rates have dropped, the savings will cover the loss on the futures contract. The effect should be that the net interest cost (subject to basis risk) would be identical. In order to hedge the interest rate exposure on an investment, financial futures would be bought. The same effect can be achieved arguably more efficiently and effectively through the use of FRAs.

The principal advantages of FRAs over other methods of hedging interest rate risk, such as futures, include:

- As FRAs do not go through a futures exchange there is no requirement for deposits or margin variation calls, with a corresponding saving in administration costs and in the costs of financing deposit and margin calls.

- Whereas futures contracts are standardised as to amount, settlement day, etc., FRAs can be negotiated to fit precisely the identified hedging requirements.

- The institution's exposure to credit risk is limited to the interest variation based on the principal and is not the full principal amount. The extent of the credit risk depends on the interest rate volatility.

- The FRA is settled by exchange of a cash sum and consequently does not gross up the balance sheet. This is in contrast to a forward deposit transaction (an agreement to place or take a deposit for a specified period at a specified value date) where funds equal to the principal of the deposit will be exchanged on the value date and the deposit will then be carried on the balance sheet throughout the hedge period.

- An FRA hedge can be closed out at any stage by entering into an equal and opposite FRA at a new price. This price will reflect the interest rate for the period at the time of closing the hedge.

- A company's borrowing rate and futures rate do not necessarily move in parallel. This basis risk can diminish the value of the hedge. FRAs can lock in a specific floating interest rate index regardless of fluctuations in other prevailing rates.
- For long-term hedging contracts, especially those having delivery dates months away or longer, the futures market is thin. It may be difficult to buy and sell in significant amounts. Futures exchanges legislate maximum allowable daily price changes causing an unfavourable contract to be illiquid during extremely volatile periods. There is the risk of not being able to enter into or close of a hedge. FRAs eliminate some of the liquidity problem as a number of intermediaries guarantee to quote FRA transactions at any time.

However, FRAs do have two disadvantages when compared with financial futures including:

- There is no formal market in which FRAs can be traded and secondary market liquidity is therefore limited in the FRA market.
- FRAs carry the credit risk (although only for the settlement amount) of the counterparty, whereas for financial futures this is covered by substitution of the clearing house which is in turn protected by the deposit of margins.

FRA VARIATIONS

There are a number of significant variations on the conventional FRA including:

- using a "strip" or a series of FRAs to lock in the interest rate over a series of interest rate reset dates;
- using a combination of FRAs and foreign exchange forward contracts to create a synthetic FRA in a foreign currency;
- Forward Spread Agreements (FSA), a relatively recent variation designed to allow parties to lock in spreads or differentials between currencies.

A strip of FRAs can be utilised to create a fixed rate loan or investment. The FRAs act as a hedge guaranteeing the interest rate on each rollover date allowing determination at the outset of the interest rate over the whole period. An example of this type of transaction is set out in *Exhibit 4.2.*

It is important to note that where a strip of FRAs is used, particularly at regular intervals, the transaction is functionally identical to an interest rate swap for the term.

FRAs are not available in every currency. However, where they are unavailable, it is feasible to synthesise an FRA in the relevant currency utilising a combination of FRAs and FX forward transactions. An example of this type of transaction is set out in *Exhibit 4.3.*

An FSA is an agreement between two parties seeking protection against potential future changes usually in the differential between London interbank interest rates for two different currencies, one of which will always be the US$ (the other one being known as the countercurrency).

The instrument is structured like a dual currency FRA but is closer to a currency swap such as a par value forward deal where the initial amount

Exhibit 4.2
FRA Strip Hedge

A borrower seeks to hedge an exposure of A$10m borrowing it on a floating rate basis for a period of 12 months ending 4 June 19X8:

Maturity dates	FRA rates %	Spot rates on maturity dates %	Net-off effect to the company A$
4.6.X8	—	12.00	—
3.9.X8	13.00	12.50	−11,589[1]
3.12.X8	12.50	13.00	+11,589
4.3.X9	12.00	13.25	+28,989
Net FRA settlement			+28,989
Effective 12 month borrowing cost[2]			12.96% pa (payable quarterly)

Notes:

1. Net-off effect of 3 September transaction =
$$\frac{10,000,000 \times 365}{(0.1250 \times 90) + 365} - \frac{10,000,000 \times 365}{(0.1300 \times 90) + 365} = A\$9,700,997 - A\$9,689,408 = A\$11,589$$

2. The effective 12 month borrowing cost is calculated as the compounded interest rates on the FRAs.

Exhibit 4.3
Synthetic FRA Transaction

A borrower wishes to lock in a two month borrowing cost in NZ$ for NZ$10m. Normally, the borrower would achieve this objective by buying a NZ$ 1×3 month FRA, that is, an FRA on two month NZ$ interest rates in one month's time. However, we assume that NZ$ FRAs are not directly available, although A$ FRAs for the required term as well as A$ and NZ$ currency forwards are available.

The current market rates are:*

A$ and NZ$	Spot:	A$1.00 = NZ$1.1660
	1 month forward	= NZ$1.1710
	3 months forward	= NZ$1.1840
A$ FRAs	1×3	13.24%

In these circumstances the borrower could synthesise a NZ$ FRA as follows:

• buy NZ$10m against a sale of A$8,539,710 for value in one month at the quoted rate of NZ$1.1710;

• sell NZ$10,334,068 against a purchase of A$8,728,098 for value in three months at the quoted rate of NZ$1.1840;

• enter into a two month A$ FRA commencing in one month at a rate of 13.24% pa.

This series of transactions would provide the borrower with a known fully hedged cost of NZ$ funds.

Exhibit 4.3—continued

Under the transaction, the borrower would draw down A$ funding for two months in one month at a rate of 13.20% pa guaranteed under the FRA. The A$ would be converted into NZ$ through the A$ and NZ$ foreign exchange contract. The A$ amount drawn down is determined by the need to generate NZ$10m of funding. At maturity, the borrower would repay NZ$10,334,668 which would be converted into A$8,728,098 through the forward contract. The A$ amount at maturity corresponds to the amount required to meet the principal and interest commitment on the A$ liability.

The overall transaction results in a guaranteed borrowing cost for NZ$10m for two months in one month's time of 20.04% pa.

* Bid/offer spreads are omitted for ease of exposition.

of currency at maturity is exchanged at the same rate as the initial exchange, and where a series of payments reflects the interest rate differential over the life of the swap. The instrument is seen as a competitor to swaps only in the short-term portion of the market where a simple structure and an even simpler type of documentation should prove advantageous.

An FSA is not designed to hedge foreign exchange risk. Typical users will be banks and corporates with assets in one currency and liabilities in another one. Such cross-currency funding entails the risk of rising interest rates in the funding currency while they decrease in the asset currency. This translates into an interest rate spread risk.

Those institutions willing to protect themselves against a narrowing of the spread between the US$ and the countercurrency interest rate will be sellers of an FSA, while those willing to hedge against a widening of the spread will be buyers of the new instrument. If the settlement spread is numerically higher than the forward spread, the seller pays the buyer the settlement sum, expressed in US$. If the settlement spread is numerically lower than the forward spread, then the buyer pays the seller the settlement sum.

An FSA trader will be receiving and paying the settlement amounts in US$. This does not involve foreign exchange exposure, but changes in the spot rate may have an impact on the profitability of a hedge. A firm hedging an interest rate spread (for example, the US$ and yen rate spread in the case of US$ assets and yen liabilities) is left with a small exposure when the settlement is made in US$. This is because the spot rate at the time of the settlement may be different from the spot rate at the time the FSA is entered into and its amount is decided upon. However, this small exposure may be hedged, as it is possible to track the influence of a move in the spot exchange rate (US$ and yen in this case) on the settlement amount made in US$.

Promoters of the FSA see a future for the product with banks or corporates running spread books as opposed to running the various legs separately. Institutions with non-US$ assets or liabilities can convert them into US$ terms and hedge that risk by combining an FSA with a US$ interest rate hedging instrument. FSAs are an alternative to forward-forward contracts, which express interest rate differentials as well, but entail a commitment in a loan or a deposit.

An example of an FSA transaction is set out in *Exhibit 4.4*.

Exhibit 4.4

Example of an FSA Transaction

On a given day, interest rates for three month deposits in Eurodollars and in Euroyen are as follows:

- for three month Eurodollars: 6.50%;
- for three month Euroyen: 4.50%.

The spread between interest rates for three month deposits in Eurodollars and in Euroyen will be −2.00% (or −200bps). If the rates are reversed, the spread will be 2.00% (or 200bps).

A two-way market spread price would be quoted as, for example:

−205 (bid price) to −195 (offer price).

On 18 May 19X7, a party (the buyer) wishing to protect a forward spread of −1.95% (or −195bps) between interest rates for three month deposits or Eurodollars and in Euroyen placed on 18 November 19X7 could enter into an FSA where the forward spread is agreed at −195bps and where the settlement date is 18 November 19X7 and the maturity date is 18 February 19X7.

On 16 November 19X7 (the fixing date) the spread between three month deposits in Eurodollars and in Euroyen for value at 18 November 19X7 would be calculated and this spread would represent the settlement spread.

When the countercurrency rate is lower than the US$ rate:

Forward spread (per cent)	Settlement spread (per cent)	Payer
−1.95000	−1.53125	Seller
−2.05000	−2.53125	Buyer

When the countercurrency rate is higher than the US$ rate:

Forward spread (per cent)	Settlement sread (per cent)	Payer
1.95000	1.53125	Buyer
2.05000	2.53125	Seller

The *settlement sum* is the amount payable in US$ by the buyer or the seller on the settlement date. It is calculated as follows:

$$\frac{A}{100} \times \frac{D}{360} \times \text{notional principal sum} = \text{settlement sum}$$

where: A = the difference, expressed in all cases as a positive number in decimal form to five decimal places, between the numerical value of the forward spread and the numerical value of the settlement spread.

D = the actual number of days elapsed from (and including) the settlement date to (but excluding) the maturity date.

For an FSA with a settlement date of 18 November 19X7 and a maturity date of 18 February 19X7 (92 days) and a notional principal sum of US$25m, where the forward spread is −195bps (or −1.95%) and the settlement spread is −1.53125%, the settlement sum (payable by the seller to the buyer) would be as follows:

Exhibit 4.4—continued

$$\frac{0.41875 \times}{100} \frac{92}{360} \times 25{,}000{,}000 = \text{US}\$26{,}753.47$$

Source: Introduction to Forward Spread Agreements (December 1986, Fulton Prebon Capital Markets in conjunction with the Hong Kong and Shanghai Banking Corporation).

Chapter 5

Caps, Floors and Collars

CAPS, FLOORS AND COLLARS

Caps, floors and collars are all different types of usually long-dated option transactions designed to hedge interest rate exposure.

Caps

An interest rate cap is an agreement between the seller or provider of the cap and a borrower to limit the borrower's floating interest rate to a specified level for a period of time.

The borrower selects a reference rate to hedge (for example, A\$ BBR or US\$ LIBOR), a period of time to hedge (for example, 12 months, two years, five years, ten years), and the level of protection desired (for example, 10.00%, 11.50%, 12.00%). The seller or provider of the cap, for a fee, assures the buyer that its reference rate will not exceed the specified ceiling rate during the terms of the agreement. If market rates exceed the ceiling rate, the cap provider will make payments to the buyer sufficient to bring its rate back to the ceiling. When market rates are below the ceiling, no payments are made, and the borrower pays market rates. The buyer of a cap therefore enjoys a fixed rate when market rates are above the cap and floating rates when market rates are below the cap.

Floors

An interest rate floor is similar to an interest rate cap agreement. An interest rate floor agreement is an agreement between the seller or provider of the floor and an investor which guarantees that the investor's floating rate of return on investments will not fall below a specified level over an agreed period of time.

The investor selects a reference rate to hedge, the period of time to hedge, and the level of protection desired. If market rates fall below the floor rate, the floor provider will make payments to the buyer sufficient to bring its rate back up to the agreed floor. When market rates are above the floor, no payments are made, and the investor enjoys market rates of return.

Collars

An interest rate collar is a variation on the ceiling rate or cap agreement. The seller or provider of the collar agrees to limit the borrower's floating interest rate to a band limited by a specified ceiling rate and floor rate.

The borrower selects a reference rate to hedge (for example, BBR or LIBOR), a period of time to hedge (for example, 12 months, five years, ten years), and the level of protection desired (for example, 8.25-10.25%, 8.00-11.00%). The seller or provider of the collar, for a fee, assures the

borrower that its reference rate will not exceed the specified ceiling rate
nor be less than the specified floor rate during the term of the agreement.
If market rates exceed the ceiling rate, the collar provider will make payments
to the buyer sufficient to bring its rate back to the ceiling. If market rates
fall below the floor, the borrower makes payments to the collar provider
to bring its rate back to the floor. When market rates are between the floor
and the ceiling, the borrower pays the market rate. The buyer of a collar,
therefore has its borrowing rate confined to a band or collar, ranging from
the floor to the ceiling, as shown below.

Settlement Mechanics

At the end of each settlement period (for example, monthly, quarterly,
semi-annually etc. as agreed depending on the type of index) during the
term of a cap agreement, the market rate is compared to the ceiling rate.
If the market rate is higher than the ceiling rate, the borrower will receive
a cash payment equal to the difference between the market rate and the
ceiling rate multiplied by the principal amount of the hedge. For example,
suppose a borrower had a $10m three month LIBOR cap at 10.00% for
two years. During a quarter when LIBOR is 12.00%, it will receive a payment
of $50,556*.

The market rate can be determined on a spot or average basis; that is,
the spot rate on the first day of the period or the daily average during
the period. The choice is usually made to match the nature of the underlying
debt obligation being hedged. Sometimes longer or shorter settlement periods
are chosen than are usually associated with the instrument being hedged
(for example, annual settlement for three month LIBOR).

The settlement mechanics for floors and collars are similar.

EXAMPLE OF A CAP TRANSACTION

An intermediary agrees to provide a customer with an interest rate cap
for an exposure of A$1m (face value borrowing) it has on a floating rate
basis at 10.00% for 12 months, based upon four 90 day rolls or interest
rate periods at 10.00%.

Maturity dates	Cap rate	Spot rates on maturity dates	Net-off effect to the company A$
3 September 19X8[1]	10	11	2,342.87[1]
3 December 19X8	10	8	—
4 March 19X8	10	7	—
4 June 19X8	10	12	4,674.52
Amount due to customer			7,017.39
Effective borrowing cost			9.04% pa

* ($10m × 2.00% × $\frac{91}{360}$).

Notes:

1. Net-off on 3 September 1984 =

$$\frac{1,000,000}{1 + \left\{ 0.11 \times \dfrac{90}{365} \right\}} - \frac{1,000,000}{1 + \left\{ 0.10 \times \dfrac{90}{365} \right\}}$$

$$= A\$973,592.96 - A\$975,935.83 = A\ \$2,342.87$$

THE RATIONALE FOR CAPS, COLLARS AND FLOORS

Caps provide protection against rising interest rates without fixing rates. With its hedge in place, the buyer continues to borrow at the short-term end of the yield curve. When the yield curve is upward sloping, borrowing short-term results in considerable cost savings compared to fixed rate alternatives such as bonds or interest rate swaps, which are priced off the term yield curve.

Locking in a fixed rate in a positive yield curve environment results in an immediate increase in interest cost. The per annum cost of a cap may be much less than this immediate increment. The fixed rate borrower has no additional risk if rates rise, but enjoys no benefit if rates decline. If rates rise only moderately, or decline, the short-term borrower with a cap will tend to achieve substantial savings without unlimited risk.

Buyers of cap agreements generally pay an upfront fee determined by the cap level, the maturity of the agreement, the instrument being hedged and market conditions (see below for a discussion on how caps are priced). Cap providers will take the fee either up front or in instalments. The front end fees will depend upon how close to current rates the cap is set and the volatility of the index.

Collars provide protection against rising interest rates without fixing rates. They can be thought of as "interest rate swaps with a band". As in the case of cap only agreements, buyers of collars continue to borrow at the short-term end of the yield curve and therefore may enjoy substantial cost savings compared to fixed rate alternatives, with only moderate upside risk. Collars are generally priced so that the all-in cost pa of borrowing at the cap rate will be somewhat more than fixed rate alternatives, while the all-in cost at the floor will be considerably less than fixed-rate alternatives. The trade-off of the cost saving to the upside risk may be as much as five to one.

The chief disadvantage of collars versus cap only agreements is that they limit the possibility of profit from a decline in rates below the floor. Obviously, interest rate expectations drive potential users toward or away from collars. Because collars are two-way agreements, they entail credit considerations similar to interest rate swaps. In fact, collars are sometimes used as a complement to, or substitute for, swaps.

As in the case of cap only agreements, buyers generally pay an upfront fee determined by the ceiling and floor level, the maturity of the agreement, the instrument being hedged and market conditions. Fees for collars are lower than for ceiling only agreements with the cap at the same level. This is because the floor has value to the provider, which is passed on to the buyer in the form of a lower front end fee. The fee depends upon how close to current rates the cap rate and floor rate are set.

The growth of these markets reflects largely the corresponding growth in the market for debt options generally, including those traded on exchanges. Caps, floors and collars represent customised options similar in a number of respects to the debt options traded on exchange rates on the relevant indexes.

Consequently, it is possible to utilise options on the relevant index traded on a futures or options exchange to replicate a cap, floor or collar agreement. The major difficulty in utilising these exchanges include:

- Exchange traded options on floating rate indexes rarely trade out for more than two years. Some contracts are limited to nine months or a year. In practice, trading depth may not be present except in the nearest months. This restricts the construction of long-term hedges which would require the hedger to rollover contracts incurring the risk of changes in rate levels and volatility as well as basis changes.

- Options, like futures contracts, are standardised and do not allow participants interested in matching dates and structures to fully match their required dates on their underlying debt obligations with the option transaction.

- There are mechanical problems involving the posting of deposits and possible margin calls on option transactions on exchanges which adds to the cost and difficulty of administration of the use of these exchange traded options.

The major advantage of exchange traded options and of utilising these instruments for hedging purposes is that they do not require the purchaser to incur the credit risk of the seller of the option.

In practice, the existence of exchange traded options undoubtedly provides the basis for the development of the market in customised caps, floors and collars as they essentially provide a mechanism by which financial intermediaries willing to enter the market as direct sellers of these customised option products hedge their own exposures.

Caps and collars are still in their infancy in corporate finance. However, it is evident that these instruments are potentially of use to any entity with an interest rate exposure which they are seeking to hedge. In this regard, these types of transactions complement other hedging transactions such as interest rate swaps and FRAs etc.

PREMIUM DYNAMICS OF CAPS, FLOORS AND COLLARS

Interest rate caps can be thought of as similar to a string of put options. The writer of the option (seller of the cap) determines a premium (fee) for the option desired based on the time remaining to the expiration of the option, the current market interest rate of the instrument being hedged, and the strike price (ceiling or cap rate). As with options, the further "out-of-the-money" the strike price is, the higher the cap is, and/or the shorter the time to expiration is, the lower the premium is.

Floors can be thought of as similar to call options. In effect in a collar agreement, a series of call options is being sold back to the provider of the cap, which reduces the premium, thus floor ceiling premiums are lower than agreements.

Providers of customised caps can price caps at almost any level. The problem for the prospective user is where to set the ceiling: tight, loose or in between. Clearly, the tighter the cap (the closer to current floating rates), the higher the fee will be and vice versa.

Borrowers using caps or collars as a substitute for fixed rate debt who are only willing to accept limited upside risk in return for cost savings if rates are stable or fall, will set their ceilings relatively close to current rates, say 100 to 150 basis points above them. The fee will be relatively high but the overall economics may be attractive. Other borrowers are more interested in "disaster insurance" that is protection against violent rate changes for a low front end fee. Such caps may be 300 to 400 basis points or more over current rates.

Because fees for caps tend to be priced in reference to options pricing theory, fees do not decrease proportionately as ceiling levels are raised. The relationship between premiums and strike prices are non-linear; for example, the premium on a put option does not decline proportionately as the strike price is raised out of the money. Therefore, the hedger does not get an equal amount of protection for its money when paying a low fee for a high cap compared to paying a high fee for a tight cap. This is a factor to keep in mind, although it may not necessarily influence the final decision, which will depend upon how much risk it is willing to bear and how much it is willing to pay for protection. The pricing of caps etc., is discussed in detail in Chapter 11.

Exhibit 5.1
Interest Rate Cap—Premium Dynamics Example

Ceiling*	Upfront fee for 3 years	Per annum cost of fee (discounted at 10.00%)	All-in borrowing cost at ceiling
8.875%	4.90%	1.97%	10.85%
9.375% (+ 0.50)	3.50%	1.45% (−0.50)	10.85%
9.875% (+ 0.50)	3.60%	1.17% (−0.28)	11.05%
10.375% (+ 0.50)	2.50%	1.00% (−0.17)	11.39%
10.875% (+ 0.50)	2.10%	0.84% (−0.16)	11.72%
11.375% (+ 0.50)	1.80%	0.72% (−0.12)	12.10%
11.875% (+ 0.50)	1.50%	0.60% (−0.12)	12.48%

*LIBOR = 7.875%

Exhibit 5.1 sets out what the total all-in cost of borrowing would be at various ceiling levels (based on three year caps on three month LIBOR when LIBOR was 7.875%). As the cap level is raised by successive 0.50% increments, the fee is decreased by smaller and smaller amounts, and, in the worst case, all-in borrowing cost at the ceiling increases.

Exhibit 5.2 sets out some sample premiums for caps and collars.

Exhibit 5.2

Sample Premiums for Caps and Collars on Three Month LIBOR

	1 year	2 years	3 years	5 years	10 years
Collars					
+ 100/0	0.5	2.4	4.2	7.6	13.5
+ 150/0	—	1.7	3.3	6.2	11.3
+ 200/0	—	1.0	2.4	4.8	9.1
Caps					
+ 100	1.0	3.6	6.0	10.4	19.4
+ 150	0.8	2.7	4.8	8.5	16.4
+ 200	0.5	1.9	3.6	6.7	13.5
+ 250	—	1.5	2.5	4.8	10.5
+ 300	—	1.2	2.1	3.7	7.6

Notes:
1. "+100/0" means a cap level of 100bps above the current spot level of three month LIBOR and a floor at the current spot.
2. "+150" means a cap only agreement with a cap level of 150bps above the current spot level of three month LIBOR.

Economics and Pricing of Swaps

Chapter 6

Economics and Pricing of Swaps: Overview

INTRODUCTION

The economics and pricing of swap transactions are central to the process of structuring, negotiating and completing such transactions. With the recent growth of the swap market, price indications for both interest rate and currency swaps in a wide variety of currencies are readily available. This increasing availability of swap prices is not matched by an equal level of understanding of key aspects of swap economics and the determinants of price for such instruments.

For example, US$ interest rate swap spreads (US$ interest rate swaps, as discussed later, are priced as margins or spreads relative to a United States Treasury bond of comparable maturity) have fluctuated significantly in the last 18 to 24 months. Similarly, in other markets, such as the yen, £ and A$, similar volatility, relative to interest rate bases, is observable. A wide variety of other discrepancies between various swap markets are also capable of being identified. For example, in NZ$ the swap prices are traditionally *below* the level for the comparable government bond. In contrast, in £, the swap spreads have moved erratically between levels above and below the £ gilt curve.

There is a widespread tendency to attribute such pricing behaviour to the relative "supply and demand conditions" in the particular market. While it is inevitably true that changes in supply and demand impact upon the pricing of such instruments, it is a truism to nominate the essential clearing mechanism, that is, the adjustment of supply or demand at a particular price level, as the cause or determinant rather than the eventual effect in the pricing of such transactions.

In seeking a clearer understanding of the economics and pricing of swaps, it is necessary to distinguish between a number of key issues:

- the economics of swaps versus pricing/yield mathematics;
- the pricing of swaps versus the pricing of swap derivatives such as LTFX, FRAs, and caps, collars etc.;
- the inter-relationships in the pricing of the various types of instruments.

It is important to distinguish between the economics of swap and related transactions and the pricing/yield mathematics of such transactions. The distinction lies in the fact that swap economics emphasises the basic parameters which form the pricing framework of swap transactions while pricing/yield mathematics emphasises the arithmetical procedures, such as the IRR or net present value concepts. The arithmetical and technical steps utilised in pricing/yield mathematics associated with swap transactions indeed are common to all financial transactions and are not peculiar to swaps. The specific yield mathematics of interest rate and currency swaps are considered in detail in Chapter 8.

While it is useful to talk generically of swap pricing, in practice it is necessary to price individual types of instrument. As discussed below, while the pricing of interest rate and currency swaps is largely dictated by capital market arbitrage factors, in contrast, a number of specific theoretical pricing mechanisms are utilised for pricing swap derivatives such as LTFX, FRAs and Caps, Collars etc. The specific pricing methodologies applicable to individual types of transactions are considered in Chapters 9, 10 and 11. In this chapter, the complex pricing inter-relationships are examined.

SWAP ECONOMICS AND PRICING INTER-RELATIONSHIPS

The economics of swap transactions vary significantly as between individual instruments although, as noted above, there are significant inter-relationships between the various transactions and consequently in the pricing between individual market segments.

It is useful to differentiate pricing mechanics as between the following categories of transactions:

- parallel or back-to-back loans;
- interest rate and currency swaps/LTFX;
- FRAs;
- caps, floors and collars.

Each of these transactions are usually priced on different bases. The parallel or back-to-back loan transactions are usually priced with reference to blocked fund situations or environments in which foreign exchange controls prevent the free movement of capital across national borders.

For example, the early parallel loans and back-to-back loan transactions arose out of the situation created both by exchange controls in the 1970s which prevented United Kingdom entities buying US$ on the spot basis and by the shortage of fixed rate £ funding for the United Kingdom subsidiaries of United States companies. Pricing of these transactions was curiously devoid of any relationship to United States or United Kingdom government bond rates. Instead, the economics of these transactions responded freely to supply and demand factors in the market. The use of these types of transactions in more recent times, usually in response to foreign exchange controls in less developed countries, has been undertaken on a purely negotiated basis as between the counterparties with the pricing/economics responding to supply and demand factors.

In contrast, the market for swaps and LTFXs is highly responsive to arbitrage between various segments of the capital market.

These transactions provide for the extension of the theory of comparative advantage from the commodity and service markets to financial and capital markets enabling institutions to borrow in markets where it enjoys a relative comparative advantage then exchanging the funds raised for funds denominated in the desired currency and/or interest rate basis through the swap transactions. In this regard, swaps are similar to parallel or back-to-back loans in that they effectively entail a "barter" transaction between counterparties trading advantages or benefits such as availability of funds and/or after tax cost.

In addition, interest rates and currency swaps must, by definition, bear a strong relationship to the forward market price for the relevant underlying commodity, namely forward interest rates or forward exchange rates. This is wholly consistent with the characterisation of interest rate and currency swaps as portfolios of interest rate and currency forward contracts.

LTFX transactions (which as discussed above can be equated to zero coupon currency swaps) provide a further level of linkage between swap transactions and money and foreign exchange markets as LTFX pricing will generally reflect current interest rates and interest differentials between currencies.

The economics of FRAs and caps and collar transactions do not directly derive from capital market arbitrage. FRA pricing usually derives from forward-forward interest rates evident in the yield curve at any particular point in time which can be replicated by cash market transactions or in the rates implied in the purchase or sale of interest rate futures contracts.

Caps and collars represent option transactions which are priced utilising option pricing theories or models whereby premiums are related to a number of factors including, in particular, the time remaining to the expiration of the option, the current rate of the instrument being hedged, the strike price (the cap or floor rate) and its relationship to the current rate, and future expectations as to the distribution and volatility of interest rates.

Although the economics of the various types of transactions are predicated, primarily on different pricing bases, a number of close inter-relationships exist between the pricing of the different instruments (see *Exhibit 6.1*). These pricing relationships are totally consistent with and are implied by the structural inter-relationships between the various instruments outlined in Chapter 2 (refer *Exhibit 2.2*).

The pricing inter-relationship between parallel or back-to-back loans with other transactions is relatively weak. However, back-to-back loans are, functionally, extremely similar to currency swaps and consequently the pricing between these two types of transactions is closely related, at least, where a blocked fund situation is not involved.

Interest rate swaps and currency swaps are closely related in a pricing or economics sense to the other types of transactions identified. For example, an LTFX transaction is functionally identical to a fixed-to-fixed currency swap and the pricing between these two transactions must be, in theory, and indeed is, in practice, closely related.

Similarly, the pricing of an interest rate swap in a particular currency is closely related to the pricing on FRAs and caps and collars in the same currency. This relationship exists because interest rate swap transactions can effectively be replicated through a series of FRA transactions coinciding with the maturity and term of the interest rate swap. Similarly, the interest rate swap is functionally identical to a collar transaction where the cap level is set at the fixed rate level on the swap with the floor level being maintained at an identical level.

FRAs in turn are related to cap and floor prices because a combination of caps and floors can be used to replicate both a bought or sold FRA. For example, a synthetic long forward or sold FRA can be created by buying a floor and selling a cap at the desired forward level. Similarly, a bought

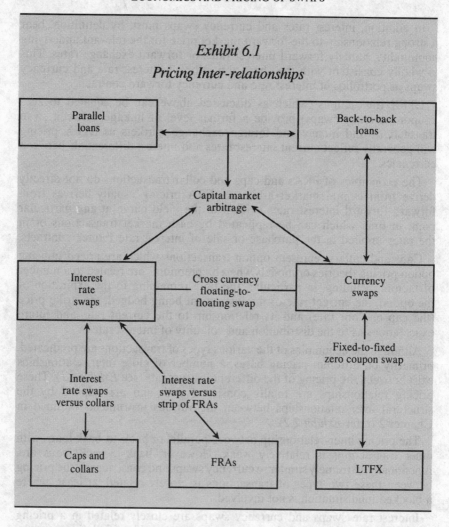

Exhibit 6.1
Pricing Inter-relationships

FRA or synthetic short forward position can be created by selling a floor and buying a put at the desired forward rate level.

The detailed pricing inter-relationship would operate in the following manner. Given yield curves in two currencies and a spot exchange rate between the currencies, it would be possible to derive theoretical prices for the full range of swap instruments. Given that swaps can be characterised as a portfolio of forward interest rate contracts, the existence of yield curves would allow the construction of interest rate swap prices in both currencies. This by implication would allow simultaneously the pricing of FRAs in the respective currencies as prices for these instruments would correspond to the forward interest rates evident in the yield curve. The availability of spot and forward interest rates could in turn form the basis of interest rate option prices for caps, collars etc., where the expected volatility of various interest rates could be supplied. Alternatively, given the capacity to characterise both interest rate swaps and FRAs as a portfolio of purchased and sold options, the prices for interest rate swaps and FRAs could be utilised as the basis for working back to option prices.

The availability of interest rates in both currencies and the spot exchange rate between the currencies would allow currency swap prices and LTFX prices also to be generated.

A striking feature of the pricing inter-relationship between the various instruments is that as forward interest rates and exchange rates are a critical component of the pricing calculation, the economics of such transactions are determined not by intermediaries or the swap market per se but rather by competition from other capital market instruments and rates and flows. These rates and flows are reflected in the yield curves and spot exchange rates which are the only information needed to determine the pricing of most swap instruments. Given that the swap is, at its simplest, a package of forward contracts, the forward rates reflected in the swap must conform to the implied forward rates in the prevailing yield curve as otherwise arbitrage will become profitable. Consequently, the process of financial arbitrage will ensure that the pricing inter-relationships described will inevitably be enforced.

The basic inter-relationships in terms of pricing and economics as outlined above may be disrupted in practice by a number of factors including: barriers to capital flow which effectively prevent replication of particular transactions in other markets and also differential treatment under accounting, taxation or regulatory standards.

In examining the pricing inter-relationships between the various types of transaction, it is important to recognise that, in practice, such transactions are often entered into, at least in the first place, by financial intermediaries rather than direct counterparties who are end users of the opposite leg of the trade. The financial intermediary enters into the transaction to provide liquidity in the relevant market, undertaking the transaction on a hedged basis in the expectation of eventually matching the transaction out with an end user or other counterpart. This requirement for temporary hedging usually means that swap transactions, of any kind, are often priced on the basis of the economics of the underlying hedge rather than the pure economics of the transaction. This type of hedge based pricing will, by definition, reflecting the choice of hedging instruments available, conform to the pricing economics described.

However, it is clear that the basic economics of each transaction cannot be violated for long periods without effectively inviting arbitrage which has the natural effect of restoring equilibrium pricing in the market. Consequently, while markets in these types of transactions may not always be in equilibrium, the basic economics dictate the framework within which the pricing of individual transactions must be effected.

The central role played by financial intermediaries in transactions involving these instruments, also facilitates the financial arbitrage which forces prices to their natural economic equilibrium. These financial intermediaries who are active in all the relevant capital market segments are ideally placed to take advantage of pricing discrepancies and to undertake transactions predicated on deviations from pricing equilibrium thereby forcing market prices towards their economic levels.

SWAP ECONOMICS AND MARKET EFFICIENCY

The fact that the swap market is predicated on the exploitation of certain arbitrage opportunities within capital markets has already been eluded to. It is useful at this point to briefly outline the meaning of the phrase "efficient markets" as it is used here and the concept of arbitrage.

An efficient market by definition is one in which prices are set at levels whereby the resources traded in the market are allocated equitably or efficiently among the participants. This highly artificial construct of economic theory requires the satisfaction of a wide range of conditions including:

- The costless availability of all relevant information to market participants.
- Highly efficient markets would, in addition, require that all participants agree on the implications of equally available information and its effect on the price of the resource or commodity being traded in the market. That is, the price import of the information would be unambiguous.
- The market structure would be such that the trading process would allow transmission of the impact of information into the price of the asset traded which implies the presence of many buyers and sellers.
- Efficient market theory requires that transaction costs, including market frictions such as taxes, regulation, or accounting impediments, are absent.

These conditions are, in practice, difficult to satisfy. The impact of taxation, regulation, and differences in these between national markets combined with differences in the perceived price impact of information, the perception of risk and the differential valuation of risk between capital markets or even segments of capital markets, create certain anomalies or inefficiencies which allow arbitrage transactions to take place.

Technically, arbitrage transactions are defined to mean one or more actions by market participants designed to exploit pricing inefficiencies or anomalies to earn profit from the inherent discrepancy in the pricing or valuation of assets as between markets. In its simplest form, arbitrage would involve the simultaneous purchase and sale of an identical asset in different markets. Where identical assets are employed in the process of arbitrage, the transaction involves no risk. However, in practise, the type of arbitrage described here entails the simultaneous purchase and sale of similar, although not identical, financial assets.

In pure arbitrage, profits are possible because of inefficiencies or differences in alternative markets for essentially the same asset. In the less restrictive form of arbitrage being considered here, profits are possible because of relative inefficiencies or differences in the pricing of *comparable* although not *identical* assets once adjustments are made for the relevant differences. That is, the transactions entail profit opportunities arising from anomalies among markets for assets that are close substitutes for each other.

By definition, arbitrage transactions operate to eliminate their own incentive. Undertaking arbitrage transactions will inevitably move prices to eradicate the initial profit opportunity. However, where the profit opportunity is implied by externally imposed action such as taxation or regulation, the mere act of seeking to take advantage of the arbitrage opportunity may not adjust market prices to eliminate the opportunity which will persist until the offending regulation etc., is eliminated.

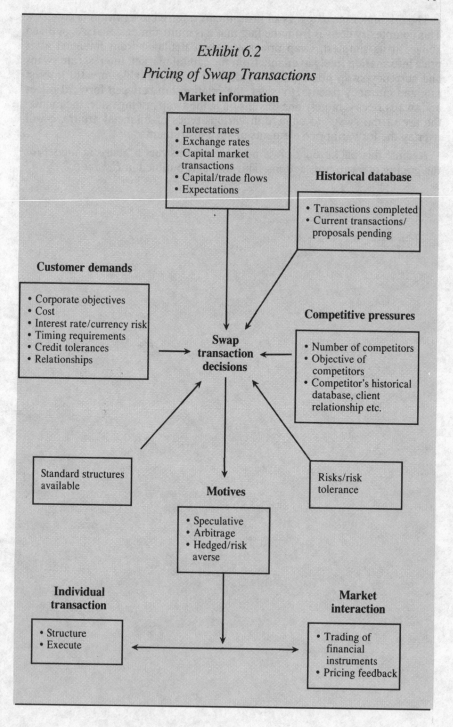

Exhibit 6.2
Pricing of Swap Transactions

Market information
- Interest rates
- Exchange rates
- Capital market transactions
- Capital/trade flows
- Expectations

Historical database
- Transactions completed
- Current transactions/ proposals pending

Customer demands
- Corporate objectives
- Cost
- Interest rate/currency risk
- Timing requirements
- Credit tolerances
- Relationships

Swap transaction decisions

Competitive pressures
- Number of competitors
- Objective of competitors
- Competitor's historical database, client relationship etc.

Standard structures available

Motives
- Speculative
- Arbitrage
- Hedged/risk averse

Risks/risk tolerance

Individual transaction
- Structure
- Execute

Market interaction
- Trading of financial instruments
- Pricing feedback

The pricing of the category of instruments referred to as swaps is complex. This complexity derives from the fact that it is multi-dimensional. As outlined above, at its simplest, swap prices may be calculated from financial asset price information freely available from the capital market. Interest rate swaps and currency swap pricings can be derived from available forward interest rate and currency prices. However, the relationship between forward prices and swap prices is merely one dimension in the swap pricing issue. In practise, the use of the swaps to engage in various types of financial arbitrage will overlay the forward price elements of such instruments.

Against this background, it is possible to construct a heuristic model for the pricing of swap transactions. This model is outlined in *Exhibit 6.2.*

Chapter 7

Economics and Pricing of Interest Rate and Currency Swaps

THE CONCEPTUAL FRAMEWORK

Popular literature on interest rate and currency swaps emphasises the ability of market participants to generate significant cost savings by combining an issue of securities with an interest rate or currency swap. The capacity to identify the source of this cost saving and a satisfying explanation of the underlying economics of such transactions is therefore essential to the pricing of swaps and also for a fundamental understanding of the market itself.

From a conceptual viewpoint, pricing of interest rate and currency swaps can be approached from two different viewpoints:

- analysing swaps as a series of forward prices;
- analysing swaps as a means for financial arbitrage.

As discussed in Chapter 6, forward interest rates and forward exchange rates are central to any interest rate and currency swap agreement respectively. It is clearly possible to characterise swap contracts as essentially a series of forward contracts which, in turn, implies that the forward rate embodied in a swap contract must correspond to the forward rates inherent in other corresponding financial instruments, primarily securities and futures contracts.

There are a number of problems with this particular approach. Attempting to price swaps on the basis of forward prices assumes the existence of the relevant forward price itself. For example, in the case of interest rate swaps, it assumes the existence of a continuous yield curve for securities of comparable characteristics, in particular, of comparable risk. In practise, such yield curves may not be available as in reality the swap may be predicated on the access or, conversely, lack of access to funding in a particular currency in a particular form. Similar considerations would apply in respect of currency swaps where the required forward exchange rates may not be available for particular market participants.

The problem of lack of availability of the relevant prices is merely symptomatic of the fact that the underlying process of arbitrage which would be required to force prices to their economic level is absent. The insufficiency of arbitrage for other than very short maturities reflects the fact that transaction costs and certain risks associated with arbitrage activity prevent the markets from operating at maximum optimal efficiency.

Transaction costs would include the bid/ask spread which in longer maturities may prevent efficient arbitrage. In a sense, the bid/ask spread is the demand for liquidity reflecting the cost of market making activities. The very wide spreads in longer maturities reflects the lack of liquidity in the market for instruments of that particular tenor. Other transaction costs include balance sheet holding costs and credit risk factors, some of which may be influenced by regulatory constraints, which once again add costs to the process of arbitrage and ultimately reduce the incentive to take advantage of price discrepancies.

An added problem in arbitrage over longer maturities is the fact that the instruments required to undertake this type of transaction would inevitably entail intermediate cash flows from holding of coupon securities which would require reinvestment. Uncertainty as to the reinvestment rate that may *actually* be achieved creates uncertainty as to the terminal cash value over the required holding period for securities which introduces an element of risk in the arbitrage transaction. This particular reinvestment problem is less acute in short-term arbitrage as generally discount instruments rather than coupon instruments are involved, eliminating any reinvestment risk.

However, even if the required forward prices were available, it is unlikely that the swap would conform to the market view of the forward price. This is because the existence of forward prices would imply that a market participant would be faced with two alternative means of achieving its objectives:

• a direct transaction to borrow funds in the relevant currency in the relevant form, that is, fixed or floating interest rates;
• an indirect transaction involving fund raising combined with an interest rate or currency swap to generate funding in the required currency and interest basis.

If swap prices were merely reflective of the forward rates which could be determined by competition from other credit market instruments, then there would be no direct cost incentive for the participant to utilise the swap as a means of obtaining its nominated objectives. There may be certain related advantages such as flexibility, particularly timing considerations, which would be difficult to quantify. These advantages of flexibility etc., may in fact also be offset by the additional credit risk assumed by the participant. This is because under the indirect option the organisation would have two levels of credit risk:

• the underlying securities transaction;
• the swap transaction.

This increased level of credit risk would impact upon the organisation's balance sheet as well as its available credit limits from banks and financial institutions. The funding transaction would be reflected on the balance sheet while the swap would be recorded as a contingent liability and both transactions would utilise credit lines available to the organisation. While the credit risk on swaps (see Chapter 30) does not equate to the notional principal amount of the swap, some credit limit utilisation would be entailed.

These problems with utilising forward prices in pricing swaps essentially mean that this price level operates as an upper bound to the pricing of interest rate and currency swaps at a given point in time. In essence, the swap price if it conforms to the forward price for either interest rates or currencies inevitably will represent an alternative means for an organisation to achieve its financing or risk management objectives which, however, does not provide any direct cost advantage.

The second approach to pricing interest rate and currency swaps is predicated on such transactions operating as a means of financial arbitrage across different capital markets. This approach implies that mutual cost savings are achievable primarily because prices in various world capital markets are not mutually consistent. Organisations can achieve lower borrowing costs by accessing particular markets with lower *relative* cost, borrowing there, and swapping their exposure, both interest rate and currency, back into their preferred form of funding, thereby achieving lower cost funding than that attainable from directly accessing the relevant markets. The basic sources of swap arbitrage include financial arbitrage, tax and regulatory arbitrage, as well as the existence of incomplete markets and the presence of transaction costs.

In summary, while from a conceptual viewpoint, it is possible to approach swap economics and pricing in terms of two different frameworks (namely, forward prices and financial arbitrage), in practice, to date, financial arbitrage has dominated swap pricing and economics. The main reason for this domination is the fact that financial arbitrage, unlike forward prices, creates a natural cost incentive for organisations to utilise swaps. If swaps were merely a means of replicating direct transactions with no cost advantage and, indeed, some level of additional cost, it is difficult to see the attraction of such transactions except for some qualitative benefits such as added flexibility.

In the remainder of this chapter, the detailed process of swap arbitrage is considered and the sources of swap arbitrage are detailed. The chapter concludes with a consideration of swap arbitrage and the A$ market to further develop an understanding of the process by which the price of such transactions evolves.

SWAP ARBITRAGE

Interest rate swap arbitrage

All swap transactions are predicated on the exchange by one party of a benefit which it enjoys in a particular market for a corresponding benefit available to another party in a different market. The basic economics of a swap transaction are best illustrated by example.

Assume that a major international bank (bank A) can issue fixed rate US$ debt for five years in the form of a Eurodollar bond issue at an interest cost of 10.50% pa; bank A pays LIBOR for its floating rate US$ funds for an equivalent maturity. Contrast that with a medium rated company (company B), which because of its lower credit standing, can only issue five year fixed rate US$ debt (if at all) at 12.00% pa; company B can, however, raise five year floating rate funds from banks at LIBOR plus 0.75% pa.

The difference between the cost of funds for bank A and company B is: 0.75% pa in floating rate terms and 1.50% pa in fixed rate terms.

5 year funding	Bank A	Company B	Interest cost differential
Floating rate	LIBOR	LIBOR + 0.75% pa	0.75% pa
Fixed rate	10.50% pa	12.00% pa (if available)	1.50% pa

This disparity between the fixed and floating rate markets provides the arbitrage which is the basis of all interest rate swaps. The discrepancy is exploited as set out in *Exhibit 7.1*. Each party borrows from the market in which they get the best relative term (bank A in the fixed rate market and company B in the floating rate market) and then exchange their interest obligations to convert into their preferred form of funding.

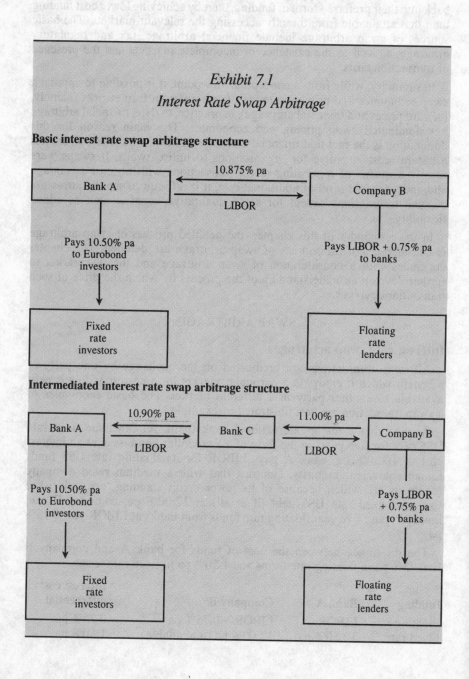

Exhibit 7.1

Interest Rate Swap Arbitrage

Basic interest rate swap arbitrage structure

Intermediated interest rate swap arbitrage structure

The net result of the transaction is as follows:

- bank A has raised floating rate US$ funds at LIBOR minus 0.375% pa, a saving of 0.375% pa;
- company B has raised fixed rate US$ fund at 11.625% pa, a saving of 0.375% pa.

Net costs	Bank A	Company B
Fixed rate outflow	10.50% pa	10.875% pa
Fixed rate inflow	10.875% pa	—
Floating rate outflow	LIBOR	LIBOR 0.75% pa
Floating rate inflow	—	LIBOR
Net cost	LIBOR −0.375% pa	11.625% pa
Alternative cost	LIBOR	12.000% pa
Saving	0.375% pa	0.375% pa

The split between counterparties is driven mainly on the basis of supply and demand and on the basis of the cost of alternative available funding which are directly related to the credit standing of each party.

In the above example, the arbitrage gains are split equally between the two parties. In addition, the transaction structure assumes no intermediation by a bank or financial institution. A more realistic transaction structure, involving intermediation, is depicted in the intermediated swap arbitrage structure illustrated in the second part of *Exhibit 7.1*.

A similar type of analysis can be utilised for currency swaps.

Currency swap arbitrage

Assume that a major multinational (company A) has access to five year fixed rate Swiss francs at 5.00% pa; company A also can raise five year fixed rate US$ at 10.75% pa. In contrast, a company well known in the US$ domestic market but relatively unknown in the Swiss market (company B) has access to five year fixed rate Swiss francs at 5.50% pa, and five year fixed rate US$ at 11.00% pa.

The discrepancy between the cost of funds clearly provides the basis of an arbitrage transaction:

5 year funding	Company A	Company B	Interest differential
Fixed rate SFR	5.00% pa	5.50% pa	0.50% pa
Fixed rate US$	10.75% pa	11.00% pa	0.25% pa

Where company A is interested in raising US$ and conversely company B is interested in raising Swiss francs, the discrepancy can be exploited as set out in *Exhibit 7.2*. Company A raises Swiss francs and company B raises US$ and they then exchange their principal and interest obligations to convert into their preferred form of funding.

Net costs	Company A	Company B
US$ fixed rate outflow	10.625% pa	11.000% pa
US$ fixed rate inflow	—	10.625% pa
SFR fixed rate outflow	5.000% pa	5.000% pa
SFR fixed rate inflow	5.000% pa	—
Net cost	10.625% pa	5.375% pa
Alternative cost	10.750% pa	5.500% pa
Saving	0.125% pa	0.125% pa

Swap arbitrage: the general methodology

The basic process of swap arbitrage can be generalised.[1] As noted above, all swap transactions are predicated on the exchange by one party of a benefit which it enjoys in a particular market for a corresponding benefit available to another party in a different market. The economics and structuring of this process are usually undertaken in a series of discreet steps:

- creating the cost/access matrix;
- determining the comparative advantage of the respective parties;
- structuring the swap;
- pricing the swap.

To facilitate the determination of swap arbitrages, it is initially necessary to construct a matrix of the relative cost and availability of access to certain markets of the different borrowers. Once this cost/access matrix is created, interest cost differentials as between the parties can be determined allowing identification of relative comparative advantage.

The process of identifying the relative comparative advantages as between the two parties entails calculation of the differential cost of access to different markets. Structuring the swap arbitrage requires that the market in which each party has a comparative advantage be identified. Once this is completed, the swap can be structured on the basis that each party borrows in the market in which they enjoy a comparative advantage and the swap is structured to exchange their interest obligations to convert their liabilities into their preferred form of funding.

The pricing of the swap operates within the swap structure implied by the comparative advantage analysis. As the market in which each party will borrow is now known, it remains to calculate the swap price itself. The swap is calculated in two distinct parts:

- the maximum swap price for each party is determined;
- the arbitrage gain is split as between the parties.

Determining the outer limits of swap prices from both partys' perspectives requires the identification of the cost of direct access into the preferred form of funding. For example, utilising the data in our interest rate swap

1. For an algebraic generalisation, see Turnbull (1987).

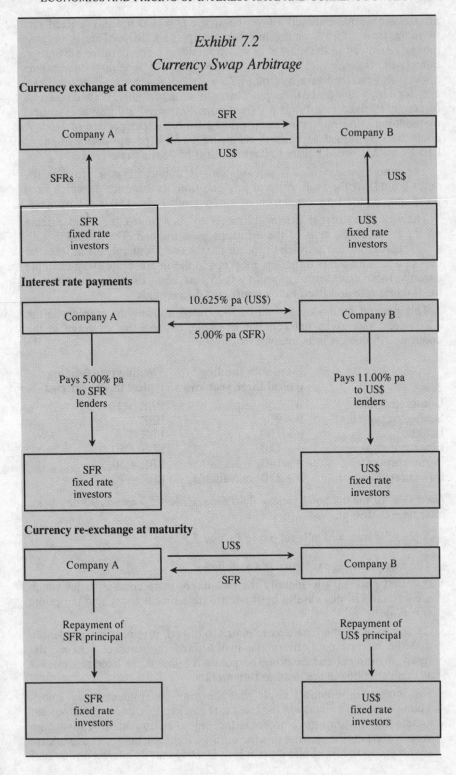

Exhibit 7.2
Currency Swap Arbitrage

Currency exchange at commencement

Company A — SFR → Company B
Company A ← US$ — Company B

SFRs ↑ Company A

US$ ↑ Company B

SFR fixed rate investors

US$ fixed rate investors

Interest rate payments

Company A — 10.625% pa (US$) → Company B
Company A ← 5.00% pa (SFR) — Company B

Pays 5.00% pa to SFR lenders

Pays 11.00% pa to US$ lenders

SFR fixed rate investors

US$ fixed rate investors

Currency re-exchange at maturity

Company A — US$ → Company B
Company A ← SFR — Company B

Repayment of SFR principal

Repayment of US$ principal

SFR fixed rate investors

US$ fixed rate investors

arbitrage example outlined above, company B would not pay a fixed rate of more than 11.25% pa against the receipt of LIBOR. This is because having borrowed in the market in which it enjoys a comparative advantage, namely the floating rate market at LIBOR plus 0.75% pa, and undertaking a swap as described at a rate of 11.25% would give it an all-in fixed rate cost for five years of 12.00% pa. This, not coincidentally, is its direct cost of access to fixed rate funds for five years. Similarly, utilising an identical methodology, the minimum swap pricing from the perspective of bank A could be determined as bank A receiving 10.50% pa against payment of LIBOR as this would equate to its direct cost of floating rate funds.

The determination of this pricing limit is important as it provides the outer bounds of the swap price at any one time as the price at which each party can create its preferred form of funding indirectly at no cost advantage.

The next part of the pricing phase is to then adjust the swap pricing on the basis of the split of the arbitrage gain implied. The arbitrage gain available for division between the parties to the swap is merely the differential cost of access to the two funding markets. In the interest rate swap example described above, the arbitrage profit is 0.75% pa, being the difference between the floating rate and fixed rate interest cost differentials.

This general methodology can be illustrated utilising an example in the A$ interest rate swap market. For example, assume the arbitrage in the domestic A$ market is as follows:

	Fixed rate funding typical three year cost	Floating rate funding typical three year cost
Commonwealth	B	BBR − 10
Semi-governments	B + 90	BBR
Banks	B + 100	BBR
Finance company	B + 140	BBR + 50
Prime corporate	B + 140	BBR + 20
Lower rated corporate	B + 250/unavailable	BBR + 70

Note: B + 40 means bond yield + 0.40% pa; BBR + 50 means 90 day bank bill rate + 0.50% pa.

A possible transaction is set out in *Exhibit 7.3*.

The swap arbitrage is structured as follows:

• It is first necessary to identify the two likely swap counterparties which are assumed in this case to be the semi-government entity and the prime corporate.

• On the basis of the cost/access matrix outlined, it is possible to identify that the interest cost differential in the fixed rate market between the semi-government and the prime corporate is 50bps in the fixed rate market as against 20bps in the floating rate market.

• The interest differentials imply that the semi-government entity enjoys a comparative advantage in the fixed rate market. It is, however, important to note that the semi-government in fact enjoys an *absolute* cost advantage in both markets. Suggesting that the semi-government enjoys a *comparative* advantage in the fixed rate market is to identify that its interest differential

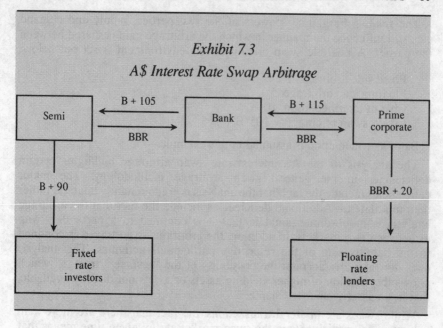

Exhibit 7.3
A$ Interest Rate Swap Arbitrage

in the fixed rate market is greater than its interest differential in the floating rate market. In this bilateral arrangement, by implication, the prime corporate enjoys a *comparative* advantage in the floating rate market which is to say that, relatively speaking, its absolute cost disadvantage is *least* in the floating rate market.

- Given the comparative cost structure, it is possible to structure the swap on the basis that the semi-government would borrow in the fixed rate funding market (the market in which it enjoys a comparative advantage) and the prime corporate would borrow in the floating rate funding market (the market in which it enjoys a comparative advantage). A swap would then be arranged whereby the semi-government would receive fixed rate and pay floating rate while the prime corporate would undertake the reverse.

- As noted above, the outer bound on the swap pricing is the level at which the two counterparties would be indifferent as to entering into the swap, that is, the swap price combined with the underlying funding equates to the cost of direct access to the respective markets. In this case, the outer bounds of the swap pricing are as follows:

  —semi-government would receive fixed rate at no lower than B + 90 and this would generate floating rate funding at its direct cost of BBR;

  —prime corporate would not pay at a rate higher than B + 120 which equates to its direct cost of fixed rate funding.

- Within this outer bounds, the arbitrage gain of 30bps will be apportioned. This 30bps is the difference between the interest differential in the fixed rate funding market (50bps) and the differential in the floating rate market (20bps).

The relative bargaining powers of the two parties, supply and demand etc., will influence the manner in which the arbitrage gain is shared between the parties. A possible swap pricing in this environment is set out below:

Fixed side arbitrage: 15
Floating side arbitrage: 5
Cost of intermediation: 10
Likely swap pricing: B + 105/B + 115

Bank intermediation is assumed in this example.

The analysis of the A$ interest rate swap arbitrage highlights certain deficiencies in the general swap arbitrage methodology. The major deficiencies include the fact that the analysis is predominantly bilateral rather than multilateral. Additional deficiencies include the fact that the arbitrage analysis is mono-dimensional in that it is confined to a particular swap as between two markets. In addition, the arbitrage as portrayed is confined to the liability side of the respective participants activities. The analysis does not take into account the possibility of the "reverse arbitrage" which allows the creation of higher yielding assets or assets not directly available, that is, an asset swap (see Chapter 18).

While swaps are bilateral transactions, the fact that there are more than two potential participants in the swap market at any given time means that the bilateral mode of analysis has a number of shortcomings. In practise, swap markets gravitate to an arbitrage driven by the two most likely participants at a given point in time. The most likely participants in swap transactions at a given time are determined by a wide range of factors including:

• the attractiveness in absolute terms of the swap arbitrage;
• the asset liability management requirements of both counterparties which may be driven by fundamental business considerations as well as interest rate and currency expectations;
• credit criteria which may limit the capacity of potential swap participants for transacting either directly or through a bank intermediary. In the latter case, the cost of intermediation essentially outweighs the benefits of the swap arbitrage;
• the investment objectives of fixed rate and floating rate investors across a wide range of currencies and their tolerance for particular credit risks as well as the state of their portfolios at a given point in time.

The major implications of a multilateral market is that the exploitation of the swap arbitrage inevitably means some change in the underlying cost/access matrix. This in a sense leads to a self-perpetuating series of evolving swap arbitrages. In essence, the swap arbitrage persists but in an ever changing form.

The second level of deficiency relates to the fact that each participant in the swap market may have options beyond those capable of being captured within the swap arbitrage methodology outlined. For example, in our A$ interest rate swap example, the semi-government entity may not find a swap where it receives B + 105bps to generate BBR—15bps attractive if it could issue US$ on a fixed rate basis and swap it first into floating rate US$

LIBOR and thence into floating rate A$ BBR at a superior rate to that achievable in the domestic A$ interest rate swap market. Consequently, while swap arbitrage methodology may give indicative pricing within the context defined, the presence of other opportunities for funding arbitrages will to some extent determine the willingness of particular participants to transact at the levels implied.

The analysis also does not recognise the capacity for other market participants to enter into reverse arbitrages creating higher yielding assets. This can be illustrated in our A$ interest rate swap example. Assume that a financial institution, for example, a State bank owned and guaranteed by the State and thereby a comparable creditor to a semi-government entity, is the intermediating bank. It is quoting a swap price of B + 105/B + 115. This would allow an investor seeking semi-government assets to buy floating rate securities yielding BBR and swap them into fixed rate A$ assets B + 105 by entering into a swap with the State bank whereby it would pay BBR and receive B + 105bps.

Provided the additional credit risk in respect of the swap is less than 15bps pa, the investor could create a higher yielding asset than that directly available in the form of fixed rate securities issued by the semi-government. This reverse arbitrage would impinge on the primary arbitrage process as essentially it would create demand for semi-government floating rate assets but decrease demand for fixed rate securities issued by semi-governments. Moreover, it would also have the effect of changing the swap pricing whereby the State bank would gradually decrease the rate it is willing to pay from B + 105 to lower levels thereby squeezing out the arbitrage for the semi-government.

This complex process of interaction is evident from the analysis of some of the deficiencies of the basic swap arbitrage methodology. Some of these interactions are examined in greater detail in the section on swap arbitrages in the A$ market later in this chapter.

The method of analysis indentified may, a number of comentators have argued, be fundamentally flawed. Turnbull (1987) argues that the type of simple comparison is misleading as a simple comparison of interest rates is insufficient if financial instruments differ in design and risk.[2] Theoretically, this proposition must be correct. However, if the financial instruments are identical (which is the implicit assumption in the method of analysis outlined) it is not clear why a simple comparison is *not* sufficient.

Turnbull (1987) introduces the concept of present value into the analysis respecifying the swap arbitrage condition as the present value of its inflows being not less than the present value of the outflows. The introduction of present value is not necessarily helpful as it requires assumptions to be made either about the absolute level of future short-term interest rates or a stochastic process by which future interest rates are generated.

In essence, the borrower must, by definition, determine whether or not it requires a fixed or floating rate liability or the currency of such a liability.

---

2. Turnbull (1987) gives the example of a comparison of issue of *callable* fixed rate debt against the issue of *non-callable* floating rate debt which is then swapped into fixed rate. The swap is, of course, inherently non-callable, although reversible at market rates.

That decision is totally separate from the swap arbitrage analysis, being governed by factors such as interest and currency rate expectations, asset liability matching requirements etc. Swap arbitrage merely assists in creating the required liability.

The more relevant problem with this methodology may be the fact that it does not incorporate the credit exposure entailed in the swap itself. If a borrower utilises a swap to create a synthetic liability, it incurs credit exposures under both the borrowing and the swap thereby utilising a scarce resource, namely access to credit. While this additional credit exposure is *not* encompassed by the methodology outlined, the oversight is inconsequential insofar as the presence of this additional risk merely dictates that there must be sufficient cost benefits in the swap to offset the credit exposure entailed. In particular it serves to highlight that while swaps can be priced as a series of forward contracts if the market traded swaps at that price there would be limited incentives for the existence of a viable swap market.

SOURCES OF SWAP ARBITRAGE

Swap arbitrage sources: a classification

Swap arbitrage methodology is predicated on the relative comparative advantages of various participants in the capital market to different sources of funding. The methodology itself is silent as to the underlying source of the comparative advantage. The theme common to all types of swaps is that they involve trading an advantage which a borrower or investor enjoys in one market for an equivalent advantage available to another company in a different market. This advantage, which drives the underlying economics, lies in one of two areas:

- post-tax cost;
- availability or access.

This principle applies equally to all types of swaps, including interest rate swaps and currency swaps. Application of this theme allows asset and liability managers to separate decisions on the market in which to invest or borrow from and decisions on the currency and interest rate basis of the investment or borrowing. In essence, the underlying swap arbitrage enables companies and investors to separate the source of liquidity from the management or the nature of the underlying asset or liability which is ultimately created.

The sources of the swap arbitrage are capable of classification into at least three separate categories:

- financial arbitrage;
- tax and regulatory arbitrage;
- miscellaneous arbitrages.

Financial arbitrage

Financial arbitrage in its purest form involves exploiting mutually inconsistent prices for securities of identical structural and issuer credit criteria in various world capital markets. The process of financial arbitrage as it applies to swap transactions entails a series of different types of arbitrage including:

- credit arbitrage (including the effect of name arbitrage and credit margin compression);
- supply and demand factors (including market segmentation, market saturation and diversification issues, sluggish communication and inadequate market liquidity etc.).

Credit arbitrage

Credit arbitrage refers to a market anomaly which is predicated on differences in risk premium requirements across capital markets or alternatively, between different segments of a particular capital market. Credit arbitrage is made possible by an *intra* or *intermarket* dissimilarity in the assessment of credit risk and the resultant discrepancies of risk premium. The examples outlined above of interest rate and currency swap arbitrage all rely to some extent on credit arbitrage.

The difference in risk pricing reflects a number of different factors operating in the respective markets or market segments.

In the case of *intramarket* credit arbitrage, such as the US\$ and A\$ interest rate swap arbitrages described above, a major factor in the differential risk pricing is the fact that the suppliers of funds are different as between the fixed and floating rate markets. The predominant suppliers of floating rate finance are banks and financial institutions. In contrast, the suppliers of fixed rate funding are direct rather than intermediated lenders, such as institutional and retail investors. The different lending groups have different capacities to assess and assume credit risk.

It is arguable that banks and financial institutions have a comparative advantage in credit risk assessment. These organisations operate sophisticated credit analysis systems and are able to analyse and accurately assess the credit risk of all borrowers. In particular, this allows them to assume credit risk in respect of lower rated borrowers more readily than direct investors.

This comparative advantage in credit risk assessment enjoyed by banks and financial institutions is certainly true in respect of retail investors who are ill-equipped to assess complex or difficult business organisations. However, capital markets have undergone significant changes in recent years with a marked institutionalisation of investment which has seen the concentration of investment decisions in professional money managers who could easily perform the evaluation of credit and investment opportunities which traditionally have been functions in which the banks have enjoyed an advantage. Consequently, while comparative capacities for credit risk assessment may explain the differential in risk pricing as between banks, financial institutions and retail investors, the argument is less compelling in respect of institutional investors.

Banks also enjoy the capacity to diversify their risk as between different borrowers, in terms of industry, geographic location etc. This allows banks to price risk premiums more competitively on a portfolio basis than investors. Again, while the diversification argument has considerable explanatory power in respect of retail investor pricing of risk, the capacity of large institutional fund managers to achieve diversification at a level comparable to that of banks and financial institutions means that the diversification argument does not fully explain the differential risk premiums as between banks and institutional investors.

The discrepancy in risk premiums between the public and bank markets, particularly in respect of institutional investors, is more probably capable of explanation in terms of the modern finance constructs of agency and contracting costs.[3] Under this approach, it can be argued that banks and other financial institutions, because of their large individual investments by way of debt funding for individual borrowers and the fact that borrowers usually deal with a relatively limited number of banks, are able to more effectively monitor loans. In contrast, the monitoring costs faced by individual institutional investors with relatively small holdings of debt securities are relatively higher and require costly contracting mechanisms such as trust deeds etc. The high monitoring cost faced by individual and institutional investors translates into a higher return required by such investors to provide loan funds to a firm of the stated risk profile relative to financial institutions giving rise to the differential in risk premiums.

Anecdotal evidence suggests that this argument is of substance. Typically, public securities issues are held in relatively small parcels of usually under A$3-5m for an individual issue and in some cases much smaller parcels. Bank loans etc. extended by individual financial institutions to a particular borrower will usually be substantially larger than individual securities holdings.

The contracting and monitoring cost argument can also be extended to enforcement issues. For example, it can be argued that the absolute cost of enforcement of a particular creditor's claim is relatively fixed and consequently translates into a higher percentage amount relative to a small individual investment in public securities relative to the percentage cost on a larger bank loan. Additional factors in this regard would include the fact that as individual borrowers may deal with a limited number of banks as distinct from a large number of security holders, banks and financial institutions enjoy a significant advantage in managing and working out problem loans.

Underlying this enforcement problem is the fundamental nature of the contracting arrangements in intermediated and direct financing. In the case of intermediated financing, the bank or financial institution accepts a deposit which it undertakes to repay at maturity together with interest. The bank then in turn on-lends the funds to a borrower. Where the borrower gets into difficulties and is unable to repay the loan or to meet interest commitments, the bank's obligations to its depositors are quite separate from and in no way linked to the performance of the loan. This separation, which is achieved through interposition of the bank in the intermediation process, provides the bank with some flexibility in the management of problem loans. This is so particularly where with a diversified portfolio it is able to service its deposits, both interest and principal payments, without jeopardising its financial viability.

---

3. For an introduction to these concepts, see Jensen and Ruback (1986), pp. 305-360.

In contrast, an institutional investor has a different contractual arrangement with the beneficiaries of the funds under management. The fund manager acts in a fiduciary capacity managing funds on behalf of individual investors. Under these contracting arrangements, a failure by a borrower to perform under its loan conditions, in terms of repayment of principal or interest or other loan conditions, will directly impact upon the investor. This is because the fund manager does not independently guarantee or ensure the payment of interest or principal as does a bank in the intermediated finance case. This more direct relationship clearly limits the discretion of the fund manager, in particular, in the case of a problem loan requiring rescheduling and restructuring. This different contracting relationship may, inevitably, tend to bias fund managers to place a higher risk premium on less creditworthy borrowers than banks and financial institutions.

These factors all have the following effects:

- Higher quality borrowers enjoy a comparative advantage in the public securities market, usually the fixed rate market, as investors for the reasons outlined are willing to pay a high price (or sacrifice yield) to purchase the securities of these entities which have a low default risk.

- Lower quality or less creditworthy borrowers enjoy a comparative advantage in the floating rate market, which is predominantly a bank or financial institution lending market, based on the fact that these institutions have certain advantages in dealing with lesser quality credits.

Both factors tend to create differential risk premiums which facilitate swap arbitrage.

Intermarket credit arbitrage is driven by slightly different factors, predominantly spread compression and name arbitrage factors.

Spread compression refers to an intermarket anomaly whereby the risk premium is significantly different as between markets. In capital markets, a hierarchy of risk is assessed by security analysts or credit rating firms and the risk premium component of the yield is related to the creditworthiness of issuers as ranked under this rating process in a more or less continuous scale of quality ratings.

For example, in the United States market a BBB rated credit would command a risk premium of say 1.50-2.00% greater than a higher quality AAA rated credit for term financing. This yield spread will vary significantly based on market conditions. However, in the European capital markets, such as Switzerland and West Germany, the risk premium between a AAA and a BBB credit may be as low as 0.40-0.60% pa. This lower risk premium may be related to the higher savings rates in particular countries, the liquidity levels in particular markets, the absolute yield levels in different currencies, as well as different normal financing practices. For example, in certain markets such as the Eurobond market, investors may be inclined to view a credit as either acceptable or unacceptable and behave accordingly in investment decisions without well-defined or serious attempts to differentiate between various degrees of creditworthiness.

This intermarket spread compression phenomena is often allied to investor focus on the *name* or reputation of a borrower as distinct from its strict creditworthiness. This phenomena of name arbitrage is particularly significant in Europe and the Euromarkets where a lower rated credit may enjoy superior access to funding at lower risk differentials than in its home market on the basis of the company being a producer of a well known and accepted product which enjoys everyday use, popularity and acceptance of the brand name. For example, companies such as Coca Cola, McDonalds and Eastman Kodak, enjoy access to European capital markets at costs very favourable, relative to their actual creditworthiness. This is particularly so in contrast to the relative cost of funding in their home markets, say the United States where the company's name and product association means far less in the credit analysis and subsequent rating of the firm's securities.

The related phenomena of spread compression and name arbitrage allows certain categories of borrowers to obtain funds in certain markets at significantly lower risk premiums than would be available in their traditional domestic or home markets, generating the comparative advantages which can form the basis of swap arbitrage.

Market segmentation

Market segmentation exists within individual national capital markets as well as between various world capital markets. Market segmentation can take the form of restrictions on investment choice imposed by regulation or internal management policy, which are dealt with in the section on tax and regulatory arbitrage.

Market segmentation exists at a number of levels. At the extreme, restrictions on cross-border capital flows create currency blockages which create attractive opportunities for participants who can circumvent capital flow restrictions by taking the opposite sides of desired transactions.

As discussed in Chapter 3, parallel and back-to-back loans, the precursors of interest rate and currency swaps, were largely an attempt to overcome government imposed currency restrictions on free cross-border capital flows. This type of market segmentation creates problems of funding availability encouraging swap arbitrage designed to exchange demand for a blocked currency for liquidity available in another capital market.

More typically, market segmentation reflects differing investor perceptions and preferences which manifest themselves in the form of risk pricing differentials similar to the spread compression issues discussed above. Market segmentation in this latter form appears to be predicated on administrative limitations on investment in certain instruments or participation in different sectors of markets.

The international market for debt security extends around the globe and is subdivided into numerous national, regional and international sectors. The major distinctions in the international bond market are between international and domestic bond issues. Domestic bond issues are offerings which are sold largely within the country of the borrower. In contrast, international bond issues are security offerings which are sold largely outside the country of the borrower. International bond issues may be further subdivided into two types of issues: Eurobonds and foreign bonds. Eurobonds are international bond issues underwritten by an international syndicate of banks and sold principally and, at times, exclusively in countries other than the country of currency in which the bonds are denominated. Foreign bonds, in contrast, are international bond issues underwritten by a syndicate of banks composed primarily of institutions from one country, distributed in the same way as domestic issues in that country, and denominated in the currency of that country.

The distinctions between the various market segments while accurate in theory are considerably more difficult to determine in practice. The major difficulty arises as a result of the nature of the securities which typically enjoy considerable liquidity as they can be freely bought and sold in an active secondary market. Consequently, one would expect that investors are able to purchase securities from different markets as and when their investment requirements dictate. This would lead to a breakdown in the strict categorisation proposed above and more importantly would lead to uniformity of pricing for comparable securities issued by the same borrower or same class of borrowers.

However, there is significant evidence to suggest that investors only participate in certain sectors of the respective markets worldwide for legal, liquidity and convenience reasons. In fact, there is evidence to suggest that nearly two thirds of the US$6 trillion total size of the international bond market (as at end of December 1985) is not readily accessible or liquid enough for active international participation.[4] This lack of freedom for international fund flows implies a significant level of market segmentation and resultant pricing anomalies which facilitate swap arbitrage.

One example of this type of market segmentation motivated swap arbitrage is in the US$ market as between the Eurodollar and Yankee bond markets.[5] The yield differential between Eurodollar and Yankee bond markets have varied significantly over time with numerous instances when yields of similarly structured Eurodollar and Yankee bonds issued by the same borrower differ by up to 0.50% pa in yield. These divergent trading patterns create significant swap opportunities for market participants.

The pricing differences as between the markets appear to be principally caused by the different credit perceptions and preferences of investors in the United States domestic and international market. These factors include:

- different maturity and issuer preferences;
- investor perceptions of credit quality of bond issuers;
- currency factors and their relevance to the investment decision.

The differing investor perceptions and preferences can be seen in the fact that bonds offered by a variety of high quality sovereign issuers, irrespective of credit rating, have generally enjoyed a less favourable reception in the Yankee market than in the Eurobond market. For example, in late 1987, debt issued by prime issuers such as the Kingdoms of Denmark, Sweden, Finland as well as the Government of New Zealand were trading at a significantly higher yield in the Yankee market than in the Eurobond market. In contrast, Canadian issuers have languished in the Eurobond market but because of the proximity of the United States and Canada, have enjoyed an excellent reception in the United States domestic Yankee market.

---

4. See Marki (1986).
5. The foreign bond sector of the United States domestic bond market.

The differential maturity preferences are evident in the fact that Eurodollar bonds with maturities over 20 years have fared very poorly in the international market. This reflects the fact that investors in the Eurodollar market have traditionally been composed of short to intermediate term security investors. This created significant pricing anomalies with the World Bank's 30 year Eurodollar bonds yielding an average of 30bps more than the 30 year Yankee bonds by the same borrower.

In addition, the Eurodollar bond market, in contrast to the Yankee market, demonstrates a high degree of sensitivity to the value of the US$. This appears to have contributed through 1986 and 1987 to wider spreads in the Eurodollar market relative to the domestic Yankee market. This differential partially reflects the fact that international (non-United States) investors in US$ view their investment as a currency as well as an interest rate play and consequently will price the same credit risk differentially according to their expectations on the future direction of the US$ relative to other major currencies.

This analysis highlights how segmentation of markets creates differential risk pricing which creates opportunities for swap arbitrages of the type described. While the discussion above has been confined to the US$ market, similar considerations apply to a significant number of other markets where similar opportunities are created by the different factors motivating investor participation in various segments of the international capital market.

Supply and demand factors

A third category of financial arbitrage relates to supply and demand factors affecting an individual issuer's securities. In particular, imbalances in the supply and demand conditions create opportunities for arbitrage.

The simplest type of supply and demand factor giving rise to financial arbitrage opportunities is market saturation or its reverse, the scarcity value of an issuer's securities. An extreme case of supply and demand imbalance exists when a given capital market is unwilling to absorb any more debt of a given issuer. In this case, if the issuer still requires financing in the currency of that particular market, proxy borrowers who are acceptable to the saturated market must be sought with the borrower's financing objectives being met by exchanging the new obligations in the required currency for more easily saleable obligations in a currency where the market continues to have demand for the debt of the particular borrower.

Market saturation relates essentially to the relative elasticity or inelasticity of the demand curve for a particular issuer's securities. It is evident that the demand curve for a particular issuer's or risk class of securities, while relatively price insensitive when limited quantities of the issuers securities are on issue, tends to become inelastic and highly price sensitive when a certain saturation point is reached. In that case, additional sales of securities by that particular issuer can only be achieved at significant increases in the risk differential required to be paid to investors. The issue of market saturation, at least from the perspective of investors, appears to relate to:

- the portfolio or credit diversification objectives of investors;
- the financing requirements of the particular issuer relative to the size of the particular capital market.

Investors on the whole seek to limit credit exposure within their investment portfolios to any particular issuer or class of issuer to a relatively small percentage of the total portfolio. This has the consequence of forcing issuers requiring substantial financing in a particular currency, beyond the capacity of that particular sector or market to provide such financing, to pay a penalty if it persists in seeking to raise funds from that particular market. In essence, at the margin, once saturation point has been reached additional net investment in that issuer's securities will only grow in proportion to the total net growth in the funds available for investment as investors are unwilling to increase their investment on a percentage basis.

Scarcity value considerations have the converse effect that investors may be willing to purchase securities issued by *infrequent* issuers in that particular market or market sector at a much higher price (lower yield) than dictated by purely economic factors on the basis of scarcity which allows the investor to achieve a greater degree of portfolio credit risk diversification.

This problem can actually be illustrated with reference to a number of supranational organisations which persist in a borrowing policy which dictates raising funds in the low coupon interest currency markets. This particular category of borrowers, primarily the World Bank, but also other development banks and the national agencies of a number of developed countries, are frequent borrowers in low coupon currencies such as Swiss francs, Deutschmarks and Japanese yen.

In the case of the larger borrowers, particularly the World Bank, the substantial size of their borrowing requirement places a heavy burden on the debt markets in these low nominal interest rate currencies. Consequently, the World Bank tends to pay a bigger penalty for its frequent borrowings in a number of low coupon currencies. This problem has led over time to the World Bank evolving a policy which dictates diversification of funding sources by issuing in a wide range of different currency markets, thereby allowing it to reach investors who would not invest in the borrower's usual currencies, and then swapping the funds raised into the institution's preferred currency and interest rate basis.

A number of institutions, primarily sovereign entities or major international banks, have also sought to diversify their funding base by issuing in a wide range of currencies allowing them to reach investors other than in their traditional currencies on the basis that the funds raised are at an attractive relative rate allowing swaps back into the desired currency at an attractive rate relative to direct market access (see discussion of new issue arbitrage in Chapter 13).

Short run supply demand imbalances, often referred to as market "windows", also create significant opportunities for swap arbitrage. Global debt markets increasingly operate on an opportunistic basis. Windows of attractive opportunities close and open as investor sentiment as to currency and interest rate outlook alters in the light of new available information. High levels of volatility in currency and interest rates as well as improved global communications and information flows means that increasingly transactions are done on the basis of the specific short-lived opportunity which is predicated on investor demand which allows a particular security transaction because the market conditions are "right" and the investors are "there"!

In this type of market, rapidly changing investor demand for particular types of securities create short-run supply imbalances which creates a premium on timing. For example, assume investor expectations in respect of a currency, say the A$, have improved dramatically in the light of market information. In this environment, investors will be seeking to purchase A$ securities for short-term capital gains as a result of currency fluctuations. This creates a short-term excess of demand over the supply of A$ securities as usually the secondary market in A$ securities cannot meet the sudden upsurge in demand for investments. Under these circumstances, an opportunistic issuer may be able to take advantage of market sentiment to issue A$ securities at a relatively advantageous cost, fulfilling the supply gap in the market, creating a comparative cost advantage which may form the basis of a swap into its preferred currency. A similar process would apply to an opportunistic issue of particular *types* of securities designed to capitalise on market opportunities.

Tax and regulatory arbitrage

Tax and regulatory arbitrage is predicated on the existence of artificially imposed restrictions on capital flows or the pricing of capital flows which artificially creates differential pricing or differential access for different classes of participants in capital markets. There are a number of classes of tax and regulatory arbitrage:

* withholding tax;
* investment asset choice;
* taxation differentials;
* subsidised funding sources.

Withholding tax

The presence of withholding taxes creates a wedge between yields on domestic securities and those on comparable securities issued outside the domestic market, primarily in the Eurobond market. The creation of swap arbitrage opportunities as a result of the presence of withholding tax relates essentially to the differential treatment of different classes of transaction under withholding tax legislation. This can be best illustrated by an example involving the A$ market.

Under currently applicable regulations, an international, that is, non-Australian investor purchasing A$ securities issued in the domestic market is subject to a withholding tax of usually 10.00% on interest payments. For example, a European investor purchasing Commonwealth government bonds yielding 13.00% pa would on each interest coupon date receive the equivalent of only 11.70% pa being the 13.00% coupon reduced by the mandatory 10.00% withholding tax. The European investor may be able to recover this withholding tax by way of a tax credit in its own country. Consequently, at best, the investor will recover the withholding by way of adjustments to its domestic tax liability which will usually entail a slight delay and some loss in yield or, at worst, the withholding will not be recoverable resulting in a significant yield loss.

Assume that the European investor can achieve its desired A$ investment objectives by purchasing A$ Eurobonds, issued by a European continental institution of high credit standing. The A$ Eurobond is free and clear of all withholding taxes as essentially it does not involve a resident to non-resident transaction for Australian tax purposes with fund flows taking place entirely outside Australia. Let us also assume that this Eurobond is priced at a yield *under* the equivalent Commonwealth government bond rate of 13.00%, say 12.50% pa. The investor will be attracted to the Eurobond on the basis that it does not realistically represent a yield loss of 0.50% pa relative to an alternative investment, the Commonwealth government bond, but rather an effective yield pick up of 0.80% pa relative to the realised yield where the investor is unable to take advantage of the tax withholding through a foreign tax credit mechanism.

In these circumstances, the issuer of A$ Eurobonds enjoys a comparative advantage in its access to A$ funding relative to domestic institutions and may, if it is not a direct user of A$, swap out of its A$ liability into another liability, say floating rate US$, which is its preferred form of funding. The swap would be effected with a domestic Australian counterparty who would exchange its floating rate US$ liability for fixed rate A$. As the domestic Australian swap counterparty would find its fixed rate debt trading at a significant margin above the Commonwealth government bond rate, the fact that the issuer has achieved a cost of funds under the bond rate should facilitate a significant cost saving in fixed rate A$ terms.

The swap arbitrage predicated on withholding tax in our example is, however, predicated on two important factors:

- the fact that the swap cash flows are free of withholding tax;
- that the Australian counterparty's underlying funding is free and clear of withholding tax.

In practice, swap payments are usually not subject to withholding tax thereby satisfying the first condition. For Australian borrowers, the US$ liability would in all probability be free of withholding tax under an alternative withholding tax exemption provision which provides for no withholding tax on transactions involving the issue offshore of widely distributed bearer securities. This exemption satisfies the second condition for the swap arbitrage involving withholding tax to be effective.

In summary, the presence of withholding tax impacts upon the pricing of capital flows across borders which may create significant differences in access and in the price of funding to different borrowers facilitating swap structures designed to arbitrage the withholding tax wedge.

Investment asset choice restrictions

Restrictions on choice of investment assets which usually limit fund managers from investing in certain types of instruments are common in a variety of markets. These restrictions are usually imposed either by regulatory authorities (both formally and informally) or by the fund itself based on prudential criteria. Restrictions usually operate on two levels:

- type of investment instrument, for example, use of futures or options may be restricted;

- currency and issuer location restrictions, for example, investment in foreign currency denominated investments or securities issued by foreign issuers may be subject to limitations.

Where such restrictions exist, particularly those imposed by regulatory authorities, fund managers often will undertake transactions designed to circumvent the limitations on investment choice to better achieve the fund's overall investment objectives. To achieve these objectives, the fund may undertake complex transactions designed to *indirectly* achieve what cannot be done *directly*. In these circumstances, the fund will inevitably undertake the transaction at a pricing level significantly above the market price level as the transaction cannot be undertaken directly resulting in arbitrage opportunities which can be exploited through swap structures.

In recent years the often byzantine nature of Japanese investment restrictions, during a period when Japanese fund managers and investors have sought to recycle substantial capital surpluses, has meant that the paradigm examples of these types of transactions entail Japanese investors. Several examples of these are outlined below. However, it is important to note that similar asset choice restrictions also pervade other markets and create equally attractive swap arbitrage opportunities from time to time.

In late 1984 and early 1985, Japanese investors sought to increase their exposure to foreign currency denominated securities. In particular, at that time, the high yields available on A$ securities made investment in A$ bonds particularly attractive. However, Japanese institutions were subject to a limitation which restricted investment in foreign currency securities to 10.00% of overall portfolios. At that time, the institutions' quota of foreign securities were close to or at the legal limit.

In early 1985, it became apparent that the 10.00% rule was subject to a minor exception. Issues of foreign currency denominated securities *by a Japanese resident company* did not, for some peculiar reason, count as part of the 10.00% foreign security quota. This exemption allied to the Japanese investors appetite for A$ securities led to two issues by Japanese banks which were placed primarily with Japanese institutional investors. These issues were undertaken at substantially lower yields than the prevailing A$ government bond rates. The yield level accepted by investors reflected the fact that a comparison with domestic A$ interest rates was largely irrelevant as under existing rules they could not, had they desired to, invest in those instruments whereas they were able to purchase the A$ securities issued by the Japanese banks. The banks in turn converted their price advantage resulting from the demand for these A$ securities within Japan into low cost US$ funding by swapping with Australian domestic institutions who in turn achieved cost effective fixed rate A$ at levels unobtainable in the domestic A$, or indeed, any market at that point in time.

Another instance of tax and regulatory arbitrage entailing circumventing investment asset choice restrictions involves dual currency bonds. Until recently, under Japanese tax law, zero coupon bonds received extremely favourable treatment as the difference between the purchase price and the face value of the bond was treated as a capital gain and taxed at the favourable capital gains rate. However, the Ministry of Finance limited the amount a Japanese pension fund could invest in non-yen denominated bonds issued by foreign corporations. In response to these conditions, a number of issuers undertook issues of a zero coupon yen bond plus a dual currency bond with interest payments in yen and principal repayment in US$.

The Ministry of Finance ruled that the dual currency bonds qualified as a yen issue for purposes of pension fund investment restrictions, even though the dual currency bond had imbedded within it a US$ denominated zero coupon bond. Effectively, the zero coupon yen bond and dual currency yen and US$ bond combined represented an investment in a normal coupon yen bond and an investment in a zero coupon US$ bond. However, this particular structure allowed issuers to capitalise on the desire of Japanese investors to diversify their portfolios internationally within the regulations imposed by regulatory authorities.

The fact that this particular structure allowed the investors to achieve an exposure otherwise not available to them, led to a pricing level which was particularly advantageous to the issuer who would usually swap the combined securities into a US$ exposure through a series of swap transactions. The cost achievable through that series of swaps was significantly better than that available from direct access to the US$ market.

In recent times, a wide variety of issue structures combining option elements with securities have appeared. These option embedded securities (which are discussed in more detail in Chapter 17) have been structured to the specifications of investors, usually Japanese, who are unable to otherwise undertake futures and options transactions to hedge or position their portfolios. The fact that the direct alternative, that is, utilisation of futures and options contracts, are not directly available to these institutions has meant that they are willing to pay above market prices for the privilege of entering into these futures and options contracts indirectly. This cost benefit has usually been translated by the issuer of these securities into cheaper cost funding in the borrowers desired currency and interest rate basis through a number of swap transactions.

A non-Japanese example relevant in this context is the issue of US$ and A$ dual currency bonds in the United States domestic market designed to cater to the requirements of certain investor groups which have provided the basis for a number of swap arbitrage opportunities in recent times.

Tax differentials

Tax driven swap arbitrage usually focuses on the dissimilarity of taxation treatment across countries for similar financial instruments. Swap arbitrage involving withholding tax effects has already been discussed. The other two major categories of tax driven swap arbitrage are:

- the differential tax treatment of types of income in the hands of investors, or conversely the different characterisations and treatments of interest, expense etc., from the perspective of the borrower or issuer of securities;
- capital allowances, such as depreciation and one off large capital consumption allowances, made available by national governments to stimulate capital investment.

The second of these two sources of swap arbitrage predicated on tax factors is discussed in the later section on subsidised funding sources.

Swap arbitrage predicated on differential treatment of revenue and/or expense focuses on the fact that investors seek to maximise *after tax* income while borrowers seek to minimise *after tax* costs of funding. Where a particular issuance format, either entailing a particular combination of cash flows or the location of the borrower or investor in a particular tax jurisdiction, is tax effective, there is a natural incentive for both borrowers and investors to gravitate towards the particular format which respectively reduces after tax cost or increases after tax returns. This potential to enhance the economics of the transaction provides the essential arbitrage profit which can be allocated between the parties through a specially structured swap transaction. This process can be best illustrated with an example.

In the early 1980s, zero coupon securities emerged as an important financial instrument. While non-tax factors, such as reduction of reinvestment risk, call protection, price volatility and duration factors, were important in the emergence of these types of debt instruments, it was tax factors which were instrumental in the upsurge of interest in zero coupon securities.

Zero coupon securities were particularly attractive for investors who were either not taxed or who were taxed at concessional rates of interest on the discount (that is, the difference between purchase price and face value which constitutes the essential return to the investor). In a number of jurisdictions, such as Japan and several European countries, the difference between the investor's sale price and the purchase price of the discount security was treated as a non-taxable capital gain. In other jurisdictions, the discount was taxed at a concessional rate which was lower than the normal rate of taxation allowing investors to achieve significant improvements in return on holdings of zero coupon securities relative to normal coupon securities. Investors, as a result of these tax factors, were willing to purchase zero coupon securities at prices which were substantially higher (implying lower yields) than conventional securities. The higher price willing to be paid reflected the willingness of investors to share part of the return benefit on an after tax basis with the issuer.

Allied to the tax factors was the preference for the investors who enjoyed tax benefits of zero coupon securities to purchase bearer securities, usually Eurobonds, which allow holders to preserve their anonymity and also the lack of any withholding tax, which also favoured Eurobond issues. The particular investors were also concerned that the issuers be of a higher credit quality satisfying not only their normal credit requirements but the additional credit risk given that the full return on the investment was "back ended".

In this environment, borrowers satisfying the identified requirements were able to access fixed rate fundings on a zero coupon basis at significantly lower yield than through other sources. This cost advantage was able to be utilised as the basis for swap arbitrages. In particular, the fact that the issuers may not have wanted to use the funding generated in the particular cash flow pattern of a zero coupon security necessitated the development of particular swap structures designed to convert this all-in cost advantage to a more acceptable or preferable form. These structures are discussed in detail in the section on accelerated and deferred cash flow swaps in Chapter 15.

Other types of tax factors which create opportunities for swap arbitrage include:

- differential rates of income tax which create incentives for cross-border financial transactions conceived to defer or avoid income taxes;
- treatment for tax purposes of hedging transactions of different types;
- differential tax policies governing cross-border transfers;
- differential foreign tax credit systems.

Often tax factors are combined with other conditions which together provide opportunities for swap arbitrage.

Subsidised funding sources

A major source of swap arbitrage opportunities derives from the fact that particular borrowers may enjoy preferential access to subsidised financing sources. Examples of such subsidised financings include:

- export credit funding;
- tax based financing structures, including leasing.

Most developed nations exporting large amounts of capital goods have established agencies to assist their exporters in financing sales overseas. These agencies which are usually government departments or statutory bodies typically provide low cost finance, or interest subsidies, as an inducement to foreign purchase of major items of capital investment. This type of export credit financing is clearly linked to the purchase of the underlying capital goods but is usually also subject to significant restrictions as to the terms and conditions of the financing, in particular the currency and interest rate basis.

A purchaser of capital goods with access to export credit financing can, therefore, find itself in the position of having access to finance on preferential terms relative to the market but in a currency or on an interest rate basis which differs from its preferred liability structure. In these circumstances, the potential arbitrage profit locked into its preferential funding sources can be mobilised through a swap structure to allow the borrower to achieve its desired mix of liabilities.

Tax based financing opportunities, particularly in the area of leasing, function in a similar way. As noted above, government policies designed to stimulate capital investment usually provide for large capital consumption allowances in the form of depreciation or immediate write offs. Potential users of equipment attracting such advantageous tax treatment, either directly through purchase or indirectly by some type of lease or hire arrangement, can usually structure financing arrangements designed to lower the all-in cost based on the available tax advantages. A limitation of this type of financing is that the tax advantage may dictate the financing being structured on a currency or interest rate basis other than the borrower's preferred liability structure. As in the case of export credits, this creates the opportunity for utilisation of swap arbitrage structures predicated on the tax based financing arrangements generating a more attractive cost structure than normal financing arrangements.

Miscellaneous arbitrages

Two other sources of swap arbitrage require mention:

- incomplete markets;
- transaction costs.

The opportunity for swaps arbitrage is also partially predicated on the incomplete nature of capital markets. In this regard, swaps contribute to the integration of financial markets by allowing market participants to fill gaps left by the unavailability of particular types of financial instruments. The use of swaps to overcome institutional market limitations is particularly apparent in Australia. For example, the institutional structure of the Australian debt market did not encompass, until very recently, a substantial long-term fixed rate corporate debt market. A factor underpinning the growth of A$ swaps is that such transactions allow corporations to generate fixed rate A$ liabilities under circumstances where such transactions are not directly available.

Transaction costs as a source of swap arbitrage are more complex. Various types of transaction costs are identifiable including the requirement for confidentiality, queuing restrictions and the opportunity to lock in gains or minimise losses on particular borrowings.

There are many reasons why a borrower may want to keep its fund raising behaviour in a particular market confidential. Where confidentiality is an issue, the borrower's objectives can be accomplished by using proxy borrowers in the desired market which forms the basis of currency and/or interest rate swaps into the borrower's preferred form of liability. In these circumstances, the advantage of confidentiality manifests itself in the form of the willingness on the part of the borrower to pay a premium for access in this particular form which can form the basis of the swap arbitrage.

The requirement of confidentiality by particular borrowers may be motivated by such factors as the desire to avoid review by rating agencies or governmental bodies.

Another form of transaction cost is the queuing procedure often applied by different national governments which dictates the timing and order of access to particular capital markets. In essence, to control the flow of investment funds, financial authorities in many countries establish a quota of financing that is available to borrowers of particular types in each financing period. Borrowers apply for permission to borrow and, if approved, are placed in a queue until their turn to borrow arrives. In certain circumstances, the queue can be extremely lengthy, being as much as one year in length.

The existence of a queuing system creates problems in the sense that borrowers must be able to anticipate market conditions and their own financial requirements considerably in advance. Given the volatility of currency and interest rate markets, it is possible that even where the financial requirement has been anticipated in advance, the period between entering into the queue and being eligible to borrow may mean that market conditions have worsened significantly from those anticipated at the time the borrowing was contemplated.

In these circumstances, borrowers can either accelerate or defer borrowings when in a queue by entering into a swap with another borrower. To accelerate its borrowing, the borrower would usually enter into a swap with a party which has currently arrived at the head of the queue. Where the borrower seeks to defer its borrowing in the particular currency or on the interest rate basis previously contemplated, the borrower having reached the head of the queue would undertake the borrowing transaction and swap out of the liability into a preferred interest rate or currency basis more in line with its expectations and requirements at the time of issue.

In these circumstances, the borrower in the queue may be willing to pay a premium to accelerate or defer its transaction creating a natural arbitrage gain which can be the basis for swap transactions. A major factor underlying swaps predicated on queuing positions is that national regulatory authorities tend to take an unfavourable view of borrowers who, having positioned themselves in a queue, upon reaching the appropriate borrowing position do not undertake the originally contemplated transaction.

The desire of borrowers to lock in currency and interest rate gains or alternatively to minimise losses from market movements also creates the basis of swap arbitrage. Unless fully hedged, currency and interest rate transactions may result in accumulated gains or losses after their inception. Rather than run the risk that an unrealised book gain will be dissipated or a book loss increased by subsequent changes in market conditions, organisations may undertake swaps to lock in the size of the gain or loss at its present level. In this context, the use of swaps becomes relevant for a number of factors:

* Alternative means of covering the exposures may not be available. For example, the borrowing may not be able to be repaid because of contractual agreements or penalties. These transaction costs create an incentive for the borrower in question to pay a premium to undertake the swap facilitating the swap arbitrage.

* Even where eligible to undertake the transaction by alternative means, market protocol may dictate that the borrower should not, in order to preserve its access to the particular sector, retire or otherwise restructure its borrowings. In these circumstances, an incentive exists for the borrower to once again pay a premium to achieve its objectives thereby indirectly, providing the arbitrage gain which can form the basis of swap transactions.

* The potential dissipation of any gain or aggravation of any loss, depending on the rate expectations of the organisation, and the likelihood of such an outcome eventuating may be so great that the borrowers are once again willing to pay a substantial premium which can provide the source of swap arbitrage.

Swap arbitrage sources: some comments

In considering the various sources of swap arbitrage, it is important to note that in a given market, several of the factors identified may coexist and combine to provide the basis of swap activity. Some aspects of this complex interaction of various elements are evident in the analysis of swap arbitrages in the A\$ market later in this chapter.

A persistent problem in seeking to explain the economics and pricing of swaps in terms of arbitrage is the problem of arbitrage erosion. In classical arbitrage, the very process of exploiting this type of opportunity would soon eliminate it. However, a careful analysis of the various sources of swap arbitrage suggests that a substantial number of them are structural in nature.

This essentially means that growth in swap activity while it may have the impact of reducing the scale of the arbitrage profit, does not of itself *eliminate* (as distinct from *reduce*) the arbitrage profit.

In the case of tax and regulatory arbitrage, in particular, there is no reason for the arbitrage opportunity to disappear, at least until the relevant tax or regulatory provisions are altered.

In summary, while opportunities for classical financial arbitrage employing swaps may be eroded by competition, several of the sources of swap arbitrage profit are embedded in the very structure of modern capital markets and, in particular, the imperfection of contracting arrangements and regulatory regimes particularly as between national markets.

SWAP ARBITRAGE IN THE A$ MARKET: A CASE STUDY

The complex process by which swap arbitrage operates in specific markets is best understood with reference to an actual example. The example utilised in this section is of swap arbitrage in the A$ market. The data utilised is hypothetical, although it is fairly typical of conditions which existed in the period 1985 to 1987 in this market.

The various cost and access opportunities relevant to A$ currency swap arbitrage are set out in *Exhibit 7.4*. *Exhibit 7.5* sets out the various cost differentials as between various participants in the market.

Exhibit 7.4
A$ Currency Swap Arbitrage Matrix

Entity	A$ fixed rate funding typical costs	A$ floating rate funding typical costs	US$ floating rate funding typical costs
Sovereigns	B − 25	BBR − 35	LIBOR − 12.50
AAA/AA + multinationals	B − 20	BBR − 25	LIBOR − 12.50
International banks	B − 10	BBR − 25	LIBOR − 6.25
Commonwealth of Australia	B	BBR − 10	LIBOR − 12.50
Semi-government instrumentalities	B + 90	BBR	LIBOR − 6.25
Australian banks	B + 100	BBR	LIBOR − 6.25
Finance companies	B + 140	BBR + 30	LIBOR + 25
Prime corporates	B + 140	BBR + 20	LIBOR + 10
Lower rated corporates	B + 250/ unavailable	BBR + 70	LIBOR + 125/ unavailable

Exhibit 7.5

A$ Swap Arbitrage: Cost Differentials (bps)

	Sovereigns	AAA/AA+ multinational	International bank	Commonwealth	Semi-government instrumentalities	Australian banks	Finance companies	Prime corporates	Lower rated corporates
Sovereigns	— —	5 (10) [0]	15 (10) [6.25]	25 (25) [0]	115 (35) [6.25]	125 (35) [6.25]	165 (65) [37.50]	165 (55) [22.50]	275 (105) [137.50]
AAA/AA + "name" multinational			10 (0) [6.25]	20 (15) [0]	110 (25) [6.25]	120 (25) [6.25]	160 (55) [37.50]	160 (45) [22.50]	270 (95) [137.50]
International bank				10 (15) [−6.25]	100 (25) [0]	110 (25) [0]	150 (55) [31.25]	150 (45) [16.25]	260 (95) [131.25]
Commonwealth					90 (10) [6.25]	100 (10) [6.25]	140 (40) [37.25]	140 (30) [22.50]	250 (80) [137.50]
Semi-government instrumentalities						10 (0) [0]	50 (30) [31.25]	50 (30) [16.25]	160 (70) [131.25]
Australian banks							40 (30) [31.25]	40 (20) [16.25]	150 (70) [131.25]
Finance companies								0 (−10) [−15]	110 (40) [100]
Prime corporates									110 (50) [115]

Notes:

1. Figures without brackets refer to cost differentials in A$ fixed rate funding.
2. Figures in ( ) refer to A$ floating rate cost differentials.
3. Figures in [ ] refer to US$ floating rate funding differentials.

Perusal of the two exhibits reveals the following distinguishing features of the cost of funding the various participants in the different market segments:

- In the A$ fixed rate funding market, there is minimal differentiation between four entities, namely, sovereign borrowers, multinational borrowers, international banks and the Commonwealth. There is also significant bunching in the typical A$ fixed rate funding costs as between semi-government instrumentalities (semis), banks (which are taken to be Australian banks), finance companies and prime corporates.

- In the A$ floating rate funding market, there appear to be three separate categories of borrower costs:

  —sovereigns, multinationals and international banks;

  —the Commonwealth, semis and Australian banks;

  —finance companies, prime corporates and lower rated corporates.

- In the US$ floating rate funding market, a number of dominant groupings emerge. These are the lower rated corporates, the prime corporates and finance companies, and all the other parties.

The differential access of the different groupings to different market segments appear to be predicated on a number of factors. One of the major determinants of the various cost differentials appears to be the distinction between onshore and offshore fund raising. For example, the A$ fixed rate and floating rate costs of sovereigns, multinationals and international banks are based on issues outside the A$ domestic market.

In the A$ fixed rate market, this distinction appears based on the presence of Australian withholding tax which leads investors outside of Australia to favour the purchase of issues structured as Eurobonds and thereby free of withholding tax in preference to the purchase of higher yielding securities issued in the A$ domestic market. The presence of withholding tax means that these investors are prepared to buy securities structured in this manner at substantial yield concessions to prevailing yields in the domestic market relative to the comparative credit standing of the parties. Additional factors include investor preference for the anonymity available in the form of bearer Eurobond securities as well as a preference for borrowers well known to the lenders. The fact that Australian organisations are not well known to the particular international investor groups attracted to A$ securities means that investors are willing to sacrifice significant yield in investing in securities issued by sovereigns, multinationals and international banks.

Similar conditions form the basis of the pricing differences of the A$ floating rate market. The substantially lower cost of A$ floating rate funding for sovereigns, multinationals etc., is predicated on the fact that these funds are supplied by offshore investors, primarily in Japan and South East Asia, seeking withholding tax-free investments in bearer form with a bias to well known issuers.

The factors identified to date do not of themselves indicate the reasons underlying the demand by overseas investors for A$ securities. This demand is clearly predicated on factors such as currency and interest rate expectations and portfolio diversification objectives. In particular, during the period in question, the fact that A$ securities yielded significantly higher nominal interest returns relative to securities denominated in other currencies, prompted investor demand on the basis that the currency risk intrinsic to the A$ investment was more than compensated for by the higher available yield.

In contrast, domestic A$ investors whose home currency is the A$ would continue to buy A$ securities for normal asset and liability matching reasons and the demand factors relevant to these investors are significantly different to those affecting international investors. The different investment motivations mean that if international investment sentiment changes, leading to a reduction in the demand for A$ securities, the different yields demanded by A$ investors in taking on A$ currency risk would change the typical A$ fixed rate and floating rate funding costs which would be reflected in the A$ currency swap arbitrage pricing.

Other factors affecting the structure of the pricing differentials include:

- the institutional structure of the A$ domestic market which dictates that no term debt market for borrowers other than primarily the Commonwealth and semis exists (at least, until very recently). This means that Australian banks, prime corporates and lower rated corporates cannot directly raise A$ on a fixed rate basis leading them to resort to swaps as a means of synthetically filling this market gap;

- the structure of international markets and investor preferences which favour non-Australian issuers of A$ securities in international markets forcing borrowers seeking fixed rate A$ to resort to swaps with borrowers such as sovereigns, multinationals etc., with preferential access to fixed rate A$;

- within the A$ market, credit arbitrage considerations which dictate that higher rated credits such as the semi-government instrumentalities enjoy preferential access to fixed rate A$ funding;

- spread compression in the floating rate US$ markets reflecting very small risk differentials predicated, in all likelihood, on excess market liquidity and competition between financial institutions seeking to obtain quality assets;

- a marked bias in the behaviour of international US$ lenders against lower rated Australian corporates.

Under these circumstances, the pricing structure as between the markets dictates that the most likely arbitrage transaction is likely to be between two groups: sovereigns, multinationals or international banks (as A$ fixed rate borrowers) and the semis, Australian banks, prime corporates etc. (as users of fixed A$ funding). The focus of the arbitrage as between these two parties is dictated by the natural preferences of both groups of borrowers and the fact that the arbitrage gain, when adjusted for the differential credit risk that must be assumed through the swap, is at a relatively high level for this type of transaction.

Assume that at this time the swap arbitrage is being driven predominantly by international banks, particularly German banks, and Australian semis. This reflects the fact that investors seeking A$ securities, primarily German investors, favour borrowers well known to them while the semis have an extensive A$ borrowing programme during the current period and they wish to diversify their sources of funding.

In these circumstances, currency swap structures similar to those set out in *Exhibit 7.6* might evolve.

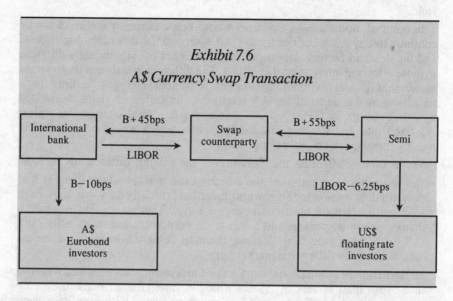

Exhibit 7.6
A$ Currency Swap Transaction

Under the structure depicted, the international bank achieves funding at LIBOR minus 55bps, while the semi achieves funding at a cost of bonds plus 48.75bps. The overall swap arbitrage gain of 100bps, reflecting the difference in the relative fixed A$ funding costs as both parties have the same US$ floating rate funding costs, is split as follows:

Semi	41.25bps
International bank	48.75bps
Swap counterparty	10.00bps

The split of the arbitrage gain between the two parties is dictated by competitive factors, supply and demand etc. In this case, the division of the swap arbitrage gain, that is, the nominated sub-LIBOR level required by the international bank to undertake the issue on the basis of a swap into floating rate US$ will be driven by other swap arbitrage opportunities available to it. For example, it may at this point in time have available to it other swap driven issues in say yen, NZ$, C$ etc. The sub-LIBOR levels available in these other markets will to a large extent determine the level required to undertake an A$ issue. The riskiness of the issue and its likelihood of success, the state of the A$ Eurobond market etc., will also be relevant. For a more detailed analysis of the factors underlying the decision to take advantage of this swap arbitrage, see the discussion of new issue arbitrage in Chapter 13.

The swap pricing in this example will also be determined by the level of competition between the semi-government and Australian banks to raise fixed A$. For example, since the arbitrage gain as between the international bank and the Australian bank is slightly higher, 110bps as against 100bps, if the credit risk of the two entities is comparable or at least the credit risk premium is less than 10bps, an opportunity exists for the Australian bank to agree a higher fixed A$ rate flow under the swap fundamentally altering the division of the arbitrage gain for the semi if it still wishes to transact the swap.

The swap transaction itself has a number of effects. In the first instance, the availability of the swap means that the A$ currency swap arbitrage matrix must be altered to reflect the changed A$ fixed rate funding cost for the semi and the altered US$ floating rate funding cost for the international bank. The change in cost structure of the matrix will result in consequential changes in the relative cost differentials as between the various parties. The matrix and the cost differentials can be reworked. The change in the relative status of different parties as a result of the undertaking of the swap transaction would of itself create new arbitrage opportunities as between various participants.

At a more fundamental level, the altered borrowing behaviour of various market participants will lead to a change in their relative borrowing costs. The increased volume of A$ securities on issue from international banks, both individually and as a group, as well as the reduction in A$ securities issued by semis in the domestic market will lead to an alteration in the pricing structure. Similar effects in the US$ floating rate market will be evident. These changes will also, by engineering changes in the relative cost differentials, lead to a reconfiguration of the arbitrage opportunities in the market.

Exogenous factors such as changed market expectations as to currency and interest rates will also impact on the process of currency swap arbitrage. For example, if A$ interest rates were expected to increase in absolute term or the A$, relative to the home currencies of the investors, is expected to depreciate, investor demand for A$ securities internationally would show a significant decrease. In terms of the currency swap arbitrage, this would manifest itself in the form of an altered A$ fixed rate funding cost for sovereigns, multinationals etc. This, in turn, will alter relative cost differentials creating a different set of arbitrage opportunities.

The behaviour of market participants also has the scope to fundamentally alter the pattern of currency swap arbitrage described. For example, the swap counterparty could fundamentally alter the pricing levels in the market if it were willing to:

- Reallocate the fixed A$ funding to other parties, say lower rated corporations. This assumes that the swap counterparty is willing to assume the higher credit risk entailed.

- The swap counterparty could seek to unbundle the arbitrage and maximise its own earnings, for example, by transacting fixed A$ against floating rate A$ swaps with lower rated corporates where the potential arbitrage profit is at a very substantial level and managing the US$ and A$ risks by floating rate A$ and US$ swaps with say semis, Australian banks, finance companies or prime corporates. In this case, the dual level of credit risk must be factored into increased potential earnings from this unbundling process.

Other categories of market participants may also intervene in the pricing process. For example, a potential fixed rate A$ investor could create higher yielding investments by purchasing floating rate US$ securities issued by international banks and swapping them into a fixed rate A$ investment with the swap counterparty at a yield of approximately bonds plus 38.75 bps. This is clearly superior to the investment return achievable by direct purchase of A$ securities issued by the international bank at bonds minus 10bps. Implicit in this analysis is that the swap counterparty and the international banks are of a similar credit quality and that the liquidity of the underlying security plus swap package is comparable to that of the A$ security purchased directly. Alternatively, the higher yield is sufficient to more than compensate for any added credit risk and/or loss of liquidity.

The process of swap arbitrage, particularly the various levels of interaction, are both complex and difficult to model accurately. This is because the basic arbitrage process itself is subject to numerous, often unpredictable, factors which, furthermore, have complex inter-relationships. The above example utilising the A$ currency swap market highlights some of the factors underlying this process of interaction which is fundamental in determining the economics of swap arbitrage.

Chapter 8

Yield Mathematics of Interest Rate and Currency Swaps

BASIC METHODOLOGY

The yield mathematics of interest rate and currency swaps encompasses the arithmetical and technical steps utilised to value swap transactions. In essence, the yield mathematics starts with a given swap price (driven by the underlying pricing economics discussed in Chapter 7) and translates it, mathematically, to an *equivalent* price for the specific swap being analysed.

The basic methodology utilised is predicated on the time value of money or net present value concept. Parties to swap arrangements usually measure the relative attractiveness of a transaction through the calculation of its "all-in cost", or its internal rate of return (IRR) in the relevant currency.*

The arithmetical and technical procedures are common to all financial transactions and are not necessarily peculiar to swaps. However, swap transactions give rise to particular complexities which are considered in detail in this chapter.

The basic complexities of pricing swap transactions utilising IRR principles arises from two sources:

• the different methods for calculating yields in different markets;
• the fact that swap transactions are seldom of a standard type.

Yield calculations vary significantly between markets as to a number of variables such as: the manner in which interest payments are made; the frequency of payments; the relevant day basis; and the compounding method used. In addition, standard market prices, such as those made available on Telerate, Reuters etc., screens, are usually confined to transactions of a standard type which in reality are rarely undertaken. The most important variations cover: commencement dates, transaction size, spreads above or below the floating rate indexes, various mis-matches, premium or discounts or reimbursement of issue fees and expenses. Price adjustments are usually necessary to accommodate these variations.

INTEREST RATE SWAPS: YIELD MATHEMATICS

Pricing conventions

The cost of a typical interest rate swap is expressed in the rates on the fixed and floating interest payments. More specifically, the price on an interest rate swap of a given maturity is quoted as a fixed rate (for example, 15.00%

---

* The discussion in this section assumes an understanding of net present value and IRR concepts.

pa) against a floating rate index, quoted flat (that is, with no margin over or under the index).

In a number of markets, the price on a generic interest rate swap is quoted as a spread over a *fixed rate* index against the floating rate index flat. For example, in US$ interest rate swaps an intermediary might quote the price on a seven year fixed rate US$ against LIBOR swap to a fixed rate payer as "the seven year Treasury rate plus 60 bps versus six-month LIBOR".

A$ interest rate swaps are priced relative to the Commonwealth government bond curve against the BBR flat as the floating rate index. A number of other markets also follow a similar quoting convention with the fixed rate being expressed usually as a margin over the appropriate government bond rate. However, in markets other than the US$ swap market, the relationship of swap rates to the comparable government securities rate is inconsistent and weak. This favours quotation on an absolute rate basis. An example of typical swap quotations in a number of currencies is set out in *Exhibit 8.1.*

Exhibit 8.1

Swap Market Quotations

INTEREST RATE SWAP QUOTATIONS

US$	Spread	Annual interest A/360
2 years	61–67	8.17–8.25
3 years	77–85	8.60–8.70
4 years	82–89	8.80–8.90
5 years	84–90	8.90–9.00
7 years	92–97	9.20–9.28
10 years	93–99	9.35–9.43

Sterling	Semi-annual interest 365/365
2 years	9.40–9.50
3 years	9.65–9.75
4 years	9.65–9.75
5 years	9.65–9.75
7 years	9.69–9.70
10 years	9.65–9.75

Swiss francs	Annual interest 360/360
2 years	4.30–4.45
3 years	4.50–4.65
5 years	4.80–4.95
7 years	4.90–5.05
10 years	5.05–5.20

Note: All fixed rates are against six months US$ LIBOR: £ rates are against six months £ LIBOR.

Exhibit 8.1—continued

Yen samurai (interest semi-annually)

2 years	4.64–4.74	5 years	5.20–5.20
3 years	4.98–4.96	7 years	5.25–5.35
4 years	5.05–5.15	10 years	5.35–5.45

DM 360/360 (interest per annum)

2 years	4.35–4.45	5 years	5.50–5.60
3 years	4.78–4.88	7 years	6.02–6.12
4 years	5.20–5.30	10 years	6.48–6.58

ECU 360/360 (interest per annum)

5 years	7.90–8.05	10 years	8.05–8.25
7 years	8.00–8.15		

Source: Euro Brokers Ltd, New York.

US MONEY MARKET INDEX SWAPS

Prime/LIBOR	Receive	Pay
2 years	P–110	P–125
3 years	P–110	P–125
5 years	P–110	P–125
Bills/LIBOR		
2 years	TB+120	TB+105
3 years	TB+120	TB+105
5 years	TB+120	TB+105
Commercial paper/LIBOR		
2 years	CP+33	CP+28
3 years	CP+36	CP+32
5 years	CP+37	CP+32

Source: Euro Brokers Ltd, New York.

AUSTRALIAN DOLLAR SWAPS

	Annual interest 360/360
3 years	14.60
4 years	14.40
5 years	14.35

Source: Commonwealth Bank of Australia.
Source: International Financing Review.

The precise definition of the government bond rate can be the subject of dispute and will normally be agreed upon at the time of committment. Generally, it is either:

• the yield on an actively traded government security with the relevant maturity; if the swap's maturity lies between that of two actively traded securities, the yield is computed as a weighted average; or

• the semi-annual yield to maturity of a specific government bond or bond with a maturity closest to that of the swap.

The second approach is often criticised because it does not exclude thinly traded securities with anomalous prices.

Under market convention, an offer (bid) swap price indicates the price at which the market is willing to receive (pay) the fixed rate under the swap. The dealer's spread is the difference between the offer and bid swap price. The terminology associated with swap price quotation is not uniform and some versions in common use are set out in *Exhibit 8.2.*

The linkage between swap rates and government bond rates merits additional comment. The relationship, which arose originally in the US$ swap market, appears to be based upon two factors:

- spreads over a risk-free rate, such as the government bond rate, act as a proxy for credit risk differentials;
- the use of government bonds to hedge swap transactions.

In highly developed capital markets, such as the US$ market, the risk premiums, embodied in spread differentials, for borrowers of different credit quality are relatively well established. Although these risk premiums change over time, the fact that they are readily determinable means that they can form the basis for swap arbitrage analysis. A result of this is that swaps, which function as a means of creating synthetic fixed and floating rate borrowings, tend to be priced "off" a benchmark risk free rate in a manner similar to that of pricing direct borrowings.

This thesis is confirmed to some degree by the fact that the relationship between swap prices and government bond rates is strongest in markets

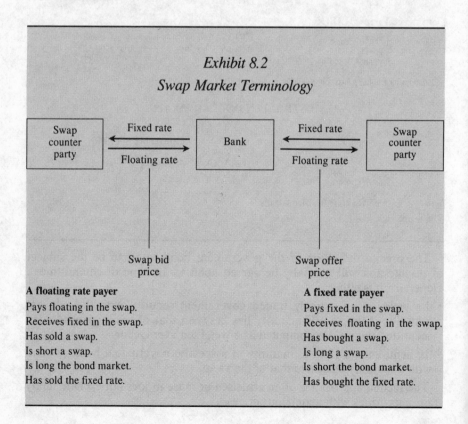

Exhibit 8.2

Swap Market Terminology

A floating rate payer
Pays floating in the swap.
Receives fixed in the swap.
Has sold a swap.
Is short a swap.
Is long the bond market.
Has sold the fixed rate.

A fixed rate payer
Pays fixed in the swap.
Receives floating in the swap.
Has bought a swap.
Is long a swap.
Is short the bond market.
Has bought the fixed rate.

with highly developed risk premium structures. In markets where certain types of securities issues are not readily possible, the linkage is significantly weaker.

Swap prices are closely tied to the cost of hedging swap exposure (see discussion Part 8). Before a swap is matched with another swap, it is generally hedged with a combination of securities, futures contracts and some form of floating rate funding such as repurchase agreements. For example, if the intermediary is the fixed rate payer on the swap, the hedge usually involves the purchase of an appropriate amount of government securities with the same maturity as the swap. The purchase of securities is in turn financed by borrowing in an appropriate market (in practice, the cash or, if available, the short-term repurchase agreement market). The government security creates a hedge against capital loss if long-term interest rates change, and also generates fixed rate income which matches the fixed payments of the swap. The floating rate income from the swap covers the floating rate cost of funding the purchase.

Swaps of shorter maturity (usually up to two years) are more likely to be hedged in the futures market. Although cash market hedges offer a wider choice of maturity and payment dates, they appear on the institution's balance sheet and potentially tie up capital. Futures contracts avoid these costs.

The use of government bonds and futures contracts to hedge swaps has an important technical effect on the mechanics of pricing swaps. As in practice, the swap counterparty will if it receives (pays) the fixed rate under the swap then seek to hedge by selling (buying) bonds or futures, the relevant bond or futures price to be used as a base will correspond to the bid (offer) price in the market for those instruments plus the relevant swap spread.

A number of other quotation conventions should be noted. The term "trade date" refers to the date on which the counterparties commit themselves to the swap.

The "effective date" on a swap is the date on which fixed and floating interest starts accruing. Normally, this is a period of up to five business days after the trade date depending upon market convention in the particular swap market. The "settlement date" is the date on which the transaction is priced for value. Normally in swap transactions this is the same as the effective date.

Swap agreements are executed on an "as of" basis; that is, the agreement is prepared and executed some time after the effective date. This custom enhances the liquidity of the swap market, but should a party fail before the contract is executed, the protection offered by the agreement, obviously, might not be present.

Valuation procedures for generic structures

The valuation methodology of interest rate swaps entails two specific and distinct phases:
- the valuation of a generic or "plain vanilla" swap;
- the factoring in of the price/cost impact of variations from the generic structure.

A generic swap structure refers to the underlying conventional swap structure which forms the basis for all swap transactions. The characteristics of a generic interest rate swap are summarised in *Exhibit 8.3*.

An important practical consideration is that the market convention as to certain key aspects of yield calculation vary significantly between various domestic and international capital markets. The main areas of difference include:

- payment of interest (whether discount or coupon basis);
- frequency of interest payments (annual, semi-annual, etc.);
- day basis factor used in accruing and compounding of interest;
- accrued interest calculations.

Yield calculation conventions in some major markets are summarised in *Exhibit 8.4*.

Exhibit 8.3
Characteristics of Generic Interest Rate Swap

Terms	Definition
Maturity	One to 15 Years
Effective date	Depending on market convention, up to five business days from trade date (corporate settlement). The effective date is such that the first fixed and first floating payment periods are full coupon periods (that is no long or short first coupons).
Settlement Date	Effective Date.
All-in-cost	Depends on market convention, but usually semi-annual equivalent of the internal rate of return of the fixed flows versus the floating index flat.
Fixed payment	
Fixed coupon	Current market rate.
Payment frequency	Either semiannually or annually depending on market convention.
Day count	Based on market convention.
Pricing date	Trade Date.
Floating payment	
Floating index	Certain money market indices.
Spread	None.
Determination source	Some publicly quoted source.
Payment frequency	The term of the floating index itself.
Day count	Based on market convention.
Reset frequency	The term of the floating index itself.
First coupon	Current market rate for the index.
Premium or discount	None

Source: Adapted from Kopprasch et al., *The Interest Rate Swap Market: Yield Mathematics, Terminology and Conventions* (1985).

Exhibit 8.4
Yield Calculation Conventions

United States Dollar[1]

	Payment frequency	Compounding	Number of days
Prime	—	—	365/360
US$ LIBOR	—	—	365/360
Money market[2]	—	A	365/360
Treasury bonds	S/A	S/A	365/365
Corporate bonds	S/A	S/A	360/360
Yankee bonds	S/A	S/A	360/360
Eurodollar bonds	A	A	360/360

West German Deutschemark

DM LIBOR	—	—	365/360
Schuldscheine	A	A	360/360
Domestic government bonds	A	A	360/360
EuroDM bonds	A	A	360/360

Swiss Franc

SFR LIBOR	—	—	365/360
Foreign Bonds (public issue)	A	A	360/360
Foreign Notes (private placements)	A	A	360/360
Domestic government bonds	A	A	360/360

United Kingdom Sterling

£ LIBOR	—	—	365/365
Gilt edged securities	S/A	S/A	365/365
Bulldog bonds	S/A	S/A	365/365
Eurosterling bonds	A	A	360/360

Canadian dollar

C$ LIBOR	—	—	365/360
Federal government bonds	S/A	S/A	365/365
Corporate bonds	S/A	S/A	365/365
EuroCanadian bonds	A	A	360/360

Japanese Yen

¥ LIBOR	—	—	365/360
Domestic government coupon bonds	S/A	A	365/365
Samurai bonds	S/A	A	365/365
Euroyen bonds	A	A	360/360

Australian Dollar

Bank bill rate	—	—	365/365
A$ LIBOR	—	—	365/360
Commonwealth/Semi-government bonds	S/A	S/A	365/360
EuroAustralian bonds	A	A	360/360
Yankee Australian bonds	S/A	S/A	360/360

Exhibit 8.4—continued

New Zealand Dollar

Prime commercial bill rate	—	—	365/365
NZ$ LIBOR	—	—	365/360
Government bonds	S/A	S/A	365/360
EuroAustralian bonds	A	A	360/360
Yankee New Zealand bonds	S/A	S/A	360/360

Notes:

1. The practice in the United States and certain other domestic bond markets is the semi-annual compounding of semi-annual bond coupons. In the Eurobond market the practice of the Association of International Bond Dealers (AIBD) is to compound annually either the annual or semi-annual bond coupons.

2. To convert rates from AIBD to United States money market basis, multiply by 360/365. To convert rates from United States money market to AIBD basis, multiply by 365/360.

3. Yield to maturity on yen bonds is calculated and quoted on a *non-compounded basis within Japan*. Outside Japan yields are usually calculated on a AIBD *or* United States basis.

The basic valuation procedure for a generic interest rate swap is predicated on the transaction being characterised as an exchange of two securities: a fixed rate and a floating rate security. The swap can, therefore, be conceptualised as follows:

• A fixed rate payer is selling a fixed rate security and buying a floating rate security.

• A fixed rate receiver is buying a fixed rate security and selling a floating rate security.

The valuation of the swap is, therefore, predicated on the valuation of the two different securities.

The two securities can be valued using traditional debt security valuation techniques based on present value concepts. Typically, the security would be valued by solving the following equation:

$$P_o = \sum_{n=1}^{n} \frac{C_n}{(1+i)^n} + \frac{P}{(1+i)^n}$$

where P_o = the current market price of the instrument.
C_n = the expected cash flow (the periodic coupon) payable to the investor in period n.
P = the principal amount payable at maturity, period n.
n = the number of periods.
i = the yield to maturity, the discount rate or the internal rate of return.

Two factors complicate the basic valuation methodology:

• The interest rate swap involves neither an investment at commencement or a final maturity payment as only coupon flows are swapped.

• The expected cash flows under the floating rate security are not certain as they are contingent on the level of future interest rates.

The first consideration is not problematic as the party undertaking the swap simultaneously buys and sells the *equivalent amount* of a fixed rate and a floating rate security. This creates a netting of the two cash flows both at commencement and at maturity creating no net cash flow effect.

The uncertainty of the floating rate cash flow stream is more difficult and can be resolved utilising different approaches. Kopprasch et al (1985) resolve this issue simply. They argue that unlike a true floating rate security, a swap has two-way cash flows: fixed versus floating. This feature allows the swap market to value the relative attractiveness of a swap's floating index by bidding the accompanying fixed rate up or down. Consequently, the floating rate security may not separately require valuation. The value of the floating rate security is incorporated into the fixed cost quoted versus the floating payments. Therefore, valuation questions for swaps focus on the hypothetical fixed rate security.

In contrast, Bicksler and Chen (1986) argue that the pricing of the swap requires valuation of the floating rate security by incorporating assumptions as to the stochastic movements of short-term interest rates.

In practice, the former approach is utilised. This is because market participants assume that the floating rate component of a swap will tend to have a value close to par (its original value) because of its frequent repricing characteristic.

Available floating rate security pricing techniques, such as the simple margin, total margin, adjusted total margin or discount margin technique, are still required to adjust the floating rate security's return by quantifying an implicit change in the floating rate whenever the note deviates from par. These adjustments generally reflect minor price effects for swaps trading with a long or short coupon where the level of the floating rate index *set* is above or below the *current* market rate for the current coupon period. An example of this type of adjustment is set out in *Exhibit 8.5*.

The basic valuation procedure for an interest rate swap with a generic structure entails calculating the internal rate of return of the hypothetical fixed security flows. For analytical purposes these flows, from the perspective of the fixed-rate payer, are the proceeds received from the sale of the hypothetical fixed rate security versus an outflow of the fixed rate payments plus the notional principal amount at maturity.

The proceeds, in this context, are not cash but instead are the value of the hypothetical floating rate security received in exchange. In a generic swap the value of the floating rate security is par. For non-generic swaps the proceeds are the net of the value of the floating rate security and any cash payment on the settlement date (see the discussion later in this chapter).

The internal rate of return (expressed as semi-annual bond equivalent) of the hypothetical fixed security is quoted as the all-in cost versus the floating flows that constitute the index flat.   The steps entailed in valuation are as follows:

- The cash flows of the two "securities" as specified in the swap contract are identified.
- Whether the floating payments are generic must be determined. If they are not, the floating cash flows must be adjusted to correspond to a stream

Exhibit 8.5

Pricing Adjustments for the Floating Rate Component of a Swap

For example, consider a swap with a floating side that resets and pays quarterly and floats off three month LIBOR. When prices with two months to the next floating payment, the discount rate should be the current two month LIBOR rate. The formula for the full price of the floating rate side, adjusted to be the index flat, is:

$$\text{Present value of the floating side} = \frac{100 + ER \times \dfrac{D_{PN}}{360}}{1 + \dfrac{CR}{100} \times \dfrac{D_{SN}}{360}}$$

where ER = the current rate in effect for the next floating coupon payment (expressed as a percentage).

D_{PN} = the actual number of days from the previous floating payment date to the next floating payment date.

CR = the current market rate of the index for the period from the settlement date to the next floating payment date (expressed as a percentage).

D_{SN} = the actual number of days from the settlement date to the next floating payment date.

The accrued interest portion of the full price of the floating side can be calculated using the following formula:

$$\text{Accrued interest on the floating side} = \frac{ER \times (D_{PN} - D_{SN})}{360}$$

The price the floating rate side of the base case swap with a settlement date of 1 June 19X5, assuming the current floating rate in effect was set at 8.9375% on 15 May 19X5, and that the current market rate for five and one half month LIBOR is 9%, the aforementioned formulas would be applied as follows:

$$\text{Full price of the floating side} = \frac{100 + \left(8.9375 + \dfrac{184}{360} \right)}{1 + \left(\dfrac{9.00}{100} + \dfrac{167}{360} \right)} = 100.377$$

$$\text{Accrued interest on floating side} = 8.9375 \times \frac{(184 - 167)}{360} = 0.422$$

Source: Kopprasch et al., *The Interest Rate Swap Market; Yield Mathematics, Terminology and Conventions* (1985).

of payments satisfying the generic standard. If the floating payments must be altered, the fixed cash flows must be adjusted by these same dollar amounts (the *adjustment flows*) so that the swap's net cash flows remain unchanged.

• The final step in the process is to determine the internal rate of return (on a semi-annual equivalent basis) of the analytical fixed flows. Because the floating cash flows were adjusted to be the generic standard, this internal rate of return is the swap's all-in-cost.

Exhibit 8.6 summarises the approach to valuation of generic swaps.

Exhibit 8.6

Generic Swap Valuation Methodology

1. Determine fixed and floating contractual flows.
2. Determine adjustment flows needed to alter floating payments to generic index flat.
3. Determine fixed and floating analytical flows equal to sum of contractual and adjustment flows plus par at maturity.
4. Find present value of next analytical floating coupon plus par discounted at current market index rate for appropriate period.

To find premium/
discount given
all-in cost

To find all-in cost
given premium/
discount

5. Find present value of analytical fixed flows discounted at all-in-costs.
6. Calculate premium/discount equal to difference between two present values computed in Steps 4 and 5.

7. Determine proceeds received by fixed rate payer equal to value of floating rate received (from Step 4) plus any discount received or minus any premium paid.
8. Find semi-annual equivalent internal rate of return of combination of proceeds determined in Step 7 and analytical fixed flow from Step 3.

Source: Kopprasch et al., *The Interest Rate Swap Market: Yield Mathematics, Terminology and Conventions* (1985).

In practice, in a generic swap which is transacted at current market rates the prices of the exchanged "securities" are equal and, thus no net cash payment is exchanged upon settlement. In non-generic swaps, the prices may not be equal. In such a case, the net of the two purchase prices would determine the cash payment upon settlement or alternatively the adjustment to the swap rates themselves.

Valuation of non-generic structures

The all-in cost of a swap can be affected by the introduction of a deviation from generic terms. Some general variations include abnormally high or low principal amounts, different amortisation structures (not a bullet loan) and long maturities for which markets are thin.

On the fixed payments side, generic terms call for a semi-annual (sometimes annual) payment frequency and a standard year basis for accruing fixed interest.

On the floating payments side, generic conventions are as follows:

- no spread above or below the floating index;
- payment frequency equal to the term of the floating index itself;
- the day count convention varies between markets but is typically either actual/360 (LIBOR) or actual/365 (BBR).
- the reset frequency is equal to the term of the floating index itself.

Other common variations include: reimbursement of fees, expenses etc., associated with a new issue of debt and/or a swap undertaken at a premium or discount. Deviations from generic features will cause the swap price to differ from the market price for a generic swap. For example, a swap may be structured to incorporate a spread of 25 bps below six month LIBOR on the floating rate side (perhaps reflecting creditworthiness considerations in the case of a highly regarded floating rate payer). To express this swap price according to market convention it should be quoted as a fixed rate against LIBOR flat. The conversion is more involved, however, than simply adding 25 bps to the all-in cost of the market price for a generic swap. The swap dealer has to take account of the different day count conventions between the fixed and floating payments side of the swap.

Mismatches in payments frequency, day count conventions or reset frequency can also cause the price on a customised swap to deviate from the quoted market price on a generic swap. In many cases the valuation of these customised details or deviations from the generic standard cannot be precisely and objectively determined but has to be negotiated between the counterparties. Such necessarily subjective elements in the pricing of swaps, together with credit risk, are a major impediment to the development of a liquid secondary market in swaps. Assignment of an existing swap with customised features, for example, may be difficult because a third party will not place the same value on non-generic terms as the original counterparties did.

To illustrate some of the problems, let us consider the case of a reset frequency mismatch. A reset frequency mismatch occurs when the reset frequency does not agree with the maturity of the floating rate index, as with monthly resets of six month LIBOR, for example. Frequent resets will generally have a valuation effect. Investors who choose a six month maturity have forsaken shorter maturities and more frequent repricing opportunities. Theoretically, on average the market's expectations for the course of interest rates over the next six months will be incorporated in the six month rate. Therefore, altering the reset frequency will generally have valuation effects relative to the generic swap structure. The specific valuation effect, however, will vary with the expectations and portfolio considerations of swap counterparties and cannot be objectively priced.

A swap may trade into the secondary market with a first floating rate payment period different from those for the remainder of the swap's life. For example, consider a generic six month LIBOR swap with four months to go until a floating rate payment. Clearly, the two months' accrued interest on both the fixed and floating rate sides of the swap must be factored into the swap price. The appropriate index to use for the floating rate over the next four months remains subject to debate, especially if the original swap was based on six month LIBOR reset monthly. There is no definitive market convention on this question. The need to negotiate these points is another impediment to secondary market liquidity.

Exhibit 8.7 sets out examples of the interest rate swap yield calculations embodying the adjustments discussed.

Exhibit 8.7
Example of Interest Rate Swap Calculations

Bond Issue Swap

Assume a US$100m bond issue with attached swap on the following terms:

Bond Issue:

Issuer:	ABC Bank (ABC)
Amount:	US$100m
Term:	Five years
Coupon:	8.00% pa (A)
Issue price:	100
Fees:	1.875% flat
Expenses:	US$125,000 or 0.125% flat
All-in issue cost:	8.51% pa (A) or 8.33% pa (S/A)
Payment:	In four weeks from launch

Interest Rate Swap

Type:	Interest rate swap
Structure:	ABC to receive fixed rate US$, pay six month US$ LIBOR
Market rate for standard:	Treasuries ("T") + 78/85 versus six month LIBOR
Swap:	T = 8.00% pa (S/A)
All-in swap quote:	8.78/8.85% pa (S/A)

Assume the swap structure requires reimbursement of fees and pricing adjustments.

The exact structure of the swap once adjusted will be as follows:

• Swap counterparty pays ABC US$2m at commencement of swap, that is, payment date.

• Swap counterparty will pay the following fixed rate versus six month LIBOR flat:

	% pa (A)
Annual swap rate[1]	8.92
Fee amortisation[2]	—0.51
Adjustment for delay[3]	+ 0.04
All-in swap payment	8.45

Exhibit 8.7—continued

Notes:

1. The 8.92% pa (A) is the annualised equivalent of 8.78% pa (S/A). The full 19bps gross up is adjusted by 5bps reflecting the added reinvestment risk to the counterparty.

2. 0.51% pa represents the recovery of the 2.00% up front payment amortised over five years. The discount rate used is the swap rate (8.97% pa (A)) but could be higher or lower reflecting the cost of funding the payment to the swap counterparty.

3. The 0.04% adjustment represents the positive carry or earning on the hedged or offsetting swap with immediate start. This represents an earning of 2.00% (based on short-term rates of 6.00% pa (S/A) versus bond rates of 8.00% pa (S/A)) which is equivalent to US$0.1538m over four weeks amortised over five years at the swap rate (8.97% pa (S/A)).

The net result of the swap is that the counter party pays 8.45% pa (A). However, the swap counterparty is required to make annual payments of 8.00% matching out the bond coupon and receives a spread under LIBOR. Consequently, the swap counterparty receives LIBOR minus 44.61bps every six months.

The 0.39bps reflect the required adjustment to adjust the swap pricing to reflect the spread below the floating rate index. This adjustment is necessary unless the fixed rate and floating rate payments are calculated on the same daycount basis and paid on the same frequency. In this example, both conditions are not met.

A structural variation to improve swap pricing might be to reconfigure the bond to be issued at a premium, that is, the issue price could be 101, the coupon 8.25%, and a comparable yield of 8.5% pa. This may allow the issuer to improve its sub-LIBOR margin where the funding cost of the fees significantly exceeds the swap rate.

CURRENCY SWAP: YIELD MATHEMATICS

The yield mathematics of currency swaps are very similar to those applicable to interest rate swaps. The cost of a typical currency swap is expressed in one of two ways:

*   as an absolute fixed rate in the relevant currency against a floating rate index, quoted flat, such as $US LIBOR;

*   as LTFX spreads, discounts or premiums to the spot currency, representing the forward exchange rate implicit in the currency swap.

The specific pricing methodologies for LTFX contracts are considered in Chapter 9.

While the basic pricing methodology and yield mathematics of currency swaps are similar to interest rate swap yield mathematics, the more complex structure of currency swaps entails a number of additional complexities:

*   different computational basis as between currencies and different market conventions;

*   the necessity to calculate equivalences as between currencies.

The necessity to adjust for different computational basis or market conventions between the different currency markets is largely similar to the process described above in connection with interest rate swaps.

The adjustments required by the necessity to ensure equivalencies as between currencies are considerably more complex. The requirement to match flows between currencies occurs in a number of contexts including: the reimbursement of issue fees, expenses etc. in one currency which must be recovered, in some cases, in another currency; and the requirement to pay spreads above or below the floating rate index in one currency.

The latter is particularly problematic as inevitably a currency swap will require one party to make payments either above or below the relevant floating rate index to avoid assuming a foreign exchange exposure. This effectively requires the other party to either borrow or lend the foreign currency. Consequently, the transaction pricing and the required adjustments from the generic currency swap case requires these borrowing and lending transactions to be encompassed in the pricing of the transaction. These spreads above or below the relevant index can be priced on the basis of either assumed borrowing or lending transactions in the relevant currencies or alternatively as a string of forward foreign exchange contracts designed to convert exposure from one currency to another.

Exhibit 8.8 sets out an example of yield calculations and adjustments for currency swap transactions.

Exhibit 8.8
Example of Currency Swap Calculations

Bond Issue Swap

Assume a A$50m bond issue with attached swap on the following terms:

Bond Issue:

Issuer:	German Bank (GB)
Amount:	A$50m
Term:	Five years
Coupon:	14.00% pa
Issue price:	101.25%
Fees:	2% pa
Expenses:	A$125,000 or 0.25% pa
Payment:	In four weeks from launch
All-in issue cost:	14.29% pa (A) or 13.82% (S/A)

Swap

Type:	A$ fixed: US$ floating currency swap
Structure:	GB to receive fixed rate A$
	GB to pay floating rate US$
Market rate:	T + 60/T + 80 versus six month LIBOR
Swap:	T = 14.00% pa
All-in swap quote:	14.60/14.80% pa (S/A)

The swap can be structured in two separate ways:

Structure 1

Under this structure, the swap counterparty partially reimburses the issue fees up to par to GB to provide it with proceeds of A$50m.
The exact structure of the swap is as follows:

- At commencement (assuming spot exchange rate of US$0.70/A$1), GB will pay over issue proceed of A$49.5m to swap counterparty; in return, GB will receive: US$34.65m. GB will also receive US$0.35m being reimbursement of fees of 1.00% or A$0.5 m.

- Over the life of the swap:

  - Every six months, GB will pay six month LIBOR less a margin (see below) upon US$35m.
  - Every year on the coupon payment date, GB will receive a payment of A$7m representing 14.00% on A$50m.

Exhibit 8.8—continued

• At maturity, GB will receive A$50 to make the principal repayment to the bond-holders; GB will pay US$35m to the swap counterparty.

The pricing of the swap will be adjusted as follows:

	% pa (A)
Annual swap rate[1]	15.03
Fee amortisation[2]	—0.30
Adjustment for delay[3]	—0.05
All-in swap payment	14.68

Notes:

1. 15.03% pa (A) is the annualised equivalent of 14.60% pa (S/A) adjusted by 10bps pa for the increased reinvestment risk.

2. 0.30% pa represents the fee reimbursement of 1% over five years at 15.25% pa (A).

3. 0.05% pa represents the negative carry or accrual (based on short-term rates of 16.00% pa (S/A) versus bond rates of 14.00% pa (S/A)) for a period of four weeks amortised over five years at 15.25% pa (A).

The adjustments yield a swap price of 14.68% pa (A).

The swap structure requires payments of 14.00% pa (A) against receipts of six month LIBOR minus a margin. This margin is 56bps.

The 56bps reflects the US$ equivalent of A$ 68bps pa. It reflects the need notionally to borrow A$ to purchase a spot US$ investment which produces the necessary US$ flows to cover the periodic US$ shortfall over the life of the swap reflected in the sub-LIBOR US$ payments.

The adjustment is calculated to equate the present value of "off-yield curve" margin in A$ at current A$ rates with an equivalent off-yield curve margin in US$ at current US$ rates. In this example, the equivalency is calculated on the basis of A$ interest rate of 15.25% pa (A) and US$ interest rates 8.00% pa (S/A) for five years.

Structure 2

This is identical to Structure 1 with the following major differences:

• In the initial exchange GB pays over A$49.5m and receives US$34.65m only.
• GB pays six month LIBOR minus a margin on US$34.65m.
• GB repays US$34.65m at maturity *but receives A$50m*.

The swap pricing adjustments are slightly different.

	% pa(A)
Annualised swap rate	15.03
Adjustment for delayed start	—0.05
Adjustment for A$ shortfall[1]	—0.15
Adjustment for lower A$ proceeds[2]	—0.14
All-in swap payment	14.69

Notes:

1. The 0.15% pa represents the amortised effect (at 15.00% pa (A)) of having notionally to invest A$ now to generate A$ at maturity to cover the extra A$ flow to GB.

2. The 0.14% represents an adjustment as the lower A$ proceeds received by the swap counterparty translates into a higher running coupon, that is,

$$\frac{A\$ \ 7m}{A\$49.5m} = 14.14\% \ pa$$

The base swap price of 14.69% pa (A) is then adjusted as before to provide GB with sub-LIBOR margin equivalent of 57bps.

Chapter 9

Pricing LTFX Contracts

LTFX PRICING METHODOLOGIES*

While the pricing of interest rate and currency swaps is largely dictated by capital market arbitrage between various borrowers and between various global capital markets, a number of specific theoretical pricing mechanisms are utilised for pricing distinct transactions such as LTFX, FRAs and Caps and Collars etc. In this chapter, the techniques for pricing LTFX contracts are discussed. Theoretical pricing mechanisms for pricing FRAs and Caps and Collars etc. are discussed in Chapters 10 and 11.

LTFX transactions are usually priced in one of two ways:

- as forward foreign exchange contracts pricing off current interest rates and interest differentials between currencies for various maturities;

- as fixed-to-fixed zero coupon currency swaps.

Selection between the two approaches is dictated by the operating philosophies and the approach to LTFX adopted by individual institutions. In practice, both approaches co-exist.

INTEREST RATE DIFFERENTIAL PRICING MECHANISMS

The conceptual basis

The conceptual basis of utilising interest rate differentials to price forward currency contracts, irrespective of maturity, is based upon the concept of arbitrage between various foreign exchange and money markets. This approach predicts that the returns obtainable in any particular currency sold in the forward markets against a base currency would normally be equal to those obtainable in the base currency. If discrepancies occur and this condition does not hold, opportunities for risk free profit exist and are quickly exploited by market participants. This process of arbitrage forces the forward rates on currencies to reflect the interest rate differential between the respective currencies.

An example of forward currency rates pricing based on arbitrage between foreign exchange and money markets is set out in *Exhibit 9.1*. In this example, market participants are faced with two choices: an investment of A$10m yielding 12.00% pa and a US$7.2m investment yielding 7.50% pa. The different amount of initial investment reflects the current spot exchange rate between A$ and US$ at which the relevant currencies could be exchanged for each other to provide the initial investment capital. The two investments

---

* The discussion of LTFX pricing techniques draws on Ant1 (1983) and Ant1, "Pricing of Long-Term Forward Foreign Exchange Contracts" in Ant1 (1986).

Exhibit 9.1
Arbitrage Between Foreign Exchange and Money Markets

Date:	28/9/X7	28/12/X7
A$ investment:	A$ 10.000[1]	
A$ return (principal and interest at 12.00% pa):[2]		10.299
US$ investment:	US$ 7.200	
US$ return (principal and interest at 7.50% pa):		7.335
Spot exchange rate:	A$1.00/US$0.72	
Forward exchange rate:		0.7122

Notes
1. All amounts are in $m
2. All rates are compounded annually and based on 365/365 day computational basis for simplicity.

respectively provide a final termination value reflecting the return of principal plus interest earned of A$10.299m and US$7.355m respectively.

This implies a forward exchange rate of A$1/US$0.7122 or a discount on spot of 0.0078. This discount equates the effective interest return capable of being earned between the two markets. This is because if the forward exchange rate does not reflect the existing interest rate differential then opportunities would exist for borrowing in one currency with a simultaneous investment in another to yield an arbitrage profit.

For example, if the forward exchange rate prevailing in the market for three months was A$1/US$0.7102, then it would be profitable to borrow A$10m, sell the currency spot for US$7.2m and lodge the US$ in an investment yielding 7.50% pa with the proceeds of the investment, both principal and interest (US$7.355m), being sold forward for value 28/12/X7 at the market forward rate. This series of transactions would provide the investor with an effective A$ termination value of A$10.328m, an increase of A$0.028m on a direct A$ investment or an effective yield of 13.16% pa which is significantly higher than the current market yield for A$ investment.

This potential arbitrage profit would encourage market participants to undertake the transaction described which would drive the market towards the equilibrium forward exchange rate as the increased supply of US$ for three months investment and also the emergence of increased numbers of forward sellers of US$ against A$ would force both the US$ interest rate and forward exchange rate to adjust.

Short-term versus long-term forward exchange contract pricing

The requirement that market participants exploit arbitrage opportunities for risk free profit holds quite well for short-term forward exchange contracts. This is particularly so between freely convertible currencies in which there are well-developed money markets, especially when international markets in the relevant currencies also exist. The fact that the international markets are unregulated and outside the control of national authorities means that they are highly efficient and that the process of arbitrage does indeed force forward rates to reflect the interest rate differentials between currencies.

However, for LTFX contracts such arbitrage is more difficult and these rates do not necessarily reflect the activity of arbitrageurs between the various capital and foreign exchange markets.

The failure of arbitrage at longer maturities reflects, in the first instance, the reluctance of market participants to undertake long-term arbitrage because of the higher transaction costs involved. These higher transaction costs entail balance sheet holding costs for assets incurred in the process of arbitrage as well as the tying up of credit lines for extended periods of time. A major factor impeding arbitrage is the difficulty in locating securities or investments which are ideally suited to the requirements of the arbitrage process.

An analysis of the above example, which illustrates arbitrage between foreign exchange and money markets over a relatively short period, highlights that a number of conditions must exist for the arbitrage to be fully effective:

- There must be available appropriate securities or investments to allow participants to borrow and invest in the appropriate currencies to undertake the arbitrage.

- The securities or investments required must have particular cash flow characteristics, that is, they must have a *known terminal value* of the investment or borrowing cost.

The latter requirement is particularly problematic. In the case of short-term forward exchange contracts, the availability of discount instruments means that the terminal value of the investment or the cost of the borrowing is known in advance. However, once this simple one payment, one period situation is replaced by either a single payment, multi-period situation, or alternatively, a multi-period, multi-payment situation, the process of determining the terminal value of the investment becomes more complex.

This reflects the fact that where investments or borrowings are undertaken for periods in excess of, for example, one year, the required borrowing or lending transaction entails intermediate cash flows in the form of coupon payments. Intermediate cash flows must be compounded in multi-period situations to provide the required maturity values for the relevant transaction. However, unless zero coupon securities are utilised (as the interest rates at which the intermediate cash flows will have to be reinvested or borrowed is unknown in advance) there is uncertainty as to the maturity value.

There are two possible solutions to this problem. Under the first, it is usually assumed that reinvestment or funding in future periods will take place at current rates. This assumption, however, is speculative and there is no assurance that the assumed rate will in fact be realised. Alternatively, it is possible to produce a series of forward rates, as discussed in Chapter 10 in the context of FRA transactions, for the contemplated maturity. Under this approach, it is possible to compound the intermediate cash flows at the assumed forward rates. However, the forward rates assumed as the basis of any reinvestment or funding transaction in future periods may not in practice be realised. This is because while it is, on the basis of empirical evidence, an *unbiased* predictor of the future spot rate, the forward rate is not necessarily an *accurate predictor* of the *actual* future spot rate.

Numerous academic studies have indicated that, given certain assumptions, the forward rate does not produce a systematically biased estimate of the future spot rate. However, a number of factors may influence the behaviour of interest rates and cause realised interest rates to differ from the implied forward rates, including:

• changes in fiscal policy;
• changes in inflation rates;
• monetary policy factors;
• changes in the country's balance of payment situation;
• political developments and uncertainties.

Where the realised forward interest rates differ from implied annual rates, a number of possibilities exist:

• It is possible that the interest rate differential between the two currencies remains constant despite the fact that the actual realised interest rates differ from implied interest rates. Under the scenario, the LTFX contract rate is likely to be approximately the same as that implied by interest differentials.

• If the interest rate differential narrows as a result of the difference between realised and implied forward interest rates, the LTFX contract rate is likely to be higher on the basis of interest rate differentials than that achieved on the basis of reinvestment of intermediate cash flows.

• If, in contrast, the interest rate differential widens, the LTFX rate implied by the interest rate differentials at the time the transaction is undertaken is likely to be lower than that actually achieved as a result of reinvestment of intermediate cash flows.

These difficulties in applying standard arbitrage techniques involving interest rate differentials mean that there are a number of competing pricing techniques for LTFX contracts. The major ones include:

• current yield curve method;
• average forward rate method;
• exchange of borrowing and currency swap method;
• fully arbitraged cash flow method.

Current yield curve method

The current yield curve method utilises the technique for short-term forward exchange contracts to calculate LTFX rates. The forward rate is based on existing interest rate differentials for the relevant maturity and assumes that the same interest rate will prevail for the entire exposure period and, consequently, compounds the required investment or borrowing at the same rate for the same period. *Exhibit 9.2* sets out an example of the current yield curve method. The exhibit indicates that the five year forward rate can be calculated as equivalent to A$1 being equal to US$0.5067 or a discount of 0.1933 (1933) on the spot rate. The forward rate is calculated as follows.

A$1m invested in A$ securities for five years at 14.25% pa should give a maturity value of A$1.9466m. This assumes reinvestment of any intermediate coupons at the assumed rate equivalent to the coupon of 14.25% pa. The same A$ amount converted in the spot market to give US$0.7m if invested for five years at 7.10% pa, the prevailing US$ rate for the maturity, would give a maturity value of US$0.9864m. The US$ maturity value also assumes compounding at the five year rate. The two investment maturity values imply a five year forward rate of A$1/US$0.5067 to prevent covered interest arbitrage between the two markets.

In this example, as in all the examples utilised in this chapter, bid/offer spreads are ignored to simplify the description of the concept. In practice, market participants would transact on either side of the implied five year forward rate with the difference between the rate at which it buys the currency and the rate at which it sells the currency representing its profit.

Exhibit 9.2
Current Yield Curve Method

Assume the following market scenario:

Spot A$/US$ exchange rate = A$1.00/US$0.70

The interest rate structure is as follows:

Year	A$ interest rates (% pa (A))	US$ interest rates (% pa (A))
1	16.00	6.25
2	14.75	6.40
3	14.50	6.60
4	14.35	6.80
5	14.25	7.10

The forward rates using the various interest rate differentials would be as follows:

	US$ per A$1.00	Discount
Spot	0.7000	—
Forwards: 1 year	0.6412	0.0588
2 years	0.6018	0.0982
3 years	0.5649	0.1351
4 years	0.5326	0.1674
5 years	0.5067	0.1933

Average forward rate method

The average forward rate method assumes that the interest rates prevailing at the time the transaction is undertaken for the longest maturity contemplated are the best reflection of future yields and that reinvestment or funding of intermediate cash flows will be at the same rates. Utilising this method, forward rates will be calculated on the basis of interest rate differentials between the two currencies for the longest relevant maturities and by applying these differentials to each of the interim maturities to compute the forward rates.

Exhibit 9.3 sets out an example of average forward rate methodology. In this case, the five year interest rates for both currencies (refer *Exhibit 9.2*) are used throughout the five year period to generate the relevant forward rates.

Exhibit 9.3
Average Forward Rate Method

Year	A$ investments	US$ investments	Exchange rate (US$ per A$1.00)	Discount
0	1.0000	0.7000	0.7000	—
1	1.1425	0.7497	0.6562	0.0438
2	1.3053	0.8029	0.6151	0.0849
3	1.4913	0.8599	0.5766	0.1234
4	1.7038	0.9210	0.5405	0.1595
5	1.9466	0.9864	0.5067	0.1933

A number of aspects of the use of the average forward rate method should be noted:

• The forward rate for five years calculated under the average forward rate method is identical to that under the current yield curve method.

• The annual discount remains constant at the interest differential, 7.15% pa, for the entire period.

Exchange of borrowing and currency swap method

Under the exchange of borrowing and currency swap method, two parties with either existing or anticipated borrowings in two different currencies agree to swap their liabilities utilising the standard currency swap structure. Under this technique, the forward rates established reflect arbitrage between the two capital markets as all cash flows are matched and the reinvestment and funding problems, described above, do not create uncertainty as to the future values of assets or liabilities. An example of exchange of the borrowing and currency swap method is set out in *Exhibit 9.4*.

Exhibit 9.4

Exchange of Borrowing and Currency Swap Method

Borrowings	A$m	US$m
Face value:	100.000	70.000
Coupon:	14.250% pa	7.000% pa
Issue price:	100.125	100.000
Borrowing costs:	2.000%	1.875%
All-in-costs:	14.810% pa	7.460%
Net proceeds:	98.125	68.6875

Cash flows

Year	A$m	US$m	Exchange rate (US$ per A$1.00)	Discount
0	98.125	68.6875	0.7000	—
1	14.250	4.9000	0.3439	0.3561
2	14.250	4.9000	0.3439	0.3561
3	14.250	4.9000	0.3439	0.3561
4	14.250	4.9000	0.3439	0.3561
5	114.250	74.9000	0.6556	0.0444

As noted in Chapter 6, the process of arbitrage implied by the exchange of borrowing technique operates on the basis that it would be possible to replicate the transaction outlined by borrowing one of the currencies, converting the proceeds into the other currency utilising the spot foreign exchange market, investing the second currency proceeds in an instrument with the same interest payment dates and selling the interest payments and principal forward against the base currency.

Fully arbitraged cash flow method

The fully arbitraged cash flow method of pricing LTFX contracts seeks to overcome some of the deficiencies of other techniques, particularly the current yield curve and average forward rate method, by devising a structure which avoids any reinvestment risk on intermediate cash flows.

The fully arbitraged cash flow method, which was first described in Antl (1983), creates a set of fully arbitraged forward rates utilising the current yield curve. This is achieved by structuring a series of borrowings or investments spread out over the entire exposure period with the amount borrowed or invested for each maturity taking into account any intermediate cash flows, interest payments, due under borrowings or investments related to exposures in other periods. In essence, the total liabilities in each period, that is, the principal plus all interest payments received, are structured to equal all assets in that same period. This creates a series of self-liquidating cash transactions whereby all currency risk and investment risk is avoided.

Exhibit 9.5 sets out an example of the fully arbitraged method. In that example, fully arbitraged forward rates are created to cover future receipts of A$1m every year for five years.

As set out in the example, the self-liquidating cover must be structured by first computing the principal amount to be borrowed for the longest period. In this example, this is equal to A$0.8753m which reflects the exposure amount of A$1m discounted at the rate of 14.25% pa. This implies a cash flow in five years from commencement of the transaction equal to A$1m, being the sum of the principal plus the interest payment. This process is then repeated for each of the shorter periods. The amount borrowed for four years reflects the fact that the sum of the interest payment from the five year loan plus the final payment for the four year borrowing must equate to A$1m. Based on a four year interest rate of 14.35% pa, this is equal to A$0.7654m. This provides a maturity value (principal plus interest)

Exhibit 9.5
Fully Arbitraged Cash Flow Method

A$ BORROWINGS (A$m)

Year	A$m receipts	1 year at 16.00% pa	2 years at 14.75% pa	3 years at 14.50% pa	4 years at 14.35% pa	5 years at 14.25% pa
0	3.3940	0.5022	0.5826	0.6685	0.7654	0.8753
1	1.0000	(0.5826)	0.0859	(0.0969)	(0.1098)	(0.1247)
2	1.0000		(0.6685)	(0.0969)	(0.1098)	(0.1247)
3	1.0000			(0.7654)	(0.1098)	(0.1247)
4	1.0000				(0.8753)	(0.1247)
5	1.0000					(1.0000)

US$ INVESTMENT (US$m)

Year	US$m investment	1 year at 6.25% pa	2 years at 6.40% pa	3 years at 6.60% pa	4 years at 6.80% pa	5 years at 7.10% pa
0	(2.3758)	(0.3515)	(0.4078)	(0.4680)	(0.5358)	(0.6127)
1	0.5112	0.3735	0.0269	0.0309	0.0364	0.0435
2	0.5455		0.4347	0.0309	0.0364	0.0435
3	0.5788			0.4989	0.0364	0.0435
4	0.6157				0.5722	0.0435
5	0.6562					0.6562

EXCHANGE RATE

Year	Borrowings (A$m)	Investment (US$m)	Exchange rate (US$ per A$1.00)	Discount
0	3.3940	2.3758	0.7000	—
1	1.0000	0.5112	0.5112	0.1888
2	1.0000	0.5455	0.5455	0.1545
3	1.0000	0.5788	0.5788	0.1212
4	1.0000	0.6157	0.6157	0.0843
5	1.0000	0.6562	0.6562	0.0438

of A$0.8753 which in conjunction with the interest payment of A$0.1247 on the five year borrowing provides the required A$ cash flow of A$1m. This process is repeated for each maturity. The total A$ borrowing can then be determined. In this example, this equates to A$3.394m.

The other side of the hedge, the investment, operates as follows. The A$ borrowing proceeds are converted into US$, at the spot rate, and invested *in the same proportion as the borrowings undertaken.* In our example, the US$ proceeds, US$2.3758m, are invested in the amounts set out. For example, the amount invested for one year US$0.3515m equates to 14.80% of the total amount available for investment. This is the same proportion as the A$ borrowing for one year (A$0.5022m) as a percentage of the total A$ borrowing (A$3.3940m).

The proceeds of the investment are equal to the sum of investments maturing in each period plus any coupons received.

The forward exchange rates are then calculated as a function of the cash flows in the two currencies, that is, the A$1m receipts divided by the US$ amounts maturing each year.

Comparison of various methods

The forward rates calculations, utilising the different techniques, are summarised in *Exhibit 9.6*.

The significant differences in the forward rates require comment. The current yield curve method creates a set of forward rates which reflect the interest rate differentials for the various maturities at the inception of the transactions. In contrast, the average forward rate method creates an annual discount of the A$ which is consistent throughout the period. Depending on the actual structure of interest rates, the current yield curve method could, conceivably, produce a set of forward rates some of which are at a premium while others reflect a discount.

Exhibit 9.6
Comparison of LTFX Rates Utilising Different Methods

Year	Current yield curve method	Average forward rate method	Exchange of borrowings	Fully arbitraged cash flow
1	0.6412	0.6562	0.3439	0.5112
2	0.6018	0.6151	0.3439	0.5455
3	0.5649	0.5766	0.3439	0.5788
4	0.5326	0.5405	0.3439	0.6157
5	0.5067	0.5067	0.6556	0.6562

Note: All rates are US$ per A$1.00.

The exchange of borrowings technique provides a set of forward rates, which merely reflect the interest rate differentials embodied in the coupons of the two respective currencies, except in the final period when the repayment of principal is affected. All rates are at a discount on the A$ reflecting the fact that A$ five year interest rates exceed US$ five year rates.

The fully arbitraged method, in the example utilised, yields forward rates with increased discounts in the initial phase which are reduced for the more distant maturities, reflecting the shape of the yield curve in the two currencies whereby the interest differentials are greatest in the shorter maturities. Depending on the shape of the current yield curves, the fully arbitraged method may yield rates similar to those computed on the yield curve base and average rate methods as they are based on a similar principle and on the same rates, although the rates are combined in a different manner.

The variety of techniques and their different results prompts the question as to the most appropriate technique to utilise. There are no simple solutions to this problem although a consideration of some of the major differences between the techniques is instructive.

The current yield curve and average forward rate methods both ignore reinvestment risk as the forward rates derived by these two methods are not fully arbitraged rates. Pricing based on the current yield curve assumes that receipts and payments in each future period may be covered by separate transactions, the price of each of which is based on the interest rate differential for that period. In contrast, the average rate method, despite the advantage of simplicity, assumes that long-term interest rates are the best available predictor of future exchange rates and thereby ignores the shape of the current yield curve. However, in both cases, reinvestment of intermediate cash flows is assumed to take place at the then current interest rate creating uncertainty as to the actual maturity value achieved.

The exchange of borrowings technique provides a set of rates that is fully arbitraged. This is because by entering into a borrowing and investment transaction, an entity can create the desired set of forward rates without incurring any currency risk or reinvestment risk. This technique is suitable primarily for institutions undertaking borrowings which they seek to exchange for borrowings in another currency, that is, the classical process of swap arbitrage. From the perspective of other types of hedges, this pricing mechanism is less appealing in that all forward rates are identical, reflecting the coupon rate differential, except at maturity where the repayment of principal is taken into account. In this regard, the forward rates established using the exchange of borrowings techniques reflect notional forward rates which merely mirror the underlying cash flows at given rates.

The fully arbitraged cash flow technique, while not universally utilised, does have the advantage of providing a fully covered self-liquidating set of forward rates. The technique does not require any reinvestment risk to be assumed. A particular advantage of the fully arbitraged technique is that it is possible to create various sets of fully arbitraged forward exchange rates, by undertaking borrowing and investment transactions in which the *proportions* of the two sides of the transactions are mismatched, in terms of amounts or maturities. This manipulation of forward rates can allow institutions to create particular cash flow patterns which have applications in structuring patterns of income and expense consistent with the organisation's financial and tax requirements.

PRICING LTFX AS ZERO COUPON CURRENCY SWAP

As noted above, LTFX transactions can be priced as fixed-to-fixed zero coupon currency swaps. The use of currency swaps as a pricing basis here is similar to but not identical to the exchange of borrowing and currency swap methodology outlined above. The major difference lies in the fact that under the exchange of borrowing approach, the intention is to create a string of outright forward prices whereas where a fixed-to-fixed zero coupon currency swap is utilised, the intention is to create a single forward rate based on the compounding of the intermediate cash flows in the currency swap.

Exhibit 9.7 sets out an example of structuring and pricing a LTFX transaction as a fixed-to-fixed zero coupon currency swap. As set out in the example, the swap entails A\$ 14.00% pa payable against receipt of US\$ 7.00% pa on principal of A\$100m based on a spot exchange rate of A\$1.00/US\$0.70. In the normal swap case, this would entail receipt of US\$4.9m annually in exchange for payment of A\$14m with the principal being exchanged at maturity. In the case of the zero coupon swap structure, intermediate cash flows are replaced with a single cash flow on maturity. The intermediate A\$ payments of A\$14m are compounded at the rate of 14.00% to give a maturity value of A\$192.541m, reflecting compounded interest together with the repayment of the original principal received under the swap. Similarly, the intermediate US\$ cash flows are compounded at the swap rate of 7.00% pa giving a maturity value of US\$98.179m, reflecting principal plus compounded interest. This would imply a five year outright currency forward rate of A\$1.00/US\$0.5099 or a discount on the spot rate of 0.1901 or 1911 points.

A number of aspects of this transaction should be noted:

- If the initial cash flows are ignored, then the cash flow pattern entailing a receipt of US\$ in exchange for a delivery of A\$ at the end of five years is identical to a five year LTFX contract entailing the sale of A\$ for US\$. For example, a US\$ borrower may have used this to hedge the principal repayment of a loan in this manner.

- The swap structure assumes compounding at the swap rate. In practice, the swap rate would have been adjusted to reflect reinvestment assumptions applicable under market conditions. This issue is discussed in greater detail in Chapter 27.

- The zero coupon currency swap is structured on the basis of exchanges of fixed rate cash flows in both currencies. This type of pricing cannot be applied to a currency swap between a fixed rate and floating rate as the floating rate cash flows are uncertain and their maturity value unknown at the time the transaction is entered into. In practice, as most currency swaps are quoted against US\$ LIBOR, the highly liquid US\$ interest rate swap market can be utilised to imply fixed US\$ rates which can form the basis of this pricing methodology.

- This technique is similar to the exchange of borrowing technique as described above, in that it reflects full arbitrage between the two capital markets in the same manner as the exchange of borrowings methodology.
- In this case, the price of the forward exchange contract for five years has been calculated. A similar methodology, utilising applicable zero coupon swap rates for the different maturities, could be utilised to engineer forward prices for all interim maturities.

Exhibit 9.7

Zero Coupon Currency Swap: Cash Flows

Assume swap rates of A$14.00% pa payable against receipt of US$7.00% pa. All rates are on an annual compounding basis.

CONVENTIONAL US$ FIXED/A$ FIXED CURRENCY SWAP CASH FLOWS

Year	Swap cash flows	
	A$m receipts	US$m payments
0	+100	−70.0
1	−14	−4.9
2	−14	+4.9
3	−14	+4.9
4	−14	+4.9
5	{ −14	{ +4.9
	{ −100	{ +70.0

ZERO COUPON US$ FIXED/A$ FIXED CURRENCY SWAP CASH FLOWS

Year	Swap cash flows					
	A$m receipts	A$m balance at start of period	Interest compounded on swap balance (A$m)	US$m receipts	US$m balance at start of period	Interest compounded on swap balance (US$m)
0	+100.000	+100.000	—	−70.000	70.000	—
1	—	114.000	14.000	—	74.900	4.900
2	—	129.960	15.960	—	80.143	5.243
3	—	148.154	18.194	—	85.753	5.610
4	—	168.896	20.742	—	91.756	6.003
5	−192.541	192.541	23.645	+98.179	98.179	6.423

Chapter 10

Pricing FRAs

APPROACHES TO PRICING FRAS

FRAs are priced off forward-forward interest rates. This forward-forward interest rate may be that implied in the cash market yield curve and capable of replication through cash market transactions, or, alternatively, through implied rates in an available interest rate futures market in the relevant currency.

Effectively, the pricing of FRAs reflects the FRA provider's capability, at least theoretically, to hedge the transaction either through the futures market or by undertaking the relevant cash market transactions.

FRAs can also be priced off a type of forward-forward arbitrage. This type of arbitrage is predicated on the fact that forward foreign exchange prices are determined by interest differentials between the relevant currencies reflecting the yield curves in the respective currencies. This therefore provides another mechanism to hedge by entering into an FRA to hedge the interest rate exposure under a covered interest rate arbitrage transaction, that is, to lock in the interest rate leg for the arbitrage.

FORWARD INTEREST RATES

Forward-forward rates

Forward interest rates can be calculated from the current yield curve. If suitably spaced yields and either synthetic or actual securities are available, then forward rates can be estimated.

The forward rates can be calculated based on the theoretical construct that securities of different maturities can be expected to be substitutes for one another.

Investors at any time have three choices. They may invest in an obligation having a maturity corresponding exactly to their anticipated holding period. They may invest in short-term securities, reinvesting in further short-term securities at each maturity over the holding period. They may invest in a security having a maturity longer than the anticipated holding period. In the last case, they would sell the security at the end of the given period, realising either a capital gain or a loss.

According to a version of the pure expectations theory, investors' expected return for any holding period would be the same, regardless of the alternative or combination of alternatives they chose. This return would be a weighted average of the current short-term interest rate plus future short rates expected to prevail over the holding period; this average is the same for each alternative.

Forward rates may be calculated from the currently prevailing cash market yield curve, as any deviation from the implied forward rates would create arbitrage opportunities which market participants would exploit. This arbitrage is undertaken by buying and selling securities at different maturities to synthetically create the intended forward transaction.

By simultaneously borrowing and lending the same amount in the cash market but for different maturities it is possible to lock in an interest rate for a period in the future. If the maturity of the cash lending exceeds the maturity of the cash borrowing the implied rate over the future period, the forward-forward rate, is a bid rate for a forward investment. Similarly, if the maturity of the cash borrowing exceeds the maturity of the cash lending, then the resulting forward-forward rate is an offer rate for a forward borrowing.

This process of generating forward rates is set out in *Exhibit 10.1*.

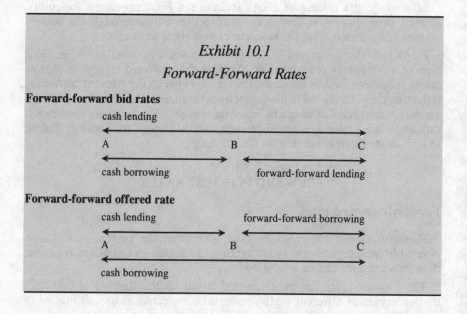

Exhibit 10.1
Forward-Forward Rates

Forward-forward bid rates

cash lending

A   B   C

cash borrowing   forward-forward lending

Forward-forward offered rate

cash lending   forward-forward borrowing

A   B   C

cash borrowing

It is important to note that forward rates, when regarded as forecasts of future short-term interest rates, require a number of theoretical and practical assumptions. From a theoretical perspective, this approach assumes the absence of transaction costs and assumes the validity of the pure expectations theory of the term structure of interest rates. In particular, the forward rate as calculated from the current cash market yield curve contains no compensation for risk and, in particular, includes no liquidity premium.

Despite these theoretical objections, there is considerable behavioural support for this methodology of pricing forward rates and, therefore, FRAs. This is reflected in consistent arbitrage undertaken by market participants to drive FRA rates toward the implicit forward rates in the current cash market yield curve. It should, however, be noted that this process of arbitrage is not costless, involving the use of balance sheets, and consequently market efficiency is strongest in the shorter maturities.

A number of practical difficulties also exist. For example, it is difficult to obtain suitably spaced yields along the complete cash market yield curve. This difficulty is partially overcome by utilising fitted yield curves with forward rates being calculated off the fitted yield curve rather than the actual cash market curve. An additional problem relates to dealing spreads or bid/offer prices (effectively transaction costs) which will naturally distort forward rates.

Despite these minor difficulties, forward rates do bear a significant relationship to the current cash market yield curve although it is useful to bear in mind that forward bid and offer rates deviate sometimes from the implied forward rates and that the more distant the future period is, the greater the spread between the bid and offer rate and the divergence from the implied forward rate.

Exhibit 10.2

Calculating Forward Rates

Maturity (months)	Interest rates (% pa)	Forward rates (% pa)
1	16.00	—
3	15.00	14.50[1] [14.31][5]
6	14.75	14.50[2] [13.98]
12	15.25	15.75[3] [14.67]
24	14.00	12.76[4] [12.76]

Notes:

1. $(1.15)^{0.25} / (1.16)^{0.0833} = 1.0228$

   $(1.0228)^6 = 1.1450$

2. $(1.1475)^{0.50} / (1.15)^{0.25} = 1.0344$

   $(1.0344)^4 = 1.1450$

3. $(1.1525)^1 / (1.1475)^{0.50} = 1.0759$

   $(1.0759)^2 = 15.75$

4. $(1.1400)^2 / (1.1525)^1 = 1.1276$

5. The forward rates indicated in brackets [] are calculated as follows: assume A$1m is invested at 16.00% pa for one month. The maturity value of this investment is A$1,013,333. If A$1m is invested at 15.00% pa for three months it gives a maturity value of A$1,037,500. The two month interest rate in one months time must be equivalent to the rate which allows the A$1,013,333 to accrete to a maturity value of A$1,037,500 where the investment term is two months.

   The second method produces different results to the first as a consequence of different reinvestment assumptions of intermediate cash flows. Neither method is superior but the second technique tends to be favoured by practitioners, reflecting as it does the actual physical transactions that must be undertaken to hedge the FRA.

Estimating forward rates

Forward rate structures are usually derived utilising the following equation:

$$(1 + R_{N-M}) = \frac{(1 + R_N)^N}{(1 + R_m)^M}$$

where: R, M, N = interest rate for maturity M or N expressed as an interest rate pa

Exhibit 10.2 sets out an example of calculating forward rates. The forward rates implied in the example by the yield curve are as follows:

1×3 (2 months in 1 months time): 14.37% pa
3×6 (3 months in 3 months time): 13.98% pa
6×12 (6 months in 6 months time): 14.67% pa
12×24 (12 months in 12 months time): 12.76% pa

On the basis of the above forward rates, FRAs would be priced at or about the implied forward rates. In practice, borrowing (investment) rates would be above (below) the implied forward rates reflecting hedging and transaction costs and the profit to the FRA provider.

FORWARD RATES IMPLIED BY SHORT-TERM INTEREST RATE FUTURES

Pricing of futures contracts

Short-term interest rate futures offer an alternative method for locking in interest rates over future periods. For example, the purchase of a bank bill 90 day futures contract secures approximately a three month investment rate as of the futures delivery or settlement date whereas the sale of the same contract secures approximately a borrowing rate over the equivalent period. Futures contracts, in this regard, represent synthetic forwards and can be used as a substitute for the borrowing and lending transactions in the cash market which can be utilised to lock in an interest rate for a future period.

In their simplest form, futures prices are prices set today to be paid in the future for goods or securities. The price of a futures contract thus depends in part on an assessment of the future price of the underlying instrument at delivery, based on information currently available in the market. Part of this market information is the fact that for some securities, one can arrange to own the underlying instrument on the delivery date by buying it today at the current market price and storing it until that time. If this opportunity is available, the cost associated with immediate purchase and storage until delivery will certainly be an important factor in the price one is willing to pay for a futures contract. Holding the futures contract enables one to avoid the investment of cash and the storage, or carrying costs, that would be incurred if the good or security is bought early and stored until delivery.

Other important factors may influence the market's assessment of the futures price of the underlying instrument. These include:

• uncertainty in the supply or demand for the deliverable security between the date in which the futures price is set and the delivery date;

- any cash flows, such as dividends or interest payments, that one would receive if the security rather than the futures contract were held;
- any risks or uncertainties that futures contract holders are exposed to that makes them willing to pay less for a futures contract than they would in the absence of such risks.

These risks include basis risk which must be borne when using financial futures. This risk arises from fluctuations in the spread between the cash and futures price. Some movement in the basis is expected over the life of a futures contract. However, the underlying motivation for hedging is that the basis is much less volatile than the prices of the underlying security.

Another risk associated with futures positions is the need to immediately make good for losses in the value of a futures contract (referred to as marking-to-market). Uncertainty with respect to the exact instrument that will be delivered and the prices at the point of each settlement can also play a role in price determination for futures.

Calculating futures prices

Prices in the futures market for short-term interest rates are driven mainly by short-term borrowing yields. This is relevant to the futures market because the arbitrage which ensures an equilibrium futures price depends in part on a cash market position financed in the short-term market. An example of the so-called cash and carry trade will help make this clear.

In a competitive market, a risk-free arbitrage should earn a return equal to the risk-free rate. Using this principle, a risk-free position combining cash and futures can be established and the futures price determined such that the return on the combined position earns the risk-free rate over the holding period. Suppose the trade consists of a short position in the bill futures maturing in three months and a long position in the six month bill. The cash bill is financed for three months (prior to its delivery into the contract) at the three month rate. In this trade, the cost of financing and the purchase price of the six month bill are known. Arbitrage will determine the futures price. In equilibrium, it will be bid to a level such that the rate of return represented by the difference between the futures price and the cash bill will be equal to the cost of financing the bill over the three month period. This calculated rate is sometimes called the break even borrowing cost.

If the futures price is greater than the equilibrium level, arbitrageurs will earn a positive return with no risk by purchasing the cash bill, selling the futures and carrying the position at the three month rate. This will drive down the futures price relative to the cash price until the holding period return equals the cost of financing the trade. On the other hand, if the futures price is below the equilibrium price, arbitrageurs will buy the futures, sell the cash and invest the proceeds at a net positive spread. This will tend to drive the futures price up relative to the cash market, again resulting in an equilibrium price such that the rate of return on the trade equals the three month borrowing rate.

In both cases, the synthetic asset consists of cash bills which are either lengthened or shortened by going long or short in the bill futures market.

A long position in futures contract or a strip of futures lengthens the cash bill by purchasing bills today for future delivery. On the other hand, a short futures position essentially sells off the back end of a cash bill, thereby shortening it.

The cash and carry trade is an example of the latter variety; a long cash bill is purchased and then delivered into a short futures position, producing a synthetic asset which matures on the expiration of the futures contract.

Assume the following scenario:

- 120 day bank bills are trading at a yield of 16.00% pa or a price of $950,026.03 per $1m face value (FV);
- the 30 day bank bill rate is 18.00% pa (that is, $985,421.17 per $1m FV);
- this implies a negative carry of 2.00% for 30 days;
- there is a 90 day futures contract settling in 30 days from today.

Utilising this data it is possible to calculate that the futures price should be equivalent to a yield of 15.11% pa or 84.89.

This futures price reflects the fact that the purchase of the 30 day bill and the purchase of the 120 day bill and the sale of a futures contract in 30 days time are equivalent transactions. For example:

Cost of 120 days bill at 16.00%   : $950,026

Proceeds from sale of bill after
30 days (that is, with 90 days to
maturity) at hedged rate of 15.11% : $964,081

                        Profit   : $ 14,055

Return on 30 day investment

$$\left(\frac{14\ 055}{950\ 026} \right) \times \left(\frac{365}{30} \right) \qquad : 18.00\%\ pa$$

This is directly equivalent to the yield on a direct 30 day investment.

If the futures price was above or below 84.89, an arbitrage transaction could be constructed.

If the futures were priced at 85.10, a cash and carry transaction could be constructed to create a synthetic 30 day investment yielding 18.62% pa, an arbitrage yield improvement of 0.62% pa.

If the futures price was 84.64, a reverse cash and carry transaction could be constructed to create a synthetic 180 day investment yielding 16.19%, an arbitrage profit of 0.19% pa.

It is important to note that the above futures price calculations do not include transaction costs such as commissions, deposits and margin calls.

Futures price and FRA prices

The relationship between the futures price and FRA prices is a complex one. The basic relationship is predicated on the FRA provider entering the futures market to hedge its exposure under the FRA itself.

For example, an FRA entered into to hedge a future borrowing or rollover entails the FRA provider having a forward purchase commitment or an exposure to rising rates which it can hedge by selling futures contracts. Consequently, the FRA provider may hedge itself in the relevant interest rate futures contract and therefore will price the FRA transaction on the basis of the corresponding price of the futures contract. However, the relationship is more complex as the terms of the FRA itself (the commencement date and its duration) may not coincide with those of the underlying interest rate futures contract being used to hedge the transaction. In this case, the futures price will be required to be adjusted to reflect these differences.

These adjustments are discussed in Chapter 28, in the context of market making in swap derivatives such as FRAs.

In summary, FRAs in any currency can be hedged utilising short-term interest rate futures contracts in the relevant currency, if such instruments are available. In fact, even if such short-term interest rate futures are not available in the relevant currency, it is in fact possible to replicate the desired instrument by a combination of futures and FRAs in a second currency and foreign exchange transactions as between the two currencies (refer Exhibit 4.3).

Chapter 11
Pricing Caps, Floors and Collars

CAPS, COLLARS ETC. AS OPTIONS

As discussed above in Chapter 5 interest rate caps, floors and collars are essentially identical to a series of options. For example, an interest rate cap can be thought of as a series of put options on the relevant index. The writer of the option (seller of the cap) receives a fee (premium) for the cap (put options) from the purchaser of the option (purchaser of the cap). Similarly, floors can be thought of as a series of call options on the relevant interest rate index. A collar, in contrast, is in effect a combination of the above transactions with the purchaser of the collar buying a series of put options or caps whilst simultaneously selling back to the provider of the collar a series of call options or floors.

Caps, collars etc. are essentially customised versions of exchange-traded options on short-term interest rates. Just as FRAs are a form of synthetic futures, caps and collars are option transactions which are customised in accordance with the requirements of purchasers.

Considerable theory exists as to the pricing of option contracts. Predictably, fees for caps, floors and collars tend to be priced with reference to option pricing theory.

OPTION VALUATION CONCEPTS

Option pricing nomenclature

In determining the value of an option, it is possible to distinguish between the *intrinsic value* and the *time value* of an option. An option's intrinsic value is based on the difference between its exercise price and the current price of the underlying debt instrument. If the option is currently profitable to exercise, it is said to have intrinsic value, that is, a call (put) option has intrinsic value if the current price of the instrument is above (below) the option's exercise price. Whether or not the option has intrinsic value, it may have time value (defined as the excess of the premium over the option's intrinsic value). The time value of the option reflects the amount buyers are willing to pay for the possibility that, at some time prior to expiration, the option may become profitable to exercise.

Three other option valuation terms merit comment:

- in-the-money;
- at-the-money;
- out-of-the-money.

It is customary for market participants to refer to particular options as belonging to one of the three groups. An option with an exercise price at

142

or close to the current market price of the underlying security is said to be at-the-money. An option with intrinsic value is referred to as being in-the-money, while an out-of-the-money option is one with no intrinsic value, but presumably with some time value.

In using this option valuation terminology in the context of caps, floors and collars, it is necessary to recognise that the relevant current market price (or yield) of the underlying debt instrument is not the spot market price for the physical security. Instead, it is the *forward price* for the relevant security which is the relevant price benchmark.

For example, consider a three year interest rate cap agreement on three month LIBOR at a cap level of 10.00% pa. This agreement represents a commitment by the writer or seller of the interest rate cap that it will compensate the purchaser if, on specified quarterly dates over the three year period of the transaction, three month LIBOR exceeds the cap level of 10.00% pa. If current three month LIBOR rates are 8.00%, then it is tempting to argue that this interest rate cap is out-of-the-money. However, the cap level (the strike price of the option) must necessarily be compared with the current actual price of the security. This requires that the cap level be compared to the *forward* three month LIBOR rates over the full three year period of the agreement.

The agreement itself represents a series of 11 put options with a strike price equivalent to a yield of 10.00% on three month LIBOR commencing in three months time and terminating at the end of 36 months. Consequently, the strike price of 10.00% must be compared to the three month forward LIBOR rates on each of the relevant quarterly periods covered by the interest rate cap. Whether each option is in- or out-of-the-money will largely be determined by the shape of the yield curve (refer to the calculation technology for forward rates discussed above in Chapter 10).

Factors affecting option pricing

The fundamental direct determinants of option value include:

- the current price of the underlying instrument;
- the exercise price of the option;
- interest rates;
- the time to expiry;
- the volatility of prices on the underlying instrument.

Other factors affecting option valuation include the type of option (that is, whether the option is American or European) as well as payouts from holding the underlying instrument.

The general effect of each of the five major relevant variables on the value of an option (where all other variables are held constant) is summarised in *Exhibit 11.1*. The effect of changes in the spot price of the instrument, option strike prices, and time to expiry on the pricing of options are relatively easily understood.

Exhibit 11.1
Factors Affecting Option Valuation

Factor	Effect of increase in factor on value of	
	Call	Put
Strike price	Decrease	Increase
Spot price	Increase	Decrease
Interest rate	Increase	Decrease
Time to expiry	Increase	Increase
		(American option only)
Volatility	Increase	Increase

In the case of a call option, the higher the price of the underlying instrument, the higher the intrinsic value of the option if it is in-the-money and hence the higher the premium. If the call is out-of-the-money, then the higher the underlying instrument's price the greater the probability that it will be possible to exercise the call at a profit and hence the higher the time value, or premium, of the option. In the case of put options, the reverse will apply.

The impact of changes in exercise price is somewhat similar. For an in-the-money call option the lower the exercise price, the higher the intrinsic value, while for an out-of-the-money call the lower the exercise price the greater the probability of profitable exercise and hence the higher the time value. A similar but opposite logic applies in the case of put options.

The impact of time to expiration and option valuation is predicated on the fact that the longer an option has to run, the greater the probability that it will be possible to exercise the option profitably, hence the greater the time value of the option.

The impact of volatility derives from the fact that the greater the expected movement in the price of the underlying instrument, the greater the probability that the option can be exercised at a profit and hence the more valuable the option or its time value. In essence, the higher the volatility, the greater the likelihood that the asset will either do very well or very poorly which is reflected in the price of the option.

The impact of interest rates is less clear intuitively. The role of interest rates in the determination of option premiums is complex and varies from one type of option to another. In general, however, the higher the interest rate, the lower the *present value* of the exercise price the call buyer has contracted to pay in the event of exercise. In essence, a call option can be thought of as the right to buy the underlying asset at the discounted value of the exercise price. Consequently, the greater the degree of discount the more valuable is the right, hence, as interest rates increase and the degree of discount increases commensurately, the corresponding option value increases. In fact, a higher interest rate has a similar influence to that of a lower exercise price.

OPTION PRICING THEORY

Approaches to mathematical option pricing

Mathematical option pricing models seek to calculate the price of particular options, utilising the identified fundamental determinants of option value and incorporating these within a defined formalised mathematical framework. The technological approach of formal valuation is the same regardless of the type of option being evaluated, whether it be an option on a share, currencies, or a debt instrument as well as futures contracts on each of these assets.

The development of mathematical option pricing models requires the following distinct steps:

- definition of certain rational arbitrage boundaries on the potential value of the option;

- specific assumptions as to the market and economic environment within which the option is sought to be valued as well as the likely price behaviour of the underlying instrument;

- derivation of a pricing solution, given the assumptions about economic environment and price behaviour within the valuation boundary constraints identified.

Boundary conditions to option values[1]

The first step in mathematical pricing is to identify certain boundaries that can be placed on the values of options based on arbitrage considerations. The concept of arbitrage in this context relies upon dominance whereby a portfolio asset is said to dominate another portfolio if, for the same cost, it offers a return that will, at least, be the same. The underlying assumption, in this context, is that if these boundary conditions are breached, arbitrage activity would force the prices of the underlying assets and options within the arbitrage boundaries as arbitrageurs would enter into transactions designed to take advantage of riskless profit opportunities.

In the interest of clarity, in this section, the boundary conditions to option value are stated with reference to generalised assets. Arbitrage conditions specific to options on debt instruments, that is, caps, floors and collars, are considered later in this chapter. However, it should be noted that the conditions discussed in this section are common to all options and the principles underlying the arbitrage conditions are fundamentally identical.

The following notation is used in outlining the boundary conditions:

S	= asset price
K	= strike price
T	= time to maturity
RF	= risk free interest rate
V	= volatility of returns from asset
C(A)	= price of American call
C(E)	= price of European call

1. This discussion on boundary conditions is based substantially upon Rowley (1987).

P(A)	=	price of American put
P(E)	=	price of European put
AB	=	arbitrage boundary
VP	=	value of portfolio
PV(K)	=	present value of amount K

There are nine major arbitrage boundaries discussed in this section. Put-call parity for options is a special arbitrage condition which is discussed later in this chapter.

AB 1

$$C(A) \text{ or } C(E) \geq 0$$

AB 1 states that the value of the call option is greater than or equal to 0. Option exercise is voluntary, consequently, investors will never undertake an option transaction if they lose money which means that call prices cannot take on negative values.

AB 2

At maturity of the option:

$$C(A) \text{ or } C(E) = 0 \text{ or } S{-}K$$
$$P(A) \text{ or } P(E) = 0 \text{ or } K{-}S.$$

At maturity, the value of a call or put option will be either 0 or its intrinsic value. If this condition is not satisfied, arbitrage opportunities exist. For example, if a call at maturity sells for less than $S{-}K$, arbitrageurs could lock in a profit by borrowing enough to purchase the call and exercising it immediately making a riskless profit after paying back the loan.

AB 3

Prior to maturity of the option,

$$C(A) \text{ will equal: } \begin{array}{l} \geq 0 \text{ or} \\ \geq S{-}K \end{array}$$

$$P(A) \text{ will equal: } \begin{array}{l} \geq 0 \text{ or} \\ \geq K{-}S \end{array}$$

AB 3 is an extension of AB 2. If at any time *prior* to maturity, an American option contract sells for less than its intrinsic value, an arbitrage opportunity exists to purchase the option and exercise immediately while buying or selling the physical asset to lock in a riskless profit.

AB 4

$$C(A) \geq C(E)$$
$$P(A) \geq P(E)$$

An American call should not sell for a premium value less than an identical European option because the American style of option provides all the benefits of the European contract with the addition of being able to be exercised at any time.

AB 5

An American call which has no intermediate cash flows should never be exercised before maturity; it is always better to sell the option.

The validity for this arbitrage can be established by constructing the following two portfolios:

> VP1: Buy C(E) and invest PV of strike price (PV(K))
>
> VP2: Buy S

The payoff from these two portfolios is set out below:

Portfolio	Current value	Value at maturity	
		Out-of-the-money $Sm < K$	In-the-money $Sm \geq K$
VP1	C(E) + PV(K)	0 + K	(Sm − K) − K
VP2	S	Sm	Sm
Relationship between portfolio values at maturity "m"		VP1 > VP2	VP1 = VP2

At maturity, VP1 is never worth less than VP2, so the current cost of VP1 can never be less than that of VP2. This implies that an American call option will usually never be exercised prior to maturity as the investor would only receive the intrinsic value of the option (S−K) which is less than $(S-K)E^{-RFT}$ for any positive interest rate. Consequently, AB 5 indicates that a rational investor will always sell a call option to somebody else rather than exercise the option.

AB 6

In the case of an American call where there are intermediate cash flows, early exercise is possible.

AB 6 is a variation of AB 5 which implies that where there are intermediate cash flows, an American option is capable of early exercise. The proof of this strategy can be established by constructing portfolios which are similar to above. The two portfolios are as follows:

> VP3: Buy C(E) and invest PV of strike price (PV (K + D))
>
> VP4: Buy S

Note that the amount invested is equal to the option's strike price and the intermediate cash flow.

Assuming that the intermediate cash flow is D, the payoff from these two portfolios will be as follows:

Portfolio	Current value	Value at maturity	
		Out-of-the-money $Sm < K$	In-the-money $Sm \geq K$
VP3	C(E) + PV(K)	0 + K + D	(Sm − K) + K + D
VP4	S	Sm + D	Sm + D
Relationship between portfolio values at maturity "m"		VP3 > VP4	VP3 = VP4

The payout table indicates that at maturity VP3 never pays less than VP4 and gives a higher return when the option expires out-of-the-money. Consequently, VP3 cannot sell for less than VP2. This means that whenever a European call is in-the-money prior to maturity the lowest value it can trade for will be equal to the stock price minus the investment required to receive an amount equal to the strike price plus any intermediate cash flow at maturity [S−PV (K + D)]. The lower limit on the value of the European call must be the lower limit on an American option's value.

This implies an optimal exercise policy for an American option on an asset with intermediate cash flows. If the lower limit on the call's value [S−PV (K + D)] is greater than the amount received by exercising (S−K), then it is better to sell than exercise. However, if [S−PV (K + D)] is less than (S−K), the American cal should be exercised rather than sold if the position is to be closed down.

In general terms, an American call should therefore only be exercised early when the discounted value of the strike price and intermediate cash flows are worth more than the strike price. In essence, it is PV(D) that determines whether the option is sold or exercised. Early exercise is therefore more probable on American options where the underlying asset has high intermediate cash flows.

AB 7

$$C(E) \text{ or } C(A) \leq S$$

A call option cannot be worth more than the underlying stock because if the option were worth more than the stock, then a riskless arbitrage profit could be made by writing a call and using the proceeds to buy the stock. If the call is exercised, the stock can be delivered and the strike price received in return, while if the call is unexercised at maturity the stock which has a positive value will be held, thereby allowing the arbitrageur to make a positive profit without incurring any risk.

AB 8

C(E) or C(A) can never be worth more than an identical option with a lower exercise price.

P(E) or P(A) can never be worth more than an identical option with a higher exercise price.

In this case, the call with the low exercise price offers a greater chance of being in-the-money, consequently, it cannot sell for a price which is lower than an option which has less chance of being in-the-money. The reverse is true for put options.

AB 9

C(E) or C(A) cannot be worth less than an identical option with a shorter time to maturity.

Intuitively, the longer the maturity on the option, the greater the opportunity for there to be a sufficiently large change in the asset price to push the option into the money. Consequently, an option with a longer maturity cannot sell for less than an equivalent option with a shorter maturity. If this condition is violated, an arbitrage can be set up whereby the arbitrageur writes the shorter dated option while purchasing the option with the longer maturity to lock in a riskless arbitrage profit.

Put-call parity

Put-call parity which defines the relationship between the price of a European call option and a European put option with the same exercise price and time to expiration is an additional arbitrage boundary on option values. Utilising the same notation as that used previously, put-call parity can be stated as follows:

$$C(E) + PV(K) = P(E) + S$$

This implies that buying a call and investing PV of K is identical to buying a put and buying the asset.

The proof of this relationship can be established by setting up two portfolios:

VP1: Buy $C(E)$ and invest $PV(K)$

VP2: Buy $P(E)$ and buy S

The payoffs on the two portfolios at maturity are as follows:

Portfolio	Current value	Value at maturity	
		Out-of-the-money $Sm < K$	In-the-money $Sm \geq K$
VP1	$C(E) + PV(K)$	$0 + K$	$(S_m - K) + K$
VP2	$P(E) + S$	$(K - S_m) + S_m$	$0 + S_m$

Relationship between portfolio values at maturity "m"

$$VP1 = VP2 \qquad VP1 = VP2$$

At maturity, VP1 is equal to VP2 irrespective of whether the option expires in- or out-of-the-money.

The put-call parity condition can be restated as follows:

Synthetic call (reversal)

$$C(E) = P(E) + S - PV(K)$$

Synthetic put (conversion)

$$P(E) = C(E) - S + PV(K)$$

Long asset/forward

$$S = C(E) - P(E) + PV(K)$$

Short asset/forward

$$-S = P(E) - C(E) - PV(K)$$

For European options, arbitrage possibilities will exist if the put-call parity conditions are not fulfilled. An example of put-call parity arbitrage is set out in *Exhibit 11.2*.

Exhibit 11.2
Put-call Parity Arbitrage

Assume that the Sydney Futures Exchange (SFE) 90 day bank bill futures contract for the near month is trading at 86.14/86.15. Call options on the contract with strike price 86.00 on the contract are trading at 0.28/0.33. Put options with an identical strike price are trading at 0.02/0.07. In these circumstances, it is possible to create a synthetic 86.00 call at less than 0.28 as follows:

• buy 86.00 put at 0.07;

• simultaneously, buy futures at 86.15;

• sell 86.00 call at 0.28.

This transaction effectively creates a call at less than the 0.28 received. This can be proved as follows: the sold call and the bought put are equivalent to a synthetic short futures position at a price of 86.00. The position creates a net cash flow to the grantor of 0.21. Of the 0.21, 0.15 is lost through the bought bond futures position at 86.15 which is above the synthetic short price of 86.00. However, the futures loss of 0.15 is more than offset by the 0.21 gain on the option.

The analysis ignores the different value of points (0.01) at different yield levels.

It is important to note that the put-call parity theorem is only valid for European options. Synthetic positions for American options are not always pure. For example, if S decreases and P(A) is exercised, then you would lose the difference between K and S immediately, not at the forward date.

This means that put-call parity for American options can be stated as follows:

$$C(A) - S + PV(K) \leq P(A) \leq C(A) - S + K$$

Mathematical option pricing models: the conceptual basis assumptions underlying option pricing model

Mathematical option pricing models can be developed to synthesise the many factors which affect the option premium within the arbitrage boundaries identified. In order to develop such mathematical option pricing models, it is necessary to make a number of restrictive assumptions, including:

• no restrictions or costs of short selling;

• no taxes or transaction costs;

• asset trading is continuous, with all asset prices following continuous and stationary stochastic processes;

• asset has no intermediate cash flows (for example, dividends, interest etc.);

• the risk free rate of interest is constant over the option's life;

• the asset price moves around in a continuously random manner;

• the distribution of the asset's return is log normal;

• the variance of the return distribution is constant over the asset's life;

• the option is European.

Most of these assumptions are self-explanatory and are consistent with efficient capital market theory. Stochastic process refers to the evolution of asset prices through time modelled as random, characterised by continuous series of price changes governed by the laws of probability as prescribed. By continuous processes, it is usually implied that the price of the underlying asset can vary over time but does not have discontinuities or jumps, that is, the price movement over time of the asset could be graphed without lifting the pen from the paper.

The stationary stochastic process, as assumed, is one that is determined the same way for all time periods of equal length. Specifically, the traditional approach to option valuation assumed at the price of the underlying asset has a particular type of probability distribution, assumed to be a log normal distribution. It is also assumed that the standard deviation of this distribution is constant over time.

The "riskless hedge" concept

The derivation of the mathematical option pricing model also requires understanding of the concept of a riskless hedge. A riskless portfolio by definition consists of an asset and a corresponding option held in proportion to the prescribed hedge ratio, continuously adjusted, whereby the portfolio is perfectly hedged against movements in asset prices as changes in the call price and the asset price are mutually offsetting. Utilising the constructs of portfolio theory or the capital asset pricing model, it is predicted that a riskless portfolio should earn no more than a risk free rate of return. It is important to note that outside the context of this riskless hedge construct, the values derived by mathematical option pricing models are not meaningful.

Certain riskless portfolio positions are set out below:

* Position for hedging:
   —long position in calls;
   —short position in calls;
   —long position in the stock;
   —short position in the stock.

* How to hedge it:
   —short stock for each call held;
   —long stock for each call issued;
   —short $(1/\Delta)$ of calls for each stock held;
   —hold $(1/\Delta)$ of calls for each stock held.

The Black and Scholes option pricing model

Black and Scholes (1973) were the first to provide a close form solution for the valuation of European call options. The mathematical derivation of the Black and Scholes' option pricing model is beyond the mathematical capabilities assumed for this text.

Black and Scholes' option pricing model is usually specified as follows:

$$C(E) = S. N (d_1) - Ke^{-RF.T} .N (d_2)$$

where: $d_1 = \dfrac{\ln (S/K) + (RF + V^2 /2)T}{v \sqrt{T}}$

$d_2 = \dfrac{\ln (S/K) + (RF - V^2 /2)T}{v \sqrt{T}}$

$N (d_1)$ and $N (d_2)$ are cumulative normal distribution functions for d_1 and d_2

ln is the natural logarithm

$Ke^{-RF.T}$ is the amount of cash needed to be invested over period or time T at a continuously compounded interest rate of RF in order to receive K at maturity

The price of a European put option can be derived by utilising put-call parity.

Binomial option pricing

The binomial option pricing model utilises an identical logical approach to Black and Scholes. However, in contrast to Black and Scholes, the binomial approach assumes that the security price obeys a binomial generating process and the relevant option cannot or will not be exercised prior to expiration (that is, the option is European).

The valuation process begins by considering the possibility that the price can move up or down over a given period by a given amount. This enables calculation of the value of the call option at expiration of the relevant period (which is always the greater of zero or the price of the instrument minus the exercise price). The riskless hedge technique starts at expiration and works backwards in time to the current period for a portfolio consisting of the physical security sold short or one sold futures contract on the relevant asset and one bought call option on the relevant asset.

Since the portfolio is riskless, it, consistent with Black and Scholes, must return the risk free rate of return over the relevant period. The derivation of the value of the call option using this approach is predicated on the fact that the call option must be priced so that the risk free hedge earns exactly the risk free rate of return.

The binomial option pricing model contains the Black and Scholes formula as a limiting case. If, for the binomial option pricing model, the number of sub-periods are allowed to tend to infinity, the binomial option pricing model tends to the option pricing formula derived by Black and Scholes.

A significant advantage of the binomial approach is that it provides a solution not only for the closed form European option pricing problem but also for the more difficult American option pricing problems when numerical simulation approaches must be employed. In essence, the binomial pricing approach is useful as it can accommodate more complex option pricing problems.

Violation of Black and Scholes[2]

The major attraction of option pricing models such as Black and Scholes and its variations include:

- the fact that all input variables, other than volatility, are directly observable;
- the models do not make any reference to the investor's attitudes to risk.

While the model plays a central role in option valuation trading, the underlying assumptions do not necessarily hold true in practice. In particular, major violations of the model's assumptions exist in the following areas:

- asset price behaviour;
- volatility measurement;
- constancy of interest rates;
- no intermediate cash flows;
- the issue of early exercise.

The key assumption that price changes are independent and log normally distributed over time with constant variance is violated in practice. The assumption of independence of asset price changes, as required by efficient market theory, is not wholly convincing. The empirical evidence and support for the log normal distribution of asset prices and its constancy over time is also not convincing. It is clear that option prices are sensitive to the stochastic processes assumed and changes in the assumptions produce significant, large percentage changes in option prices.

The violation of the asset price behaviour assumptions underlying Black and Scholes has prompted the development of variations on the basic model which make use of alternative stochastic processes, including absolute diffusion, displaced diffusion, jump processes and diffusion-jump processes. Empirical tests have tended to show that these alternative models are not able to provide better predictions of actual prices than the Black and Scholes type of model on a consistent basis. The price differences resulting from differing assumptions as to the underlying asset price movements in fact are *no* greater than the price differences that result from different assumptions of volatility.

The asset price volatility factor required as an input to option pricing models must be "forward looking", that is, a forecast of the probable size (although not necessarily the direction) of asset price changes between the present and the maturity of the option. The problem in volatility estimation (the determination of the true constant volatility of the asset price) is, in practice, sought to be overcome by utilising two types of volatility: historical and implied.

Historical volatility is based on past prices of the underlying asset computed as the standard deviation of log relatives of daily price returns (usually annualised) over a period of time. Utilising historical volatility requires the selection of the period over which price data is to be sampled. It is possible to utilise price information over long periods (up to five years or longer)

---

2. This discussion is based substantially on Das (1987).

to derive the volatility estimate. This assumes that volatility is constant over long periods. It is also possible to use a much shorter period (less than 30 days) to get a good estimate of the current level of volatility. It is necessary to adjust the volatility input into the option pricing formula on a regular basis where short-term volatility is used on the basis that the volatility actually varies significantly.

Implied volatility is determined by solving an option pricing model (such as Black and Scholes) in reverse, that is, calculating the volatility which would be needed in the formula to make the market price equal to fair value as calculated by the model. Where this method is used, the implied volatility equates the model premium to the actual premium observed in the option market. An interesting problem with implied volatility measures is that options with different strike prices but with the same maturity often have different implied volatility.[3]

Historical volatility is a measure of past, already experienced, price behaviour. To the extent the option pricing model is validated, implied volatility reflects market expectations of future price behaviour during the life of the option. Both measures are important, and comparing the two can reveal interesting insights into the market in the underlying asset. However, no normative rule for derivation of the volatility estimate is available. This means that in reviewing option premiums, particularly where the value of the option in question is sensitive to the volatility estimate utilised, any option price suggested by an option pricing model must be regarded with caution.

Some attempted solutions to the volatility measurement model have sought to explicitly take into account the stochastic nature *of volatility* itself by using multi-factor numerical techniques which utilise two stochastic variables, namely, the asset and the volatility.

The model assumption regarding constancy of interest rates is also problematic. While option prices are relatively insensitive to interest rate fluctuations, Beenstock (1981) concludes that if interest rates are uncertain, Black and Scholes tend to underprice by approximately 4.00%.

The assumption that interest rates are constant is particularly problematic in the case of options on debt instruments. This is because interest rate changes drive asset price changes where the asset itself is an interest bearing security. In addition, the volatility of asset prices in the case of debt instrument is a function of remaining maturity and, in turn, interest rates which reflect the shape of the yield curve. As maturity diminishes, the volatility of the asset diminishes and constant variance cannot be assumed.

The impact of intermediate cash flows depends on the pattern of payments and the certainty with which the cash flows can be predicted. The Black and Scholes model does not appear to be very sensitive to assumptions about intermediate payouts which are certain. Where the intermediate cash flows are uncertain, however, the closed form Black and Scholes approach appears to break down and it is particularly difficult to compute American call prices.

3. This discussion of volatility is based on Jarratt (1987).

The Black and Scholes model sets a lower limit for the price of the American call, but the model does not encompass the additional problem of determining the optimal time to exercise the option where the possibility of early exercise is not excluded. However, the model provides a reasonable approximation for the prices of American options.

Empirical tests of the Black and Scholes model indicate that the model is remarkably robust and provides accurate pricing for at-the-money options with medium to long maturity. The model appears to systematically misprice out-of-the money and in-the-money options and also options where volatility increases or time to maturity is very short. In general, however, the model appears to successfully capture the essential determinants of option prices and United States studies show that traders cannot make consistent above normal returns on an after tax, post commission basis by setting up hedged portfolios.

Different models, which seek to overcome some deficiencies of Black and Scholes, essentially introduce new assumptions and do not necessarily produce improvements in pricing predictions.

The increased effort in improving and developing variations on available theoretical option pricing models creates the added problem of model selection. Clearly, there is no simple basis for selecting between the various techniques as the actual benefit from a particular model will depend on the user's objective. The selection of any model, practically, depends on the user's assumptions concerning the underlying asset price process. As there is no universal or true underlying process of asset prices, there can be no universal option pricing model and therefore no definitive fair value price for options.

The strength of the various option pricing models may ultimately lie in their capacity to compress the four observable variables into one other variable, implied volatility, which can then be interpreted. However, the problem of model pricing performance has led to option grantors utilising risk management techniques to manage the risk of writing options.

Hedge ratios: comparative statics

Mathematical option pricing models not only provide a neat closed form means of valuing option contracts, but, in addition, these models provide a wealth of additional data with respect to the various formula variables. For example, the delta, that is, the derivative of C with respect to S, provides investors, portfolio managers or market makers with the exact hedge ratio required to hedge their portfolio position in options or in the underlying assets.

These derivatives allow market participants to identify the short-term sensitivity of option premiums to changes in the underlying security price, volatility, time to expiration etc. In mathematical terms, these sensitivities are derivatives of the premium with respect to these parameters.

These derivatives include:

- Price delta (delta): the change in the premium given a unit change in the underlying price. Deep out-of-the-money options have deltas close to zero because they are not very responsive to changes in the underlying asset price; deep in-the-money options have deltas close to 1 because they move in step with the underlying price; at-the-money options tend to have deltas close to 0.5 because of the interaction between time value and intrinsic value.

- Price gamma (gamma): the second derivative of the premium (delta is the first derivative) with respect to the underlying security price. It indicates how quickly delta will change as the underlying price changes, that is, the change in the price delta given the unit change in the underlying price. Gamma is generally maximised for at-the-money options which are close to expiration.

- Volatility delta (vega): the change in the premium given a one percentage change in the implied volatility. The absolute change in the option price for a given change in volatility is largest when the option is at-the-money with a long time to expiration.

- Time delta (theta): the decline in the premium given a one day passage of time. Theta increases as the option approaches expiry as this means that the time value of an option falls much more quickly as the time remaining to expiration diminishes.

Exhibits 11.3, 11.4, 11.5 and 11.6 set out sample plots of the various derivatives and their behaviour over time.

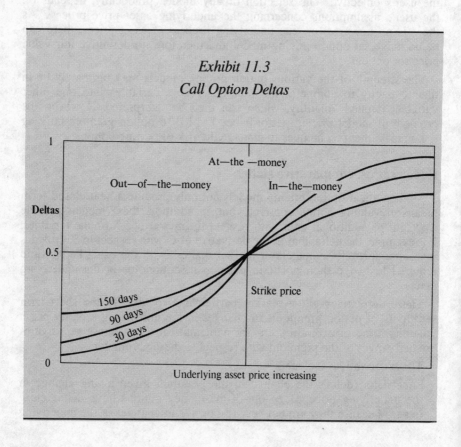

Exhibit 11.3

Call Option Deltas

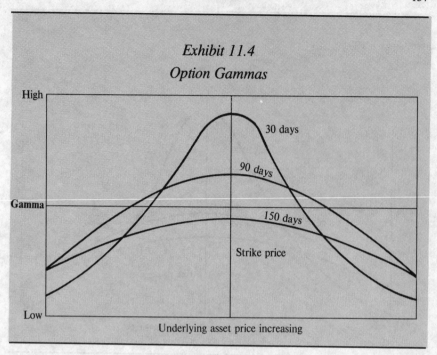

Exhibit 11.4
Option Gammas

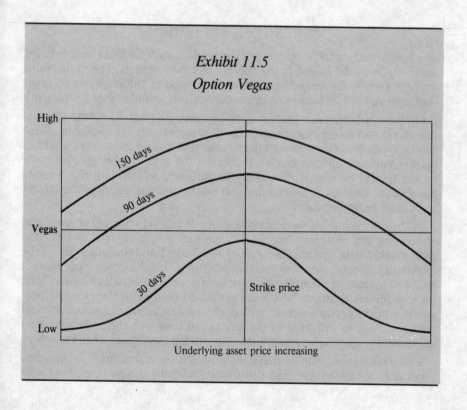

Exhibit 11.5
Option Vegas

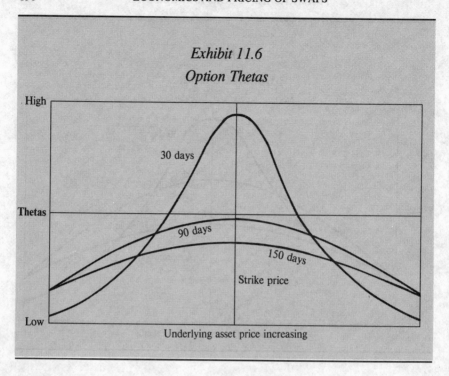

Exhibit 11.6
Option Thetas

PRICING OF DEBT OPTIONS

The basic mathematical option pricing models, such as Black and Scholes, were originally developed in the context of equity options. The basic model requires significant amendments where it is used to value options on other instruments, such as futures contracts, currencies and also debt instruments.

Options in both cash market debt instruments (that is, actual physical securities) and futures on the relevant debt instrument are available. These similar types of options co-exist despite the fact that a cash market, a futures market and one options market (either on the cash market instrument or on the futures contract) will usually be sufficient to fulfill all risk transfer possibilities since the option on the cash market and the option on the futures market serve similar functions.

In distinguishing between options on cash market debt instruments and options on the corresponding futures market, it is important to note that cash market debt options, because of the limited and declining life of the underlying security, present special problems. Unlike other cash market financial assets (for example, shares or foreign currencies) which have infinite lives or futures contracts which are not based on a particular, wasting debt security, but rather on a security with particular characteristics, actual physical debt securities are affected by the passage of time with the underlying debt instrument getting closer to maturity as the option itself approaches expiration.

This feature necessitates that a debt option on cash market instruments takes one of two forms: fixed deliverable, whereby a debt instrument with specified characteristics is required to be delivered; or variable deliverable, whereby a specified existing debt issue is required to be delivered.

For instance, a six month call option on a 90 day bank bill (the 13.50% May 1994 Commonwealth government bond) which requires delivery of a bank bill with 90 days to maturity (the 13.50% May 1994 bond—irrespective of remaining term to maturity) is an example of a fixed (variable) deliverable option.

These features of debt instruments must be incorporated into the pricing of debt options. The key differences relative to other types of options which must be incorporated in the pricing mechanism of debt options include:

- The underlying security in the case of debt instrument usually involves payouts in the form of interest during the life of the option.
- The rate of interest cannot be assumed to be constant as interest rate changes drive price changes in the underlying asset.
- The volatility of the underlying debt instrument depends on maturity, therefore, constant variance cannot be assumed.

The presence of these factors will vary depending on whether the underlying asset for the debt option is a cash market debt security or a futures contract on the relevant debt instrument. Where the option is on a futures contract on the relevant debt instrument, the fact that there are no coupon interest payments and that the maturity of the particular debt security is fixed, means that the general pricing technology applicable to options on futures contracts can be utilised. However, where the option is on the physical debt security, the presence of these three factors is problematic.

The assumption made by models such as Black and Scholes that there are no intermediate cash payouts can be relaxed using a modification of the formula that allows for payouts that are proportional to the price of the underlying security. However, the normal type of adjustment utilised may not be appropriate in the case of debt options. Where the option is on an underlying security which bears a coupon, the accrued interest is continuously added to the full price of a bond representing a continuous payout to the holder of the debt security. As the coupons are fixed in dollar amounts not proportional to the price of the underlying debt security, this type of modification proposed is inappropriate.

The effect of changes in interest rates and in the time to expiration are even more complex. For options on assets, such as shares, as the risk free rate increases, the value of the call option increases as the present value of the exercise price in the event of exercise declines; that is, if the call option and the security itself are regarded as different ways for an investor to capture any gain on the security price, as rates rise the increased cost of carry on the underlying security will make the call more attractive leading to an increase in its value. However, in the case of debt options, it is unreasonable to assume (as is usually done in the case of equity options) that the price of the underlying debt security is independent of the level of interest rates. Significant movements in the prices of debt instruments will occur as a result of changes in interest rates and, in general, any cost of carry consideration will be minor relative to the change in the value of the underlying security. For example, it would be reasonable to assume that rate increases will usually have a *negative* impact on the price of call options on debt instruments as a rise in interest rates will most likely cause a fall in the price of the underlying instrument or futures contract.

Since interest rates are the driving variable behind the price of debt securities, assumptions made in respect of interest rates in deriving option values must be consistent with the possible price effects on the underlying security. A number of complex option pricing models, involving the modelling of the yield curve movements, can be utilised to calculate debt option prices. In some cases, these models assume that the short-term rate, necessary to calculate the riskless hedge earnings, is a known function of the rate or price of the underlying security. More complicated yield curve movements, such as parallel shifts, snap ups and snap downs, can also be incorporated into various models. While these more complex models may be more theoretically correct, they are in practice difficult to implement and, unfortunately, require additional assumptions to be made.

The effect of changes in time to expiration is also problematic. For options on assets with unlimited lives, an option with a longer time to expiration will be worth more than a comparable option with a shorter term to expiry on the basis that it has all the attributes of the nearer option plus more benefits for the holder, that is, there is greater probability that the option can be profitably exercised. This pricing property need not necessarily hold for debt options, particularly variable deliverable options, as depending on the relative magnitudes of the time value and the intrinsic value, it is conceivable that, under certain circumstances, an option with the longer time to expiration may be worth less than one with a shorter term. This would reflect the fact that securities usually begin to trade closer to par as the instrument approaches maturity. This greater price stability may distort the value of the option.

In practice, the pricing of debt options falls into two categories:

• Options on futures where the underlying asset is a standardised debt instrument: these types of options are valued in a manner consistent with the valuation of futures options as the problems of intermediate cash flows and uncertain term to maturity can be minimised.

• Options on physical debt instruments: these are more problematic and usually entail the use of various numerical, usually binomial, option pricing models.

PRICING CAPS, FLOORS AND COLLARS

The discussion to date has focused on the generalised theory of option pricing as well as the pricing of general debt options. Within this framework, the pricing of cap, floor and collar agreements usually takes a definite form. The approach to pricing of such contracts reflects the fact that they are essentially European options on short-term interest rates. Consequently, they are analogous, for the most part, to European options on futures or forward contracts on short-term interest rates. This basic intuition is reinforced by the fact that caps, floors and collars are essentially simple, customised versions of options on short-term interest rate futures. There is considerable interaction between the two markets whereby the sellers of caps etc., utilise the futures and options on futures markets to hedge risk positions.

This approach to pricing allows these contracts to utilise Black's version of the original basic Black and Scholes' model for a premium paid European option on a futures contract:

$$C(E) = e^{-RF.T}[F.N.(d_1) - K.N.(d_2)]$$
$$d_1 = \frac{\ln(F/K) + (1/2\ V^2\ T)}{V\sqrt{T}}$$
$$d_2 = d_1 - V\sqrt{T}$$

All notation is as used elsewhere in this chapter except as follows:

F = forward or future prices of the underlying asset

The intuition behind the Black reformulation of the Black and Scholes option pricing model in the context of futures is that:

- Investment in a futures contract requires no commitment of funds (deposits, margins etc. are ignored), whereas investment in the physical asset, for example, a share in the case of an equity option, imposes a cost. Consequently, nothing is paid or received (up-front) in setting up the hedge which entails buying or selling the futures contract.

- The value of a call option on a futures contract should be lower than the value of a call option on the physical asset, as the futures price should already impound the carrying costs associated with the physical commodity.

That is, the futures price is in essence the forward price which will naturally reflect any carry costs over the relevant period.

The price of a put option on the futures contract can be derived utilising standard put-call parity as follows for European put options:

$$P(E) = C(E) - (F - K)e^{RF.T}$$

The usual qualifications concerning early exercise of American options will, of course, apply.

The computational method for the price of the relevant options will differ depending on the type of margining system applicable. When the margining system dictates that proceeds are not paid up-front to option writers (for example, on the London and Sydney Futures Exchanges) prices have to be higher to compensate the seller for the fact that the premium is not received at the beginning and consequently it is not available for investment. If it is assumed initially that the premium is paid over to the seller of the option only at maturity, the premium would have to be increased by the additional interest that could have been earned over the life of the option if the premium was available for investment. Consequently, the value of the call option will become:

$$C(E) = F.N(d_1) - K.N(d_2)$$

In addition, the put-call parity relationship, where proceeds are not paid up-front for open futures contracts, is different:

$$P(E) = C(E) - F + K$$

In practice, the adjustment process is not simple, because if nothing changes, part of the premium will be paid over to the writer of the option and the time value decays to zero over the life of the option.

Pricing caps, floors and collars utilising this approach entails the following steps:

- The cap, floor or collar agreement is analytically separated into a series of option contracts. For example, an interest rate cap agreement may be split up into a series of put option contracts on the relevant interest rate index.

- Each separate option is then valued utilising the identified model. In determining the price of each option, it is important to note that the input for the current spot price of the index is not the physical market price at the time the agreement is entered but the then current futures or forward price on the relevant index.

- The option premium for each contract is calculated and then summed to give the actual price for the overall contract. In the case of a collar, as the seller is simultaneously writing a series of put options while buying a corresponding set of call options from the purchaser of the collar, the price to the purchaser represents the value of the put options reduced by the value of the call option written.

An example of the calculation of cap, floor and collar prices is set out in *Exhibit 11.7*.

Exhibit 11.7

Cap and Collar Pricing Example

Assume a bank is asked by one of its clients to quote on an interest rate cap and a collar on the following terms:

Amount:	per A$1m
Term:	3 years (maturing 1/6/X6)
Cap level:	14.50% pa (300bps over the spot rate)
Reference rate:	180 day BBR
Settlement:	SA
Settlement date:	1/6/X3

The bank is being asked to structure the following series of options for the client:

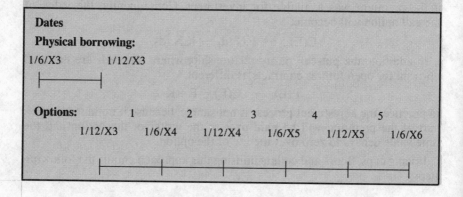

Exhibit 11.7—continued

On 1/6/X3, the following interest rate structure prevails:

Date	Maturity (year)	Yield to maturity (% pa)	Forward rates (% pa)
1/12/X3	0.5	11.50	12.50
1/6/X4	1.0	12.36	12.90
1/12/×4	1.5	12.55	14.52
1/6/X5	2.0	13.27	14.61
1/12/X5	2.5	13.55	13.15
1/6/X6	3.0	13.63	—

In this example, the bank is required to price five put options which it will grant to its customers. To evaluate this commitment the bank needs to determine the forward interest (calculated from the yield curve—see above) and the volatility of interest rates. The option premium (the cap cost) is then determined utilising the Black and Scholes option pricing model modified for an option on a forward or futures contract:

Expiry date	Option type	Quantity	Strike rate	Forward rate	Volatility	Option price
1/12/X3	cap	1.00	14.50	12.50	15.00	0.05
1/6/X4	cap	1.00	14.50	12.90	15.00	0.22
1/12/X4	cap	1.00	14.50	14.52	15.00	0.86
1/6/X5	cap	1.00	14.50	14.61	15.00	0.96
1/12/X5	cap	1.00	14.50	13.15	15.00	0.53

The total premium is 2.62% flat (in percentage terms). The dollar value of the cap depends on the value of each point (0.01%) and the total amount sought to be hedged.

The collar is priced in a similar manner. The main difference being that, in addition to the cap the floor element of the contract must necessarily be priced. Assuming that the floor is set at the level of the current spot rate for six months (11.50% pa), the floor price would be as follows:

Expiry date	Option type	Quantity	Strike rate	Forward rate	Volatility	Option price
1/12/X3	floor	1.00	11.50	12.50	15.00	0.15
1/6/X4	floor	1.00	11.50	12.90	15.00	0.21
1/12/X4	floor	1.00	11.50	14.52	15.00	0.09
1/6/X5	floor	1.00	11.50	14.61	15.00	0.13
1/12/X5	floor	1.00	11.50	13.15	15.00	0.37

The total premium is 0.95% flat for the floor.

On this basis the bank would quote its client, the following cap and collar prices. Cap set at 300bps above spot of 11.50% pa: 2.62%; collar-cap at 300bps above spot of 11.50% pa; and floor set at spot: 1.67%.

The effect of variations in cap and floor levels as well as volatility on cap and floor premiums for the transaction in this example are as follows:

	Volatility (% pa)	
	12	15
Cap		
14.50	1.98	2.63
13.50	3.39	4.09
Floor		
11.50	0.53	0.95
10.50	0.14	0.35

Part 4

Evolution of the Swap Market

Chapter 12
Evolution of the Swap Market

EVOLUTION OF THE SWAP MARKET: OVERVIEW

The emergence of interest rate and currency swaps as an important instrument of finance has been among the most exciting developments in capital markets in recent times. The sheer size of the market is, in part, evidence of its central role in capital market activity. However, the growth in the absolute size of the market for swaps tends to mask the subtler changes in the nature of the market; in particular, the shifts in the use of swaps as a financial instrument.

The development of swap financing has been influenced by a number of key factors, including:

• regulations and the regulatory environment;
• capital markets arbitrage;
• the volatility of interest rates and exchange rates.

Changes in the pattern of swap financing have largely been a response to changes in these key factors.

The evolution of the swap market is reflected in developments in a number of areas:

• the uses of swap financing;
• the technical evolution of swap structures;
• the development of swap markets in a wide range of currencies;
• the wide variety of participants active in the swap market.

Each of the above developments are closely inter-related. It is sometimes difficult to decipher the cause-effect relationships in the evolution of the swap market.

For example, the change of emphasis in the utilisation of swaps from pure capital market arbitrage to asset liability management resulted from the decreased arbitrage profits available from capital market arbitrage transactions and also the increased volatility of currency and interest rates which promoted the use of swaps as techniques of risk management. The erosion of profits from capital market arbitrage led to the development of various security issue structures designed to arbitrage capital markets which required the corresponding development of new swap structures to translate these arbitrage profits into the issuer's desired currency and interest rate basis. The search for new arbitrage profits also prompted the opening of swap markets in a wide range of currencies. Simultaneously, the increased use of swaps as asset liability management tools prompted a number of financial intermediaries to enter into swaps on a principal basis while managing the risks entailed in swap trading through various hedging techniques.

In this chapter, the evolution of the swap market is analysed with respect to:

- the key factors underlying the evolution of the market;
- the changes in the use of swap transactions;
- the technical development of swap structures;
- the development of a global swaps market; and
- the entry into the market of various types of organisations.

EVOLUTION OF THE SWAP MARKET: KEY FACTORS

The key factors underlying the evolution of the swap market as noted above, include regulatory factors, capital market arbitrage and the volatility of currency and interest rates.

The impact of regulatory factors on the evolution of the swap market is both direct and indirect. As discussed in Part 3 the economics of swap transactions derive, at least in part, from the existence of regulations. An example of direct regulatory influences which have shaped the swap market include governmental prohibitions on cross-border capital flows. The British government levied a tax on foreign exchange transactions for overseas investment which was designed to discourage the flow of British capital abroad. This led to the development of parallel and back-to-back loans which were used as a means of circumventing the government's restrictions on the currency. This type of structure still continues to have relevance in allowing organisations to deal with the problems of blocked funds. Governmental regulation also has influenced the evolution of the swap market indirectly through the imposition of restrictions on cross-border capital flows, such as withholding taxes, and restrictions on asset portfolio choice.

Capital market arbitrage as a basis for the development of the swap market has operated on a number of bases:

- classical financial arbitrage;
- tax and regulatory arbitrage.

Classical financial arbitrage across different capital markets has and continues to be one of the basic factors driving the development of the swap market. This type of financial arbitrage is based on the fact that prices in various world capital markets are not mutually consistent and issuers can lower their borrowing costs by accessing the capital market with the lowest relative rates, borrowing there, and then swapping their exposure back into the desired currency thereby achieving lower cost funding than obtainable directly from borrowing in that market. For example, the development of interest rate swaps was predicated on a form of credit arbitrage based on the differential pricing of identical risks in between the fixed and floating rates debt markets.

The second type of arbitrage, tax and regulatory arbitrage, as noted above, relies on externally imposed restrictions on capital flows or investment choice. An important aspect of the development of the swap market has been the evolution of some extremely creative swap structures designed to in effect unbundle the currency and interest rate exposure from the regulation and tax rules applicable in certain markets. A number of instances of tax and regulatory arbitrage are discussed in Chapter 7.

An additional factor driving the development of the swap market was the increased volatility in currency and interest rates. Throughout the late

1970s and, in particular, the 1980s, financial markets experienced unprecedented volatility in currency and interest rates. In this environment, the capacity of swaps to allow firms to manage exposures to interest rates and/or currencies was quickly recognised. The capacity of interest rate swaps to function as forward interest rate contracts extending beyond the scope of futures markets in interest rates was increasingly useful to market participants as a means of managing asset and liability exposures. Similarly, the role of currency swaps in replicating conventional LTFX contracts, usually more efficiently, allowed the currency swap to be utilised as an instrument for the management of corporate foreign exchange exposures over extended periods.

THE EVOLVING FUNCTION OF SWAPS

Historically, swap transactions evolved in response to regulatory factors and opportunities for capital market arbitrage. Initially, swap transactions were, in the main, predicated on the exchange by one party of a benefit which it enjoyed in a particular market for a corresponding benefit available to another party in a different market. This advantage could be one of access or effective after tax cost.

Consequently, the swap market functioned as a new funding market utilised by a wide range of organisations to lower the cost of raising *new* funds.

The classical interest rate swap, for example, arbitraged the different risk and reward criteria of fixed rate investors against those of floating rate lenders. However, as in any type of arbitrage, the continuous and active exploitation of an identifiable arbitrage opportunity gradually eroded the arbitrage. For example, in the case of interest rate swaps, the market actions embodied in the transaction should result in the following:

• Direct fixed rate borrowing costs to fixed rate issuers (such as banks) would increase as they borrow more in the fixed rate market.

• Direct floating rate costs to fixed rate issuers would decrease as they borrow less in the floating rate market.

• Direct fixed rate costs to the lower rated companies would decrease as they borrow less in the fixed rate market.

• Direct floating rate costs to lower rated companies would increase as they borrow more in the floating rate market.

The actual outcome of market actions, for example, in the US$ market, corresponds closely to the predictions of the theory. The use of interest rate swaps appears to have caused the predicted changes in pricing relationships.

The most obvious impact of such transactions has been in the Eurobond market. As the cost savings of funding via a fixed rate bond issue with an interest rate swap or (if appropriate) a currency swap attached became apparent, banks, particularly those with good credit standings, switched from the floating rate markets to the fixed rate market as a source of funds.

The switch had dramatic consequences for pricing relationships. In the floating rate markets traditionally used by banks to raise floating rate funds (primarily US$), such as the floating rate note (FRN) and floating rate certificate of deposit market, the absence of new issues meant that prices on existing issues increased with banks being able to issue new paper at lower spreads relative to LIBOR than ever before. Through 1985 and 1986, the margins on FRNs issued by prime quality issuers plummetted, precipitating a collapse of the FRN market in late 1986. In the fixed rate bond markets, the increased volume of new issues by bank names meant a marked increase in the yields demanded by investors to purchase bank issued fixed rate Eurobonds. The relative deterioration of the banks' collective standing in the Eurobond market was a factor of not only the increased supply of bank paper but of investors' belief that many bank Eurobond issues were being unrealistically priced to accommodate the swap integral to the transaction.

An associated, but not often recognised factor, which affected at least the US$ interest rate swap market over this period was the abolition of the United States withholding tax on interest rate payments to overseas investors in United States domestic securities. While the change, implemented in July 1984, did not spell the end, as indeed some had predicted, of the Eurobond market, which continued to survive and even prosper as a result of its qualities of innovation and superior speed relative to the United States market, it did reshape some historic pricing relationships.

The previously existing pricing differences between anonymous, bearer Eurodollar bonds and registered United States bonds were eroded as foreign purchases of United States government and corporate securities grew. The previous pricing pattern which had favoured virtually all creditworthy borrowers in the Eurobond market was reversed as most international borrowers attracted comparable and sometimes higher yields on their Eurodollar bonds than the yield on United States government Treasury bonds of a comparable maturity.

New Eurodollar offerings are no longer expected to trade consistently at lower yields than United States Treasury bonds and the borrowers that can issue Eurobonds at yields below United States Treasuries are extremely rare. Even the most coveted borrowers in the Eurobond market have seen their issues outperformed consistently by Treasuries during the period since the abolition of withholding tax. For example, Eurodollar bonds with five year maturities issued by a selected group of United States corporations have traded, on average, at a yield of approximately 0.30% pa above five year United States Treasuries since the change, compared to an average yield of 0.70% pa below comparable United States Treasuries prior to the repeal of the withholding tax.

The increase in yields on Eurobonds has eliminated, to a very significant degree, the advantage previously enjoyed by major international borrowers who could issue at a substantial margin under comparable United States Treasuries and swap into floating rate US$ funds against a fixed rate borrower (usually a United States corporation of medium to low credit standing) pricing off Treasuries as a benchmark to determine the alternative cost of US$ fixed rate funding.

The erosion of the arbitrage through market actions and the increased yields evident in the Eurobond market as a result of the change in United States withholding tax laws combined to reduce the gains from interest rate swaps. For example, whereas the first swap transactions routinely generated floating rate funds for banks at LIBOR less 0.625% pa to 0.75% pa, those same banks would now be struggling to achieve funding at LIBOR less 0.125% pa to 0.25% pa through a straight Eurodollar bond issue with an interest rate swap attached. As the arbitrage spread narrowed, the savings to fixed rate borrowers, who were utilising swaps to generate fixed rate funds, also diminished.

While the above analysis has focused primarily on interest rate swaps, a similar erosion in the arbitrage savings from currency swaps was evident, as the arbitrage was exploited by market forces.

However, as the process of arbitrage erosion became evident, the swap market itself adapted by undergoing certain fundamental changes. The market developed in two different but complementary directions. The first development involved the search for "new" arbitrage opportunities and the development of transaction structures designed to exploit identified discrepancies to provide net economic gains to the parties involved. The second development was a change in the purpose for which swaps were utilised; instead of merely being an attractive way of reducing the cost of *new* funds to be raised, swaps were increasingly used as an instrument for actively managing an organisation's *existing* liabilities.

The search for new arbitrage opportunities primarily entailed increased effort to understand the economics of swap transactions and to identify the underlying comparative advantages which enable the arbitrage to be undertaken. As already noted, swap transactions are predicated on the central principle of the exchange of an advantage which a party enjoys in one market for an advantage enjoyed by a counterparty in a different market. Importantly, the advantage need not be absolute, it need only be comparative, that is, one party may in fact have an absolute advantage in both markets, but may have a comparatively greater advantage in one market. That advantage can be in terms of cost of borrowing and/or availability of funds.

As market forces eroded the initial credit arbitrage between fixed and floating rate markets, the search for new opportunities focused on both temporary and sustainable arbitrage opportunities between various markets. Some short-lived arbitrage opportunities which appeared intermittently focused on the creation of securities issues and associated swap structures which appealed to niches of investors and borrowers at particular times. The experience of the Eurobond market, where it is common to think of the market in terms of "windows" (the term being used to characterise the moments in time when a particular type of security can be issued because the investors are "there") rapidly became equally relevant to the swap market.

Popular innovations of this type (at least for a time) included zero coupon bond swaps, debt warrant swaps and dual currency bond swaps. Just as the type of security and related swap changed in line with investor and borrower preferences, the relevant sector of the bond market which provided the most attractive swap also changed. During recent years, markets as widely varied as the Eurosterling, Euroyen, European Currency Unit (ECU), EuroCanadian dollar, EuroNew Zealand dollar, Eurolira, EuroFrench franc, Eurokrone and the EuroAustralian dollar market have at various times been the basis of the most attractive swap transactions.

A particular feature of this change in the basic arbitrage nature of swap transactions was an unbundling process, primarily in straight interest rate swaps, whereby the securities issue used to raise the underlying debt and the swap transaction were separated in a timing sense. A borrower would issue into a particular market at the time when the market was most receptive to its issue with the swap being separately entered into later when the swap market was most attractive for the swap transaction. The order of transactions could also be reversed with the swap being put in place prior to the fund raising.

The process of unbundling or swap timing also saw borrowers seeking to engineer currency swap transactions in stages. For example, a borrower seeking to swap from fixed rate £ to fixed rate A$ would first swap from fixed rate £ to floating rate US$ (this transaction being timed to ensure the maximum position achievable under LIBOR) and subsequently swap from floating rate US$ to fixed rate A$ (the second transaction also being timed to optimise the fixed rate achieved).

In this regard, floating rate US$, usually priced relative to LIBOR, emerged as a useful medium through which a large proportion of cross-currency swaps were transacted. This was, at least in part, a result of the emergence of a select group of currency swap market makers (see discussion below) who were willing to quote prices relative to US$ LIBOR, that is, an institution may make prices in Japanese yen whereby it would pay (receive) fixed rate yen in return for receiving (paying) US$ LIBOR.

The process of new issue arbitrage involving swap transactions is examined in detail in Chapter 13.

As the classic arbitrage advantage of swaps diminished, there was, in addition to seeking out new arbitrage opportunities, a fundamental change in the purposes for which swaps were utilised. Currency and interest rate swaps came to be utilised as an instrument for the active management of an organisation's existing liabilities. At the same time, swap applications relevant to the asset side as opposed to the liability side of the balance sheet came increasingly to be recognised, enabling portfolio or investment managers to use interest rate and currency swaps to create synthetic securities which were otherwise unavailable, to provide both yield pick-up and portfolio diversification.

For the borrower, interest rate swaps have four major applications:

• to lock in the cost of floating rate debt;
• to create term floating rate debt;
• to unlock the cost of existing high coupon fixed rate debt; and
• to actively manage the cost of an organisation's fixed or floating rate debt in a manner consistent with interest rate expectations.

The continued use of interest rate swaps to generate a synthetic fixed rate liability, even when they are not necessarily a method of creating liabilities at rates more advantageous than a conventional capital market transaction (such as a direct fixed rate bond issue), highlights the increased focus on factors other than cost savings in the decision to utilise swaps. The flexibility, speed and anonymity of swap transactions are increasingly major considerations in utilising swaps.

The flexibility of swaps derives from the fact that the swap transaction is separate from the underlying funding to be transformed. Swap transactions are also more flexible from a timing viewpoint. Unlike a major public bond issue, swaps may be specifically tailored to a company's exact requirements. For example, whereas a public issue requires the rate to be set at a single point of time (creating problems in timing the issue to obtain the most attractive interest cost), a strategy whereby a series of swaps is undertaken, perhaps incorporating some timing options (see Chapter 15), can enable an organisation to achieve a blended rate which may result in a lower average all-in cost.

Swap transactions, unlike a conventional fixed rate issue, also allow the underlying floating rate source of funds to be varied, for example, by switching between US$ LIBOR based funding and United States CP funding, to take advantage of variations in the cost of funds to further reduce the overall cost to the borrower.

The primary feature of swaps is that they, unlike direct borrowings, are highly flexible and can be reversed. Effectively, unlike most public issues, swaps provide a borrower with an at-the-market call on its fixed rate debt enabling the company to manage its interest cost more actively than previously feasible. The fact that the restrictions in terms of covenants etc. that swap transactions place on a borrower, are less onerous relative to loan documents, enhances this added flexibility.

In addition to their inherent flexibility, the speed with which swap transactions can be undertaken is relevant. The emergence of a select group of market makers, who are willing to transact swaps as principals as distinct from agents structuring on behalf of other counterparties, has enabled swap transactions to rapidly become a financial commodity with transactions being completed over the telephone. The relative simplicity of swap documentation, relative to the requirements of other financial transactions and the lack of major regulatory requirements for swap transactions, such as the formal registration, prospectus, reporting etc. requirements usually associated with public issues, also contributes to the speed with which transactions can be completed.

The fact that swaps enjoy a high degree of anonymity by virtue of the fact that they are private transactions is also a consideration. Rating agencies tend to view swaps in a neutral manner, treating them as fixed rate obligations of the appropriate maturity and the relatively uncomplicated accounting and tax treatment of such transactions makes swaps an attractive financing alternative.

The above comments are equally relevant for currency swaps. However, as it encompasses a currency exchange, a swap provides a mechanism for managing long-term foreign currency exposure. For example, a currency swap can be used to transform the currency denomination of its borrowing relatively easily to lock in unrealised gains on foreign currency liabilities incurred during a period of favourable exchange rates or created by a rise in interest rates relative to the level at which the borrower obtained the foreign liability. By executing a currency swap, the borrower, depending on the currency into which the liability is transformed, alters or eliminates the exchange risk for the remaining life of the liability and therefore protects itself from a possible reversal of the gain or increase in any loss due to further currency and interest rate fluctuations.

For the investor, swaps have emerged as an instrument for creating synthetic assets and as a means for more active portfolio management. Interest rate swaps can be utilised to effectively create a fixed rate investment using floating rate securities, or transform a fixed rate asset into a floating rate investment. Interest rate swaps can also be used to lock in capital gains or minimise losses arising from the impact of interest rate fluctuations on investment portfolios.

For portfolio managers, the impact of swap transactions on investment strategies in respect of holdings of debt securities is subtle. The active investment management approach of many portfolio managers seeking improved performance means that swaps have not altered their *approach* to portfolio management but rather changed the *way* in which active portfolio management may be undertaken. Swaps have emerged as an alternative technique whereby existing investments can be transformed through swaps into selected currencies and/or interest rate basis without the need to physically trade the underlying security.

The use of swaps and swap derivatives in asset liability management is considered in Chapter 14.

TECHNICAL EVOLUTION OF SWAP STRUCTURES

The evolution of the function of swap transactions from its original role as a tool of new issue arbitrage to a general asset liability management technique was accompanied by significant innovations in the technical structures of swaps. The technical evolution of swap structures was evident in three separate areas:

- development of new liability swap structures;
- development of asset swaps;
- the emerging differentiation between primary and secondary market swaps.

The new liability swap structures evolved in response to the demand for enhancements to the classical swap structure to accommodate more complex asset liability management structures as well as structural innovations designed to accommodate the swapping of new types of securities issues structured to capitalise on available tax and regulatory arbitrages. A number of the new liability swap structures are set out in Chapters 15, 16, and 17.

While many banks and corporations were competing fiercely to swap their liabilities into desired currency and interest rate bases, the realisation that assets could be swapped as readily and easily as liabilities prompted the development of the asset swap market.

The term asset swap generally refers to an interest rate or currency swap combined with an asset designed to transform the interest rate and/or currency basis of the investment.

The development of the asset swap market was driven by two separate influences:

- yield considerations;
- asset management considerations.

The early impetus to the asset swap market came from the potential to create higher yielding securities than those available directly. This was the direct reverse of the liability arbitrage which had originally created the currency and interest rate swap market. However, as the active exploitation of the asset swap arbitrage saw potential profits diminish, the asset swap became accepted as a technique for enhancing the flexibility and management of asset portfolios.

Asset swaps are considered in detail in Chapter 18.

The technical evolution of the swap market as well as the altered function of swaps effectively created a two-tier market: a primary and a secondary market.

A *primary market* transaction usually refers to a transaction between two counterparties. In contrast, a *secondary market* transaction refers to subsequent transactions involving the original contract between the counterparties.

This secondary market in swaps has emerged for two reasons: first, the emergence of market makers (see below) who must eventually move to square the temporary risk position (protected by hedges), created by entering into one side of the swap, by entering into an equal and opposite swap which provides the only perfect hedge; and secondly, the move by borrowers to actively manage their asset or liability portfolios by entering into swaps then subsequently unwinding their initial position.

Both types of transactions envisaged can be accomplished by one of two methods. Under the first, the reversal is accomplished by entering into a mirror or identical but reverse position at current market rates, while under the second, the reversal is done by effectively selling, at the prevailing market rate, to another participant the swap obligation entered into by the party now wishing to reverse its initial position.

The economic consequences of this reversal, irrespective of the method adopted, will depend upon market conditions with the party showing a gain or loss depending upon the original transaction structure, the side of the transaction the party was on, and the movement in rates since the initial transaction was entered into. The difference between the two techniques is that under a reverse swap, the profit or loss is usually recognised over the remaining life of the mirror contract whereas, if it sells or assigns the original contract, this profit or loss may be recognised immediately.

The secondary market in swaps therefore includes three distinct types of transactions:

- swap sales (or assignments) to a new counterparty;
- voluntary swap terminations; and
- reverse swaps.

Of these only swap sales are directly analogous to the secondary market in securities. One estimate puts the secondary market (sales, terminations and reversal) at 30.00% of the total market. Sales and terminations both involve a cash payment and the extinction of the seller's swap obligations. Reverse swaps are merely new swaps arranged as a perfect or near-perfect offset to existing swaps. Some define the secondary market to include only sales and terminations, which together are estimated to constitute 20.00% to 25.00% of the market.

Until recently, the purpose of swap sales and terminations was typically to realise the capital gain on a swap. If, for example, a fixed rate receiver entered into a five year swap one year ago when rates were, say, 14.00% and four year swap rates today are 11.00%, the swap has accrued a capital gain. The receiver can realise this gain (at least, in part) by assigning the rights (and obligations) to a third party or by negotiating a termination of the swap with the counterparty, each in exchange for a cash payment. Alternatively, the receiver can lock in the gain by entering into an offsetting swap in which 11.00% fixed rate is paid for four years.

The secondary market for swaps has developed unevenly. The volume of swap sales or assignments has reportedly remained low. There are a number of reasons for this. The original counterparty to a potential swap assignment may, and often does, object to the assignment because it would assume a different counterparty credit risk. The assuming counterparty may be unacceptable for some reason or outstanding credit lines to that counterparty may be fully utilised. Assignment clauses must be drafted to ensure that all rights are properly transferred and documented. In addition, many swap contracts are highly customised, making assignment cumbersome or making it difficult to find parties willing to assume the swap at all.

Standard documentation, standardised pricing indexes or benchmarks, sizes and maturities as well as standardised measures of counterparty risk in swap transactions are also clear prerequisites to increasing the depth and liquidity of the secondary market.

DEVELOPMENT OF GLOBAL SWAP MARKETS

As swap transactions increasingly unbundled the process of fund raising, separating the decision to raise funds in a particular market and the process of conversion of the funds raised into the desired currency and interest rate basis, all the major global bond markets increasingly became arbitrage markets. With an ever higher percentage of issues being swap driven, the pricing in almost every segment of the international bond market came to be arbitrage driven: the relevant pricing being not the absolute interest cost of an issue per se, but the pricing achievable in US$ terms in either fixed rate terms relative to United States Treasuries, or more often, in floating rate terms as a margin under LIBOR.

As the classic credit arbitrage in the Eurodollar sector of the Eurobond market eroded, each sector of the international bond market came to be regarded as a potential source of swap-driven issues. At various times, the Eurosterling, the Euroyen, the ECU, EuroCanadian dollar, EuroNew Zealand dollar, Eurolira, EuroFrench franc, Eurokrone and the EuroAustralian dollar markets became the focus of large volumes of issues as borrowers, without a legitimate direct interest in the market, used the issue as an arbitrage-based vehicle to generate lower cost overall funding taking advantage of the particular circumstances that prevailed.

As the major global bond markets increasingly became swap driven, swap markets in a wide variety of currencies also developed. The development of bond markets, in particular, Eurobond markets in a wide variety of currencies, were dependent on the simultaneous development of corresponding currency swap markets. The liquidity in the bond and swap markets came to be closely related with the pricing in one being closely related to pricing in the other.

Against this background, currency and interest rate swap markets developed in a wide range of currencies. The US$ interest rate swap market continues to remain the largest single swap market. The outstanding volume of currency swaps while less than that of interest rate swaps is showing greater growth. Principal currency swap markets include: Swiss francs, Japanese yen, deutschmarks, ECUs, £, C$, A$ and NZ$. The currency swap market is complemented in most of these currencies by a corresponding interest rate swap market as well as cross-currency floating-to-floating swap markets.

A detailed analysis of global swap markets is undertaken in Part 7 of this book.

SWAP MARKET PARTICIPANTS

There are two broad classes of participants in the swap market: end users and intermediaries. An end user is a counterparty which engages in a swap in order to change its interest rate or currency exposure for some economic or financial reason. An intermediary (or a dealer) enters into a swap in order to earn fees or trading profits. In principle, end users and intermediaries are distinguished by their motivations. In practice, however, some institutions are active in both capacities.

A wide variety of end users are involved in the swap markets today. Banks and corporations around the world, savings and thrift institutions, insurance companies, government agencies, international agencies and sovereign entities have all been active.

End users utilise the swap markets for a number of reasons:

* to obtain low cost financing;
* to obtain high yield assets;
* to hedge interest rate of currency exposure generated from the structure of normal business;
* to implement short-term asset liability management strategies; and
* to speculate.

The World Bank was a major driving force in the development of the currency swap market. It sought low interest rate borrowings, mainly in Swiss francs or deutschmarks, since it wished to make loans in these currencies. The World Bank borrowed considerable amounts directly but at times wished to issue more debt in the Swiss and German markets than could be absorbed easily. On the other hand, it could borrow relatively cheaply in the larger US$ markets. These circumstances created a natural opportunity to carry out swaps with counterparties who had European currencies or good access to borrowings in Europe, but who needed US$ financing. Indeed, the currency swap between the World Bank and IBM in August 1981 described in Chapter 1 was a catalyst to the modern development of the currency swap market.

In the early days of the swap market, most intermediaries merely brought together the two swap parties and arranged swaps. At times, they also provided letters of credit or other forms of credit enhancement for weaker credits. As the variety of end users on both sides of the market increased, potential counterparties grew increasingly reluctant to accept the credit risks involved in a purely brokered swap. This created the opportunity for large commercial and investment banks to take on the role of the intermediary by entering into two offsetting swaps. Today most large intermediaries act almost exclusively as counterparties, and frequently the intermediary is a more acceptable counterparty credit risk to both end users in the swap chain. A few of the largest end users with high credit ratings, however, continue to enter into swaps directly with other highly rated end users, eliminating the need for intermediaries.

The largest intermediaries in the swap market are major United States money centre banks, major United States and United Kingdom investment and merchant banks, and major Japanese securities companies. Commercial banks in Australia, New Zealand, Canada, France, Japan, Sweden, Switzerland and the United Kingdom are also active. These institutions have undertaken dealing in swaps in order to earn fee income and to profit from trading opportunities. For both commercial and investment banks, swaps were, until recently, an attractive source of off-balance sheet earnings as well as a product which facilitated other types of business (for example, underwriting securities).

Commercial banks and investment banks have different approaches to the swap market. Commercial banks tend to view swaps as an extension of more conventional banking business. For example, when a bank combines a floating rate loan with a swap, it is creating the equivalent of a fixed rate loan for a borrower. In the past, banks have found it difficult to extend fixed rate loans outright because their fixed rate funding costs have been high, sometimes as high as those faced by some of their customers. Moreover, they felt obliged to accept prepayments on fixed rate loans when rates had moved to the disadvantage of the borrower. By unbundling the components (the floating rate loan and the swap) banks can price each more efficiently. Commercial banks stress that as swap market intermediaries they offer a large customer base and expertise in assuming long-term market and credit risks.

Investment or merchant banks tend to view swaps as tradable securities. They are at the forefront of efforts to standardise swap contracts and market practices in order to improve the liquidity of the swap market. Investment banks also attempt to equalise the credit exposure on all swaps by incorporating collateral provisions in the contract. These provisions give the investment bank (and sometimes the other counterparty) the right to call for an amount of collateral equal to the credit exposure on the contract. As intermediaries, investment banks seek to offer competitive pricing because of their trading and hedging expertise.

By mid 1985 there was an active market in swaps between swap dealers that served to match end users in much the same way that the interbank Eurocurrency market connects non-bank depositors with ultimate borrowers. Thus, for example, a bank (which is not a swap specialist) may enter into a swap with an end user for which it has arranged a bond issue. It covers itself by entering into an offsetting swap with a dealer, who in turn enters into an offsetting swap with another dealer. This second dealer may then find a bank which wants to offset a swap it is arranging with an end user. In this example, a swap between two end users has given rise to four intermediate swaps.

The move by intermediaries to act as principal or direct counterparties in swap transactions had two separate aspects. The intermediary could either be a genuine market maker in swaps willing to trade more or less continuously offering a relatively tight bid/offer spread or alternatively could enter into the swap utilising its balance sheet and then square its position with a market-making house.

Relatively few financial intermediaries sought to act as market makers in swap transactions routinely quoting two-way prices on swaps. The major emphasis amongst market makers was on interest rate swaps, particularly US$ interest rate swaps, although specialist market makers in interest rate swaps in a number of liquid swap currencies also developed. Simultaneously, a much smaller group of institutions emerged as market makers in cross-currency swaps in and between, inter alia, Swiss francs, deutschmarks, ECU, Japanese yen, £, C$, A$, NZ$ and US$.

The smaller number of market makers in currency swaps reflected the smaller transaction volume and the complexity and difficulty of hedging and managing positions in this type of transaction.

The emergence of market makers in swap transactions required the development by the institutions concerned of techniques to manage the large temporary risk positions created in a variety of currencies where the institution transacted swaps as a principal when there was no immediately available counterparty. The risk confronting a swap market maker is that in providing one side of a swap transaction, it may not be able to profitably cover the other side in the market. This temporary risk position can be in the form of position taking in the swap market as a natural extension of position taking in other fixed interest markets, or alternatively, it can be viewed as a transient unmatched position, not entered into as an interest rate or currency (in the case of currency swaps) bet, but, with the exposure to interest rates or currency values being hedged either through the physical securities market (for example, bonds, deposits, borrowings, etc.) or in a corresponding futures market on the relevant underlying physical security. The latter is often referred to as swap "warehousing".

The development of marketmaking capabilities in interest rate swaps has two distinct implications for the potential swap participant:

• The availability of institutions willing to commit to an interest rate or currency swap without necessarily having a counterparty in position makes possible a *prompt execution* capability which eliminates the delay necessitated where it was necessary to have precisely matched counterparties to complete a transaction.

• The availability of market makers making two-way prices on swap transactions provides the flexibility required to allow companies to *reverse or unwind a swap* transaction at the current market rate facilitating the use of swaps as a dynamic asset liability management instrument.

Marketmaking in swaps and swap derivatives is examined in detail in Part 8 of this book.

SUMMARY

The emergence of deep and relatively liquid markets in swaps, with transactions being undertaken for reasons other than the pure capital market arbitrage which motivated early transactions, represents perhaps the most significant development in corporate finance in recent times. The adaptability of the basic concept to different market conditions seems likely to ensure the future of swap transactions in international capital markets.

Part 5

Utilising Swaps

Chapter 13

New Issue Arbitrage

THE CONCEPT OF NEW ISSUE ARBITRAGE

As outlined in Chapter 12 swaps can be utilised as an instrument for new issue arbitrage as well as an efficient asset and liability management device. New issue arbitrage refers to the role of swaps as a cost competitive *new* fund raising technique whereby combining the issuance of debt with the concurrent interest rate or currency swap can create a synthetic liability that, in the specific circumstances, can provide financing at a cost less than that available through conventional direct access to the relevant market.

The possibility of new issue arbitrage is self-evident in the basic origin of swaps and in the fundamental economics of swap transactions. In essence, new issue arbitrage usually refers to the fact that the swap transaction allows the party seeking to raise funds to arbitrage differential access and relative cost across different markets. Where the borrower wishes to raise funds in a market where the terms available to that specific borrower are *relatively* less favourable, it may be less expensive to issue debt in a market where the terms are more favourable and combine the issuance of new debt with an interest rate or currency swap thereby creating a liability corresponding to the borrower's favoured form of funding.

Analysis of the process of new issue arbitrage requires consideration of three major issues:

* the approach and economic criteria for profitable new issue arbitrage;
* the concept of arbitrage funding, an extreme form of new issue arbitrage; and,
* the impact of these techniques on the primary debt markets and on the practices of borrowers and financial institutions.

APPROACH TO NEW ISSUE ARBITRAGE

New issue arbitrage transactions, at their simplest, entail the issuance of new debt combined with a swap transaction. The basic types of arbitrage involve:

* transactions in the same currency involving swapping fixed-to-floating and vice versa;
* transactions across currencies involving swapping of debt in a particular currency to another, usually, at least initially, into US$ floating rate funding.

A basic pattern permeates the types of new issue arbitrage undertaken. The predictions of the economic theory of swaps would suggest that highly rated borrowers would utilise their comparative advantage in fixed rate markets to swap their liabilities to a more cost effective floating rate basis within the same currency or, alternatively, issue in a foreign currency then exchange the liability for funds in the desired form in its own currency. Similarly, the theory would predict that lower rated borrowers would generally raise floating rate funding and swap it into fixed in the same currency or, alternatively, into floating or fixed in a foreign currency. These predictions are consistent with actual market practice where this pattern is evident.

The analysis of new issue arbitrage tends, on the whole, to focus on term borrowings. The process of arbitrage, however, can exist in short-term markets. An obvious example of this type of transaction would entail the issue of say 90 day short-term securities in one currency with the simultaneous execution of a spot and forward currency contract to convert the liability into a different currency on the basis that the all-up achieved cost is superior to direct access to the relevant currency.

The process of new issue arbitrage also tends to over emphasise the role of securities. For example, it is commonplace to talk about swap-driven primary issue markets or swap-driven securities issues. This reflects the fact that the basic debt underlying swap transactions has in recent times involved the issue of securities. This reflects general trends in capital markets where the use of securities, particularly for highly rated borrowers, has become commonplace. The fact that the highly rated borrowers who, arguably, provide the driving force to new issue arbitrage enjoy strong access on cost advantageous terms to securities markets throughout the world is an important factor in this association. However, the whole concept of new issue arbitrage operates independently of the underlying source of the funding, although it should be noted that the basic access to direct funding through securities issue is, at least in part, the basis of the cost differences which allow the process of arbitrage to take place.

The process of new issue arbitrage, as its very title exemplifies, is primarily cost-driven. However, in practice, the process of new issue arbitrage is considerably more complex. The factors motivating new issue arbitrage include:

- minimisation of borrowing cost;
- diversification of funding sources;
- the success of the borrowing transaction and ensuring continued market access;
- specific factors inhibiting access to particular capital markets;
- flexibility of liability management.

The identified factors operate in a number of ways. Minimisation of cost operates as a first order factor which provides the initial incentive for new issue arbitrage. In contrast, the other identified factors act as qualifications to the basic cost minimisation objective and usually serve to set up minimum arbitrage profit targets which must be satisfied before a new issue funding involving a swap can be undertaken.

The cost minimisation objective is self-evident. However, this objective alone is not satisfactory because it does not of itself provide guidance as to the desirability of a transaction per se. For example, the concept of cost minimisation only has significance within a defined asset liability management requirement profile. Only where the relevant currency and interest rate exposure basis of the borrowing has been specified can cost be considered a factor. The overall specification of the asset liability management profile is usually generated by the nature of the underlying assets that are being funded. Other relevant factors may include the desired maturity profile of debt and liquidity considerations.

An additional problem in cost minimisation as the basis for new issue arbitrage is the need to set a minimum improvement on the cost of funds before undertaking the swap-driven new issue arbitrage transaction. This is because the cost minimisation argument in extremis would dictate that even a very marginal improvement in cost would dictate undertaking a swap-driven transaction. However, given that a particular funding transaction may have implications for future access to the market and hence future arbitrage possibilities, it is necessary to consider some of the other identified factors.

A further consideration is that at a given point in time a number of competing swap-driven arbitrage opportunities may exist. The borrower may have the choice of a number of issues in various formats which can be swapped to provide cost effective funding. The likelihood of success of individual transactions in terms of market reception etc. may vary significantly. Consequently, the complexity of the cost minimisation objective increases as the risks of a transaction must be considered against the potential cost savings of individual transactions.

A critical factor shaping the process of new issue arbitrage appears to be the desire on the part of borrowers to diversify their sources of funding on a global basis. The need to diversify the sources of funding for a particular borrower through broadening the investor base in its debt is self-evident. This problem is exacerbated in the case of a number of borrowers whose borrowing requirements relative to the size of their domestic capital market are large. Given that this type of imbalance is one of the key factors underlying swap arbitrage profits (see Chapter 7) the process of new issue arbitrage must seek to balance carefully the supply and demand for an issuer's debt both on a global and a market by market basis.

The issue of diversification of investor base is a complex and controversial one. In theory, distinctions between markets, particularly given the increased trend towards global markets, should not be severe. The nature of debt securities (which are bonds which typically enjoy considerable liquidity being able to be freely bought and sold in an active over the counter secondary market) should of itself ensure distribution to the potential investors. This is so despite restrictions involving registration and listing etc. which, theoretically, impede the distribution process into selected markets. There is evidence to suggest that investors are able to purchase securities from different markets as and when their investment requirements dictate. This would, in theory, lead to an automatic diversification of a borrower's investor base as individual suppliers of capital would diversify their portfolios in terms of borrower credit risk by buying the existing securities on issue of a particular borrower irrespective of which market the securities were originally issued in.

However, there is evidence to suggest that international investors only participate in certain sectors of the respective markets. This appears to be motivated primarily by reasons of legal restrictions, liquidity and convenience factors. In fact, there is evidence to suggest that nearly two thirds of the total size of the international bond market (in 1985 estimated at US$6 trillion) is not readily accessible or liquid enough for active international participation. This lack of freedom for international fund flows means that borrowers can tap different classes of investors by issuing in different currencies and utilising different instruments as well as by adopting different issuing formats in an attempt to appeal to particular investor clientele. These factors dictate that borrowers need to identify potential clientele for their securities and specifically seek to target these investor bases with the objective of finely balancing supply and demand to each segment with a view to maximising their arbitrage profits.

The availability of continued market access is particularly relevant. This dictates that an issue must be perceived as successful by the market at large to allow the borrower to return to access this particular investor base at a future point in time. This requirement while largely vouchsafed by borrowers has in recent times been sadly neglected with issuers grossly mispricing issues to accommodate their cost targets with resultant investor backlash. This issue is discussed in detail below.

The need to ensure success of the transaction and to maintain continued market access relates to the desire of borrowers to maximise their arbitrage gains from a particular market segment which is receptive to it in terms of credit worthiness etc. over a medium to long time horizon.

In looking at the underlying forces of new issue arbitrage, it is vital to recognise a number of restrictions which may impact upon individual institutions' capacities to enter into certain types of transactions. The major restriction of relevance is regulatory factors such as registration requirements in particular markets which must be satisfied as a precondition to the issue of debt securities. For example, an issue in the United States domestic market requires a full Securities and Exchange Commission registration, an onerous and time consuming process. In contrast, the self-regulated Eurobond market does not require such registration processes and the documentary and listing requirements are considerably less onerous than in certain domestic markets. An additional factor may be the operation of a queuing system whereby issuers must formally register their intention to undertake a securities transaction in the particular market.

In certain jurisdictions taxation factors, like the imposition of withholding tax, may limit the capacity to enter into new issue arbitrage transactions. In the case of Australian borrowers, the need to get an exemption from withholding tax under the provisions of s. 128F of the *Income Tax Assessment Act* 1936 (Cth) means that the issue must satisfy certain structural constraints. This may have the effect of inhibiting certain types of arbitrage transactions.

An additional factor relevant to the new issue arbitrage decision is the difference in flexibility between a direct borrowing and a borrowing combined with a swap. This difference in flexibility may derive from a number of sources and may be both positive or negative in impact.

For example, where a fixed rate debt issue is swapped into floating rate funding, in the same or a different currency, the rollover or repricing timing of the floating rate debt is fixed at the time at which the original swap transaction is undertaken. There are minor exceptions to this as the timing of the repricing dates can be varied either through a separate swap, special arrangements within the swap transaction itself, or by utilising other instruments such as actual direct borrowings and lendings or future/forward interest rate transactions. This underlying inflexibility may detract from a party entertaining a new issue arbitrage transaction which must be matched up against an existing portfolio of assets whose characteristics do not align totally with those of the synthetic liability being created.

The use of a swap may also enhance flexibility. Where floating rate funding is swapped into fixed rate funding, the opportunity to vary the underlying source of liquidity can be seen as adding flexibility for the borrower. Other issues relating to flexibility include the potential to terminate both types of transaction as well as the opportunities for early redemption etc. which may vary between a direct borrowing and a synthetic liability entailing the use of a swap.

The complex series of factors which underlie the process of new issue arbitrage necessarily dictate that the decision to undertake a particular arbitrage transaction requires a balance between these competing considerations. In practice, these factors are summarised in a target swap level set relative to a particular funding benchmark. Common funding benchmarks in this regard include US$ LIBOR, A$ BBR, US$ CP rates as well as fixed rates relative to government securities such as United States Treasuries and Australian government bonds.

In deference to the complexity of determining the pricing of any new issue arbitrage transaction, swap targets are set at levels, in cost terms, substantially below the level of funds available from alternative sources. This additional arbitrage margin which is built in is designed essentially to capture in quantitative terms factors such as diversification, the utilisation of scarce market access, restrictions of access to particular markets as well as flexibility concerns. These benchmarks evolve over time reflecting the changing conditions in the capital market in general with benchmarks usually being adjusted up or down primarily as a result of changing market opportunities for arbitrage funding.

The whole approach to new issue arbitrage can be best understood in the context of a special category of borrower, referred to as arbitrage funders, who represent an extreme case of new issue arbitrage practices.

ARBITRAGE FUNDING

Arbitrage funding: the concept

The concept of arbitrage funding is merely an extreme case of new issue arbitrage. Specifically, it refers to the practice by a borrower of a highly opportunistic borrowing strategy which entails accessing almost any market at short notice on the basis that the issue proceeds will be swapped into the borrower's desired form of funding at a cost lower than a nominated benchmark. The basic concept is best exemplified by the title of an article published in *Euromoney* in 1985, "How SEK Borrows at Fifty Below (LIBOR)".

The concept is best illustrated by example. In essence, it involves a highly rated borrower who is attuned and exposed to market innovations and movements and is prepared to take advantage of short-term windows to issue debt in particular forms, currencies and/or structures with a view to generating cheaper funding elsewhere. The common operational benchmark in this regard is US$ floating rate LIBOR. Arbitrage funders usually nominate a margin *under* LIBOR as the relevant benchmark which must be surpassed if they are to transact. For example, to take the example of SEK, given a benchmark of LIBOR minus 50bps, SEK would be prepared to issue say NZ$ securities provided the accompanying swap could generate US$ floating rate funding at a cost of LIBOR minus 50bps or better.

The clearest distinguishing feature of arbitrage funding is the willingness of the borrower to issue debt on a swapped basis almost totally unfettered by asset liability management considerations. For example, the maturity of the debt or the availability of offsetting assets may not be major constraints on particular new fund raising structures. In particular, arbitrage funders may borrow on a purely opportunistic basis to optimise their costs of borrowings irrespective of asset funding requirements with the resultant funds being matched against specifically acquired investments which are later exchanged for normal business assets such as loans or other infrastructure required for the relevant business.

These requirements for effective use of arbitrage funding limit the types and numbers of entities which can engage in the practice. A number of key requirements to undertake arbitrage funding activities can be readily identified.

The most important criteria would appear to be that the borrower enjoy a very high credit standing, usually an AA or AAA rating. This limits the scope of arbitrage funding for entities other than major money centre banks, sovereign or quasi-sovereign entities and a select group of corporations.

An additional important requirement is the capability for setting targets in terms of universally acceptable interest rate benchmarks. The setting of a benchmark such as LIBOR minus 50bps implicitly assumes that such a cost is, first, relevant to the institution in question, and, second, that the nominated cost level is a realistic estimation of a significant cost advantage.

The need to nominate this benchmark immediately assumes that the entity has assets priced off the same benchmark in the case of financial institutions or, in the case of non-financial institutions, that the benchmark represents an alternative source of funding for the borrower.

The benchmark issue is clear cut in the case of banks who may have substantial portfolios of loans etc. priced off a number of indexes against which they can match opportunistic borrowings which represent significant cost savings relative to alternatives to funding these assets. However, in the case of non-financial institutions, the argument is more complex as it assumes that the funding cost achieved is better than an alternative source of funding priced against the same benchmark but has little to say about the relative attractiveness of a number of benchmarks. This difficulty arises largely because non-financial institutions tend not to have financial assets on the asset side of the balance sheet thereby creating more complex asset liability management matching requirements.

The benchmark issue also assumes that the borrower has a relative diverse range of funding facilities or instruments available allowing the borrower to establish alternative costs of borrowing directly in a number of markets.

This tends to limit arbitrage funding practices, once again, to highly rated borrowers.

As noted earlier, the traditional benchmarks for arbitrage funding are nominated relative to indexes such as US$ LIBOR or the relevant floating rate benchmark in a particular currency. Alternatively, the benchmark may be represented as a spread above or below the relevant government bond rate in the currency.

The important role of US$ LIBOR in arbitrage funding necessitates comment. Its role derives partially from the fact that it is a major market benchmark of interest rates but also that the entities which practice arbitrage funding usually have loan assets or, alternatively, can readily acquire loan assets priced relative to this index creating the opportunity to match off opportunistic borrowings against these investments.

An additional reason underlying the use of LIBOR in this particular role relates to the fact that US$ LIBOR functions very much as a central hub against which all currency swaps are transacted. As discussed in Part 8 currency swaps tend to be quoted as a fixed rate against US$ LIBOR.

Adoption of arbitrage funding approaches requires that the borrower is of a critical portfolio mass which allows it to readily absorb new opportunistic borrowings into its overall balance sheet with little dislocation or additional mismatches.

For example, a very attractive funding opportunity may be less attractive if the particular pattern of repricings etc. on the floating rate funding generated creates significant mismatches against the borrower's asset portfolio. The resultant exposure on the portfolio may more than offset the cost advantage achieved. This means that borrowers with substantial portfolios are at a distinct advantage in using this pattern of financing as their portfolios are likely to be large enough to absorb particular fundings without creating this type of additional exposure. In addition, such borrowers are likely to be less sensitive as to the types of liability, maturity, rate reset details etc., as the marginal effect of a new borrowing on the overall portfolio is limited.

An additional requirement may be the capacity of such entities to take on new liabilities because of their attractive pricing and to match them off against specifically purchased investments to lock in the arbitrage spread between the borrowing and the investment. This type of activity can be undertaken on a short-term basis with the intention of ultimately selling off the short-term investments with a view to acquiring the basic assets required to be funded. This necessity means that the borrower's balance sheet must be capable of absorbing significant size transactions without creating undue gearing or other balance sheet pressures.

A critical element in utilising arbitrage funding is the capability of responding flexibly and, most importantly, quickly to market opportunities. This requires a management structure which is market sensitive and capable of reacting to short-lived opportunities in capital markets. A key requirement in this regard is a management team with the necessary knowledge and experience to work with financial intermediaries and to tap into market linkages whereby they have sufficient exposure to market innovations and information to take advantage of opportunistic borrowing possibilities.

The range of borrowers who can be truly called arbitrage funders is relatively limited. The group is primarily limited to a number of major banks and sovereign or quasi-sovereign issuers. As mentioned above, borrowers such as SEK, the Swedish Export Agency, and the Kingdom of Denmark have largely developed this concept. A number of major money centre banks are also practitioners of these types of funding techniques.

In Australia, most of the major banks and State government central borrowing agencies operate on the basic principles of arbitrage funding although the nature of their portfolios and range of activities provide some limits to the extent to which they can operate as purely opportunistic borrowers.

The extent of new issue arbitrage by these types of borrowers can be seen from a summary of some of the issues undertaken by major practitioners of this technique. *Exhibit 13.1* sets out the issues undertaken by SEK in recent years on a swapped basis. *Exhibit 13.2* sets out issues undertaken by two major Australian arbitrage funders, the Australian Industries Development Corporation (AIDC) and the Commonwealth Bank of Australia.

Exhibit 13.1
Swapped Issues Undertaken by SEK

General policy

SEK operates an arbitrage funding strategy with most public issues being linked to interest rate and currency swaps to generate floating rate US$ at substantial margins under LIBOR. Central to this policy is:

• receptivity to new issue structures and instruments as evidenced by the various innovations (such as the Mini-Max Notes, T-Bill Based Floaters, Bull-Bear Bonds, Ice-Bear Bonds, Naked Currency Options, A$/DM Dual Currency Securities, MOOSE Bonds etc.) introduced by SEK. Many of these pioneering transactions have attracted international attention as "Deals of the Year";

• willingness to raise funds at short notice with excess liquidity being invested at a positive spread in anticipation of future disbursements in export credits;

• using swaps to manage SEK's total debt portfolio.

The extent of this policy is evident from the following table which summarises SEK's debt portfolio, before and after currency swaps:

SEK's LONG-TERM BORROWING—1986

Currency	Distribution before currency swap (%)	Distribution after currency swap (%)
US$	48.4	83.5
¥	26.6	—
SFR	10.3	1.7
ECU	4.5	4.5
FRF	6.0	6.0
DKr	2.8	2.8
LUF	1.5	1.5

Source: SEK *Annual Report* 1986.

Exhibit 13.1—continued

Public issues—SEK 1985-1988

Issue	Summary of terms	Final maturity	Lead manager
US$100m	10.75% "adjustable rate notes	1991	Morgan Stanley International (MSI)
£50m	11.375% notes	1992	Lloyds
US$125m	Mini-max floating rate notes	1992	Goldman Sachs
US$150m	Floating rate notes priced off US$ T-bills	1990	Merrill Lynch (ML)
DKr200m	11.75% notes	1990	MSI
US$100m	10.00% notes (initial tranche of a $500m "tap" issue)	1992	Goldman Sachs
NZ$50.00	16.00% notes	1990	Goldman Sachs
¥13.50 billion	Zero coupon notes	1990	Nikko
A$40m	13.00% notes	1998	Bankers Trust (BT)
NZ$50m	17.375% notes	1990	ML
DKr50m	10.00% notes	1992	Kredietbank
¥ 20 billion	8.00% notes	1996	Yamaichi
US$100m	9.625% notes	1993	Daiwa
ECU60m	8.625% notes	1993	MSI
US$100m	9.25% notes	1993	Daiwa
DKr300m	9.625% notes	1993	Privatbanken
¥10.1 billion	6.625% notes	1996	Nikko
US$200m	8.625% notes	1991	BT
US$200m	8.625% 40 year bonds	1991	BT
FRF500m	8.75% notes	1996	CCF
¥10 billion	6.00% notes	1991	Sanwa
US$100m	7.50% notes	1993	LTCB
¥10 billion	Bull-bear bonds linked to the Nikkei-Dow stock index	1991	Daiwa
US$50m	8.00% ice-bear bonds with redemption linked to 30 year United States Treasury yields	1989	Bank of Tokyo
US$100m	7.25% notes	1991	Daiwa
A$50m	14.50% notes	1990	Country NatWest
—	Currency warrants	—	BT
US$100m	6.75% notes	1990 ⎫	Pru-Bache
US$100m	7.50% notes	1991 ⎬	Securities
US$125m	7.00% notes	1991	BT
DKr300m	10.75% notes	1990	Privatbanken
—	Currency warrants	—	BT
A$220m	9.50% DM/A$ dual currency notes	1992	S. G. Warburg

Exhibit 13.1—continued

US$100m	Multiple option on the stock exchange (MOOSE) 8.00% fixed notes with warrants on the American Stock Exchange	1990	Union Bank of Switzerland (UBS)
A$50m	14.125% notes	1989	Swiss Banking Corporate (SBC)
—	Currency warrants	—	BT
A$50m	14.125% notes	1989	Salomon Brothers
SFR 100m	4.75% notes	1999	Citicorp
¥20 billion	4.50% notes	1992	Mitsubishi Finance
¥15 billion	4.125% notes	1991	Daiwa/Tokai
ECU40m	7.375% notes	1992	Nikko
ECU50m	7.50% notes	1994	Daiwa
£50m	9.125% notes	1992	S. G.Warburgs
NZ$50m	17.125% notes	1990	Hambros
SFR100m	Serial promissory notes coupons 4.00-4.00%	1990-1994	S. G. Warburg Soditic
DKr100m	9.625% notes	1993	Privatbanken
DM300m	5.375% notes	1993	MSI
—	Currency warrants	—	MSI
—	Currency warrants	—	BT
US$250m	8.375% notes	1991	BT
US$200m	8.125% notes	1992	Daiwa
ECU100m	7.375% notes	1992	Paribas
£60m	9.50% notes	1993	BT
C$150m	Zero coupon notes	1995	Wood Gundy
A$75m	12.25% notes	1993	Paribas
US$200m	7.50% notes	1989	Kidder Peabody
US$200m	7.625% notes	1989	BT
ECU50m	7.375% notes	1992	Paribas
A$50m	13.25% notes	1991	Wood Gundy
ECU50m	7.375 notes	1992	ML
US$250m	9.00% notes	1993	Daiwa
ECU100m	7.50% notes	1991	Paribas
US$200m	9.50% notes	1991	IBJ
DFL150m	0.50% fixed rate notes with currency warrant	1993	ABN
US$100m	8.875% notes	1990	Nikko
ECU40m	7.50% notes	1991	Paribas
C$100m	10.25% notes	1990	BT
US$70m	8.50% notes	1989	MSI

Sources: Various. The list of issues, while comprehensive, may not be totally complete.

Exhibit 13.2

Swapped Issues Undertaken by AIDC and Commonwealth Bank

General issue policies

Both the AIDC and Commonwealth Bank have funding requirements primarily in A$ (fixed or floating rate) or US$ (floating). Consequently, most issues undertaken by both institutions are swapped into their preferred form of funding. The major exception would be some fixed rate A$ issues which may be maintained in primary issue form for balance sheet purposes.

An additional aspect of such swap-driven issues may be that the funds raised via these issues become part, once the transaction is completed, of a fungible liquidity pool. This liquidity may be the subject of further secondary swaps designed to alter the nature of the funding as liquidity, maturity and currency needs and interest and/or currency rate expectations dictate.

Public issues—AIDC 1983-1988

Issue	Summary of terms	Final maturity	Lead manager
US$75m	11.00% notes	1989	MSI
US$100m	11.875% notes with harmless warrants into 11.50% notes	1990	MSI
US$100m	8.375% notes	1996	MSI
C$100m	10.00% notes	1991	Canadian Imperial Bank of Commerce
FRF600m	7.875% notes	1993	BNP
¥20 billion	6.00% notes	1996	Nomura
A$30m	14.50% notes	1988	Orion Royal Bank (ORB)
A$30m	14.00% notes	1988	ORB
A$40m	12.875% notes	1988	ORB
A$42m	12.125% notes	1990	ORB
A$50m	12.75% notes	1990	ORB
A$30m	Zero coupon notes	1992	ORB
A$50m	14.00% notes	1992	ORB
A$75m	12.75% notes	1991	Commerzbank
C$100m	10.125% notes	1993	Wood Gundy
A$100m	12.875% notes	1993	Nomura
DM200m	6.125% notes	1998	Commerzbank

Public issues—Commonwealth Bank 1984-1988

Issue	Summary of terms	Final maturity	Lead manager
US$100m	12.375% notes	1989	CSFB
A$35m	12.625% notes	1989	ORB
£40m	11.00% notes	1992	Hambros
A$50m	13.25% notes	1990	ORB
A$125m	12.875% notes* (fungible with issue marked *)	1990	SBC
US$100m	10.00% notes	1993	CSFB
SFR50m	5.125% notes	1992	SBC
SFR70m	Zero coupon notes	1992	SBC

Exhibit 13.2—continued

A$150m	13.80% notes	1991	ML
SFR100m	4.75% notes	1991	SBC
A$100m	13.00% notes	1989	ML
A$125m	Zero coupon notes	1991	ORB
DM120m	5.25% notes	1991	Deutsche Bank
A$75m	12.875% notes	1990	ORB
C$100m	9.50% notes[+] (fungible with issue marked [+])	1992	UBS
A$125m	Adjustable rate notes	1992	SBC
¥15 billion	8.00% notes	1992	Salomon Brothers
A$75m	14.00% notes	1994	ORB
SFR80m	4.50% notes	1994	SBC
NZ$50m	17.25% notes	1990	Hambros
£50m	9.625% notes	1993	Baring Brothers
C$50m	9.50% notes[+]	1992	UBS
A$100m	12.625% notes	1993	Hambros
NZ$60m	14.000% notes	1991	Hambros
US$100m	9.25% notes	1993	CSFB
US$300m	US$300m floating rate note	Perpetual	CSFB
US$400m	US$400m floating rate note	Perpetual	CSFB

Source: Information on public issues supplied by AIDC and the Commonwealth Bank.

In each case, a perusal of the list of issues undertaken highlights the fact that the currencies and issue structures utilised are totally at odds with the basic currency and interest rate basis of each entity's lending. These discrepancies could only be explained on the basis that the issues are primarily designed to generate lower cost funds in each entity's preferred currencies (US$ and Krone in the case of SEK and US$ and A$ in the case of the AIDC and the CBA) at a lower cost than achievable through the direct issuance of debt in those currencies.

Arbitrage funding: a case study*

Background

The process of arbitrage funding is best illustrated by use of an example. In this section, an example of a Euroyen bond issue with accompanying currency and interest rate swap is used as the basis for discussion of a number of general issues relevant to arbitrage funding.

---

* The author would like to acknowledge the assistance of Stephen Sloan (AIDC) in the preparation of this case study.

Assume that the borrower or issuer in this example is a major Australian bank. The bank operates both in Australia and internationally and has substantial asset portfolios, primarily loans, denominated in two main currencies: A$ and US$. The bank is an opportunistic borrower willing to access a variety of markets to obtain cost effective funding to support its asset portfolio.

Major sources of funding for the bank (apart from shareholders' equity) include the following facilities:

* Domestic borrowings:
    —negotiable certificates of deposit (NCDs) issued into the wholesale money market at a pricing of approximately BBR for the relevant maturity;
    —retail and wholesale interest bearing deposits primarily for short terms up to six months at rates at least 30 to 40bps below BBR;
    —sundry issues of term certificates of deposit and private placements to generate funds at the Australian government bond rate plus a margin of between 60 to 90bps.
* International facilities:
    —public issues, primarily Eurobond issues in a variety of currencies as well as some foreign bond issues, primarily in Switzerland, swapped into usually US$ or A$. The margins on these borrowings achieved have been in the range US$ LIBOR minus 25bps to US$ LIBOR minus 45bps;
    —inter-bank US$ deposits at around LIBOR;
    —a Euro-Commercial Paper (ECP) facility, allowing for the issue of ECP or EuroCDs at rates around US$ LIBID/LIBID plus 4 to 6bps;
    —a US CP programme which generates very short-term 30 to 45 day funding at a small margin under US$ LIBOR. The margin varies according to the US CP/LIBOR funding spread.

The major restrictions on the bank undertaking an international securities issue on a swapped basis include:

* the need to satisfy s. 128F of the *Income Tax Assessment Act* to obtain exemption from Australian withholding tax which requires the borrower to satisfy the widely spread debenture issue requirements of the legislation;
* the fact that the bank does not have a current registration in the United States domestic market and consequently cannot undertake a domestically targeted issue in that and certain other markets.

The specific opportunity which currently exists involves the issue of a Euroyen bond with an accompanying swap into US$ LIBOR to produce funding for the bank at LIBOR minus 38bps. The transaction has been originated by a Japanese securities house which has approached the bank with the full package: bond and swap.

In practice, the opportunity could have arisen in a different manner. For example, an approach by a securities house or investment bank to undertake a Japanese yen issue may have provoked interest whereupon the bank may have made enquiries about Japanese yen/US$ LIBOR swap rates. Alternatively, a particularly attractive or aggressive swap opportunity may have led the bank to pursue the question of undertaking a securities issue on the back of the particular swap.

In this case, the transaction satisfies the general asset liability management requirements of the bank and there is a reasonable assurance of a successful reception for the issue. The bank has decided to proceed with the transaction.

The details of the proposed yen issue and the accompanying swap are detailed in *Exhibit 13.3*.

Exhibit 13.3

Structure of Euroyen Bond Issue and Accompanying Swap

Bond swap structure

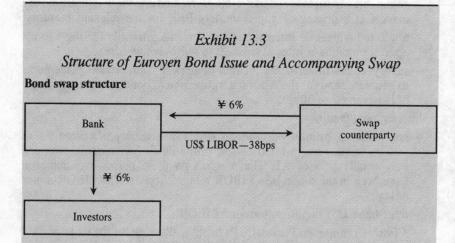

Detailed cash flows

Date	Bond issue	Swap		Net
		Receipts	Payments	
	(¥ billion)	(¥ billion)	(US$m)	(US$m)
26/3/X6	+19.675[1]	−19.675	+139.54[2]	+139.54
26/9/X6	—	—	(−LIBOR − 38 bps)[3]	(−LIBOR − 38bps)
26/3/X7	−1.2[4]	+1.2	(−LIBOR − 38bps)	(−LIBOR − 38 bps)
26/9/X7	—	—	(−LIBOR − 38bps)	(−LIBOR − 38 bps)
26/3/X8	−1.2	+ 1.2	(−LIBOR − 38bps)	(−LIBOR − 38 bps)
26/9/X8	—	—	(−LIBOR − 38bps)	(−LIBOR − 38 bps)
26/3/X9	−1.2	+ 1.2	(−LIBOR − 38bps)	(−LIBOR − 38 bps)
26/9/X9	—	—	(−LIBOR − 38bps)	(−LIBOR − 38 bps)
26/3/X0	−1.2	+ 1.2	(−LIBOR − 38bps)	(−LIBOR − 38 bps)
26/9/X0	—	—	(−LIBOR − 38bps)	(−LIBOR − 38 bps)
26/3/X1	−1.2	+ 1.2	(−LIBOR − 38bps)	(−LIBOR − 38 bps)
26/9/X1	−20.0	+20.0	−139.54	−139.54

Notes:

1. The initial yen receipts are calculated based on an issue amount of ¥20 billion, issued at 100.375 with fees of 2.00% giving net issue proceeds of ¥19.675 billion (¥20 billion × 98.375%).
2. The US$ amount on initial exchange is calculated at an exchange rate of US$1.00/¥141.00
3. The US$ LIBOR flows are based on a US$ borrowing of US$139.54. For example, assuming LIBOR of 7.875, the actual interest payment for the relevant six month period is approximately US$5.229m.
4. Based on yen interest rate of 6.00% pa.

Negotiating and executing the transaction

Negotiating the terms of the bond package is more complex because the two elements must be separately negotiated but must correspond to fuse together into a seamless cohesive funding transaction.

The key elements in negotiating the actual bond issue include the following:

- Selection of lead manager: selection of the lead manager will depend upon the particular borrower's attitudes. Some borrowers may have established lead managers in particular markets whom they will try to utilise for this particular transaction. Alternatively, the borrower may award the mandate to a reputable investment bank on the basis of its all round abilities despite the fact that the borrower has no relationship with this bank in this particular market segment. The institution which has brought the opportunity to the attention of the bank will usually be awarded the mandate. "Deal shopping" is not well regarded by market participants and may lead to the borrower not being shown future attractive borrowing possibilities by the relevant institution.

- Pricing and negotiating details of the bond issue: the lead manager bringing the deal to the attention of the bank will inevitably provide indicative pricing which will be progressively refined as the deal nears execution. The focus will be on the all-in borrowing cost which in this type of transaction will inevitably mean the final sub-LIBOR margin achieved by the bank.

  The bank may in fact seek a second opinion on pricing for the bond issue from another independent investment bank with whom it has a relationship in this particular market. This is usually done to mitigate the risk of a mispriced transaction. The strategy is risky as each house may try to denigrate its competitors and will tend to talk its own "book".

  Important terms and conditions such as default conditions, negative pledges as well as the issuing vehicle to be used and credit support, such as guarantees (if applicable), must be agreed upon.

  The negotiation process will inevitably lead to the lead manager providing firm final pricing prior to agreement to undertake the issue. The need to provide firm pricing inevitably requires the transaction to be structured as a "bought deal", that is, the lead manager submits a firm offer to the borrower with an underwriting syndicate to be formed only after the borrower has accepted this offer. The technique of the bought deal is designed to transfer the entire market risk from the borrower to the lead manager to ensure that the securities transaction underlying the swap is assured. A "best efforts" or classical "open priced" bond transaction to be swapped would expose the issuer to a market risk of price movements on the bond and/or swap which most borrowers regard as unacceptable.

  Typical offer and acceptance telexes for the Eurobond component of the transaction are set out in *Exhibit 13.4*.

Exhibit 13.4
Euroyen Issue Terms

Issuer:	Bank
Lead manager/book runner:	Japanese securities company
Co-lead managers:	Up to three co-lead managers recommended by the lead manager
Principal amount:	Yen 20 billion
Maturity:	26 March 19X1
Coupon:	6.00% pa
Issue price:	100.375
Gross commissions:	2%
Out-of-pocket expenses:	Reimbursable lead managers expenses to be a maximum of US$60,000
Form and denomination of notes:	To be specified
Optional redemption:	None, except in the event of the imposition of withholding taxes and then in whole but not in part
Payments:	All payments of principal and interest will be made without deductions or withholding for, or on account of, any present or future taxes or duties of whatever nature
Governing law:	The law of England
Conditions precedent:	Japanese Ministry of Finance approval to proceed with issue

- Selection of Eurobond management group for the Eurobond issue: it is currently usual to offer the provider of the swap to the bond issue the opportunity to join the lead management group for the securities transaction. Other lead managers may be selected by virtue of their market presence in the relevant sector or relationships with either the issuer or the book running lead manager.

  Underwriters and co-managers will be selected similarly with regard to relationships with the borrower and lead manager as well as with reference to their placement power and market making capabilities in the particular market. Frequent borrowers to a particular market segment will have favoured co-management groups based on experience gained through the course of a number of transactions. Additions and deletions from this co-management group may be designed to create flexibility for particular transaction structures as well as to create incentives for improved performance.

  The key points of negotiation on the swap component of the transaction will include a range of equally important but significantly different issues. These include:

- Acceptability of counterparty: it will be necessary to assess the creditworthiness of the swap counterparty as the issuer will be exposed, in a credit sense, to the swap counterparty for the life of the transaction.
- Negotiating pricing, terms and conditions: as in the case of the bond issue, the bank will negotiate the terms and conditions as well as the pricing of the swap leading up to final commitment. A particular problem may be getting swaps on truly comparable terms because of the variety of swap structures that can be utilised in connection with a particular issue

(see further comments below). In addition, where a complex series of swaps are entailed, the necessity to match different elements of the securities transaction, the initial swap and any subsequent swap creates an extra level of complexity. For example, in this example, the bank could swap the yen issue into US$ LIBOR and then subsequently swap into A$ either on a fixed or floating basis.

A key issue in negotiating the important terms and conditions of the swap will be the necessity from the view point of the borrower to ensure that the swap is conditional on the successful closing of the underlying securities transaction to minimise any market exposure for the bank. Swap counterparties usually attempt to resist this condition as it merely transfers the market risk from the issuer to the swap counterparty.

An additional issue may be the question of structuring the swap to provide for front end recoupment of issue expenses. A number of borrowers who seek to minimise tax expenses in a given year will seek recovery of issue expenses and costs. The issue of front end recoupment is discussed in the context of the yield mathematics of swaps in Chapter 8.

Once the final negotiations are completed and prices are agreed upon, the parties will exchange telexes detailing the terms of the swap agreed upon. A sample of this type of swap telex is set out in *Exhibit 13.5*.

Exhibit 13.5

Yen/US$ Currency Swap Terms

(Valid until February 28, Tokyo time.)

Yen payer:	A counterparty acceptable to bank (counterparty)
US$ payer:	Bank
Commencement date:	26 March 19X6
Maturity date:	26 March 19X1
Optional redemption:	Non-callable
Initial yen amount:	Yen 19.675 billion
Initial US$ amount:	US$ equivalent of yen 20 billion for delivery on 26 March 19X6 as determined between bank and counterparty 10 am Tokyo time on launching date
Annual yen payments:	Yen 1.2 billion corresponding to yen coupon payments payable by bank on its Euroyen issue
US$ payments:	Semi-annual payment on 26 March and 26 September in arrears based on 38bps less than six month LIBOR (the arithmetic mean of six month LIBOR quoted two London business days before start of each semi-annual interest payment period in Reuter LIBO page rounded upward to the nearest one bps) and calculated on the US$ amount
Principal re-exchanges:	1. On 26 March 19X1 bank to pay counterparty yen 19.675 billion (as above) and counterparty to pay bank the US$ amount (as above) 2. On 26 March 19X1 bank to pay counterparty the US$ amount (as above) and the counterparty to pay bank the Yen 20 billion
Governing law:	The law of England
Condition precedent:	Successful closure of bank's yen 20 billion Eurobond issue.

It is customary for both offers on the securities and swap transactions to be confirmed by a return telex by the borrower agreeing to the terms on which the whole transaction is proposed to be undertaken.

The timing in negotiating a particular arbitrage funding transaction can vary significantly. In this particular case, the yen issue plus currency swap were negotiated in a period of approximately two to three days. However, for a first issue, the process may take several months depending upon the organisational and management styles of the parties and the specific transaction being proposed. The normal period of negotiation for experienced arbitrage funders is extremely short and would not be longer than three days and may be as short as a few hours for a specific transaction.

Frequent issuers, who utilise arbitrage funding practices, usually seek indicative pricing from particular market segments on a regular basis, usually weekly for major markets and on a more opportunistic basis in other markets. This means the borrowers are well attuned to market movements and are well placed to react to particular opportunities within a relatively short time frame.

Exhibit 13.6
Timetable for the Issue

Day	Activity
-3	Identify a specific opportunity for an issue and swap Check alternatives Price negotiations and obtain internal approvals
0	Agree final terms and conditions Form syndicate group
5	Japanese Ministry of Finance approval obtained Launch of issue Oral invitation to and acceptances from selling group
6	Formal telex to invite selling group Obtain quotes for fiscal agency services
8	Appoint fiscal agent
9—22	Receive draft documents—review and negotiate
10	Formalise any necessary internal approvals
11	Submit taxation applications • s. 14c, *Taxation Administration Act* 1953 (tax haven) certificate • s. 128f (IWT), *Income Tax Assessment Act* 1936 opinion (comfort letter)
20	Obtain s. 14c certificate and s. 128f opinion letter
22	Sign subscription agreement Receive first audit comfort letter Exchange legal opinions
22—28	Finalise documents to be signed at the closing
28	Closing of the issue • sign fiscal agency and swap agreements • issue temporary global note • receive proceeds of issue • receive second audit comfort letter • exchange of principal amounts on swap transactions and any necessary rate sets • appoint process agent

Source: Massey (1987).

The timetable for the particular issue completed by the bank is summarised in *Exhibit 13.6*. The transaction will also entail a significant level of documentation and housekeeping. Some of the key documents required to be completed as well as some major housekeeping tasks required to be undertaken by the bank in our example are outlined in *Exhibit 13.7*.

Exhibit 13.7

Bond/Swap Documentation and Housekeeping

Pre-closing

1. Appointing fiscal agent:
   * competitive quotes;
   * appointment;
   * documentation.

2. Telexes:
   * offer and acceptance, both for issue and swap(s);
   * selling and underwriting group;
   * allotment.

3. Agreements:
   * subscription;
   * selling and underwriting group;
   * fiscal agency;
   * trustee (if applicable);
   * swap(s);
   * masters.

4. Taxation approvals:
   * interest withholding tax opinion;
   * s. 14c (Tax Haven) Certificate (if necessary).

5. Other documents:
   * legal opinions domestic and foreign counsel;
   * extel cards and prospectus;
   * stock exchange listing requirements;
   * consent for service of process;
   * press release.

6. Auditors comfort letters:
   * on signing subscription agreement;
   * at closing.

7. Housekeeping:
   * agree and ensure receipt of correct proceeds from the issue;
   * agree and settle swap(s) up-front cash flows.

Post-closing

1. Note printing:
   * temporary global note;
   * definitive notes.

2. Section 128f withholding tax certificate.

3. Box advertisement (London Stock Exchange only).

4. Tombstones:
   * issue;
   * swap(s).

Exhibit 13.7—continued

5. Maintain diaries:
   • reset dates for interest rate and/or currency fixes;
   • payments to noteholders and swap counterparty;
   • for callable issues:
     —redemption notice dates;
     —prepare draft public notices.

Source: Massey (1987).

Some of the key problems and difficulties encountered with arbitrage funding transactions include:

• Price negotiations: a key to price negotiations is the capacity to compare a wide variety of offers on a standardised basis. This is particularly so where bidding is relative to a benchmark.

For example, US$ issues as well as US$ interest rate swaps are usually quoted at a spread to United States Treasuries of a comparable maturity. However, because of potential significant differences between the benchmark, that is, United States Treasury bond rate, assumed by different institutions quoting the transaction, the actual all-in rate for both swap and bond issue may not be clear and thereby inappropriate conclusions can be drawn.

Exhibit 13.8

Swaps—Standardised Basis for Comparison

Firm prices quoted in relation to United States Treasury bonds
as at 10.00 am London time

Counterparty	Rate (spread to United States Treasuries)
A	+ 88
B	+ 87
C	+ 90.5 ⎫ spread = 0.5bps
D	+ 90 ⎭
E	+ 89
F	+ 84
G	+ 86

Based on these results C and D were invited to rebid their final absolute rate (against which the issuer would pay LIBOR.)

Counterparty	Bid rate
C	8.77 ⎫ difference = 6bps
D	8.71 ⎭

Solution may be to buy reference United States Treasuries and sell to successful counterparty on swap.

Source: Massey (1987).

An example of swap prices quoted in relation to United States Treasuries is set out in *Exhibit 13.8*. In this particular case, the final bids received are anomalous as the major market makers in United States Treasuries quote standard bid/offer spread of approximately 1.5bps. Consequently, the difference between the two quotes of 6bps is inexplicable given that the maximum can only, by definition, be approximately 3bps.

The variation between the relative and absolute bids can, in these circumstances, also be the result of different interest rate assumptions in the interest rate calculation for the absolute rate, different assumptions as to day counts as well as different discount rates used when up-front payments or other swap structure refinements are incorporated.

- Issue pricing: a critical consideration for a regular issuer in the particular market segment may be the requirement that the issue be regarded as fairly priced and trade successfully. This is a particularly vexed issue and is commented on separately below. However, one approach to overcoming these difficulties should be noted. A number of borrowers now disaggregate the securities issue and the swap, with the book running lead manager not being allowed to bid for the swap. This disaggregation is intended to provide fair pricing for both elements of the transaction as the lead manager is not allowed to cross-subsidise one element of the transaction with profits on the other.

- Legal issues: some of the particular problems in arbitrage funding relate to a number of legal considerations including differences in default conditions in the securities transaction and the swap as well as jurisdictional differences between the securities transaction and the swap. Care should be taken to ensure that required linkages between the swap and the issue are inserted into the documentation. Tax effects of the transaction must also be carefully considered.

- Returning to the market sector: most frequent issuers will wish to preserve the opportunity to return to a particular sector to undertake a future issue. Consequently, issuers inevitably analyse and rate the performance of participants in a particular transaction. Both the issue and the swap performance are analysed with reference to independent benchmarks. The performance of the management group on the securities transactions as well as the swap provider must be recognised and rewarded or punished as merited. One problem may be dealing with unsuccessful bidders as well as those parties not invited to form part of the management group for the issue, a particular problem for a well-received transaction.

The risks of arbitrage funding

While the use of opportunistic arbitrage funding practices can be utilised by high quality borrowers to achieve significant cost savings, the practice also has inherent risks.

The major risk is rigid adherence to target spreads without flexibility. This may encourage mispricing of securities transactions resulting in poor secondary market performance and poor distribution ultimately damaging the borrower's reputation and capacity to access the market over a longer time frame. In essence, the argument is that a rigid arbitrage funding approach with insufficient emphasis on the success of the underlying borrowing transaction may reduce borrowing costs in the short-term but may, in fact, through reduced longer term market access, cause the borrower's cost of funding to rise. This problem may be exacerbated where the borrower is slow in adjusting target spreads in rapidly moving market conditions.

An often bitter controversy surrounding the borrowing programme of the Kingdom of Denmark highlights some of the risks in respect of arbitrage funding.

The Kingdom of Denmark has established a reputation as one of the premier borrowers in international markets. Denmark approached the Eurobond market alone 32 times in 1986 raising the equivalent of krone 45 billion. Denmark established a reputation as a highly opportunistic arbitrage funder utilising swap-driven securities issues as a means of lowering its all-in cost of borrowings. The debt strategy of Denmark is highlighted in a explanatory note which was released by the Ministry of Finance and is set out as *Exhibit 13.9*.

Exhibit 13.9
Kingdom of Denmark Foreign Debt Management Strategy

The Kingdom of Denmark (KoD) is one of the most important sovereign borrowers with, in 1986, its gross foreign borrowing reaching a record of US$6.5 billion.

The KoD, that is the Ministry of Finance, does not go abroad to finance the budget (which showed a surplus for 1986) but is a residual or buffer borrower.

The Danish authorities do not want to adapt domestic economic policies to whatever change there may be in private capital movements which are free, except for certain short-term financial transactions.

Private capital movements have, indeed, shown big shifts, for example, from 1985 to 1986 when foreign borrowing by Danish businesses and movements of securities, especially domestic Danish krone bonds, made a swing of about US$7 billion. Furthermore, the borrowing activity in recent years had been enlarged because of prepayments ranging from US$1.5 billion to more than US$3 billion. In 1984, the KoD in fact reduced the outstanding debt whereas in 1987 net borrowing will amount to US$3 billion, assuming that there will be no private capital net inflow.

By the end of 1986 the total foreign debt of the KoD was US$15 billion, corresponding to 18.00% of GDP. For the country as a whole net foreign debt amounted to US$33 billion or nearly 40.00% of GDP.

The KoD and the Euromarket

The Euromarket has developed remarkably during the last few years. Because it is flexible and characterised by non-bureaucratic requirements for documentation, it is here that the growing competition among banks has been most visible and here that changes in borrowing techniques and product have gone furthest. The KoD has, since 1983, raised between 80.00% and 85.00% of its new funds in the Euromarket and we see no reason for immediate change.

"Normal" loans and "profit" loans

The KoD conceptually divides its borrowings into two parts, the so-called "profit loans" and the "normal loans". The profit loans are those which would be undertaken even in the absence of a financing need, because it would be possible to place the proceeds at a higher yield. Unfortunately only something like one quarter to one third of the borrowing needs have been covered in this way, and it has been necessary to supplement these with normal market

Exhibit 13.9—continued

transactions. The difference in the cost of funds between the two types of borrowing was around 40bps in 1986.

It might be asked whether it would not have been better to relax the target for profit borrowing somewhat and thus increase the volume forthcoming, but it has been found that when the KoD through normal transactions had covered the substantive needs it could set relatively high standards for further transactions and exploit its unusually quick decision process to take advantage of possibilities cropping up in the markets.

Use of swaps to cheapen and balance the debt

Until 1983 the KoD used relatively traditional instruments in fund raising. The tremendous development in the swap markets and the willingness, indeed eagerness, of banks to make firm offers for an issue have changed the situation dramatically. Therefore, a borrower can tap the markets where its relative advantage is greatest and reach the desired currency and interest structure through swaps, knowing in advance precisely what the result will be.

The KoD made its first swap-driven new issue in 1983. In the beginning most transactions were fixed rate US$ issues transformed into floating rate money. In later years there has been a rise, especially in swap transactions from yen but also A$, NZ$ and C$. Altogether one third of the amounts raised by the Kingdom in the period 1983-1986 have been through transactions with simultaneous swaps mostly into floating rate US$.

This has left the KoD with a big proportion of dollars in the debt. To avoid the risk which lies in having too much debt in one currency, the KoD in 1986 began to make secondary market swaps out of floating rate dollars into fixed rate European currencies, with a view to a combination of relatively low interest rates combined with the low risk of dramatic exchange rate increases. In 1986 through May 1987 the KoD has swapped more than US$2 billion.

Even stronger change has been caused by the decline in the dollar exchange rate so the KoD's dollar debt fell from 67.00% in 1983 to 46.00% at the end of 1986. Since then it has been further reduced to 40.00%. It is difficult to determine where to go from there, but tentatively it is felt that the share of US$ in present circumstances should be reduced still further, perhaps to around one third of the debt.

While most of our deutschmark and Swiss franc debt has been raised through swaps from US$, ECU debt is provided through direct issues in the Eurobond market. This is due to the fact that it is cheaper getting ECU directly than through swaps. The KoD has normally only raised ECU when the interest rate has been lower than the one which could be theoretically calculated on the basis of the market rates for debt in the component currencies.

Avoiding being seduced by options

Many offers look advantageous because the underlying issue has some particular feature in which there is, at least temporarily, a special investor interest, for instance options, especially warrants. Our view is, however, that proceeds from the sale of the warrants cannot be deducted when determining the cost of the loan unless the warrants are covered in some way. This is not to say that the KoD will in no circumstances issue warrants which are harmless but to say that the question is whether the price for the warrants is high enough to cover the risk. The KoD has made seven transactions with attached warrants, of which five have been harmless.

Eurokrone market stabilisation

In 1985 the KoD began raising funds in the Euromarket for its own currency, the krone. It was not caused by a wish to include Danish krone in the portfolio, but rather to reduce the possibilities for arbitrage operations in which a foreign (or other Danish) entity would make Eurokrone issues and place the proceeds in domestic krone bonds at a higher yield. So whenever the interest differential between the Euromarket and the domestic market exceeds a certain level the KoD is disposed to move with a view to reduce the spread.

Source: (1987) (No. 673, 16 May) *International Financing Review* 1596, 1597.

The opportunistic borrowing strategies of Denmark made it the "darling" of investment bankers in the Eurobond market. Denmark's willingness to undertake innovative borrowing structures provided certain cost targets could be met provided these bankers with the opportunity to introduce innovations in security structures and accompanying swaps into the Euromarkets through 1985 and 1986. However, by 1986, there were disturbing signs suggesting some difficulties with this particular strategy.

Denmark through 1986 brought to the market a series of aggressively priced transactions. The result was a series of securities which, by general consensus, performed particularly poorly both in syndication and in secondary market trading. The difficulties encountered appeared to be motivated by a combination of factors including:

- aggressive pricing, often irrationally so, from underwriting banks competing for international bond business and "league table" status;
- Denmark's use of competition among Eurobond underwriters to lower its borrowing costs.

While Denmark utilised market conditions brilliantly, arguing that the banks making such aggressively priced offers to it must be the ultimate arbiter of how its securities could be sold and distributed in the international market, there was by the end of 1986 signs that the strategy had the potential to damage Denmark's reputation with the investor community and capital markets generally.

These signs were manifested in two particular ways:

- private indications from a number of major investment banks to the effect that they had no wish to lead manage or indeed participate in any Danish issue while this particular type of debt strategy prevailed;
- the recurrent appearance of a series of repackaged, usually asset swapped, Danish securities issues at pricing levels which were clearly undermining Denmark's future price levels in certain market segments.

The two factors were clearly inter-related. The willingness of Denmark to issue in response to aggressively priced offers from major investment banks led to a series of sometimes ill-conceived transactions which proved profitable only to the lead manager or, in a number of cases, to nobody other than Denmark. Problems of structure and pricing rapidly led to other underwriters and market makers becoming extremely reluctant and reticent to participate in Danish issues which resulted in poor syndication and poor subsequent secondary market trading performance. The poor trading performance allowed financial institutions to repackage Danish securities at very attractive prices *to the investor*. By early 1987, these repackaged issues included the following transactions:

- a US$300m fixed rate issue from Morgan Stanley International which represented a remarketing of a US$300m fixed-to-floating issue undertaken late in 1986;
- a US$200m synthetic FRN, dubbed TOPS, created by Bankers Trust International out of a US$1 billion two year fixed rate Eurobond launched late in 1986 by Shearson Lehman Brothers International;
- an elegant repackaging by Morgan Guaranty Limited of a historic US$1 billion ten year FRN priced at 0.125% *under* LIBID (the lowest priced

FRN in history) into deutschmarks and £ FRNs respectively totalling DM300m and £100m.

Apart from these public repackagings, a series of privately repackaged Danish issues was also placed amongst investors. In each case the repackaging was made feasible by the poor original syndication of the host debt as well as its poor secondary market trading. The secondary market trading suggested that the real price for Danish securities was much lower than that being obtained by Denmark's relentless use of competitive pressures to clinch the tightest terms each time it came to market. The poor secondary market performance was, however, translated through the repackaging exercises into market clearing levels at which the issues, at least in their repackaged form, could be placed with genuine investors.

However, what was particularly disturbing was that the repackaged issues, whether private or public, merged at a much higher yield than what market sources estimated Denmark would have attained on any direct borrowing in the particular market segment. For example, on the repackaged deutschmark and £ FRNs (known as Stars and Stripes) the coupons were set at 0.1875% pa and 0.20% pa over deutschmark and £ LIBOR respectively. These levels, at the time, were significantly above the levels at which Denmark could have issued directly on a floating rate basis in deutschmark and £.

Essentially, the terms of the repackaged debt had dramatically impacted on Denmark's ability to tap those market segments in future as investors had available to them a supply of richly priced assets of Danish risk against which any future Danish transaction would be compared. The repackaged issues were essentially determining Denmark's future pricing in the relevant markets.

The repackagings also have implications for the relationship between Denmark and its investment bankers, underwriters and investors. Its use and reliance on unfettered competition between market participants has inevitably eroded any direct loyalty between borrower, intermediary, and lender. This is evident in the fact that in the case of the repackagings, the transactions were undertaken with minimum consultation with Denmark. Consequently, Denmark had effectively largely lost control of the secondary market trading and repackaging of its debt which ultimately would influence the terms on which Denmark could hope to access particular markets in the future.

Denmark issued a strongly worded reply to these allegations. This reply is reproduced in full in *Exhibit 13.10.*

However, despite this refutation defending its behaviour, there was evidence that Denmark was aware of the problems in this regard and was looking at means of ensuring a more orderly market for its securities transactions.

The case of the Kingdom of Denmark's debt strategy and the controversy surrounding it is not presented as a particular paradigm or case of particular notoriety. However, the controversy does highlight some of the risks of arbitrage funding. It is difficult, however, to disentangle the problems of Denmark's debt strategy from the particular market environment which prevailed in 1985 and 1986. During this period, intense competition between financial institutions seeking to carve out market shares in the highly competitive international bond business as well as unprecedented growth

Exhibit 13.10

"Is the Kingdom of Denmark's Debt Strategy Going Badly Wrong": A Reply

"If 'Big firms' do not want to do business with the Kingdom, it would be more business-like to tell us so directly, rather than do it in a defaming way under the cover of IFR. We have never received a message like that from any bank. On the contrary several prime banks have strongly asked us to be invited to bid for the next deal. By the way, only in eight out of 32 issues made in 1986 competitive bidding was used.

Furthermore, your article touches upon the performance of our issues when they come to market. As everybody knows forecasting the reception of the market is very difficult. However, that key point in bond issuing cannot be avoided so it is no wonder that banks in the market put their very best resources to tackle those problems. From time to time the market is not as good as expected but I fail to see how we are to be blamed, especially when considering that our knowledge and feeling of the market cannot be as deep as is the case for the prime banks.

That brings us to the next issue. Is it true that Danish bonds perform poorly in the secondary market? We do not think so. If you consider the major fixed rate issues we did in 1986, we think they perform reasonably satisfactorily. As far as the US$1billion Morgan Guaranty FRN is concerned, we must admit that it has never performed well. But we think, as you also mention in the article, that there has been some special reasons for that, especially the United Kingdom super-jumbo FRN a few days later and the general development in the FRN market.

Thirdly, the question of repackaging our issues, which the article take[s] as writing on the wall. It should be noted that a lot of repackaging takes place in the market. It is not only bonds of the Kingdom of Denmark that are involved in such operations. Even the FRN from the United Kingdom has been used in such an operation. We do not think that repackaging operations necessarily is a bad thing. The Euromarket has over the years been very successful. One of the reasons is that the players accept innovations and arbitrage and repackaging is precisely an effort to overcome imperfections of the market. Looking from the borrowers' point of view repackaging could have a positive effect since the neutralising of the repackaged bonds may make it easier for us to sell new issues.

The article mentioned that we are considering to ask the Danish Central Bank to act as 'a purchaser of last resort'. For information, I can say that our line of thinking is different. The purpose of such operations would be to improve the market efficiency and to make a profit by making purchases in some of the old illiquid outstanding issues.

To sum up it is our conclusion that our strategy has been fairly successful. Quite often in the past the IFR has quoted sources saying that our strategy would backfire and make it difficult for us to place new issues at reasonable prices. Consistently this view has been shown to be erroneous since subsequent issues have been on advantageous conditions. We believe that it will be no different in the future. Quite another matter is that the ultra competitive phase of the markets may well pass so that profit margins for the banks will improve."

Source: (1987) (No. 663, 7 March) *International Financing Review* 781.

in capital market activity and generally favourable markets conditions may have to a large extent influenced events. With the market downturn in late 1987, following the collapse of global equity markets, the change in market environment, from a borrower's market to a lender's market, may dictate changed attitudes which mitigate the more extreme aspects of arbitrage funding.

However, there is little doubt that the opportunistic basis of arbitrage borrowings will continue to exist as a legitimate part of borrowers' strategies as it essentially derives from the basic economic fundamentals which give rise to these types of transactions in the first place. In essence, despite the risks of arbitrage funding, its impact on primary debt markets and the way in which new borrowing activity is conducted is not likely to change significantly.

IMPACT OF NEW ISSUE ARBITRAGE ON PRIMARY DEBT MARKETS

Swap-driven primary issues

As swap transactions increasingly unbundle the process of fund raising, separating the decision to raise funds in a particular market and the process of conversion of the funds raised into the desired currency and interest rate basis, all the major global debt markets increasingly became arbitrage markets. This resulted in the development of a unique class of debt instruments that could be characterised as "swap-driven primary issues". By definition under such structures, despite the fact that the primary issuance of debt involved may well be a standard, publicised securities issue, the borrower acquired an exposure in a currency and interest rate basis other than that of the borrowing.

The emergence of swap-driven primary issues had two major implications:

* the pricing approach to the issuance of new debt changed radically;
* swap-driven primary issues resulted in a radical change in the currency distribution of international bond issues.

With an ever higher percentage of issues being swap-driven, the pricing in almost every segment of the international bond market came to be arbitrage driven with the relevant pricing being *not* the absolute interest cost of an issue per se, but the pricing achievable in US$ terms in either fixed rate relative to United States Treasuries, or more often, in floating rate terms as a margin under LIBOR. In this regard, as noted above, floating rate US$, usually priced relative to LIBOR, emerged as a useful medium through which a large proportion of cross currency swaps were transacted. The exact pricing in US$ terms, be it in fixed or floating rates, did not matter as the existence of deep liquid markets in US$ interest rate swaps meant that floating rate could be converted to its fixed rate equivalent and vice versa.

Exhibit 13.11

Currency Swap-Driven Issues in International Bond Markets 1983-1988

Share of currency swap-driven issuance in the international bond markets, 1983—1988 (US$ billions or equivalent)

	1988	1987	1986	1985	1984	1983
US$ issuance	77.239	62.980	118.979	100.676	69.114	40.610
% swapped	35.000%	19.000%	7.000%	3.000%	4.000%	4.000%
Non-dollar issuance	142.689	110.983	101.779	64.864	39.495	32.695
% swapped	18.000%	30.000%	26.000%	25.000%	9.000%	6.000%
Total issuance	219.928	173.963	220.58	165.540	108.609	73.305
% swapped	24.200%	25.900%	16.000%	12.000%	5.000%	5.000%

Source: Salomon Brothers estimates.

The extent to which markets came to be swap-driven is evident from *Exhibit 13.11* which illustrates an explosive growth in swap-driven issues. However, the true extent of swap-driven transactions is even higher as the statistics in *Exhibit 13.11* only consider *currency swap*-driven issuance. *Exhibit 13.12*, which records the extent of swap-driven Eurobond transactions in 1987, reveals the percentages to be even higher. This is particularly so in a number of market segments such as EuroUS$, ¥, A$ etc. where the percentage of issues which are swapped are very high.

These conclusions are reinforced by the data presented in *Exhibit 13.13* which shows the currency distribution of fixed rate international bonds swapped. The data in *Exhibit 13.13* also highlights how the emergence of swap-driven primary issues of debt have led to the development of international bond markets in a number of currencies, previously unknown outside their national markets. For example, international debt markets in A$, NZ$, ECU, French francs, Danish krone, etc. owe, at least, their rapid expansion to the existence of substantial currency swap markets which provide the basis for new issue activity in these market sectors. Consequently, allied to financial deregulation and liberalisation in many key markets, the emergence of swap-driven new issues had a dramatic impact in the distribution of currencies utilised in international finance.

The impact on the primary debt markets, however, extended well beyond these factors and included certain effects on the characteristics of bonds which themselves started to evolve in response to their function as the host debt for, often complex, swap-driven fund raising exercises. The primary changes to the characteristics of the bonds included:

- the increased use of non-callable bullet maturities designed to help match counterparties in the swap transaction;
- the issuance of securities in odd amounts in order to match the proceeds of the borrowing to the underlying swap because if one side of a currency swap is kept to a round amount, it produces, almost inevitably, an odd total in the other swapped currency;

Exhibit 13.12

Swap-Driven Eurobond Issuance 1988

	Swapped issues as % of total issues
US$	39
¥	50
DM	4
SFR	15
A$	37
ECU	16
C$	41
£	9

Source: Salomon Brothers estimates.

- the emergence of a series of "exotic" security structures designed to appeal to small groups of investors with specific objectives, which were structured around the underlying swap transactions, which were increasingly complex and designed to insulate the issuer from some of the characteristics of the securities being issued;
- the phenomena of increasingly aggressive and tight pricing on swap-driven primary issues reflecting both the demand for the specific issuer's debt in the primary market being accessed but also aggressive bidding by investment banks and underwriters who were seeking to maximise their profits on a larger set of transactions, which included both the securities issue and the accompanying swap transactions.

Impact on the new issue business

The emergence of swap-driven primary issues also had a profound impact on how the new issue business itself operated. The increased realisation that issuers saw the actual securities issuance or debt transaction as the basis for an accompanying swap, meant that the financial institutions active in raising new funds for clients had to increasingly acquire a new set of skills. For intermediaries traditionally strong in the issuance of securities, it meant the acquisition of swap skills while for a number of major innovators in the swap market, it provided an opportunity to increase their new issue business on the back of their swap prowess. Financial institutions like J. P. Morgan, Banque Paribas Capital Markets and Bankers Trust are powerful examples of the second group.

Exhibit 13.13
Currency Distribution of Fixed Rate International Bonds Swapped in 1988 (1987)

	Total swapped	Total issues	% of issues swapped	Share of all swaps by value
	(US$ billions equivalent)			
US$	27.2(12.2)	73.3(59.0)	37.1(21)	52.1(27.5)
¥	6.8(10.4)	16.9(22.4)	40.2(46)	13.0(23.5)
SFR	3.8 (2.8)	25.4(23.5)	15.0(12)	7.3 (6.3)
A$	3.0 (6.6)	7.6 (8.4)	39.5(79)	5.7(14.9)
ECU	2.0 (2.9)	12.2 (7.3)	16.4(40)	3.8 (6.5)
C$	5.3 (3.0)	13.2 (6.1)	40.2(49)	10.2 (6.8)
DM	0.9 (1.0)	24.0(13.5)	3.8 (7)	1.7 (2.3)
FRF	0.3 (0.3)	2.9 (2.3)	10.3(13)	0.6 (0.7)
NZ$	0.5 (1.7)	1.2 (2.7)	41.7(63)	1.0 (3.8)
£	2.0 (2.7)	13.3(12.8)	15.0(21)	3.8 (6.1)
DKr	0.1 (0.2)	1.3 (1.4)	7.7(14)	0.2(0.5)
Dfl	0.2 (0.1)	3.6 (1.5)	5.6 (7)	0.4 (0.2)
Others	0.1 (0.4)	6.8 (1.2)	1.5 (3)	0.2 (0.9)
Total	52.2(44.3)	201.7(162.1)	25.9(27.3)	100(100)

Source: Salomon Brothers estimates.

As the practice of arbitrage funding, involving bond swap packages as well as easily defined funding targets developed, the basic approach to originating securities transactions and investment banking business was forced to evolve.

In the first place, the financial institutions were increasingly required to provide the total package with an all-up cost of funds stated as a margin under US$ LIBOR. In addition, as markets became increasingly volatile with issuance opportunities or windows opening and closing at relatively short notice and as swaps evolved from highly structured counterparty driven corporate finance transactions to standardised commodity products dealt off trading desks, the origination business moved rapidly into a trading room environment.

The whole process of originating securities transactions which had previously often stretched out over a period of months and in some cases years involving the client being courted by investment bankers gave way to highly opportunistic securities transactions on a swapped basis driven by the existence of short-lived opportunities. These opportunities came increasingly to be offered to potential borrowers through the medium of small units working closely with the securities issuance or syndicate desk and swap desks to develop all-in funding packages.

These units, referred to variously as "debt transactions group" (Merrill Lynch), "capital market services" (Salomon Brothers), "frequent issuers desks" (Citicorp and Nomura Securities), "financing desk" (Shearson Lehman Brothers) etc., would stay in touch with the borrower advising them of changing opportunities in the international capital markets and, in particular, the relatively rapid changes in estimated arbitrages available via primary market transactions in various currencies.

As the practice of arbitrage funding on a purely opportunistic basis grew, a number of financial institutions focused almost exclusively on these borrowers offering them various opportunities as and when they arose. This type of approach to the new issue business is evident from an advertisement in *Euromoney* in late 1987 placed by Bankers Trust Company which was headed: "If your bank has never delivered money at 200 points below LIBOR, try the one that has." The advertisement also indicated that: "over the last two years, Bankers Trust has lead managed 10 issues for SEK. We were book runners not only on their history-making US$200 million Eurobond issue at more than 200 basis points below LIBOR, but also on the US$200 million 40 year Eurobond issue—the longest term ever done."

Given the status of SEK as perhaps the premier arbitrage funder in the world, this strategy of Bankers Trust of centralising its resources to originate capital markets transactions by focusing the attention of various specialists, in a small unit delivering bond swap packages to key arbitrage funders is self-evident.

However, the impact on the new issue business of swap-driven primary issues also has a darker, more disturbing aspect. The emergence of primary issues which were swap-driven changed forever the profit equation on capital market business. As there were two sources of earnings, the securities issue and the swap, the financial institution involved had the opportunity to maximise its own earnings from the transaction by separating the pricing of the two elements to its own advantage. Increasingly through 1985 and 1986, the underlying securities issue was often priced aggressively, sometimes beyond the tolerance of the market, reflecting aggressive pricing by the book running lead manager who, if it provided the swap, used the swap fees to compensate for the terms on the bond and who was essentially relying on competition for market share by co-managers to limit the lead manager's underwriting commitment and therefore its risk of loss on the securities transaction.

This changing profit equation led increasingly to mispriced issues which traded poorly and were not effectively distributed. These mispriced issues allowed substantial opportunities for asset swap transactions and repackaging of issues into alternative formats, usually involving a swap, to be undertaken. This aspect is considered in detail in the context of asset swaps in Chapter 18.

This practice is particularly true of the EuroAustralian dollar bond and swap market where lead managers take their earnings on the swap, which is clearly accruing to them, while structuring a tightly priced securities issue with the objective of syndicating the risk to lower any potential risk on placement of the securities.

However, the historical pattern of mispricing on the bond side with the lead manager laying off bonds on the syndicate and making money on the swap has undergone some revision in recent times. The swap has more often recently become the vehicle for the subsidy. This has been particularly true, indeed for some years, in certain swap market segments such as the Japanese yen where subsidies on the swap as a means of "buying business" has been a common, though often heatedly denied, practice.

As issuers, concerned with market reputation and the desire to maintain longer term access to debt markets, dictate terms on the securities transactions to guard against mispricing, financial institutions, given that the borrower still wishes to satisfy certain cost targets, must increasingly build the subsidy into the swap. This shift in the profit equation has an interesting subsidiary effect as lead managers can only subsidise to the extent of the proportion of the new issue they control. This has resulted in book runners tending to control and distribute a very high percentage of issues with allotments to other underwriters and selling group participants being confined to relatively small amounts.

This was evident in a celebrated case where Credit Suisse First Boston pulled out of a syndicate for an issue lead by County Natwest for the Kingdom of Belgium on the basis that County, the book running lead manager, was holding back too much of the issue for itself in order to offset the reputedly substantial subsidy on the swap it had provided to win the particular mandate.

This change in the distribution of profits between the securities and the swap is not without its critics who point out that it might be more desirable to take a loss on the mispriced bonds than to book an offmarket rate swap because the latter is a term commitment which will stay on the books of the particular institution and will require capital to be held against it over the full term.

The fundamental underpinning of the securities issuance business by swap-driven primary issues has required market participants to adjust their business practices to the new environment. While the changes to market environment necessitated by changes in market conditions following the collapse of global equity markets in 1987 may, in the medium term, lead to some changes in the origination process for new transactions, the basic impact of swaps is likely to persist. This reflects the fact that while the continued growth of swap-driven primary issuance is not likely to continue at the explosive pace of growth recorded in the immediate past, it is nevertheless an established and important part of the structure of the international capital market and financial institutions operating in this market must necessarily recognise and adapt to it.

Chapter 14
Asset and Liability Management

SWAPS AND ASSET LIABILITY MANAGEMENT

The use of swaps in asset and liability management is predicated on the capacity of such instruments to convert fixed rate exposures to floating rate and vice versa, and, in the case of currency swaps or LTFX, to convert assets and liabilities from one currency to another. This capability makes swaps an important potential means of managing interest rate and currency exposures on *existing* assets and liabilities. In contrast to new issue arbitrage which focuses on utilising swaps to create synthetic liabilities on the basis of cost advantages, where swaps are used as instruments of asset and liability management, the economic or price benefit is subsumed to other objectives. In this regard, swaps function, as noted above, as an over the counter futures or forward contract on interest rates and currencies.

The key factors in the emergence of swaps as an asset liability management instrument include:

- The incomplete nature of market structures whereby swaps are utilised to fill in gaps in the range of available instruments.
- Swaps allow unbundling of funding (or investment decisions) from currency or interest rate basis determination.
- Non-economic benefits such as flexibility, lower critical transaction size, execution speed, anonymity, ease of documentation and absence of regulatory requirements.

The primary focus of this chapter is to outline some potential uses of swaps in the active management of asset and liability portfolios. The use of interest rate and currency swaps are considered in detail first. The use of swap derivatives, such as FRAs, LTFX, caps and collars, etc., are then considered. The discussion, in respect of utilising the swap derivatives, focuses on the major differences between these derivatives and interest rate and currency swaps which usually motivate the use of these instruments.

The use of swaps as an instrument for active *asset* management requires some preliminary observations.

As the fundamental changes in the swap market began to manifest themselves, swap applications relevant to the asset side of the balance sheet came increasingly to be recognised. This enabled portfolio and investment managers to use interest rate and currency swaps to create synthetic securities which were otherwise unavailable and to provide both yield pick-up and portfolio diversification. The detailed structure and market for asset swaps is considered in detail in Chapter 18. However, in this chapter, the use of swaps as a means for *active* management of asset portfolios is considered.

The difference between a liability and an asset swap is minimal. The advantages of flexibility, speed and anonymity, which are significant considerations in liability swaps, are equally relevant to asset swap transactions. An added dimension, however, is the opportunity to trade swaps in a manner similar to more traditional debt instruments.

The use of swaps as a surrogate debt instrument for the purposes of investment and trading are predicated on their cash flow similarities to fixed interest securities. Under certain circumstances, the yield advantage on swaps (where they are at attractive margins relative to comparable debt securities), the absence of significant funding costs as well as favourable treatment (in some jurisdictions) from the perspective of withholding tax makes swaps attractive when compared to conventional securities.

For the investor, swaps have emerged as an instrument for creating synthetic assets and as a means for more active portfolio management. Interest rate swaps can be utilised to effectively transform a fixed rate asset into a floating rate investment. Interest rate swaps can also be used to lock in capital gains or minimise losses arising from the impact of interest rate fluctuations on investment portfolios.

Currency swaps, against underlying asset and investment portfolios, enable portfolio managers to create fixed or floating rate securities in currencies different to that of the underlying securities in which funds are invested. They can also be used to manage the foreign exchange risk of investments as well as protecting portfolios from possible reversals of gains arising from investments made during a period of favourable interest or exchange rates.

Swaps against assets and investments may be utilised to generate improvements in yields relative to conventional investment alternatives or to structure investments of a type not otherwise available. Even where higher yields and/or security availability is not a consideration, factors such as the flexibility, speed and anonymity of portfolio operations entailing swaps instead of purchases and sales of securities, have increasingly forced portfolio managers to view swaps as an investment management instrument. For example, the problems of an illiquid security held in a portfolio can be overcome, in part, by utilising swaps against that asset.

UTILISING INTEREST RATE AND CURRENCY SWAPS

Liability based interest rate swaps: examples

Interest rate swap transactions can be utilised as an instrument for managing liabilities as follows.

Creating synthetic fixed or floating rate liabilities

The classic use of interest rate swaps is to create synthetic fixed or floating rate liabilities.

For example, where a corporate treasurer believes interest rates will increase, a swap can be used to create a synthetic fixed rate liability. Under the swap, the corporation pays a fixed rate and receives a floating rate thus locking in the cost of short-term debt (see *Exhibit 14.1*).

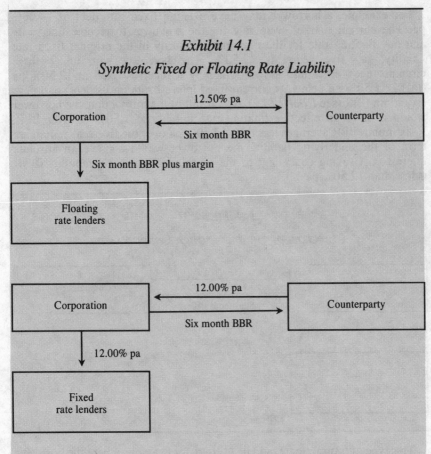

Exhibit 14.1

Synthetic Fixed or Floating Rate Liability

Note: All interest rate swap examples are in A$ terms with six month BBR being utilised as the floating rate index. In the case of currency swaps, all rates are quoted as fixed A$ against six month LIBOR. Bid/offer spreads are not included for simplicity of exposition.

The converse of this transaction entails the swap being undertaken against a fixed rate issue or borrowing to create synthetic floating rate term debt (see *Exhibit 14.1*). This type of transaction may be undertaken where a corporate treasurer believes that floating interest rates (given that these are priced at the shorter end of the yield curve) will provide the borrower with lower interest cost funding over the relevant time horizon.

Unlocking the high cost of existing fixed rate liabilities

An interest rate swap can be utilised to unlock (or unhinge) the cost of existing high coupon debt, enabling a company to achieve significant cost savings. This can be achieved either where the previous fixed rate debt was the result of a borrowing on fixed rate terms or, alternatively, was the result of an earlier swap transaction to convert floating rate liabilities to fixed rate.

For example, a borrower may have existing fixed rate debt at 14.00%
pa. The current market swap rate for the borrower to receive fixed rate
and pay floating rate for the remaining maturity of the original fixed rate
liability, say five years, is 12.50%. The borrower can, under these
circumstances, enter into a swap whereby it receives fixed at 12.50% pa
(that is, 1.50% pa below its current fixed interest rate on its debt) and pays
six month BBR (see *Exhibit 14.2*). As a result of the transaction, the borrower
would achieve an effective floating rate liability at 1.50% pa over BBR.
If six month BBR averages less than 12.50% pa over the five year remaining
term of the underlying liability the borrower would achieve an absolute
interest cost saving equivalent to the margin by which six month LIBOR
is less than 12.50% pa.

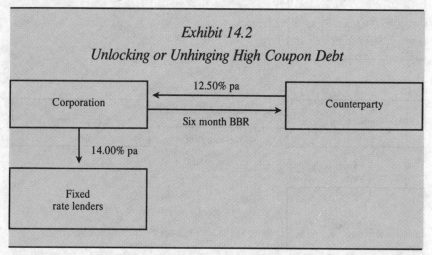

Exhibit 14.2

Unlocking or Unhinging High Coupon Debt

This type of transaction would be utilised, for example, where the borrower
expected that a floating interest rate would provide it with lower cost funding
for the relevant term. The use of a swap to unlock the high cost of existing
fixed rate debt may be particularly attractive where the relevant borrowing
cannot be repaid and, subsequently, refinanced or alternatively, where the
pre-payment penalties applicable and/or the costs associated with refinancing
would be significant.

Managing the cost of floating rate liabilities

Interest rate swaps can be utilised by a borrower to manage the cost
of its existing floating rate liabilities. For example, where a borrower is
currently borrowing on a floating rate basis in the expectation that this will
minimise its interest cost in a normally sloped yield curve environment,
interest rate swaps can be utilised to lower its floating rate interest cost.

Transaction 1. The borrower enters into an interest rate swap where it
pays a fixed rate in exchange for receiving BBR. The initial swap is then
reversed at a later date by the borrower entering into a further swap where
it *receives* a fixed rate in exchange for *paying* BBR. Provided that fixed
interest rates have risen to a level above the rate at which the initial swap
was entered into, the borrower would achieve a lower floating rate cost
(see *Exhibit 14.3*).

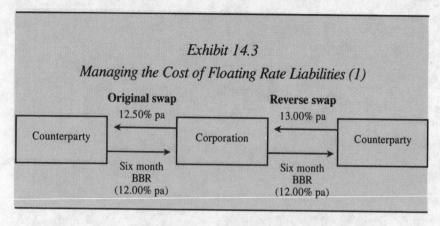

Exhibit 14.3

Managing the Cost of Floating Rate Liabilities (1)

For example, if the fixed rate payable under the first swap was 12.50% pa and the swap could be reversed at a rate of 13.00% pa, the borrower would achieve a floating rate funding at 0.50% *below* BBR.

This cost saving represents the difference between the rates payable on the successive swaps. However, the all-up benefit must be calculated by the basis of factoring in the higher interest cost incurred during the period the borrower pays fixed rates under the first swap. This cost will vary depending on the shape of the yield curve, the period between the initial swap and its reversal and the remaining term of the borrowing.

In the above example, if six month BBR was 12.00% pa at the time the transaction was entered into, the time elapsed between the first and second transaction was six months, and the remaining term of the borrowing was five years, the net cost saving after factoring in the higher interest cost for six months would be equivalent to 0.43% pa below BBR.

Transaction 2. Where the borrower is currently borrowing on a floating rate basis, it bears the risk of a change in the shape of the yield curve, particularly an inversion of the yield curve.

For example, where the yield curve is negatively sloped, that is, six month BBR is at 15.00% pa while the swap rate for a party to pay fixed rate is 12.50% pa, the borrower could lower its funding cost by entering into a swap under which it pays a fixed rate of 12.50% pa and receives six month BBR. When the yield curve returns to a normal positive slope, the initial swap can be reversed by entering into an offsetting swap where the borrower receives fixed rate in return for paying six month BBR (see *Exhibit 14.4*).

The saving achieved (in this example 2.50% pa) is realised as long as the fixed rate for the remaining maturity of the swap has not moved significantly from its previous level. For example, in the example used, if the initial transaction was for a maturity of three years and was reversed after six months, the borrower would realise an interest cost saving as long as the rate at which the reversal was achieved was greater than 11.91% pa.

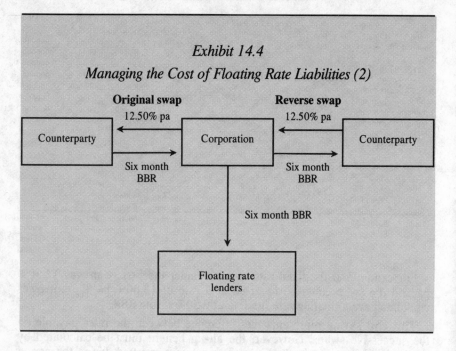

Exhibit 14.4

Managing the Cost of Floating Rate Liabilities (2)

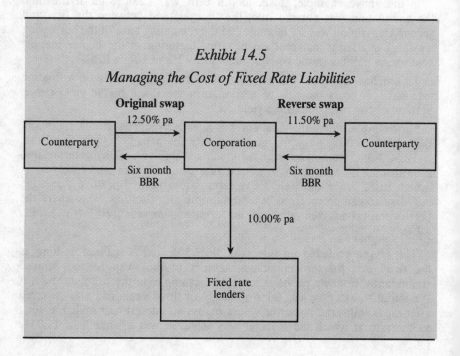

Exhibit 14.5

Managing the Cost of Fixed Rate Liabilities

Managing the cost of fixed rate liabilities

Interest rate swaps can be used by borrowers to also manage the cost of its *fixed rate* borrowings, created as a result of either a fixed rate borrowing or a previous interest rate swap.

For example, assume a borrower has fixed rate debt at 10.00% pa with a remaining term to maturity of five years. Current market fixed interest rates for five years are 12.50% pa but are expected to decline. The borrower normally would pay BBR plus a margin of 0.50% pa for its floating rate borrowings.

The borrower can, in these circumstances, utilise interest rate swaps to manage the cost of its fixed rate funding as follows. The borrower initially enters into a swap where it receives a fixed rate and pays six month BBR. This effectively generates floating rate funding at 2.50% *under* BBR enabling it to achieve a saving of 3.00% on its usual floating rate interest cost. If after six months, fixed rates decline as expected, to say 11.50% pa for four and a half years, the borrower can reverse the initial swap, swapping back into fixed rate funding. The reversal effectively generates fixed rate funding at 9.00% pa (see *Exhibit 14.5*).

This particular transaction enables the borrower to preserve the value of its below market fixed rate funding even in a declining rate environment.

Liability based currency swaps: examples

Currency swap transactions, whereby an interest rate exchange is combined with a currency exchange, can be utilised to expand the range of possible uses of swaps as follows.

To hedge foreign currency exposures

For example, where the borrower has an existing liability in a currency, say US$, which is expected to strengthen, it can hedge its exposure by entering into a currency swap to convert the currency denomination of its liability into say, A$.

Currency swaps can also, of course, be used to lower the cost of debt by converting existing liabilities in a particular currency to a liability in a different currency on either a fixed or floating rate basis in line with expectations on foreign exchange and interest rates.

To "lock in" foreign currency gains or minimising losses on foreign currency borrowings

For example, if the borrower had borrowed in US$ and the US$ has depreciated (appreciated) against the A$ since the liability was incurred, the borrower could enter into a currency swap whereby it converted its exposure from US$ into A$ and would, by virtue of the fact that the initial currency exchange and subsequent re-exchange would be undertaken at the then prevailing US$/A$ exchange rate, enable the foreign exchange gain (loss) to the borrower to be locked in (limited) irrespective of subsequent movements in the exchange rate.

The use of currency swaps to manage existing liabilities is illustrated by an example set out in *Exhibit 14.6*.

Exhibit 14.6

Managing Foreign Currency Liabilities Utilising a Currency Swap

The example relates to a US$/A$ currency swap. The company involved has an outstanding US$ issue which it now seeks to convert into an A$ liability in order to lock in the economic gains resulting from favourable movements in currency and interest rates since the liability was incurred.

The counterparty's A$ issue is specifically designed to match the principal amount, maturity and interest payment dates of the outstanding US$ issue. The terms of the borrowers' respective borrowing are as follows:

	Company's existing US$ issue	Counterparty's new A$ issue
Principal amount (millions)	US$50,000	A$75,000
Exchange rate (at time of issue)	A$1.50/US$1.00	—
Maturity (years)	5	5
	(Remaining life of existing 8 year US$ issue)	
Interest:		
Coupon rate	8.25%	12.50%
Payment frequency	Annual	Annual
Sinking fund	None	None
Issue price		100.00%
Less:		
Issuing and other issue expenses		2.125%
Net proceeds to issuer		97.875%
Net cost of money (annual)		13.11%

Assume that the counterparty has a US$ target rate of 10.00% pa. However, under the swap agreement, the counterparty will service the company's 8.25% US$ issue. Therefore, the counterparty will be required to compensate the company for the rate differential. In order to avoid any currency exposure, the compensation is in the form of an initial transfer payment.

Through its A$75m borrowing, the counterparty obtains net proceeds of A$73,406,250. By converting these proceeds in the spot market (at A$1.25/US$1.00), the counterparty obtains US$58,725,000. However, the net present value of the US$ payment stream to be assumed discounted at the counterparty's 10.00% pa target rate, is US$46,683,062. Therefore, the counterparty must pay the difference, A$15,052,423 (or US$12,041,938) to the company. This initial transfer payment effectively raises the counterparty's all-in US$ cost while lowering the company's A$ cost.

This initial transfer payment to the United States company represents the net present value (@ 10.00% pa) of the following:

* the difference between the current interest rate on US$ debt of the relevant maturity 10.00% pa and the coupon on the existing US$ issue of 8.25% pa;
* the exchange gain on the borrowing arising from the fact that the A$/US$ rate has moved from A$1.50/US$1.00 when the borrowing was undertaken to A$1.25/US$1.00.

The all-in US$ cost to the company is determined by translating the US$ principal amount of the seasoned issue into A$ at the spot rate and adjusting this amount to reflect original issuance costs (A$73,406,250, assuming issuing costs of 2.125%). In addition, the company must take into account the initial transfer payment which it receives from the counterparty (A$15,052,423) and the A$ payments it has agreed to make to cover the counterparty's A$ obligations of A$9,375,000 in years one through four and A$84,375,000 at maturity. The company would therefore effectively raise A$ at an all-in cost of 8.00% pa.

Exhibit 14.6—continued

The all-in US$ cost to the counterparty consists of the US$ proceeds of US$58,725,000 resulting from its own A$ issue less the US$ transfer payment it makes to the company (US$12,041,938) and the US$ payments it has agreed to make to cover the company's US$ obligations of US$4,125,000 in years one through four and US$54,125,000 at maturity. The counterparty thus effectively raises US$ at an all-in cost of 10.00% pa.

Year	Cash flow on outstanding US$ issue	Effective A$ flow
0	(46,683,062)	(88,458,673)
1	4,125,000	9,375,000
2	4,125,000	9,375,000
3	4,125,000	9,375,000
4	4,125,000	9,375,000
5	54,125,000	84,375,000

Asset based interest rate swaps: examples

Interest rate swap transactions can be utilised as an instrument for managing investment portfolios as follows.

Creating synthetic fixed or floating rate assets

The classic use of interest rate swaps in asset or investment based transactions is to create synthetic fixed or floating rate securities which best satisfy return and portfolio requirements.

For example, a portfolio manager can transform existing or newly acquired floating rate investments (such as a bank deposit, FRN, floating rate CD or other variable rate asset) into a term fixed rate of return by entering into an interest rate swap whereby it pays a floating rate and receives a fixed rate (see *Exhibit 14.7*).

In the example, the transaction transforms the floating rate asset to provide an effective rate of return equal to 12.75% pa while maintaining the flexibility and liquidity of the underlying asset. An investment manager may undertake this type of transaction to increase the yield on its floating rate portfolio in a positively sloped yield curve environment.

The converse of this transaction entails an investor undertaking a swap, whereby it pays a fixed rate in return for receiving a floating rate, to transform the yield on a fixed rate asset (such as a bond, fixed rate CD or other fixed rate asset) into a floating rate (see *Exhibit 14.7*). This type of transaction may be undertaken where an investor believes short rates are going to rise and/or a negative yield curve is going to prevail or, alternatively, to change the mix of the investment portfolio. For example, in the example below, the investor generates an effective return of BBR plus 1.25% pa.

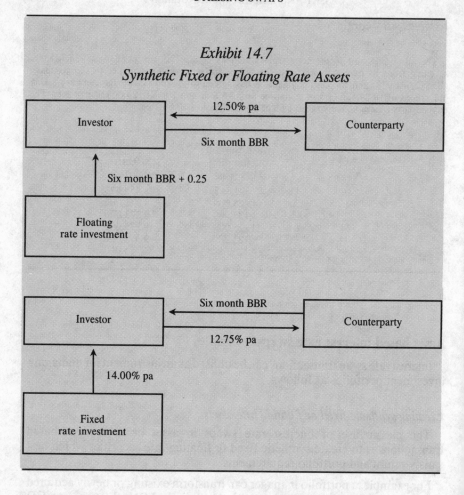

Exhibit 14.7
Synthetic Fixed or Floating Rate Assets

"Locking in" gains and minimising losses on fixed rate investments

Interest rate swaps can be utilised to "lock in" unrealised profits (or minimise losses) on the capital value of fixed rate investments resulting from interest rate fluctuations, irrespective of whether the underlying asset is a fixed rate security or a synthetically created fixed rate asset.

Transaction 1. For example, where the investor is holding fixed interest securities, yielding say 12.00% pa, and interest rates have fallen to 10.00% pa, the investor can protect itself from a possible reversal of the gain due to further rate fluctuations as follows. The investor enters into an interest rate swap where it pays a fixed rate of 10.00% pa and receives a floating rate, six month BBR. This effectively generates a floating rate return of 2.00% pa over BBR. If rates for the relevant maturity increase to say 12.00% pa, it can reverse the original transaction by entering into a swap where it receives 12.00% pa and pays six month BBR. The net effect of the transaction is to provide the investor with a yield of 14.00% pa thereby using the swap transactions to "lock in" the unrealised capital gain to boost portfolio yield (see *Exhibit 14.8*).

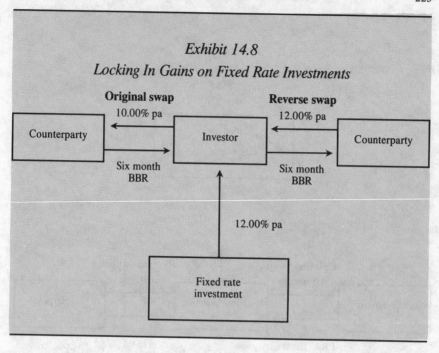

Exhibit 14.8
Locking In Gains on Fixed Rate Investments

The improvement in portfolio yield achieved is affected by the period between the two swaps and the slope of the yield curve, that is, the yield loss (if any) during the period that the investor has a floating rate asset. In the above example, if six month BBR averages 12.00% pa during the period until the first swap is reversed, no yield loss results. Assuming that the period between the initial swap and its reversal is six months and the underlying fixed rate investment was for a maturity of three years, the six month BBR rate would have to average less than 3.58% pa for the transaction to result in an overall loss of portfolio yield.

Transaction 2. Where the slope of the yield curve changes, interest rate swaps can be used to insulate the portfolio against capital losses.

For example, where a trader holds fixed interest securities by funding its investment through shorter term borrowings, an inversion in the yield curve would result in the trader sustaining a loss as its cost of funding would, at least during the period the yield curve remained negatively sloped, exceed the earnings on the fixed interest security. Under these circumstances, the investor could protect itself by entering into a swap, whereby it receives a floating rate, six month BBR, in exchange for paying a fixed rate, as such a transaction would enable it to match its short-term funding cost with short-term investments. The initial transaction could then be reversed by a swap, whereby it pays six month BBR and receives a fixed rate, when the yield curve reverts to its normal slope (see *Exhibit 14.9*).

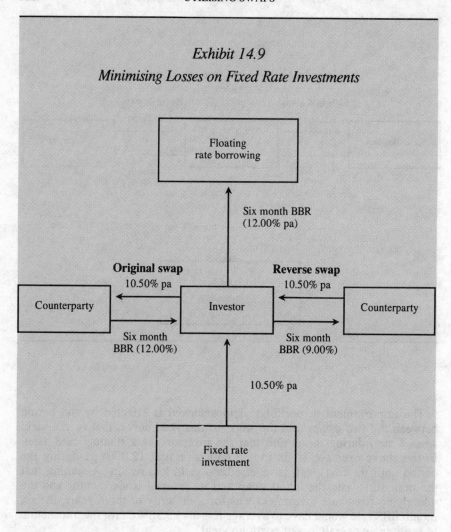

Exhibit 14.9

Minimising Losses on Fixed Rate Investments

The risk for the investor is that the fixed interest rate on the swap transactions may move adversely in the period between the time when the original swap is entered into and its reversal. This risk must be weighed against the saving in funding costs during the period during which the yield curve is inverse. In the present case, assuming that the original fixed rate investment was for three years, and the period between the two swaps was six months, the rate payable on the second fixed rate swap would have to be less than 10.05% pa (a decrease of 0.45% pa) for the transaction to result in a loss to the investor.

An alternative means of achieving similar objectives would be to undertake yield curve (or maturity) switches utilising interest rate swaps rather than physical purchases and sales of securities (see discussion below). This would lengthen or shorten the term of the portfolio consistent with rate expectations to maximise the gains and/or minimise the losses resulting from yield curve changes.

Improving investment performance

Interest rate swaps can be utilised by investment managers, to improve portfolio performance on both fixed rate and floating rate assets.

Transaction 1. Where an investor has an underlying portfolio of floating rate investments it can boost the investment yield on these assets by undertaking and then reversing interest rate swaps (see *Exhibit 14.10*). The investor would initially enter into a swap where it pays a floating rate, say six month BBR and receives a fixed rate of 11.50% pa. This swap is later reversed by a subsequent transaction whereby the investor receives six month BBR and pays a fixed rate. If the fixed rate paid under the second transaction is lower than the fixed rate on the first transaction, the investor enhances the return on its floating rate investment. For example, if the reversal is done when the fixed rate is 10.50% pa, the effective return after the two transactions to the investor is BBR plus 1.00%. Where the yield curve is positively sloped, the investor may, in addition, benefit from the increased earnings received under the swap during the period until the initial swap is reversed.

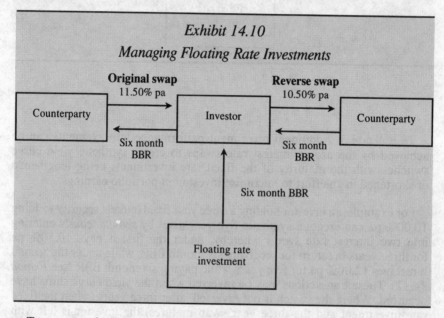

Exhibit 14.10
Managing Floating Rate Investments

Transaction 2. Conversely where the investor has a fixed rate investment portfolio, it can enhance portfolio return by initially entering into a swap where it pays a fixed rate and receives six month BBR. This transaction is then reversed by a new swap under which the investor receives a fixed rate and pays floating rate. If the fixed rate paid under the initial swap was 10.50% pa and the fixed rate received at the time of the reversal is higher, say 11.50% pa, the investor will have achieved an effective increase in portfolio yield from 10.50% pa to 11.50% pa (see *Exhibit 14.11*). The yield pick-up achieved is affected by the slope of the yield curve and the period between the two swap transactions. Where the yield curve is positively sloped the investor will incur a loss in earnings as it will receive the lower floating interest rate until the initial swap is reversed.

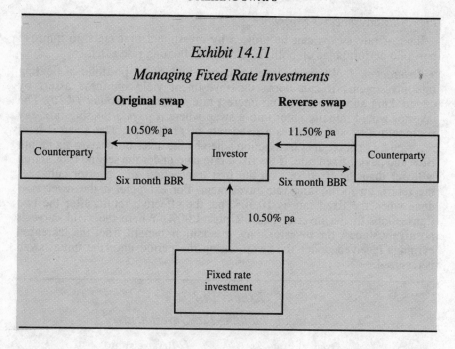

Exhibit 14.11

Managing Fixed Rate Investments

Transaction 3. Additional investment performance improvements can be achieved by the use of interest rate swaps to create synthetic yield curve switches with the maturity of the fixed rate investments being lengthened or shortened in an effort to maximise investment portfolio earnings.

For example, an investor holding a three year fixed interest security yielding 10.00% pa can create a synthetic five year asset by *simultaneously* entering into two interest rate swaps whereby, under the first it pays 10.50% pa for three years in return for receiving six month BBR, while under the second it receives 12.00% pa for five years while paying six month BBR (see *Exhibit 14.12*). These transactions may be reversed when the yield curve shifts have occurred. Where the switch is not reversed, after three years (when the fixed rate investment and the three year swap matures) the investor is left with the outstanding two years to maturity of the original five year swap. This swap can be left as a "naked" interest rate position or converted into a two year fixed rate security by the investor utilising the proceeds of the maturing investment to purchase floating rate securities yielding a rate relative to BBR which will generate a fixed return of 12.00% pa for two years.

Conversely, an investor can shorten the maturity of its investment portfolio using two interest rate swaps. As in the case of a lengthening switch, the swap transactions can be reversed, for example, when the anticipated yield curve shifts have occurred. Where the switch is not reversed, at the end of three years the investor is left with a floating rate investment yielding BBR (see *Exhibit 14.13*).

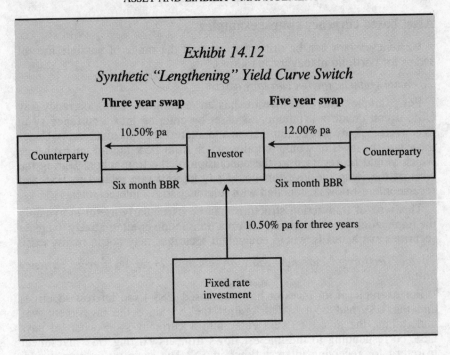

Exhibit 14.12
Synthetic "Lengthening" Yield Curve Switch

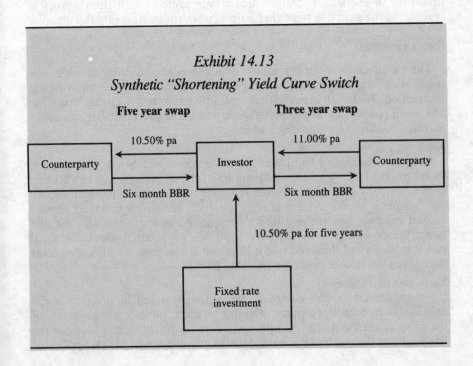

Exhibit 14.13
Synthetic "Shortening" Yield Curve Switch

Asset based currency swaps: examples

Currency swaps can be utilised to expand the range of possible uses of swaps for portfolio managers as follows.

To create synthetic foreign currency assets

For example, where an investor has an existing asset in a currency, say US$, it can create a synthetic A$ asset by entering into a currency swap to convert the currency denomination and interest receipts of its assets. Under the swap, the investor would initially switch from US$ into A$, an exchange which would be reversed at the conclusion of the transaction. During the term of the swap the investor would pay interest rate related to US$ and receive interest flows calculated with reference to A$ interest rates.

This type of transaction structure may be particularly useful in avoiding the implications of withholding tax on a transaction or alternatively to create securities synthetically where equivalent securities may not in reality exist.

To lock in foreign currency gains or minimise losses on foreign currency investments

For example, if an investor had purchased US$ fixed interest securities and the US$ had appreciated against the A$ since the investment was undertaken, the investor could enter into a currency swap where it pays US$, corresponding to the interest flows from its existing US$ investment in return for receiving interest flows in A$. The swap transaction would, by virtue of the fact that the initial currency exchange and subsequent re-exchange would be undertaken at the then prevailing US$/A$ exchange rate, thereby eliminate any exchange risk for the investor for the remaining life of the investment. Therefore the investor protects itself from a possible reversal of the gain due to further currency and/or interest rate fluctuations.

Swap reversals

The use of swaps as an instrument of active asset or liability management requires the capacity to enter into and subsequently reverse the original transaction. Where an organisation trades its swaps to effectively neutralise any swap position so as to capitalise on market opportunities, it can either reverse or sell swap transactions as follows.

Reversing swaps

Assume a company completes the swap described below (the original swap) paying 10.50% pa and receiving BBR, and all rates increase by 50 bps. If the company wished to reverse the swap in the new rate environment, the company would write a reverse swap, under which it would receive a fixed payment and make a BBR payment. When combined with the first swap, the company would achieve a 50 bps pa profit between the fixed rate it receives and the fixed rate it pays and would pass the BBR it receives through as the BBR it pays (see *Exhibit 14.14*).

Swap sale or assignment

As an alternative, the company could assign or sell its position in the existing swap to a third party. The fair market value (cash payment) of the swap is determined by the present value of the difference between the fixed rate on the original contract (10.50% pa) and the fixed rate applicable to a new contract (11.00% pa). In this example, because interest rates have risen since the original swap was priced, the company could realise a substantial cash payment by selling the original swap (see *Exhibit 14.14*).

The difference between the two techniques is that under a reverse swap, the company will recognise its profit or loss over the remaining term of the mirror contracts whereas if it sells or assigns the original contract, this profit or loss will be recognised immediately. It should also be noted that the market tends to value the two techniques differently.

The assignment structure may be advantageous for reasons of income recognition in the current period, prepayment or sale of the underlying asset or liability being hedged, and interest cost management. It also eliminates the original credit exposure whereas the swap reversal structure creates an additional credit exposure.

The rationale behind the vast majority of assignments has been recognition as income of the cash payment in the current period. The assignment technique is particularly advantageous where the front end cash payment receives a favourable tax treatment, for example, as a capital amount.

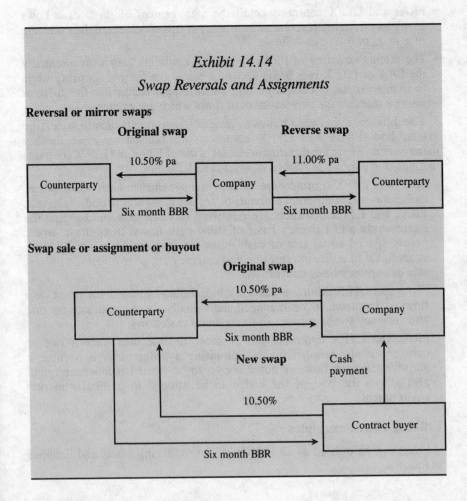

Exhibit 14.14

Swap Reversals and Assignments

Reversal or mirror swaps

Swap sale or assignment or buyout

The practice of income recognition in the current period has come under the scrutiny of the Financial Accounting Standards Board and the Federal Home Loan Bank Board in the United States, both of whom have discouraged the current period recognition of income or expense except when the underlying asset and/or liability has been eliminated. They recommend that any gain or loss be recognised over the remaining life of the underlying asset or liability to which the swap was tied. Accounting treatment elsewhere in the world is still relatively undefined.

UTILISING FRAs AND LTFX CONTRACTS

FRAs and LTFX versus interest rate and currency swaps

FRAs and LTFX contracts have similarities with interest rate swaps and currency swaps respectively. Consequently, it would be expected that FRAs and LTFX contracts could be utilised in a manner analogous to the use of these instruments for asset liability management purposes. The major difference between the two classes of instruments include:

- FRAs and LTFX contracts entail the management of *single* cash flows as distinct from interest rate and currency swaps which entail the exchange of a *series* of future cash flows.

- The pricing structure of FRAs and LTFX contracts vary with essentially the FRA or LTFX rate being above or below the current spot rate while in an interest rate or currency swap, this difference is built into the different interest rates on the two sets of cash flows which are exchanged.

The differences between the two classes of instruments dictate, to a large extent, how FRAs and LTFX contracts are utilised in asset liability management. There are three main classes of use of FRAs and LTFX contracts in managing existing portfolios of assets and liabilities:

- FRAs and LTFX contracts are ideal to manage uneven cash flows. Where cash flows are of different amounts or are not at regular periodic intervals, FRAs and LTFX contracts are relatively more flexible in changing the interest rate and currency basis of these cash flows. In contrast, where evenly spaced equal sets of cash flows are involved, it is usually more economical to utilise interest rate and currency swaps to effect the interest rate or currency basis conversion.

- FRAs and LTFX contracts allow each cash flow, where a stream of cash flows is involved, to be managed individually. In contrast interest rate and currency swaps convert all the relevant cash flows.

- FRAs and LTFX contracts can be more flexible than interest rate or currency swaps in adjusting or optimising a hedge. This is because it allows each cash flow, as noted above, to be treated independently but also allows the cost of the hedge to be attuned to particular market environments.

Utilising FRAs: examples

FRAs can be utilised as an instrument for managing assets and liablities as follows.

Locking in future borrowings

FRAs can be utilised to lock in or fix or guarantee a future rollover rate or repricing on either a loan or an investment. Generally, the underlying loan or investment will be on a floating rate basis with the FRAs being utilised to lock in future borrowing or investment rates on the relevant repricings on the loan.

The FRA could be utilised, as noted above in Chapter 4 to fix the borrowing or investment return for a single period or, alternatively, a series of FRAs can be utilised to lock in the rates on a series of repricing dates to lock in investment or borrowing rates for an extended period.

Creating exposures to floating interest rates

FRAs can also be used to create an exposure to floating rates for an investor or borrower with a fixed rate investment or borrowing. A borrower with fixed rate debt can create synthetic floating rate exposure for the period of the borrowing by selling FRAs. Similarly, a fixed rate investor can create a synthetic floating rate investment by buying FRAs. As in the case of interest rate swaps, due to anomalies in the forward markets, it may be possible to create cheaper borrowings or high yielding investments through these strategies.

Locking in future reinvestment rates

FRAs can also be utilised to lock in future reinvestment rates on intermediate cash flows, such as interest coupons, on a term borrowing. In this context, the FRAs function in a manner similar to zero coupon swaps where a periodic coupon flow is swapped for a lump sum amount payable at maturity. This type of strategy is applicable not only to investment managers seekng to eliminate reinvestment risk within their asset portfolios but also to corporate liability managers creating sinking funds for the repayment of future liabilities.

Trading static yield curves

A more complex strategy utilising FRAs entails using FRAs to trade a static yield curve. Where interest rates are expected to be static at or about current levels, investors and borrowers can both potentially benefit from utilising FRAs under certain circumstances. This type of strategy is predicated on the fact that the forward rate yield curve lies above or below the current physical market yield curve.

For example, if the yield curve is normal or upwards sloping, the forward rate yield curve lies above the cash market yield curve. Where the yield curve is inversely shaped or downwards sloping, the forward rates lie below the cash market yield curve. In an environment where the yield curve is not expected to change significantly, borrowers and investors can benefit where they plan to undertake short-term borrowing or lending activities.

In the case of investors, where the forward rate curve lies above the cash market yield curve, it may be profitable to lock in forward investment rates as if the yield curve does not change significantly, then the forward rate achievable will be higher than the likely cash market rate at the time the investment must be undertaken. For borrowers, the reverse applies with borrowers being able to benefit by locking in lower forward borrowing costs for short time frames than would be physically possible in the cash market, provided that the inverse yield curve which prevails is not expected to shift significantly. It should be stressed that these strategies are not riskless but entail a form of limited risk yield curve trading or asset liability management.

Trading against interest rate swap

A more sophisticated kind of transaction would entail trading FRAs, usually a strip of FRAs against an interest rate swap. This type of strategy is predicated on the fact that the real cost of an interest rate swap for a payer of fixed rate is the difference between the fixed rate paid and the average floating rate cost over the life of the transaction. Where an inverse yield curve prevails, a fixed rate payer under an interest rate swap may simultaneously execute a series of sold FRA positions to lock in a fixed rate, usually higher than the swap rate for at least a part, sometimes a substantial part, of the life of the interest rate swap. This would lock in a spread between the rate being paid under the swap and the rate locked in through the sold FRAs. As the full term of the underlying interest rate swap is not covered, a residual exposure towards the latter end of the life of the swap, the "tail", will remain exposed.

Exhibit 14.15

FRAs versus Interest Rate Swap Arbitrage

Assume the following market rates are available:

- A$ interest rate swaps for three years are quoted at 14.00/13.90% pa versus 180 day BBR flat.
- Current BBR is 16.00% pa.
- The following FRAs are available:

6 × 12:	15.10/15.00
12 × 18:	14.85/14.75
18 × 24:	14.35/14.25

A financial institution (F) undertakes the following transaction:

- F enters into an interest rate swap where it pays 14.00% pa against receipt of BBR.
- F simultaneously sells three FRAs:
  one 6 × 12 at 15.00% pa
  one 12 × 18 at 14.75% pa
  one 18 × 24 at 14.25% pa

The net results of the FRA sales when combined with current BBR of 16.00% pa means that F has locked in a fixed rate of 15.00% pa for two years as against payments under the swap of 14.00% pa.

On a present value basis (assuming a discount rate of 15.00% pa) this locked in spread between the fixed rate being received and paid is valued at 1.77% at the commencement or a future value equivalent of 2.34% pa.

This implies that where the *net* payment in year three under the swap is *less than* approximately 2.62% pa (assuming a reinvestment rate for year three of 12.02% pa) then F will gain. For example if BBR averages 12.00% in year three, then F will pay 2.00% pa (14.00% pa less 12.00% pa) under the swap generating net cash inflow of approximately 0.62% pa.

In essence, the party undertaking the transaction is speculating that the spread locked in over the initial period of the swap will not be lost over the tail period where it must pay the fixed rate under the swap. In a reversal of the strategy, particularly where a positive yield curve exists, a transaction where the entity receives the fixed rate under the swap and offsets part of the risk exposure through buying FRAs, at least over part of the life of the swap, can be devised. Examples of this type of strategy are set out in *Exhibit 14.15*. It should be understood that these strategies are also not risk free but entail the assumption of certain risks related to the shape of the yield curve as well as underlying interest rate expectations.

Utilising LTFX: some examples

LTFX contracts can be used as a substitute for currency swaps in a manner analogous to that of using FRAs as a surrogate for interest rate swaps. LTFX transactions can be utilised for managing assets and liabilities with great effect in the following situations:

• LTFX contracts can be used to change the currency basis of future cash flows in a particular currency. An LTFX contract can be utilised in respect of a future payment due on a loan or receipts generated from an investment. As with FRAs, a series of LTFX contracts can be simultaneously transacted to lock in the currency rate on payments or receipts relative to a base currency.

• A sophisticated use of LTFX contracts may be to undertake a type of risk arbitrage between currency swaps and a series of LTFX contracts. This particular technique is discussed in detail in the context of hedging LTFX books or marketmaking in respect of LTFX contracts (see Chapter 27).

The main advantage of using LTFX contracts in preference to currency swaps is the capacity to alter the currency basis of *some* but not *all* cash flows in a foreign currency. An added advantage which is equally applicable to FRAs relates to the flexibility available to reverse hedges in line with evolving market expectations of future currency and interest rates. In the case of LTFX contracts, as each contract relates to a specific cash flow, individual payments can be hedged and unhedged. In contrast, under a currency swap, the whole swap must be lifted or reversed necessarily unwinding the hedge in respect of *all* future cash flows.

The method of pricing LTFX contracts, whereby they are priced in terms of points reflecting premiums and discounts relative to the spot exchange rate can provide potential advantages. For example, the cost of the hedge can be optimised in terms of points lost or gained rather than transferring the cost of the hedge to the interest rate differential received or paid in the case of a currency swap. This may provide potential advantages depending on the shape of the yield curve in the two relevant currencies which may create potential advantages for using LTFX contracts over currency swaps. This method of pricing LTFX contracts can also be particularly useful in accelerating or deferring income or expense items invoiced in different currencies for purposes of taxation treatment as well as balance sheet presentation.

UTILISING CAPS, COLLARS AND FLOORS

Symmetric versus asymmetric risk management instruments

Caps, collars and floors as species of options on interest rates belong to a class of asymmetric risk management instruments. This characteristic of caps, floors and collars necessarily means that there are some significant differences as well as similarities in their use in managing asset and liability portfolios. In particular the risk profiles and payoffs to buyers and sellers of these instruments are fundamentally different. As with all options, the purchaser of the cap, floor or collar enjoys the insurance features of such a transaction which limits their risk from adverse changes in interest rates but without the need to give up any potential benefits from a favourable movement in rates. In contrast, the seller of a cap or floor assumes a potentially unlimited liability, dependent only on movements in the benchmark rate, in exchange for a reward equal to the premium or fee received. These differences in payoffs dictate to a large extent the uses of this particular class of instrument in asset liability management.

There are two general classes of uses in caps and floors:

- Purchasers of caps and floors utilise these instruments as an alternative to price fixing mechanisms such as interest rate swaps and FRAs. The basic intention is to establish a *maximum* cost of borrowings or *minimum* rate of return on investments while maintaining the possibility of lower costs or higher returns if favourable movements in the rate structure occur.

- Sellers of caps and floors seek to gain (particularly in stable market environments) from the premium received from option writing activities which can be speculative or written against offsetting portfolio positions. The premium acts as a means of lowering borrowing costs or enhancing investment returns while providing a cushion or limited hedge against minor market movements.

An example of the first type of transaction would entail a borrower taking out a cap as an alternative to swapping floating rate debt into a fixed rate liability as protection against potential increases in interest rates. Some examples of the sale of caps and floors as a technique for portfolio management are considered in detail below.

Caps and collars versus swaps

A fundamental issue in utilising symmetric versus asymmetric risk management instruments is the relative attractiveness of each technique under different market scenarios. *Exhibit 14.16* compares the cost of a number of hedging alternatives for a particular borrowing transaction.

The results of the selected hedging alternatives (outlined in *Exhibit 14.16*) at various rate levels indicate that there is no single preferred hedging strategy. Fixed rates prove to be the best protection against very high interest rates in the future, while no hedge appears to be the best strategy if rates fall. Caps or collars provide protection against high costs at high rate levels but allow the borrower to participate in falls in interest rates. While break evens at any particular rate level are simple to ascertain, the true benefits of these alternative hedges can only be determined with reference to actual interest rates achieved over the life of the transaction. As future interest rates cannot be forecast accurately, many organisations seek to diversify the hedge by blending techniques. Alternatively, it is possible to simulate outcomes over time utilising different interest scenarios.

A possible means of analysing these hedging positions is to take a probablistic approach to future interest rate scenarios. By utilising assumptions of the future mean and volatility (standard deviation) in the level of interest rates, it is theoretically possible to calculate the expected cost or benefit of any particular hedging strategy. For example, in *Exhibit 14.16*, the problem of hedging floating rate debt against the potential increase in interest expense as a result of increasing interest rates can be analysed in terms of first establishing the economics of each hedging alternative and then calculating expected values for the outcome with various instruments. Applying this approach, it is necessary to first specify the actual economic cost of each alternative. The economics of the various hedging alternatives considered can be summarised as follows:

Exhibit 14.16
Utilising Caps and Collars versus Interest Rate Swaps

The following example compares the costs of four hedging alternatives on a five year, six month LIBOR based obligation. (All-in cost calculations do not include the borrower's credit spread, which would be the same in all cases; front end fees are converted to per annum equivalents using a discount rate of 11.00% pa.) At the time of the example six month LIBOR was 8.81% and five year Treasuries were yielding 10.88%.

Alternatives

- No hedge.
- Interest rate swap (fixed rate of 11.68%, semi-annually, against six month LIBOR).
- Ceiling rate agreement, cap at 11.31% (2.5% higher than spot rate), fee 5.1% (equivalent to 1.37% pa).
- Floor-ceiling rate agreement, cap at 11.31%, floor at 8.81% (spot), fee 3.2% (equivalent to 0.87% pa).

All-in borrowing costs per annum

Market rate						
(six month LIBOR)	6.00%	8.00%	10.00%	12.00%	14.00%	20.00%
No hedge	6.00%	8.00%	10.00%	12.00%	14.00%	20.00%
Interest rate swap	11.68%	11.68%	11.68%	11.68%	11.68%	11.68%
Cap rate agreement						
Market rate	6.00%	8.00%	10.00%	12.00%	14.00%	20.00%
Cap rate refund	—	—	—	(0.69%)	(2.69%)	(8.69%)
Fee amortisation	1.37%	1.37%	1.37%	1.37%	1.37%	1.37%
Total	7.37%	9.37%	11.37%	12.68%	12.68%	12.68%
Collar agreement						
Market rate	6.00%	8.00%	10.00%	12.00%	14.00%	20.00%
Cap rate refund	—	—	—	(0.69%)	(2.69%)	(8.69%)
Floor rate payment	2.81%	0.81%	—	—	—	—
Fee amortisation	0.87%	0.87%	0.87%	0.87%	0.87%	0.87%
Total	9.68%	9.68%	10.87%	12.18%	12.18%	12.18%

- The economics of a swap into a fixed rate can be specified in terms of a borrower incurring a cost if the floating rate remains *below* the fixed rate, on average, for the term of the swap. Conversely, an economic gain to the borrower accrues where the floating rate averages a level above the fixed rate paid under the swap.

- The economics of the purchase of a cap relates to the cost of the cap with an economic gain accruing to the borrower if the floating rate remains above the cap rate on average for the term of the transaction, after adjustments for the fee.

- The economics of the collar is similar to the economics of the cap combined with the sale by the borrower of the floor. The sale results in a premium being paid to the borrower which partially offsets the cost of the cap with an economic loss arising if the floating rate index remains below the floor rate agreed under the collar agreement.

In each case, for the purpose of constructing a mathematically analytical model, the expected loss or gain over the life of each transaction can be calculated based on an assumed probability distribution of interest rates for the relevant index.

The calculation of expected values of hedging with the different instruments would take the following form:

- In the case of the interest rate swap, the expected gain or loss equals the floating rate minus the fixed rate swap multiplied by the probability of that level of floating rate occurring. The total expected gain or loss of the swap will equal the probability weight of the sum of the gains and losses for all possible levels of the floating rate. This expected value will be a function of the mean level of the floating rate index, the current level of the floating rate and its volatility, or standard deviation.

- For the interest rate cap or collar, the expected gain or loss will be a function of the floating rate minus the cap rate or the floor rate minus the floating rate multiplied by the probability of that floating rate occurring. Once again, the expected overall gain or loss is equivalent to the probability weight and sum of the gains or losses for all possible interest rate levels.

This type of probablistic analysis enables comparison of the relative cost effectiveness of different hedging strategies as a function of interest rate expectations using different probability estimates and levels of confidence. The framework allows outcomes to be simulated, utilising techniques such as monte carlo simulation.

Utilising caps and collars: examples

Caps, floors and collars can be utilised as an asset liability management technique in a number of ways.

Structured caps and collars

Sophisticated insurance structures involving deferred or staggered caps can be devised. Under this type of arrangement, borrowing interest rates, for example, could be capped at increasing or decreasing levels or banded within upper and lower limits for individual periods within the overall term of the liability. This type of structuring can be utilised to achieve two objectives:

• To protect the borrower's cash flow capacity or interest cost levels relative to its resources by essentially insuring via the purchase of the cap or collar, that certain interest cost and/or cash flow levels are maintained. For example, caps and collars are utilised extensively in connection with real estate projects as well as leveraged buy-outs in the United States for these types of reasons.

• To adjust the cost of protection at levels consistent with the project's or borrower's capacity to bear risk.

Creating synthetic floating rate liabilities

A fixed rate borrower can create an exposure to a floating interest rate index by purchasing a floor at a level equal to the cost of its fixed rate debt. If interest rates fall, the borrower benefits by an amount equivalent to the difference between the market level of the index relative to the floor level, adjusted for the amortised purchase price of the floor. This type of strategy means that the borrower participates in any rate declines below the floor level on the relevant index, while having no exposure to rate increases because if the floating rate index exceeds the floor level, its cost of funds equate to its fixed rate debt costs. This type of strategy is illustrated in *Exhibit 14.17*.

A conceptually similar strategy can be utilised by a fixed rate investor holding a portfolio of fixed rate assets, such as bonds, who engineers an exposure to floating rates by purchasing a cap where the cap level is set at the level of interest receipts on the fixed rate portfolio. If interest rates on the relevant index increase, the investor receives cash inflows equal to the excess of the index above the cap rate level (adjusted for the premium) thereby allowing it to participate by way of increased interest earnings if rates increase while maintaining a floor on portfolio interest earnings as the portfolio will earn a minimum of the fixed interest rate accruing on the portfolio.

Exhibit 14.17

Purchasing Floors to Create a Synthetic Floating Rate Liability

Assume a borrower has a five year fixed rate borrowing at 14.00% pa. The borrower purchases a five year floor on BBR at a floor level of 14.00% pa for a fee of 5.00% (equivalent to 1.46% pa utilising a discount rate of 14.00% pa).

All-in borrowing costs per annum

Bank bill rate	10.00%	12.00%	14.00%	16.00%	18.00%
Fixed rate borrowing	14.00%	14.00%	14.00%	14.00%	14.00%
Floor rate agreement					
Fixed rate borrowing	14.00%	14.00%	14.00%	14.00%	14.00%
Floor rate refund	(4.00%)	(2.00%)	—	—	—
Fee amortisation	1.46%	1.46%	1.46%	1.46%	1.46%
Total	11.46%	13.46%	15.46%	15.46%	15.46%

This type of strategy can also be utilised by investors who may buy deferred or staggered floors or collars designed to guarantee minimum portfolio earnings or cash inflows to match expected liabilities in particular periods.

Selling caps and floors

A floating rate borrower can seek to lower its cost of borrowing while simultaneously achieving a modicum of protection from rate increases by selling floors against its liabilities. Under this type of strategy, if interest rates decline, the borrower does not participate in the fall in interest rates beyond the floor level as it must make payments to the purchaser of the floor which brings its cost of funding to the floor level adjusted to the premium received. If rates increase, however, the borrower has limited protection equal to the amortised premium level which partially offsets increased costs. However, if rates increase sharply, the borrower is exposed to increased interest cost under the strategy. An example of this type of transaction is set out in *Exhibit 14.18*.

In an asset based variation of the last strategy, an investor holding a portfolio floating rate assets may seek to enhance the yield on the portfolio by selling caps. Under this strategy, if interest rates increase above the cap level, the investors return is limited to the level of the cap adjusted for the premium received. However, if rates drop, the investor earns the market interest rate adjusted for the premium which allows it to earn a margin above the usual floating rate earnings that would accrue to the investor.

The above strategies outlined are not comprehensive. The use of caps, floors and collars are still in their infancy in corporate finance. As understanding of these instruments increases, additional uses and strategies for asset liability management utilising caps, floors and collars are likely to emerge.

Exhibit 14.18

Selling Floors to Manage Floating Rate Liabilities

Assume a borrower has floating rate liabilities for five year pricing "off" to 180 day BBR. The borrower sells a five year floor on BBR at a floor level of 12.00% pa for a fee of 2.40% (equivalent to 0.67% pa utilising a discount rate of 12.00% pa). The current level of BBR is 13.00% pa.

All-in borrowing costs per annum

Bank bill rate	10.00%	12.00%	14.00%	16.00%	18.00%
Floating rate borrowing	10.00%	12.00%	14.00%	16.00%	18.00%
Sale of floor rate agreement					
Floating rate borrowing	10.00%	12.00%	14.00%	16.00%	18.00%
Floor rate payments	2.00%	—	—	—	—
Fee amortisation	0.67%	0.67%	0.67%	0.67%	0.67%
Total	11.33%	11.33%	13.33%	15.55%	17.33%

Part 6

Non-generic Swap Structures

Chapter 15

Liability Swaps: Non-generic Structures

NON-GENERIC SWAP STRUCTURES: AN OVERVIEW

The conventional swap structures discussed in Part 2 of this book form the basis of *all* swap transactions. However, an increasing proportion of swaps embody a wide variety of variations on the conventional swap concept. These variations are usually referred to as non-generic swap structures.

Non-generic swap structures represent a response to the increased variety of uses to which swap transactions are put. These variations reflect, primarily, two factors:

- The variations in structure designed to accommodate the special features in underlying borrowings and securities transactions which were originated to take advantage of capital market arbitrage opportunities.
- The need to incorporate additional flexibility within the basic swap structure to cater for various asset liability management strategies.

The non-generic structures include both liability and asset swaps. While asset swaps do not necessarily require specific variations to the basic swap formula, it is useful to view asset swaps as a variation on the original liability swap idea.

Non-generic swap structures can be classified as follows.

Variations on conventional swaps

These involve simple variations on the basic parameters of interest rate and currency swaps such as: amortising notional principal; variations of the commencement date, such as deferred takedown swaps and forward swaps as well as spread locks; and, deferred or accelerated cash flow swaps such as zero coupon, deferred coupon, premium/discount and deferred coupon FRN swaps.

Structural variations to accommodate miscellaneous issue structures

These entail the use of usually conventional swap structures or a series of swaps in combination to accommodate particular securities issue structures such as dual currency bonds and bull or bear FRNs.

Basis swaps

These are floating-to-floating swaps in the same currency, almost exclusively in US$, which represent a unique component of the global swap market.

Variations in the form of execution of swaps

Swap transactions are usually entered into with a principal, or, alternatively, arranged by a financial institution or broker which locates an appropriate counterparty. In recent times, a number of innovative execution strategies including tender processes and revolving swap facilities have also evolved to accommodate particular requirements of certain swap counterparties.

Options on swaps

These transactions represent a combination of options and swaps. They include such structures as options on swaps or swaptions, callable, putable, extendible swaps and contingent swaps.

Option swaps

Option swaps are somewhat of a misnomer as they need not necessarily include a swap component at all. These transaction structures evolved out of a number of innovative security structures, involving embedded options, which evolved, particularly in the Euromarkets, in the period since 1985. The security structures required an option element to be stripped and securitised. This requirement was usually met through a variation on basic swap structures. Options securitised through this particular technique include options on interest rates, currencies and stock indexes.

Asset swaps

Asset swaps are the converse of liability based swaps. This category of transactions is distinguished primarily by the fact that the underlying cash flows being transformed, whether in terms of currency or interest rate basis, are generated by an investment asset.

The first four non-generic swap structures are considered in the remainder of this chapter. Options on swaps are analysed in detail in Chapter 16. Option swaps are discussed in Chapter 17. Asset swap structures are described in detail in Chapter 18.

It should be noted that the non-generic swap structures as described in this part of the book are *not* comprehensive, but rather represent the major types of variations to the basic swap concept. In addition, the grouping or classification of the various non-generic structures is subjective.

VARIATIONS ON BASIC SWAP STRUCTURES

Amortising swaps

Amortising swaps entail swap transactions based on amortising (decreasing or increasing) notional principal amounts. This type of structure is used in connection with all types of non-bullet maturity assets and liabilities.

Amortising structures are feasible for both interest rate and currency swaps. The discussion below focuses primarily on interest rate swaps, for ease of exposition, but the basic concepts developed are equally applicable to amortising currency swaps.

Amortising swap transactions are relevant wherever non-bullet asset and liability structures are involved. For example, the conversion, in terms of interest rate or currency basis, of an amortising loan, either from the viewpoint of the borrower or the lender, would require an amortising swap structure to be utilised. A common example is lease transactions where lease rental payments include both a principal and interest component, often combined with a "balloon" residual value payment at maturity. Lessees can convert fixed rate lease rentals to a floating rate basis (or vice versa) while lessors can match fund lease receivables through amortising swaps to achieve the lowest cost funding available.

Asset funding for specific projects often entails a series of future drawdowns under a funding facility. Swaps with increasing principal balances can be utilised to fix the interest cost of the future schedule of liabilities. The most common application of this type of structure relates to construction funding where increasing notional principal swaps are used to fix the rate on a project which is to be funded with a floating rate facility. Where the construction funding facility has a specific principal amortisation schedule, the amortising swap may include both an increasing and decreasing principal basis giving rise to a "roller coaster" swap.

Other uses include asset swaps whereby amortising swap structures are used to convert amortising (via sinking fund or early redemption provisions) fixed interest securities into floating rate securities, or amortising swaps structured to match the expected prepayment schedule of mortgage backed securities or receivable backed securities to reduce reinvestment risk. Analytically, an amortising swap, whether an interest rate or currency swap can be replicated by a *series* of bullet notional principal swaps. *Exhibit 15.1* sets out, diagrammatically, the cash flow patterns for a five year amortising swap for a notional principal of A$50m with 20.00% annual (A$10m) straight line amortisation.

Consistent with this characterisation, amortising swaps are priced using current market swap spreads over the duration of the amortisation schedule. Within this framework, there are a number of available pricing approaches.

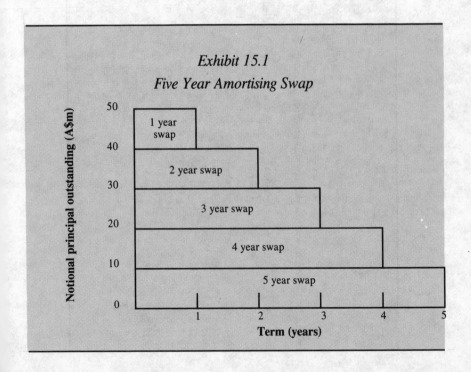

Exhibit 15.1

Five Year Amortising Swap

Exhibit 15.2
Pricing an Amortising Swap

Pricing for a US$50m swap whose notional principal is amortising at the rate of US$7,142,857 every six months.

Date	Tenor (years)	Notional (US$)	Amortisation (US$)	United States Treasury bond (% pa)	Spread (% pa)	All-in swap rate (% pa)	Tenor amount (US$)	Tenor rate amount (US$)
30.06.X5		50,000,000						
31.12.X5	0.50	42,857,143	7,142,857	7.27	0.60	7.87	3,600,782.71	283,381.599
31.12.X6	1.50	35,714,286	7,142,857	7.54	0.60	8.14	10,743,639.71	874,532.272
31.12.X7	2.50	28,571,429	7,142,857	8.43	0.60	9.03	17,886,496.71	1,615,150.653
31.12.X8	3.51	21,428,572	7,142,857	8.79	0.57	9.36	25,048,923.18	2,344,579.209
31.12.X9	4.51	14,285,715	7,142,857	9.26	0.54	9.80	32,191,780.18	3,154,794.457
31.12.X0	5.51	7,142,858	7,142,857	9.46	0.42	9.88	39,334,637.18	3,886,262.153
31.12.X1	6.51	0	7,142,858	9.68	0.38	10.06	46,477,500.68	4,675,636.569
			50,000,000				175,283,760.34	16,834,336.91

Weighted average rate: 9.604% pa

- Blended rates: whereby the swap is treated as *a number of separate* swaps with the total swap price reflecting a weighted average of these individual swap rates. *Exhibit 15.2* sets out an example of a blended rate pricing of a US$ floating-to-fixed interest rate swap. Under a variation to this technique, the transaction can be treated as a series of zero coupon swaps (see discussion below) and priced accordingly.

- Duration or half life pricing: under this approach, the maturity characteristics of the amortising notional principal is reduced to a single measure. This measure is either the duration or the average life of the amortising swap (for an example of an average life calculation for an amortising swap see *Exhibit 15.3*). Once the duration or average life of the swap is calculated, the swap is then priced as a *bullet* swap with the maturity corresponding to the duration or half life of the amortising swap. For example, if as in *Exhibit 15.3*, the average life of the amortising swap was eight years, the swap would be priced on the basis of a normal eight year bullet swap.

The blended rate technique whereby the amortising swap is treated as a series of bullet swaps is preferable primarily because it more accurately reflects the manner in which an amortising swap is matched off against offsetting counterparties. In practise, it is also common to include in the pricing a small additional risk premium which is based on the frequency or irregularity of the decline or increase in the notional principal balance.

Exhibit 15.3

Calculating Average Life of Amortising Swap

	Amount:	A$25m	
	Tenor:	ten year	
	Grace:	five year	

Tenor (years) (A)	Balance (A$) (B)	Prepayment (A$) (C)	(D) = (A) × (C) (D)
0	25,000,000	0	0
1	25,000,000	0	0
2	25,000,000	0	0
3	25,000,000	0	0
4	25,000,000	0	0
5	25,000,000	0	0
6	20,000,000	(5,000,000)	(30,000,000)
7	15,000,000	(5,000,000)	(35,000,000)
8	10,000,000	(5,000,000)	(40,000,000)
9	5,000,000	(5,000,000)	(45,000,000)
10	0	(5,000,000)	(50,000,000)
		(25,000,000)	(200,000,000)

$$\text{Average life} = \frac{(200,000,000)}{(25,000,000)} = 8.000 \text{ years}$$

Timing variations

A conventional swap usually entails the transaction commencing within a short period after the agreement between the counterparties. Similarly the fixed rate payable under the swap is agreed to at the time the transaction is entered into. Both these terms of the swap can be varied.

Under a deferred takedown or delayed start swap (also known as a forward commencement swap), if funding is not necessary immediately or a party wishes to more precisely match either a rollover date or an underlying borrowing, then a swap can be structured at a slight premium over the current fixed rate with accrual to begin at a mutually agreed rate, usually within six months. Under the deferred takedown structure, the fixed rate is agreed upon with accrual to commence at an agreed date in the future.

A forward swap is conceptually similar to a deferred takedown swap with the exception that the commencement date is usually deferred for a significant time frame, up to two to three years in the future (see discussion below).

Such deferred takedown swaps are usually priced as a standard swap with pricing adjustments reflecting the carry cost (the difference between the fixed rate on the swap and short-term rates) from the execution date to the forward start date.

This adjustment can be priced either as the difference between the current swap yield and current short-term rates or alternatively as the cost of undertaking a securities hedge and funding it. *Exhibit 15.4* sets out an example of pricing of a deferred takedown swap.

A spread lock or deferred *rate setting* swap is fundamentally different. Under the spread lock structure, an institution may agree to provide the swap over a defined period (generally less than six months) at an agreed upon *spread* over a reference rate comparable to the maturity of the anticipated swap. The spread lock is useful in guaranteeing the vailability of the swap at a known *margin* over the relevant reference rate enabling the borrower to take advantage of any expected decrease in interest rates or movements in the swap spread. It is important to note that under a spread lock, the party gaining the benefit of the spread lock is obliged to enter into the swap. It merely has the option of determining the timing of setting the base fixed rate.

The pricing of the spread lock is quite complex. For example, a swap counterparty may have paid out at bonds plus 45 for five years against six month BBR. It may have hedged this position by buying the appropriate amount of five year government securities. It can then enter into a deferred rate setting swap whereby it agrees to enter into a swap whereby its client pays and it receives bonds plus 60, with, however, the bond rate not being set for three months. In this case, the swap counterparty has locked in a spread profit of 15bps but is required to hold the hedge, that is the government securities, for up to three months. The deferred rate set or spread lock is then priced at the holding or carry cost of the bond for the relevant period.

These types of variations on standard swap structures are also available for currency swaps. For example, it is possible to have deferred takedown or spread lock arrangements on a currency swap. However, where these

Exhibit 15.4
Pricing a Deferred Takedown Swap

Assume on 8 May 19X7 company A (A) approaches a bank (B) to enter into a five year swap whereby A pays fixed rates against receipt of six month BBR. The transaction will commence on 7 June 19X7, as against a normal spot start of 9 May 19X7. Current market rates are as follows:

> Five year swap rates: 13.40/13.50% pa (S/A)
> Five year bond rates: 13.00/13.02% pa (S/A)
> Six month BBR: 12.00% pa
> One month BBR: 11.50% pa

If B enters into the deferred takedown swap it has two options:

1. It can enter into an offsetting *spot* start swap with another counterparty (C).

2. It can sell bonds to hedge its price risk and enter into an offsetting swap in 31 days' time.

Option 1

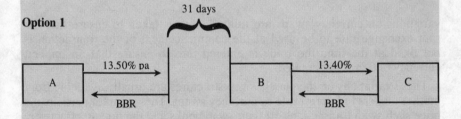

Under this structure, B is paying 13.40% pa for one month but *not* receiving the offsetting fixed rate accrual. Instead, assume that B earns the equivalent of the one month BBR rate. The earning difference is as follows:

Fixed swap rate:	13.40% pa (S/A)
One month BBR (adjusted to a S/A rate basis)	11.78% pa (S/A)
Difference	1.62% pa
or	13.76bps

$$(1.62 \times \frac{31}{365})$$

This difference is then amortised over the term of the swap at a discount rate equivalent to the swap offer rate (13.50% pa (S/A)) as a pricing adjustment of approx 4.56bps pa. Consequently, the deferred takedown swap price quoted to A would be 13.55% pa (S/A) for a one month delayed start.

Please note:

• The discount rate is subjective and should reflect B's borrowing or investment opportunity cost.

• The price adjustment does *not* cover any risk of mismatches in reset dates, including the first BBR set, arising from the delayed start.

Exhibit 15.4—continued

Option 2

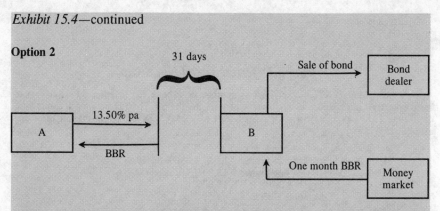

Under this structure, B sells bonds and reinvests the proceeds at one month BBR, thereby lowering its interest accrual from the bond rate (13.02% pa) to one month BBR (11.78% pa). This negative carry of 1.24 pa or 10.53bps over 31 days equates, when amortised at the swap rate, to 2.96bps or a one month deferred takedown swap price of 13.53% pa (S/A).

This later structure, while it should cover any date reset mismatch risk does not protect B against movements in the swap spread.

variations on currency swaps are utilised, care is taken to ensure that the spot exchange rate to be used at the commencement of the transaction is not fixed at the time the trade is entered into to ensure that an implicit currency option is not created.

These variations on the classic swap structures are usually available from market makers in interest rate or currency swaps. These market participants price such swap transactions off their swap books and the pricing effectively reflects the cost of putting on the position and hedging it in conjunction with any profit margin to the swap provider. This is because it is unusual to be able to match out these specialised variations against capital market issues or against a direct counterparty. These variations are often also means by which these market makers manage certain mismatches within their swap books (see Part 8).

Forward swaps

Concept of forward swaps

A forward swap is an interest rate swap which commences at a specified time in the future. For example, an A$ interest rate swap commencing in two years from the time the transaction is entered into with final maturity three years from commencement or five years from the time the transaction is entered into is usually termed a forward swap.

As in a normal interest rate swap transaction, the party entering into the transaction can use the swap to convert floating rate liabilities into fixed rate liabilities or vice versa. There are two types of forward swaps:

• *forward swaps* in which the party entering into the transaction is a fixed rate payer;

• *reverse forward swaps* in which the party entering into the transaction is a payer of the floating rate.

Utilising forward swaps

Forward swaps are utilised for two general categories of transactions:

- forward rate setting transactions;
- structured capital market transactions, in particular, refinancing high coupon bonds.

Forward swaps are utilised, in the first type of transaction, to lock in fixed rates commencing at a specified time in the future. This type of rate setting is utilised in connection with projects with a known schedule of drawdowns extending several years into the future or to lock in a known fixed cost of funds for future funding. The rationale in both cases is the expectation that the general level of interest rates will increase between now and when the funding is required.

Forward swaps can also be used to extend existing swaps or fixed rate liabilities to suit a changing asset or liability profile. A reverse forward swap is utilised to convert an existing fixed rate liability into a floating rate liability at a point of time in the future. It is usually undertaken to take advantage of changes in the shape of the yield curve, changing spread differentials as between swaps and fixed rate liabilities, and existing profits or value in an entity's current portfolio of liabilities.

The second category of applications evolved in early 1986 when a marked decline in US$ interest rates resulted in a corresponding increase in the value of call options on existing fixed rate bonds. In all cases, the call option on existing debt could not be exercised until some time in the future. This delay in the exercise of the call meant that its value was uncertain as an increase in interest rates between early 1986 and the time the option was capable of being exercised would erode or eliminate the value of the option.

In this environment, two particular types of transactions evolved:

- transactions which entailed ordinary callable fixed rate bonds; and
- transactions involving callable fixed rate bonds which had been swapped to generate sub-LIBOR floating rate funds.

In the first case, the issuers entered into a forward swap coinciding with the call option on the outstanding securities with the intention of calling the bond and simultaneously refinancing with new floating rate funds which, by virtue of the forward swap, would generate fixed rate funds at the current lower interest rates.

The second type of transaction was more complex. The borrowers had uncrystallised value from two sources: the value of the call and the value in the original interest rate swap written at rate levels above current market rates. In this environment, the borrower could call the original bond leaving it with an above market rate swap.

The value of the swap was realised by entering into a forward swap in which the borrower made payments to the forward swap counterparty corresponding to its fixed rate receipts from the original swap counterparty in return for receiving floating rate LIBOR payments which it passed onto the original swap counterparty. The forward swap simply reversed the original swap between the call and final maturity of the original fixed rate issue. This reversal left the borrower with a profit representing the movements in interest rates between the time the two swaps were entered into.

The value of the reversal was capable of being crystallised in a number of ways:

- as a periodic flow being the difference between the two swap rates; or
- as an up-front payment representing the present value of the future cash flows.

In one case, the difference was taken as a subsidy on a new issue and swap dramatically reducing the cost of funds to the borrower. In that case, the borrower chose to effectively prefund its call by issuing debt, swapped into floating rate funds, with a maturity coinciding with that on the original issue. The value of the forward reversal of the original swap was applied to the new issue. This prefunding of the call resulted in the borrower having additional cash for the period until the call on the original issue which was consistent with its financing requirements.

A number of these type of transactions, including a much publicised one for SEK, were concluded in early 1986.

Forward swap structures compete with deferred call debt warrant issues as a means of crystallising the current value in a call option not capable of being exercised until some time in the future.

Under the deferred call debt warrant structure, a borrower with a callable high coupon bond securitises the call option by issuing debt warrants. The warrants are exercisable, on the call date, into the borrower's debt on terms coinciding closely with the original callable issue. If interest rates fall the warrants are exercised. The borrower simultaneously calls the original issue being left with funding on largely identical terms but with a lower effective cost as a result of the premium received from the issue of warrants. If interest rates increase the warrants will expire unexercised, with the borrower using the premium received to lower its all-in borrowing cost.

The forward swap structure and the debt warrant were effectively different financial engineering techniques designed to achieve similar economic objectives. The choice between the techniques is usually a purely mathematical decision based on the market conditions and the resulting economics of the debt warrant and forward swap transactions.

Key market factors include:

- the shape of the swap yield curve which affects the pricing dynamics of the forward swaps;
- the value characteristics of the debt warrant which will be dependent upon:

—the warrant exercise period (that is, the period until call);

—the life of the back bonds underlying the warrants;

—the exercise period for the warrant (that is, if the warrant is a "window" warrant designed to avoid doubling up of outstanding debt).

The attitude of the borrower is also critical. In particular, the issuer's attitude to doubling up debt until call etc., is important in determining the choice between the two techniques.

It is important to recognise that the concept of a forward liability can be replicated in the cash market by a borrowing, the proceeds of which are reinvested until needed to finance the call on the original bond. The technique of using physical instruments has the effect of increasing on-balance sheet commitments which may not be tolerable and also may be economically less attractive as a result of a negative spread between the borrowing and lending rates.

The pricing dynamics of forward swaps

Forward swaps can be priced using one of two general approaches:

- constructing the forward swap as two separate but offsetting swaps mismatched as to maturity;
- treating the forward swap as a conventional swap with an extended takedown period.

The offsetting swap approach is illustrated in *Exhibit 15.5*.

Exhibit 15.5

Pricing a Forward Swap

Assume company C (C) wishes to enter into a three year forward swap commencing in two years from the time of execution. The transaction can be broken up into two separate swaps as follows:

- a five year swap where C pays a fixed rate and receives BBR;
- a two year swap where C receives a fixed rate and receives BBR.

Assuming that the swap rates are as follows:

Two years:	12.50/12.60% pa (S/A)
Five years:	13.60/13.70% pa (S/A)

the cash flows (A$m) to C for a A$100m forward swap would be as follows:

Period (years)	Receives 12.50% pa	Pays BBR	Pays 13.70% pa	Receives BBR	Pays	Receives
0.5	+6.250	−BBR	−6.850	+BBR	−0.600	—
1.0	+6.250	−BBR	−6.850	+BBR	−0.600	—
1.5	+6.250	−BBR	−6.850	+BBR	−0.600	—
2.0	+6.250	−BBR	−6.850	+BBR	−0.600	—
2.5			−6.850	+BBR	−6.850	+BBR
3.0			−6.850	+BBR	−6.850	+BBR
3.5			−6.850	+BBR	−6.850	+BBR
4.0			−6.850	+BBR	−6.850	+BBR
4.5			−6.850	+BBR	−6.850	+BBR
5.0			−6.850	+BBR	−6.850	+BBR

Where C does not wish to cover the cash flow shortfalls over the first two years, it may utilise a bank (B) to undertake the two swaps and create a customised forward swap for C. B will need to adjust the yield on the forward swap to reflect the funding required as a result of the shortfall from the combined swaps.

In this example, assuming that B uses a funding rate equivalent to the *five year* swap offer rate, the yield adjustment spread would be approximately 1.11% pa. This yield adjustment has the same net present value as the residual two year cash flow. Consequently, B would quote a rate of 14.81% pa (S/A) for a three year forward swap commencing in two years' time.

The all-in rate for the forward swap is calculated by allocating the net cash flow deficit in the first two years to the payments over the three years of the forward swaps on a present value basis using the swap rate as the relevant discount rate. The cost of the forward swap is dependent on the shape of the yield curve which determines the shortfall between the two swaps.

A reverse forward swap is priced in a similar manner. However, the price behaviour of a reverse forward swap is more attractive in a positive yield curve as there is a cash flow surplus in the early years of the swap which reduced the cost of the reverse forward swap by increasing the fixed rate inflow over its life.

Treating the forward swap as a deferred takedown conventional swap usually entails pricing the swap on the basis of the expected cost of the hedge. This approach is illustrated in *Exhibit 15.4*.

In the case of a forward swap, the swap counterparty would usually hedge by selling or shorting bonds. The price of the hedge would reflect the difference in investment yield as between the bond sold and the alternative short-term investment reflecting the deferred start of the swap. Where the yield curve is positive (negative), the lower (higher) investment return would translate into a higher (lower) forward swap rate relative to a conventional swap with an immediate start.

In the case of a reverse forward swap, the logic is identical. However, the hedge would be effected by purchasing bonds and the forward swap rate would reflect the positive or negative carry cost on the holding.

The two approaches are comparable and would usually yield comparable forward swap rates. However, the shape of the physical security yield as compared to the swap yield curve and differences in transaction entailing physical securities such as differential funding costs investment opportunities as well as the balance sheet impact of physical transactions create divergences between the two approaches.

Forward currency swaps

Forward currency swaps are theoretically feasible. However, in practice, such transactions are unbundled into a series of LTFX contracts and a forward interest rate swap in one currency.

For example, consider the case of a borrower seeking to engineer a forward A$ fixed rate against US$ LIBOR floating rate swap where it wishes to pay floating rate US$. The transaction is to commence in two years with a final maturity three years from commencement. The cross-currency forward would take place in two stages.

• The borrower would create a three year deferred synthetic US$ liability commencing in two years by entering into a series of LTFX contracts (buying A$ and selling US$) which would convert the A$ cash flows into a synthetic US$ liability. This liability would have a known fixed cost as the US$ outflows to generate the A$ to fully cover the A$ outflows would be known at the outset. This known US$ cost could be translated into a yield or IRR figure which would then form the basis of the second part of the operation.

- The borrower would enter into a three year US$ forward swap commencing in two years to convert the fixed rate US$ liability into floating rate US$.

Deferred or accelerated cash flow

Types of deferred or accelerated cash flow swaps

An important variation on the conventional swap structure, both interest rate and currency, involves swaps with significant changes in the structure of coupons relative to the even coupon cash flow associated with normal transactions.

The major types of deferred or accelerated cash flow swaps include:

- zero coupon swaps;
- deferred coupon swaps;
- deferred coupon FRN swaps;
- premium and discount swaps.

Applications of deferred or accelerated cash flow swaps

The demand for this type of swap structure is driven by three separate influences:

- unusual coupon structures of securities issues;
- taxation factors;
- cash flow considerations.

In recent times, a number of securities issues have been structured with unusual coupon payment patterns. In the extreme, securities which pay no interest until maturity (zero coupon bonds) have been issued. Other variations include graduated coupon bonds as well as high premium or high discount bond structures. These securities have generally been created to satisfy demand from investors seeking protection from reinvestment risks or seeking to take advantage of some particular tax treatment on discounts or premiums.

The *issuers* of these securities have generally, however, sought to be protected from the reinvestment or funding requirement implied by the security structure. This desire on the part of issuers has prompted the development of deferred and accelerated cash flow swaps which are designed to shield the issuer from the cash flow peculiarities of the issue while translating the overall yield advantage achievable through these securities into the desired currency and interest rate basis.

Tax factors have also played an important part in the restructuring of swap cash flows. Such structures involving either the deferral or acceleration of interest receipts or payments have primarily been utilised to influence the tax liabilities of the counterparty.

Tax-driven applications of deferred or accelerated cash flow swaps can be illustrated with the example of a tax loss company. The tax loss company may have available tax credits which are due to expire shortly. In these circumstances, the tax loss company can "refresh" its existing tax losses utilising the swap structure depicted in *Exhibit 15.6*.

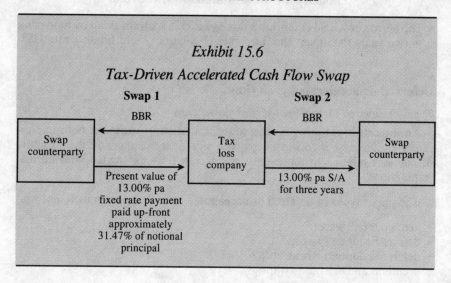

Exhibit 15.6
Tax-Driven Accelerated Cash Flow Swap

Under the structure, the tax loss company receives, in effect, a tax free lump sum on settlement which is sheltered by tax losses. The company essentially repays this payment by way of the fixed rate payments under the swap over its full maturity. These payments, which are assumed to be deductible, allow the tax loss company to essentially renew its tax losses. Where, for example, the tax loss company hopes to return to profitability and tax paying status in future years, an additional element of tax arbitrage arises from the asymmetric treatment of the lump sum and the fixed rate swap payments which are respectively tax free and tax deductible.

This type of structure requires *sets* of swaps to be undertaken to essentially offset the floating rate exposure otherwise created by the transaction. Alternatively, this floating rate exposure can be notionally hedged against floating rate receipts from day to day investment operations or by hedging BBR utilising futures agreements.

Such tax driven applications of accelerated or deferred cash flow swaps are predicated on the treatment of swap payments on a cash (that is, due and payable) as against an accrual basis. Where taxation on swap payments is on a cash basis, as in the case of Australia for most corporations, deductions (assessable income) on payments (receipts) arise when the swap payment is incurred. This allows the type of transaction described to be undertaken to manage tax liabilities. The position is less clear for entities deemed to be market makers or traders in swaps, such as financial institutions, including banks.

There are widespread differences between the tax treatment of payments under swap agreements, particularly as to timing, across jurisdictions. For example, in Australia most banks report swaps on a cash basis although some report on an accruals basis. It is believed, although the matter cannot be clarified, that the Australian Tax Office treats swaps as cash basis items. In contrast, in several countries, including the United States, in the case of transactions undertaken by professional traders, swap payments are treated on an accruals basis.

Irrespective of any tax impact, the capacity of accelerated and deferred cash flow swaps to generate or conserve cash flow has been a significant factor in their utilisation. For example, in early 1987, Westfield Capital Corporation arranged a funding package to finance its investments in a number of companies including Coles Myer and ACI.

As the dividend yields on the investments were well below the interest coupons on the debt financing, Westfield utilised a zero coupon interest rate swap to generate fixed rate funding on which no payment was due until five years in the future. The zero coupon swap deferred the cash outflow, overcoming the problem of the negative spread in the short run and was consistent with Westfield's objective of achieving capital growth on its share investments.

Pricing of deferred or accelerated cash flow swaps

These structural departures from conventional interest rate or currency swaps effectively require the swap provider to either assume reinvestment risks or alternatively to fund payments to the swap counterparty which are then recovered over the life of the swap. The latter type of transaction can be equated to a loan transaction by a swap provider to the party entering into the swap. The pricing of these deferred and accelerated cash flow swaps reflects the assumptions as to reinvestment rates and funding costs.

The simplest way of pricing a zero coupon swap is to utilise the forward rates implicit in the prevailing yield curve. Under this approach, intermediate cash flows under the swap are reinvested at these forward rates, which, theoretically are unbiased estimators of expected forward rates. An example of this technique is set out in *Exhibit 15.7*.

Exhibit 15.7

Pricing a Zero Coupon Swap

Assume that the three year A$ interest rate swap market is priced at 14.85/14.95% pa (S/A) versus six month BBR. Bank A (A) is requested to quote on a A$10m zero coupon swap where it pays the fixed rate.

The swap is to be priced on the basis of the implicit forward reinvestment rates in the government securities yield curve which are as follows:

Maturity	Interest rates (% pa S/A)	Forward rates (% pa S/A)
0.5	15.25	14.75
1.0	15.00	13.50
1.5	14.50	12.51
2.0	14.00	14.75
2.5	14.15	14.75
3.0	14.25	—

Exhibit 15.7—continued

These forward rates are then used to reinvest the cash flows to determine the zero coupon swap pricing:

Maturity	Fixed rate swap flow	Interest at forward rate	Accumulated balance
0.5	0.7425	—	0.7425
1.0	0.7425	0.0548	1.5398
1.5	0.7425	0.1039	2.3862
2.0	0.7425	0.1493	3.2779
2.5	0.7425	0.2417	4.2622
3.0	0.7425	0.3143	5.3190

This equates to a compounded swap rate on the zero swap rate of 14.73% pa (S/A) as against 14.85% pa (S/A) for a conventional swap (a cash difference of A$0.050m).

This type of pricing does not of course guarantee that the predicted return on the transaction is realised because the actual reinvestment rates achieved may differ substantially from the prevailing forward rates at the time the transaction was entered into. The risk can be sought to be managed in a number of ways:

- utilising pricing adjustments whereby conservative reinvestment rates or high borrowing rates are assumed;
- neutralising reinvestment risks by entering into hedging transactions and locking in the required maturity value. This may entail entering into, for example, forward rate agreements or forward swaps against the exposure created by the accelerated or deferred cash flow swap.

Some of the structures in respect of these transactions discussed in detail below seek to minimise the swap provider's exposure to these risks.

While the focus hitherto has been largely on interest rate swaps, the methodology in respect of currency swaps is identical. This reflects the fact that accelerated or deferred cash flow structures affect the coupons *in each currency*. Consequently, the currency basis of the transaction is not strictly speaking affected by the manipulation of the coupon flow. However, once a zero coupon swap rate has been established for the particular currency, it is still necessary to translate that into the specific cash flows of the transaction. An example of the pricing of a zero coupon currency swap is set out in *Exhibit 15.8*.

It should be noted that a zero coupon swap, as noted above, is structurally identical to an LTFX contract.

Zero coupon swaps

Under certain conditions in the early 1980s, yields on zero coupon Eurodollar bonds were significantly lower than full coupon conventional bonds because of strong demand by foreign investors wanting to, for example, lock in relatively high yielding US$ interest rates (avoiding the reinvestment rate risk implicit in a normal coupon paid bond or take advantage of favourable tax treatment of the discount).

For example, in August 1984, a prime quality borrower would have been able to issue a ten year Eurodollar bond at an all-in cost of 30bps pa over a comparable United States Treasury bond and swapped the fixed debt for floating debt at 55bps over a comparable United States Treasury bond resulting in a cost of 25bps under LIBOR. The same company could have issued a ten year Eurodollar zero coupon bond at an all-in cost of at least 60bps pa *below* a comparable United States Treasury. This significant saving on issuing yield on a zero coupon bond was available for swap transactions but required a special structure constructed to match the cash flow characteristics of a zero coupon security.

Two possible types of zero coupon interest rate swap structures are outlined in *Exhibit 15.9* and *Exhibit 15.10*. Both transactions are designed to enable a borrower to issue zero coupon bonds and to enter into swaps such that the borrower's net cash flow is largely identical to that it would have had if it had instead issued a low cost coupon paid floating rate instrument.

The transaction outlined in *Exhibit 15.9* entails the borrower issuing a zero coupon Eurobond, for example, a ten year issue, net proceeds of US$50m, and a face value of US$135.7m which implies an interest rate of 10.50% pa on an annual basis. This issue is then swapped in two stages entailing two distinct transactions:

- *Transaction A.* Whereby the issuer enters into a conventional interest rate swap (with counterparty A) based on a notional principal amount of US$50m for a term of ten years under which the issuer pays floating rate interest at a margin under LIBOR while it receives fixed rate interest payments annually at a rate of 10.60% pa.

Exhibit 15.8

Pricing Zero Coupon NZ$ Issue and Cross-Currency Swap

Assume that the five year zero swap rate for fixed NZ$ and US$ LIBOR is 16.50% pa (A) versus six month LIBOR flat.

Also assume that the current spot exchange rate is NZ$1/ US$0.58. For a NZ$ zero coupon issue with face value of NZ$100 with a maturity of five years yielding 16.50% pa (A), the current price of the issue would be NZ$46.5983 giving net proceeds of US$27.027.

All-in issue pricing would be as follows:

Net proceeds:	US$27.0270m =	NZ$46.5983m
Reserve fund to generate sub-LIBOR margin:[1]	US$ 0.2698m =	NZ$ 0.4651m
Expense (US$125,000):	US$ 0.1250m =	NZ$ 0.2155m
Issue fees: (1.375%):	=	NZ$ 0.6591m
Total:	=	NZ$47.9380m
Swap fee:	US$0.500m =	NZ$ 0.8621m
		NZ$48.8001m

The gross proceeds required for the issue is therefore NZ$48.8001.

This translates into an issue yield of 15.43% pa (A) for a five year NZ$100 issue.

Note:

1. Based on sub-LIBOR margin of 25bps which equates to US$67,568 pa (0.25% of US$27.027). This is then discounted at 8.00% pa (A) (the current US$ interest rate) for five years to produce a present value amount of US$0.2698m.

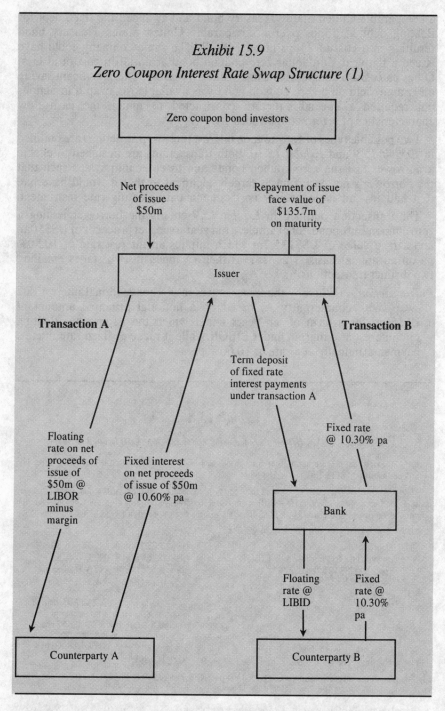

Exhibit 15.9
Zero Coupon Interest Rate Swap Structure (1)

- *Transaction B.* Whereby the issuer reinvests the fixed interest rate payments received under the interest rate swap to guarantee a maturity value equal to the face value of the bonds to meet the repayment obligation to bond holders at maturity. Transaction B effects this as follows: the required maturity value is generated by the issuer entering into a commitment to deposit each fixed rate interest receipt under the swap with a bank. The bank in turn enters into an interest rate swap (with counterparty B) to fix the yield on the floating rate deposit. The size of the deposit increases and the corresponding notional principal under the swap increases over the term of the transaction. The swap with counterparty B enables the bank to guarantee the issuer a fixed rate on its deposits which continue to roll forward until the final maturity of the bond.

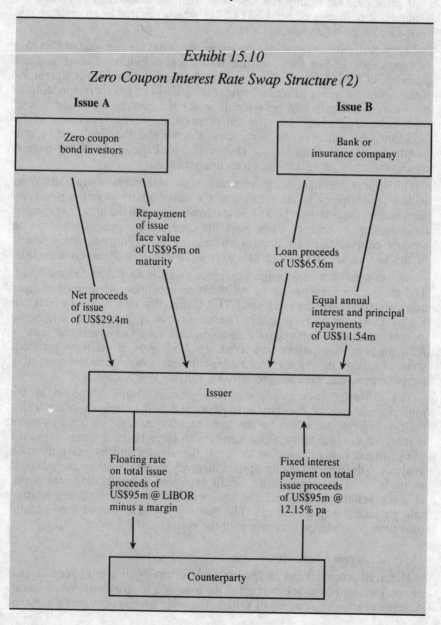

Exhibit 15.10
Zero Coupon Interest Rate Swap Structure (2)

Issue A

Issue B

Zero coupon bond investors

Bank or insurance company

Repayment of issue face value of US$95m on maturity

Loan proceeds of US$65.6m

Net proceeds of issue of US$29.4m

Equal annual interest and principal repayments of US$11.54m

Issuer

Floating rate on total issue proceeds of US$95m @ LIBOR minus a margin

Fixed interest payment on total issue proceeds of US$95m @ 12.15% pa

Counterparty

Exhibit 15.10 sets out an alternative structure. The transaction entails two separate issues:

- *Issue A*. An issue (usually public) of zero coupon Eurobonds, for example, ten year, net proceeds of $29.4m (after fees), and a face value of US$95m which implies an interest rate of 12.44% pa on an annual basis.

- *Issue B*. An annuity loan (usually arranged as a private placement) whereby the amount of the loan is repaid at the end of each year until maturity by equal level repayments composed of interest and annual redemption of principal, for example, a ten year loan for US$65.6m repayable by annual instalments of net US$11.54m which equates to an interest rate of 11.85% pa on an annual basis.

The overall package provides the issuer with total net proceeds of US$95m (net proceeds US$29.4m from the zero coupon Eurobond issue and net proceeds of US$65.6m from the annuity loan), an annual commitment for nine successive years to make payments of US$11.54m (corresponding to the interest and principal repayments under the annuity loan) and a final repayment of US$106.54m after ten years (equalling the repayment of the US$95m face value of the zero coupon issue and the final US$11.54m instalment of the annuity loan). The overall package implies a net interest cost to the issuer of 12.15% pa on an annual basis.

The insurer then undertakes a conventional interest rate swap transaction with a counterparty to the effect that the counterparty pays the issuer, on each annual interest date, US$11.54m corresponding to the instalments under the loan annuity and the issuer pays the counterparty every six months an amount equivalent to six months interest on the aggregated net proceeds of the two issues (US$95m), at a rate equalling LIBOR minus a margin.

An example of a zero coupon currency swap is set out in *Exhibit 15.11*. The transaction depicted is an A$200m zero coupon A$ Eurobond issue and associated currency swap and LTFX transaction undertaken by Eastman Kodak Company in early 1987. The transaction is particularly interesting in that it entailed two separate swap transactions to convert the issuer's A$ zero coupon exposure into fixed rate US$. Part of the issue proceeds were swapped utilising a zero coupon currency swap, while the remaining net issue proceeds were hedged into A$ utilising LTFX contracts.

The difficulty in creating the zero coupon swaps lies both in the reinvestment risk for the fixed rate payer and in the credit exposure which the floating rate payer has on the fixed rate payer, since no fixed payment is received until maturity. Some banks with large balance sheets avoid the reinvestment risk by ignoring the cash flow issues and by using duration analysis to determine the appropriate maturity for an offsetting conventional swap. In order to minimise the credit exposure of the floating rate payer, in some instances trust vehicles were established into which the floating rate payments would be made. The floating payments would then be held over time with interest accruing until the maturity of the swap.

Deferred coupon bond swaps

Deferred coupon bond swaps are architecturally similar to zero coupon swaps. Deferred coupon bonds entail the issue of a security with, say, maturity of seven years with a coupon of 8.00%. The issue structure requires a payment

Exhibit 15.11
Zero Coupon Currency Swap Structure

Initial exchange

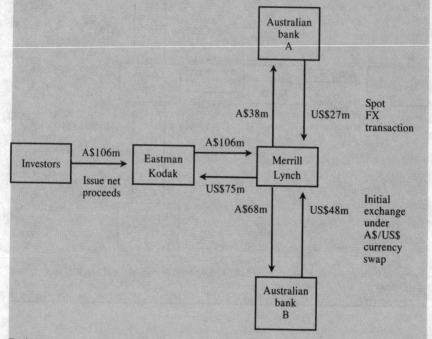

Exchange rate is US$0.7075/A$1.00.

Interest payments

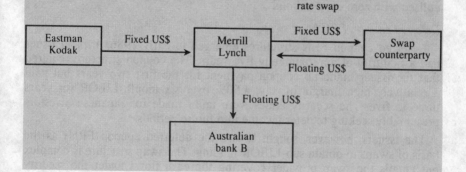

Exhibit 15.11—continued

Final exchange

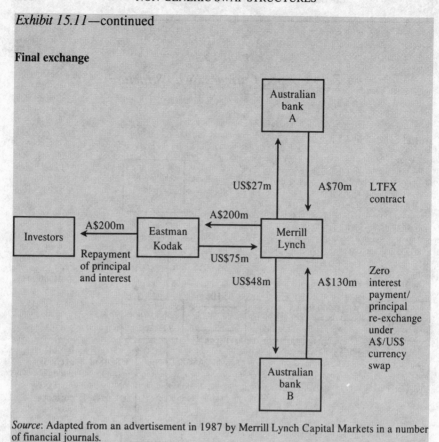

Source: Adapted from an advertisement in 1987 by Merrill Lynch Capital Markets in a number of financial journals.

of the coupon for the first four years at the end of that period as a rolled up lump sum of 32.00% of the principal value of the bond with level 8.00% coupon payments thereafter. Designed to circumvent regulations against the purchase of zero coupon securities by Japanese investors, deferred coupon bonds had similar cash flow characteristics to zeros, at least for the first part of its life, and the swap structures utilised were largely similar to those utilised with zero coupon bonds.

Deferred coupon FRN bond swaps

Deferred coupon FRN structures emerged in early 1986. Typical issues had a maturity of approximately five years. The coupon structure required that the issuer made no coupon payment for the first two years but paid a relatively high margin of, say, 4.50% over six month LIBOR for years three to five. The security issues were tailor-made for Japanese investors presumably seeking to defer income into future periods.

The issuers, however, sought to use the deferred coupon FRNs as the basis of swaps to obtain sub-LIBOR funding. The swap structure is complex but entails the swap provider covering the cash flows under the security issue in return for receiving a substantial margin under LIBOR throughout the five years. Under the structure, the swap provider has a positive cash flow initially followed by a negative cash flow. This cash surplus which turns into a deficiency presents the swap provider with a reinvestment risk. This risk can be partially managed, potentially, by utilising the positive cash flow in years one and two to purchase zero coupon securities maturing in the later period so as to service the 4.50% spread.

A variation on the deferred coupon FRN structure is the high initial spread FRN which reverses the cash flow pattern with large payments in the early years and absent or very low payments in the distant years. These transactions were similarly swapped but provided the opposite problem for the swap provider in that it required it to fund large payments in the early years which were recovered in the latter half of the transaction.

Premium or discount swaps

Premium or discount swaps entail either an up-front payment by the swap provider in return for higher running coupon payments or its reverse, that is, swaps entailing an up-front payment to the swap provider in return for lower subsequent swap payments. The basic rationale for such transactions is the acceleration or deferral of interest payment for cash flow or tax advantages.

An example of an off-market swap is set out in *Exhibit 15.12*.

Exhibit 15.12

Structuring an Off-market Interest Rate Swap

Assume current markets for five year A$ interest rate swaps are 13.25/13.35% pa (A). A borrower (B) wishes to transact an interest rate swap where it pays fixed rate of 15.00% pa (A) on A$25m for five years.

The value of the 15.00% pa swap at current market rates is as follows:

Period (years)	Generic swap flows (A$m)	Off-market swap flows (A$m)	Difference (A$m)
0	+25.00	+25	—
1	−3.338	−3.75	0.413
2	−3.338	−3.75	0.413
3	−3.338	−3.75	0.413
4	−3.338	−3.75	0.413
5	−28.338	−28.75	0.413

Utilising the offered swap rate (13.35% pa) as the relevant discount rate, the off-market swap is valued at A$26.439 which implies a payment of A$1.439m *to* B. This can be arrived at by discounting back the difference @ 13.35% pa *or* discounting back the off-market swap flows @ 13.35% pa and subtracting the value of a generic swap (A$25m).

As the swap counterparty is essentially lending B the up-front payment to be recovered via the higher than market swap payments, a higher discount rate may be appropriate. A discount rate of 14.35% pa (the offered swap rate plus 1.00% pa) reduces the up-front payment to A$0.553m.

SWAP STRUCTURES PREDICATED ON ISSUE STRUCTURES

Dual currency bond swap structures

A dual currency bond involves an issue where the interest coupon is denominated in a different currency to the underlying principal of the bond. For example, a dual currency Swiss franc bond would have interest payable in Swiss francs and the principal in US$. Dual currency markets can be an inexpensive source of US$ financing where the investors are speculating on the strength of the US$.

Alternative structures include dual currency bonds with interest payable in US$ and principal in Japanese yen (often referred to as a reverse dual currency bond as it contrasts with the usual structure whereby the coupon is payable in a low interest rate currency) which are designed to appeal to Japanese investors' eagerness to enjoy high current yield while minimising exposure to possible long-term devaluation of the US$ against the yen.

Other dual currency bond structures have been undertaken in: C$ and Swiss francs; A$ and yen; NZ$ and yen; Dutch guilders and US$.

The structure of a swap against a dual currency issue entails a number of separate steps usually involving separate currency or interest rate swaps and a series of LTFX contracts. For example, for a dual currency issue with coupons denominated in Swiss francs and principal in US$, the swap would entail the following separate transactions: a series of LTFX contracts to hedge the Swiss francs into US$ to create a synthetic US$ liability which could then be swapped into floating rate US$ through an interest rate swap or into an alternative desired currency or interest rate basis through a currency swap. Alternatively, the US$ principal could be hedged back into Swiss francs to create a synthetic Swiss franc liability which could then be swapped into US$ through a Swiss franc and US$ swap.

In the case of a reverse dual currency bond issue, the swap structure would include a conventional US$ interest rate swap to convert the borrower's interest commitment to floating rate US$ and a long-dated foreign exchange forward contract purchasing Japanese yen against US$ to lock in the fully hedged floating rate US$ cost to the issuer.

Exhibit 15.13 sets out an example of a yen and A$ dual currency bond issue undertaken in 1987 with the proceeds being swapped first, into US$ and, finally, into fixed rate A$.

The dual currency bond swap layers a complex initial transaction with a series of foreign exchange and swap transactions basically designed to generate, at least initially, cost effective floating rate US$ funding.

Bull and bear FRN swap structures

In early 1986, during a period of sustained decreases in interest rates, investors seeking the benefit from expected declines in short-term interest rates sought an instrument whose yield increased as interest rates fell. The "bull" or reverse FRN was one such instrument. The bull FRN carried an interest coupon which was a fixed rate (say, 17.25% pa) less six month US$ LIBOR. As LIBOR decreases, the return payable under the note increases commensurately. However, the instrument held little attraction for issuers

Exhibit 15.13

Yen/A$ Dual Currency Bond and Swap Structure

In early 1987, an Australian borrower undertook a ¥/A$ dual currency bond issue on the following terms:

Amount:	¥10 billion
Term:	five years
Issue price:	102.50%
Interest rate:	8.00% pa payable in yen and calculated on the yen denominated principal
Redemption amount:	A$119.2m (implied redemption exchange rate of A$1/ ¥83.92)
Fees:	2.00% flat

The borrower did *not* want a yen exposure but wished to create a synthetic A$ liability utilising the dual currency bond issue as the basis for an arbitrage funding transaction.

The issue was swapped in three stages:

1. The following series of LTFX contracts to create a synthetic fixed rate US$ liability:
   - sell spot ¥10.05 billion and buy US$70m;
   - buy forward at yearly intervals ¥800m and sell US$5m;
   - buy 5 year forward A$119.2m and sell US$68m.

2. A US$ interest rate swap to convert the fixed rate US$ liability into floating rate US$ as follows:
   - receive US$5m annually for five years;
   - pay LIBOR minus a margin (M) semi-annually for five years plus US$2m at maturity.

3. An A$ fixed to US$ floating currency swap to convert the floating US$ liability into fixed rate A$ as follows:
   - at commencement pay US$70m and receive A$100m;
   - over the life of the transaction receive US$ LIBOR-M semi-annually for five years and pay A$ fixed rates at the Australian bond rate (B) plus a margin (M*);
   - at maturity, receive US$70m and pay A$100m.

The overall effect of the forward contracts and swaps is to convert fixed yen payments to, first, fixed US$ payments, then to floating rate US$ payments and finally to end up with fixed A$ payments at an effective Commonwealth bond rate + M*. This rate represented a significant cost saving to the borrower.

The cash flows for the total transaction are set out in the table below:

CASH FLOWS

Period (years)	Bonds	LTFX contracts ¥m	US$m	Receive US$m	Swap 1 Pay US$m	Swap 2 Pay A$m	Receive US$m
0	+ ¥10,055m	−10,055m	+70	—	—	−US$70.0m	+A$100m
0.5					−LIBOR−M	B + M*	+LIBOR−M
1.0	− ¥800m	+800	−5.0	+5.0	−LIBOR−M	B + M*	+LIBOR−M
1.5					−LIBOR−M	B + M*	+LIBOR−M
2.0	− ¥800m	+800	−5.0	+5.0	−LIBOR−M	B + M*	+LIBOR−M
2.5					−LIBOR−M	B + M*	+LIBOR−M
3.0	− ¥800m	+800	−5.0	+5.0	−LIBOR−M	B + M*	+LIBOR−M
3.5					−LIBOR−M	B + M*	+LIBOR−M
4.0	− ¥800m	+800	−5.0	+5.0	−LIBOR−M	B + M*	+LIBOR−M
4.5					−LIBOR−M	B + M*	+LIBOR−M
5.0	⎧ − ¥800m	+800	−5.0	+5.0	−LIBOR−M	B + M*	+LIBOR−M
	⎩ −A$119.2m	+A$119.2	−68.0		+US$2.0m	−A$100m	+US$70.0m

who would be disadvantaged if short-term interest rates fell. However, a particularly ingenious swap structure designed to protect the issuer from increases in its effective cost of funds was devised. Under this structure, the issuer undertook conventional interest rate swaps for *double* the amount of the FRN issue to create a synthetic floating rate liability. The bull or reverse FRN issue and swap structure are set out in *Exhibit 15.14*.

Exhibit 15.14

Bull or Reverse FRN Issue and Swap Structure

The issue structure entails a FRN issue on the following terms:

Amount:	US$100m
Term:	five years
Interest payment:	The issue carries an interest rate of 17.25% (calculated on bond basis, payable S/A) less six months US$ LIBOR flat. At no time will there be negative interest for the investor, that is, if US$ six month LIBOR reaches 17.25% pa or above, the investor will not be required to make any payment to the issuer
Fees:	0.25% flat

The issue structure is designed to provide investors with an investment on which the return increases as short-term interest rates decline.

The underlying FRN issue is swapped utilising the following swap structure:

Transaction structure:	Conventional US$ interest rate swap
Notional principal amount:	US$200m
Issuer pays swap counterparty:	LIBOR − 0.125% pa
Issuer receives from swap counterparty:	8.625% pa S/A

The total transaction can be depicted as follows:

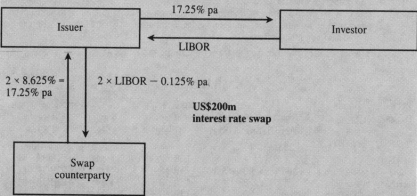

US$100m Bull FRN issue

The net effect of the transaction is to generate LIBOR less 25bps on a principal borrowing of US$100m for the issuer.

Importantly, this result is achieved so long as LIBOR is less than 17.25% pa, that is, the basic fixed interest coupon on the FRN issue. Where LIBOR exceeds 17.25% pa S/A, the sub-LIBOR margin to the issuer is eroded. At a LIBOR level of 17.25% pa S/A, the issuer achieves funding at a level equivalent to LIBOR, that is, the sub-LIBOR margin is eroded.

The underlying cash flows of the issue and related swaps are set out in the following table.

Exhibit 15.14—continued

(1) Level of six month LIBOR (% pa S/A)	(2) 17.25% pa S/A on US$100 (S/A payment)	Issue cash flows (3) Six month LIBOR on US$100m (S/A payment)	(4) Cost to issuer (return to investor) [(2)−(3)]	(5) Issuer receives 8.625% pa S/A on US$200m (S/A payment)	Swap cash flows (6) Issuer pays US$ six month LIBOR minus 0.125% pa on US$200m (S/A payment)	(7) Net swap cash flow [(5)−(6)] (S/A payment)	(8) Net cost to issuer [(4)−(7)]
4.0625	8,625,000	2,031,250	6,593,750 (13.1875% pa S/A)	8,625,000	3,937,500	+ 4,687,500	1,906,250 (3.8125% pa S/A LIBOR − 25bps)
8.1250	8,625,000	4,062,500	4,562,500 (9.125% pa S/A)	8,625,000	8,000,000	+ 625,000	3,937,500 (7.875% pa S/A LIBOR − 25bps)
12.1875	8,625,000	6,093,750	2,531,250 (5.0625% pa S/A)	8,625,000	12,062,500	− 3,437,500	5,968,750 (11.9375% pa S/A LIBOR − 25 bps)
17.2500	8,625,000	8,625,000	0	8,625,000	17,125,000	− 8,500,000	8,500,000 (17.00% pa S/A LIBOR − 25 bps)
17.5000	8,625,000	8,625,000	0	8,625,000	17,137,000	− 8,750,000	8,750,000 (17.50% pa S/A LIBOR)
21.5625	8,625,000	8,625,000	0	8,625,000	21,437,500	−12,812,500	12,812,500 (25.625% pa S/A LIBOR + 406.25bps)

The basic concept was varied with the "bear" FRN which carried a coupon of two times LIBOR minus a fixed rate which was designed to appeal to investors concerned about future increases in short-term interest rates.

The bear FRN structure together with accompanying swap is set out in *Exhibit 15.15*. Under this structure, as in the bull FRN, the issuer is insulated from any interest rate risk as a result of fluctuations of interest rates achieving floating rate funding related to LIBOR at an all-in cost below its normal floating rate funding cost.

Miscellaneous swap structures

The extraordinary flexibility of swap structures have made them relevant to a wide variety of new issue structures. A particular example of this was an issue by Halifax Building Society undertaken in May 1987. At that time, the best interest rate swaps in £ were available in three year maturities. But the Bank of England did not allow Eurosterling issues with maturities of less than five years. Consequently, Halifax Building Society issued £50m of debt based on a fixed coupon for the first three years and a variable rate over LIBOR for the remaining two years. The building society which was seeking floating rate funding then swapped the first three year fixed rate coupon to floating. The three year swap was extremely attractive and allowed Halifax to swap into floating rate funding at a sufficient margin under LIBOR to generate sub-LIBOR funding for the whole five year life of the transaction.

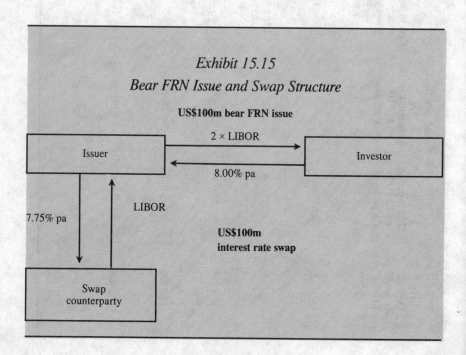

Exhibit 15.15

Bear FRN Issue and Swap Structure

US$100m bear FRN issue

Issuer

2 × LIBOR

8.00% pa

Investor

7.75% pa

LIBOR

US$100m
interest rate swap

Swap
counterparty

BASIS SWAPS

Basis swaps developed as an important subset of classical interest rate swaps since they allow parties to swap from one floating rate instrument to another, thereby allowing them to tap markets which may not directly be available to them.

Basis swaps (or floating-to-floating interest rate swaps) entail the conversion of one floating rate index into another in the same currency. Basis swaps function in much the same way as a fixed or floating interest rate swap, except that instead of one rate being held constant for the life of the transactions, both rates are reset throughout, relative to the agreed notional principal amount. As with a conventional interest rate swap, the notional principal is never exchanged.

The market in basis swaps, which is almost exclusively confined to US$, originally developed primarily between the United States prime rate and LIBOR. These transactions arose because non-United States banks were often members of lending syndicates with prime based (priced) loan assets which had to be funded in the LIBOR market, which was their traditional funding source. By entering into a swap where they paid a specified margin under United States prime and, in return, received LIBOR, these banks were able to match their assets and their liabilities and lock in the profit margin on the prime related loans.

The other forms of basis swaps developed in and between, inter alia, LIBOR, United States Treasury bills (T-Bills), commercial paper (CP), certificate of deposit (CD) rates, bankers acceptance (BA) rates, Federal Funds rates, etc. *Exhibit 15.16* sets out the basic market quotations for the main types of basis swaps.

Exhibit 15.16

Basis Swap Quotations

UNITED STATES MONEY MARKET INDEX SWAPS

Prime/LIBOR	Receive	Pay
2 years	P—110	P—125
3 years	P—110	P—125
5 years	P—110	P—125
T-Bills/LIBOR		
2 years	T—Bills+120	T—Bills+105
3 years	T—Bills+120	T—Bills+105
5 years	T—Bills+120	T—Bills+105
Commercial Paper/LIBOR		
2 years	CP+33	CP+28
3 years	CP+36	CP+32
5 years	CP+37	CP+32

Source: Euro Brokers Ltd, New York.

The various basis swap markets vary significantly as to liquidity and debt. The LIBOR and CP and the LIBOR and T-Bills are by far the most common markets. This reflects the popularity of United States CP as a form of short-term funding for high quality borrowers who use these short-term funds as the underlying liquidity for US\$ interest rate swaps. In the case of T-Bills, the requirements of a number of prime borrowers, such as Sallie Mae, for T-Bill funding provides this market with liquidity.

The initial application of basis swaps entailed borrower's obtaining funding in particular markets without the necessity for specifically entering those markets directly. For example, some non-United States companies utilised LIBOR and CP swaps to convert LIBOR funding to a CP base without needing to qualify themselves (for example, obtaining rates etc.) to issue in the CP market. Conversely, United States companies with available CP lines used these swaps to generate LIBOR based funding for their European operations. Financial institutions were particularly active in basis swaps, using their relative funding power in different markets to generate funding at attractive rates in other markets to better match asset liability portfolios.

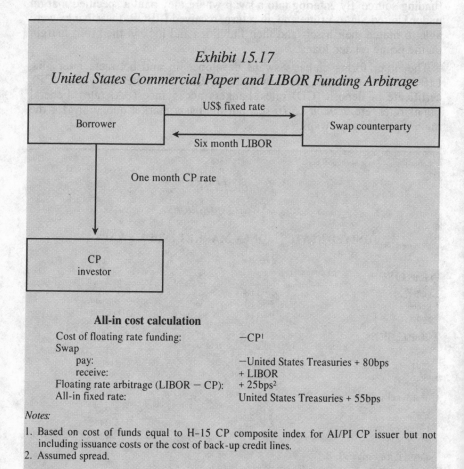

Exhibit 15.17
United States Commercial Paper and LIBOR Funding Arbitrage

All-in cost calculation

Cost of floating rate funding:	−CP[1]
Swap	
pay:	−United States Treasuries + 80bps
receive:	+ LIBOR
Floating rate arbitrage (LIBOR − CP):	+ 25bps[2]
All-in fixed rate:	United States Treasuries + 55bps

Notes:

1. Based on cost of funds equal to H-15 CP composite index for AI/PI CP issuer but not including issuance costs or the cost of back-up credit lines.
2. Assumed spread.

The second application was predicated on the fact that when transforming a floating rate liability into a fixed rate basis the all-in fixed rate cost ultimately generated consists of two components: first, the fixed rate payment flow under the swap; and second, the spread between the floating rate payment flow under the swap and the floating rate funding cost. Where the latter is positive, that is, if the cost of the borrower's underlying variable rate funds is lower than the floating rate payment received from the counterparty, the fixed rate cost to the borrower is reduced.

A substantial market developed in transactions whereby companies fixed for several years the cost of short-term borrowings through the United States CP market. The interest rate swaps used, however, were linked to LIBOR rather than the CP rate allowing the borrower to lower its fixed cost where its cost of CP is below the LIBOR floating rate payment it receives under the swap. As the swaps are generally linked to six month LIBOR but are effectively funded by 30 day CP and as six month LIBOR has exceeded the cost of 30 day A1/P1 CP, the borrower could, provided the historical pattern of rates is replicated during the term of the swap, sometimes achieve funding at a rate under the equivalent United States Treasury rate at the commencement of the transaction. *Exhibit 15.17* sets out an example of this type of swap structure.

This transaction structure entails the borrower running the basis risk that CP rates will rise relative to LIBOR and, more importantly, that the shape of the yield curve may change, for example, an inverse yield curve where 30 day CP rates are above six month LIBOR, will increase its effective cost. The latter risk, in some transactions, is sought to be eliminated through a particular type of basis swap known as a "reset" swap which moderates the maturity risk that the cost of borrowing for 30 days will rise between the six monthly rate setting dates for LIBOR by sampling the six month LIBOR at more frequent (usually monthly) intervals. For example, a typical five year interest rate swap against six month LIBOR would entail ten LIBOR rate setting and payment dates. A reset swap will have ten payment dates but the rate that is paid every six months will be the average of six monthly (a total of 60) rate settings of six month LIBOR.

An alternative means of taking basis risk unhedged entails arbitraging the yield spreads between various floating rate indexes and the pricing margins on basis swaps. For example, where the spread between LIBOR and the CP rate narrowed and was accompanied by a lower than usual swap spread in switching from LIBOR based to CP based funding, a borrower could take advantage of its expectation that the spread between LIBOR and CP would widen by transacting a swap under which it receives LIBOR and pays CP plus a margin.

This form of risk controlled arbitrage is increasingly the rationale for basis swaps, with borrowers and investors shifting to floating rate indexes which they believe will be more attractive over a particular time horizon. For example, if the heavy indebtedness of the United States banks to Third World countries raises the spectre of painful adjustments that could have an adverse impact on the LIBOR rate, then borrowers who have structured their borrowings with a LIBOR benchmark would experience an increased cost of funding. These borrowers may be able to obtain more attractive funding by entering into a basis swap which effectively converts their existing

LIBOR linked funding to one tied to other benchmark rates, such as the United States Treasury bill or CP index.

Basis swaps were also entered into by borrowers seeking to diversify away from a single floating rate index. For example, if a European corporate with extensive United States CP borrowings wishes to decrease its sensitivity to fluctuations in CP rates, it may do so by employing basis swaps which convert the debt into United States Treasury bills or US$ LIBOR. It can thereby diminish its basis risk through diversification.

Swaps, which allow a borrower to convert three or six month LIBOR funds to one month LIBOR funds or vice versa, are a subset of basis swaps. These types of basis swaps are used extensively by banks. For example, the Australian Industries Development Corporation initiated one of the first basis option swaps when it requested that banks provide it with bids for a US$ interest rate swap against either one, three or six month LIBOR payments. This swap provided the Australian Industries Development Corporation with the option to pay on any of three floating rates.

In September 1987, AIG Financial Products engineered a swap involving an *arrears* reset on floating rate US$ LIBOR. Under the arrears reset structure, floating rate payments were based on LIBOR set *two days before the payment date*, whereas on a normal swap, LIBOR would be set *six months and two days prior to the payment date*.

The arrears reset structure was designed to create value from a positively sloped yield curve where implied forward rates lie successively higher above the physical yield curve. However, higher implied forward rates are only an unbiased estimate of actual future interest rates, and the actual spot rate at the relevant future date may differ from that implied by the forward rate.

This means that the arrears reset structure may be attractive to a counterparty who expects that short-term rates will remain stable or decrease. Such a counterparty would under this structure receive fixed rates under the swap against payment of floating rates receiving the benefit of the higher implied forward rate, in the form of a higher fixed rate flow under the swap. If, however, LIBOR increases from one payment period to the next, the savings on the arrears reset structure could be offset by the higher LIBOR rate. This feature dictates that the arrears reset structure is unsuitable where the borrower is seeking to match fund assets.

Several major international banks already run active books in basis swaps. Since basis swaps involve only a net interest exchange equal to the difference in short-term rate indices, the associated default risk is extremely low. Market makers write such basis swaps against residual positions or mismatches arising from other swaps. For example, a market maker could have two swaps whereby it received fixed against six month LIBOR but had paid fixed against one month CP. The market maker could then write a basis swap paying CP against receipt of LIBOR to close off its mismatch. *Exhibit 15.18* sets out an example of the construction of a basis swap involving the United States prime rate and US$ LIBOR.

Pricing of basis swaps thus tends to be on the basis of existing swap position mismatches as well as the market arbitrage positions. In addition, the historical relationship between the two floating rate indexes is also relevant.

MISCELLANEOUS VARIATIONS ON BASIC SWAP STRUCTURES

An interesting variation on basic swap structures focuses on the mechanism by which swap transactions are executed. Conventionally, swaps are executed either directly with a counterparty, inevitably a financial institution, or through the medium of an arranger who procures a counterparty. In recent years,

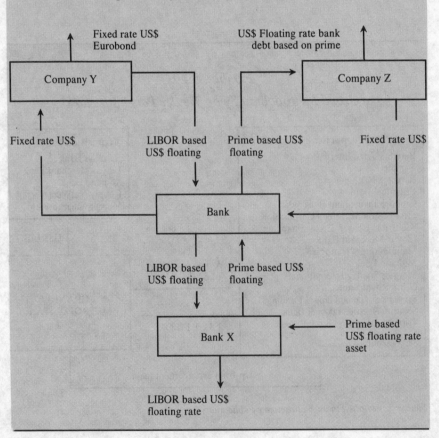

Exhibit 15.18

Engineering a US$ Prime and LIBOR Basis Swap

Bank X, which has access to floating rate funds through the London interbank market, has a prime based asset for which it seeks matched funding. It then enters into a swap whereby it receives an amount linked to LIBOR and pays an amount related to prime. The two offsetting counterparties could be company Y, swapping between a fixed rate and LIBOR, and company Z, swapping between prime and a fixed rate. The two fixed rates can then be arranged to cancel each other, leaving a residual position which is prime against LIBOR.

a number of innovative arrangements have been developed to arrange swap transactions reflecting, primarily, the size and complexity of the particular entities swap requirements.

Innovations in the area of swap execution commenced in 1984 when Morgan Grenfell arranged a US$50m Euronote facility for the Export Finance and Insurance Corporation of Australia. The facility included a tender panel which allowed members to bid for the right to swap the floating rate debt raised by the notes into fixed rate funding.

Subsequently, the Export Credit Guarantee Department in the United Kingdom and Grand Metropolitan, both of whom were faced with very large swap programmes, utilised a swap arranger to put together swap programmes with a number of counterparties.

The Grand Metropolitan transaction illustrates the basic concept. The company was faced with the need to put a programme of US$ interest rate swaps totalling US$750m. In order to avoid the administrative complexity of dealing with separate counterparties, given certain timing constraints, Grand Metropolitan appointed Warburg Securities, a United Kingdom investment bank, to arrange the programme. The structure of the Grand Metropolitan swap tender panel is set out in *Exhibit 15.19*.

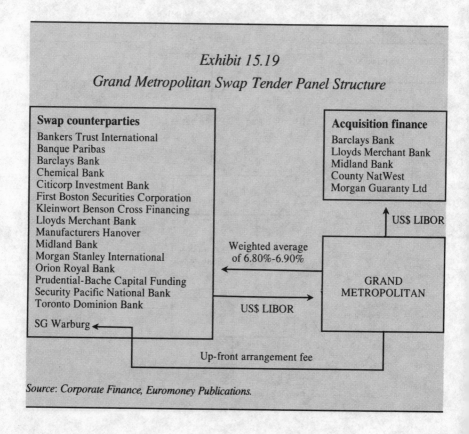

Exhibit 15.19
Grand Metropolitan Swap Tender Panel Structure

Swap counterparties

Bankers Trust International
Banque Paribas
Barclays Bank
Chemical Bank
Citicorp Investment Bank
First Boston Securities Corporation
Kleinwort Benson Cross Financing
Lloyds Merchant Bank
Manufacturers Hanover
Midland Bank
Morgan Stanley International
Orion Royal Bank
Prudential-Bache Capital Funding
Security Pacific National Bank
Toronto Dominion Bank

SG Warburg

Acquisition finance

Barclays Bank
Lloyds Merchant Bank
Midland Bank
County NatWest
Morgan Guaranty Ltd

US$ LIBOR

Weighted average of 6.80%-6.90%

US$ LIBOR

GRAND METROPOLITAN

Up-front arrangement fee

Source: Corporate Finance, Euromoney Publications.

Warburg Securities were also instrumental in developing the revolving swap facility. In this case, the transaction was arranged for Booker, the international food distribution and health products business company, which had an ongoing need to convert US$ assets into £. The structure of the revolving currency swap facility is set out in *Exhibit 15.20*. In late 1987, the Mass Transit Railway Corporation of Hong Kong arranged a similar revolving currency swap facility to convert liabilities from a variety of other currencies into Hong Kong dollars.

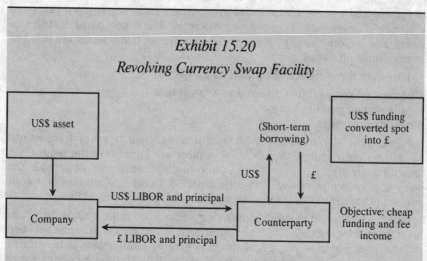

Exhibit 15.20
Revolving Currency Swap Facility

The company:
- pays US$ LIBOR and receives £ LIBOR minus a spread;
- pays the US$ principal amount and receives the £ principal amount at maturity;
- determines the date where the swap is entered into (the facility is drawndown);
- determines the date where the swap is terminated.

The counterparty arranges the maturities of its funding so as to match possible termination dates chosen by the company.

Source: *Corporate Finance, Euromoney Publications.*

Chapter 16

Liability Swaps: Options on Swaps

INTRODUCTION

Coincidental with the growth in the market for swaps, substantial markets in futures and options on financial instruments, including interest rates and currencies, developed. Transaction structures which combined features of swaps and options rapidly emerged. These types of instruments are referred to as options on swaps.

There are three classes of options on swaps:

- options on swaps (often referred to as swaptions);
- callable and putable swaps;
- contingent swaps.

While generally regarded as distinct and different types of transactions by market participants, the above structures are largely overlapping. Each structure effectively represents an option to either enter into or provide the swap at a known price over a specified period. In essence, options on swaps combine the features of interest rate options with swap transactions.

It should be noted that the terminology associated with options on swaps is far from standardised. There are significant differences in usage as between jurisdictions. For example, as discussed in greater detail below, in the United States a putable swap would imply an option whereby the holder, a payer of fixed rates under a swap, would have the right to terminate a swap. In contrast, a callable swap would imply the right of the holder to enter into a swap as a payer of fixed rates. In London, terminology is exactly opposite with a callable swap giving the right to terminate the swap arrangement.

OPTIONS ON SWAPS (SWAPTIONS)

An option on a swap usually entails an option on the fixed rate component of a swap. It is designed to give the holder the benefit of the strike rate (that is, the *fixed* rate specified in the agreement) if the market rates are worse, with the flexibility to deal at the market rates if they are better.

An option on a swap provides the purchaser or holder of the option with the right, but not the obligation, to enter into a swap where it pays fixed rates against receipt of a floating rate index. The reverse type of transaction where the holder of the option on the swap will, if the option is exercised, receive the fixed rate is also feasible.

The terminology associated with options on swaps is as follows:

- American style: a swap option which can be exercised on any business day within the swap option exercise period.

278

- European style: a swap option which can be exercised only on the expiry date.
- Exercise or strike price: the specified rate at which the buyer has the right to enter into the swap.
- Premium: the consideration paid by the buyer for the swap option.
- Expiry date: the last date on which the swap option can be exercised.

Options on swaps primarily offer protection against interest rate uncertainty in a manner analogous to a conventional debt option. The user of options on swaps is able to limit its downside risk in switching from fixed to floating interest rates or vice versa, without limiting potential benefits associated with unforeseen *favourable* interest rate movements. In return for this opportunity, the purchaser of an option on a swap pays a fee, that is, the swap premium.

An important aspect of options on swaps is that for certain classes of borrower, where they would ultimately be users of swaps, the emergence of options on swaps provides them with greater flexibility and certainty in managing their assets or liabilities. This can be seen from the fact that before the emergence of these instruments, the only management tool for asymmetric risk management available to customers were exchange traded options, usually on government bond rates or, to a lesser extent, over the counter markets in options on government bond rates.

Options on swaps are much more flexible than exchange traded options markets with the user being able to specify exercise dates, amounts, specific exercise rates and other structural aspects without the constraint of standardised exchange options and their administrative procedures such as deposits and margins. A particular advantage of options on swaps for borrowers or investors who traditionally use swaps to manage their portfolios is that such structures provide an option on the all-in fixed costs of funds and, consequently, avoid the risks associated with changing spreads between swap rates and underlying government bond rates on which exchange traded and over the counter options are available.

Two examples of utilising options on swaps are set out in *Exhibit 16.1*.

Exhibit 16.1

Using Options on Swaps

Example 1

Company A (A) has a six month US$ LIBOR facility for US$100m. The company is tendering to construct a plant estimated to cost US$100m.

The project manager needs to submit a fixed cost of funding this project to the finance director on 15 January 19X6. However, studies will not be completed until 31 March 19X6, and the contract will not be awarded until 15 April 19X6. The project manager needs to fix the cost of five year funds based on current information for a project that will not begin for at least three months, and will not necessarily be awarded to the company.

Exhibit 16.1—continued

On 15 December 19X5 it was decided that there was no need to buy a swaption because of wasted time value. The swaption could be purchased, it was decided, next month at a lower premium. One month later the finance director agreed to buy a European style swaption at a premium of 2.00% of the principal. The company on exercise will pay a fixed interest rate of 10.00% pa and will receive LIBOR semi-annually for five years. The exercise date is 15 April 19X6.

On 15 April 19X6 the contract is awarded to A. The pay off to A in this case would be as follows:

Scenario 1

Interest rates increase to 12.00% therefore A agrees to exercise swaption.

Current interest rate:	12.00%
Swaption rate:	10.00%
Benefit from exercising swaption:	2.00%
2.00% × $100,000,000 × five years	US$10,000,000
Less cost of premium	−US$ 2,000,000
Total savings (on an undiscounted basis)	US$ 8,000,000

Cost of swap funding will be approximately 10.55% pa, 1.45% less than the current interest rate of 12.00%. A has ensured through the swaption that the cost of funding for the project will not be greater than the presumably acceptable level of 10.55% pa.

Scenario 2

Interest rates decrease to 8.00%. A abandons the swaption and enters into a swap transaction at a fixed rate of 8.00%.

Cost of funding achieved is 8.50% by taking advantage of lower interest rates.

Example 2

Interest charges on the US$ floating debt of company B (B) increased in the past year. B is considering actions to rectify this situation, but is unwilling to swap the floating debt into fixed debt because it believes interest rates will drop.

On 15 January 19X6 B purchases a European style option on a rate of 10.00% whereby the company on exercise will pay an annual fixed rate of 10.00% and will receive LIBOR semi-annually for five years. The premium is 2.00% of US$25m. The exercise date is 1 July 19X6.

On 1 July 19X6, B decide to exercise the option because rates have increased to 14.00%. This will allow B to fix its swap cost of funds for five years at 10.00%.

The benefits of this strategy are as follows:

4.00% × $25,000,000 × five years	US$5,000,000
2.00% premium	−US$ 500,000
Total savings (on an undiscounted basis)	US$4,500,000

The company achieves fixed rate funding at a rate of 10.58% pa after incorporation of the premium cost. If rates had fallen, B could have let the option lapse taking advantage of lower available market swap rates. For example, if swap rates fell to 6.00% pa, B would achieve an all-in swap cost of 6.47% pa.

While the discussion to date has focused on options on interest rate swaps, similar structures involving options on interest rates on a particular currency can be devised in currency swaps. Such structures can entail an interest rate swap alone or, where the exchange rate on the currency swap at which the initial and final exchange are to be transacted are known in advance, an option on currencies can also be created. This type of option is usually structured as a contingent swap which is discussed in detail later in this chapter.

CALLABLE AND PUTABLE SWAPS

A callable or putable swap is a natural extension of the concept of an option on a swap. As noted above, the terminology in this context is potentially confusing. Accordingly, it is necessary at the outset to define the various transaction structures.

From the perspective of a fixed rate payer:

- A *callable swap* allows the fixed rate payer to enter into, at its option, swaps, up to a maximum amount, at a known cost, up until the end of the expiry of the option, in which it pays a fixed rate and receives a floating rate (that is, this is similar to the option on swaps described above).

- In the case of a *putable swap* a fixed rate payer has the option to terminate the swap at some future date without further penalty by selling it to the provider of the putable swap.

A number of other terms are also used to describe these types of transactions. For example, a putable swap is often referred to as a "cancellable" or "terminable" swap. A variation is the extendible swap which allows a fixed rate *receiver* to, at its option, enter into a swap at or up until some future date.

The party entering into the callable (putable) swap usually compensates the swap provider, for the additional flexibility of the call (put) provision, either by payment of an upfront premium or an adjustment built into the swap rate (reflecting the amortisation of the premium at a nominated funding cost).

Callable and putable swap structures have been utilised, primarily, in two situations:

- in conjunction with capital market issues which have implicit call and/or put options on the underlying debt security;

- in conjunction with asset swaps where the underlying fixed rate security has an uncertain life, as a result of call options embedded in the original issue terms.

Callable and putable swaps have been utilised usually in conjunction with callable or putable capital market issues. In this regard, these transactions represent the initial attempts to securitise the value of options embedded in debt securities, a process which has culminated in the option swaps described in detail in Chapter 17.

For example, a number of floating rate payers entered into transactions allowing them to enter into additional amounts of a swap, under which they received fixed rates in return for paying floating rates, during a specified period of sometimes up to five years. One of the first such swaps allowed the counterparty to call additional amounts of the swap when fixed rates fell in the future. These swaps were created to allow issuers to undertake bond issues with attached warrants for additional bonds. If the warrants were exercised, additional amounts of the swap could be called to convert the fixed rate funds into floating rate debt. The counterparty, who was effectively providing a call option, received an up-front premium for providing the option in return for absorbing the risk that rates might fall and the warrants would be exercised. The callable swap served to guarantee the borrower's spread below LIBOR on the additional funds raised. Debt warrant swaps are examined in Chapter 17.

These early callable and putable swap structures were eventually combined with issues of callable debt in highly sophisticated and complex transactions designed to effectively arbitrage the value of interest rate options between various markets. In 1986 and 1987 and again in early 1989, a significant volume of transactions, primarily in US$, combined a callable issue of debt securities with an associated putable swap.

The basic structure entailed a borrower issuing say five, seven or ten year debt securities which were non-callable for three or five years. After the expiry of the call protection period, the borrower could redeem the issue usually at par or with the payment of a very slight premium. The borrowers, in these cases, utilised these fixed rate issues as a basis for creating a synthetic floating rate borrowing. Consequently, the borrower would inevitably enter into a simultaneous swap wherein it received fixed rates and paid floating rates. The interest rate swaps, however, had an additional feature whereby the swap counterparty, paying fixed rates, had the right to terminate the swap at a future date, coinciding with the call date of the underlying bond. For example, in the situation described above, the five year issue might be swapped with the counterparty who agreed to pay fixed rates for five years and receive floating rate but with the added right to cancel the swap after three years.

The economics of such transactions was predicated on the swap counterparty paying a premium to the borrower who thereby achieved a lower floating rate cost of funding. If interest rates fell, the swap counterparty would exercise its put option and cancel the agreement. Simultaneously, the borrower would then have the right to terminate the overall borrowing by exercising its call option on its debt securities. If, however, interest rates rose, the swap counterparty would be unlikely to terminate the swap which would run its full term and the borrower would have achieved a cheaper cost of funding than it might otherwise have had available to it over the full five year term.

The internal economics of these transactions relied on the borrower's call option on its debt essentially offsetting the put option on the swap that it was creating in favour of the swap counterparty. Logically, investors should demand a higher yield on callable bonds because of the interest rate risk they assume and it would be expected that this increase in yield would offset any premium received from the swap counterparty for the cancellation rights. However, the fact was that the amount investors charged, by way of higher yields on the securities, for providing the borrower with a call option was substantially below what the swap counterparties were willing to pay for the right to cancel the swap. Consequently, the opportunity existed to securitise the call option on the debt securities via the putable swap to effectively allow the borrower to achieve a lower all-in cost of funding.

The counterparties for these swaps were borrowers seeking to hedge interest rate risk but also seeking some capacity to benefit from a favourable rate movement. However, some counterparties entered into such putable swaps merely to buy the underlying call option on interest rates implicit in the putable swap.

For example, in November 1987, Salomon Brothers, in a difficult market, brought approximately US$1.85 billion of fixed rate debt involving putable swaps to market. While the rationale for these transactions was not made public, observers speculated that the transactions were driven by an internal need by Salomon Brothers to purchase call options on United States Treasuries. Under one theory, the US Investment Bank was using the options to hedge positions in its proprietary option book whereby it had previously sold Treasury bond options or interest rate cap positions. Under an alternative theory, Salomon Brothers was using the putable swaps to hedge prepayment of mortgage backed securities, either in its own portfolio, or a portfolio which it had sold to a client.

An example of a transaction involving a putable swap is set out in *Exhibit 16.2*.

Exhibit 16.2
Callable Bond Issue Combined with Putable Swap

Terms of bond

Issue date:	15/10/X1
Maturity:	15/10/X8
Coupon:	10.00% pa
Call provisions:	At par on 15/10/X6 and 15/10/X7
Issue price:	100

Terms of putable swap

Maturity	15/10/X8
Fixed rate:	10.00% pa
Floating rate:	LIBOR−25bps
Put provisions:	At par on 15/10/X8 and 15/10/X7
Swap premium:	1.25% pa flat

The combined transaction results in the following case flows for years one to five of the transaction:

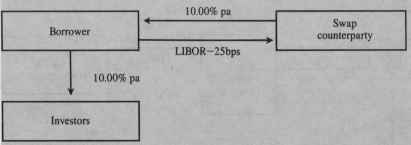

The all-in cost of funds to the borrower, after the proceeds of the up-front premium are factored in, is LIBOR−51bps (assuming a discount rate of 10.25% pa).

If the swap is cancelled under the put on the swap, the borrower calls the underlying bond which means it achieves lower cost funding but for a shorter period:

6 years:	LIBOR−54bps
5 years:	LIBOR−58bps

In early 1987, Banque Nationale de Paris (BNP) undertook an interesting variation on this basic structure which also coincidentally was one of the first callable interest rate swaps denominated in £. In this transaction, BNP issued a seven year £ bond with a coupon of 10.00%, callable after five years at 100.25, with the call premium declining by 0.125% pa. BNP simultaneously entered into a five year £ swap to generate floating rate £ funding. The only unusual feature of this swap was that it was for a period of *five years*. BNP also entered into a forward £ interest rate swap commencing in five years' time for a period of two years. This forward swap commenced at the call date of the underlying bond and at the maturity of the five year £ interest rate swap. Both swaps were on identical terms.

The provider of the £ forward swap, Kleinwort Benson, simultaneously purchased the right to terminate a two year interest rate swap in five years' time. This putable option on the swap somewhat confusingly allowed Kleinwort to put or terminate the swap with BNP. In effect, if Kleinwort

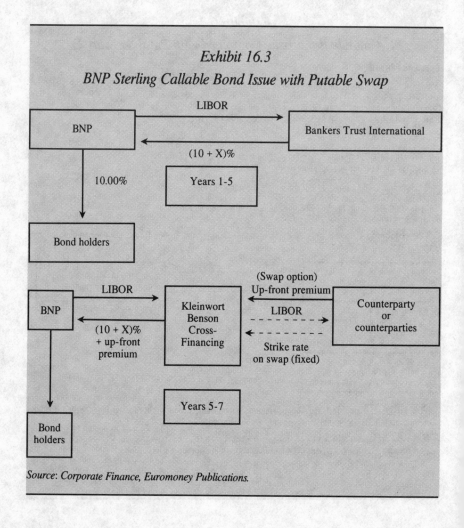

Exhibit 16.3

BNP Sterling Callable Bond Issue with Putable Swap

Source: Corporate Finance, Euromoney Publications.

Benson chose at the end of five years not to enter into the two year swap, BNP would merely call its underlying £ bonds, thereby eliminating any exposure as a result of the expiry of the original swap. From the perspective of BNP, the premium received for the provision of this putable swap was significantly greater than the higher yield it paid on the bonds for the right to retire the securities after five years. This allowed BNP to achieve significant reductions in its overall cost borrowing in this transaction. The BNP transaction is set out in *Exhibit 16.3.*

Other variations include issues of callable fixed rate debt (say seven year with a call right as at year 3 combined with a *3 year* swap under which it receives fixed rate and pays a floating rate. Simultaneously, the issuer sells the option for a counterparty to pay fixed rates under a swap *commencing at year 3*. If interest rates fell and the option to enter into the swap at year 3 was not exercised, then the issuer called the underlying debt. If the option on the swap was exercised, then the issue was *not* called and the issuer enjoyed floating rates for the full term of the issue at a favourable rate. This type of structure is particularly attractive in an environment when borrowers seek protection against potential interest rate increases but are anxious to preserve the opportunity to benefit from decreases in rates.

Putable swaps have also been utilised in asset swapped transactions where the underlying asset is a callable bond. The putable swap allows investors to enter into transactions whereby a fixed rate bond, which is callable, is swapped into a floating rate basis. If the bond is called, the investor can terminate the original swap by cancelling or putting the swap to the provider of the putable swap option. This allows the investor to terminate the swap at the time the underlying fixed rate security is called away.

Such asset based putable swap transactions were extremely important in the development of this particular type of swap structure. As discussed in detail in Chapter 18, asset swaps where synthetic floating rate assets at attractive spreads relative to LIBOR are created have been an important component of the growth of the swap market. However, there has been a limited universe of non-callable fixed rate bonds. As a result many of the bonds used in the asset based swaps have embedded call options.

When in 1986, interest rates fell sharply, the assets were called away with investors being left with interest rate swap positions with high fixed coupons. In the lower interest rate environment, similar quality, high yielding replacement assets were not available and the swaps were expensive to reverse, creating losses for investors. Putable swaps were structured as a means of mitigating these losses resulting from early redemption in asset swap transactions.

In addition, this type of structure can be utilised to swap assets which have uncertain lives. This can be particularly important in structuring asset swaps against mortgage and receivable backed securities. An example of an asset based putable swap is set out in *Exhibit 16.4.*

Exhibit 16.4
Asset Based Putable Swaps

Terms of bond

Maturity:	15/3/X7
Coupon:	10.00% (S/A)
Call provisions	
(date and price):	15/3/X4 to 14/3/X5 @ 103
	15/3/X5 to 14/3/X6 @ 102
	15/3/X6 to 14/3/X7 @ 101
	15/3/X7 @ 100
Bond price:	102.50

Terms of putable swap

Maturity:	15/3/X7
Up-front payment:	2.50 paid to investor
	(swap buyer pays fixed)
Fixed coupon:	10.00% (S/A)
Floating coupon:	LIBOR + 136
Put provisions	
(date and price):	15/3/X4 to 14/3/X5 for three points
	15/3/X5 to 14/3/X6 for two points
	15/3/X6 to 14/3/X7 for one point
Option type:	Deferred American
All-in cost of non-putable swap:	8.00%
Cost of put option:	24bps

The initial cash flows under this transaction are as follows:

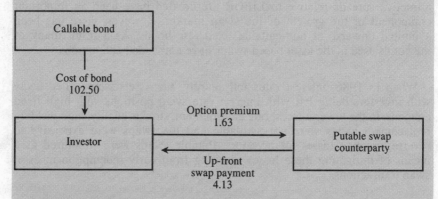

Net up-front payment to investor: 4.13 − 1.63 = 2.50.
Net cost to investor: 102.50 + 1.63 − 4.13 = 100.00.
The up-front payment of 2.50% to the investor represents the net of the up-front swap payment that the investor would *receive* for agreeing to pay what is effectively an above market fixed coupon, and the fact that the investor must *pay* for the put option on the swap.

Exhibit 16.4—continued

The investor's cash flow on each interest payment date will be as follows:

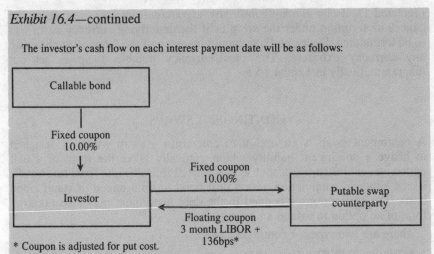

* Coupon is adjusted for put cost.

Note that, in fact, the 136bps amount is based on the assumption that the investor exercises its right to put the swap if and only if the underlying bond is called. However, the investor may be able to exercise its put option, even if the bond is not called, and buy another swap at more favourable terms. It may also be possible that when the issuer calls the bond, the investor would do better by selling the swap in the market than by exercising its put to cancel the swap.

If the bond is called as per the schedule, say on 15 March 19X4, the investor is paid 103.00% by the issuer, but passes 3.00% to the swap counterparty for the right to cancel the swap. This effectively gives the investor back its initial investment of 100.

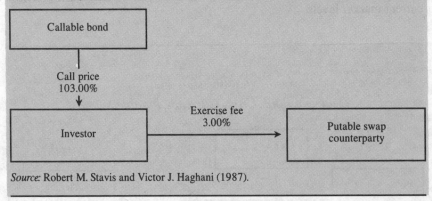

Source: Robert M. Stavis and Victor J. Haghani (1987).

While the discussion to date has been confined to callable and putable swaps in one currency, it is possible to extend the concept to currency swaps. For example, in 1987, Deutsche Bank undertook an issue of £75m for ten years. The issue was callable after seven years. Deutsche Bank swapped the sterling funds raised into US$ LIBOR by entering into a *ten year* £/US$ LIBOR currency swap. Kleinwort Benson, the swap counterparty, however, required the right to terminate the swap after seven years. Deutsche Bank received a substantial up-front premium in return for selling Kleinwort the right to terminate the swap, presumably utilising the proceeds to lower its cost relative to US$ LIBOR. The call option implicit in the £ bond issue protected Deutsche Bank against any exposure from the exercise of the cancellation option under the swap as if the underlying currency swap was to be terminated, Deutsche Bank would merely call the £ bonds to eliminate any currency exposure. The cross-currency putable swap is set out diagrammatically in *Exhibit 16.5*.

CONTINGENT SWAPS

A contingent swap is an option to enter into a swap which is designed to hedge a contingent liability which generally takes the form of a call option on debt instruments, such as warrants exercisable into fixed rate bonds, issued either in conjunction with a host bond or on a naked or stand alone basis. The call option embedded in the debt instrument may also take the form of an option to extend an existing issue.

There are two types of contingent swaps:

- a contingent interest rate swap;
- a contingent currency swap.

The contingent interest rate swap entails purely an interest rate option. A contingent currency swap may entail either a purely interest rate option, or alternatively a combined interest rate and currency option.

A contingent swap structure designed to hedge a naked debt warrant issue illustrates the mechanics of a contingent swap. In this example, a contingent swap is tied to debt warrants exerciseable at interest rates below current market levels.

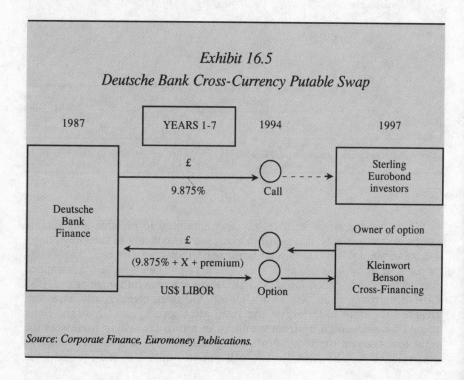

Exhibit 16.5
Deutsche Bank Cross-Currency Putable Swap

Source: *Corporate Finance, Euromoney Publications.*

When the warrants are issued, the two parties enter into a contingent swap agreement and the fixed rate payer receives an up-front fee from the issuer of the warrants. The swap becomes effective if and when the warrants are exercised and is identical to a traditional interest rate or currency swap.

If interest rate levels rise or remain constant, it is likely that the warrants will expire unexercised and the contingent swap provider will keep the commitment fee. If, however, interest rates fall, the warrants are likely to be exercised and the two parties will enter into the swap as the contingent swap is triggered.

The contingent swap structure generates significant savings compared to a standard swap. This saving is generated from two sources:

- The fixed interest rate on a contingent swap is generally substantially below the current market level.
- The fixed rate payer receives an up-front commitment fee which, if the warrants expire unexercised, will be retained as income or, if the warrants are exercised, will lower the all-in cost of the swap.

The issuer of the warrants, meantime, is insulated from the fixed rate level on the swap. If the warrants are exercised it immediately translates its fixed rate funding into floating rate funds, usually at a predetermined margin under a floating rate index, which compares favourably to its alternative cost of floating rate funds.

An example of a naked warrant issue and accompanying contingent swap is set out in *Exhibit 16.6*.

Exhibit 16.6
Naked Warrants Issue and Contingent Swap Structure

Institution A (A) issues warrants exercisable into A$ bonds on the following terms:

Back bonds

Amount:	A$50m
Term:	Five years
Coupon:	14.00% pa (A)

Warrants

Number of warrants:	50,000 (based on assumed exchange rate) each exercisable into A$1,000 bonds on above terms.
Assumed exchange rate:	US$0.70/A$1.00 (see discussion below)
Warrant price:	(See discussion below)
Expiry date:	The warrants will expire, unless exercised approximately one year after issue (that is, February 19X7). The warrant can be exercised at any point in time before expiry

Institution B (B) provides a contingent currency swap on the following terms:

Amount:	A$50m
Term:	Five years
B to pay A:	14.00% pa (A)
B to receive from A:	Six month LIBOR
Up-front fee:	(See discussion below)
Commencement date:	The swap can be triggered at any time within one year after issue (that is, by February 19X7) at the option of A

Exhibit 16.6—continued

The rationale for the transaction is as follows:

- issuer (A) is indifferent as, if warrants are exercised, it triggers contingent swap to achieve margin under LIBOR;
- purchaser of warrant gets a highly leveraged A$ interest rate play (possibly a currency play if exchange rate is fixed: see below);
- contingent swap provider (B) must get attractively priced funding if the contingent swap is called upon.

From B's perspective:

- B can obtain funding at say 14.70% pa (S/A) (15.24% pa (A)) for six years (the A$ bond rate);
- B can obtain funding for one year (the swap option period) at 17.00% pa (S/A);
- consequently, if B can obtain funding at less than 14.24% (S/A) (14.75% pa (A)) in one year from now, it can effect a cost saving.

The pricing dynamics of the transaction are complex. Assume:

- A requires LIBOR minus 25bps; and
- B requires 13.75% pa (A) (13.25% pa (S/A)) if warrants and contingent swap are triggered to undertake the transaction.

Given these assumptions, it is possible to structure the transaction:

- B requires 25bps under 14.00%:

  —25bps on A$50m = A$125,000 pa;
  —discounted back at 15.24% pa (A) (the bond rate) this equates to A$416,649 (US$291,654 at the assumed exchange rate);
  —however, the swap may not be exercised for up to a maximum of one year, that is, B gets investment earning at 15.24% pa (A) for this period, therefore allowing the up-front payment to be reduced (PV at 15.24% pa) to A$361,549 (US$253,084);
  —therefore, depending on assumption of timing of warrant and swap exercise, B would need between US$253,084 to US$291,654 to achieve 13.75% pa (A).

- A requires 25bps under LIBOR:

  —25bps on US$35m (A$50m @ US$0.70/A$1.00) = US$87,500;
  —discounted back at 10.00% pa (A) this equates to US$331,694;
  —depending on assumption of timing of warrant and swap exercise (see above discussion) A would need between US$301,540 and US$331,694 to achieve 25bps spread under LIBOR.

Given the size of the up-front payment to A and B the warrants would have to be sold for at least:

$$\left[\frac{(US\$253,084 + US\$301,540)}{50,000} \right] = US\$11.09$$

$$\left[\frac{(US\$291,654 + US\$331,694)}{50,000} \right] = US\$12.47$$

Any price over and above that amount would be profit for the investment bank structuring and executing the transaction.

B may, in fact, require a considerably higher payment to enter into the contingent swap if it analyses the transaction in terms of option theory to price the implicit interest rate option it is creating.

Assume that the warrants are sold for US$24.00 per warrant (net of fees, commissions and expenses). This will result in a net inflow of US$1,200,000 (50,000 warrants @ US$24.00 each). The warrant proceeds received are utilised as follows:

- A is paid US$331,694 for acting as the issuer of the warrants.
- B is paid US$291,654 for entering into the contingent swap.
- The surplus of US$576,652 is retained by the investment bank.

Exhibit 16.6—continued

The position for all participants in this transaction under different interest rate scenarios, is as follows:

Scenario	Warrant holder or buyer	Warrant issuer or seller	Contingent swap provider
Bond rates increase above 14.00% pa (A)	Warrants not exercised	Retains up-front payment US$0.30m	Retains up-front payment of US$0.25-US$0.30m
Bond rates decrease below 14.00% pa (A)	Warrants exercised	Obtain funding at LIBOR less 25bps	Obtain fixed rate funding at 13.75% pa: A provided it funds at LIBOR flat; *only* if rates have gone below 13.75% pa for five years would B register an *opportunity* loss

For the contingent swap provider, the opportunity loss may not be relevant, say where it has an ongoing need for substantial fixed rate funding or is running an asset liability gap, for example, for a bank with high yielding fixed rate loans on its books, it may be happy to take on the liability at an appropriate rate in any case.

As a variation, the A$/US$ exchange rate on exercise of the warrant can be fixed at or near the spot rate on the date of launch or settlement.

This has the following effects:

- The purchaser of the warrants has a currency option as well as an interest rate option, that is, if the A$ appreciates irrespective of interest rate movements, the warrant may have value. The purchaser gives up the opportunity of paying less US$ to buy the bond if the A$ depreciates, but the decline in A$ is reflected in the lower US$ value of the underlying bond.

- The issuer is indifferent because it knows the maximum cost of US$ funding it is obtaining, if the exchange rate is not fixed:
  —if the A$ appreciates, it gets less US$ and achieves a higher margin under LIBOR;
  —if the A$ depreciates it gets more US$ and achieves a lower margin under LIBOR.

- The contingent swap provider is in this case granting a foreign exchange option on the A$/US$ rate. Consequently, it has an exposure to an appreciation in the A$ where it would suffer a loss as it would receive less A$ or conversely it would have to borrow more US$ to support the currency swap if it was to be triggered.

Contingent swaps have special appeal to organisations with specific fixed rate financing targets below current market levels. A contingent swap entered into at the target level can provide such organisations with attractive fixed rate funding. Alternatively, organisations with large swap requirements can use contingent swaps as one component of a swap programme.

The concept of an interest rate swap which is contingent is easily extendible to a currency swap. However, the translation of the contingent swap concept into the domain of currency swaps need *not* entail a foreign exchange option. However, where the underlying debt warrants are exerciseable into foreign currency bonds and say the US$ amount required to buy the relevant bonds is fixed at the outset, the warrants entail both a specific interest rate and currency option which is usually covered by the contingent currency swap.

In late 1985 a true currency option swap was created by Credit Commercial de France (CCF). CCF structured such a swap by issuing a US$ floating rate note for the first counterparty with attached warrants into an ECU issue. A contingent swap was then written with a second counterparty who wished to borrow ECU. If the warrants are exercised, then the contingent swap is invoked and the second counterparty pays the fixed rate coupons on the ECU bonds. The first counterparty then pays US$ LIBOR to cover the second counterparty's interbank funding cost. The investors purchased the warrants for a premium which reflected their estimation of the potential currency and interest rate option value. Since the ECU bond warrant premium is shared by both counterparties, the first party effectively raises dollars at a sub-LIBOR rate while the second counterparty raises fixed rate ECU at a borrowing cost well below current market levels, assuming that the warrants are exercised.

The earliest type of currency option swaps were those written by banks which allowed a corporate counterparty to increase the face amount of a currency swap at any time during the first six to 12 months of the transaction. The primary value of this type of option is that it gives the counterparty the opportunity to wait until spot currency rates are favourable. Although the interest rates on additional amounts of the swap remained unchanged under these transactions, the incremental principal amounts were calculated at the new exchange rates. Thus they can perhaps best be referred to as interest rate option swaps and not true currency option swaps.

Contingent currency swaps involving deutschmarks were also pioneered by CCF with an issue of 250,000 warrants to buy a 6.375% deutschmark bond attached to a US$250m floating rate note issue. If the warrants are exercised, a swap is automatically triggered whereby a counterparty agrees, in return for an option premium, to assume the fixed deutschmark liability on CCF's behalf and receive US$ coupon payments. CCF has thus hedged its currency exposure into US$ should the warrants be exercised. Similar deals were undertaken by Swedbank and PK Banken.

More recently the swap market has developed the concept of contingent swap off-warrant issues into a more pragmatic structure, providing both corporations and banks with the opportunity to convert liabilities from one currency into another if they choose over a period of time. One variation on the contingent swap theme is the contingent basis swap, where floating debt in one currency may be exchanged for floating debt in another currency.

PRICING OPTIONS ON SWAPS

Options and swaps represent combinations of the primary features of swaps and options on interest rates. Consequently, the pricing of options on swaps, predictably, is based on traditional option pricing theories. In essence, an option on a swap is the purchase or sale of an option on the fixed rate component of the swap.

The pricing of options on swaps reflects the underlying options embodied within the swap structure. This option price is usually captured as the option premium on an appropriate put or call option on government bonds in the relevant currency. This reflects the fact that these options are typically used to hedge positions created by writing options on swaps.

For example, where a counterparty provides a corporation with a putable swap, it may hedge its exposure by purchasing a call option on the appropriate government security. Similarly, a market maker may hedge its exposure under a callable swap by purchasing an appropriate put option on a government security.

It is important to note that the purchase of options on government securities is not necessarily a perfect hedge as effectively options on swaps entail separate options on interest rates on government securities and on the swap spread. The option on the swap spread is usually more difficult to hedge.

The primary determinants of the price or premiums payable on options on swaps include:

- the effective fixed rate level;
- swap maturity;
- exercise payments;
- time outstanding until exercise.

The level of effective fixed rates on the swap are one of the key determinants of the value of the option on the swap. For example, the higher the effective fixed coupon (fixed rate minus any spread relative to the variable index) under the swap, the greater the value of being able to put the swap back to the counterparty and, conversely, the lower the value of being able to enter into the swap. Consequently, if all other parameters are held constant, the higher the fixed rate payable under the swap, the more valuable (less valuable) is the option to, at some future date, terminate (enter into) the swap for a fixed exercise fee.

However, the net effect on the total cost to a borrower or investor is more complex. For example, in the case of a putable swap, while the value of the put option rises as the effective fixed rate on the swap is increased, the premium generated up-front by a higher effective coupon on the underlying swap increases at a faster rate. Consequently, although an increase in the fixed rate raises the cost of the put option, the net effect on the package may be a decrease in the up-front fee paid by the purchaser of the putable swap.

The greater the exercise payment that must be paid to exercise the option, the lower is the value of the option on the swap. In essence, a large positive exercise payment can be equated to an increasingly out-of-the-money option with the consequent impact on the value of the option on the swap.

Generally, the longer the time to final maturity of the underlying swap as at the exercise date of the option on the swap, the more valuable the option on that swap will be. This reflects the increased price sensitivity of the swap with the longer maturity.

The impact of outstanding time until exercise in the case of options on swaps can be complex. For example, if the time to expiration of a European swap option is extended, holding the maturity of the swap constant, a variety of factors begin to influence its value. While the increasing period to expiration of the option increases the premium, the fact that the underlying swap is ageing over the life of the option may, in fact, lower the value of the put option. In the limiting case, where the expiration date of the option equals the maturity date of the swap the option will, in theory, have no value.

Chapter 17

Option Swaps

OPTION EMBEDDED SECURITIES TRANSACTIONS AND OPTION SWAPS

The term option swaps refers to transactions involving the purchase or sale of options on financial instruments and commodities. The structures essentially entail the securitisation of options embedded in securities issues.

Option swaps are strictly speaking not classical swap transactions as they primarily entail a series of option trades. However, they are included for the following reasons:

* It is very common to incorporate a swap within the overall transaction structure to change the currency or interest rate basis of the borrowing as the option element in the transaction is merely designed to create the basis for a lower cost borrowing transaction for the issuer.
* These option swaps are usually originated, structured and executed by the swap desks of financial intermediaries.
* The basic underlying premise of such transactions, involving arbitrage between various sectors of the capital market, as discussed below, is identical with the rationale of other types of swap transactions.

The swap incorporated in such transactions, either interest rate or currency, involves a considerable degree of structuring in itself. For example, it is common to utilise a premium or discount swap structure or a swap with accelerated or deferred cash flows to match the uneven pattern of cash flows generated by the underlying option embedded security.

As noted above, these types of swaps have their origin in a whole new class of securities which emerged in international capital markets in about 1985. The majority of these securities have been structured with options embedded in the basic security structure. The options embedded in these capital market issues include options on debt instruments and interest rates, currencies and stock indexes. In most cases, from the viewpoint of the issuer, the transaction structure is predicated on the necessity of shielding the borrower from the option elements of the security itself. This is achieved through the option swap which inevitably accompanies the securities transaction.

These types of structures have elicited considerable interest from investors and issuers. From the viewpoint of issuers, the fact that they typically have no exposure to the option ffectively created has meant that high quality issuers have utilised these types of securities issues as the vehicle for classical new issue arbitrage. In contrast, investors have been attracted to these securities for more complex reasons including:

294

- The inability of certain key groups of investors, such as Japanese institutions, to purchase or write options on financial instruments because of regulatory restrictions which have the effect of restricting their portfolio management strategies.
- Several investors have sought to use these types of securities to hedge offsetting positions in the underlying commodity or instrument.
- Such transactions typically create options for longer periods than otherwise available thereby increasing the risk transfer opportunities for various market participants.

An important aspect of utilising capital markets to create these particular types of options is that these transactions are usually based upon arbitraging various segments of the market seeking to capitalise on the differing values placed on the same option by different participants.

It is evident that on a number of occasions investors have created options implicit in securities below their theoretical economic price. This has allowed option writers to lock in a profit by granting an option from its own portfolio and hedging the risk position with the option purchased from the underlying capital market issue. For example, in a number of the currency option transactions involving capital market issues, high option premiums in the short-term market have allowed option purchasers to strip off and buy the option created through the issue and recoup the bulk of the premium by granting options different in maturity as part of an ongoing granting programme.

The anomalous pricing features of these transactions are not capable of ready explanation. One argument often offered is that investors may view the purchase of an option linked security fundamentally differently to the granting of options. Key factors in this regard include the relative liquidity of the instruments, the income stream attaching to a security as distinct from an option, as well as attitudes towards and capacity to absorb risk.

It is important to distinguish these option embedded securities transactions and the accompanying option swaps from a totally different class of securities issues which emerged primarily in late 1986 and early 1987. During this period, a significant number of transactions entailing the issue of debt accompanied by commodity or currency warrants appeared in various capital markets. These transactions were designed to take advantage of particularly attractive spreads between so-called wholesale or institutional option prices and what retail customers and investors were willing to pay for similar options. For example, in late 1987, a number of United States investment banks arranged issues of foreign currency options, mainly US$ and yen or US$ and deutschmark currency options in the United States domestic market. The issuers in each case hedged their own exposure under the foreign currency option by buying an identical option from a small group of institutions willing to write such options. The profit from these transactions resulted from the fact that buyers at a retail level for these options were willing to pay up to say 9.00% option premiums which was significantly higher than the price at which the issuer could cover its exposures by the purchase of an identical option in the interbank or wholesale market, usually between say 5.00-6.00% premiums.

There are basically three types of option swaps, reflecting the three categories of option embedded securities transactions:

- interest rate option swaps;
- foreign exchange or currency option swaps;
- stock index option swaps.

INTEREST RATE OPTION SWAPS

Interest rate option swaps involving embedded options on debt instruments and interest rates, include issues of capped FRNs and certificates of deposit (CD), issues of debt warrants, either on a stand alone (or naked) basis or, in conjunction, with the issue of debt securities, and issues of securities where the redemption amount is linked to fluctuations in the value of an identified debt security.

Capped, mini-max and floor FRNs

In the case of capped FRN and CD issues, typically, the issues were seven to 12 year FRN or two to five year CD issues with ceilings on interest payments undertaken by highly rated borrowers, primarily banks or sovereign entities. Investors in the issues, in return for accepting a ceiling on their yield, received a higher than normal current coupon or margin on the FRNs and CDs.

Capped FRN issues were initially undertaken in June 1985 in US$ in the Euromarkets. This was followed by the emergence of a capped floating rate CD market which has enjoyed more sustained interest. The capped FRN concept has also been extended beyond US$ with a series of issues in deutschmarks and in Dutch guilders. Later variations include delayed cap FRNs where the maximum interest rates do not operate for the first three to four years.

A variation on the capped FRN structure was the maximum rate notes (MRNs). MRNs involved the issue of fixed rate debt combined with a nominated cap rate on a floating rate index (such as six month LIBOR). If six month LIBOR exceeds the cap rate, the fixed rate coupon decreases by the same amount. Functionally, MRNs operate in the same way as capped FRNs.

The concept of a capped FRN issue has been utilised in Australia. In late 1987, the State Electricity Commission of Western Australia issued a capped FRN in A$ with effectively, a cap on the Australian BBR. The cap implicit in the transaction was securitised in much the same way as similar issues in other markets. A number of other private transactions in the Australian domestic market are known to have been contemplated.

The ceiling, which is structurally identical to a put option on the underlying short-term interest rate index, is sold to third parties with the proceeds of the sale, the option premium, in effect, lowering the issuer's borrowing cost, usually below market rates. Where the market rates exceed the capped rate, the investor's return is limited to the specified ceiling allowing the purchaser of the cap to receive the difference between the cap and market rate from the issuer, thereby allowing it to establish a known maximum cost of funding.

The detailed structure of the transaction is more complex. For example the Banque Indosuez transaction, arranged by Shearson Lehman Brothers, which opened this market, was an issue of 12 year US$200m FRNs carrying an interest coupon of 0.375% over three month LIMEAN capped at 13.0625%. Shearsons arranged for the sale of the cap to a United States corporation. Indosuez pays out LIMEAN plus 0.375%, or 13.0625% to the holders of the FRNs if three month LIMEAN exceeds 13.0625%. For example, if rates go to 14.0625%, Indosuez pays 13.0625% to the FRN holders and 1.00% to Shearsons who passes it on to the purchaser of the cap to compensate it for rates rising above the cap level. Indosuez is compensated for the cap by a payment of 0.375% pa of the principal amount. Indosuez wanted this flow as a continuous quarterly flow, although it could have received it as a discounted lump sum. This brought Indosuez's cost of funds down to LIMEAN. To avoid any credit risk, the purchaser of the cap paid Shearsons a lump sum which was reinvested in some Treasury zero coupon securities which produced the quarterly income stream equivalent to 0.375% pa.

The structure of such a transaction is set out in *Exhibit 17.1.*

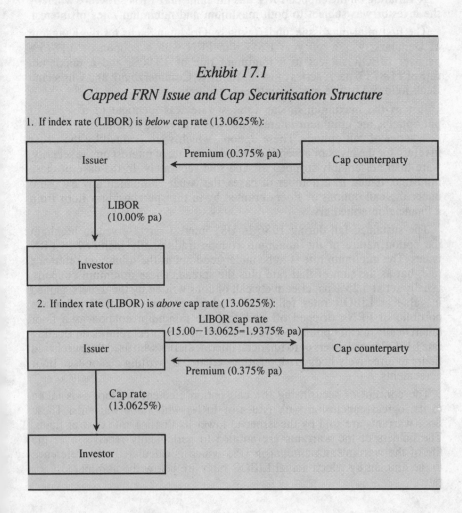

Exhibit 17.1
Capped FRN Issue and Cap Securitisation Structure

1. If index rate (LIBOR) is *below* cap rate (13.0625%):

Issuer ← Premium (0.375% pa) ← Cap counterparty

LIBOR (10.00% pa)

Investor

2. If index rate (LIBOR) is *above* cap rate (13.0625%):

Issuer → LIBOR cap rate (15.00−13.0625=1.9375% pa) → Cap counterparty

Issuer ← Premium (0.375% pa) ← Cap counterparty

Cap rate (13.0625%)

Investor

In an extension of this concept, an issue of securitised caps, effectively an issue of put options or warrants, was arranged by Banque Paribas Capital Markets in early 1987.

The structure of the capped FRN and its derivatives is that the issue was engineered such that the investors created out-of-the-money caps or put options on the underlying interest rate index. Analytically, the investor has written a *series* of put options expiring every three or six months until maturity on the underlying index. The premium paid to the investor is the higher spread on the FRN.

Studies undertaken to evaluate the pricing structure have concluded that the values implied for the caps are all low compared with theoretical values derived from historical levels of volatility. This undervaluation provided a significant arbitrage opportunity whereby certain organisations active in writing customised caps, usually by creating synthetic options (see discussion in Chapter 29) for higher premiums, purchased these caps stripped from the FRNs, etc. to effectively hedge their risk exposures.

A variation on the capped FRN was the mini-max FRN structure whereby the investor was subject to both maximum and minimum rates of interest.

The first mini-max issue, undertaken by Goldman Sachs for the Kingdom of Denmark, was a ten year US$250m FRN with a coupon of 0.1875% pa over LIBOR subject to a minimum rate of 10.00% and a maximum rate of 11.875% pa. A series of issues for SEK, Commerzbank and Christiana Bank followed before investor interest evaporated.

Just as the maximum or cap interest rate was identical to a series of put options, the minimum interest rate was analytically identical to a floor or a series of call options. These options, which were granted by the issuer in return for the investor accepting a maximum rate of interest on the security, were then presumably stripped off and sold separately. In the case of these mini-max issues, in a number of cases, the issuer eliminated any exposure under the call options or floors granted by in turn purchasing a floor from a financial intermediary.

The sustained fall during 1986 in US$ interest rates served to highlight the option nature of the minimum coupon traditionally included in FRN issues. The minimum rate is to be understood not as the minimum reference rate, but as the sum of that rate plus the spread. These minimum coupons, usually set at 5.25% pa, effectively call options written by the issuers, gained in value as LIBOR rates fell. In a number of cases, investors holding a portfolio of FRNs stripped off and sold the minimum coupon as a floor (analytically, a call option) to investors seeking to protect returns on floating rate LIBOR based assets or to financial intermediaries who used the purchased floors to effectively hedge risk positions created by writing customised floor agreements.

The concept of securitising the call option element or floor was taken to its logical conclusion with issues of FRNs with floor warrants. These floor warrants are sold by the issuer to lower its floating rate cost of funds. The holders of the warrants are entitled to periodically receive, over the life of the warrants, an amount in US$ which is calculated with reference to the amount by which actual LIBOR rates are below the nominated floor rate.

The concept was introduced in February 1986 by Banque Paribas in an issue for BATIF which was repeated in July 1986. An issue for Bank of Montreal, via Morgan Guaranty, was undertaken in June 1986.

The put and call options created by the capped, mini-max, etc. issues were, in fact, bought, substantially, by institutions active in the creation and sale of customised debt option facilities, usually in the form of floor, cap or collar agreements. The securitised options were purchased to match out the portfolio risk exposures of the market makers, allowing them to unwind (or reverse out of) other less efficient hedges.

Debt options and warrants

In recent years, a number of issues have entailed the offering of fixed rate bonds with attached warrants. The holders of the warrants acquire the right to purchase *further* fixed rate bonds of the issuer on predetermined terms. Issues of naked warrants, not linked to an issue of debt securities but usually accompanied by a contingent swap, have also been undertaken (see Chapter 16).

The warrants are effectively call options on the debt of the issuer created in exchange for the receipt of an explicit or implicit premium (that is, the premium may be built into a lower than market cost on a related issue of debt). From the borrower's viewpoint, the sale of warrants produces cash which reduces the cost of the borrower's total funding programme. This advantage can be translated into floating rate funding or funding in other currencies through a series of swaps, specially structured to accommodate the warrant issues.

In most transactions involving the issuance of debt options and warrants, the underlying funding has been swapped. The specific swap structure used can vary significantly depending on the overall structure of the debt warrant package. There are basically three general categories of swaps.

The first category is usually associated with naked warrant issues where a contingent swap is arranged (see Chapter 16).

The second and third categories of warrant swaps relate specifically to issues of warrants in conjunction with debt utilising one of two alternative arrangements:

- where the total package has an uncertain level of proceeds over its life and/or an uncertain maturity;
- debt warrant packages where the amount of debt remains relatively constant and the cost to the issuer does *not* change when and if the warrants are exercised.

The latter two categories of debt warrant swaps require elaboration.

For example, during 1984, expectations of falling rates saw a number of issues entailing the offering of fixed rate bonds with attached warrants which allowed the holder of the warrant the right to further purchase fixed rate bonds of the issuer at a predetermined coupon. The warrants which had lives of anywhere between one and seven years allowed the cost of the initial fixed rate debt to be reduced by the proceeds of the warrants. This resulted in a saving in yield of between 50 and 100bps relative to a conventional issue. The issuer was simultaneously exposed to issuing further

debt at a coupon cost equal to that of the fixed rate bonds into which the
warrants can be exercised which is generally 25 to 50bps lower than the
host coupon bond. Given that there are no issuance costs or fees on issuance
of the warrant bonds, the cost of the warrant bond can be 70 to 100bps
below the issuer's current fixed rate cost.

The overall yield savings (anywhere up to 100bps compared to a
conventional fixed rate offering) was achieved at the expense of not being
able to determine in advance how many of the warrants which create
additional debt will be exercised, or indeed when they will be exercised.
The issuer therefore had a known cost of debt, but an uncertain amount
of debt over the life of the transaction. For fixed rate issuers with absolute
interest rate targets, the uncertainty regarding the amount of debt was not
problematic. However, certain issuers were only attracted to a warrant issue
on the basis of the underlying issue being swapped into floating rate US$.

If the borrower could insulate against the cost of the prospective issuance
of additional fixed rate debt as a result of the warrants being exercised,
by being able to swap it into floating rate, then both parties could be
accommodated simultaneously. The borrower no longer has an exposure
to fixed interest rates, only to the uncertain amount of debt which might
be outstanding at any time.

The perfectly matched interest rate swap allowed the issuer to swap the
host issue immediately into floating rate US$ and provided for the swap
facility to be increased at any time to accommodate further amounts of
fixed debt created by the exercise of warrants. In the first few transactions
of this type, the warrant issuer was matched against a United States company
with a sizeable requirement to swap from floating to fixed rate funds which
had set itself interest rate hurdles at which it was willing to fix its cost
of funds. It was then willing to effectively create a series of out-of-the-
money call options on interest rate swaps whereby it was committed, where
a bond holder exercised a warrant, to enter into a swap with the bond issuer
on predefined terms, regardless of interest rate levels prevailing in the market
at the time the warrant was exercised. This structure allowed the issuer
to substantially shift the exposure of warrant exercise to the swap counterparty.

The cost of creating a swap which can be increased in size at a fixed
known interest rate level could, however, outweigh most or even all of the
advantages gained by issuing warrants. Consequently, the structure of warrant
swaps increasingly began to trade off the quantum of the spread below
LIBOR and warrant exercise risk. Typical warrant swap structures designed
to provide cost savings and limit risk would feature a seven year host bond
issue callable at par at any time after four years with attached warrants
with a life of four years. This structure was predicated on the assumption
that warrants are not usually exercised until near to their expiry date and
at their expiry date the host issue can be called. This capacity to call the
host bond, allows the issuer to have a degree of control over the amount
of debt outstanding, enabling it to keep the total volume of paper on issue
constant. The issue is combined with a standard seven year swap to convert
the fixed rate into floating with the value of the warrants being used to
subsidise the cost of the swap.

While originally the warrant swap structures proved popular, such
transactions required the willingness of a prime counterparty to commit

to a swap with a call option and as these counterparties found alternative outlets, the underlying warrant structures had to be considerably refined. The structure developed was the harmless debt warrant.

Pioneered by the Kingdom of Denmark, debt and warrant issue packages were created to ensure that the amount of the debt outstanding remained relatively constant and the cost of the issue did not change significantly if the warrants were exercised. The host bond was made callable at any time should warrants be exercised to ensure that the amount of debt outstanding remains constant enabling a standard interest rate swap to be executed. This alternative entails a higher cost of the host issue in terms of both coupon (approximately 0.125% pa) and call premium (approximately 1.00%). However, depending on the value of the attached warrants, the floating rate cost obtainable with this structure can be considerably better than a standard fixed rate issue without warrants. Under this structure, a conventional interest rate or (if applicable) currency swap could be utilised as the security issue's cash flows resemble a straight bond issue. This type of issue structure has increasingly gained in popularity.

This structure essentially gave borrowers access to cheap funds designed in most cases to be swapped into floating rate at extremely competitive levels with extremely limited exposure to the implicit call option. This is illustrated in *Exhibit 17.2* with the example of an issue for Westpac Banking Corporation.

A variation of the traditional warrant issue is the case of the putable bond or, its securitised extension, an issue of "put" warrants. Based on similar rationale to debt warrants, the proceeds of the implicit or securitised put option is designed to lower the borrower's cost of funds. As these issue structures provide the investor with the mechanism whereby, at its option, it can sell the bond back to the issuer at an agreed price, the structure creates a maturity uncertainty which is impossible to immunise. Where such issues have been swapped, the issuer would, where the basic debt is swapped, seek to protect its own exposure under the swap with an agreement with the swap counterparty to terminate the swap where the underlying debt was put back to the borrower.

Interest rate linked securities

The concept of embodying options on interest rates in capital market transactions has been extended in recent times to transactions where the implicit option is engineered through a variable redemption amount (originally introduced in the form of Treasury Indexed Notes).

This type of option swap is best illustrated by an example. The basic transaction entails the issue of debt securities bearing a higher than market coupon. However, the redemption amount, that is, the amount repaid to the investor at maturity, is linked to price fluctuations (and by implication yield movements) on an identified debt instrument, usually the 30 year United States Treasury bond. In a typical transaction, the coupon was 10.00% pa (approximately 200 to 250bps above the market yield) for three years with the redemption formula being as follows: if the benchmark 30 year United States Treasury bond at the end of three years (the maturity of the debt instrument) is at a break-even yield (say 7.10% pa) the bonds are redeemed

Exhibit 17.2

Westpac "Harmless" Debt Warrant Issue and Swap

The Westpac issue was on the following terms:

- US$100m ten year (maturing 1996) 10.00% pa coupon issued at 100 7/8 with 2.00% fees; issue callable after five years at 101 1/2, declining by 0.50% pa to par.

- 200,000 warrants @ US$50 each; two warrants are exercisable after five years into one 11.25% non-callable bond due 1996 at par (that is, US$100 per bond); during the first five years, the warrants pay 10.00% interest, and, if not exercised, they are each redeemable @ US$50 in 1996.

The table below shows the cash flow (US$m) to Westpac if the warrants are, or are not, exercised. It is assumed that the host bonds will be called if the warrants are exercised in years six to ten; the warrants will automatically be redeemed at maturity if they are not exercised.

Year warrants are exercised
(assume warrants exercised at year end)

Year	Not exercised	5	6	7	8	9	10
0	108.875	108.875	108.875	108.875	108.875	108.875	108.875
1	−11.000	−11.000	−11.000	−11.000	−11.000	−11.000	−11.000
2	−11.000	−11.000	−11.000	−11.000	−11.000	−11.000	−11.000
3	−11.000	−11.000	−11.000	−11.000	−11.000	−11.000	−11.000
4	−11.000	−11.000	−11.000	−11.000	−11.000	−11.000	−11.000
5	−11.000	−12.500	−11.000	−11.000	−11.000	−11.000	−11.000
6	−10.000	−11.250	−11.000	−10.000	−10.000	−10.000	−10.000
7	−10.000	−11.250	−11.250	−10.500	−10.000	−10.000	−10.000
8	−10.000	−11.250	−11.250	−11.250	−10.000	−10.000	−10.000
9	−10.000	−11.250	−11.250	−11.250	−11.250	−10.000	−10.000
10	−120.000	−111.250	−111.250	−111.250	−111.250	−111.250	−111.250

All-in cost to Westpac as margin relative bps pa to United States Treasuries:

	43	43	27	13	0	−8	−8

Note: Assumes host bonds are called from the end of year five. In the no-exercise case, warrants are redeemed at $50.

From the table, it is apparent that *the issue is structured such that the issuer is guaranteed a maximum rate, which can only decrease if the warrants are exercised.* Through this structure Westpac paid a *maximum* of 9.82% pa (9.59% S/A, or T + 43), a saving of approximately 20-25bps.

The issue was swapped into, at least initially, floating rate US$ LIBOR using a conventional US$ interest swap which *may* have been structured to accommodate the unusual cash flow pattern.

at par (100), but if the yield is above (below) the break-even yield, the amount received by the investor will be less (greater) than par. In any case, the redemption amount cannot be less than zero.

Implicit in the variable redemption formula inherent in this particular structure are (European) options on the 30 year United States Treasury bond with a maturity of three years. The structure of the transaction entails the investor granting a put option on the 30 year bond with a strike yield of 7.10% pa and simultaneously purchasing a call option with an identical strike yield.

The option granted by the investor is securitised through the option swap to effectively insulate the issuer from the risk of variations in the redemption amount. The swap usually generates funding at an attractive margin relative to a floating rate index such as LIBOR.

The economic logic underlying the transaction would appear to be as follows: the investor (in the example) would usually be writing a put which was substantially in-the-money (by about 40bps) and buying an out-of-the-money call (for example, by the same margin). The swap provider would sell the put on the 30 year bond at a higher premium than the outlay needed to purchase the call with the difference being used to subsidise the higher than usual payments on the swap (remembering that the issue coupon would be substantially above the market). The swap thus behaves like a high coupon premium swap transaction.

The swap structure could be simulated, as an alternative to trading options, by holding an appropriate amount of 30 year bonds purchased at market price (the yield would be approximately 7.50% pa) for the three years and liquidating them at market rates at the end of that period. The variable redemption structure would lock in the 40bps profit on the bonds which could be used to subsidise the swap.

The fact that the swap structure can be simulated through a long forward position with the underlying securities, merely reflects the fact that a transaction which involves the simultaneous purchase of a put option and the granting of a call option is equivalent to a short forward position in the relevant security.

Where the issuer does not wish to alter the currency or interest rate basis of the borrowing, the transaction need *not* technically be a swap, but merely a series of option trades. This is basically a consequence of the fact that buying put options and selling call options at the same strike price is economically identical to paying fixed rates under a swap.

The concept was introduced in two issues launched in April 1987 by Nomura International for GMAC and Mitsui and Co. (USA). The GMAC issue was subsequently withdrawn due to tax regulations. The basic concept has been extended to other structures, including dividing the issue into two tranches with one tranche providing the upside potential and the other the downside potential to better attune the structure to individual investor's interest rate expectations.

The detailed underlying transaction logic for such transactions is illustrated utilising a transaction for Quatrain, a vehicle guaranteed by the South Australian Financing Authority, set out in *Exhibit 17.3.*

FOREIGN CURRENCY OPTION SWAPS

Foreign currency option swaps securitising the option component of securities featuring embedded foreign currency options have also been undertaken.

In 1985, an issue of indexed currency option notes (ICONs) saw for the first time the combination of a conventional fixed rate debt issue with a currency option. The ICON structure is very similar, conceptually, to and, in fact, predated the Treasury Indexed Note structure described above.

The initial issue, for the Long Term Credit Bank of Japan, entailed the issuer paying the investor a higher than usual coupon, in return for which the investor creates what is effectively a currency option. The investor, in that case, granted a European style ten year yen and US$ call option with a strike price of ¥169.

Exhibit 17.3

Treasury Indexed Security and Option Swap Structure

Quatrain Co., through Nomura International, made a three year, 10.00% US$100m issue of Treasury indexed bonds on 15 May 1986. Redemption value is linked to the 9.25% of 2016 series of United States Treasury bonds via the following formula:

$$R = US\$100,000,000 \times (\frac{MIP - 26.491782}{100})$$

where

    R = redemption value in US$

    MIP = market index price of the 9.25% of 2016 United States Treasury bond at maturity of the issue

This exposure to 30 year Treasuries is passed on by Quatrain to Nomura via the option swap.

Nomura can hedge its exposure, equivalent to taking on a short forward Treasury position, through either the purchase of a 30 year Treasury bond which is then funded and held for three years or by entering into a simultaneous forward commitment to buy US$100m 9.25% 2016 bonds in three years' time. Assume Nomura purchases the underlying Treasury and funds it for three years at a rate not higher than the yield on the 30 year bond. Nomura can buy the 30 year Treasuries at the current market yield of 7.65% pa and lock in a corresponding three year funding cost, probably through a repurchase agreement, at or less than 7.65% pa.

The profit dynamics are as follows:

• Assume 30 year United States Treasury bond yield is 7.65% pa; and three year United States Treasury bond yield is 7.50% pa.

• Nomura's net profit position from the purchase which is offset by the short forward position (bond price of US$118 equivalent to a yield of 7.65% pa) is:

$$\text{Profits} = US\$100,000,000 \times (\frac{I - 118}{100}) + \$100,000,000 \times (\frac{126.491782 - I}{100})$$

$$= US\$100,000,000 \times (\frac{8.491782}{100})$$

$$= US\$8,491,782 \text{ at maturity}$$

where I = MIP at maturity

• Nomura's US$8,491,782 profit is equivalent to a US$2,628,526 annuity for three years at an interest rate of 7.50% pa. This annuity of US$2,628,526 can be used to reduce the Treasury indexed bond's interest cost from US$10m (that is, 10.00% of $100m) to US$10,000,000−US$2,628,526 = US$7,371,474, so that effective interest cost is S$7,371,474/US$100,000,000 or 7.37% pa, which is *below* the equivalent three year Treasury rate.

• In reality, the annuity stream will only be used to reduce the effective cost to a level at which the issuer's sub-LIBOR target is satisfied with the surplus representing Nomura's profit from the transaction.

• The accompanying US$ interest rate swap will entail Quatrain receiving the fixed rate equivalent of US$10m or 10.00% pa and paying LIBOR minus the agreed margin. Notice the off-market rates necessitated a premium swap structure.

The redemption structure of the ICON effectively simulated the characteristics of a call option on yen (which can also be expressed as a put option on US$ relative to yen) with the investor (the grantor of the option) losing as the yen strengthens relative to the US$ and conversely the purchaser gaining.

The currency option was implicit in the redemption terms of the issue whereby notes were to be redeemed at par (100) if the yen and US$ rate was equal to ¥169 or more at maturity. If the US$ was below ¥169 at maturity, the redemption amount received by the investor was reduced on a sliding discount from par.

Analytically, the investor had granted a foreign currency option in exchange for the higher coupon on the transaction (approximately 55 to 65bps pa) which represented the option premium.

The net result of the transaction is that the issuer, Long Term Credit Bank of Japan, has purchased a ten year European put option on the US$ against the yen with the strike price of US$1/¥169 from the investors in the security. Given that it was interested in securitising the option, using the proceeds from the sale to reduce its borrowing costs, the issuer is likely to sell the option position to a financial intermediary, such as the originator of the transaction. The purchaser will compensate the issuer for the option either in the form of an up-front payment or, usually, through an annuity payment which will be designed to lower the all-in funding costs of the issuer. This will usually be built into the accompanying swap for the transaction.

The financial intermediary purchasing the option has a number of alternatives to securitise this currency option:

- The intermediary can, in turn, sell this currency option.
- Given that the market for long-dated currency options is limited, as an alternative to selling the option on identical terms, the intermediary could write short-term US$ put options against the yen and roll the position at maturity of each series of options. In this case, while the high level of premium for short-term options may allow the financial intermediary to recover the price it pays for the option in a relatively short time, the cash flow mismatches suggest that it may not be able to ensure a profit from the transaction and, in fact, it may even incur a loss if exchange rates move substantially against it, given that it cannot effectively exercise the currency option securitised through the ICON issue.
- Alternatively, the financial intermediary can utilise the US$ put option position as part of the hedge for a straight Euroyen debt issue for a counterparty who wants US$ funding.

The final structure noted is almost inevitably the most attractive means of securitising the option. This structure is set out, in the case of the ICON issue, in *Exhibit 17.4*.

A variation on this basic structure was undertaken in an issue for IBM (nicknamed "Heaven and Hell") whereby in return for taking a risk of loss if the yen strengthens beyond US$1/¥169, the investor would receive a higher redemption payment if the yen is weaker than US$1/¥169 at maturity.

Exhibit 17.4

ICONs and Option Swap Structures

The ICON issue was lead managed by Bankers Trust (BT) for the Long Term Credit Bank of Japan (LTCB). The issue was for US$120m for ten years with coupon of 11.50%. The redemption value was calculated according to the following formula if the ¥ strengthened beyond ¥169/US$1:

$$R = US\$120,000,000 \times (1 - \frac{169 - S}{S})$$

where

R = redemption value in US$

S = ¥/US$ spot exchange rate on 21/11/1995

If the ¥/US$ exchange rate was weaker than ¥169/US$1, investors would receive the face value of the notes.

Under the terms of the accompanying US$ interest rate swap, LTCB achieved an all-in cost of approximately LIBOR minus 40-45bps. The swap structure effectively securitises the currency option. BT purchases this US$ put option against the ¥ on US$120m at a strike price of ¥169/US$1.

To securitise the option position, BT will arrange either directly or indirectly for a ¥ issue at 6.65% pa for ten years for ¥24,240m, exchange the proceeds for US$120m on the spot market, hedge the interest commitments forward, leave the capital redemption unhedged and charge the counterparty 10.70% for the US$120m loan.

The profit dynamics of the transaction are as follows:

- Assume ten year United States Treasury bond rate is 10.50% pa; yen risk free rate (the ten year Japanese government bond) is 6.50% pa; ¥/US$ spot exchange rate as at November 1985 was ¥202/US$1.

- Assume forward exchange rates were:

1 year forward	¥194.6878/US$1;	6 year forward	¥161.911/US$1;
2 year forward	¥187.64/US$1;	7 year forward	¥156.05/US$1;
3 year forward	¥180.8476/US$1;	8 year forward	¥150.401/US$1;
4 year forward	¥174.3013/US$1;	9 year forward	¥144.956/US$1;
5 year forward	¥167.9918/US$1;	10 year forward	¥139.956/US$1.

- At maturity, the worst case exchange rate BT will have to repay its ¥ commitment is ¥169/US$1, therefore the shortfall in ¥ amount on that date if the worst case rises is: ¥24,240,000,000 − ¥20,280,000,000 = ¥3,960,000,000. This shortfall translates into an annual payment of ¥293,454,573.

- Therefore, BT has to hedge the interest payment of ¥1,611,960,000 + ¥293,454,573 = ¥1,905,414,573 forward annually.

- Cash flows from the ¥24,240m debt issue are as follows:

Year	Yen interest commitment (¥)	Annuity for capital redemption (¥)	US$ amount to hedge cash flows (US$) @¥202/$1	Counterparty interest payments (US$)	BT's profits (US$)
0	24,240,000,000	———————→		120,000,000	
1	1,611,960,000	293,454,573	9,787,026	12,840,000	3,052,974
2	1,611,960,000	293,454,573	10,154,629	12,840,000	2,685,371
3	1,611,960,000	293,454,573	10,536,024	12,840,000	2,303,976
4	1,611,960,000	293,454,573	10,931,729	12,840,000	1,908,271
5	1,611,960,000	293,454,573	11,342,307	12,840,000	1,497,693
6	1,611,960,000	293,454,573	11,768,284	12,840,000	1,071,716
7	1,611,960,000	293,454,573	12,210,282	12,840,000	629,718
8	1,611,960,000	293,454,573	12,668,896	12,840,000	171,104
9	1,611,960,000	293,454,573	13,144,779	12,840,000	−304,779
10	1,611,960,000	293,454,573	13,638,443	12,840,000	−798,443
	24,240,000,000	−3,960,000,000	@¥169/$1	120,000,000	

Exhibit 17.4—continued

- BT's profits from the above transaction, at a discount rate of 10.50% pa, will, after ten years, be US$25,564,688, equivalent to a US$1,566,024 annuity over ten years.
- This annuity can then be used to reduce LTCB's borrowing cost from US$13,800,000 (11.50% of US$120m) to US$12,233,976 pa (US$13,800,000−US$1,566,024) which translates to an effective interest rate of US$12,233,976/US$120,000,000 or 10.20% pa, a rate under the equivalent United States Treasury rate if all the profits are distributed to the issuer (an unlikely scenario).

The redemption arrangements analytically constitute a yen and US$ call granted by the investor and the simultaneous purchase of a yen and US$ put. Both options have a strike rate of US$1/¥169 and a term of ten years. In the IBM transaction the issue was structured in two tranches: a fixed rate and a floating rate issue. In the fixed (floating) rate portion, the investor received approximately 70bps (25bps) in extra yield in return for the variable redemption arrangement. In this structure, a two-way currency option was created, one written by the investor and one by the issuer. Both options again were capable of being sold separately to reduce the overall borrowing cost of its issues.

The detailed structure of the Heaven and Hell issue and accompanying currency option swap is set out in *Exhibit 17.5*.

Exhibit 17.5
"Heaven and Hell" Notes and Option Swap Structure

The first issue of Heaven and Hell notes was lead managed by Nomura International for IBM Credit Corporation. The IBM issue was to raise US$50m for ten years, with a maturity date of 4 December 1995. To entice investors to invest in this bond, IBM had to pay a rich coupon of 10.75% pa, payable in US$, which was equivalent to 84bps over Treasuries. In a prior comparable issue, IBM had only paid 14bps over Treasuries for a straight Eurodollar issue. The redemption amount for the issue, payable in US$, will vary according to the following formula:

$$R = US\$50,000,000 \times (1 + \frac{S - 169}{S})$$

where

R = redemption amount in US$

S = ¥/US$ spot exchange rate at maturity of the bonds

If the ¥/US$ exchange rate at maturity was stronger than ¥84.5/US$1, investors will get no principal return.

IBM securitises the options implicit in the transaction to Nomura in return for payments which effectively lower its cost of funds.

From the IBM Heaven and Hell debt issue, Nomura will have a short US$ position in ten years time at a forward price of ¥169/US$1 for US$50m. To utilise this forward position effectively, Nomura will issue ¥10,212,500,000 at 6.70% pa for a counterparty who wants 10 year US$ funds. Nomura would exchange the ¥ proceeds on the spot market, hedge the interest commitments forward and leave the final capital redemption amount unhedged. Nomura will charge the counterparty approximately 10.25% pa for the US$ funds.

Exhibit 17.5—continued

The profit dynamics of the issue are as follows:

- Assume ¥ ten year risk free interest rate is 6.50% pa; ten year United States Treasury interest rate is 10.00% pa; ¥/US$ spot exchange rate is ¥204.25/US$1.

- Assume forward exchange rates were:

  1 year forward ¥197.751/US$1;   6 year forward ¥168.230/US$1;
  2 year forward ¥191.459/US$1;   7 year forward ¥162.877/US$1;
  3 year forward ¥185.367/US$1;   8 year forward ¥157.695/US$1;
  4 year forward ¥179.469/US$1;   9 year forward ¥152.677/US$1;
  5 year forward ¥173.759/US$1;   10 year forward ¥147.819/US$1.

- At maturity, Nomura will exchange the US$ into ¥ at the rate of ¥169/US$1. This will give Nomura ¥8,450,000,000 to repay the ¥10,212,500,000 ¥ loan, leaving a shortfall of ¥1,762,500,000. This shortfall translates into an annual payment of ¥130,609,517 at the risk free rate of 6.50% pa.

- Nomura has therefore to enter into an annual forward agreement to hedge ¥814,847,017 annually (¥684,237,500 + ¥130,609,517).

- The cash flows involved are as follows:

Year	Yen interest commitment (¥)	Annuity for capital redemption (¥)	US$ amount to hedge cash flows (US$)	Counterparty interest payments (US$)	Nomura's profits (US$)
			@ ¥204.25/US$1		
0	10,212,500,000		———————→	50,000,000	
1	684,237,500	130,609,517	4,120,571	5,125,000	1,004,429
2	684,237,500	130,609,517	4,255,987	5,125,000	869,013
3	684,237,500	130,609,517	4,395,858	5,125,000	729,142
4	684,237,500	130,609,517	4,540,322	5,125,000	584,678
5	684,237,500	130,609,517	4,689,524	5,125,000	435,476
6	684,237,500	130,609,517	4,843,649	5,125,000	281,351
7	684,237,500	130,609,517	5,002,837	5,125,000	122,168
8	684,237,500	130,609,517	5,167,234	5,125,000	−42,234
9	684,237,500	130,609,517	5,337,065	5,125,000	−212,065
10	684,237,500	130,609,517	5,512,465	5,125,000	−387,465
	10,212,500,000 −1,762,500,000		@ ¥169/US$1 ———→	50,000,000	

- Nomura's profits from the above transaction, using a discount rate of 10.00% pa, will, at the end of ten years, be US$7,291,912, equivalent to a US$457,534 annuity over ten years.

- The annuity will be used to reduce IBM's annual interest cost of US$5,375,000 (10.75% of US$50m) to US$4,917,467 (US$5,375,000 − US$457,533) which will reduce IBM's interest cost down to US$4,917,467/US$50,000,000 = 9.835% (a rate below United States Treasuries).

- However, because investors of the IBM Heaven and Hell issue also purchased a US$ put option with a strike price of ¥84.5/US$1, Nomura will be left with a residual foreign currency risk should the ¥/$US exchange rate strengthen beyond ¥84.5/US$1. Nomura can leave this position unhedged or hedge this residual exposure, by buying a customised US$ put option with a strike price of ¥84.5/US$1 or it could delta hedge the position to create a synthetic option.

The currency options implicit in these transactions are effectively securitised usually through a swap transaction structurally similar to that described above in connection with the Treasury Indexed Note structure.

The ICON type structure which yields currency options which are securitised and on-sold has been extended in a number of directions, for example:

- variability linked to currency rates has been extended to coupon amounts thereby creating a stream of currency options;
- mini-max notes where the variable redemption amount operates *only* if the currency rates are outside a stated band;
- inclusion of ICON features in dual currency issues; and
- variable redemption structures linked to both currency and interest rates.

The ingenuity of these currency linked variable redemption bonds and also their creators, primarily, the Japanese securities houses, is best illustrated by two examples. *Exhibit 17.6* sets out the intricate and elegant combination of an issue by OKB and BFCE which allowed simultaneous foreign currency options to be securitised. *Exhibit 17.7* sets out the structure of "duet" bonds where the linkage to currency rates has been extended to coupon amounts.

Exhibit 17.6

Yen/US$ Variable Redemption Reverse Dual Currency Bond and Option Swap Structure

On 15 April 1986, Oesterreichische Kontrollbank (OKB) issued a ¥20 billion, ten year variable redemption bond. The coupon was 8.00% pa payable in ¥. Redemption was in US$ based on the following formula:

$$R = US\$114,155,252 \times (1 + \frac{S - 169}{S})$$

where

R = redemption amount in US$

S = ¥/US$ spot exchange rate at maturity of the bonds

If ¥ strengthens beyond ¥84.5/US$1, investors will not receive their principal back.

On the same date, Nomura also lead managed a reverse dual currency bond issue worth ¥20 billion, with a maturity of ten years for Banque Française du Commerce Exterieur (BFCE). This issue involved BFCE paying a 7.50% pa coupon, payable in US$ at a fixed exchange rate of ¥179/US$1. Redemption amount, payable in ¥, is at par as long as exchange rates are above ¥84.5/US$1, declining below par as ¥ strengthened beyond ¥84.5/US$1. The foreign currency options implicit in the two issues were securitised by Nomura.

The OKB and BFCE issues complement one another as the redemption amount in the OKB issue is in US$ while the redemption amount of the BFCE issue is payable in ¥. The redemption formula of both issues *jointly* give a short US$ position at a forward price of ¥169/US$1.

Interest payment of the OKB issue is in US$ but that of the BFCE issue is in ¥, therefore, if BFCE wants US$ funding, Nomura will have to hedge the ¥ interest commitments of the BFCE issue forward. To capitalise on the short US$ position obtained from both issues, Nomura would not hedge the capital redemption of OKB's ¥ redemption amount forward.

The profit dynamics of the transaction are as follows:

- Assume ¥ ten year risk free interest rate is 6.50% pa; United States ten year Treasury interest rate is 8.50% pa; ¥/US$ spot exchange rate is ¥175.2/US$1.
- Assume forward exchange rates were:

1 year forward	¥171.97/US$1;	6 year forward	¥156.69/US$1;
2 year forward	¥168.8/US$1;	7 year forward	¥153.81/US$1;
3 year forward	¥165.65/US$1;	8 year forward	¥150.97/US$1;
4 year forward	¥162.63/US$1;	9 year forward	¥148.19/US$1;
5 year forward	¥159.64/US$1;	10 year forward	¥145.46/US$1.

Exhibit 17.6—continued

- Interest flows for BFCE are as follows: assuming OKB pays Nomura the equivalent of 8.30% pa (a rate under United States Treasuries), BFCE pays an interest flow to Nomura of [(¥20 billion/175.2) × 8.30%] = US$9,474,886. Nomura will have to pay investors [(¥20 billion x 7.50%) ¥179/US$1] = US$8,379,888. Therefore, Nomura will obtain an annual profit of US$1,094,998 from this part of the transaction.

- Interest flows for OKB are as follows: assuming it pays Nomura the equivalent of US$ 8.30% pa, BFCE will pay Nomura US$9,474,886 [(¥20 billion/175.2) × 8.30%] and Nomura will have to pay investors ¥1,600,000,000 [¥20 billion × 8.00%]. Nomura will have to hedge this obligation forward to limit any losses.

- The interest flows under the OKB transaction are as set out below.

Year	OKB ¥ interest commitment (¥)	US$ amount to hedge cash flows (US$)	OKB's interest payments (US$)	Nomura's profits (US$)
1	1,600,000,000	9,303,949	9,474,886	170,937
2	1,600,000,000	9,478,673	9,474,886	−3,787
3	1,600,000,000	9,656,588	9,474,886	−181,722
4	1,600,000,000	9,838,283	9,474,886	−363,417
5	1,600,000,000	10,022,551	9,474,886	−547,685
6	1,600,000,000	10,211,245	9,474,886	−736,379
7	1,600,000,000	10,402,445	9,474,886	−927,579
8	1,600,000,000	10,598,132	9,474,886	−1,123,266
9	1,600,000,000	10,796,950	9,474,886	−1,322,084
10	1,600,000,000	10,999,588	9,474,886	−1,524,722

- Nomura's net profit position from the two transactions is:

Year	Profit from BFCE (US$)	Profit from OKB (US$)	Net profit (US$)
1	1,094,998	170,937	1,265,935
2	1,094,998	−3,787	1,091,211
3	1,094,998	−181,722	913,276
4	1,094,998	−363,417	731,581
5	1,094,998	−547,685	547,313
6	1,094,998	−736,379	358,619
7	1,094,998	−927,579	167,419
8	1,094,998	−1,123,266	−28,268
9	1,094,998	−1,322,084	−227,086
10	1,094,998	−1,524,722	−429,724

- At the US$ risk free interest rate of 8.50% pa, the compounded value of this net profit cash flow at year 10 is US$8,368,408.

- Redemption amount which OKB and BFCE will pay Nomura at maturity = US$114,155,252 × 2 = US$228,310,504.

- Premium from OKB issue ¥300,000,000 and for BFCE, it is ¥350,000,000 which totals to US$3,710,045 at ¥175:US$1 (both issues were made at premiums to par).

- Total amount of cash available to Nomura to repay investors = US$8,368,408 (Nomura's profit) + US$228,310,504 (principal repayments in US$ by OKB and BFC) + US$3,710,045 (issue premium) = US$240,388,957.

- Amount owed by Nomura to investors of both issues at maturity if spot exchange rate is weaker than ¥84.5/US$1 depends on the following formula:

$$R = ¥20 \text{ billion}/179 \times \left(1 + \frac{S - 169}{S}\right) + ¥20 \text{ billion}/S$$

where

     R = redemption amount in US$

     S = ¥/US$ spot exchange rate

Exhibit 17.6—continued

Therefore, Nomura's profit is as follows:

Spot rate (S)	Cash available to Nomura (US$)	Redemption amount (US$)	Gain (US$)
300	240,388,957	227,188,083	13,200,874
200	240,388,957	229,050,280	11,338,677
150	240,388,957	230,912,477	9,476,480
100	240,388,957	234,636,872	5,752,085
90	240,388,957	235,878,337	4,510,620
85	240,388,957	236,608,610	3,780,347
84.5	240,388,957	236,686,391	3,702,566
80	240,388,957	235,937,500	4,451,457
60	240,388,957	197,222,222	43,166,735

• From the above profit table, we observe that it is possible for Nomura to reduce the cost of borrowing of both entities to below United States Treasuries and still not incur a loss on the capital redemption amount at maturity.

Exhibit 17.7

Duet Bond and Option Swap Structure

The first duet bond was issued for the Kingdom of Denmark and managed by Dai-Ichi Kangyo Bank (DKB). It was a five year debt issue worth US$1m issued on 8 August 1986. The coupon, payable in US$, is based on the following formula:

$$C = \$100,000,000 \times 0.165 - \left[\frac{\yen\,16,300,000,000 \times 0.065}{S} \right]$$

where

C = coupon payable in US$

S = ¥/US$ exchange rate at coupon date

The capital redemption amount, also payable in US$, is calculated using the following formula:

$$R = US\$100,000,000 \times 2 - \left[\frac{\yen 16,300,000,000}{S} \right]$$

where

R = redemption amount in US$

S = ¥/US$ exchange rate at maturity of the bonds

From the formula, it is clear that Denmark has an exposure to the ¥/US$ exchange rate on each coupon date and at maturity of the bonds. These currency options were securitised by DKB.

Under the swap structure, Denmark effectively sells the options implicit in the structure to DKB. DKB assume an annual exposure to ¥ coupon payments as a result of the duet bond's coupon payment formula. In addition, DKB will have a short US$ forward exposure for US$100m in five years' time, at a forward rate of ¥163/US$1.

To capitalise on this position, DKB arranges a ¥ issue, for a counterparty wanting US$ funding, with an annual coupon payment equivalent to ¥1,059,500,000. If the ¥ interest rate on the issue is 5.20%, then DKB will have to issue ¥20,375m, principal amount pa of bonds.

The duet bond, because of the amount issued, will only support US$100m or ¥16,300m of the ¥ issue to be perfectly hedged, therefore, ¥4,075m from the ¥ issue will be unhedged. DKB has to undertake a five year forward agreement to purchase ¥ to hedge this exposure.

Exhibit 17.7—continued

The profit dynamics of this transaction are as follows:

- Assume five year ¥ interest rate is 5.00% pa; five year US$ interest rate is 7.50% pa; spot exchange rate is ¥163/US$1; the five year forward rate is ¥144.9078/US$1.
- Therefore, DKB will require ¥4,075,000,000/ ¥144.9078 = $28,121,329 to hedge the ¥4,075,000,000 ¥ forward exposure.
- If DKB charges counterparty 7.70% pa for US$ funding, the borrower will therefore have to pay DKB US$9,625,000 (7.70% of US$125,000,000) and DKB will be committed to pay ¥1,059,500,000 (at ¥163/US$1) (5.20% of ¥20,375,000,000) for the straight ¥ debt. The duet bond coupon formula will cover this, leaving DKB with US$3,125,000 (US$9,625,000-US$6,500,000) annually for the next five years. This will accumulate to US$18,151,222 at the end of five years, at the interest rate of 7.50% pa.
- At maturity, DKB will have US$125m to pay off the ¥20,375m straight ¥ debt. The duet bond will hedge ¥16,300m (equivalent to US$100m) and the forward agreement will hedge the remaining ¥4,075m. This amount will be covered by the US$18,151,222, from the coupon receipts and US$25m, from the capital redemption amount. This will leave DKB with US$25,000,000 + US$18,151,222 − US$28,121,329 = US$15,029,893 profits at maturity.
- This profit at maturity (US$15,029,893) would be used to reduce the duet bond's interest cost. The US$15,029,893 plus the US$1,625,000 premium from the issue of duet bonds will give an annuity of US$2,989,260 over five years at 7.50%. Interest cost of the duet bond = 10.00% of US$100,000,000 = US$10,000,000. Effective interest cost of the bond after deducting the annuity is: (US$10,000,000 − US$2,989,260)/US$1,000,000,000 = 7.02%, a rate under the equivalent United States Treasury bond rate, if the full benefit is passed onto the borrower.

STOCK INDEX OPTION SWAP

The concept of creating and subsequently securitising options embedded in capital market transactions has been extended to stock index options.

Stock indexes utilised to date include the New York Stock Exchange Index, the Tokyo Nikkei Stock Average, the German FAZ Share Index, the Swiss SBC Index, the Hong Kong Hang Seng Index as well as the Sydney All Ordinaries Stock Index. Transaction structures involving individual stocks are also clearly feasible.

By utilising a variable redemption structure similar to that used in Treasury Indexed Notes and ICONs and linking the redemption amounts to the value of an identified stock index, call and put options on the relevant indexes have been created. To date, the few issues undertaken have not always *created* options but rather entailed, usually through the swap arrangement, the *purchase* of stock index options.

A number of structures have appeared. Some transactions linked to the Nikkei Stock Index have been similar to the Treasury Indexed Notes and ICON structure with redemption above or below par, depending on the maturity value of the index. Other structures include:

- the creation of offsetting tranches designed to appeal to bullish and bearish investors which produces a known maximum cost of funds for the issuer;
- a below market coupon issue with a redemption value which provides for potential gains if the relevant index appreciates (but no reduction in the redemption value below par) which effectively replicates the purchase of a call on the index which in turn is hedged by the swap provider who grants the option.

There are currently two main categories of stock index option embedded capital market transactions meriting discussion. The first of these is the so-called bull and bear bonds. The second is the variable redemption structures discussed above where the redemption amount is linked to a stock index. It is important to note that the first category are not true options while the second are designed to fully replicate the pay off profiles of options on the relevant stock index.

Bull and bear bonds in all currencies have been structured to include offsetting tranches with the redemption value of each tranche being directly linked either positively (in the case of the bull bond) or inversely (in the case of the bear bond) to the value of the relevant index. From the viewpoint of the investor in a bull or bear bond, the fact that the redemption value upon maturity is determined by the level of the relative index at some point of time in the future allows the investor to participate in index movements consistent with its expectations. It is however important to note that in almost all bull and bear bonds, the structure embodies a cap on the final pay out as well as a floor. In this regard, the characteristic pay off of a bull or bear bond *approximates* but is *not* a true option.

From the perspective of the issuer, there is no underlying risk to movements in the relevant index. This is because the two tranches are designed to be perfectly offsetting and to provide the issuer with a known fixed stream of cash flow payments into the future. The issuer effectively assumes no risk to movements in the relevant index as changes in the redemption value in one tranche (say the bull tranche) are offset by the asymmetric changes in the redemption value generated by the other tranche (in our example the bear tranche).

An example of the type of stock index bull-bear issue involving the Nikkei Keisai Shimban Index on the Tokyo Stock Exchange is set out in *Exhibit 17.8.*

From the perspective of the issuer, the only reason for undertaking a bull or bear bond is that the overall locked in fixed cost of funds generated is significantly lower than that achievable by a straight conventional transaction in the relevant market. That is, the issuer thus takes no final redemption risk (although the investor does) and is able to lock in a cheaper cost of borrowing no matter what the level of the relevant index is upon maturity.

This lower cost of borrowing achievable through the bull or bear bond can be translated across markets. That is, the issuer could effectively swap out of the currency or interest rate basis of the underlying bull or bear transaction to generate an attractive alternative cost of funds in its desired currency or interest rate basis.

It is important to note that, from the viewpoint of the issuer, there is nothing apart from the relative cost to distinguish a bull or bear transaction from a conventional borrowing and the swap transaction is entirely conventional.

The only variation from a standard interest rate or cross-currency swap may flow from differential coupons etc. (relative to market levels). For example, in one issue for SEK, the coupon on the bonds was an above market 8.00% pa (relative to the market rate that would have had to be

Exhibit 17.8

Yen Bull and Bear Bonds Linked to Nikkei Stock Index and Option Swap Structure

AB Svensk Exportkredit (SEK) on 25 July 1986 issued a series of ¥ bull and bear bonds. The SEK issue involved two tranches, each for five years. The bull tranche involved an issue of ¥10,000m and pays a rich coupon of 8.00% to compensate investors for the additional risks that they have undertaken. The redemption value of the bonds were indexed to the Nikkei Keisai Shimbun index in the following manner.

For the bull bonds:

$$R = ¥10,000,000,000 \times (1 + \frac{I - 26,067}{22,720})$$

For the bear bonds:

$$R = ¥10,000,000,000 \times (1 + \frac{I - 19,373}{22,720})$$

where

$$R = \text{redemption value in } ¥$$
$$I = \text{Nikkei stock average at maturity of the bonds}$$

R is subject also to the following constraint: if I is greater than 28,461 at maturity, $R = ¥6,000,000,000$; if I is less than 16,979 at maturity, $R = ¥11,054,000,000$.

SEK's net position is a function of the underlying option position created which was securitised by Daiwa Securities, the lead manager of the issue.

For Daiwa, the bull bonds represent a five year (European) bear option spread where Daiwa purchased a call with a strike price of 28,461 and wrote a call with a strike price of 16,979, both of which expire in five years' time. The bear bonds resemble a bull spread for Daiwa where the strike price of the purchased call is 16,979 and the strike price of the written call is 28,461.

The offsetting nature of the two tranches allows Daiwa to stay perfectly hedged with no exposure to the stock index. Mathematically, this can be represented as follows:

- Redemption value of both the bull and bear tranches where I is the index at maturity is:

$$¥10,000,000,000 \times [(1 - \frac{I - 19373}{22720}) + (1 + \frac{I - 26067}{22720})]$$

$$= ¥10,000,000,000 \times (\frac{22720 - I + 19373}{22720} + \frac{22720 + I - 26067}{22720})$$

$$= ¥10,000,000,000 \times (\frac{38746}{22720})$$

$$= ¥17,053,697,183$$

- Therefore, profit for Daiwa

$$= ¥20,000,000,000 - ¥17,053,697,183$$

$$= ¥2,946,302,817$$

- For example, profit if the Nikkei Index is greater than 28,461 is:

—for Bear bond: ¥10,000,000,000 − ¥ 6,000,000,000 = ¥4,000,000
—for Bull bond: ¥10,000,000,000 − ¥11,054,000,000 = ¥1,054,000

Profit for Daiwa   = ¥ 2,946,000

Exhibit 17.8—continued

- Profit if Nikkei Index is less than 16,979 is:

  —for Bear bond: ¥10,000,000,000 − ¥11,054,000,000 = −¥1,054,000
  —for Bull bond: ¥10,000,000,000 − ¥ 6,000,000,000 = ¥4,000,000

  Profit for Daiwa   = ¥2,946,000

  The profit dynamics of the issue are as follows:

- The bull bear bonds pay a rich ¥ coupon of 8.00% which, in ¥ terms is: ¥20,000,000,000 × 0.08 = ¥1,600,000,000

- At a five year ¥ risk free rate of 6.50%, the profit of ¥2,946m translates into an annuity of ¥517,419,347 for five years.

- Therefore, effective interest cost to SEK is ¥1,600,000,000 − ¥517,419,347 = ¥1,082,580,653 which translates into 5.413% pa (¥1,082,580,653 / ¥20,000,000,000).

- From the above derivation, we observe that the bull and bear structure can reduce interest cost to below the ¥ risk free rate. In fact, the all-in cost achieved represented a saving of approximately 55bps on a comparable Euroyen issue. SEK, desiring floating rate US$ funding, undertook a ¥/US$ swap generating funds at an attractive margin under LIBOR.

paid by SEK of 6.00%). This higher coupon was compensated for by an effective redemption value at maturity of less than par (once the offsetting tranches were taken into account). If SEK had desired to undertake a swap against this bond issue then the peculiar high coupon cash flow structure would have had to be matched under the corresponding swap.

It is important to note that several important variations on the basic bull and bear structure are feasible such as undertaking a transaction where the linkage between the relevant index and the redemption value of the bond is structured on the basis that the maturity of the bond is longer than the period over which the final pay out to be distributed to the investors in the various tranches is determined. For example, a number of transactions have been undertaken on the basis that on a five year maturity bond, the final redemption amount is determined by the movement in the index for a period of say one year. Under this structure, if the index appreciates, the bull tranche investor has a higher redemption value which crystallises and is guaranteed after one year although not payable until maturity of the bond. Conversely, the exact opposite applies to an investor in the bear tranches.

The alternative structure is closer to that of Treasury index notes or ICONs. This type of instrument, which creates a true option on the stock index for the investor, is more complex.

This type of stock index linked bond is best illustrated with an example. In November 1986, Bankers Trust Australia Limited (BTAL) launched an issue of A$50m of All Ordinaries Share Price Riskless Index Notes (ASPRINs). The issuer was the New South Wales Treasury Corporation.

The essential structure of the investment in this instrument was as follows. The transaction was for a maturity of four years and carried a zero coupon. The investor is guaranteed return of its initial investment. That is, if A$100 is invested at maturity, then the investor receives at least A$100. The investors final cash receipt, that is, the redemption amount, is linked to the all ordinaries share price index such that if the index appreciates over a stated level (1,372) and stands at this level upon maturity of the security, the investor receives a redemption amount which is calculated as the face value amount multiplied by the all ordinaries index at maturity divided by the initial share index level of 1,372. Thus, if the index doubles over the four year life of the bonds, investors simply double their original investment; if the index declines under the strike price, investors will receive back their original investment.

The economic logic of the transaction would appear to be as follows: the investor in ASPRINs is effectively giving up current coupon income, that is, the dividend yield of the stock which make up the all ordinaries index which is around 3.00% but in return is able to participate in any further appreciation of the Australian share market without putting capital at risk. The issuer on the other hand would normally have been able to obtain funds at the market rate at the time of the issue of 14.50 to 15.00% pa. Thus, the issuer saves approximately 14.50 to 15.00% pa, that is, the full coupon on conventional debt. However, the issuer takes on a final redemption risk as it has an exposure to the level of the all ordinaries share price index at maturity. The issuer uses a substantial portion of its saving on interest cost to purchase an option which effectively hedges its exposure of the final redemption amount on the securities. The New South Wales Treasury Corporation purchased a (European) option on the all ordinaries index at a strike price of 1,372 with a maturity date of four years. It is understood that after payment of the option premium to the option writer, the New South Wales Treasury Corporation achieved funding at around 50bps under its alternative cost of funds through a conventional transaction. That is, the option writer received up to 40.00 to 42.00% flat for granting the option on the index.

The options were arranged by BTAL and were apparently written by institutions against their equity portfolio as part of a covered call writing strategy. BTAL provided the New South Wales Treasury Corporation with the option and in turn purchased an offsetting option from the institutions. BTAL's earnings from the transaction was the difference between the price at which it bought the option and the price at which it sold the option to the issuer.

Chapter 18
Asset Swaps

THE CONCEPT OF ASSET SWAPS

The underlying concept of liability swaps can be extended to transactions involving the creation of synthetic assets.

"Asset swap" is a generic term for the repackaging of a security paying fixed interest rates into floating interest rates, or from floating into fixed, or from interest and principal payments in one currency to interest and principal payments in another currency.

The market for synthetic assets exists primarily for one of two basic reasons:

- An arbitrage (similar to a liability arbitrage) exists to enable the creation of a higher yielding security than one directly available in the market.
- The unavailability of a particular security with the desired credit, interest rate or currency characteristics in conventional form creates the opportunity to generate a synthetic security.

In essence, asset swaps are predicated on the fact that investors often require a set of *cash flows* that is unavailable directly in capital markets. In order to create the desired cash flow, the investor combines existing cash market instruments with an accompanying swap to create the synthetic asset.

In this chapter, techniques for structuring asset swaps, the market for synthetic assets, as well as private and public securitised asset swap structures are examined. The focus in this chapter is typically on transactions in which the asset and the accompanying swap have the same maturity, being designed to fully hedge the investor's underlying exposures into an acceptable form. However, it is clearly possible to structure transactions to provide any particular mismatch the investor requires and in practise, market timing or outlook, or any combination of both can greatly influence the structure of a synthetic asset transaction.

STRUCTURING AN ASSET SWAP

Asset swap mechanics

The basic mechanics of an asset swap are very similar to those of a liability swap. The asset swap will usually entail three distinct phases:

- the underlying physical security is purchased for cash;
- the cash flows, both interest and principal (in the case of a cross-currency asset swap), are linked to either an interest rate or a currency swap to change the interest rate or currency denomination of the investment into the desired form;
- the overall package is then held by the investor or, if assembled by a financial institution, is sold to an ultimate investor as an asset in its synthetic form.

Exhibit 18.1 sets out the basic structure of an asset swap involving an interest rate swap. The underlying transaction in this case is the purchase of a fixed rate US$ bond with a maturity of three years and a coupon of 10.00% pa. The fixed rate US$ bond is then swapped into a synthetic FRN, yielding LIBOR plus 25bps through an interest rate swap.

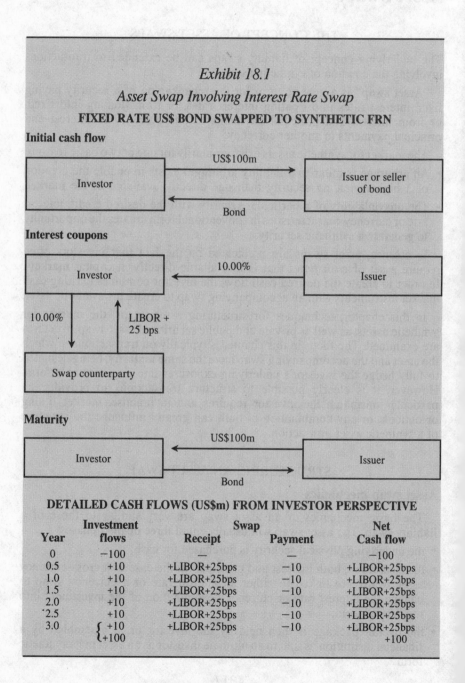

Exhibit 18.1
Asset Swap Involving Interest Rate Swap
FIXED RATE US$ BOND SWAPPED TO SYNTHETIC FRN

DETAILED CASH FLOWS (US$m) FROM INVESTOR PERSPECTIVE

Year	Investment flows	Swap Receipt	Payment	Net Cash flow
0	−100	—	—	−100
0.5	+10	+LIBOR+25bps	−10	+LIBOR+25bps
1.0	+10	+LIBOR+25bps	−10	+LIBOR+25bps
1.5	+10	+LIBOR+25bps	−10	+LIBOR+25bps
2.0	+10	+LIBOR+25bps	−10	+LIBOR+25bps
2.5	+10	+LIBOR+25bps	−10	+LIBOR+25bps
3.0	{ +10	+LIBOR+25bps	−10	+LIBOR+25bps
	{ +100			+100

Exhibit 18.2 sets out the basic structure of an asset swap involving a currency swap. In this case, the underlying transaction is an investment in an A$ bond where the return is swapped to create a synthetic US$ FRN. The underlying A$ bond is for three years with a coupon of 14.00% pa which when combined with an A$ and US$ LIBOR currency swap results in the creation of a US$ asset yielding LIBOR plus 45bps.

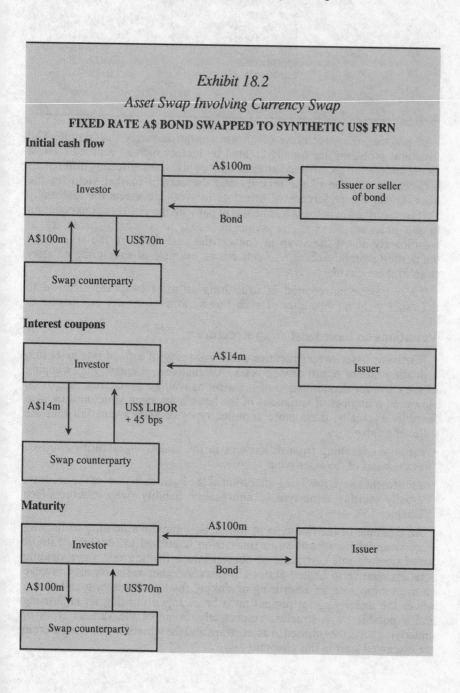

Exhibit 18.2

Asset Swap Involving Currency Swap

FIXED RATE A$ BOND SWAPPED TO SYNTHETIC US$ FRN

Initial cash flow

Investor — A$100m → Issuer or seller of bond

Investor ← Bond — Issuer or seller of bond

A$100m ↑ / US$70m ↓ Swap counterparty

Interest coupons

Investor ← A$14m — Issuer

A$14m ↓ / US$ LIBOR + 45 bps ↑ Swap counterparty

Maturity

Investor ← A$100m — Issuer

Investor — Bond → Issuer

A$100m ↓ / US$70m ↑ Swap counterparty

Exhibit 18.2—continued

DETAILED CASH FLOWS FROM INVESTOR PERSPECTIVE

Year	Investment flows ($Am)	Swap Receipt (US$m)	Payment (A$m)	Net Cash flow (US$m)
0	−100	−70	+100	−70
0.5	+7	LIBOR+45bps	−7	LIBOR+45bps
1.0	+7	LIBOR+45bps	−7	LIBOR+45bps
1.5	+7	LIBOR+45bps	−7	LIBOR+45bps
2.0	+7	LIBOR+45bps	−7	LIBOR+45bps
2.5	+7	LIBOR+45bps	−7	LIBOR+45bps
3.0	{ +7 { +100	LIBOR+45bps +70	{ −7 { −100	{ LIBOR+45bps { +70

In practise, the structuring of an asset swap is rarely this simple. The structural problems are usually created by factors such as accrued interest on the underlying security and any discount or premium reflecting differences between the coupon of the security and the current market yield for the asset. Given the preference of investors in synthetic assets for essentially a clean security where the investment is at par with the yield coupons equating to the purchase yield of the synthetic asset, it is usually necessary to significantly adjust the swap to convert the cash flows of the security to the desired pattern. *Exhibit 18.3* sets out an example of structuring an asset swap in these circumstances.

The adjustments required in structuring an asset swap are identical to the usual yield mathematics of such transactions as set out in Chapter 8.

Variations on basic asset swap structure

The basic asset swap structures entail swapping of a fixed rate asset into a floating rate of return or vice versa. Alternatively, it entails the swapping of the currency denomination of the asset as well as the interest rate basis. However, a number of variations of the basic asset swap structures are also feasible. Typically, these more complex types of asset swaps fall into the following categories:

• variations resulting from differences in the underlying securities utilised as the basis of the asset swap;

• adjustment swaps involving alteration of the basic cash flow of the security, usually utilising some type of non-generic liability swap structures (see Chapter 15).

An example of the first type of transaction may be a floating-to-floating asset swap where a basis swap transaction is utilised to convert a LIBOR based floating rate certificate of deposit into a floating rate asset yielding a return relative to United States CP rates. Another variation may involve an asset swap with an amortising or sinking fund provision or a call option where the underlying instrument must be swapped utilising an amortising and a putable swap structure respectively. Some of the various types of underlying securities utilised in asset swaps and the variations resulting therein are discussed later in this chapter.

Exhibit 18.3

Structuring an Asset Swap

Assume the following scenario exists as of 19 May 19X7:

- A semi-government bond is currently available in the secondary market on the following terms:

Amount:	A$10m
Maturity:	15/8/19X2
Coupon:	12.50% pa (S/A)
Yield:	14.90% pa (S/A)
Settlement:	26 May 19X7
Price:	91.4402 or A$9.1440m
Accrued interest:	3.4530 or A$0.3453m

- The A$ interest rate swap market for the relevant maturity is showing the following price: 14.30% pa/14.00% pa versus three month BBR.

An investor decides to purchase the bonds and swap them into a synthetic A$ FRN as follows:

- On 26 May 1987, the investor pays A$9.4893m to purchase the bonds.
- The investor simultaneously enters into a structured swap on the following terms:

—Swap counterparty pays A$0.3453m (accrued interest) on 26 May 19X7.
—Investor pays swap counterparty A$0.625m every 15 February and 15 August commencing 15 August 19X2 ending 15 August 19X2. Note that the first payment reflects the full coupon rather than the accrual from settlement.
—Investor receives from swap counterparty, a margin over three month BBR based on a notional principal of A$9.1440m (the original investment).
—At maturity, investor makes a payment of A$0.8560m to swap counterparty reflecting the difference between purchase price and face value of bond.

The margin relative to BBR is determined as follows:

	% pa (S/A)
Swap rate	14.30%
Actual fixed rate receipts[1]	−13.67%
Adjustment for principal payment at maturity[2]	+1.12%
Adjustment for carry cost on coupon[3]	− 0.04%
Adjusted margin:	1.71% pa

Notes:

1. Calculated as A$6.25m ÷ A$9.1442 or 13.67% pa.
2. Calculated as A$0.8560m amortised over each coupon date at the equivalent of 16.00% pa (S/A) on assumed principal of A$9.1442m.
3. Assuming a negative 4.00% pa over the 81 days to the first coupon on A$0.3453m amortised over each coupon date at the swap rate.

The concept of an adjustment swap is more complex. Typically, certain types of investors for reasons such as tax or accounting treatment may prefer to change the cash flow characteristics of the underlying security. For example:

- An investor buying a fixed rate bond or FRN at a substantial discount may seek to convert it into a par security by entering into an interest rate swap in which the investor pays fixed or floating at a rate equal to the coupon on the security. This rate will usually be less than the market rate on the swap of that maturity and in return for paying less than a market return, the investor will make a one-time up-front cash payment to the swap counterparty equal to the difference between the par value and the purchase price of the security. This difference compensates the swap counterparty for receiving a submarket coupon with the up-front payment being repaid to the investor over the life of the swap in the form of a premium on the swap payments it receives.

• In the opposite situation, an investor buying a bond at a premium may choose to pay an above market rate on the swap equivalent to the bond coupon in return for an up-front payment from the swap counterparty equal to the premium on the bond. This payment is recovered by the swap counterparty by the fact that the investor pays an above market coupon under the swap.

These types of adjustment swaps, which are increasingly common, allow investors to smooth out and adjust the cash flows connected with specific investments. In essence, swap coupons can be set equal to bond coupons while margins above or below market coupons can be exchanged for up-front or, in some cases, backended payments allowing the investor to rearrange cash flows from an investment into a structure that, for any reason, the investor finds more attractive.

Some examples of these types of adjustment swaps include:

• Par/par flat swap where a customer wishing to invest in a par asset at a stated return with no accrued interest needs to convert a security trading at a discount through this specific swap structure (for example, see *Exhibit 18.3*).

• A zero coupon issue swapped into a three or six month floating rate coupon.

• A discount floating rate coupon swapped to full floating coupon, for example, where a FRN can be bought at a substantial discount to par but the investor wants current income and therefore wants to buy the bonds at par and receive the current market yield to maturity spread rather than the difference between the purchase price and face value of the notes at maturity.

• A zero coupon bond swapped to a full fixed coupon, for example, where the zero coupon is priced attractively but the investor desires to shorten the duration and improve the cash flow of the investment.

Exhibit 18.4 illustrates an adjustment swap involving swapping of the discount on a FRN to a full floating coupon.

THE MARKET FOR ASSET SWAPS

The structure of the market

The concept of asset swaps is best understood with reference to the underlying market for these types of transactions. The market for asset swaps which has evolved over the period since 1982 has a number of clearly identifiable dimensions:

• the type of asset swap transaction, classified by category of investor;

• types of underlying securities utilised in structuring the asset swap;

• private asset swap structures versus public or securitised asset swaps. Private asset swap structures themselves can be separated into two further categories: investor made swaps and synthetic securities.

Exhibit 18.4

Adjustment Asset Swap

An investor has the opportunity to buy the following FRN:

Amount:	US$5m
Maturity:	30/6/X9
Interest rate:	six month LIBOR, net and payable semi-annually
Price:	98.90
Yield to maturity spread:	LIBOR + 34bps
Current coupon:	7.3125%
Settlement date:	30/6/X5

However, the investor has a preference for current income and thus would prefer to purchase the FRN at par and receive the current market yield to maturity spread as coupon income. The investor achieves this by entering into an asset swap whereby:

• The investor pays the counterparty six month LIBOR flat semi-annually as well as an up-front payment of 1.20% or US$60,000.

• In return, the investor receives six month LIBOR plus 35.14bps semi-annually over the life of the transaction.

The spread over LIBOR earned by the investor equates to the 1.20% being amortised over the outstanding life of the security at an assumed reinvestment rate of 8.80% pa (S/A).

The basic asset swap structures utilised are largely dictated by the interaction of these various structural dimensions.

Types of asset swaps

The types of asset swaps that are usually undertaken are dictated almost totally by the investor base for such synthetic assets. In turn, the investor base for these types of asset swaps is motivated to enter into such transactions for some clearly identifiable reasons.

The main factor in this context has been the increasing securitisation of capital markets which has led to borrowers increasingly issuing securities to raise money on more competitive terms than available by borrowing from financial intermediaries, primarily banks. This has created a significant shortage of conventional loan assets. As a result many banks face a dwindling asset base as they lose their historic customer base to the securities markets.

An additional factor which is relevant was the substantial improvement in yields that were achievable by creating synthetic assets relative to the purchase of direct investments. In essence, the right conditions existed for a basic arbitrage which created the opportunity for yield pick-ups where, importantly, there was a ready-made market for these synthetic assets primarily among banks.

Since the origins of these markets, similar factors have attracted other more traditional investors such as institutions, pension funds etc. to this market.

The basic types of asset swaps include:

• assets denominated in any currency which are swapped into synthetic US$ LIBOR based FRNs which are sold primarily to banks;

- asset swaps which entail the creation of synthetic fixed rate bonds, in currencies such as yen, utilising either fixed or floating rate securities in a variety of currencies for sale to Japanese institutional investors;
- asset swaps designed to create synthetic FRNs in currencies other than US$ to match demands for non-US$ floating rate assets;
- a number of variations on the above usually entailing special structured transactions including:

  —insurance company deposit transactions;

  —matched zaitech transactions.

Asset swaps involving the creation of synthetic US$ LIBOR based FRNs constitute by far the most significant sector of the asset swap market. It constitutes probably 80.00% of all asset swaps undertaken. The predominance of this type of structure primarily reflects the nature of the underlying investment demand which comes from commercial banks seeking floating rate loan assets which can be match funded. The continued need for high quality and relatively high yield assets by a large group of commercial banks (such as Japanese, Australian and New Zealand banks becoming active in international markets) seeking asset growth, provides a significant impetus to this particular market segment.

The extent of the yield improvements achievable by investing in asset swaps as against direct purchase of floating rate assets can be gauged from the analysis set out in *Exhibit 18.5*. As indicated, the synthetic assets not only offer substantial yield pick-ups compared with the return available on equivalent direct investments but as an additional incentive they offer an investor greater flexibility to diversify its portfolio by allowing investment in issuers who do not usually undertake FRN issues.

It is also worth noting that part of the attraction of synthetic US$ FRNs relates to the call features on normal FRNs which allow the borrower to redeem the issue prior to maturity. In recent years, the absence of high quality assets and competition among financial intermediaries has led to decreasing levels of call protection on FRN issues. For example, in the first half of 1986, a number of major FRN borrowers exercised their calls and retired outstanding FRN issues and utilised alternative sources of funding to refinance—primarily, the rapidly developing Euro CP market. As a result, FRNs with protection against calls have tended to trade at substantial premiums to par therefore causing a significant erosion in margins as well as causing certain cash flow mismatches which may be unattractive to investors. Against this background, synthetic FRNs have proved particularly attractive as the underlying asset has in most cases provided significantly higher levels of call protection.

The creation of fixed rate bonds for sale, in the main to Japanese investors, has been a more recent, and often transient, phenomenon. The essential motivation here is the substantial yield improvements achievable for these institutions by directing investment funds to synthetic as against direct yen assets. The concept of creating fixed rate bonds in a particular currency through an asset swap is not unique to the yen market and transactions involving other currencies have also been completed.

From time to time, substantial demand for non-US$ floating rate assets has existed. This has primarily reflected the asset demand of various banks with attractive funding in usually their home currency. Added demand has come from investors seeking to take advantage of currency fluctuations without necessarily creating a simultaneous interest rate exposure. The paradigm example of the creation of synthetic FRNs in other currencies is the Stars and Stripes transaction involving the creation of two synthetic FRNs, in deutschmark and £ (see discussion below).

The concept of creating synthetic assets has particularly found a market in specially structured transactions involving demand for specific assets to match a particular investor requirement. This investor requirement is usually dictated by an offsetting transaction elsewhere in the investor's portfolio or by regulatory considerations. While technically these types of transactions are similar to the other transactions described they nevertheless represent an interesting variation on the basic asset swap concept.

One of the earliest examples of this type of specially structured asset swap were insurance company deposit transactions. In this case, Japanese insurance companies were the primary factor behind such transactions because of their need to invest substantial volumes of funds in assets

Exhibit 18.5
Return Comparison of Synthetic versus Direct US$ FRN

Issuer	Rating	Maturity (years)	Margin over six months LIBID in basis points		
			Estimated in public FRN market	Available on synthetic FRN	Absolute yield pick-up
Republic of Austria	AAA	6(1)	−5.0 (0)	+22.5(+27)	+27.5(+27)
Bank of Tokyo[1]	AA	5(7)	+4.0(+30)	+25.0(+47)	+21.0(+17)
Credit Anstalt Bank Verein		5(5)	+5.0(−5)	+27.5(+23)	+22.5(+28)
Kingdom of Denmark	AA+	6(3)	−5.0 (0)	+25.0(+39)	+30.0(+39)
Industrial Bank of Japan[1]	AAA	6	+3.0	+25.0	+22.0
Royal Bank of Canada		6(6)	+6.0(+6)	+27.5(+27.5)	+21.5(+21.5)
Osterreichische Landesbank		3(3)	+5.0(+5)	+25.0(+25)	+20.0(+20)
Mitsubishi Corporation	AAA(AA+)	8(5)	+12.5	+30.0(+42)	+17.5(+42)
PK Banken		5(5)	+6.0(+10)	+27.5(+30)	+21.5(+20)
Deutsche Bank	AAA	9(9)	−2.0 (0)	+27.5(+30)	+29.5(+30)
Development Finance Corporation (New Zealand)	AA	9(9)	0.0(5)	+30.0(+55)	+30.0(+60)
			+2.5(+5.7)	+26.5(+34.6)	+24.0(+28.9)

Average return on public market FRN portfolio	+2.5bps (+5.7bps)
Average return on synthetic FRN portfolio	+26.5bps (+34.6bps)
Increase in average return	+24.0bps (+28.9bps)

Note:

1. Similar returns are available on corporate bonds with bank guarantees.
2. The return comparison is based on 1986 market conditions. The numbers within brackets indicate comparative returns available as at May 1988.

Source: Citicorp.

denominated in currencies other than yen. This particular investment requirement could usually not be satisfied directly because:

- the institution in question could not actually undertake foreign investments and was limited to domestic investments within Japan, such as bank deposits;
- these institutions, despite the fact that they were allowed to invest overseas, had already reached or were near the maximum limit imposed by the Ministry of Finance, which in the early half of the 1980s was 10.00% of their overall portfolio;
- direct investment in a foreign market was problematic because of unfamiliarity with the credit quality of issuers of the underlying securities, settlement difficulties and the impact of withholding tax on cross-border interest flows.

In these circumstances, a number of ingenious transactions were developed to circumvent some of these difficulties. In a typical transaction, an insurance company would make a deposit in the desired currency, say C$, with a Japanese bank. The Japanese bank in turn would buy a matching synthetic asset in C$ which provided the necessary cash flows to make interest payments and repay the original principal invested by the institution. The synthetic C$ asset would usually consist of floating rate US$ assets, either a US$ FRN or US$ CD which were rolled over on maturity, combined with a US$ LIBOR and C$ fixed currency swap.

This particular structure satisfied all the necessary requirements. For instance, the deposit with the Japanese bank was usually within the allowable investment categories of the investor and, moreover, the deposit with the Japanese bank did not usually constitute a foreign security for Ministry of Finance purposes and therefore did not represent utilisation of the 10.00% foreign asset allocation. It should, however, be noted that this rule deficiency was later rectified.

An additional benefit of this structure was that the Japanese bank, usually one of the major city or trust banks, was in a better position to assess the underlying credit of the security purchased as well as the credit of the swap counterparty. Settlement was also made relatively easy and the swap cash flows were not usually subject to withholding tax. This type of transaction involving deposits was undertaken in a wide variety of currencies including C$, A$ and NZ$.

The practice of zaitech transactions is a more recent phenomenon relating particularly to the period 1986 to 1987. The term zaitech derives from the Japanese word *zaiteku* which means financial engineering. The practice of zaitech financing referred to the activities of major Japanese corporations who increasingly found themselves involved in financial arbitrage transactions to generate profits to subsidise basic business earnings in a period when the appreciating yen led to severe downturns in the profitability of their export businesses.

A popular practice during this time was for these companies to undertake borrowing transactions where the funds raised were immediately reinvested at usually a higher return to provide a locked in annuity stream of earnings for the issuer. One form of this transaction was the issue of bonds with attached equity warrants which because of the equity option element led to the cost of financing being significantly reduced for the issuer, allowing it to generate substantial spread earnings by reinvesting the funds raised. In extreme cases, particularly in 1987, a number of borrowers actually were able to generate a negative cost of funds in yen. The funds raised were usually reinvested in yen assets. Some of these yen assets were, in fact, asset swaps, usually with the final synthetic asset being a fixed rate yen bond.

An example of an insurance company deposit transaction is set out in *Exhibit 18.6*. An example of a matched zaitech transaction is set out in *Exhibit 18.7*.

Types of securities used in asset swaps

The availability of the underlying securities is essential to the asset swap process. It is also essential that there be a discrepancy in the price of the asset and/or the relationship between the asset yield and swap prices. These discrepancies form the basis of the higher returns available on synthetic asset transactions.

The discrepancies in asset prices may arise from differential pricing between various market segments. This may reflect different credit criteria or restrictions on asset choice which create supply and demand imbalances leading to asset prices which provide opportunities for arbitrage. For example, in 1986, the margins on FRNs were bid to unsustainably low levels as the supply of FRNs dwindled and the opportunity for short-term capital gains attracted a variety of investors. As similar factors were not present in the fixed rate market, a discrepancy between the prices of assets emerged as between the FRN and fixed rate market creating the opportunity for arbitrage entailing the creation of synthetic FRNs which yielded significant margins over those available on comparable FRNs trading in the market.

Discrepancies in the relationship between asset yields and swap prices are more complex. Opportunities for arbitrage emerge when asset yields move to a level which allows them to be swapped, given the prevailing structure of swap rates, to generate a coupon stream in excess of that on equivalent non-synthetic securities. The process effectively is one of transferring the particular security from one market segment to another to equalise supply and demand at a given price.

As in the liability swap market, a major factor in asset swap arbitrage is the leads and lags between various market segments in the same currency. For example, lags between the domestic United States and Eurodollar market can sometimes be as long as two days. Just as a nervous or bearish United States Treasury market opens the conventional liability swap window allowing issuers to swap their fixed rate new issues into sub-LIBOR funds, a rallying or bullish United States Treasury market with United States Treasury yields and swap rates falling, creates fixed-to-floating asset swap opportunities. If this asset swap is attractive vis-à-vis the conventional floating rate asset market, the asset swap arbitrage is undertaken.

The types of securities used in asset swaps are readily identifiable:

- ex-warrant debt component of a bond with equity warrants issue;
- illiquid or mispriced bonds available in the primary or secondary market;

- mortgage or asset backed securities;
- new issues specifically designed to be asset swapped.

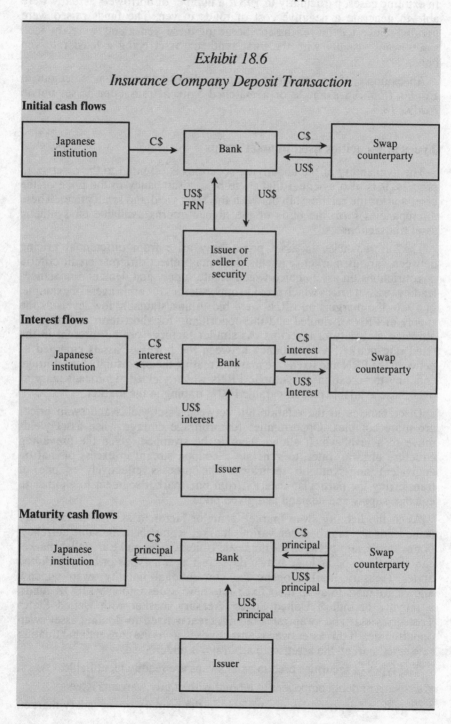

Exhibit 18.6

Insurance Company Deposit Transaction

Exhibit 18.7
Zaitech/Yen Equity Warrant Swap

Assume that a Japanese corporation undertakes a US$ debt with equity warrants issue for a five year maturity with a coupon of 1.00% pa.

Assume that the following market rates are applicable:

US$ swap rate:	8.00% versus six month LIBOR
¥/US$ swap rate:	4.77% versus six month LIBOR
US$/¥ spot:	140.00
US$/¥ five year forward:	114.80%

Under these conditions, the issuer's ¥ cost is equal to approximately −2.03% pa [4.77%−(8 × 0.85) where 0.85 is the ¥/US$ conversion factor].

The issuer can undertake the swap in one of two ways:

• A series of interest rate and currency swaps.

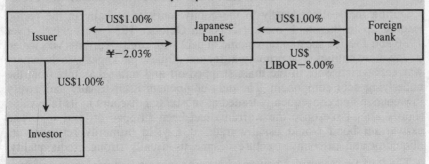

• A combination of LFTX contracts and a structured interest rate swap.

Year		Year	
0	US$100m	0	US$100m
1	1% × US$100m	1	1% × US$100m
2	1% × US$100m	2	1% × US$100m
3	1% × US$100m	3	1% × US$100m
4	1% × US$100m	4	1% × US$100m
5	1% × US$100m + US$100m[1]	5	1% × US$100m + US$30m

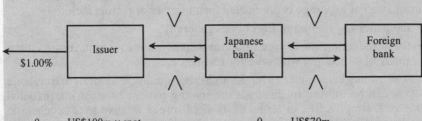

0	US$100m × spot	0	US$70m
1	2% × ¥14 billion	1	LIBOR flat × US$70m
2	2% × ¥14 billion	2	LIBOR flat × US$70m
3	2% × ¥14 billion	3	LIBOR flat × US$70m
4	2% × ¥14 billion	4	LIBOR flat × US$70m
5	2% × ¥14 billion + ¥14 billion	5	LIBOR flat × US$70m

The issuer would then purchase a fixed rate ¥ asset to lock in a spread.

Exhibit 18.7—continued

Note:

1. Japanese bank makes up the $70m difference ($100m − $30m) by selling ¥. Five year forward: $70m × (140 − 25.2) = ¥8 billion.

Source: *Corporate Finance, Euromoney Publications.*

By far the largest source of securities for asset swap transactions has been the ex-warrant debt component of a debt with equity warrants issue package where, in the main, the issuer is a Japanese corporation. In many cases, the Japanese issuer's own credit is enhanced by the availability of a bank guarantee or letter of credit securing the debt component of the issue.

During the sustained rally in the equity markets globally in the period leading up to the stock market crash in October 1987, particularly over 1986 and 1987, a substantial volume of debt with equity warrants was issued by Japanese entities. The primary attraction of these packages was the equity warrants which were in the main stripped off and sold separately from the underlying debt component. The debt component itself usually had a very low coupon and consequently traded at substantial discount to its face value shortly after issue once the warrants had been stripped off and sold. The ex-warrant bond would usually trade at a yield primarily reflecting its illiquidity and discount structure despite its usually strong credit quality.

The Japanese securities houses who were the main financial intermediaries arranging these equity warrant issues essentially became involved in the process of repackaging many of these issues for sale primarily to commercial bank investors as high yielding US$ LIBOR based FRNs. As discussed more fully below, the swapping of ex-warrant bonds formed the basis of the large market in public or securitised asset swap structures which grew up primarily through 1987.

A major source of securities for asset swaps have been relatively illiquid or mispriced Eurobond issues. This lack of liquidity which facilitates the asset swap of arbitrage is predicated on a number of factors including:

• the pattern of trading in Eurobonds generally;

• the introduction into the securities markets of innovative security structures, many of which met with investor resistance.

The trading behaviour of a liquid, high credit quality, US$ straight Eurobond issue, can be utilised to illustrate the trading pattern of most international bonds. During its life, in terms of its yield spread relative to a benchmark, such as United States Treasuries, the trading history of the security generally approximates the following pattern.

The spread, which is totally credit related, is greatest at issue date and declines over the life of the transaction to almost zero close to maturity when the credit risk is negligible. This assumes an issue which is originally successfully priced and placed and has considerable liquidity reflecting the underlying size of the issue, the quality of the issuer and the presence of a substantial number of major market makers willing to make consistent two-way prices in the issue throughout its life.

However, more typically, most bonds while they may be launched at the same spread relative to Treasuries as the above liquid issue are less popular with a resultant drift to wider spreads over time vis-à-vis the underlying benchmark. This usually reflects the lack of liquidity in the issue which itself is a function of the size and the quality of the issuer, as well as the lack of market makers in the particular issue.

As the price of these issues falls relative to more liquid and better traded issues, the high yield on these bonds facilitates the asset swap arbitrage. This arbitrage is particularly facilitated by the fact that the investors in floating rate assets will traditionally be commercial banks or other financial intermediaries who match fund their assets, usually through the short-term money market at a cost relative to LIBOR. These institutions are also seeking high quality loan assets and therefore will be less concerned about the factors which are leading to the bond's poor performance in the secondary market.

While the above example focuses on US$ Eurobonds, the situation is similar with bonds denominated in other currencies where the problems identified above are usually more acute in their influence on secondary market performance.

An additional factor assisting in the availability of asset swap fodder in recent years has been the competitive environment in international capital markets which has seen a consistent pattern of mispriced bonds being brought to market primarily to accommodate the new issue swap arbitrage, on the liability side, for the issuer. Many new issues now traditionally begin to trade shortly after launch at substantial spreads below issue price. Such aggressively priced, poorly syndicated and, most importantly, poorly distributed issues have tended to have a particularly poor trading performance as they have failed to attract any investor interest (the celebrated "dog" or "canine" issue).

An additional factor has been the incredible array of security structures which have been introduced into various markets in recent years as investment bankers have sought to create completely new types of securities to satisfy perceived investor requirements, usually predicating the issuer's involvement on the basis of a new issue arbitrage. Many of these issues have not attracted significant investor support. These issues on the whole have proved difficult to sell in their original form and have been combined with swaps to create a synthetic asset which is more attractive to investors.

A good example of this type of repackaging of what would otherwise have been unsaleable securities is the case of the bull FRN. As discussed in Chapter 15 these types of issues were designed to appeal to investors seeking to benefit from falling short-term rates. A number of these issues proved to be disastrously unsuccessful as investors shunned the structures. Such issues were usually repackaged as floating rate assets for commercial bank investors. *Exhibit 18.8* sets out such a repackaging of a bull FRN for an investor.

An increasingly important source of securities for asset swapping is mortgage backed securities. Mortgage backed and asset backed securities have been particularly important sources of assets for such transactions

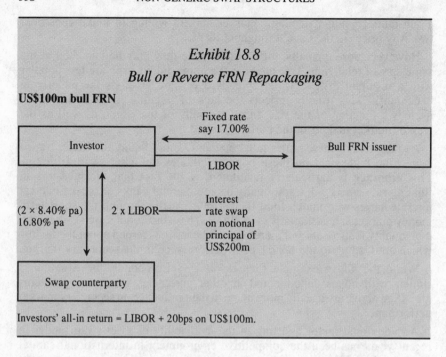

Exhibit 18.8

Bull or Reverse FRN Repackaging

US$100m bull FRN

Fixed rate
say 17.00%

Investor

Bull FRN issuer

LIBOR

(2 × 8.40% pa)
16.80% pa

2 x LIBOR

Interest
rate swap
on notional
principal of
US$200m

Swap counterparty

Investors' all-in return = LIBOR + 20bps on US$100m.

because they have typically offered much higher yields than comparable corporate or financial institution paper. This added return, however, has been in return for the investor in the securities accepting an additional element of risk relating to the risk of prepayment. If interest rates fall, the underlying mortgages or assets tend to be prepaid effectively resulting in the mortgage backed security itself being called.

However, this risk of prepayment has not precluded the use of these securities for asset swapping with the underlying prepayment risk being essentially hedged through the use of putable swaps to convert the mortgage backed security to a floating rate asset (see description of putable swaps in Chapter 16). The fact that the spread differential between the coupon on the mortgage backed security and the fixed rate payable on the swap has in fact been consistently wide enough to create a substantial spread over LIBOR (even after immunising, usually within certain boundaries, the prepayment risk utilising a putable interest rate swap) has continued to make this particular type of asset swap extremely attractive. An example of this type of asset swap is set out in *Exhibit 18.9*.

A final category of securities used in asset swaps are new securities issues specifically designed to be sold in synthetic asset form. Over the last several years, a number of asset swap-driven issues have been brought to market. These issues are usually for less creditworthy names allowing them to tap the fixed rate market from which they would be otherwise precluded with the fixed rate bond being sold in synthetic form as a US$ LIBOR FRN primarily to bank investors. *Exhibit 18.10* sets out an example of an issue specifically designed to be asset swapped.

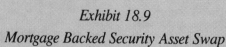

Exhibit 18.9

Mortgage Backed Security Asset Swap

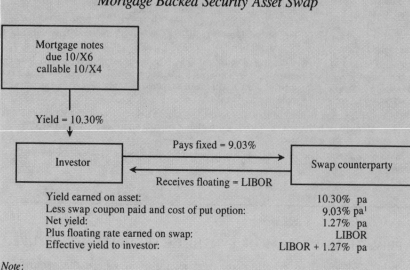

Mortgage notes
due 10/X6
callable 10/X4

Yield = 10.30%

Pays fixed = 9.03%

Investor

Receives floating = LIBOR

Swap counterparty

Yield earned on asset:	10.30% pa
Less swap coupon paid and cost of put option:	9.03% pa[1]
Net yield:	1.27% pa
Plus floating rate earned on swap:	LIBOR
Effective yield to investor:	LIBOR + 1.27% pa

Note:
1. The payments include 0.40% for the put and 8.63% for the swap.

Source: Salomon Brothers.

Exhibit 18.10

New Issue Designed to be Asset Swapped

Hotel Parker Meridien Capital Corporation

Guarantor:	Mitsubishi Bank
Amount:	US$60m
Maturity:	ten years (due 11 February 1997)
Coupon:	8.375%
Issue price:	10.25
Yield:	8.34% (gross), 8.55% (less selling concession)
Amortisation:	Bullet
Call option:	Of the issuer—for tax reasons only. Callable by the guarantor in certain circumstances at par
Listing:	Luxembourg
Denominations:	US$5,000 and US$50,000
Commissions:	2.00% (management, underwriting 0.625%, less 0.125% praecipum; selling 1.375%)
Expenses:	US$100,000
Stabilisation:	IPMA recommendations
Selling deadline:	9 January
Payment:	11 February
Governing law:	New York

Exhibit 18.10—continued

Negative pledge:	Of the issuer only
Cross-default:	Of the guarantor only
Pari passu:	Yes
Lead managers:	Morgan Guaranty (books), Mitsubishi Finance
Co-managers:	BBL, Bear Stearns, Chemical Bank Int., Fuji Int., LTCB Int., Mitsubishi Trust Int., Mitsui Trust Int., Societe Generale, Sumitomo Trust Int., SBCI
Pre-market price:	Less 1.75, less 1.50

Launched at 144bps over Treasuries, this deal is asset swappable producing AAA floating rate paper at around 20bps over LIBOR (although lead manager MGL reported some success in placing bonds in their pristine form). The deal amounts to a placement as the amount is obviously too small to provide liquidity.

The issuer is a special purpose company formed to finance the construction of the eponymous hotel in Manhattan by the Jack Parker Corporation. A first mortgage on the property has been assigned to the guarantor.

In an overall good performance, the bonds were quoted at less 1.75, less 1.50 by the lead manager Wednesday.

Source: International Financing Review.

PRIVATE ASSET SWAP OR SYNTHETIC SECURITY STRUCTURE

A critical element in creating an asset swap, even where the security is available and an investor for the synthetic asset can be located, relates to the specific structuring of the swap in a form acceptable to the investor. The asset swap can be on a private or synthetic security basis or, alternatively, a public or securitised asset swap structure can be utilised. In this section, private asset swap structures are considered.

Where the asset swap is to be structured as a private transaction, there are two possible structures:

• a private or investor made asset swap;
• the creation of a synthetic security.

Exhibit 18.11 sets out, in diagrammatic form, the two structures.

Under the investor manufactured asset swap structure, the investor specifically purchases the underlying cash or physical security and enters into the swap to convert the return into its preferred form. The implications of this particular structure include:

• The investor is responsible for multiple sets of cash flows, including the coupon on the bond and the flows under the swap.

• The credit risk on this transaction is quite complex with the investor having credit risk on both the issuer *and* the swap counterparty. Conversely, the swap counterparty has a risk on the investor and will usually treat the transaction as an allocation of credit lines to the investor, potentially imposing a constraint on future transactions.

• The accounting and most importantly the revaluation structure of this package will be complex as both the bond and the swap will need to be treated separately. This may result, depending on the accounting techniques used, in discrepancies which distort the reporting of the investment.

- The liquidity of this investment will be a factor of both the liquidity of the bond and the swap. The cost of liquidating the investment will essentially be the sum of the cost of the bid/offer spread for both the bond and the swap. Depending on the liquidity of the underlying security, the cost of selling the bonds may range from 0.50% to 1.00% of the price of the bond. Similarly, the cost of reversing the swap will typically be between 0.10% and 0.20% pa or up to 1.50% flat of the notional principal value of the swap, depending, of course, on maturity. The combined cost of liquidating both the bond and swap can therefore range from 1.30% to as much as 2.50% of the principal value of the transaction.

These factors dictate that investor manufactured asset swaps are usually the preserve of highly sophisticated investors with the expertise to assemble and account for these structures and who moreover have no significant need for any secondary market liquidity of the package.

The synthetic security structure is specifically designed to overcome some of the difficulties of the first structure and to provide investors with the benefit of a simpler structure, lower transaction costs and enhanced liquidity.

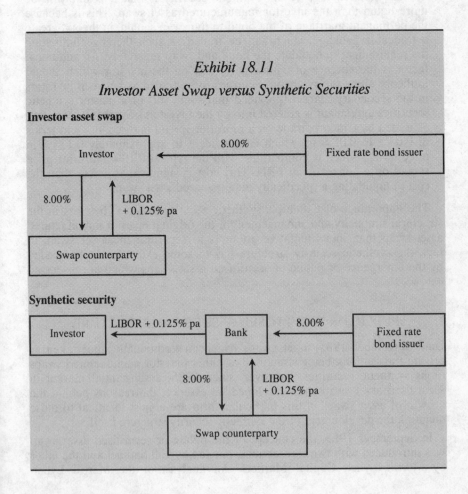

Exhibit 18.11

Investor Asset Swap versus Synthetic Securities

The synthetic security structure was originally developed by Citicorp Investment Bank Limited (Citicorp). Under the structure, Citicorp effectively interposes itself between the issuer and the investor with regard to the cash flows of the transaction. Citicorp strips and collects the fixed coupon from the bond and simultaneously arranges the swap, usually with an internal swap "warehouse". Under the structure Citicorp pays the investor a synthetic floating rate coupon.

The major structural advantages of the synthetic security include:

• The cash flows are considerably simplified by the marriage of the bond and the swap resulting in only one cash flow for the investor.

• The credit risk factors are, effectively, identical to a normal asset swap.

• The accounting and revaluation requirements for the investor are greatly simplified and the investor should, in most cases, be able to account for, and revalue the synthetic FRN as a normal FRN. This may have certain administrative advantages as existing accounting procedures and systems may be capable of being utilised for the investment.

• The major advantage of the synthetic security is that it is likely to be more liquid than the investor manufactured asset swap. This is because the permanent marriage of the bond to the swap should, in theory, create a tradeable package which can be traded as such thereby eliminating the requirement to liquidate the bond and swap separately. An additional factor is the absence of counterparty risk on the investor which should in theory allow the synthetic securities to be traded as between investors in the secondary market (provided that some sort of a master synthetic securities agreement is entered into by the investors). Synthetic securities, as traded by Citicorp, trade on a bid/offer spread in discount yield terms of 0.03% to 0.05% pa which is equivalent to approximately 0.125% in price terms, which is comparable with the typical 0.10% bid/offer price spread on a conventional FRN. This cost is significantly lower than the cost of liquidating a specifically manufactured asset swap.

The importance of Citicorp's synthetic security structure lies less in the structural simplicity and enhancement of the original investor manufactured asset swap than in its tentative attempts to securitise the asset swap. In fact, the synthetic security structure has to some extent been superceded by the emergence of public or securitised asset swaps which are discussed below.

PUBLIC OR SECURITISED ASSET SWAP STRUCTURE

Until September 1985, asset swaps had been traditionally undertaken as private transactions, being structured as either investor manufactured swaps or as synthetic securities. However, since 1985, a substantial market in securitised asset swaps has developed. In essence, the reasons behind the growth of asset swaps in this particular form are almost identical to those dictating the development of the synthetic security structure itself.

In September 1985, the concept of the public or securitised asset swap was introduced with two transactions, one led by Hill Samuel and the other by Merrill Lynch Capital Markets. An analysis of the Merrill Lynch transaction provides an insight into the mechanics of the securitised asset swap.

Towards the end of September 1985, the United Kingdom raised US$2.5 billion through the issuance of seven year FRNs, due October 1992. The notes were originally priced at 99.70% of face value, net of fees, with a coupon of three month US$ LIBID and were non-callable for three years from the time of issuance. Following the launch of this issue, the sales force of Merrill Lynch, a United States investment bank, noted that there was considerable interest from its investors in *fixed rate* United Kingdom government US$ denominated debt. In particular, the sales force had reported a coupon of approximately 9.375% pa for a three year maturity as acceptable to these investors. However, no fixed rate United Kingdom government debt denominated in US$ was available. Consequently, the Merrill Lynch swap and Eurobond syndicate desk set about designing, at that time, the largest securitised asset swap.

The structure of the transaction was as follows:

• Merrill Lynch bought US$100m of United Kingdom FRNs.

• The US$100m of United Kingdom 1992 FRNs were then sold into a special purpose vehicle known as Marketable Eurodollar Collateralised Securities Limited (MECS).

• Simultaneously, Merrill Lynch arranged a swap with Prudential Global Funding Corporation between MECS and the swap counterparty under which MECS made payments of US$ LIBID every three months in return for Prudential making payments equivalent to 9.375% pa to MECS. This effectively converted the floating rate US$ cash flow that MECS trust earned from the United Kingdom FRNs into a fixed rate US$ flow.

• Merrill Lynch then arranged a Eurodollar bond issue in the name of MECS with a coupon of 9.375% pa and a final maturity of October 1988. The bonds issued by MECS were collateralised with the assets of the trust which was a holding of US$100m of United Kingdom FRNs and also the contingent liability reflecting the interest rate swap with Prudential. Essentially, the package constituted a high quality (AAA) credit risk.

This structure is set out in *Exhibit 18.12.*

The two transactions undertaken, both involving the United Kingdom government US$2.5 billion 1992 FRN, clearly demonstrated the advantages of securitising the underlying asset swap to improve the liquidity and marketability of the investment.

However, the market for public asset swap structures remained stagnant for almost one year. In September 1986, Morgan Guaranty Limited undertook a US$250m repackaging of a subsequent US$4 billion United Kingdom FRN. Significantly, in September 1986, Banque Paribas Capital Markets undertook the first securitised synthetic asset transaction involving a currency swap whereby, utilising a vehicle known as Republic of Italy Euro Repackaged Asset Limited (dubbed Ferraris), the French Investment Bank utilised approximately ECU200m of Italy 1993 Treasury certificates as the basis of a synthetic asset US$, paying a coupon of LIMEAN.

It was in early 1987 that the securitised asset swap market entered its growth phase. Bankers Trust International undertook two transactions within

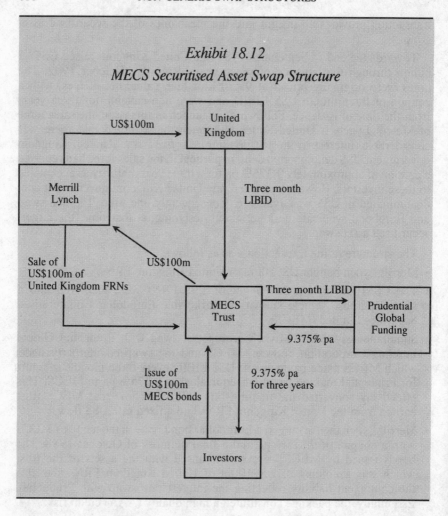

Exhibit 18.12

MECS Securitised Asset Swap Structure

one month of each other which created the environment for rapid growth in these transactions. Utilising a vehicle know as Trust Obligation Participating Securities (TOPS), Bankers Trust first repackaged Kingdom of Denmark 7.00% 1988 bonds into US$200m of two year FRNs paying a coupon of LIBOR plus 0.0625% pa and, perhaps more significantly, swapped a portfolio of Japanese bank guaranteed ex-warrant bonds into a US$100m five year US$ FRN paying LIBOR plus 0.125% pa. The structure of the second transaction was significant in that for the first time it utilised ex-warrant bonds, mainly from Japanese issuers with, usually, bank guarantees, in a public securitised asset swap transaction.

The structure of the TOPS 2 transaction was extremely complex because the package of ex-warrant bonds contained a variety of maturities requiring the issue of FRNs to incorporate a complex sinking fund provision which detracted from its underlying liquidity. However, the transaction aroused sufficient interest from Japanese regional banks seeking US$ floating rate assets to allow further transactions to be undertaken.

In the period January to December 1987, approximately US$4 billion of public securitised asset swap transactions were undertaken. These transactions fell into two distinct categories:

- the repackaging of Japanese ex-warrant bonds for sale to commercial bank investors;
- other usually more complex transactions involving a variety of currencies.

The main factors operating in the market at this time appeared to be:

- the unsustainable decline in yields in the FRN market and the subsequent calamitous fall in and loss of liquidity in the main FRN market;
- the huge volume of Japanese equity warrant issues being brought to market creating vast amounts of ex-warrant bonds which were proving increasingly difficult to sell;
- an interest rate environment where expectations of increased interest rates, primarily in US$, was forcing investors to seek refuge in floating rate assets.

The combination of these factors served to create a particularly conducive environment to this type of securitised asset swap activity. The repackaging of Japanese ex-warrant bonds into US$ FRNs for placement with bank investors quickly became a highly standardised issue structure dominated by the Japanese securities houses and the subsidiaries of Japanese banks who were the primary players in the equity warrant markets themselves. Initial problems involving the varieties of maturities requiring repackaging was solved simply and elegantly by bringing bunches of equity warrant issues with the same maturity and coupon dates to actually facilitate the repackaging process. The availability of a number of market makers willing to structure discount swaps to generate the required even coupon and maturity date cash flows also assisted in this process.

The other category of securitised asset swaps was considerably more complex. In particular a large part of the activity appeared to be repackaging of originally unsuccessful issues into saleable form.

The most notable example of this type of transaction was the repackaging of the hallmark Kingdom of Denmark 1996 US$ FRN which had carried a coupon of 0.125% pa *below* LIBID, the lowest coupon on a US$ FRN in history. The transaction which met with considerable criticism appeared, ultimately, never to have found sufficient favour to be considered firmly placed with end investors. The original lead manager, Morgan Guaranty, elegantly repackaged the issue to produce deutschmark and £ synthetic FRNs by combining the original US$ FRN with a deutschmark and US$ floating-to-floating currency swap and a £ and US$ floating-to-floating currency swap respectively.

Taking advantage of a weakening US$, the general depression in FRNs and a window in the currency swap market, Morgan Guaranty placed the two synthetic assets, nicknamed Stars and Stripes, with different investor groups. The deutschmark FRN was mainly distributed into Europe, including German funds, while the £ FRN, was sold to some banks as a commercial banking asset but also met with substantial demand from British building societies requiring floating rate assets.

Interestingly, subsequent repackaging included the restructuring of a number of highly complex dual currency bond transactions undertaken earlier (see discussions in Chapter 17) which were repackaged in more conventional form.

Ironically, the repackaging of bonds to create a tradeable instrument itself came under severe criticism for one of two reasons:

• The argument that the repackaging in the public or securitised asset swap form created liquidity rapidly disintegrated as investors tended to hold the security as a term asset thereby limiting the development of a secondary market.

• The repackaging activity was seen by a number of observers as a means of improving individual investment banks' standing in the "league table" (comparisons in terms of volume of new issues brought to market). In particular, there was an element of double counting as investment banks essentially got credit for the original bond issue as well as the repackaged security, where the latter was publicly syndicated.

Exhibit 18.13 sets out the major publicised Euromarket securitised asset swaps undertaken. *Exhibit 18.14* sets out Eurobond league tables comparing the relative positions of different investment banks where such securitised asset swaps are first included and second specifically excluded from the calculation of volumes of business undertaken.

ASSET SWAPS: IMPLICATIONS FOR CAPITAL MARKETS

The emergence of asset swaps as an important aspect of capital market activity has considerable implications for issuers, investors, and financial intermediaries.

For borrowers, the significance of asset swaps lies in the fact that effectively it points to the existence of a particular investor clientele seeking to purchase securities issued by the relevant borrower but in a form other than that currently available. Consequently, one possible response would be for the borrower to issue a security similar in substance to the synthetic asset directly to the investor base.

The potential for asset swaps entailing securities issued by a particular borrower also points to potential arbitrages and mispricing of issues. By definition, a synthetic security should not be possible at least where the borrower has issued similar instruments which are outstanding in the market unless the investors could through the asset swap obtain a higher return. In this way, asset swaps point to potential mispricing of transactions.

Asset swaps also often allow borrowers to undertake transactions which would otherwise not be feasible. For example, a low rated corporation may not have direct access to fixed rate bond markets. However, where a high yielding fixed rate bond can be swapped into a synthetic FRN which would be attractive to certain investors, the borrower may be able to proceed with the direct fixed rate bond issue which otherwise would not be feasible. However, inevitably in these cases the transaction undertaken is inefficient from an economic and pricing viewpoint as the issuer pays a premium to gain this type of access to particular market segments.

Exhibit 18.13

Euromarket Securitised Asset Swaps

Announcement date	Issue	Amount	Maturity (years)	Interest rate (% pa)	Underlying assets	Lead manager
1985						
September	BECS	US$100m	3	9.375	US$102m of UK1992 FRN	Hill Samuel
	MECS	US$100m	3	9.375	US$102m of UK 1992 FRN	Merrill Lynch
1986						
September	FLAGS	US$250m	5	7.00%	US$252m of UK 1996 FRN	Morgan Guaranty Ltd
	FERRARIS	US$204m	7	LIMEAN	ECU200m of Italy 1993 Treasury certificate	Banque Paribas
1987						
January	TOPS 1	US$200m	2	LIBOR + 0.10%	Denmark 7.00% 1988	Bankers Trust International
February	TOPS 2	US$100m	5	LIBOR + 0.125%	Japanese bank guaranteed bonds	Bankers Trust International
	LIVES	US$150m	5	LIBOR + 0.125%	Japanese bank guaranteed bonds	Nomura
	STARS	DM300m	9.5	DM LIBOR + 0.1875/0.25%	Denmark 1996 FRN	Morgan Guaranty Ltd
	STRIPES	£100m	9.5	£ LIBOR + 0.20/0.25%	Denmark 1996 FRN	Morgan Guaranty Ltd
April	SABRE	¥20 billion	5	5.00%	US$137m of UK 1996 FRN	Yamaichi
	LIVES 2	¥17 billion	5	3.99%	US$97m of Denmark 1992	Nomura
May	FERRARIS II	US$330m	6	LIBOR + 0.1875%	ECU182m of Italy 1992/93 Treasury certificate	Banque Paribas
	CIVAS	US$100m	5	LIBOR + 0.1875%	Japanese ex-warrant bonds	Nikko
	TOPS 3	US$100m	5	LIBOR + 0.15%	Japanese ex-warrant bonds	Bankers Trust International
	TOPS 4	US$130m	5	LIBOR + 0.15%	Japanese ex-warrant bonds	Bankers Trust International

Exhibit 18.13—continued

Month	Name	Amount	Term	Rate	Description	Lead manager
June	LIVES 3	¥11 billion	9	5.00%	Eurofima 8.00% dual currency bond 1996	Nomura
	LIVES 4	¥8 billion	9	5.00%	Postipanki 1996 dual currency bond	Nomura
	LIVES 5	¥16 billion	9	5.00%	OKB 1996 dual currency bond	Nomura
	STARS 2	DM300m	11	DM LIBOR + 0.30%	Ireland 1988 FRN	Morgan Guaranty Ltd
	TOPS 5	US$150m	5	LIBOR + 0.15%	Japanese ex-warrant bonds	Bankers Trust International
July	CIVAS 2	US$100m	5	LIBOR + 0.17%	Japanese ex-warrant bonds	Nikko
	SABRE 3	US$200m	5	LIBOR + 0.1875%	Japanese ex-warrant bonds	Yamaichi
	CARP 5	US$100m	5	LIBOR + 0.1875%	Japanese ex-warrant bonds	Pru-Bache
	JEWEL	US$100m	5	LIBOR + 0.1875%	Japanese ex-warrant bonds	Daiwa
	CARPS 2	US$80m	5	LIBOR + 0.15%	Japanese ex-warrant bonds	Pru-Bache
	MASTERS FUNDING	US$32.1m	5/6	LIBOR + 0.16%	Japanese ex-warrant bonds	IBJ
	JETS	US$55m	5	LIBOR + 0.1875%	Japanese ex-warrant bonds	Mitsubishi Finance
August	SMART	US$50m	5	LIBOR + 0.1875%	Japanese ex-warrant bonds	Sumitomo Finance
	SABRE 5	US$185m	5	LIBOR + 0.1875%	Japanese ex-warrant bonds	Yamaichi
	CANVAS	US$50m	5	LIBOR + 0.22%	Japanese ex-warrant bonds	Mitsui Trust
	CIVAS 4	US$200m	5	LIBOR + 0.23%	Japanese ex-warrant bonds	Nikko
	SMART 2	US$50m	5	LIBOR + 0.21%	Japanese ex-warrant bonds	Sumitomo Finance
September	CIVAS	¥9 billion	7	LIBOR + 0.19%	Hokuriko Electric Power Co. 1994 4.50% bonds	Nikko
	FLASH 1	US$50m	5	LIBOR + 0.21%	Japanese ex-warrant bonds	Samwa
	JETS 2	US$55m	5	LIBOR + 0.24%	Japanese ex-warrant bonds	Mitsubishi Finance
	SPRINT	US$30m	5	LIBOR + 0.20%	Japanese ex-warrant bonds	Fuji International Finance
October	MASTERS FUNDING 3	US$38.7m	7	LIBOR + 0.20%	Eurogen bonds	IBJ
	SABRE 6	US$72m	5	LIBOR + 0.25%	Japanese ex-warrant bonds	Yamaichi
	SPRINT 2	US$35m	5	LIBOR + 0.20%	Japanese ex-warrant bonds	Fuji International
	WING 1	A$129m	8.5	8.6875%	Various dual currency bonds	Mitsui Finance International
	SPRINT 3	US$35m	5	LIBOR + 0.20%	Japanese ex-warrant bonds	Fuji International
	WINGS 1	US$37.5m	5	LIBOR + 0.25%	Japanese ex-warrant bonds	Mitsui Finance International

Exhibit 18.13—continued

October	CANVAS II	US$30m	5	LIBOR + 0.20%	Japanese ex-warrant bonds	Mitsui Trust
November	FLASH 2	US$35m	5	LIBOR + 0.21%	Japanese ex-warrant bonds	Sanwa International
	SPRINT 3	US$30m	5	LIBOR + 0.24%	Japanese ex-warrant bonds	Fuji International Finance
	FLASH 3	US$35m	4	LIBOR + 0.18%	Japanese ex-warrant bonds	Sanwa International
	FLASH 4	US$30m	5	LIBOR + 0.20%	Japanese ex-warrant bonds	Sanwa International
December	FLASH 5	US$30m	5	LIBOR + 0.21%	Japanese ex-warrant bonds	Sanwa International
	WING 3	US$37.4m	5	LIBOR + 0.30%	Japanese ex-warrant bonds	Mitsui Finance
	FERRARIS III	US$300m	7	LIBOR + 0.125%	Treasury certificates of Italy	Banque Paribas
1988						
January	WING IV	A$195.4m	9	7.00%	US$120m fixed rate notes	Mitsui Finance International
February	FIGHTER	US$80m	5	LIBOR + 0.24%	Japanese ex-warrant bonds	New Japan Securities
	JEWELL III	US$150m	5	LIBOR + 0.23%	Japanese ex-warrant bonds	Daiwa
	SPRINT 4	US$36m	5	LIBOR + 0.25%	Japanese ex-warrant bonds	Fuji International Finance
March	FIGHTER II	US$70m	3	LIBOR + 0.23%	Japanese ex-warrant bonds	New Japan Securities
	FLASH 6	US$33.2m	2	LIBOR + 0.23%	Japanese ex-warrant bonds	Sanwa International
April	JETS 3	US$42m	5	LIBOR + 0.25%	Japanese ex-warrant bonds	Mitsubishi Finance
	FLASH 7	US$36m	4	LIBOR + 0.18%	Japanese ex-warrant bonds	Sanwa International
	JETS 4	¥5.44 billion	5	5.0625%	Japanese ex-warrant bonds	Mitsubishi Finance
	NOEL II	US$40m	5	LIBOR + 0.25%	Japanese ex-warrant bonds	Norinchukin International
	HEART	US$30m	5	LIBOR + 0.23%	Japanese ex-warrant bonds	DKB International
	SPRINT 5	US$30m	5	9.35%	Japanese ex-warrant bonds	Fuji International
May	SEA OTTER	US$53m	5	LIBOR + 0.25%	Japanese ex-warrant bonds	NKK Europe
June	SMART 3	¥4.3 billion	5	5.25%	Japanese ex-warrant bonds	Sumitomo Finance
	NOEL III	¥5 billion	5	5.00%	Japanese ex-warrant bonds	Norinchukin International
	FLASH 8	US$38.2m	5	LIBOR + 0.22%	Japanese ex-warrant bonds	Sanwa International
	CIVAS VII	US$100m	5	LIBOR + 0.25%	Japanese ex-warrant bonds	Nikko

Exhibit 18.13—continued

July	CIVAS VIII	US$100m	5	LIBOR + 0.25%	Japanese ex-warrant bonds	Saitama International
	LIVES 14	US$70m	5	LIBOR + 0.23%	Japanese ex-warrant bonds	Nomura
	FLORA 2	US$58.8m	5	LIBOR + 0.25%	Japanese ex-warrant bonds	LTCB International
	SABRE 8	¥5 billion	5	¥ LIBOR + 0.0625%	Japanese ex-warrant bonds	Yamaichi
August	SPRINT 6	¥6.372 billion	5	Zero coupon bonds yielding 4.72%	Japanese ex-warrant bonds	Fuji International
	SABRE 9	US$52m	5	LIBOR + 0.25%	Japanese ex-warrant bonds	Yamaichi
	SABRE 10	US$24m	4	LIBOR + 0.25%	Japanese ex-warrant bonds	Yamaichi
September	FLASH	US$33.34m	4	9.50% (for 2 years) LIBOR + 0.22% (for 2 years)	Japanese ex-warrant bonds	Sanwa International
	SMART 5	¥10 billion (in 3 gamle)	4	(1) ¥6.5 billion at 5.4375% (2) ¥2.5 billion of step up notes 3.00% for years 1 and 2, 8.00% thereafter (3) ¥1.0 billion at LIBOR + 0.25%	Japanese ex-warrant bonds	Sumitomo Finance
October	FLASH, SERIES B	US$30.2m	5	LIBOR + 0.21%	Japanese ex-warrant bonds	Sanwa International
	FLASH, SERIES C	US$37m	4	LIBOR + 0.21%	Japanese ex-warrant bonds	Sanwa International
December	TRIPS	US$23m	4	LIBOR + 0.175%	Japanese ex-warrant bonds	Toyo Trust International
	FLASH, SERIES D	US$30m	4.5	LIBOR + 0.18%	Japanese ex-warrant bonds	Sanwa International

Source: International Finance Review.

Exhibit 18.14

Eurobond "League Tables"—With and Without Repackaged Issues

ALL EUROBONDS

Book runners only

1 January-18 December 1987

	Managing bank or group	Number of issues	Total US$m	Share %
1	Nomura	122	18732.63	13.22
2	CSFB	77	9486.76	6.70
3	Deutsche Bank	69	8205.67	5.79
4	Nikko	60	7977.17	5.63
5	Yamaichi	71	7249.22	5.12
6	Daiwa	71	6894.56	4.87
7	Morgan Stanley	35	5079.66	3.58
8	Morgan Guaranty	47	5058.97	3.57
9	Paribas	44	4478.45	3.16
10	Salomon Brothers	36	4413.48	3.11
11	IBJ	40	4133.73	2.92
12	Warburg Securities	37	3965.07	2.80
13	UBS (Securities)	28	3188.89	2.25
14	Commerzbank	28	2744.00	1.94
15	Dresdner Bank	21	2422.01	1.71

EXCLUDING ALL "REPACKAGED BONDS"

Book runners only

1 January-18 December 1987

	Managing bank or group	Number of issues	Total US$m	Share %
1	Nomura	115	18074.60	13.26
2	CSFB	77	9486.76	6.96
3	Deutsche Bank	69	8205.67	6.02
4	Nikko	54	7113.50	5.22
5	Daiwa	69	6694.56	4.91
6	Yamaichi	66	6550.05	4.81
7	Morgan Stanley	35	5079.66	3.73
8	Morgan Guaranty	44	4536.46	3.33
9	Salomon Brothers	36	4413.48	3.24
10	IBJ	36	4027.13	2.96

Source: IFR Bondbase.

In contrast, for investors, the emergence of a significant market for asset swap allows them to purchase or create investments yielding higher than normal returns or, alternatively, customised to precisely match the cash flow requirements of the particular investor. An additional advantage for investors is that the presence of asset swaps allows a greater degree of portfolio diversification by allowing investors the opportunity to better manage the composition of credit risks in a portfolio without necessarily being constrained by the types of securities actually on issue.

However, advantages have to be traded off against the problems of liquidity and added credit risk that must sometimes be assumed in purchasing synthetic assets as investments. In particular, the wide variety of synthetic asset structures and their differing liquidity dictates that investors must be discriminating in their choice of synthetic asset *structure* in order to be able to liquidate the investment in a timely and cost effective manner. The differences in credit risk between the structures also dictates that various types of synthetic asset structures must be evaluated with a view to optimising the utilisation of available credit lines.

A less obvious consequence of the growth of asset swaps is that the emergence of this market provides an upper bound to the price fluctuations or yield differences of securities held in a particular portfolio. The fact that bonds can have their basic structure altered through swaps and therefore be placed with a different group of investors tends to place bounds on its value. For example, a fixed rate bond will have its trading performance bounded by its relativity to swap market spreads as if the yield on the bond increases too rapidly then the bond can be repackaged as a floating rate asset at an attractive spread and placed with a particular investor who will accept the issuer's credit risk but would prefer the asset in a floating rate form. This influence on the trading performance of securities is of significance not only to investors but to financial institutions.

The first category of financial institutions affected by asset swaps are investment banks active in new issue markets or in trading bonds in the secondary market. Essentially, the value bounding process of the underlying asset arbitrage means that relatively illiquid issues or offerings which have for a variety of reasons performed poorly and proved difficult to place can be repackaged for sale in a new form to a group of investors to whom the security in its new form is attractive. This effectively creates a new option for investment banks to reduce their risk in new issue activity and in trading as it, at least in theory, provides them with an additional mechanism for selling and distributing securities.

For financial institutions active in swaps, the emergence of asset swaps provides an interesting new dimension in their activities. At the most basic level, asset swap activity creates additional transaction volume which increases the underlying liquidity of the relevant swap market. It provides the other end to the liability swap arbitrage and thereby creates an incentive for swap activity during periods when the liability swap arbitrage window is not operating. This additional liquidity improves the pricing performance and efficiency of the basic swap market.

In essence, the asset and the liability swap can, in many instances, be the opposite ends of the same transaction. This is because many new issues, as discussed previously, are undertaken on a fixed rate basis with an accompanying swap whereby the issuer receives the fixed rate to service the issue and pays floating rates. The pattern of payment under the liability swap, in this new issue arbitrage, is exactly the opposite side of the swap needed to generate synthetic assets, whereby, usually the purchaser of the asset will choose to pay a fixed rate in return for receiving a floating rate of return. Essentially, the presence of the asset swap therefore enables financial institutions active in swaps, particularly in swap warehousing and market making, to operate more or less continuously in the expectation of liquidity generated from both ends of the arbitrage.

For swap counterparties, the evolution of the form of the asset swap is also significant. Of particular significance is the development of the public or securitised asset swap structure. The major advantage to swap counterparties is the changing credit risk implications of this particular structure.

From the swap counterparties perspective, the public or securitised structure through a special purpose vehicle significantly reduces its exposure to the investor. This is because the issue vehicle is almost always collateralised by the bonds being repackaged and the swap counterparty usually has first call on that collateral. This allows swap counterparties to enter into the structuring and sale of synthetic assets to investors whose credit may not have been acceptable to the swap counterparty directly. In essence, under the public or securitised asset swap structure, the investor takes a risk on the swap counterparty but the swap counterparty removes exposure to the investor. This absence of credit risk which would otherwise be present essentially improves the pricing efficiency of the swap market quite considerably.

Part 7

Global Swap Markets

Chapter 19

Global Swap Markets

OVERVIEW OF GLOBAL SWAP MARKETS

Like most other new financial instruments, swap transactions are not executed in a physical market. Participants in the swap market vary in terms of location, character and motivations in undertaking swap transactions. However, the total sum of activities of participants in the swap market gives it some of the characteristics of a classical financial market connected to an integrated underlying capital, money and foreign exchange market.

As swaps are counterparty transactions, any structure or currency is possible for which there is a participant with an offsetting requirement. However, characteristics of most transactions are within the following ranges:

- Currencies:

    —United States dollars;
    —Japanese yen;
    —pounds sterling;
    —Deutschmark;
    —Swiss francs;
    —European Currency Unit;
    —Australian dollars;
    —Canadian dollars;
    —New Zealand dollars;
    —Dutch guilders;
    —French francs;
    —Luxembourg francs;
    —Swedish kroner;
    —Dutch kroner;
    —Belgian francs;
    —Hong Kong dollars;
    —Italian lira.

- Maturities of two to ten years (depending on currency).
- Amounts of US$5-200m (equivalent).

Increasingly, liquid markets in interest rates and currency swaps are available in this wide variety of currency. Active parallel markets in swap derivatives, primarily LTFX and FRAs and, less frequently, caps, floors and collars, have also developed.

THE STRUCTURE OF SWAP MARKETS

The mainstream swap markets tend to operate at two levels: an interest rate swap and a currency swap market. The distinction between these two market segments arises from the fact that the interest rate swap market, particularly in US$ and, to a lesser extent, in other swap currencies, behaves as a highly liquid and well-traded market paralleling fixed interest markets in the relevant currency. In contrast, the currency swap market tends to be a less liquid, more structured market driven by new issues entailing the exchange of comparative advantages in terms of price and/or access to the market segment.

The difference between the two tiers of the swap market largely reflects the character of participants in the two different segments. The fact that a significant number of participants trade or make markets in interest rate swaps generates considerable liquidity in the interest rate swap market. This reflects the use of interest rate swaps as a highly flexible mechanism for positioning, arbitrage and portfolio management activities. This generates considerable liquidity as both a primary and secondary market in interest rate swaps operate.

In contrast, the currency swap market operates as a primary market with limited secondary market activity. Although, in recent years, secondary market currency swap activity entailing restructuring and hedging of current debt portfolios, cash flows or investments has emerged, the currency swap market continues to be biased towards the primary market entailing the issue of securities accompanied by a swap to generate more attractive funding than that available directly.

A primary influence in the difference is the fact that market making in currency swaps, although growing, is still not as widespread as in the interest rate swap market. This reflects the difficulties in managing open currency swap positions. In particular, the difficulty of covering the interest rate risks in certain currencies while the swap is in position is considerable (see Part 8).

For example, a currency swap market maker can cover the foreign exchange risks associated with writing a position in a given currency. However, the market maker may not be able to cover against a movement in interest rates for that currency or is often forced to use poor surrogate cover as currency swap rates, in a given currency, may not move parallel to movements in local government bond market rates. This reflects the fact that in a number of currency swap markets, currency swap rates reflect the laws of supply and demand rather than relationships to interest rate movements in the relative market.

This means that the currency swap markets tend to be driven by liquidity in the underlying bond markets with a relatively lower proportion of secondary market activity.

The swap market in each currency would usually have at least three components:

- an interest rate swap market in the currency;
- a cross-currency market usually between the fixed rate in the currency and US$ LIBOR;
- a cross-currency floating-to-floating swap market.

This structure reflects the basic nature and objectives of participants in each swap market. While generally reflecting the pattern described, there are significant variations between markets which should be kept in mind.

The interest rate swap market usually reflects credit arbitrages in the local domestic capital market. In extreme cases, such as Australia and New Zealand, the absence of a substantial corporate bond market may foster the development of an interest rate swap market.

The cross-currency fixed to US$ floating market reflects the development of the Eurobond market in a wide number of currencies. The development of these multi-currency Eurobond markets in turn reflects the desire for portfolio diversification, in currency terms, by investors as well as investor preferences for Eurobonds or other types of international bond issues in preference to accessing domestic markets directly. This may reflect market frictions, such as withholding taxes, or investor preferences dictated by convenience and policy (see Chapter 7).

In addition, this type of cross-currency swap component reflects the existence of a wide variety of highly rated issuers who may be characterised as arbitrage funders. These issuers, primarily sovereigns, supranationals, and banks, are willing to issue in a wide range of currencies provided the issue can be swapped to generate funding at a rate, usually expressed as a margin relative to LIBOR. This margin, usually under LIBOR, reflects the desired degree of cost saving by the issuer relative to other sources of borrowing, which will prompt the issuer to lend its name to a bond issue in a particular currency or utilising a particular structure (see Chapter 13).

These two developments have dictated the development of a cross-currency market where a floating rate leg usually paid by the issuer is priced relative to US$ LIBOR. The fact that US$ LIBOR based funding is increasingly available to most borrowers in almost every national market, allows these borrowers to utilise the other side of such swaps to obtain fixed rate funding in the relevant currencies at significant cost savings.

The floating-to-floating cross-currency swap structure is generally a by-product of the first two components of the swap market. For example, in Australia, this type of swap is usually utilised to cover the mismatch between A$ floating rate payments and US$ LIBOR receipts. However, on occasions, deliberate floating-to-floating cross-currency swaps have been engineered. The most notable example of this was the issue of A$ and NZ$ floating rate notes at significant margins under the A$ and NZ$ BBRs in the two countries in the Yankee market in 1986 and, briefly, in 1987.

While the structure of global swap markets has traditionally been dictated by the activities of liability managers, increasingly, asset swaps have come to influence these structures. In particular, asset swaps have, as discussed in Chapter 18, to a large extent contributed to the enhanced liquidity in certain segments of the swap market. This increased liquidity is most apparent in the interest rate swap and the cross-currency market between the fixed rate in one currency and US$ LIBOR. Asset swaps have generated a significant volume of fixed rate payers in these two market segments, reflecting the preference for the major category of investors in synthetic assets, commercial banks, for floating rate assets. This paying interest, in fixed rate terms, has provided an alternative supply of fixed rate payers under the swap, at times, particularly, when traditional paying interest from corporations or other borrowers has been absent due to either the absolute level of interest rates or the level of actual swap spreads.

The other major component of swap markets is the basis swap. Again, the basis swap tends to be a residual position generated as a by-product of other swap activities, particularly mismatches in floating rate books of market makers in the relevant swap currency. The major basis swap market is in US$ reflecting the wide diversity of indexes in use in the US$ market.

In all swap markets, the bulk of activity entails standard or plain vanilla swaps, usually with minor variations to accommodate particular end user requirements. The alternative types of swap structures usually constitute a relatively small portion of the total swap market. In particular, these enhancements are responses to market situations, usually investor demand for particular types of securities issues, which generally have short life spans.

The generic structure of individual swap markets is set out, in diagrammatic form, in *Exhibit 19.1*.

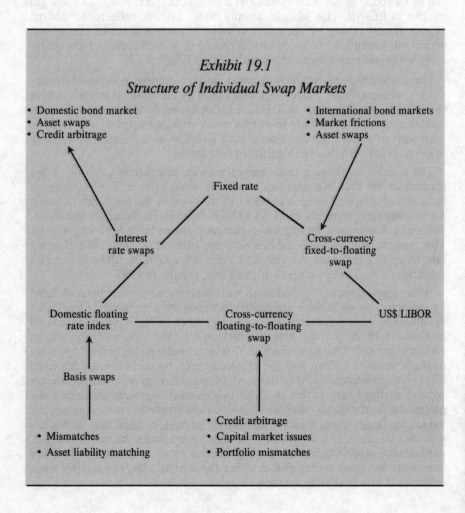

Exhibit 19.1

Structure of Individual Swap Markets

• Domestic bond market
• Asset swaps
• Credit arbitrage

• International bond markets
• Market frictions
• Asset swaps

Fixed rate

Interest rate swaps

Cross-currency fixed-to-floating swap

Domestic floating rate index — Cross-currency floating-to-floating swap — US$ LIBOR

Basis swaps

• Mismatches
• Asset liability matching

• Credit arbitrage
• Capital market issues
• Portfolio mismatches

INDIVIDUAL SWAP MARKETS: OVERVIEW

The largest swap market in the world, although ironically not the oldest sector, is the US$ interest rate swap market. The most important currencies in the currency swap market in rough order of magnitude are Japanese yen, Swiss francs, deutschmarks, ECU, £, C$, A$ and NZ$.

The Swiss franc, yen and deutschmark swap markets derive their impetus from their relatively low interest rates and the relative ease of access by a wide range of issuers to private and public debt in the international and domestic markets for these currencies. Many supranational and sovereign borrowers find their access to the debt markets of such currencies constrained relative to their sometimes very large requirements and therefore make active and frequent use of the currency swap market. These entities usually lend in these currencies and are therefore covering or matching assets with liabilities or are trying to diversify their debt portfolios away from the US$.

In contrast, the ECU swap market is predicated on the value of the ECU as a currency hedge for both investor and borrower and the fact that access to the ECU bond market is limited to a relatively small number of prime quality borrowers who provide the bulk of the fixed rate bond issues against which swap transactions are undertaken.

The high interest currencies, such as A$ and NZ$, £ and C$, derive their role in the swap market primarily as speculative vehicles for aggressive debt portfolio managers or companies in the local market which would have to pay a premium to access fixed rate debt. These phenomena account for the very rapid development of Eurobond markets in these currencies and the corresponding development of relatively liquid currency swap markets.

The currency swap market is still dominated by the US$ on one side of the swap but increasingly, many direct currency combinations are developing rapidly. The most important among these include yen and Swiss franc, yen and ECU, deutschmark and Swiss franc etc.

Parallel markets, in each of these currencies, for swap derivatives have also developed. Often driving off mismatches or opportunities within overall swap books, substantial markets in FRAs and LTFX have developed complementing growth in mainstream markets in interest rate and currency swaps. In recent times, markets for long-dated interest rate options, in the form of caps, floors and collars, have also started to emerge.

In the chapters which follow in this part, the major swap markets in individual currencies are discussed. A separate chapter also analyses the market for swap derivatives.

Chapter 20

North American Swap Markets: US$ and C$

US$ SWAP MARKET

Overview

The US$ interest rate swap market is the largest single element of the global swap market. Current annual volume of transactions is in excess of US$350 billion. There is naturally no currency swap market in US$ as the US$ itself functions as the other side of almost all currency swaps.

The vast size of this market reflects a number of factors including the size of the United States capital market itself and particularly the size of the market for fixed rate obligations, primarily United States Treasuries but also a very sizeable corporate bond market both within the United States and outside in the Eurobond market. An additional factor contributing to the size of the US$ interest rate swap market is the fact that a large proportion of global financing flows continue to be denominated in US$. The infrastructure which provides the US$ interest rate swap market with its depth and liquidity depends on these factors.

For example, the presence of a substantial number of market makers in US$ interest rate swaps contributes to the size and liquidity of the market. Their presence in turn, is predicated largely on the existence of a substantial and sophisticated market in United States Treasuries and United States Treasuries futures which allows these participants to hedge their risk position in unmatched swaps. The practice of pricing US$ obligations as a margin relative to United States Treasuries also contributes to the capacity of these market makers to trade or warehouse interest rate swaps and also, in a number of cases, make substantial capital commitments to the swap market.

The US$ interest rate swap market exhibits many of the characteristics of a mature financial market:

- a large number of participants with relatively clearly defined roles;
- the presence of several subsectors within the market;
- the presence of both a primary and secondary market; and
- the existence of considerable depth and liquidity.

In this regard, this market is by far the most sophisticated and structurally well developed of global swap markets.

Market structure

The US$ interest rate swap market can be broadly classified into two sectors:

- The primary market, which itself can be further subdivided into two distinct segments in terms of maturity—under two to three years and over.

356

- A secondary market.

The distinction within the primary market is largely predicated on the factors driving activity, pricing and the method of hedging risk positions in these two segments. The under two to three year sector functions as an extension of financial futures markets in US$ interest rates. The key participants in this short-term sector are a group of United States and non-United States banks, both of which provide fixed rate US$, usually through their access to fixed rate Eurodollar deposits or to the fixed rate CD market in London and New York. They also act as payers of the fixed rate in these swaps. The activity in this area is largely driven by the structure of the bank's asset liability portfolio and the primary motivation is either balance sheet management or speculative in nature.

The pricing in this segment of the market largely reflects the hedging practice whereby risk positions in the short swaps are usually managed by executing futures transactions in US$ interest rate futures in the United States and London financial futures markets. Market makers in the short swaps traditionally utilise Eurodollar futures markets as the standard hedging vehicle for short-dated interest rate swaps. For example, a dealer entering into a swap whereby it receives fixed rate and pays floating rate for say two years will offset the risk on the swap by positioning a series of sold or short Eurodollar futures positions, that is, a "sold Eurodollar futures strip".

This segment of the market tends to be extremely volatile in price largely reflecting its close proximity in maturity to the volatile US$ money markets. This price volatility of financial futures based swaps requires a high level of execution skills to undertake transactions in markets susceptible to very quick and sharp movements. A particular characteristic of this section of the market is a very substantial level of speculative interest whereby experienced dealers take positions on both absolute rate movements as well as spread movements between various indexes.

This type of speculative trading usually relates to the triangular relationship in this segment of the market between:

- the yield on the relevant United States Treasury note;
- the implied rate on the Eurodollars futures strip;
- the prevailing swap spread over the Treasury note.

In view of the fact that given any two of these variables, the remaining one is uniquely determinable, traders often trade the spread between the two year Eurodollar strip and two year United States Treasury note. The primary objective of this type of trading is to profit from a correct prediction of the change in the spreads of the two or three year Treasury note relative to the implied rate on the two or three year Eurodollar strip (in the jargon of the market: "trading the TED (Treasury Eurodollar) spread"). For example, if a trader expects the TED to narrow, he or she would buy Eurodollar futures and sell two year Treasury notes, while conversely, if the trader expected the spread to widen he or she would sell Eurodollar futures and buy two year Treasury notes.

This type of activity, which requires participants to establish and unwind these positions rapidly to maximise profits, has greatly increased the liquidity in the futures markets and, indirectly, contributed to the depth and liquidity in these types of swaps. *Exhibit 20.1* sets out the relationship over recent years between the two and three year Eurodollar strip and the two and three year Treasury note.

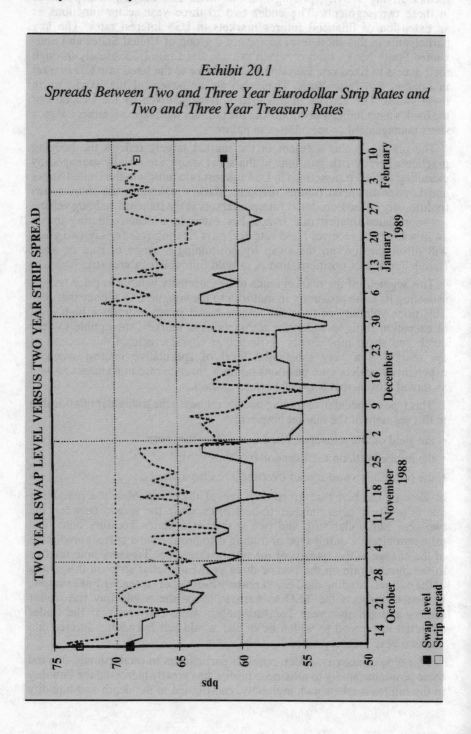

Exhibit 20.1

Spreads Between Two and Three Year Eurodollar Strip Rates and Two and Three Year Treasury Rates

Exhibit 20.1—continued

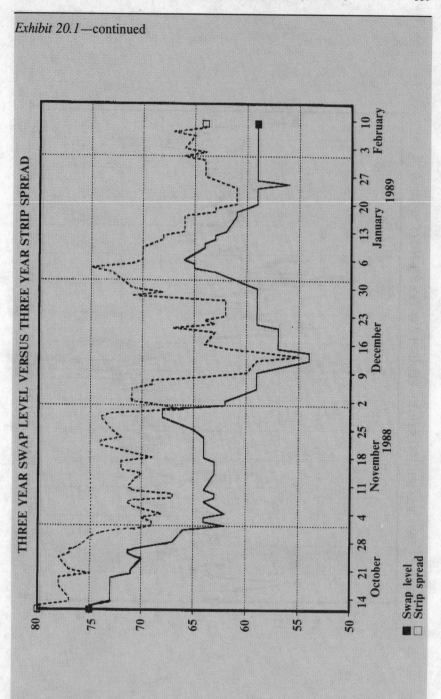

Exhibit 20.1—continued

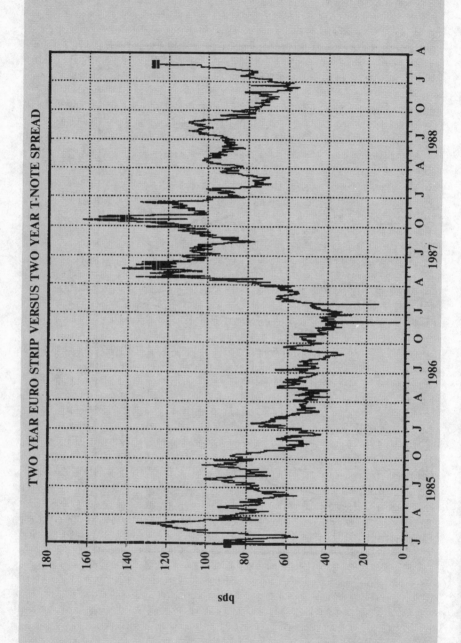

Exhibit 20.1—continued

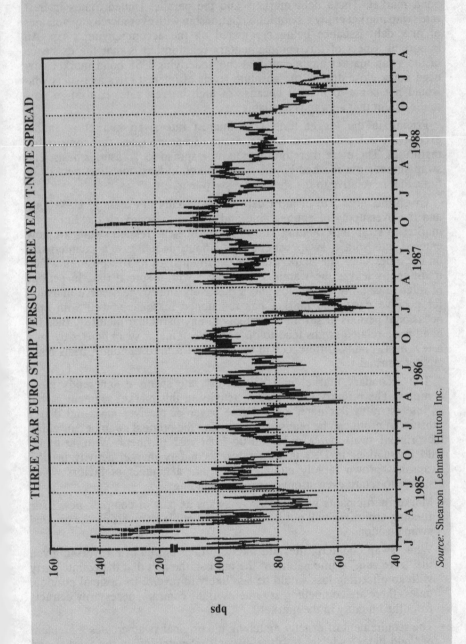

THREE YEAR EURO STRIP VERSUS THREE YEAR T-NOTE SPREAD

Source: Shearson Lehman Hutton Inc.

The longer maturities, beyond two to three years, in the US$ interest rate swap market are dominated by securities transactions, primarily the issuance of fixed rate bonds in the United States domestic and Eurodollar bond market. These debt markets and the parallel United States interest rate swap market enjoy a symbiotic relationship with ever increasing volumes of new debt issuance being predicated on the accompanying swap. An important aspect of this complementary relationship is that the existence of the swap market has meant that the underlying US$ bond market now need never close despite the absolute levels of interest rates as issuers who would not come to market because of high interest rates can do so now to the extent that a swap is available.

Pricing in the longer term US$ interest rate swap market is almost exclusively related to the United States Treasury rates for comparable maturities. These are therefore quoted on a spread to Treasuries basis. The swap spreads are marked by relative stability, at least for short periods of time, that is, relative to the short-term swap markets.

Given the large size of most debt issues, usually in excess of US$100m, and the oversupply of entities able and willing to approach the Eurobond market to swap into floating rate funds, most issue related swaps are now entered into with a swap warehouse without, necessarily, a counterparty on the other side. The market maker usually hedges its risk position which traditionally leaves the warehouse manager with a spread risk. In periods of relative stability of spreads and a positively sloped yield curve allowing for positive carry, the market has functioned reasonably well with only occasional periods of severe oversupply in any particular maturity. Bids for bond issue related swaps tend to differ between major swap houses by only a few basis points, differences in the order of a third or fourth basis point are not unusual.

The secondary market in US$ interest rate swaps is inherently more complex. The primary rationale for activity in this market segment is that as interest rates fluctuate, a fixed rate payer or receiver may find that a substantial profit can be realised by reversing the original swap or cancelling the original swap in return for an up-front cash payment. With, at times, wild fluctuations in US$ interest rates, secondary market activity in US$ swaps has grown rapidly although there are a number of factors which continue to retard even stronger growth including:

- Market participants who undertake swaps as part of complex new issue funding arbitrages will not usually be susceptible to reversing the original swap position.

- While swap counterparties are likely to take profits in a reversal, given the "zero sum" game nature of the market, the fact that the counterparty with an offsetting loss would be less likely to reverse its original position, unless there are compelling arguments to the contrary, necessarily detracts from the liquidity in the market.

- The requirement of exactly matching the original swap creates a problem of "odd dates" which are often difficult to match off in the market and the pricing adjustments necessitated may erode any profits in the transaction.

Despite these problems, secondary market liquidity in swaps is constantly growing. A major factor in this regard is the increasing sophistication of market makers in US$ interest rate swaps who can accommodate the structural complexities of such reversals. The move by such swap houses from perfect matching to portfolio approaches to swap book management has largely contributed to this development (see Chapter 27).

The US$ interest rate swap market offers a wider variety of swap structures than almost any other swap market. The maturity of the market together with the presence of a substantial number of market makers with large swap portfolios means that, increasingly, non-generic swap structures as well as more complex transactions involving options on swaps are available. A major factor in this regard is the existence of substantial markets in options on United States Treasuries which allow the hedging of certain risks entailed with options on swaps. A major aspect of the US$ interest rate swap market is the presence of a substantial and rapidly developing market in basis rate swaps in and between the various US$ interest rate indexes. A hetrogenous population of participants and the resultant mismatches created in the books of swap market makers have fueled to a large extent the growth in this segment of the market.

In 1987, Salomon Brothers Bond Market Research published an analysis of US$ interest rate spreads (see Evans, Ellen and Parente (1987)). The research identified a number of key influences:

- Yield levels and spreads and movements in these parameters, particularly for corporate borrowers in public debt markets such as the United States domestic corporate, Yankee and Eurodollar bond markets, were a major factor in swap spread levels. Specifically, swap spreads approximate the spreads over United States Treasuries on investment grade corporate securities, usually in a 20 to 30bps range defined by AA and A rated spreads.

- Swap spreads appeared to be influenced by interest rate expectations. For example, as set out in *Exhibit 20.2*, the historical data on changes in the absolute levels of rates show that swap spreads move inversely to Treasuries: swap spreads tend to widen when Treasury yields fall and narrow when Treasury yields increase.

- The changing use of swaps and the evolving cast of participants, particularly the development of asset swaps, by influencing the supply and demand of fixed rate payers, has been a major determinant of swap spreads.

- Technical factors, such as hedgings costs, have influenced spread changes.

Exhibit 20.2

US$ Swap Spread Movements Relative to US$ Interest Rate Movements

Period	Type of market	Change in United States Govt. yields		Change in Euro$ bond yields		Change in Dom Corp. bond yields		Change in Euro$ bond spreads v. Govts.		Change in Dom Corp. bond spreads v. Govts.		Change in interest rate swap spreads v. Govts.	
		5 year	7 year	5 year	7 year	5 year	7 year	5 year	7 year	5 year	7 year	5 year	7 year
		bps	bps	bps	bps	bps	bps	bps	bps	bps	bps	bps	bps
3 Oct. 84-5 Nov. 84	Bull	-116	-113	-64	-75	-75	-53	52	38	13	33	3	1
29 Jan. 85-22 Feb. 85	Bear	71	82	34	40	44	56	-37	-42	-24	-17	-2	-2
15 Mar. 85-19 Apr. 85	Bull	-96	-85	-91	-87	-92	-79	5	2	4	6	-1	0
5 Jul. 85-2 Aug. 85	Bear	69	65	51	45	69	71	-18	-20	0	5	4	2
2 Aug. 85-23 Aug. 85	Bull	-40	-46	-35	-34	-41	-34	5	12	-1	13	0	0
6 Sept. 85-1 Nov. 85	Bull	-55	-57	-38	-25	-29	-49	17	32	26	7	-6	-2
6 Dec. 85-27 Dec. 85	Bull	-60	-63	-49	-54	-11	-42	11	9	49	21	3	3
10 Jan. 86-28 Feb. 86	Bull	-104	-121	-69	-80	-85	-84	35	41	20	37	1	4
18 Apr. 86-30 May 86	Bear	112	118	95	98	65	57	-17	-20	-4	-31	-1	-7
30 May 86-18 Jul. 86	Bull	-99	-99	-75	-79	-65	-11	24	20	34	88	11	14
29 Aug. 86-19 Sept. 86	Bear	68	72	56	42	29	14	-12	-30	-39	-58	-2	-2
9 Jan. 87-13 Feb. 87	Bear	25	24	10	8	14	5	-15	-16	-12	-19	-8	-8
13 Mar. 87-24 Apr. 87	Bear	128	129	124	125	119	96	-4	-4	-9	-34	15	17
22 May 87-19 Jun. 87	Bull	-55	-47	-48	-57	-42	-23	7	-10	13	24	-6	-10
10 Jul. 87-31 Jul. 87	Bear	22	23	18	23	12	-2	4	0	-19	-36	0	0

Source: Salomon Brothers Inc.

Exhibit 20.3 sets out the swap spread curve at various periods since late 1984. *Exhibit 20.4* sets out the historical levels of swap rates and spreads in a number of key maturities.

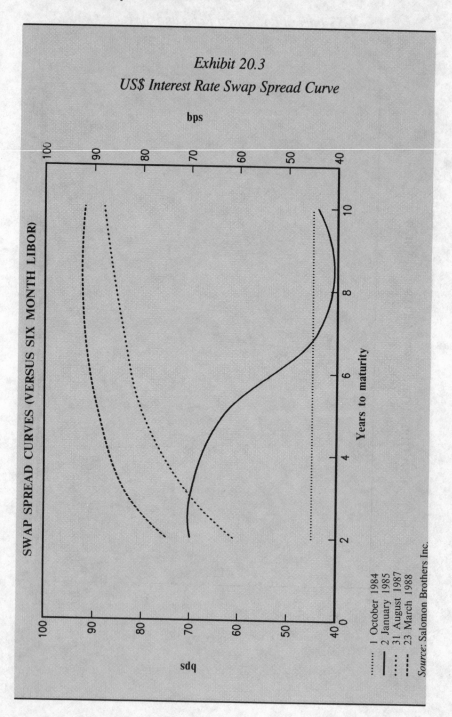

Exhibit 20.3

US$ Interest Rate Swap Spread Curve

SWAP SPREAD CURVES (VERSUS SIX MONTH LIBOR)

Years to maturity

1 October 1984
2 January 1985
31 August 1987
23 March 1988

Source: Salomon Brothers Inc.

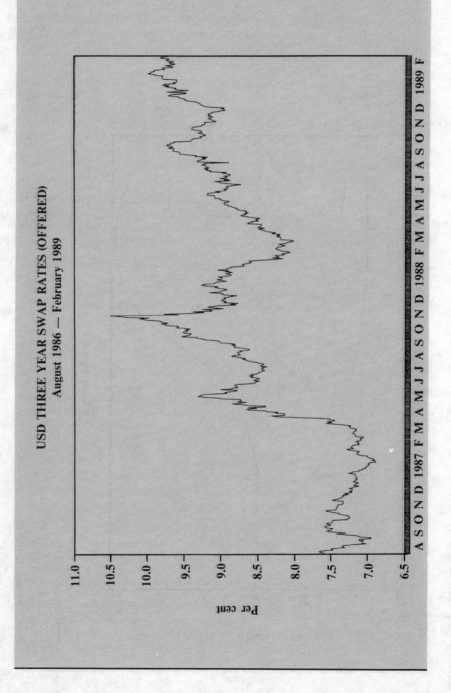

Exhibit 20.4

US$ Interest Rate Swap Rates and Spreads

Exhibit 20.4—continued

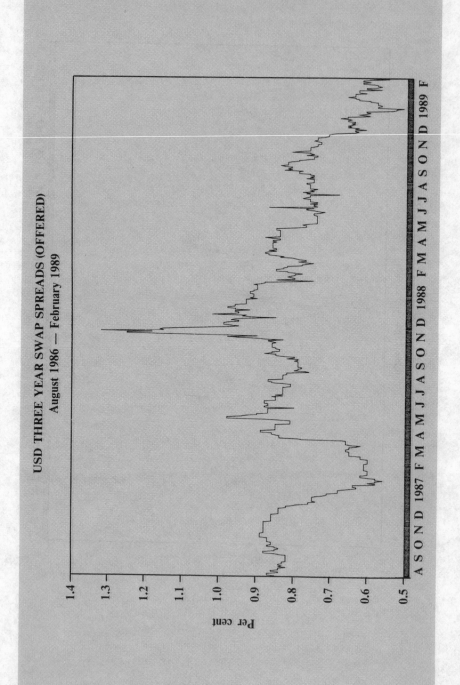

USD THREE YEAR SWAP SPREADS (OFFERED)
August 1986 — February 1989

Exhibit 20.4—continued

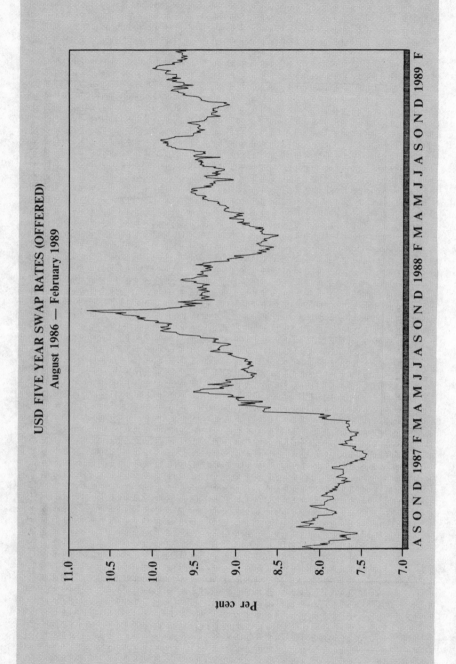

USD FIVE YEAR SWAP RATES (OFFERED)
August 1986 — February 1989

Exhibit 20.4—continued

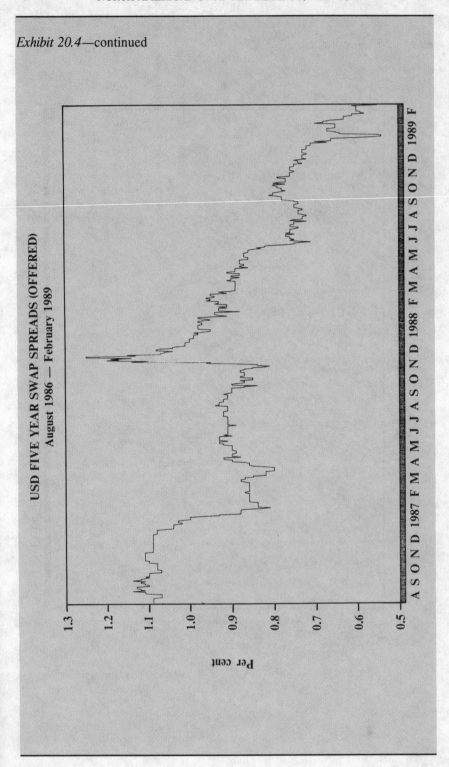

USD FIVE YEAR SWAP SPREADS (OFFERED)
August 1986 — February 1989

Exhibit 20.4—continued

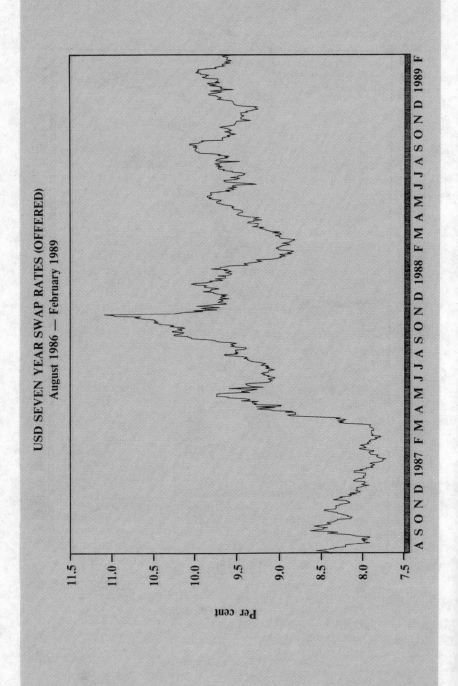

USD SEVEN YEAR SWAP RATES (OFFERED)
August 1986 — February 1989

Exhibit 20.4—continued

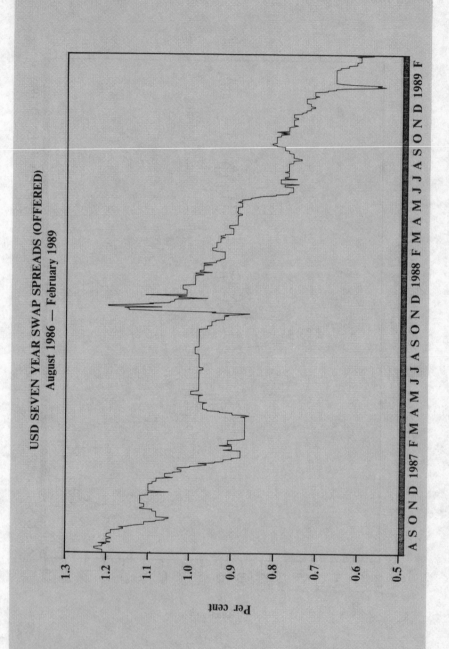

USD SEVEN YEAR SWAP SPREADS (OFFERED)
August 1986 — February 1989

Exhibit 20.4—continued

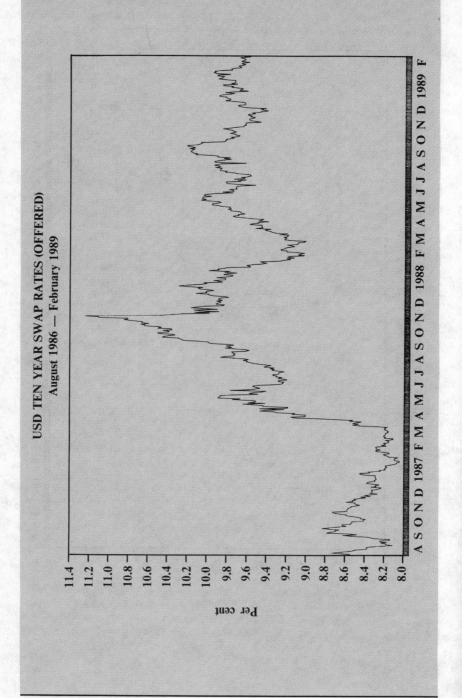

USD TEN YEAR SWAP RATES (OFFERED)
August 1986 — February 1989

Exhibit 20.4—continued

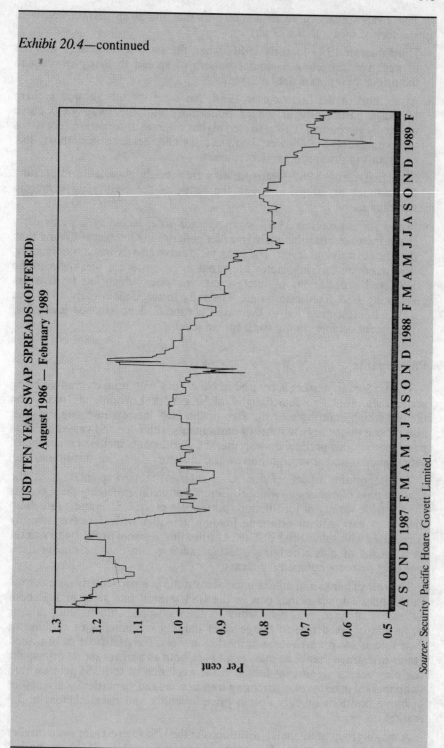

USD TEN YEAR SWAP SPREADS (OFFERED)
August 1986 — February 1989

Per cent

Source: Security Pacific Hoare Govett Limited.

The swap spread curve data indicates that the swap market has been characterised by a number of phases:

- Third quarter 1984 to early 1986, when the swap spread curve was flat or negative, reflecting a similar pattern of spread to that prevailing in the primary corporate debt markets.
- At the end of the first quarter 1986, the swap spreads showed a sharp increase, particularly at longer maturities, with the swap yield curve gradually steepening. This reflected higher volumes of corporate debt issues to take advantage of lower absolute rates and increases in maturity risk premiums in the corporate debt market.
- In the first quarter 1987, swap spreads were exceedingly volatile, fluctuating by as much as 20bps, although the shape of the swap yield curve did not change.
- In the second quarter 1987, swap spreads rose, including a particularly sharp increase after the equity market collapse in October 1987 and then declined to previous levels. The swap yield curve also flattened significantly. The major underlying factor appeared to be persistent weakness in the US$ and expectations of interest rate increases which led to investors shunning US$ fixed rate issues. The rally in the US$ in early 1988 and easier interest rates led to increased corporate debt issuance levels and significant declines in the swap spread levels.

Participants

The US$ swap market is centred in New York with primary trading being undertaken in the "golden triangle" of New York, London and Tokyo. The factors which contribute to the size of the US$ interest rate swap market also dictate that a large number of participants with wide and varied interests participate in this particular swap market. Participants include corporations, supranational and sovereign borrowers, investors, financial institutions etc.

An important aspect of the US$ interest rate swap market is the participation of entities of widely different nationalities. Highly rated credits from a wide variety of jurisdictions participate in the US$ interest rate swap market as part of their arbitrage funding activities while less creditworthy corporates with substantial US$ debt utilise this segment of the swap market as a means of either hedging existing floating rate debt or raising fixed rate debt on more competitive terms.

The role of banks and other financial institutions is particularly noteworthy. Banks play a fundamental part in the US$ interest rate swap market both as issuers of fixed rate debt which is then swapped into floating rate or as payers of fixed rate to hedge asset liability mismatches in addition to their role as swap warehouses or market makers. The participation of United States investment banks as market makers, both as brokers and as principals, has also been a significant factor in the evolution of the US$ interest rate swap market in terms of distributing transactions and, in particular, the ability to move positions quickly due to price volatility and risks inherent in the market.

A major group of financial institutions in the US$ interest rate swap market are United States thrifts. The entry of thrifts into the US$ swap market to manage asset liability mismatches contributed significantly to the liquidity of the market. Their entry was in large part made possible by the creativity of United States investment banks, who pioneered collateral of swaps with high quality securities, enabling the participation of these less creditworthy institutions in the swap market.

Reflecting the maturity of the product itself and the depth and liquidity of the US$ interest rate swap market, the range of applications is very broad. New issue arbitrage as well as sophisticated asset liability management and interest rate risk management purposes is evident. An increasingly significant factor in the US$ interest rate swap market is the emergence of a substantial asset swap market in US$. The evolution of this particular market segment has provided greater liquidity to the US$ swap market overall as it has increased the supply of fixed rate payers, primarily commercial banks, who swap fixed rate assets into high yielding floating rate assets for portfolio purposes.

Market evolution

Initially, the US$ interest rate swap market was driven by two factors:
- the presence of United States withholding tax;
- a classic credit arbitrage.

The presence of United States withholding tax essentially allowed prime rated United States corporates to issue Eurodollar bonds for much of the early part of the 1980s at spreads under or comparable to United States Treasuries. This discrepancy facilitated the initial growth of the swap market. Allied to this fact was the almost traditional absence of banks and highly rated financial institutions from the fixed rate sector of the Eurobond market. These institutions who had little or no use for term fixed rate funds were attractive as issuers of fixed rate debt because of their scarcity values as investors sought to diversify the credit risk elements in their portfolio.

The initial growth of US$ interest rate swaps saw these banks and financial institutions enter the market as issuers of fixed rate debt which was then swapped into floating rate US$ funding consistent with their general asset liability management requirements. However, the exploitation of the arbitrage as well as the legislative changes in United States withholding tax, led to this original rationale for US$ interest rate swaps declining in importance. It is clear that sub-LIBOR spreads available to issuers declined as the market became more efficient in pricing the relative value of the swap. While in the initial phase of the market, a AAA issuer could reasonably expect to achieve up to 75 to 100bps below LIBOR on a US$ straight bond issue and accompanying swap, by 1986, the same issuer might only expect to achieve a spread of 25 to 30bps below LIBOR on a plain vanilla bond issue and swap.

The change in the arbitrage profits was also influenced by a number of less obvious factors. First, the growth of non-US$ international bond markets saw United States entities seeking fixed rate funds turning to sectors other than the US$ as a means of achieving the most cost effective US$ funding. In essence, the US$ interest rate swap market competed as an arbitrage market with other available opportunities in different currencies.

An additional factor was the change in relationship between the United States CP and LIBOR rates. The CP and LIBOR spread which was approximately 100bps in 1984 narrowed significantly. This meant that the situation whereby a United States corporate could pay 60bps over Treasuries on a swap and receive LIBOR whilst being funded in the CP market at or about LIBOR minus 100 thereby allowing it to achieve an all-in cost of funds of Treasuries minus 40bps, evaporated.

The final factor was the decline in interest rates during the 1985 to 1986 period which led to an oversupply of fixed rate payers with borrowers crowding in to fix debt costs at the lower absolute rates. A basic structural change also occurred with the increasing importance of asset swaps which added to the oversupply of fixed rate payers in the US$ interest rate swap markets.

Under these pressures, the fundamental structure of US$ swap rates changed dramatically, predominantly showing both an increase in the spread levels as well as a significantly higher degree of volatility in the swap spreads. Perversely, the changing pattern of swap spreads and the increase in underlying volatility of these spreads prompted innovations such as options on swaps, options on swap spreads, spread locks etc. The volatility also attracted trading interest, initially from United States investment banks, who came to view swaps as another trading instrument which, via the medium of the spread, allowed them to trade the relativities of different sectors of the capital market.

However, this basic speculative or positioning interest still needed to be fed by activity in the primary segment of the US$ interest rate swap market which inevitably meant the engineering of new issues. The primary focus in this regard was the creation of bond structures which offered the fixed rate issuer lower costs and therefore a better spread below LIBOR which in turn required additional engineering on the basic interest rate swap.

In addition to this requirement of creativity was a more highly developed sense of timing in bringing issues to market and in executing the accompanying swap. While finding a window in primary debt markets has always been a feature of a successful issue, with the advent and development of the US$ interest rate swap market, the Eurodollar bond market began to function in terms of a complex interaction of investor demand and swap spread windows. Given that the long-term US$ interest rate swap market operated on a relatively stable, at least in the short-term, spread level versus US$ Treasuries, issuers sought to locate a spread window for a particular type of issuer usually predicated on timing leads and lags in the behaviour of various sectors of the markets, such as reaction lags as between the US$ domestic and Eurodollar markets.

In summary, it is useful to distinguish between two phases in the history of the US$ interest rate swap market.

- An initial period when substantial arbitrage gains provided the primary driving factor behind the growth of the market.
- A second, necessarily more complex, phase when in the face of declining arbitrage profits but ironically increasing depth and liquidity as various participants entered the market, the structure of the market broadened

to widen the range of instruments available as well as basing the activity in the primary level of the market on development of new and innovative bond structures or on timing considerations.

C$ SWAP MARKET

The involvement of United States banks and corporations in Canada and vice versa made the emergence of a C$ swap market inevitable. A natural demand for cross-currency swaps, primarily between C$ and US$, existed and interest rate swaps soon followed and now predominate.

The C$ swap market commenced in about 1980. The initial participants were the Canadian banks who sought to use swaps as a means of managing mismatches between assets and liabilities within their own portfolios. Currency swaps were also used to hedge foreign exchange positions. The growth in the market from these tentative beginnings was initially slow with the banks being followed into the market by the Crown agencies, such as the Federal Business Development Bank, who sought to utilise swaps as a method of generating cheaper floating rate funds to replace liabilities such as CP. The initial impetus to a faster rate of growth in the market came from a period of increased interest rates in the early 1980s when Canadian corporations and, more recently, trust and insurance companies entered the market. The participation of this last group was to primarily utilise swaps as a method of interest risk management as well as currency risk management.

Structurally, the fixed rate side of the C$ swap market is dominated by the EuroCanadian dollar bond market. As in the case of a number of minor currencies, the availability of swaps has helped create a deeper C$ bond market, both domestically and internationally, while, simultaneously, the growth of the bond market has been critical to the further development of the swap market. Since 1985, increased international appetite for C$ securities, primarily in the form of EuroCanadian dollar issues, has helped sustain the C$ swap market. Investors have sought C$ investments as a yield pick-up relative to the US$ market or as an alternative to high yielding currencies such as the A$, NZ$ or £.

Alternative sources of fixed rate funds for swap transactions have come from specially structured one off issues in the domestic Canadian market such as a home oil index debenture issued in 1986 or, until recently, the presence of a substantial fixed rate preference share market. As discussed in Chapter 18, C$ swaps have also been utilised in deposit based asset swap transactions primarily in Japan.

However, with about half of the EuroCanadian issues currently being undertaken by non-Canadians, the primary driving force behind the growth of the market remains the continuing international demand for C$ securities.

Canadian dollar swaps are usually quoted on the fixed rate side as a margin over the yield on government of Canada bond issues of comparable maturities. The floating rate side is usually set in relation to the C$ bankers acceptances floating rate index, typically for 30, 60 or 90 days or, as against US$ LIBOR set every three or six months, in the case of cross-currency swaps. The typical spread between the bid and offer price is 0.15% pa.

Exhibit 20.5 sets out the historical levels of swap rates and spreads for C$ swaps in a number of key maturities.

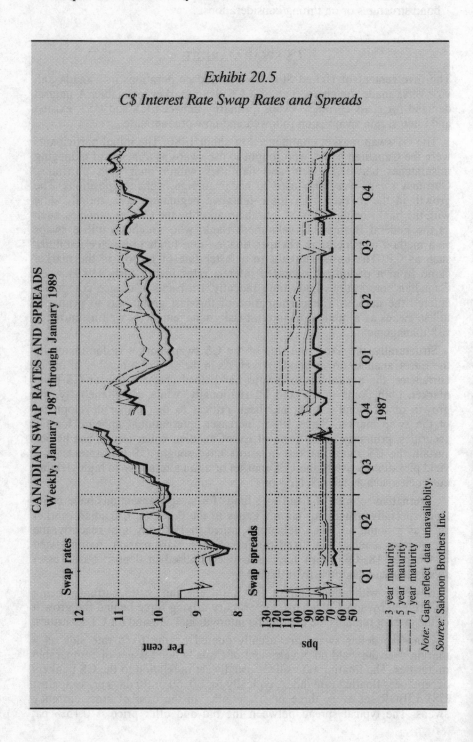

Exhibit 20.5

C$ Interest Rate Swap Rates and Spreads

Swaps vary hugely in size, ranging from C$5m to over C$100m. The normal size for a domestic transaction is in the range C$10-50m while Eurobond related swaps in C$ start at C$50m. Among the bigger transactions completed in recent years include a C$200m five year EuroCanadian issue for Nippon Telephone and Telegraph which was swapped into, first, sub-LIBOR US$ and then finally into yen.

The nature of the investor base in C$ securities as well as the pattern of non-Canadian issuers has dictated the presence of some curious currency swap combinations between, inter alia, C$, yen, deutschmarks, Swiss francs, ECUs, £ and, at least on one occasion, A$. Inevitably, however, the transactions involve a US$ LIBOR leg.

As at 1988, the outstanding C$ denominated swap transactions was estimated at C$150-200 billion. Annual volume is estimated at between C$30-40 billion per year. Much of this activity has been in liability related swaps done on behalf of issuers although a growing part of the market is now asset based.

The market is dominated by the major Canadian banks such as the Royal Bank of Canada, CIBC, Toronto Dominion and the other chartered Canadian banks with the major foreign participants being the United States banks with substantial activities in Canada, such as Citibank and Bankers Trust.

Chapter 21

Asian Swap Markets: Yen and HK$

JAPANESE YEN SWAP MARKETS

Overview

The Japanese yen swap market is probably the second largest swap market in the world, although the lack of exact comparable statistics makes a precise ranking impossible. Currency swaps conducted between yen and other currencies totalled the yen equivalent of approximately US$35-40 billion in 1988, while yen interest rate swaps total a similar or perhaps even larger amount.

While the yen swap market enjoys many structural similarities with other major swap markets around the world, there are also significant differences in structure. A major difference is that the arbitrage which drives swap transactions in yen tends to be more structural than the traditional forms of credit or other arbitrages which drive swaps in other markets.

A key factor underlying this type of structural arbitrage is the rigid regulatory framework governing the activities of financial institutions within Japan. For example, the classification of Japanese financial institutions between city banks and long-term credit banks creates an artificial segmentation which leads to asset liability mismatches which to some extent have been arbitraged utilising swap transaction structures. Similarly, the regulation of interest rates and the complex inter-relationships between various interest rates within the Japanese market also underly the basic swap arbitrages undertaken.

History, development and participants

The history and development of the yen swap market can be divided into two distinct phases: pre- and post-liberalisation and deregulation of the Euroyen bond market in 1984.

The earliest yen swaps were arranged in the early 1980s. During this period, the yen swap market consisted of back-to-back transaction mostly related to investment or borrowing transactions whereby large multinational corporations sought to hedge their forward payables or receivables of a commercial, rather than a financial nature.

In 1981, this was followed by a series of bond issues, primarily by French institutions, which were swapped into yen. The motivation for these transactions was primarily a large French foreign exchange borrowing requirement which the French authorities preferred to handle through private placements. Consequently, a public or private placement would be arranged; simultaneously, a swap into yen would be executed with Japanese investors who would thereby create an artificial yen asset.

At the same time, a number of Japanese entities created synthetic yen liabilities. For example, Japan Development Bank and Japan Airlines issued bonds in 1981 in US$ which were swapped into yen. The source of the yen for these swaps were largely airline leases. For example, in one of these early transactions, a United States airline with a yen-based lease transaction, desiring to swap into US$, provided the yen part of one transaction. During this period the overall liquidity of the market was extremely low with spreads of over 1.00%.

The major expansion of the yen market came in 1984 with the liberalisation and deregulation of the Euroyen bond market. While the Euroyen market had begun in spectacular fashion in 1977 with an issue by the European Investment Bank, the Japanese Ministry of Finance only authorised six issues per year. In December 1984, non-Japanese residents were permitted access to the Euroyen market. Supranationals, sovereigns, government agencies and local governments with an A rating or better and all corporates with a AA rating or better as well as some lesser corporates were allowed to issue Euroyen bonds. Simultaneously, non-Japanese houses and subsidiaries of Japanese banks were allowed to lead manage Euroyen issues. The Ministry of Finance also allowed, for the first time, swaps on Euroyen issues.

These measures led to a dramatic increase in the volume of issues denominated in yen. This growth is evidenced by the fact that the yen rapidly became the second major currency, after the US$, in the international bond market.

In April 1986, further liberalisation took place with eligibility for Euroyen borrowers being relaxed further. The rule that Euroyen bonds could not be sold into Japan until 180 days had elapsed since issue was also replaced with a shorter restriction period of 90 days. More recently, foreign commercial banks were allowed to undertake Euroyen transactions. In July 1986, Euroyen subordinated bonds were also approved.

This expansion of the Euroyen market and in the resulting volume of yen funds that were being supplied led to a rapid expansion of the yen swap market. The impetus came primarily because almost 90.00% of Euroyen issues launched were swapped, primarily, into US$. In fact, because of the presence of withholding tax as well as a direct prohibition on some Japanese issuers undertaking borrowings, the Euroyen market until recently was primarily used by borrowers who utilised the yen funding as part of arbitrage funding practices to generate cheap funding in a variety of currencies. The legitimacy of the yen swap market was well and truly established in 1984 when a transaction was arranged for the World Bank, whereby it swapped an existing US$ liability into yen.

The majority of these swaps were undertaken by the issuers of Euroyen securities with the Japanese banks, in particular, the trust banks. These banks were the main payers of yen in any swap. The factors underlying the ultimate utilisation of the fixed rate yen funding generated are, however, more complex. The Japanese banks themselves are significant users of the fixed rate funds for their own asset liability management purposes. Similarly, the clients of the banks utilised significant quantities of this fixed rate yen funding, either directly through a swap against an existing liability or alternatively in the form of a fixed rate yen loan provided by a bank.

In recent years, a significant portion of the demand for yen funding via these swaps has come from Japanese corporations who have increasingly raised capital, denominated in non-yen currencies, outside Japan. For example, in 1987, Japanese corporations, primarily industrial companies or trading houses, raised more than US$20 billion *through equity warrant linked issues alone*. In 1988, despite the generally weaker global equity markets, the strength of the Japanese stock market saw issues at a level comparable to 1987. In 1989, for the month of January alone, over US$8 billion of equity warrant linked issues were brought to market for Japanese entities. The vast majority of the US$ liabilities created were then swapped into fixed rate yen, as discussed in Chapter 18, on some occasions, particularly in the heady days of 1987, at negative rates of interest.

Foreign borrowers have also utilised swaps as a vehicle for accessing fixed rate yen funding. The reasons for this are largely structural and relate to the eventual effective cost of the yen liability. For example, the World Bank has been a significant user of yen swaps because of its continuing high levels of demand for fixed rate yen funding.

The nature of the investor base in Euroyen securities has largely limited issuers to sovereign, semi-sovereign or prime corporate entities. The full range of borrowers allowed access have never, in fact, enjoyed this privilege. The conservative nature of the investor base and their concern about changing financial conditions within the corporate sector has led over time, at least once the rarity value of corporate bonds decreased, to great limitations on the range of issuers whose securities were purchased. This has meant that a number of corporate borrowers, seeking yen funding, have found it more advantageous to utilise swaps to generate fixed rate yen liabilities.

Structure of yen and US$ swap market [1]

There are two distinct and separate yen and US$ swaps markets, both of which are linked to either the Euroyen or the Eurodollar bond markets:

- the fixed yen versus floating rate US$ swap market;
- the fixed yen versus fixed US$ market (that is, the LTFX market).

These two markets are not closely connected because of the different ways the swaps are constructed and the different pricing variables.

Fixed yen and US$ LIBOR swaps

The typical structure of a fixed yen and US$ LIBOR swap against an issue is set out in *Exhibit 21.1*.

---

1. This discussion of the structure of yen swaps draws heavily on "The Explosive Growth of the Yen/Dollar Swap Market" (1986).

The structure of this segment of the market is largely dictated by the type of participants while pricing is closely linked to their ability to borrow long-term yen funds.

Pricing for fixed yen and floating US$ swaps is determined principally by the long-term prime rate (LTPR). The LTPR is part of the regulated interest rate structure within Japan, and is connected to the Japanese government bond coupon via the bank debenture rate. An overview of the Japanese interest rate structure is set out in *Exhibit 21.2*.

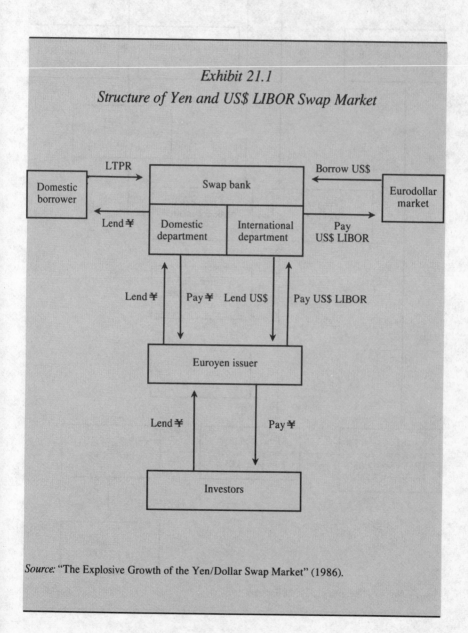

Exhibit 21.1
Structure of Yen and US$ LIBOR Swap Market

Source: "The Explosive Growth of the Yen/Dollar Swap Market" (1986).

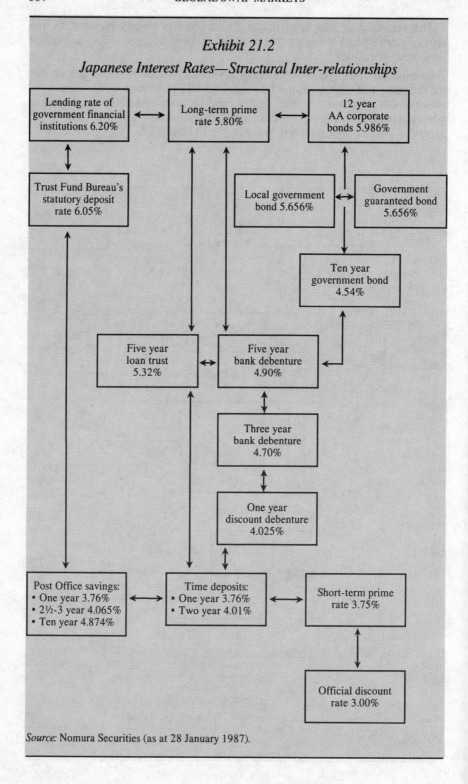

Exhibit 21.2

Japanese Interest Rates—Structural Inter-relationships

Source: Nomura Securities (as at 28 January 1987).

The rate the swap bank will pay is typically a margin below LTPR (say 10-15bps). The final rate may depend upon expectations of future movements in the domestic bond market and LTPR. Consequently, swap rates depend very heavily on current demand from borrowers which, in turn, depends upon market expectations.

There is a division between certain types of banks within the Japanese domestic market. City banks have access to short-term (up to two years) funds which has meant that they have historically concentrated on short-term lending. The long-term banks and trust banks, in contrast, have access to long-term debt primarily through the issue of bank debentures and they have specialised in providing long-term loans to industry. Therefore the long-term and trust banks predominate as payers of fixed rate yen. More recently, however, in order to create fixed rate long-term yen liabilities to match their domestic long-term loans the city banks have played a more active role as payers of fixed rate yen in fixed yen and floating US$ swaps.

The principal source of potential arbitrage is the differential between the LTPR and Euroyen bond yields. The LTPR is dependent upon domestic Japanese government bond market conditions whereas Euroyen bond yields are subject to conditions in both the Japanese government bond market and the international bond markets as well as exchange rate expectations. Further, as Euroyen bond yields are substantially more volatile than the LTPR, the interest differentials between these two rates can widen substantially to create attractive swap arbitrages for Euroyen issuers.

The volatility of yen swap rates is evident from *Exhibit 21.3*. The relationship between yen swap rates and the benchmark Japanese government bond is also set out in *Exhibit 21.3*.

The reverse of the first type of transaction is where the swap bank receives fixed rate yen, typically to convert a Eurodollar bond or "sushi" issue into fixed rate yen funding. This type of structure is set out in *Exhibit 21.4*.

In these cases, city banks are in a better competitive position as they can fund the yen receipts by utilising their very cheap deposit base. The banks are often prepared to risk the asset liability maturity mismatch for historical as well as strategic reasons. Trust banks and long-term banks will either match their long-term lending (via the swap) to their long-term funding or use their deposit base like the city banks.

There were a number of sources of arbitrage in these transactions. The swaps were often "hara-kiri" swaps; that is, the swaps were priced at off-market rates.

It was often assumed by non-Japanese observers, including other financial institutions, that the swap bank was making a loss. In reality, the bank providing the hara-kiri swap was not making an actual loss, but an "opportunity" loss (that is, it could have lent the funds at a higher rate), as the banks' funding cost (via cheap deposits) was below the rate at which they were lending via the swap.

An additional factor here was that the swap bank usually sought to time its entry into a swap to coincide with the large interest cost differential between the Japanese domestic and the Euroyen market. For example, there were two periods when the volume of swap-driven issues rocketed. The

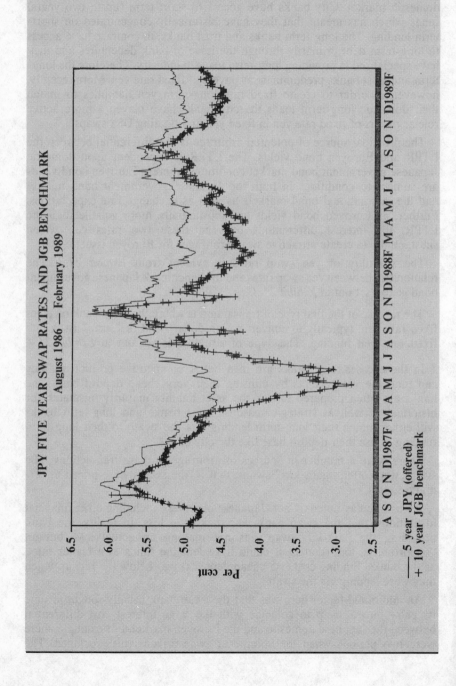

Exhibit 21.3
Yen Swap Rates and Spreads

Exhibit 21.3—continued

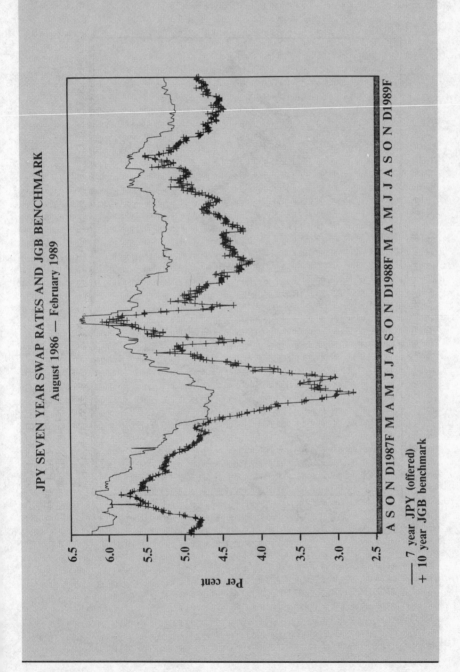

JPY SEVEN YEAR SWAP RATES AND JGB BENCHMARK
August 1986 — February 1989

— 7 year JPY (offered)
+ 10 year JGB benchmark

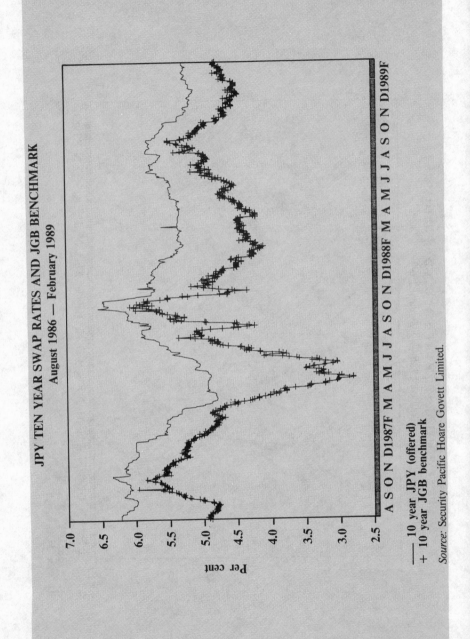

Exhibit 21.3—continued

JPY TEN YEAR SWAP RATES AND JGB BENCHMARK
August 1986 — February 1989

Per cent

— 10 year JPY (offered)
+ 10 year JGB benchmark

A S O N D1987F M A M J J A S O N D1988F M A M J J A S O N D1989F

Source: Security Pacific Hoare Govett Limited.

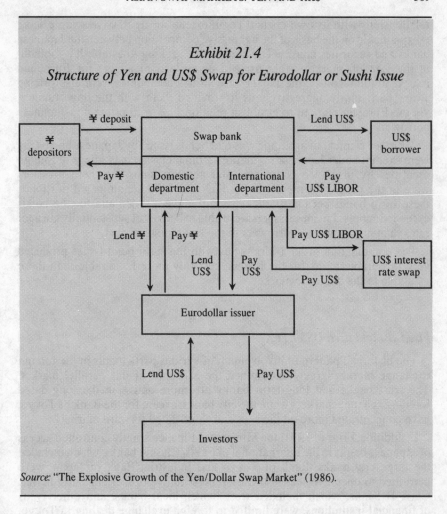

Exhibit 21.4

Structure of Yen and US$ Swap for Eurodollar or Sushi Issue

Source: "The Explosive Growth of the Yen/Dollar Swap Market" (1986).

first being between December 1985 and January 1986 when there was a wide gap between LTPR and the cost of Euroyen issues. At this time, LTPR was expected to rise and so Japanese corporations rushed to borrow from the banks. Similar conditions prevailed again in March and April 1986. During these periods, what may have appeared to the observer as extraordinarily aggressive yen swap rates were primarily temporary imbalances in the supply and demand of fixed rate yen funding creating attractive swap opportunities.

An additional more nebulous consideration is that as the lending rate is virtually determined by the bank, it is necessary to consider whether the Japanese banks were able to manipulate LTPR to essentially prevent large losses from their aggressive swap positions.

It is also clear that the so-called hara-kiri swaps were typically provided to obtain a coveted co-lead management position in a Eurodollar issue for a Japanese corporation (a sushi issue), and/or to maintain or improve relationships with its own clients. To an extent, the aggressive swap pricing is explainable on the basis of the aggressive competition between the Japanese banks and securities houses. The banks were seeking to establish a foothold in the London market either as lead or co-lead managers for Eurobond issues. Simultaneously, the Japanese securities companies were also pricing swaps particularly aggressively as it provided them with the opportunities, via the Euroyen market, to establish relationships with prime non-Japanese borrowers.

A further element of arbitrage was that bonds issued by Japanese borrowers were exempt under Japanese regulations from inclusion in holdings of foreign securities by insurance companies and pension funds. As these investors were in the process of rapidly expanding their US$ denominated portfolios these sushi bonds became particularly attractive. As demand for the bonds exceeded supply, Japanese issuers were able to borrow at substantially cheaper rates than non-Japanese borrowers in the Eurodollar market.

The combination of hara-kiri swaps with the sushi bond issues produced very favourable terms for the issuers, certainly more favourable than those available in the domestic market.

Fixed yen and fixed US$ LTFX

The historical pattern of involvement of various participants in the foreign exchange market largely determined the existence of this parallel market. The trust banks and long-term banks are more active in the long-dated foreign exchange markets while the city banks, except for the Bank of Tokyo, have concentrated more on the spot and short-dated forward markets.

In addition, prior to 1971, the Ministry of Finance strictly controlled access of Japanese banks to the international markets. Class A banks, which included the large city banks, Bank of Tokyo and Industrial Bank of Japan, were permitted to open overseas branches, representative offices and subsidiaries. Class B banks, which included trust banks, local banks, and other types of financial institutions, were limited to foreign exchange dealing in Tokyo, trade financing and correspondent bank relationships.

The trust banks and long-term banks have used their long-dated foreign exchange dealing capabilities to develop their corporate relationships, both within and outside of Japan, and are therefore often prepared to offer attractive LTFX swaps if they are linked to public Eurobond transactions.

Pricing for fixed yen and fixed US$ swaps is determined principally by the interest rate differential between United States Treasury bonds and Japanese government bonds, although because the yen and US$ LTFX market is relatively illiquid, it is also dependent to a large extent on supply and demand. Because of lags between price and yield movements in the United States Treasury market, which is relatively volatile, and movements in rates in the LTFX markets, which are relatively stable, it is possible to pick up attractive arbitrage opportunities.

The source of the arbitrage, therefore, is the US$ and yen interest differential implicit in the yen and US$ spot and forward rates and the yield on United States Treasuries.

Structure of the yen interest rate swap market

The yen interest rate swap market is the most recent stage of development of the Japanese yen swap market. The yen interest rate swap market evolved in the middle of 1986 and by the end of 1986 had become an important component of the Japanese capital market.

The growth in yen interest rate swaps is predicated on the following factors:

- the structure of the banking system within Japan;
- the asset liability management requirements of Japanese corporations.

Central to the growth of yen interest rate swaps has been the tacit approval by the Ministry of Finance to these types of transactions which implicitly portend crossing of traditional banking divides within Japan. These types of transactions have been utilised by the Japanese city banks as an entree into long-term lending, an area, as noted above, to which they have previously been denied access. These city banks have utilised swaps as a means of generating synthetic fixed rate funding to match off their exposure on fixed rate lending to Japanese corporations. The long-term trust banks, at least in theory, should provide the opposite side to these transactions as they are able to generate floating rate funding, pricing off short-term interest rates to fund their growing short-term lending business.

This role of yen interest rate swaps in bank asset liability management contributes to the fact that approximately 70.00% of activity is between financial institutions. However, there is a growing interest among Japanese corporations in utilising yen interest rate swaps. Liability management concerns predominate in attracting these participants into the yen interest rate swap market.

The participation of non-financial institutions in yen interest rate swaps is usually based on one of the following reasons:

- Fixed rate funding opportunities for companies with lower credit ratings. This is precisely the type of credit arbitrage which dominates many other swap markets. For example, steel and shipping companies as well as leasing companies have been active as payers of fixed rates in yen interest rate swaps.

- The use of interest rate swaps to unhinge high coupon yen borrowings into floating rate liabilities to lower the absolute interest levels on outstanding loans. This particular type of transaction has been popular because of the reluctance of Japanese corporations to repay existing loans at high fixed interest rates because of the complex relationship between lenders and borrowers in Japan. Against this background, by converting long-term fixed rate liabilities into floating rate through the swap market, Japanese corporations have sought to reduce their annual interest cost without having to risk falling out with their traditional house relationship bank.

- As liquidity has developed, corporations have sought to trade interest rates by entering into interest rate swaps to take advantage of the differential between fixed and floating interest rates and also to seek to capitalise on interest rate movements. The fact that swaps are off-balance sheet transactions requiring no margin calls or cash payment has made this type of positioning activity increasingly popular.

Approaches to yen swap pricing and arbitrage

Despite the fact that the yen swap market is now second only to the US$ swap market, the more complex factors driving swap arbitrages in yen means that the approaches to pricing yen swaps is not as readily identifiable as in the US$ market. Instead, the market is dominated by mismatches and arbitrage or position-driven pricing relationships.

One of the most serious obstacles to liquidity and the development of the market is the difficulty that market makers in yen swaps have in hedging their swap positions. Unlike other markets such as the US$ market, the number of hedging tools available are limited. While there is a substantial Japanese government bond market and an increasingly liquid yen bond futures contract traded in Tokyo, certain structural factors limit the potential to use these instruments to hedge swap positions. The primary obstacles include:

- The low correlation between swap yields and the Japanese government bond yield. For example, statistical work undertaken shows that the correlation between swap yields and government bond yields on a daily basis is less than 30.00%. In contrast, correlation between swap rates and LTPR is greater.

- Structural restrictions mean that it is almost impossible to short Japanese government bonds, except through the futures market.

- The lack of continuous supply of government bonds has meant that no consistent yield curve exists over which swaps can be quoted making relative valuation more difficult and creating inefficiencies in market pricing mechanisms.

In practice, swap market makers tend to either take positions onto their books *unhedged* or alternatively utilise the futures market in yen government bonds which necessarily means the market maker assumes a significant amount of basis risk on the transaction.

Additional inefficiencies result from the method by which, for example, yen interest rate swaps are quoted. Currently, yen interest rate swaps are quoted on the basis of fixed yen interest rate payments against *Euroyen LIBOR*. Given that Euroyen LIBOR does not exactly correspond to the short-term funding rates for Japanese banks, there is necessarily a mismatch when such swaps are utilised to create synthetic assets or liabilities.

These structural problems within the yen swap market have led to two particular responses from the financial institutions who dominate activity in this area:

- A large number of participants maintain substantial swap books acting as market makers or warehouses for yen swaps.

- The development of new approaches to yen swap arbitrage primarily by the Japanese securities houses who, hitherto, have largely refrained from entering into such swaps on a market making or trading basis, although this practice is now undergoing some change.

The approach to yen swaps by institutions has also been dictated by declining profitability and changes in the pattern by which swaps are transacted. Initially, the earnings from yen swaps were approximately 0.50% flat on the total notional principal of the swap and the spread between the bid and offer was 30 to 40bps pa. However, as the market developed, these spreads were rapidly squeezed and the profitability for financial institutions declined significantly. Simultaneously, while initially, the market had operated on an indicative basis with open timing, speed of execution rapidly became necessary to effect the underlying arbitrages.

Against this background, the larger Japanese city and long-term credit banks began to maintain large swap warehouses in yen. A number of foreign banks, including Citicorp, Bankers Trust, Morgan Guaranty, Security Pacific, Salomon Brothers and Paribas, one suspects drawing on their experience in other global swap markets, also operate marketmaking facilities in yen swaps.

However, the Japanese securities houses, primarily Nomura Securities, initially the most aggressive of the Japanese securities houses in swap transactions, rapidly evolved a totally new approach to the yen swap market. This approach was predicated on a very complex process of multivariate risk management and a marked emphasis on innovation.

Nomura's approach to swap arbitrage was predicated on the fact that a swapped new bond issue, especially across currencies, provided numerous prospects *to exploit market opportunities.*

For example, in a Euroyen issue swapped into deutschmark there are typically six variables which directly determine the final deutschmark cost of funds to the issuer, including:

- Euroyen bond yields;
- yen and US$ spot rates;
- yen and US$ forward rates;
- United States government Treasury note yields;
- US$ fixed and float swap spreads;
- fixed deutschmark and floating US$ swap rates.

Not only is the number of variables that can be arbitraged larger in a cross-currency swapped bond issue than in a single currency swapped issue, but their inter-relationships are also significantly more complex.

The inter-relationship between the variables for a fixed rate Eurodollar bond issue swapped into floating rate US$ are relatively stable over a typical 24 to 48 hour period. However, in the case of a fixed rate Euroyen issue swapped into a European currency, the relationship between the variables within the period of one working day is potentially very volatile.

Nomura would price and underwrite to the issuer the sum of the swaps (but not necessarily individual swaps) at an agreed break-even rate on cost to the borrower. The break-even rate could also be termed the natural arbitrage and is the statistically most probable economic relationship between the variables over a specified period of time. Nomura would take this multivariate risk onto its books.

Nomura would not normally lock in all the swap arbitrages or the swaps simultaneously. The reasons for this are complex.

First, in Euroyen issues, there is a time delay (originally three to ten days, now reduced to 48 hours) between being awarded a mandate and the Japanese Ministry of Finance giving approval for the issue to be launched. In addition the time overlap between the major swap countries is limited. It would be common in a single transaction for the fixed yen and fixed US$ swap to be concluded in Japan, the US$ interest rate swap to be concluded in the United States and the floating US$ and fixed deutschmark to be concluded in Europe.

Second, and more importantly, time delays create not only additional risks, but also opportunities to improve both the borrower's cost of funds and the investor's yield. The variables have a different level of intercorrelation, that is, particularly over a period of 12-24 hours, some of the variable inter-relationships will be stochastic. For example, within one day, the implied interest differential inherent in the yen and US$ spot and forward rates are unlikely to widen or narrow precisely in line with changes in the yields of United States government Treasury bond and Japanese government bonds.

Over a specific period of time, the movements of the variables tend to be cyclical and are likely to return to the natural arbitrage position. The swaps or the swap arbitrages will therefore be locked in at the optimum point during the cycles of adjustment between the variables.

Nomura's approach involved the *positioning* and *trading* of the underlying swap arbitrages in a way designed to optimise the pricing of the swaps for the issuer as well as seeking to provide the best terms to the investor. Explicit in the approach was the fact that Nomura wished to maintain the ability to benefit from or conversely not lose from changing market conditions. This risky strategy was only possible because of Nomura's capacity to operate globally with detailed knowledge of individual markets as well as using time zones to its advantage wherever possible.

The second approach which was developed contemporaneously was the introduction of a number of innovations in securities structures. Many of the swap structures, described in Chapter 17, involving securitising options on swaps are a direct outcome of these efforts. Each of the instruments identified were designed to meet specific investor portfolio requirements while providing borrowers with a competitive cost of funds, usually in floating rate US$. The investors in question were clients of the major European, Japanese and United States investment banks who were regular investors in a wide variety of assets. However, the approach was to identify particular portfolio requirements and to develop hybrid debt instruments to satisfy these requirements. Inevitably, the instruments combined conventional bond structures with arbitrage instruments, primarily forwards and options, which were then securitised through the swap specially structured for that specific purpose.

This development in yen swaps was an important response to the structural uncertainties of the yen market because from the viewpoint of the financial institutions the fact that they could be firmly placed at launch, as they were specifically matched to identified investor requirements, meant that they were not subject to the vagaries of short-term market movements of more conventional swap structures.

Interestingly, this combination of approaches has allowed the major Japanese securities houses to operate highly successfully as mainstream *arrangers* of swaps in the yen market.

HK$ SWAP MARKET

The only other Asian swap market of note is in HK$. The HK$ swap market developed rapidly throughout 1985 and 1986. Market estimates suggest that the volume as at the end of 1988 was approximately HK$10-15 billion, as against HK$1-2 billion in 1984. The swap market in HK$ has been one of the key factors behind the rapid development of Hong Kong's domestic capital markets.

Structurally, the HK$ swap market is dominated by interest rate swaps which total between 80.00% and 90.00% of overall volume. Participants in the market tend to fall into two clear categories:

- banks and financial institutions which issue fixed rate CDs which are then swapped into cost efficient floating rate funding, usually at a rate under the Hong Kong Interbank Offered Rate (HIBOR);

- corporations who utilise HK$ interest rate swaps to generate fixed rate liabilities off the back of substantial volumes of floating rate funding.

The primary impetus to HK$ swaps has been corporate appetite to lock in fixed rate funding, primarily at a time of very low interest rates. When long-term prime rates fell from a peak of 17.00% pa in 1980 to only 7.00% pa at the end of 1985, a number of large Hong Kong companies, with substantial debt portfolios, sought to carry out swaps to lock in their cost of funding over the medium to long-term.

This demand for fixed rate funding prompted the growth of the corresponding market in fixed rate CDs, issued primarily by financial institutions, seeking sub-HIBOR funding for their loan portfolios. The use of fixed rate CDs to match out corporate demand for fixed rate funding, via swaps, is evident from the following facts: in 1984, only 16.00% of the HK$1.685 billion of CD issues were fixed rates, while a year later, fixed rate issues accounted for 84.10% of the HK$6.3 billion CD issues, and in the first eight months of 1986, 89.70% of the HK$8.435 billion of CD issues were fixed rate. Estimates suggest that at least 80.00% of these fixed rate CD issues were swap-driven.

The market in HK$ swaps is largely driven by the big corporate swap users including Hong Kong Land, Mass Transit Railway Corporation, China Light and Power, Jardine Mathieson, KESCO and Eastern Energy. However, the substantial corporate demand has prompted a significant interbank swap market to develop. Approximately 20 banks actively participate in the interbank market with a number acting as market makers.

The pricing of HK$ swaps tends to be driven by investor demand for bank issued fixed rate CDs. The pricing tends to be a function of the rate achievable on a fixed rate CD adjusted for the sub-HIBOR margin required by the issuing bank. This tends to create an absolute rate market, where the fixed rate is quoted against HIBOR.

Development of the HK$ swap market has been impeded to some extent by the lack of available hedging instruments for professional swap market makers. Currently, the only avenue for hedging is through the fixed rate CD market by purchasing or shorting physical securities. The proposed introduction of a HK$ interest rate contract on the Hong Kong futures exchange will assist in providing an alternative to the physical market for hedging swap positions.

An additional structural difficulty has been the limited number of corporations with sufficient debt to entertain swaps. For example, in 1987, the demand for corporate fixed rate funding through swaps was largely concentrated in relatively long maturities, five to ten years, which did not coincide with the fixed rate CD market which is largely in the five year and under category.

Despite these technical difficulties, the HK$ swap market has reflected global swap market trends towards both standardisation and innovation. For example, more advanced swap structures such as deferred and forward swaps in HK$ were introduced in 1987.

Chapter 22

European Swap Markets: Swiss Franc, Deutschmark, £ and ECU

OVERVIEW

The European swap market is made up of a large number of separate markets in different currencies which have a complex pattern of similarities and discrepancies. The main European swap markets are the Swiss franc, deutschmark, £ and ECU markets. Each of these markets are discussed in greater detail below.

In addition to these major European swap markets, in recent times, markets for swaps have developed in a wide range of European currencies including: Dutch guilders, French francs, Luxembourg francs, Swedish and Danish kroner, Belgian francs, and Italian lira. These new emerging swap markets are driven by a complex series of factors including:

- the development of international, primarily Eurobond, markets in a number of these currencies;
- the development of futures markets in some of these currencies;
- special regulatory factors which affect financial transactions in the currency.

A number of the minor European swap markets owe their existence to the recent development of bond markets, primarily outside the domestic market, driven by international investor interest in securities denominated in the particular currency. For example, international bond markets in Luxembourg francs and Swedish and Danish kroner have recently emerged as international investors have sought easy access to securities in these currencies. A number of arbitrage funders have sought to issue securities in these currencies on the basis of an accompanying swap into "cheap" US$ floating rate funding at attractive margins relative to LIBOR. The main counterparties to these swaps have been institutions, primarily in the domestic markets, seeking cost effective fixed rate funds in the particular currency.

Against this background, these particular swap markets have developed on the back of periodic investor appetite for international securities denominated in the particular currency.

The recent introduction in a number of markets of futures contracts on interest rates has facilitated the development of shorter term swap markets in the relevant currency. For example, the emergence of MATIF in France has allowed a number of financial institutions to offer short-dated swaps denominated in French francs with the risk positions being offset in the futures market.

An additional factor influencing these minor European swap markets has been the regulatory framework within the individual currency. For example, in Italy, until recent changes, the presence of substantial foreign exchange

397

controls created segmented markets where a small group of institutions, the powerful state agencies, have been able to transact currency swaps off the back of international lira issues.

These factors are in addition to more traditional swap arbitrages such as the standard credit arbitrage between the fixed and floating segments of the capital market as well as market frictions such as withholding tax which have created opportunities for swap arbitrage.

SWISS FRANC SWAP MARKET

The Swiss franc market is one of the oldest "modern" swap markets. As described in Chapter 1 the hallmark swap between the World Bank and IBM involved Swiss francs.

However, despite this long history, the Swiss franc swap market is a relatively limited market which operates primarily off new issues in Swiss francs. Structurally, the market is dominated by two groups:

- A group of Swiss franc bond issuers, usually highly rated corporations or sovereigns as well as a number of popular, well known United States and Japanese corporations with good name recognition among investors, who utilise the issue as a basis for an arbitrage into a more desired currency, primarily US$ and, to a lesser extent yen.

- A group of swap counterparties, primarily supranationals and some lower rated sovereign borrowers, who provide the major interest in paying fixed rate Swiss francs under the swaps.

The receptivity of the Swiss franc market to some types of borrowers on terms not directly related to their credit rating has for many years formed the basis of the fundamental credit arbitrage which underlies this market. For example, a wide variety of well known United States corporations which are household names among the traditional retail investor base within Switzerland have been able to issue bonds denominated in Swiss francs on yield differentials which are substantially below the risk premiums they would have had to pay in other markets, such as the US$ market. These institutions have utilised this differential access to Swiss franc funding to generate cheaper US$ debt. While the precise cost savings vary from time to time, cost savings for these lower rated United States corporates has often been up to 50bps, although the more typical number is 15-30bps.

Some very highly rated sovereign borrowers with no direct requirement for Swiss francs have also been periodic issuers as part of swap transactions. These borrowers, whose paper carries considerable scarcity value, have been able to generate cost savings in other markets through the vehicle of the Swiss franc issue from time to time.

The payers of fixed rate Swiss francs in the swaps have in the main been supranationals, such as the World Bank and Asian Development Bank, who have from time to time been able to use swaps to generate more cost effective Swiss franc funding. The substantial demand from such borrowers for low coupon funding has meant that a strategy of diversifying their source of funds and converting some of their non-Swiss franc liabilities into Swiss francs through swaps has proved an important aspect of their liability management.

Another group of swap counterparties are lower rated sovereigns and corporations who cannot undertake direct issues of debt. This group, including a number of South East Asian countries, have swapped against liabilities, usually US$ borrowings, diversifying the currency basis of their governmental debt portfolios.

Paying interest in fixed rate Swiss francs can be a function of Swiss interest rates and expectations about the value of the Swiss francs versus a number of other currencies. For example, falling interest rates in Switzerland in early 1986 and 1987 allowed swaps to be written off old debt where borrowers swapped relatively expensive foreign debt into Swiss francs. In addition, the steady rise of the yen against the Swiss franc has also meant that a number of Japanese borrowers who have been favourites in the Swiss market for a long time, have undertaken a number of Swiss franc swaps to take advantage of the expected strength of the yen.

The underlying structure of the Swiss franc market, in particular, its new issue orientation, has meant that there is little secondary market activity and consequently limited liquidity in these types of swaps. However, the presence of a number of swap market makers, primarily the "big three" Swiss banks as well as a number of other institutions, such as Citibank, Morgan Guaranty, Paribas, etc., has added to the depth of the market though liquidity and activity levels remain tied largely to new issue levels and swap arbitrage windows.

Swiss franc swaps have no uniform benchmark interest rate over which they are priced. Consequently, the market is an absolute interest rate market where movements in the swap rate are largely tied to interest rate levels in the new issue market, the level of paying interest by swap counterparties and the availability of comparable new issue arbitrage opportunities in other segments of the international bond market. Shorter dated swaps, primarily under three to four years, tend to follow domestic interest rates.

Exhibit 22.1 sets out historical data on Swiss franc swap rates.

DEUTSCHMARK SWAP MARKET

The deutschmark swap market is similar to the Swiss franc swap market, although it is of more recent origin. The deutschmark swap market has its origins in the German Bundesbank's decision in 1984 to deregulate the deutschmark debt markets and lift a specific prohibition on deutschmark issues intended to be swapped. Prior to this period, a number of banks had, however, disregarded the rules. During the initial phase of deregulation, Bundesbank restrictions, such as a new issue calendar and a registration process to be completed two days before the end of the month preceding the launch, greatly restricted the flexibility of this market. However, recent changes greatly liberalising the issue procedures have given the market considerable impetus.

Statistics released by the Bundesbank provide an indication of the size of the deutschmark swap market. As at the end of 1988, German banks had a total of approximately DM250 billion outstanding in swap transactions of which DM170 billion was interest rate swaps. The value of swaps arranged by German domestic banks was DM152 billion of which DM113 billion

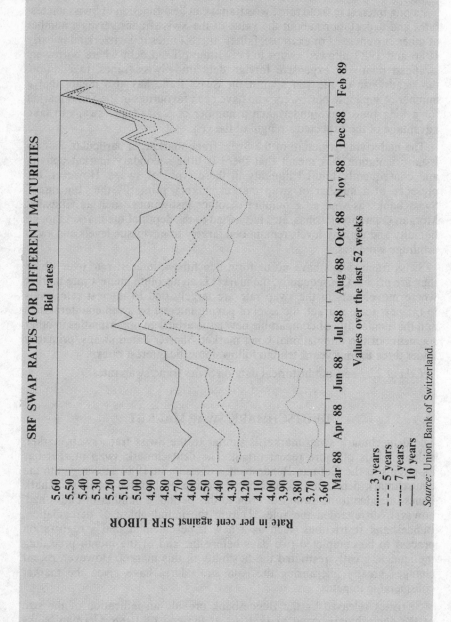

Exhibit 22.1
Swiss Franc Swap Rates

was in interest rate swaps. Roughly DM88 billion was booked by German bank offices or subsidiaries abroad of which DM57 billion was in interest rate swaps. Considerable care should be taken in using these figures to infer the actual level of deutschmark swap activity as these volume statistics undoubtedly include swaps in other currencies transacted by the German banks where it acts as an intermediary between two counterparties.

The structure of the deutschmark swap market is very similar to that of the Swiss franc market with swaps being transacted primarily against new issues. The primary receivers of fixed rate deutschmark are either highly rated sovereign or corporate names sought after by investors and well known, but not necessarily highly rated, United States corporate names which enjoy good access to this particular market segment. This pattern in the new issue market reflects the fact that a significant portion of investors in deutschmark issues come from the traditional Swiss franc investor base.

The pattern of swap counterparties is also similar to those active in Swiss franc swaps. Supranationals as well as lower rated sovereigns often utilise deutschmark swaps to either achieve more cost efficient deutschmark funding or alternatively to avoid excessive access to this market segment. However, there is an additional group of fixed deutschmark payers who are primarily motivated by asset liability management concerns. For example, a typical counterparty might be a Dutch company with heavy US$ borrowings and significant deutschmark assets. Another typical counterparty may be a German company seeking fixed rate deutschmark debt without accessing the public deutschmark markets. Both groups are highly active from time to time in the deutschmark market. The level of activity tends to be driven by the absolute levels of deutschmark rates as well as the deutschmark:US$ exchange rate.

Like the Swiss franc swap market, the new issue emphasis of the deutschmark swap market dictates a relative lack of depth and liquidity in secondary market deutschmark swaps. However, over recent years, liquidity has significantly increased with the emergence of a number of major market makers, primarily the major German banks.

Secondary market activity in deutschmark swaps has grown rapidly, in part because of the development of a deutschmark government bond futures contract which facilitated the hedging of swap positions. Since 1987, there has been a bond index future for Dutch government bonds in Amsterdam which was used as a surrogate for deutschmark bond price movements (reflecting the close inter-relationships between the two markets). This superseded the use of a synthetic hedging technique whereby United States Treasury Notes and US$ and deutschmark foreign exchange contracts were used to hedge deutschmark swaps. More recently, since late 1988, the London International Financial Futures Exchange (LIFFE) has traded a deutschmark government bond futures contract. The liquidity of the bond futures contract and the low bid/offer spread in the futures market relative to the cash market for bonds has made the contract a popular hedging mechanism for market makers in deutschmark swaps.

As the deutschmark swap market has matured, swaps are increasingly being quoted against the domestic German index known as Schuldscheine. Schuldscheine are fixed rate promissory notes issued by German banks and corporations with maturities of one to ten years, rather like CDs. They show a real interest rate reflecting current market conditions and the availability of these securities allows market makers to hedge positions in deutschmark swaps. The advantage of pricing of Schuldscheine is that for potential participants, the swap rate can be related to current market levels for direct issuances of debt by that particular company facilitating comparisons.

Schuldscheine has emerged as a benchmark swap index because of the structure of the German bank funding system. Under this system, a bank making a market in deutschmark swaps must ensure that the price it quotes for a deutschmark swap in exchange for floating rate US$ is linked to the cost of funds in the domestic market.

Exhibit 22.2 sets out some historical data on deutschmark swap rates and their spread relationship to the deutschmark bond market.

£ SWAP MARKET

The £ swap market is an important European swap market which differs significantly from the Swiss franc and deutschmark swap markets in a number of respects. Reasonably active markets for £ interest rate swaps as well as cross-currency swaps into US$ exist.

The £ swap market has its origins in the foreign exchange restrictions in the late 1960s and early 1970s when a thriving back-to-back or parallel loan market involving £ on one side developed. The modern £ swap market has its origins in the early 1980s when local authorities were being offered cheap subsidised fixed rate funds from the public works loan board. The subsidised nature of the funding provided the basis of a very attractive arbitrage for these public authorities into floating rate £ allowing them to make significant savings or realise an immediate profit on a positive yield curve. While government action removed this pricing distortion, the £ swap market has continued to develop. In recent years, an increasing market for Eurosterling bond issues has been a major component in the growth of the corresponding swap market. However, rather uncharacteristically, the swaps of Eurosterling issues are not necessarily exclusively into floating rate US$ with a number of issues being swapped instead into floating rate £.

The Eurosterling market itself is far from constant, operating spasmodically in response to the differential between £ interest rates and comparable interest rates on certain low coupon currencies as well as the future outlook for the £ in foreign exchange markets. Investor demand for £, particularly outside the United Kingdom, tends to be driven by a mixture of portfolio diversification and short-term trading objectives. Expectations of interest rate falls or appreciation in the £ creates short-term demand pressures for £ assets which are usually quickly satisfied by bringing Eurosterling issues to market.

The issuers of Eurosterling securities on a swapped basis include typical arbitrage funders as well as the United Kingdom branches or subsidiaries of international banks and United Kingdom building societies. The foreign bank branches and building societies are primarily motivated by asset liability matching considerations and are seeking to generate cost effective floating rate funds in £ at a cost better than that achievable directly. In recent times, issues have been swapped into floating rate £ at margins of up to 40bps

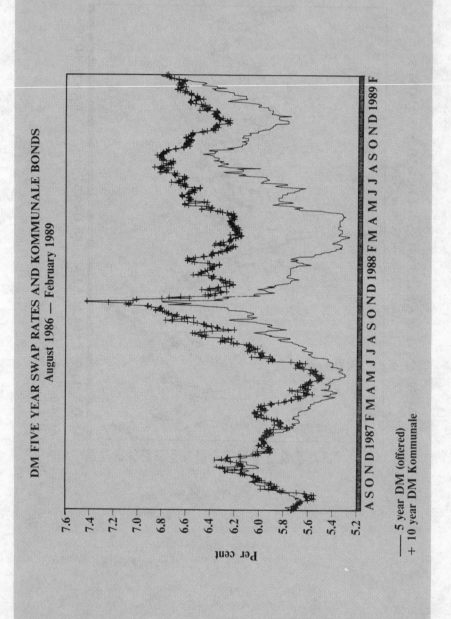

Exhibit 22.2
Deutschmark Swap Rates and Spreads

Exhibit 22.2—continued

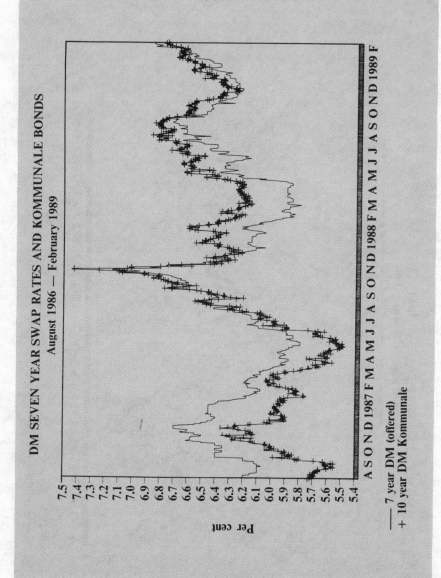

DM SEVEN YEAR SWAP RATES AND KOMMUNALE BONDS
August 1986 — February 1989

Exhibit 22.2—continued

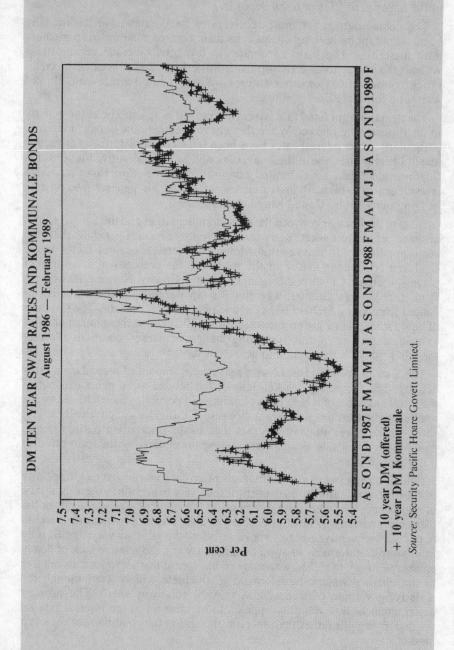

DM TEN YEAR SWAP RATES AND KOMMUNALE BONDS
August 1986 — February 1989

—— 10 year DM (offered)
+ 10 year DM Kommunale

Source: Security Pacific Hoare Govett Limited.

under £ LIBOR although savings of around 15-25bps are more usual. For United Kingdom building societies, in particular, £ interest rate swaps represent an alternative form of funding to more traditional techniques, such as the issuance of CDs or retail deposits.

The counterparties for these receivers of fixed rates have traditionally been corporations seeking to lock in their cost of funding over medium term maturities. The main corporates in this group include organisations without the ability to directly tap the Eurosterling market because of credit rating considerations or other entities whose funding requirements do not warrant a full scale Eurobond issue.

The demand from fixed rate payers has proved as spasmodic as the activity in the Eurosterling market. While there have been periodic bursts of interest, particularly when interest rates have been felt to be at historically attractive levels, interest rates above these levels as well as a conservative bias towards floating rate funding has limited corporate use of swaps. However, there is evidence that there is increased use of swaps for general interest rate hedging purposes by United Kingdom corporates.

Despite the linkage between the Eurosterling market and the £ swap sector, absence of Euromarket activity does not necessarily mean that the corresponding swap market shuts down completely. A major factor in the fluid and continuous nature of the market is the presence of a number of players such as Citicorp, Morgan Guaranty, County Natwest Investment Bank and Morgan Grenfell who run £ swap warehouses and a number of United Kingdom merchant banks active in arranging £ swaps. The presence of liquid markets in £ government securities (gilts) allows these intermediaries to hedge unmatched positions pending changes in market conditions allowing the other side of a transaction to be executed.

The £ swap market also shows a reasonable amount of secondary market activity. The secondary market activity has tended to be generated out of the interbank market where banks holding gilt portfolios have utilised swaps to effectively short the gilt market. Because of difficulties in physically selling short, banks have, utilising the fact that swaps price off a particular gilt, paid out the fixed side as an alternative means of creating the short physical position.

Pound sterling swaps are traditionally priced at a margin over a gilt security of the relevant maturity. However, despite this benchmark, there is a lack of consistency and general agreement on the particular relevant gilt in the particular maturity as most gilts stand at a significant premium or discount to par. Consequently, margins above or below the gilt may vary significantly from swap counterparty to swap counterparty and the relative lack of depth, compared to say the US$ swap market, has meant that swap spreads relative to the gilt benchmark have tended to fluctuate widely even though the underlying volume of transactions may be relatively small. The primary determinant of this volatility appears to be changes in the interest rate on the underlying gilt rather than specific changes in the conditions of the swap market.

The level and pattern of swap spreads and spreads in the £ market are depicted in *Exhibit 22.3*. The inter-relationship between changes in the swap rate and £ interest rate movements is set out in *Exhibit 22.4*.

Exhibit 22.3
£ Swap Rates and Spreads

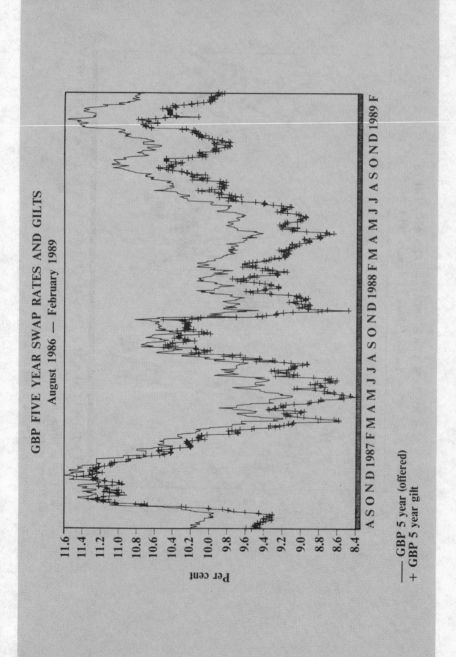

GBP FIVE YEAR SWAP RATES AND GILTS
August 1986 — February 1989

A S O N D 1987 F M A M J J A S O N D 1988 F M A M J J A S O N D 1989 F

Per cent

— GBP 5 year (offered)
+ GBP 5 year gilt

Exhibit 22.3—continued

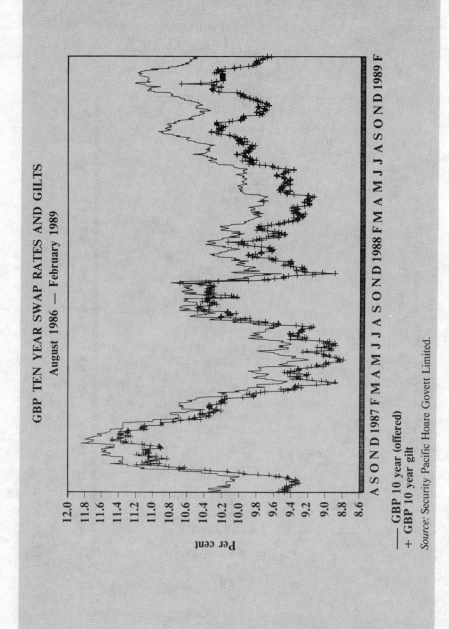

GBP TEN YEAR SWAP RATES AND GILTS
August 1986 — February 1989

— GBP 10 year (offered)
+ GBP 10 year gilt

Source: Security Pacific Hoare Govett Limited.

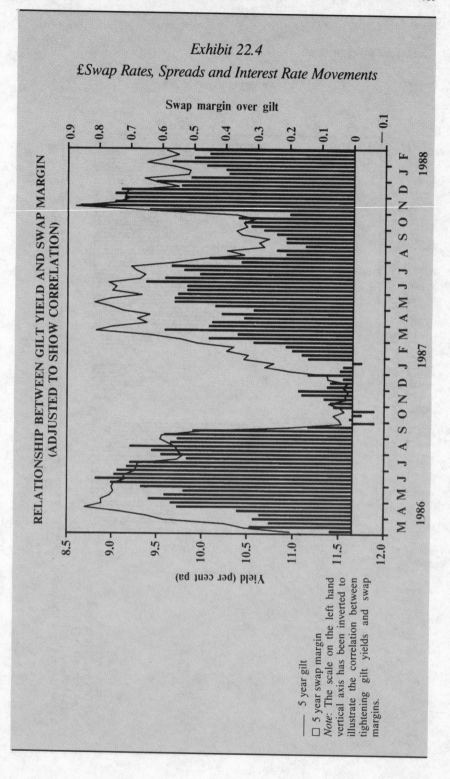

Exhibit 22.4
£Swap Rates, Spreads and Interest Rate Movements

RELATIONSHIP BETWEEN GILT YIELD AND SWAP MARGIN
(ADJUSTED TO SHOW CORRELATION)

Swap margin over gilt

Yield (per cent pa)

—— 5 year gilt
☐ 5 year swap margin
Note: The scale on the left hand
vertical axis has been inverted to
illustrate the correlation between
tightening gilt yields and swap
margins.

Exhibit 22.4—continued

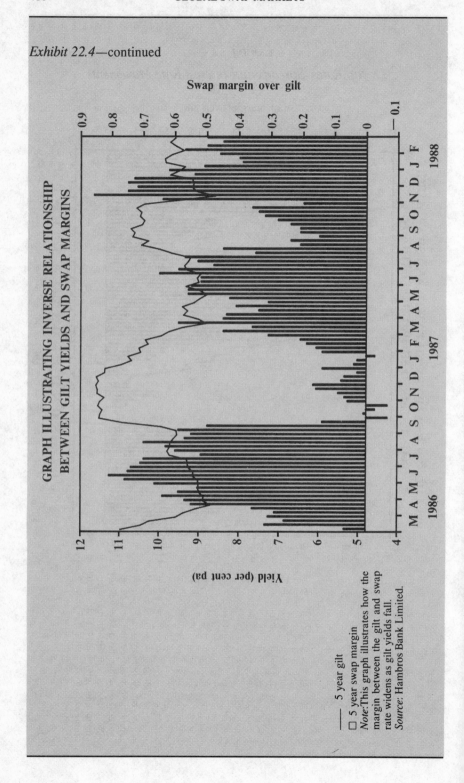

GRAPH ILLUSTRATING INVERSE RELATIONSHIP
BETWEEN GILT YIELDS AND SWAP MARGINS

Swap margin over gilt

—— 5 year gilt
□ 5 year swap margin
*Note:*This graph illustrates how the margin between the gilt and swap rate widens as gilt yields fall.
Source: Hambros Bank Limited.

The emergence of an asset swap market in £ has been a feature of this sector of the global swap market. For example, in late 1987 a number of issues were brought to market with the specific intention of being sold on an asset swap basis.

The £ swap market is also highly sophisticated in that more complex non-generic swap structures are available including options on swaps. In 1988, a number of local authorities sought to raise cash and generate profits by aggressively selling £ swaptions.

ECU SWAP MARKET

The ECU swap market has a number of unique features although in its emphasis on new issue swap activity it demonstrates considerable similarity with the Swiss franc and deutschmark swap markets. This unique status derives from the fact that because of the artificial nature of the ECU, unlike most other bond markets, there is no natural benchmark against which absolute swap rates can be quoted as there are no ECU government bonds. Structurally, this creates a problem insofar as ECU swaps are inherently difficult to hedge with the resultant effect that most transactions are counterparty driven.

The structure of the ECU swap market is predicated largely on the characteristics of the end users of fixed rates ECUs. The main borrowers of ECUs include:

- Various official entities of the European Common Market, including supranational entities such as the European Investment Bank, as well as member countries such as France, Italy and Ireland. This group are largely motivated by the need to support the concept of the ECU as part of the EEC concept, the capacity to borrow outside their domestic market with a currency linked to their own and generally at a cheaper cost.

- Sovereign and semi-sovereign borrowers from a wide variety of countries, including Australia, who are motivated by objectives of diversification in terms of both currency and investor base.

- Corporations, both European and non-European, that have European assets and are seeking to incur liabilities in ECU as a means of match funding their balance sheets.

- A small group of opportunistic entities seeking to arbitrage the ECU versus other domestic markets. This type of activity is based on the fact that the ECU can often represent an opportunity to generate liabilities in currencies which cannot be obtained directly and, above all, offers the possibility to take advantage of discrepancies between yields of the component currencies and the ECU rate itself.

Potential borrowers in ECU do not, however, enjoy equal access to ECU funding. The major investor base in ECU, which in recent times has included a substantial Japanese element seeking a yield pick-up relative to the deutschmark (given that the deutschmark is a major component of the ECU), are highly credit sensitive. This means that access to the ECU bond market itself is available only to a relatively select group of borrowers. This necessarily means that several of the identified users of ECUs, primarily corporations seeking ECU funding either for asset liability management purposes or as an arbitrage to a component currency as well as some lesser rated sovereign borrowers seeking diversification, are forced to utilise ECU swaps usually against receipt of floating rate US$ to achieve their desired ECU exposures. Their interest in paying fixed rate ECU essentially drives new issue activity in the ECU Eurobond market.

The issuers of ECU Eurobonds are predominantly new issue arbitrage funders seeking cheap US$ floating rate funding. For example, the World Bank in 1986 undertook an ECU150m issue which was partially swapped into yen. The type of issuer is influenced by investor demand which has from time to time favoured good quality United States names with good investor recognition. The fact that these often lesser ranked but well known borrowers can obtain funding on relatively attractive credit differentials in the ECU market relative to other borrowing avenues allows them to issue relatively cheap ECU debt which is then swapped into cheaper floating rate US$.

The structure of the market dictates that the majority of transactions are undertaken on a counterparty basis with investment banks obtaining mandates from issuers based on an all-in cost target in the swapped currency and then seeking to take advantage of ECU bond market conditions and the availability of swap counterparties to engineer the transaction.

While the primary market related swaps dominate, increasingly a tentative secondary market in ECU swaps has developed. A number of financial institutions, primarily Banque Paribas as well as to a lesser extent Bankers Trust, Morgan Guaranty and Chase Manhattan, have begun to provide liquidity by running unmatched warehousing operations allowing participants to transact swaps unrelated to a new issue. The financial institutions making markets in ECU swaps have either taken positions on their own books seeking to profit from movements in ECU rates or alternatively have arranged surrogate cover for the swap positions. For example, on occasions, these financial institutions would buy deutschmark bonds to hedge the swap position. The risk linked to this activity is substantial because the only means to generate a short position in ECU itself is to launch an ECU issue which is subject to favourable market conditions.

A relatively recent feature of the ECU swap market, which has prompted increased trading activity, is a complex arbitrage between ECU Eurobonds and Certificates di Credits del Treroro (CTE) denominated in ECU issued by the Republic of Italy.

This arbitrage transaction operates as follows: a borrower issues ECU Eurobonds and simultaneously enters into an ECU and US$ currency swap with a bank active in ECU swaps whereby it receives fixed rate ECU and pays US$ LIBOR. The bank generates the mirror reverse side of the swap by purchasing ECU CTEs and repackaging them via an asset swap into a US$ LIBOR FRN and placing the asset with an investor. The asset swap requires the investor to pay fixed rate ECU (the receipts from the CTEs) and receive US$ LIBOR neatly covering the bank's exposure under the original ECU swap.

The yield differential between ECU CTEs and AAA rated Eurobonds can be as much as 100bps pa, resulting in attractive swap arbitrage opportunities. This arbitrage differential may allow issuers to generate US$

funding at up to 40-50bps under LIBOR and investors to generate Republic of Italy assets at up to 40bps over LIBOR.

The crucial element driving CTE based swaps is withholding tax factors. CTEs issued prior to 20 September 1986 are tax exempt; issues prior to August 1987 are taxed at the rate of 6.25% on the coupon payment; all issues after August 1987 are taxed at a withholding tax rate of 12.50%. Investors in certain countries are exempt under a withholding tax exemption agreement between the Republic of Italy and the relevant country or, alternatively, are eligible to recover any withholding tax via a tax credit.

However, despite this emergence of some trading activity, the ECU market continues to be strongly dependent upon the primary bond market with up to 80.00% of the ECU Eurobonds being swapped. The cycles in ECU swaps being largely explainable on the basis of this interdependence. For example, at a given time, the exchange rate levels would trigger strong demand from counterparties wishing to convert their debt into ECU and this would, if market conditions were favourable, be met by a number of swapped bond issues. Usually, a surfeit of issues would create an oversupply in the primary bond market and force primary market yield to a level which would close off this particular arbitrage. Conversely, at other times, the demand for ECU bonds could rise to such a level that the lack of swap counterparties would induce a shortage of bond issues and an exaggerated decrease of primary market yields.

Despite this lack of maturity, the ECU swap market has grown impressively in recent years with volume touching ECU25-30 billion in 1988. *Exhibit 22.5* sets out ECU swap rates relative to theoretical ECU interest rates for a number of maturities.

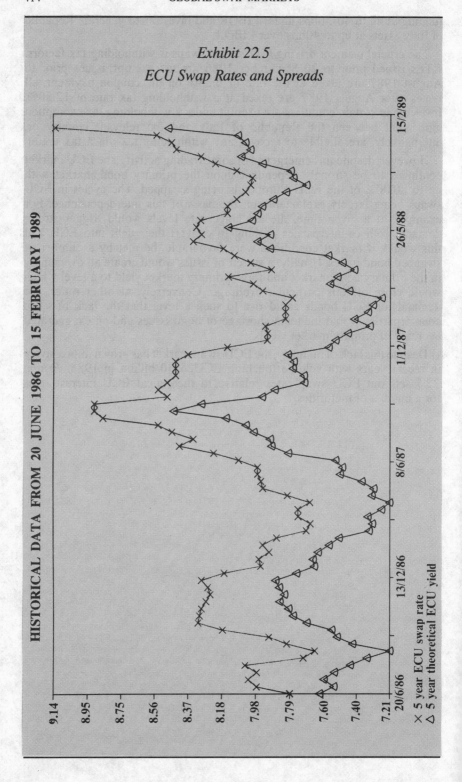

Exhibit 22.5
ECU Swap Rates and Spreads

HISTORICAL DATA FROM 20 JUNE 1986 TO 15 FEBRUARY 1989

× 5 year ECU swap rate
△ 5 year theoretical ECU yield

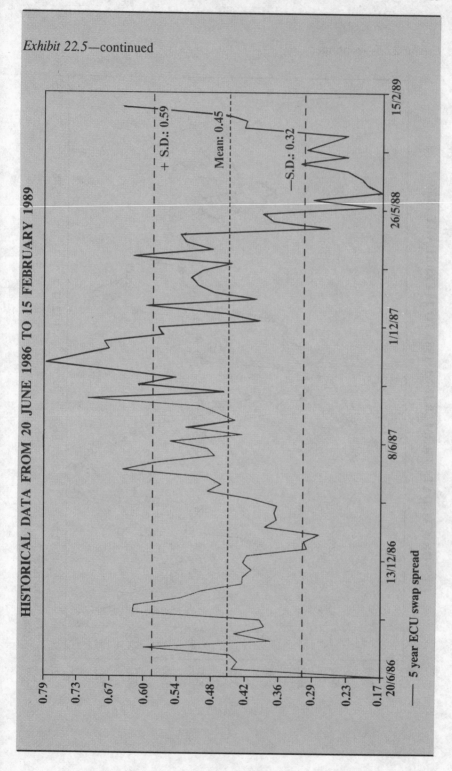

Exhibit 22.5—continued

HISTORICAL DATA FROM 20 JUNE 1986 TO 15 FEBRUARY 1989

Exhibit 22.5—continued

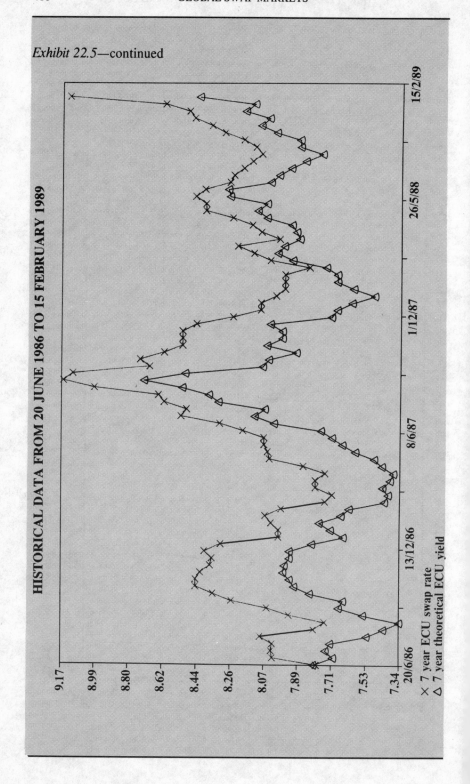

HISTORICAL DATA FROM 20 JUNE 1986 TO 15 FEBRUARY 1989

× 7 year ECU swap rate
△ 7 year theoretical ECU yield

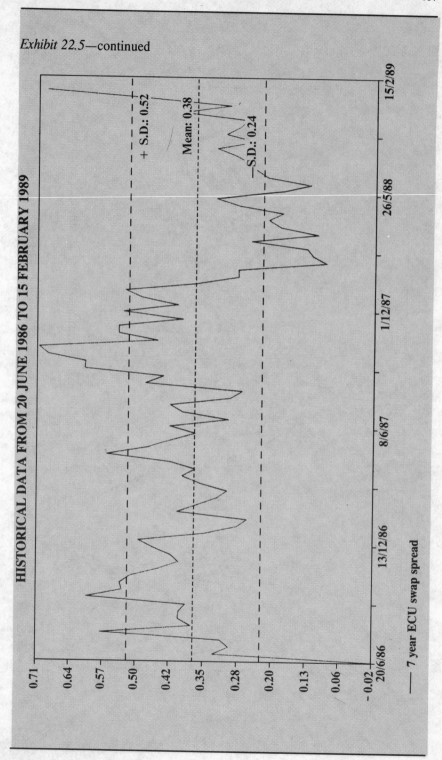

Exhibit 22.5—continued

HISTORICAL DATA FROM 20 JUNE 1986 TO 15 FEBRUARY 1989

— 7 year ECU swap spread

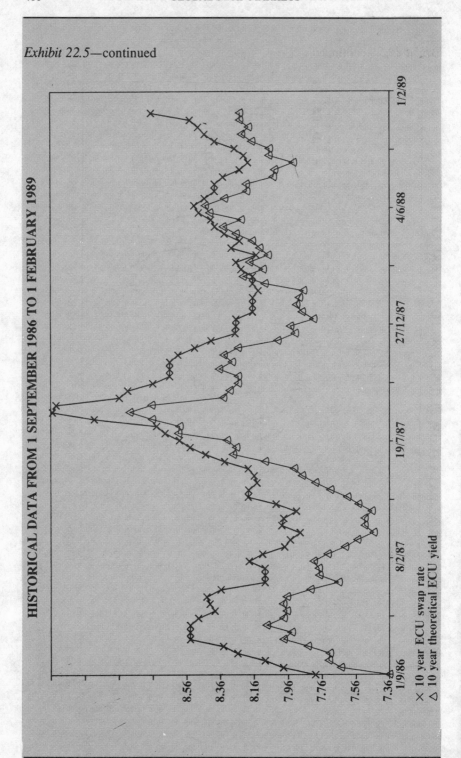

Exhibit 22.5—continued

HISTORICAL DATA FROM 1 SEPTEMBER 1986 TO 1 FEBRUARY 1989

× 10 year ECU swap rate
△ 10 year theoretical ECU yield

Exhibit 22.5—continued

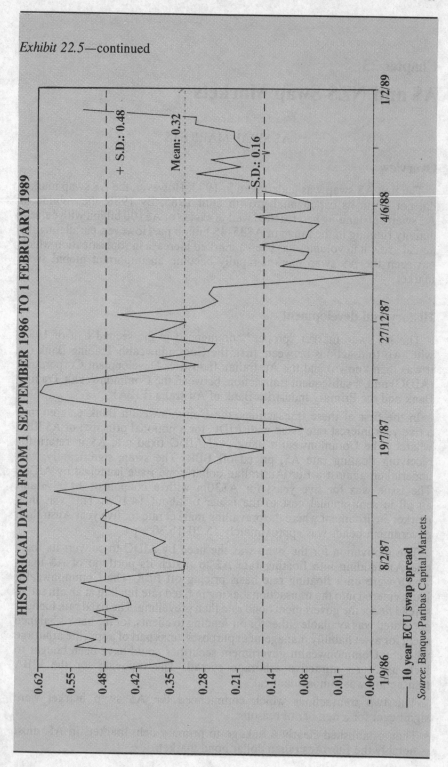

HISTORICAL DATA FROM 1 SEPTEMBER 1986 TO 1 FEBRUARY 1989

— 10 year ECU swap spread

Source: Banque Paribas Capital Markets.

Chapter 23

A$ and NZ$ Swap Markets

Overview

The first A$ swap was undertaken in 1983. However, the A$ swap market did not begin its exponential growth until 1985. By 1988, the volume of A$ swap outstanding had reached well in excess of A$100 billion with current activity running in the range of A$35-45 billion pa. However, paralleling the actual growth in volumes has been a marked increase in sophistication which has seen the A$ swap market rapidly become an important global swap market.

History and development

The A$ swap market "proper" commenced in the second half of 1983, with two transactions between, first, the Commonwealth Trading Bank (as it was then known) and the Australian Industries Development Corporation (AIDC) and, a subsequent transaction, between the Commonwealth Trading Bank and the Primary Industries Bank of Australia (PIBA).

In the first of these transactions, the Commonwealth Bank entered into a five year interest rate swap with AIDC for a notional principal of A$30m, whereby the Commonwealth Bank paid AIDC fixed rate A$ in return for receiving floating rate A$, priced off BBR. The swap, significantly, was undertaken against a EuroAustralian dollar bond issue launched by AIDC. The issue was for five years for A$30m with a coupon of 14.00% and an all-in semi-annual cost to the issuer of about 14.10%. This was in a market environment where the prevailing market rate for five year Australian government bonds was approximately 15.20-15.30% pa.

The motivation for the swap was the need by AIDC to convert its fixed rate A$ funding into floating rate A$ to match its portfolio of A$ loans which were on a floating rate basis pricing off BBR. The Commonwealth Bank entered into the transaction locking in fixed rate funding at an attractive spread *under* the government bond rate then prevailing. The fixed rate funding generated was available either for on-lending to clients, for the bank's balance sheet for asset liability management purposes, or as part of a specific arbitrage whereby Commonwealth government securities could have been bought to lock away an attractive arbitrage spread. The rationale for the PIBA transaction was almost identical.

The two transactions which commenced the A$ swap market were significant for a number of reasons:

- They established clearly a linkage to primary debt markets in A$, most notably the EuroAustralian dollar bond market.

- They highlighted an unsatisfied requirement for instruments to enable a wide category of institutions to better match their asset liability portfolios.
- The transactions pinpointed a number of pricing anomalies as between the domestic A$ and offshore A$ markets.

It is highly significant that these concerns which allowed the initial transactions in the A$ market to be undertaken have continued to dominate this sector of the global swap market. An interesting aspect of these transactions was that the A$ swap market commenced with *interest rate swaps* rather than currency swaps which have historically opened swap markets in a number of currencies.

It should be noted that prior to August 1983, more precisely since 1981, a substantial market in short-term interest rate swaps had already existed within Australia. These were transactions involving the purchase and sale of bills at fixed rates, that is, essentially interest rate swaps. These forward sales and purchases of bills were undertaken by a small number of financial institutions with the price risk being hedged through the 90 day bank bill interest rate futures contract which had traded on the Sydney Futures Exchange since October 1978.

The development of the A$ swap market can be divided into two distinct phases:

- 1983 to 1984 when the major receivers of fixed rate A$ in swap transactions were AIDC, PIBA and the Australian Resources Development Bank (ARDB) as well as semi-government institutions;
- post 1984 when the major receivers of fixed rate A$ were non-Australian issuers of A$ securities in the Eurobond and, more recently, Yankee markets.

The distinction between the two periods is, in practice, less clearly delineated than might be assumed. In particular, in periods when primary market issuance activity in A$ securities outside Australia has diminished or ceased altogether, the pattern of 1983 and 1984 has re-emerged.

The key factor underlying the evolution of the A$ swap market has been the development of an international market in A$ securities. Although international purchases of A$ securities commenced in the mid 1970s, until 1985 the primary issuers were Australian entities with a genuine demand for A$ funding. For example, during 1983 and 1984, AIDC and PIBA issued over A$200m of securities in the Eurobond market. These two issuers accounted for almost half the EuroAustralian dollar issues in that period. Both entities used their access to these cost effective fixed rate A$ to generate floating rate funding to support their asset portfolio utilising A$ interest rate swaps. Both PIBA and ARDB also swapped off the relatively cheap domestic fixed rate retail funding basis which they possessed.

During this period, the other major receiver of fixed rates in the A$ swap market were the semi-government authorities. These entities which enjoyed good access to fixed rate funding in the domestic market had predominantly fixed rate debt portfolios and a number of innovative statutory authorities took the opportunity to convert some of their debt into a floating rate basis via interest rate swaps as part of an overall restructuring of the interest rate bases of their debt.

During this period, the primary interest in paying fixed rates came from financial institutions interested in raising fixed rate funding to close out gaps in their asset liability portfolios and from corporations without alternative access to fixed rate A$ funding. Given that for much of this period the yield curve was sharply inverse, a natural cost incentive existed for undertaking such transactions.

However, in 1985 international demand for A$ securities reached an unprecedented level. Attracted by the high level of A$ interest rates as well as seeking, to a lesser extent, currency diversification, successive waves of investors began to purchase A$ securities, primarily in the form of EuroAustralian dollar bonds, in unprecedented volumes. These investors included European retail and institutional investors, Japanese institutions, and United States institutions.

Within Europe itself, interest in A$ securities expanded from investors in the Benelux countries to other more substantial investors groups, such as retail German investors and the Swiss market.

This evolution in the investor base created a bias which prompted further growth in the A$ swap market. The new investors in A$ securities had a preference for bearer Eurobonds, free of any withholding tax, issued by organisations with which the investor base was familiar. This investor preference dictated to a large extent the form (Eurobond) and the type of issuer which now came to dominate the international A$ market. When in 1986, United States investors joined the numbers of investors seeking A$ securities, this clientele effect was also evident because United States domestic investors had a strong preference for United States Securities Exchange Commission registered issues, criteria which very few Australian borrowers could satisfy.

This shift in the structure of the A$ securities market meant that A$ borrowers ceased, almost totally, to directly borrow in A$, relying instead on a swap undertaken with an issuer who utilised the A$ securities issue as part of a new issue arbitrage transaction. These new issuers included a number of sovereign and supranational borrowers including the World Bank and Sweden, a number of international banks, primarily German banks reflecting the underlying investor demand within Germany, as well as a number of well known United States corporations with good name recognition among European retail investors. Examples of the last category include companies such as Pepsico, McDonald's and IBM.

International interest in A$ securities after the initial surge proved to be volatile, although the A$ established itself as a significant, though minor, international currency. Interest rate movements, particularly interest rate differentials relative to the other major currencies and the behaviour of the A$ exchange rate shaped the pattern of investment and disinvestment from this sector of the international bond market. For example, in the second half of 1985, 1986 and 1987, A$ Eurobond activity slowed and, on a number of occasions, ceased completely. During these periods, borrowers with access to domestic fixed rate A$, primarily the semi-government authorities, moved quickly to resume their roles as major receivers of fixed rate A$ in swap transactions.

Structure of A$ swap market

The structure of the A$ swap market corresponds closely to that of the US$ market. The market is essentially split into two segments:

- short-dated interest rate swaps, primarily under two years;
- longer dated swaps, usually with maturities between three and ten years, with a marked concentration in the three to five year range.

The difference between the two segments lies in the hedging mechanisms utilised and the consequent price behaviour. As in the United States market, the short-dated swaps tend to be hedged through the A$ interest rate futures market, as identified above. This market is both liquid and volatile with interest rates showing a close correspondence to changes in money market conditions and movement in short-term interest rates. The long-term swap market is priced off Commonwealth government bonds and hedged by buying and selling these securities.

The A$ swap market, particularly in the over two year segment, is made up of three separate segments:

- fixed A$ and US$ LIBOR currency swaps;
- fixed A$ and floating A$ interest rate swaps; and
- floating A$ and floating US$ currency swaps.

The structure of the A$ swap market is set out in *Exhibit 23.1*.

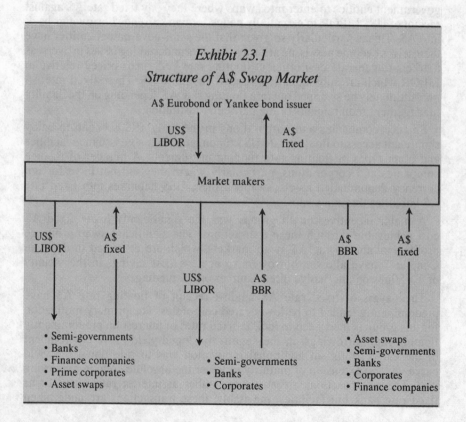

Exhibit 23.1
Structure of A$ Swap Market

A$ Eurobond or Yankee bond issuer

US$ LIBOR · A$ fixed

Market makers

US$ LIBOR · A$ fixed · US$ LIBOR · A$ BBR · A$ BBR · A$ fixed

- Semi-governments
- Banks
- Finance companies
- Prime corporates
- Asset swaps

- Semi-governments
- Banks
- Corporates

- Asset swaps
- Semi-governments
- Banks
- Corporates
- Finance companies

The participants in each sector of the swap market are slightly different. The receivers of the fixed rate A$ flows in these swaps tend to be predominantly the issuers of A$ securities in international markets, whether it be the EuroAustralian dollar market or in the Yankee A$ market. In the instances where these markets are inactive, the semi-government authorities may act in this role. The receivers of fixed rate A$ do not change between the various market segments.

The payers of fixed rate A$, however, vary significantly between the various market segments. The main payers of fixed rate A$ against receipt of US$ LIBOR tend to be financial institutions, semi-government authorities, finance companies or a number of major corporations. In the case of financial institutions, the swap may be taken on as part of the bank's own balance sheet funding or alternatively as a position which will be shifted to clients either directly or indirectly by unbundling the swap into various components. The participation of semi-governments as fixed rate payers is considerably more complex. Historically, many of the semi-government entities borrowed offshore in foreign currencies. The marked depreciation in the A$ in the 1985 to 1986 period led the semi-government entities, which had suffered severe currency losses, to change their liability management practices to undertake new funding, primarily in A$, as well as hedging their existing foreign currency exposures. These entities also have annual allocations to borrow overseas which they have sought to utilise to achieve a greater degree of diversification of their funding sources. These factors have driven the semi-government entities to enter into swaps where they pay fixed rate A$ against receipt of US$ LIBOR to essentially hedge foreign currency borrowings back into A$. This is particularly so given that the semi-government entities have themselves become new issue arbitrage funders undertaking issues in overseas markets to generate cost efficient floating rate US$ funds priced relative to LIBOR which are subsequently swapped back into A$. These fixed rate A$ may ultimately be swapped out into floating rate A$ depending on the liability management requirements of the particular institution.

Finance companies and corporations in the early 1980s began to enjoy significant access to floating rate US$ funding through note issuance facilities and other types of floating rate funding instruments. A number of finance companies and corporations, particularly where they did not have foreign currency denominated assets, swapped these US$ liabilities into fixed rate A$ liabilities through swaps.

A major incentive for all groups was the significantly lower fixed A$ cost achievable through these transactions. The significant swap arbitrage profits available in the A$ swap markets, which are discussed in detail in Chapter 7 have allowed borrowers to achieve cost savings in the vicinity of 40-50bps on alternative direct sources of A$ funding.

The payers of fixed rate A$ against receipt of floating rate A$ have predominantly tended to be lower rated corporates. The primary motivation for this group is their need to lock in fixed rates of interest on predominantly floating rate borrowings. In the negatively sloped yield curve environment of the early 1980s, an additional motivation was to ride down the yield curve with an extension of maturity to lower the absolute coupon borrowing cost. These transactions are structured either as interest rate swaps or as fixed rate bank bill facilities. Inevitably, these transactions are undertaken with a swap market maker, usually a bank or financial institution, on one side.

The floating US$ and floating A$ currency swap market has been dominated primarily by financial institutions, mainly banks, semi-government entities as well as a number of Australian corporates. This group enjoys access to relatively cost effective US$ funding, either through note issuance facilities, EuroCP facilities in the international money markets or United States CP programmes. A number of this group have converted these floating rate US$ liabilities into floating rate A$ liabilities on a term basis utilising this type of swap. Again, the all-in cost of floating rate A$ raised in this manner is typically lower than the cost of raising A$ in the domestic market.

A major impetus to this particular segment of the market came from the banking regulations applicable (now changed) which dictated that funds raised outside Australia did *not* attract the statutory reserve deposit reserve requirement. This made it particularly attractive for Australian banks to raise US$ overseas and swap them in this way into term A$ funding. However, recently announced changes which will see the phasing out of the statutory reserve deposit requirement will make this particular factor less relevant.

The floating US$ and floating A$ swap market enjoyed a brief but spectacular period of growth in early 1986 when a series of A$ denominated FRNs, bearing margins substantially under BBR, were launched in the United States domestic market. These issues were swapped with Australian domestic institutions, primarily banks, who utilised the swaps to generate cost effective A$ floating rate funding for their portfolios. Investor demand for these securities proved short-lived, closing this window very rapidly.

A substantial asset swap market in A$ provides a considerable volume of transactions whereby financial institutions pay fixed rate A$ against receipt of either A$ BBR or US$ LIBOR. The underlying assets being swapped are primarily fixed rate bonds, issued by finance companies and, to a lesser extent, semi-governments and corporations which are swapped into a floating rate basis as banking loan assets for a wide variety of financial institutions, primarily, a number of new licensed banks operating in Australia since 1985 and a significantly larger number of merchant banks that have commenced operations in the same period. Pricing anomalies in the highly illiquid secondary market for EuroAustralian dollars and Yankee A$ securities have also created sporadic asset swap opportunities which have fueled activity in the A$ swap market.

An increasing factor in the overall activity levels and structure of the A$ swap market has been interest in purely trading interest rate swaps. For example, during late 1986 and again in late 1987 when the EuroAustralian dollar bond market closed, a number of corporates unwound existing swaps to realise a capital profit to utilise the benefits as a subsidy on their net cost of funding. The windfall profits often gained motivated a number of entities to begin trading swaps purely and simply on the basis of expected appreciation dictated by interest rate and, to a lesser extent, currency movements.

An additional source of volume has come from banks with substantial fixed asset portfolios held for reserve ratio purposes who have sought to hedge their investments against capital losses by entering into swaps to effectively create short positions against their bond portfolios in periods of increasing interest rates.

Pricing and marketmaking in A$ swap

Australian dollar interest rate swaps are priced off Commonwealth government bonds and are quoted as a spread relative to a comparable benchmark security. Interest rates are quoted against the 90 or 180 day BBR, usually determined with reference to Reuters Screen "BBSW". Cross-currency swaps are quoted with reference to 90 or 180 day US$ LIBOR. The shorter end of the swap market is priced primarily off a strip of interest rate futures contracts.

Spreads relative to government bonds can be volatile. Despite increased liquidity, the A$ swap market, in common with a number of other global swap markets, operates spasmodically in terms of windows. Australian dollar interest rate swap rates and spreads (relative to both physical government bonds and also the 10 year government bond futures contract) are set out in *Exhibit 23.2.*

The volatility of the spreads reflects a number of factors including:

• activity level and pricing in the primary debt markets, both internationally and domestically;

• the supply and demand for payers and receivers of fixed rate A$.

These factors are complicated by the fact that corporations, who are predominantly payers of fixed rates, tend to operate on the basis of *absolute rate* targets creating a bunching effort of either significant or nil paying interest. An additional complication is the funding pattern of semi-government entities which dictates that they have annual borrowing targets which must be completed by set dates. These institutional factors tend to exacerbate the volatility of A$ swap spreads.

The emergence of a number of A$ swap market makers and warehouses has been critical to the growth of the market. These institutions, which include Citibank, Bankers Trust, the Commonwealth Bank, ANZ Merchant Bank, Westpac, Macquarie Bank and Security Pacific, have injected a degree of liquidity which has in turn assisted the new issue market. The availability of a reasonably liquid government bond market and an even more liquid A$ government bond futures contract has allowed these institutions to hedge their exposures from swap marketmaking activities.

A key aspect of the A$ swap market has been the capacity of these market makers to provide more complex swap structures. For example, a wide variety of variations on the basic structure including deferred and accelerated cash flow swaps, forward swaps etc. are now available indicating the growing maturity of the market.

NZ$ SWAP MARKET

The NZ$ swap market bears a close resemblance to the A$ swap market although it is a fraction of its size.

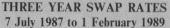

Exhibit 23.2
A$ Swap Rates and Spreads

THREE YEAR SWAP RATES
7 July 1987 to 1 February 1989

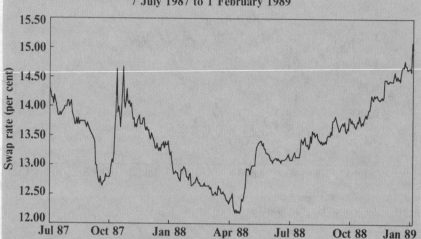

FIVE YEAR SWAP RATES
7 July 1987 to 1 February 1989

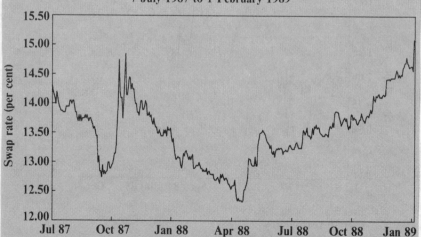

Exhibit 23.2—continued

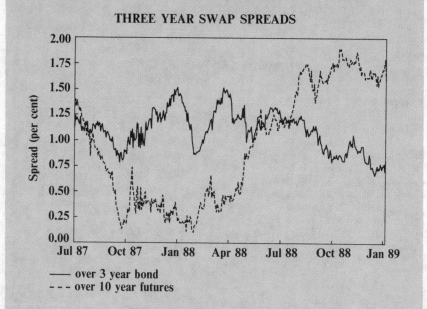

THREE YEAR SWAP SPREADS

—— over 3 year bond
- - - over 10 year futures

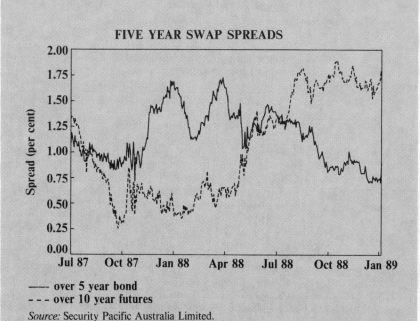

FIVE YEAR SWAP SPREADS

—— over 5 year bond
- - - over 10 year futures

Source: Security Pacific Australia Limited.

Exhibit 23.2—continued

THE THREE YEAR SWAP RATE AS A SPREAD OVER THE MARCH 1992 BOND

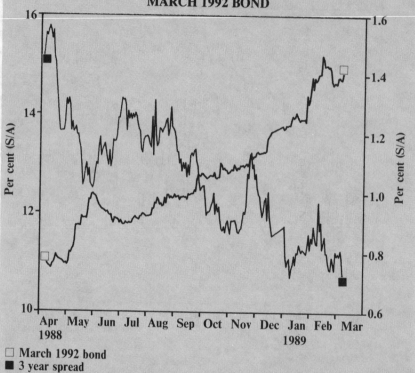

□ March 1992 bond
■ 3 year spread

Note: Swap rate is the best overnight payer of fixed rate and in return for US$ LIBOR flat.

Exhibit 23.2—continued

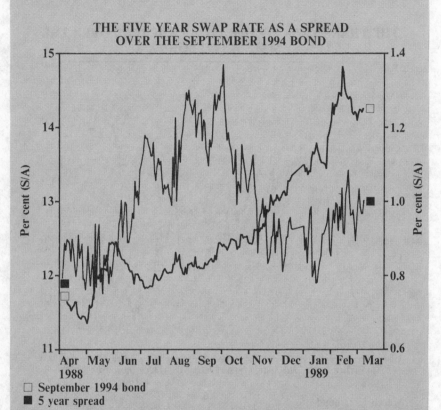

**THE FIVE YEAR SWAP RATE AS A SPREAD
OVER THE SEPTEMBER 1994 BOND**

□ September 1994 bond
■ 5 year spread

Note: Swap rate is the best overnight payer of fixed rate and in return for US$ LIBOR flat.
Source: Hämbros Bank Limited.

Exhibit 23.2—continued

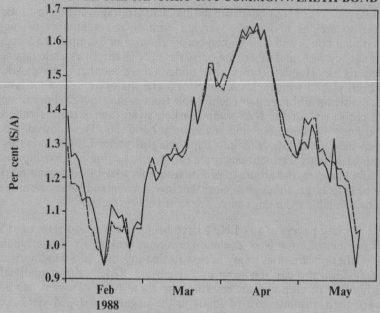

THREE AND FIVE YEAR SWAP RATES AS A MARGIN OVER THE JANUARY 1991 COMMONWEALTH BOND

— — 3 year swap
——— 5 year swap

Note: Swap rate : Payers of fixed rate A$ in return for US$ LIBOR flat.

Source: Hambros Bank Limited.

The NZ$ swap market, from a structural viewpoint, is primarily a currency swap market of fixed rate NZ$ against US$ LIBOR with a limited interest rate swap and an even more limited floating US$ and floating NZ$ currency swap component. A major reason for this particular structure is the relatively undeveloped state of the New Zealand domestic market where no clear dominant floating rate exists, although the prime commercial bill rate has increasingly begun to take on this role.

The NZ$ swap market tends, like its A$ counterpart, to be dominated by new issues of NZ$ Eurobonds as well as NZ$ Yankee issues. Driven by spasmodic investor interest in NZ$ securities from European and United States investors attracted by the high yields on NZ$ bonds, the market is largely predicated on the presence of 15.00% interest withholding tax, which creates significant pricing anomalies, and the lack of alternative sources of fixed rate NZ$ funding.

Primary issuers of NZ$ bonds are the classical arbitrage funding institutions such as sovereigns and semi-sovereign entities and a number of major international banks and well known corporations. For example, the Swedish export agency, SEK and BP are major issuers of NZ$ securities while Japanese institutions like Honda Finance have undertaken a number of issues which have been placed with Japanese investors. The major attraction for issuers is the significant arbitrage gains achievable from issuing in NZ$. For example, in the early days of the NZ$ swap market, swap rates were a significant margin *under* the corresponding government bond rate. This allowed issuers to swap their fixed rate NZ$ into huge margins under LIBOR; margins of around 80-100bps were not unknown. While the pricing relationships have gradually changed, the arbitrage profits from this sector of the swap market continue to be large, although inconsistent investor demand means the amount of funds available from this source are relatively restricted.

The primary payers of fixed NZ$ have been New Zealand state agencies and a number of large New Zealand corporates seeking fixed rate funding. Most of these institutions enjoy access to floating rate US$ funding which they transform through the swap into fixed rate NZ$. A major motivation for a number of corporations entering into these types of swaps has been to lower their absolute cost of funds in the negatively sloped yield curve environment which has persisted in the NZ$ market in recent years. In addition, in the early days of the NZ$ swap market, a number of financial institutions merely undertook swaps on their own books purchasing government bonds as an offsetting investment to lock in margins of up to 1.00 to 1.25% pa.

While NZ$ swaps are, in theory, priced off New Zealand government rates, sometimes at a negative margin to the government bond rate, the volatility of the spread as well as the lack of liquidity in the NZ$ bond market dictates that the market primarily operates as an absolute rate market with prices being quoted relative to US$ LIBOR and, in the more limited interest rate swap market, against prime commercial bill rates.

The behaviour of NZ$ swap rates and spreads is set out in *Exhibit 23.3*.

The emergence of a number of market makers in NZ$ swaps, primarily the Bank of New Zealand, Development Finance Corporation and South Pacific Merchant Finance, have added considerably to the depth and liquidity of the market and in turn, as in the case of A$ swaps, assisted in the growth of the EuroNew Zealand dollar bond market. However, the relative illiquidity of the NZ$ government bond market as well as high short-term rates, create problems of significant negative carry on holdings of bonds taken on to hedge swap positions, restricting the activities of these market makers.

Exhibit 23.3

NZ$ Swap Rates and Spreads

**NEW ZEALAND THREE YEAR SWAP RATE VERSUS
THREE YEAR NEW ZEALAND GOVERNMENT BOND**
(1987 - 1988)

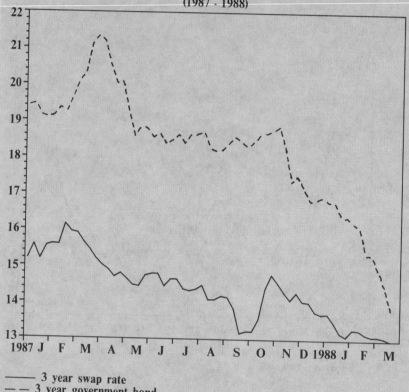

———— 3 year swap rate
— — 3 year government bond

Exhibit 23.3—continued

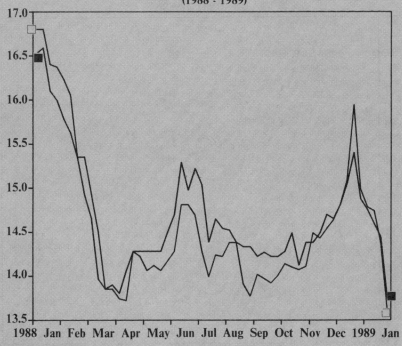

NEW ZEALAND THREE YEAR SWAP RATE VERSUS
NEW ZEALAND THREE YEAR GOVERNMENT BOND
(1988 - 1989)

■ 3 year swap rate
□ 3 year government bond

Exhibit 23.3—continued

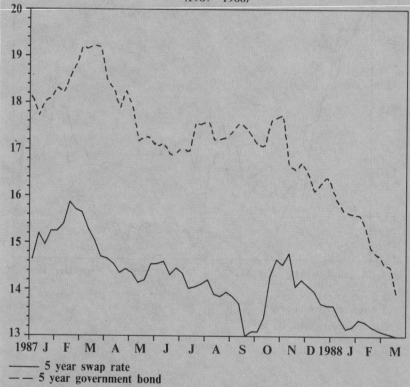

**NEW ZEALAND FIVE YEAR SWAP RATE VERSUS
FIVE YEAR NEW ZEALAND GOVERNMENT BOND**

(1987 - 1988)

———— 5 year swap rate
— — 5 year government bond

Source: Hambros Bank Limited.

Exhibit 23.3—continued

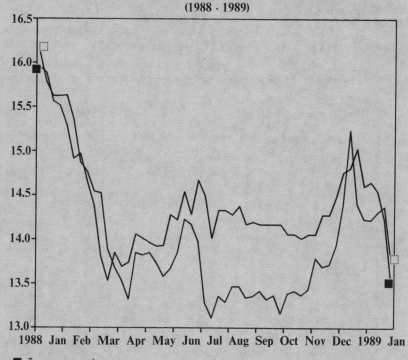

NEW ZEALAND FIVE YEAR SWAP RATE VERSUS NEW ZEALAND FIVE YEAR GOVERNMENT BOND
(1988 - 1989)

■ 5 year swap rate
□ 5 year government bond

Source: Hambros Bank Limited.

Chapter 24

Global LTFX, FRA and Cap and Collar Markets

OVERVIEW OF SWAP DERIVATIVE MARKETS

The markets for swap derivatives all have highly individual histories. For example, markets in LTFX contracts and FRAs have, in many cases, predated markets in interest rate and currency swaps in that currency. However, despite these historical nuances, it is evident that the market for these types of swap derivatives has grown strongly, paralleling the growth in mainstream swap instruments.

This growth has been accompanied by the development of significant inter-relationships between the various market segments. These inter-relationships cover a number of areas including:

* pricing relationships;
* consolidation of the trading in the various instruments into integrated units within financial intermediaries which quote and deal in the full range of swap instruments with a concentrated focus on utilisation of these instruments for corporate finance and risk management applications;
* the integration of the instruments allowing each to be used to complement others and to create and manage risk positions in one through activities in another instrument. For example, utilising a cap transaction to hedge an open risk position in the swap.

LTFX MARKETS

The LTFX market has operated largely parallel to and in some cases has predated the currency swap market in the relevant currency. The market participants usually include corporations and government institutions as well as financial intermediaries. Most corporations or government institutions enter into LTFX contracts for a number of reasons including:

* hedging capital market transactions;
* hedging trade flows;
* hedging capital flows denominated in other currencies associated with projects or capital acquisitions in other countries;
* hedging of asset exposure from cross-border investments.

The development of reasonably liquid markets in currency swaps has significantly reduced the use of LTFX contracts in connection with capital market transactions. Some minor exceptions persist due to institutional or structural reasons. However, LTFX contracts continue to be used for the other applications. The major advantage of LTFX contracts relative to currency swap transactions is the capacity to tailor them to hedging uneven, in terms of amount and timing, currency cash flows. This capacity of LTFX contracts to be tailored to a specific size and date requirement has meant that LTFX contracts have continued to complement currency swap structures.

The main providers of LTFX contracts have been financial institutions, primarily commercial and investment banks. A number of these institutions quote prices between, inter alia, US$, deutschmarks, Swiss francs, yen, £, French francs, A$ and NZ$ for various maturities up to ten years although for a number of currencies, only quotes for much shorter periods are available. In addition, there is an active broker market for LTFX contracts.

Up to approximately 1982, almost all LTFX transactions were perfectly matched counterparty-driven transactions with participants seeking to cover foreign exchange exposures on future cash flows related to capital or trade transactions but in opposite directions. However, since that time, a number of institutions have started transacting LTFX business without necessarily having an offsetting position. In fact, currently in excess of 90.00-95.00% of LTFX transactions are executed by financial intermediaries without having an offsetting counterparty. In view of the inter-relationship in pricing terms between swaps and LTFX contracts, most major financial intermediaries active in the area have integrated their LTFX and currency swap activities.

However, despite this increased participation by financial intermediaries which has added to the depth and liquidity of the market, the LTFX market, defined as all forward foreign exchange contracts with a maturity beyond one year, is considerably less efficient and liquid than corresponding markets in foreign exchange forward contracts with shorter maturities. A principal reason underlying this reduced level of liquidity is the difficulty of undertaking arbitrage in longer term markets and the absence of speculators who contribute to market depth.

The volume of LTFX transactions is significantly lower than that for short-dated foreign exchange forward contracts. The average size of an LTFX contract is US$10-20m with maturities concentrated in the three to five year range. A small group of financial institutions, primarily the United States money centre banks and a number of major investment banks as well as the major foreign exchange banks in each currency, are the principal participants in the LTFX markets. The increased participation by a range of institutions has contributed to the development of a growing interbank market in LTFX wherein banks can offset positions created through customer-driven transactions.

Pricing on LTFX contracts is generally based on interest rate differentials between the relevant currencies. Analysis of actual bid/offer spreads as well as comparison of *actual* forward market prices against theoretical market spreads suggests a highly efficient market. In general, the *actual* forward market prices could not profitably be made by making a market through covered interest arbitrage. This suggests that financial intermediaries do not use covered interest arbitrage but rather match offsetting LTFX transactions. The matching transaction can be a currency swap which is unbundled into its LTFX components by the financial intermediary. Actual LTFX bid/offer quotes suggest that the prices are largely similar to the calculated theoretical forward rates utilising the current yield curve method. Commission rates between dealers are similar with little differences in spreads between the major participants in the market.

An active secondary market in LTFX contracts is gradually developing with corporations trading their existing LTFX contracts as their underlying exposure positions alter or if market movements necessitate restructuring of the hedge.

A small but growing market in A$ and US$ LTFX contracts has developed. In its initial phase, the market was driven by counterparties—the sellers of US$ usually being exporters with long-term periodic US$ cash flows while the purchasers of US$ were Australian corporations with significant overseas borrowings. In more recent times, the driving force for these contracts has been trade or balance sheet hedging considerations with the offsetting risk being laid off against the liquid A$ currency swap market.

FRA MARKETS

There has been, in recent times, significant growth in the market for FRAs. The market globally is estimated at over US$500 billion annually as at the end of 1988, compared with only US$50 billion for 1985. FRAs denominated in US$, A$, £, Swiss francs, yen, deutschmarks, Dutch guilders, C$, NZ$, French francs and ECUs are all available. The growth in these markets reflects the underlying volatility of interest rates which has forced borrowers and lenders to seek some form of risk protection on short-term interest rate exposures.

United States dollar FRAs are by far the largest segment of the market, totalling between 60.00 and 70.00% of the total FRA market. Initially, FRAs were only available for round periods such as three against six months. However, as the US$ FRA market matured, the range of dates for which FRAs are quoted has broadened substantially. Currently, for US$ FRAs it is possible to obtain quotes for practically any period, although the greatest liquidity is, predictably, with standard periods. Similarly, the size of deals that the market can accommodate has grown. Initially, transactions of US$5-10m were the norm. By late 1985, US$ FRAs of up to US$20m were quite common. In the current market environment, US$ FRAs amounting to US$50-200m can be readily executed.

London is the main centre for US$ FRAs, accounting for about 40.00% of the market, although this proportion is falling as activity increases elsewhere. New York is next in importance with about 25.00% of the total.

The principal market makers are the large United States banks, British merchant banks and some British clearing banks. Italian and Dutch banks are fairly consistent participants in the market while participation by Belgian, French, Canadian and Scandinavian banks is more inconsistent. Japanese banks have been slow to begin trading FRAs, although they are expected to become more active. German banks appear to have used FRAs only infrequently.

The FRA market in US$ has a significant interbank element, with about half the contracts arranged through brokers. Most banks also conclude a significant volume of FRAs with non-bank customers, who almost always use FRAs to cover future borrowing rather than deposit rates. Few contracts with non-banks are arranged through brokers.

British, Italian, Dutch, Australian and New Zealand banks offer FRAs to non-bank customers as a form of over-the-counter futures contract. The attraction to the customer is that the FRA can be tailored exactly to its requirements as far as amounts, dates and interest rate basis are concerned, and without margining requirements.

In the United States, use of exchange traded futures contracts by non-banks is well established and the FRA is, therefore, comparatively less attractive. There is apparently little sign of investment bank involvement in FRAs, either for their own account or as market makers. Commercial banks use FRAs for their own account.

The A$ FRA market is a substantial proportion of the global FRA market. This market, which operates out of Sydney, is quoted against the physical market for bank accepted bills. The A$ FRA market differs from the US$ FRA market in that there is a substantial end customer, usually borrower, element in the pattern of participation. This reflects the fact that while a FRA most closely resembles a customised interest rate futures contract, it is typically used by Australian borrowers as a short-term interest rate swap.

The growth of FRAs has been assisted by the relative ease with which commercial banks have been able to provide FRAs for clients by combining this activity with their own deposit taking and lending operation. Banks have particularly utilised FRAs to shorten or lengthen their own liability profile. The availability of usually liquid markets in short-term interest rate futures in a number of currencies has allowed financial institutions to write FRAs which are then hedged through the futures markets.

Market pricing of FRAs in each currency reflects the cost of alternative ways of constructing a similar hedge either through a combination of the cash deposit and lending market, the interest rate futures market and the term interest rate swap market itself. Bid/offer spreads on FRAs have narrowed from approximately 0.10 to 0.125% pa in early 1986 to 0.05 to 0.075% pa currently (for major currencies).

There is no evidence that widespread profitable arbitrage opportunities exist between the FRA and deposit markets after taking into account transaction costs. Nevertheless, the FRA rate in any of the available currencies can at times be sufficiently different from the implied forward-forward rate for one means of hedging to be preferable to the other.

Arbitrage opportunities involving placing and taking of deposits do appear to exist for the banks active in writing FRAs, allowing these banks usually to fund themselves at relatively attractive rates under the interbank rate. This appears to be particularly the case for longer maturities such as nine against 12 months. This type of arbitrage involving deposits is not usually attractive, however, for banks with return on asset requirements since the interest differential can only be enjoyed for three months while the transaction would have to be placed on-balance sheet with consequent gearing and reserve costs for a full 12 month period.

Interestingly, in recent times, swap market makers and warehouses have emerged not only as writers of FRAs but as users of the instrument. These market makers have utilised FRAs to hedge their own risk positions or to reallocate the risk arising from mismatches within their swap books.

CAP AND COLLAR MARKET

The market for caps, floors and collars is predominantly a US$ market. Over 80.00-90.00% of volume in these types of instruments transacted are denominated in US$. Cap markets also exist, to varying extents, in C$, yen, deutschmarks, £, French Francs and A$.

The difference between the US$ sector and the other currencies is most marked in terms of:

- size, depth and liquidity of market which outside the US$ sector is severely constrained;

- maturities, features and special structures which again outside the US$ sector are limited. For example, cap markets in currencies other than US$ are mainly confined to very short maturities usually two to three years and under.

For the remainder of this section, the primary focus will be on the US$ cap market reflecting its status as the premier mature currency segment of this market.

United States dollar caps, floors and collars have a significant history. The market originated in the early 1980s in the form of insurance against increases or decreases in interest rates. In the early 1980s, Merrill Lynch was one of the first institutions to offer a cap facility utilising the proprietary title "Interest Rate Protection". Other financial institutions such as Citicorp and Salomon Brothers joined Merrill Lynch as providers of this type of facility. A number of commercial banks and, interestingly, a number of insurance companies and commodity brokers also began providing these types of facilities. However, for many of these participants, the experiment was short-lived in that a number of providers of caps ultimately discontinued their involvement. However, their early efforts created the basis for the market itself to develop and ultimately prosper.

The growth in the cap market reflects the complex interaction of a number of factors including client demand for these types of risk management instruments as well as the increased availability of providers. However, the rapid development of options markets generally and in particular exchange traded options on interest rates have assisted in the overall growth. The emergence of exchange traded options has been critical in that it has allowed participants in the cap market who act as providers of these instruments to, at least partially, reallocate their risk through the exchange rated options market. In this regard, the cap market operates in a manner which is largely analogous to the relationship between the futures markets in short-term interest rates and FRAs.

Customer demand for caps, floors and collars has been motivated primarily by the asymmetric risk profile of the instrument. The capability of these caps or collars to provide protection against adverse movements in interest rates while allowing the user to benefit from favourable movements has become particularly attractive given the sharply increased *volatility* of interest rate structures in the global capital market.

Typical users of caps etc. have included:

- companies involved in leveraged buyouts and leveraged acquisitions;
- real estate developers concerned with capping construction interest costs;

- project financing sponsors;
- financial institutions utilising them for asset liability management;
- floating rate borrowers who have sought to place a cap on borrowing costs for specific periods of time based on rate expectations, exposure levels or as an alternative to interest rate swaps.

A key factor in the growth of the cap market has been the increased availability of providers of these types of facilities. Ironically, as noted above, many of the early participants in the market have ceased to participate due in no small part to losses sustained in the early 1980s when interest rates rose sharply.

The ranks of providers of caps, at least in a principal capacity, are dominated by a handful of commercial and investment banks. These include Citicorp and Salomon Brothers who dominate the US$ cap business, although a number of other institutions also participate in the market. The less active participants may act as brokers, marking up a cap provided by another principal or by supplying caps stripped from a debt issue in the market (see discussion below). An important factor limiting the range of cap providers is credit risk. Given that the cap provider must be able to make payments over a number of years when and if market rates exceed the cap rate, the provider of the cap must be of very high credit standing. This naturally limits the range of financial institutions who would be acceptable as a counterparty to such transactions.

The main attraction to providers of these types of instruments include:
- the fact that there is no credit risk by the purchaser of the cap allows these financial institutions to deal with a wider range of market participants;
- potential profit from these particular transactions has been perceived as being significant;
- caps etc. complement other risk management services offered by these institutions;
- developments in hedge technology have allowed a number of these participants to create mechanisms for reallocating the risk of managing cap portfolios within acceptable risk limits.

The providers of caps, floors or collars fall into one of a number of categories:
- brokers or matched back-to-back providers;
- traders or positioners;
- customised cap providers utilising theoretical delta based or synthetic option hedge strategies;
- providers of stripped caps who distribute the cap element from capital market issues that they have originated;
- synthetic swap providers.

The brokers or matched providers of caps or floors usually source their supply of caps etc. either from stripping operations related to capital market issues or with genuine customer demand for the offsetting form of the transaction. In the case of financial institutions, often the customer is the bank's own treasury which seeks to write options as part of their asset and liability management process. A number of providers write caps, floors and collars purely based on interest rate expectations, seeking to profit from a view that the floor or cap level will not be breached during the life of the transaction.

The third category of provider is by far the most dominant one. This group is made up of a number of financial intermediaries who utilise option theory, in particular, delta hedging, whereby they hedge the cap positions utilising a mixture of cash, securities and futures contracts. For shorter maturities, these financial intermediaries often utilise exchange rated options markets to cover their own exposures and the cap or collar agreements.

As discussed in Chapters 11 and 29, the risks associated with providing caps on this basis are not inconsiderable. While theoretically tractable, this type of technique has a number of practical problems which can lead to losses particularly where interest rates prove volatile, as in the 1980s. These problems have led a number of participants to initially enter and ultimately withdraw from the market. Of these participants, only Citicorp and Salomon Brothers have been capable of continuing to write a growing volume of transactions, usually on the basis of absorbing the risk into their total securities dealing operations. In addition, the sheer volume of these institutions' securities businesses and the size of the their balance sheets allow them to ride out volatility better than smaller rivals.

These institutions have nevertheless been frustrated by a number of factors including:

- the fact that caps have proved too cheap in the market relative to theoretical option values;
- the need to provide for hedging and transaction costs.

The need to factor in the fair value of the option plus the requisite mark up for risk and transaction costs has made the prices of these financial institutions for caps and collars relatively expensive and out of the market. This problem has in recent times been exacerbated by the emergence of a substantial market in stripped caps.

This market developed in June 1985 when capped FRNs were introduced. As discussed in Chapter 17 in the context of securitising options through option swaps, these capped FRN issues embodied cap and/or floor elements which were capable of being separated and sold in securitised form. In the second half of 1985, in excess of US$4 billion of floating rate paper with caps were issued. These caps were then stripped and sold into the market.

The emergence of the stripped caps provided institutions active in writing customised caps using delta hedging technology with significant competition. These competitive pressures derived from the fact that the presence of stripped caps attracted a whole new class of participants. The fact that these caps involved no positioning or trading risk allowed a variety of financial institutions to act as brokers distributing these caps to end customers. While the emergence of stripped caps and the entry of new participants assisted in greatly increasing the awareness of these instruments among potential corporate and financial institution clients, the fact that the premiums for these stripped caps tended to be consistently lower than those quoted by financial institutions for customised transactions created a new source of competitive pressure.

The stripped caps available were, in reality, not ideal for corporate or investor risk management applications. Typical stripped caps available were of two varieties:

- Seven or 12 year caps with a strike level of around 12.50-13.25% pa with the reference index being three or six month LIBOR. These caps were stripped off capped FRN issues in the Euromarkets.

- Three or five year caps with strike levels of 11.875-12.50% pa again with the reference rate being LIBOR. These caps were stripped off variable rates CD issues primarily undertaken by Japanese banks in the New York or Far East market.

The caps provided by these issues were often too high or too long in maturity for most corporate applications. For example, the early evidence suggests that the FRN caps were bought by United States thrifts. In addition, the lack of flexibility as to term, structure and level available make the stripped caps relatively unattractive. Inability to customise the transaction to the end customer's need in terms of a client's rollover dates on its underlying borrowing, variable settlement bases, a choice of indices as well as special features such as deferred starts, amortisation, variable principal, etc. to a large extent mitigated the competitive impact of the stripped caps.

The supply of stripped caps from capital market issues has also been less than consistent. Supply from this source is dependent upon investor willingness to create securities with the requisite features. In fact, shortly after this market was born, investor demand for capped Eurocurrency FRNs and, to a lesser extent, for variable rate CDs evaporated significantly creating a shortage of supply from this particular source. The difference between the customised caps sold by financial institutions and the stripped cap market should not be overstated. This is because, in fact, the bulk of caps created by capital market issues were, in fact, bought by financial institutions which utilised these caps as hedges against open positions in their own cap books.

A growing source of cap providers have been financial institutions who are active in providing interest rate swaps on a principal basis through their swap warehouses. This is because, as outlined in Chapter 2, an interest rate swap can be characterised as a simultaneous purchase and sale of a cap and a floor with the same strike price. Utilising this basic economic relationship, a number of swap warehouses have started to write caps and collars while simultaneously hedging the inherent risks through their swap books. This area promises to be a growing source of supply of these types of instruments.

A limited interbank market in caps and collars, primarily in New York and London, has emerged. The market is dominated by three to four participants who are the primary market makers. An additional 15 to 20 financial institutions also participate in this market. A number of commodity traders, such as Cargill of Minnesota, are also active in this market. A number of active brokers also participate. The market is primarily in three to five year caps and the depth and liquidity of the market is increasing. The global swap market has been estimated at approximately US$250 billion in 1988 (compared to US$50 billion in 1986), the majority of which is US$ caps. The geographical distribution of all cap activity irrespective of currency, is interesting with the United States dominating with a total of 65.00% of total activity. The other major centres include the United Kingdom (20.00%), France and Germany (both approximately 5.00%) and the remainder of the world, which includes Europe and Australasia contributing the remainder.

An interesting feature of the global cap market is the significant differences in the way a number of these markets, at least initially, commenced. For example, the deutschmark and Dutch guilder cap markets were purely created off the back of capped FRN issues in those particular currencies.

A small A$ cap and collar market emerged in the middle of the 1980s. The market is concentrated in the less than two to three year maturity spectrum. A few institutions provide customised caps hedging their exposure with a mix of options on the bank bill interest rate futures contract or utilising delta hedging techniques. In late 1987, the first capped domestic FRN was issued creating an additional source of supply of these instruments.

Part 8

Swap Marketmaking and Warehousing

Chapter 25

Swap Marketmaking and Warehousing

COUNTERPARTY TRANSACTIONS VERSUS MARKETMAKING IN SWAPS

Many of the developments in swap markets, in terms of both the greater range of swap structures that have emerged and the changes in the way swaps are used, were made possible by fundamental changes in the way the market operated.

The earliest transactions were purely counterparty transactions where a commercial or investment bank structured a transaction on behalf of two (or more) counterparties with matched but mirror reverse requirements. However, as the market matured, the major participants in the market moved to being principals in transactions rather than only agents structuring transactions on behalf of counterparties. This shift accelerated the creation of a secondary market in swaps as these institutions began to act as market makers routinely quoting two-way prices on swaps.

The change in emphasis from counterparty transactions to intermediated transactions, where financial institutions enter swaps as principals, took place on two separate levels:

* bank intermediation in a matched counterparty transaction;

* principal trading without matching counterparty.

These two different approaches were predicated on quite different considerations. Bank intermediation in a matched transaction was utilised as a form of credit enhancement. In contrast, principal trading entailed marketmaking, that is, willingness to buy or sell swaps at a price. Marketmaking was usually undertaken as part of positioning and arbitrage strategies or on a fully hedged basis, involving entry into a temporary unmatched swap position until a counterparty could be located while hedging the risks entailed.

Principal trading can, but need not necessarily, merge the marketmaking function with the credit intermediation role.

Against this background it is possible to set out a taxonomy of swap arrangement techniques. Swap arrangers can act in any of the following capacities:

* *Brokers* instantaneously arrange perfectly matched swaps acting solely as agents by introducing complementary swap partners to one another. Brokers collect a small arrangement fee for their services.

* *Intermediated swap arrangers* serve as principals to instantaneously priced, exactly matched swap counterparties. This technique merges the credit intermediary and broker functions. The intermediary bears no market risk but does assume credit risk, that is, if one counterparty to a matched transaction fails, the principal must continue to service the other counterparty.

449

- *Dealers* make continuous two-way markets and hedge open swap positions in the cash securities or futures market. These positions are later matched with opposite swaps and placed in the dealer's matched book. The dealer merges a marketmaking function with the credit intermediation role.

- *Arbitrage swaps* involve a long or short swap position versus an opposite position in another financial instrument, for example, a bond or bond futures contract. Here, the motivation is to exploit inefficiencies between markets.

Virtually every major institution involved in the swap market, with minor, although notable, exceptions, participates in the swap market as market makers or dealers. This analysis of swap marketmaking and warehousing, therefore, focuses primarily on this type of principal trading in swap transactions without matching counterparties.

THE RATIONALE FOR SWAP MARKETMAKING

The emergence of swap marketmaking reflects a response to a number of developments in the swap market, including:

- the increased range of applications of swap transactions;
- the increased desire for prompt execution on the part of users;
- the requirement of structural flexibility in swap transactions;
- the profit potential from marketmaking in swaps;
- the development of adequate hedging technology;
- the potential synergy of swaps with other activities such as new issues and sales and distribution of securities.

The cause and effect relationship in the emergence of swap marketmaking is not easily discernible. The relationship is symbiotic. The development of market makers assisted in the actual further development of the swap market, while these developments, in turn, required participants who would act as marketmakers.

One of the major factors prompting the emergence of market makers was the evolution of the swap market from a market emphasising new issue arbitrage to a market focusing on asset liability management. This increased emphasis on asset liability management required the development of a relatively liquid swap market. The emergence of market makers providing two-way prices on swap transactions allow users of the swap market the requisite flexibility to reverse or unwind swap transactions at the current market rate, facilitating the increased use of swaps as an asset liability management technique.

As the swap market evolved, the users of the swap market came increasingly to expect, demand and receive instantaneous pricing and transaction structures tailored to their needs. The original structure of the market, essentially a broker market predicated upon arranging counterparties, was not capable of meeting these demands. This is because the intermediary in question could not guarantee that it would be able to locate and instantaneously price a perfectly matched swap with a counterparty. This resulted in the swap market becoming increasingly dominated by market makers.

The market makers provided both the required prompt execution and structural flexibility. The availability of intermediaries willing to commit to a swap without necessarily having a counterparty in position made possible a prompt execution capability which eliminated the delay where it was necessary to have a precisely matched counterparty to complete a transaction.

The market makers also provided enormous structural flexibility. As new issue structures grew more complex, usually to exploit identified arbitrage opportunities, the required swap structures grew correspondingly more complex. In addition, swaps utilised in asset liability management situations, increasingly needed to be tailored to the cash flow characteristics required by the client. This lead to the increasing necessity of swap structures which departed significantly from the generic swap structure. The existence of market makers who were willing, for a cost, to absorb slight cash flow mismatches and to tailor the swap to specifically match client requirements thus provided the basis for the further development of the swap market.

Market makers also allowed complex multiparty swap transactions to be structured in a way which allowed each counterparty to exactly achieve their required objectives without the necessity of undertaking multiple swap transactions or entering into a number of swaps. The emergence of multiparty swaps, or cocktail swaps, greatly expanded the number of counterparties that could potentially be involved in any one transaction. The difficulty in persuading each counterparty to transact on perfectly matched terms as at the relevant dates meant that the interposition of a market maker to warehouse the various components of the swap, usually, for short periods, allowed such transactions to be undertaken.

The emergence of swap market makers also reflected the changing remuneration basis in the swap market. Originally, swaps were structured on the basis of substantial arrangement fees with some ongoing "drip" income in the form of an annuity (from the difference between the cash flows on both sides of a matching swap trade). As the market developed and competition increased, the market rapidly evolved to a spread market with intermediaries earning the spread between the rate they paid on one side of the swap and the rate they received on the matching counterparty trade, usually, the fixed rate component of the swap.

This change in the pricing of swap transactions became evident with the emergence of the first market makers. With the emergence of these market makers, other intermediaries not willing to act as principals or market makers were placed in a position of significant competitive disadvantage.

An organisation's policy not to position swaps resulted in two fundamental constraints in the organisation's swap operations. The intermediary effectively became a *price taker*, that is, buyers at the offered side of the market and sellers at the bid side of the market. The intermediaries were further disadvantaged as they were dependent on locating market makers who had to be persuaded to trade instantaneously and to match the specifications of their client.

These prerequisites for entering into swap transactions severely impacted on the non-marketmaking intermediary's price levels, price turnaround time, etc. This naturally inhibits volume and confines the intermediary's swap activities to delivering its client to another intermediary to get the order filled. An added problem, in this type of operation, is that it practically hands over the intermediary's client to a swap market maker, virtually inviting the client to go directly to the swap market maker for future transactions. The brokering fee earned in such transactions is significantly lower than one that could have been earned from entering into the swap as a principal, for example, 0.03 to 0.15% *flat* versus 0.05 to 0.125% *pa* for principal trades on interest rate swaps (for currency swaps the amounts are slightly higher).

In this situation, the non-marketmaking intermediary could book the swap with the swap market maker as principal and then deal as principal with its clients. This would serve to disguise the identity of the ultimate swap provider from its client. However, the intermediary would be required to mark-up its price to cover balance sheet usage. This effectively would add a credit intermediation fee of say 0.05% to 0.10% pa to the swap market maker's bid/offer price. This would mean that the actual swap quote is significantly above the actual dealer market price. The result is usually low volume and client dissatisfaction with the non-marketmaking intermediary's swap prices and turnaround time. Increasingly, many end users of the swap market refuse to be brokered through, either directly or indirectly, to another swap market maker.

Consequently, once a small group of market makers in swap transactions emerged, it effectively forced other participants in the swap market to also commence marketmaking in such transactions to avoid placing themselves at a significant competitive disadvantage.

The move to marketmaking by intermediaries was also prompted by the potential to earn significant profits. This profit was primarily generated by changing the position of the intermediary from that of a *price taker* to a *price maker*. The basic profit strategy was for the intermediary to opportunistically position and execute round lots trades (usually $50m to $100m), which can be transacted at the most advantageous prices, at the time of its choice and to subsequently re-offer or bid the opposite side of the transaction on a continuous basis in smaller parcels (say $5 to $10m). This capacity to break down large positions into retail size and to distribute these smaller parcels combined with the opportunity to trade at the time of the intermediary's choice allows the intermediary to influence the market by letting the market come to it. This usually facilitates buying at the bid side of the market and selling at the offer side greatly increasing the volume of profitable transaction put through its swap book.

Opportunities to buy swaps at the bid side tend naturally to occur through new securities issues which are then re-offered to market participants seeking to synthetically create fixed rate liabilities. This pattern of activity is largely true for a wide range of markets, including the US$ and A$ swap market.

The profit potential from this type of activity can be viewed as earning the spread between the buy and sell side of the market, supported by adequate hedging technology to manage the risks of booking open positions. Alternatively, the profit potential of the operation can be sought to be enhanced by operating the book, at least partially, in a speculative manner designed to take advantage of swap spread and interest rate movements.

The development of an adequate hedging technology was crucial in the emergence of swap market makers. Recognition, over a period of time, of the fact that the risks entailed in booking open swap positions were not substantially different to the risks entailed in the management of bank treasury or securities dealing operations allowed institutions to adapt existing technology to the management of swaps operations.

In addition, the realisation that a large swap book with a locked in earnings spread and resulting income stream would, on an actuarial basis, allow a swap warehousing operation to operate on a profitable basis, after adjustment for risk, prompted a number of financial institutions to enter the market as principals.

The emergence of swap market makers can also be traced to potential synergies arising from the natural linkages of swap transactions with new issues of securities and the sales of securities. Increasingly, intermediaries were attracted to act as market makers in view of the fact that swaps were an essential complement to their new issue securities business. Alternatively, for institutions lacking a strong new issue business, such as commercial banks, swaps represented an opportunity to further develop their new issue business.

Intermediaries were also quick to realise that the ability to continuously make markets in swaps of all sizes and maturities greatly enhances the marketability of seasoned securities contributing to the liquidity of their security sales and distribution activities. As discussed in Chapter 18, asset swaps are increasingly utilised to transform securities, in terms of currency and/or interest rate basis, greatly expanding the universe of potential investors. In the US$ market, this type of technique has been instrumental in expanding the investor base for mortgage backed securities in particular. In addition, both US$ and currency swaps have been utilised to package seasoned Eurobonds for sale to suitable investors.

SWAP MARKETMAKING APPROACHES

Different types of institutions have significantly different approaches to swap marketmaking. The principal differences in approach have developed as between commercial banks and the investment or merchant banks. These differences reflect both the different client bases and also differences in the purpose for which these types of institutions utilise swaps.

Investment banks view swaps as a natural adjunct to their strong position in the new securities issue and security sales and distribution businesses. In addition, investment and merchant banks seek to exploit their historical client basis. For example, United States investment banks have based part of their swap business on their historically strong relationships with thrift institutions, which use swaps primarily to create fixed rate liabilities which are difficult for them to raise in the capital markets directly. In the United Kingdom, merchant banks dominate the building society sector of the swap market, based on their natural and historically strong relationship with these institutions.

In contrast, commercial bank swap dealers depend on the flow of swap transactions from the following sources:

- the liability management needs of corporations;
- general bank balance sheet management;
- swap and Eurobond combinations, usually introduced by an investment bank.

In each case, the swap activity is seen to naturally and profitably complement the entity's other businesses.

The difference between commercial and investment banks also reflects very different philosophies. The investment banks see swaps as another trading and arbitrage vehicle in their trading portfolios while commercial banks view swaps as akin to longer term commitments such as an extension of credit.

This difference can be graphically illustrated by examining market practice in the US$ swap market. Traditionally, the US$ swap market tends to operate as follows. When rates fell, United States corporates, for example, usually sought to fix the cost on their debt. These corporates would enter into swaps which the swap market makers would simply place on their books, hedged by shorting Treasuries. The basic strategy by the swap market maker would be to take on the position at a relatively high spread as against the appropriate government bond. The market maker would then move to square its position by swapping out against a fixed rate securities issue, usually one in the Eurobond or US$ Yankee market and usually with a bank, financial institution or sovereign borrower seeking to generate sub-LIBOR floating rate funds. The swap market maker would seek to time the issue to take advantage of a spread window in the new issue market to allow it to satisfactorily close out its open swap position whilst satisfying all client needs and, hopefully, ensuring a successful bond issue.

The major difference would be that once both sides of the transaction were in place, the commercial banks would usually choose to stand in the middle of the swap transaction until its maturity. In contrast, the investment banks would generally, although there are a number of exceptions, commit to the swaps on a right of assignment basis allowing them to step out of the middle of the swap transaction and allowing the ultimate counterparties to directly deal with each other. In our example, this would be achieved by the investment bank assigning the original swap with the United States corporate to the issuer of the securities in the bond transaction.

The difference in approaches reflects the perspective of the investment bank which seeks to trade the spreads on swaps and new issues as against a commercial bank which sees the swap as a service to its corporate client in achieving a fixed rate cost on its debt.

As the market in swaps changed, a large number of financial intermediaries started to operate what came popularly to be referred to as *swap warehouses*. These warehouses were merely the marketmaking units within organisations which entered into the swap hedging the risk until a counterparty could be located. The advent of warehousing saw significant changes in the way swap business was conducted. The shift was one away from large swap origination teams located throughout the globe seeking to identify matching counterparties to smaller teams managing a number of warehouses in different currencies with the origination function being shifted to the corporate finance or general banking staff of financial institutions.

The most extreme case of this switch from counterparty to dealer trading in swaps is Citibank/Citicorp. Citicorp operates a large number of warehouses in a wide range of currencies including US\$, C\$, A\$, NZ\$, yen, £, deutschmark, Swiss franc and Dutch guilder. A number of other participants also run swap books in a number of currencies, although most participants tend to specialise in one or a few currencies. The largest number of market makers are in US\$ while a number of banks specialise in particular market niches. For example, a number of Australian banks run swaps books in A\$ reflecting their client base and their operational strengths.

In actual fact, it is difficult to accurately determine the number of market makers in swaps as it is not always possible to determine whether or not a participant is a true market maker or is merely acting as an intermediary broking through the trade to another swap trader.

A number of factors are identifiable as prerequisites to enable a participant to act as a market maker in swaps. These include:

- a strong distribution system to locate and market swaps to counterparties;
- a presence in the new issue markets to create wholesale swap positions;
- an active trading operation in the relevant government securities market, giving the swap book ready and efficient access to, and funding for, large securities positions needed to hedge and unwind swap positions;
- reasonable inventories of securities which can be sold in combination with swaps providing liquidity for both the securities and swap traders;
- a substantial capital base allowing the institution to deal, in a credit sense, with other swap counterparties.

The majority of major market makers in swaps have most, if not all, of the above qualifications.

The emergence of a select group of institutions willing to act as principals in interest rate and currency swap transactions, while important, is often overstated. While adding flexibility in terms of execution of transactions and while undertaking complex cocktail swaps entailing a series of cross-currency, fixed-to-floating, amortising permutations, the additional costs of hedging and warehousing as well as the necessity to commit capital and earn acceptable returns on risk where the institution acting as principal in a swap transaction effectively assumes a term commitment means that intermediated swaps are often uneconomic. In particular, the erosion of arbitrage margins dictates that intermediation in swap transactions, at least where the institution acting as a principal is adequately compensated for the risk assumed, does not always add value to the transaction.

Consequently, an active agency market in swaps where financial institutions arrange swap counterparties and design the transactions has continued to exist. Where the counterparties are mutually acceptable, the institution merely structures and arranges the swap acting as principal and intermediating the transaction only for credit enhancement reasons or where it otherwise makes economic sense. The emergence of a number of swap brokers, usually traditional Euromarket broking firms, with extensive data bases on potential swap counterparties has also helped ensure the continuance of direct counterparty transactions.

The emergence of marketmaking in swap derivatives follows an identical pattern. However, there are also some minor differences.

LTFX marketmaking was a natural extension of making two-way prices in the spot and short-dated forwards in the foreign exchange market. Given that the relevant hedging technology was already understood and capable of extension, albeit with greater risks as the maturity of contracts became longer, a number of financial institutions developed LTFX marketmaking capabilities. As the currency swap markets developed, the fact that currency swaps and LTFX contracts could be utilised to replicate very similar economic consequences forced the marketmaking function in these instruments to be combined.

Marketmaking in FRAs to some extent predated the advent of swap warehouses. The fact that commercial banks could effectively replicate FRAs through borrowing and lending activities allowed these institutions to begin making prices as principal to clients. The emergence of warehouses, however, had an impact on FRAs as the portfolio of swaps allowed the institution to create FRAs either as a by-product of swaps or, alternatively, to hedge risks, particularly, mismatches within the swap portfolio.

Marketmaking in caps, floors and collars remains relatively infrequent, with only a few market makers of substance being active. The relative immaturity of the cap market, the problems of pricing and the considerable risk of failure of hedging techniques are all factors constraining the increase in cap marketmaking.

SWAP MARKETMAKING: THE "PLAYERS"

By the end of 1986, swap marketmaking had become an established practice. The swap market makers are capable of classification into three separate categories:

- US$ swaps;
- reserve currency swaps;
- other currency swaps.

The US$ swap market has by far the largest number of market makers, with a large number of commercial and investment banks participating. Market makers in the other major reserve currencies (yen, £, Swiss francs and deutschmarks) are available, although hedging difficulties constrains liquidity.

In other currencies, marketmaking in swaps in varying degrees takes place. In currencies like A$, NZ$, C$, etc., active and often highly liquid markets for swaps are maintained by a limited group of financial institutions. In the remaining swap currencies, liquidity is limited with transactions being undertaken on a substantially matched basis with marketmaking being limited to very short-term positioning or, alternatively, the booking of positions *purely* for speculative purposes.

The individual swap market makers in the respective markets reflect the following pattern:

- The diversity of market makers in the US$ market is significantly greater than in other markets.

- In the reserve currencies, the principal market makers are typically major banks or financial institutions resident in the domestic market place of the currency supplemented by a limited number of foreign institutions, usually United States money centre banks or investment banks with a global presence.

- In non-reserve currencies, swap marketmaking is almost totally the preserve of major local banks resident in the relevant currency.

- Very few financial institutions, with the most notable exception being Citicorp, are active market makers in greater than three to four currencies.

Exhibit 25.1 identifies the major market makers in the US$ market. *Exhibit 25.2* identifies the major market makers in the other swap markets. *Exhibit 25.3* sets out the estimated volume of swaps undertaken by some of the leading swap market makers.

These "beauty contests" and statistics are not wholly reliable and must, as a result be treated with caution. However, they do provide a basic indication as to the major participants.

A number of major developments in swap market makers require comment:

- increase in specialisation;

- the emergence of "pure" swap market makers;

- the advent of specialised swap brokers.

Consistent with the maturing of the market, a number of swap market makers have sought to specialise both by currency segment and, also increasingly, by type of transaction (usually, the high value added structured transactions). For example, Prudential Global Funding, Klienwort Benson Cross Financing and AIG Financial Products have sought to focus on highly structured, non-generic US$ swaps. This increase in specialisation seems likely to continue.

Exhibit 25.1

Major Market Makers in US$ Swaps

Rank	Bank
1	Security Pacific
2	Bankers Trust
3	Citicorp
4	Morgan Guaranty
5	Banque Paribas
6	Chemical Bank
7	Chase Manhattan
8	Deutsche Bank
9	Salomon Brothers
10	SBCI

Source: Euromoney.

Exhibit 25.2

Major Market Makers in non-US$ Swaps

Yen
- Japanese trust banks and some major city banks (such as Bank of Tokyo).
- The big four Japanese securities houses (primarily as arrangers but increasingly as principals).
- Some foreign banks (Citicorp, Morgan Guaranty, Paribas, Salomon Brothers).

Deutschmark
- Major German universal banks (for example, Deutsche Bank and Commerzbank).
- Foreign banks (Morgan Guaranty, Citicorp).

Swiss franc
- Big three Swiss universal banks.
- Foreign banks (Citicorp, Morgan Guaranty, Paribas).

£
- United Kingdom merchant banks.
- Investment bank subsidiaries of United Kingdom clearing banks (such as County Natwest).
- Foreign banks (Citicorp, Morgan Guaranty, Security Pacific).

ECU
- Banque Paribas, Bankers Trust.

C$
- Canadian chartered banks (in particular Royal Bank, CIBC).
- Foreign banks (Citicorp, Bankers Trust).

A$
- Major Australian banks (Commonwealth Bank, ANZ, Westpac).
- Foreign banks (Citibank, Bankers Trust, Security Pacific).

NZ$
- BNZ, DFC, South Pacific Merchant Finance.

HK$
- Manufacturers Hanover, Wardleys.

Note: Only principal traders not swap arrangers are included.

Exhibit 25.3

Volume of US$ Swaps Undertaken by Major Maket Makers: 1986

	US$ billion
Citibank Bankers Trust Salomon Brothers[1]	30-45
Morgan Guaranty Chase Manhattan Chemical Bank First Chicago Prudential Bache	15-25
First Boston[1] Bank America Security Pacific Kleinwort Benson	13-15
Manufacturers Hanover Merrill Lynch[2] Banque Paribas[3] UBS Nomura[1]	10-12
SBCI Lloyds First Interstate Morgan Stanley DKB Morgan Grenfell Drexel Burnham Lambert	4-10

Notes:

1. Estimated as these banks refused to disclose their volume.

2. Data excludes swaps of less than two years maturity, swaps executed for internal funding, and asset swaps.

3. Only transactions as principal are included.

Source: Euromoney.

The emergence of "pure" swap market makers represents major structural changes in the swaps markets. The two major participants in this category are Prudential Global Funding (owned by the Prudential Insurance Group) and AIG Financial Products (owned by the American International Group). Both Prudential Global Funding and AIG operate as swap market makers with no substantive parallel commercial or investment banking business, although Prudential has become increasingly associated with Pru-Bache, the United States based investment bank, also owned by Prudential Insurance.

Both entities act as principals in swaps and run active books primarily in US$ interest rate swaps. Backed by their highly rated insurance parents, the two groups are rated AAA by the major rating agencies, allowing them to act as counterparties to transactions involving even the most credit sensitive of participants. The move by these two groups is part of a trend whereby top rated insurance companies can use their capital strength to generate revenues unaffected by the capital adequacy constraints which restrict rival commercial and investment banks active in swaps.

A number of specialised swap brokers, such as Tullet & Tokyo, Capital Market Services, Tradition Financial Services, etc. have emerged. These specialised brokers have improved the liquidity of the swap market.

Chapter 26

Risks in Swap Marketmaking

RISK DIMENSIONS*

Swap warehouses are operated on the basis that the intermediary can enter into a swap contract without a matching counterparty being available. In entering into unmatched swaps, the intermediary incurs an exposure to movements in interest rates and, in the case of currency swaps, exchange rates. The principal purpose of swap portfolio management is to preserve the value of the swaps booked on the bid or offer side by hedging against the risk of loss from interest rate and/or currency movements created by temporary open swap positions in the portfolio.

It is useful in this context to differentiate between the *pre-closeout* period and the *post-closeout* period.

The pre-closeout period is typically up to a maximum of three months, depending on the size and liquidity of the swap market, during which the open position is maintained and hedged until it is closed out by an equal and opposite swap. The post-closeout period (typically up to ten years) is the period until maturity of the two matched swaps.

The risks as between the pre- and post-closeout period differ significantly. The primary risk in the pre-closeout period may be characterised as market risk, that is, the risk to movements in interest or currency rates, while the post-closeout period is characterised principally by counterparty default or credit risk.

The distinction while conceptually tenable is less clear in practice. For example, it is possible, although unlikely, for a default on credit grounds to take place during the pre-closeout period. Similarly, certain types of market risk are evident in the post-closeout period, including certain mismatch risks which must be assumed for the full term of the swap.

In this part, the focus is primarily on market risk. Credit or default risk considerations in swap transactions are considered in detail in Chapter 30.

The market risk in swap warehousing operations can itself be classified into:

- interest rate risk;
- currency risk;
- mismatch risk.

These individual types of market risk are considered in detail below.

---

* The discussion of swap marketmaking risks draws on William P. Lawton and Douglas Metcalf, "Portfolio Approach to Interest Rate Swap Management" in Antl (1986) Vol. 2.

INTEREST RATE RISK

Interest rate risk in swap marketmaking usually encompasses any actual exposure related to changes in interest rates as well as the risk associated with hedging that exposure.

In booking an open swap position, the intermediary creates interest rate exposures which are similar to exposures that can be created in the cash market for these instruments. The typical exposures are as follows:

- Receiving fixed rate and paying floating rate is equivalent to being long fixed rate bonds and short floating rate bonds.
- Paying fixed rate and receiving floating rate is equivalent to being short fixed rate bonds and long floating rate bonds.

It is usual in analysing the risks on swap transactions to decouple the fixed rate flows from the floating rate flows since these, in general, belong to different markets and must be managed separately. It is also common to focus attention on the management of the fixed rate flows rather than the floating rate flows as the value of the latter is more stable because it reprices more frequently and consequently trades at a level closer to par than the fixed rate component of the swap.

It is also customary to separate the interest rate risk component into two separate elements:

- the base interest rate risk;
- the spread risk.

The base risk usually refers to movements in the base rate off which swaps are priced. This is usually a government bond interest rate, such as US$ Treasuries or A$ government bond rates. The base risk is usually hedged by undertaking cash or financial futures transactions in the relevant securities.

The spread risk on swaps relates to the fact that swaps are priced as a margin relative to the fixed rate base or government bond. The risk in this context is that, for unmatched swap positions, the market spread will move against the intermediary and result in originating a matching position at a spread lower or higher than originally anticipated.

The swap market operates largely as a spread risk market since a common objective in swap marketmaking is to lock in a positive spread on matched transactions. For example, a position may be booked to receive fixed rate at a spread of 60bps over a relevant five year government security, and hedged in anticipation of finding another counterparty to receive at the five year government bond rate plus 50bps. Assuming the *base rate* hedge is efficient, the intermediary's exposure is to changes in the spread and, in our example, an increase in the bid rate in the market or an increase in the overall spread structure could potentially produce a negative spread for the life of a matched transaction.

Spread risk cannot usually be hedged and since positions may be in inventory for some time before matching, swap market makers are sensitive to volatility in swaps spreads. In essence, swap portfolios are essentially managed as spread portfolios with market makers seeking to identify potential shifts in swap spreads before they occur to minimise potential loss and take maximum advantage of spread shifts to benefit the swap portfolio.

Swap spread movements largely reflect the underlying arbitrage factors and changing supply and demand factors. The changing supply and demand in the swap market in turn reflects changes in anticipated volumes, directions, types of counterparties, levels of interest rates, new issue volumes, activity in parallel markets and maturity preferences.

Swap spreads in recent times in the US$ market as well as in the £, A$ and NZ$ market have been notoriously volatile. The risk of changes in spread levels is greatest for shorter rather than longer maturity positions. Longer swap spreads are *relatively* more stable because transactions are normally linked to new issues and changes in swap spreads reflect changes in new issue spreads. Shorter maturity swap spreads are significantly more volatile, primarily reflecting the fact that these swap spreads are determined by swap and futures arbitrage, with changing prices of short-term interest rate futures contracts and particularly futures strip prices causing swap price changes. While the outer limits spread range are approximately predictable, the swap spread is still relatively volatile.

The behaviour of swap spreads in individual swap markets are analysed in Part 7.

As noted above, spread risk cannot be hedged. Protection against changes in the value of warehouse swap positions is a particularly vexed issue. Shorter positions are more vulnerable and are consequently usually taken on more cautiously, although this varies between markets, with very short swaps, such as positions in the US$ market, only being positioned at extremes of historical bid/offer range. Swap market makers seek to compensate for spread risk by maintaining an appropriate bid/offer spread in the relevant maturity. However, the fact remains that the best method to minimise spread risk, across all maturities, is to limit hedge positions by maturity and match them out relatively quickly.

CURRENCY RISK

Currency swap transactions entail interest rate risks, as described above, as well as exposures to movements in currency rates. Booking currency swap positions exposes the intermediary to movements in the currency as the swap entails effectively being short or long the relevant currencies.

Typical exposures from currency swaps can be seen from the following example:

- Receiving fixed A$ and paying floating rate US$ is equivalent to being long A$ fixed rate bonds and short US$ floating rate bonds.
- Paying A$ fixed rate and receiving US$ floating rate is equivalent to being short A$ fixed rate bonds and long US$ floating rate bonds.

The currency exposures entailed in currency swap transactions are conceptually straightforward. It is important, however, to note that currency risk and interest rate risk are clearly interwoven. This requires that a combined hedge for the interest rate and currency risk is usually sought to be structured. This, in practice, entails either borrowing or lending the appropriate currency as well as seeking the appropriate interest rate risk cover through buying or selling an appropriate fixed rate instrument.

A particularly important source of currency risk is coupon mismatches in currency swaps. As outlined in Chapter 8, currency swap structures invariably require one party to make payments above or below the relevant interest rate index, most typically the floating rate index, in the particular currency. These spreads relative to the index entail clearly identifiable exposures to movements in exchange rates and must be hedged accordingly.

MISMATCH RISK

Swaps have a number of factors which, if they are not matched or managed properly within the portfolio, have the potential to inflict substantial economic loss. It is incumbent on the portfolio manager to measure and manage this mismatch risk. The management of mismatch risk is arguably the single most important aspect of swap portfolio risk management.

Mismatches usually occur from the market maker's attempt to accommodate customer preferences. In practice, if a market maker insists on matching every swap in all its aspects, compensation will have to be paid to the other counterparty as an incentive to accept the required structure, which may be significantly different from its precise requirements. In addition to this reduction in margins, the institution must be willing to carry a large hedged inventory position for potentially longer periods while searching for the identical match thereby incurring hedging and spread risk.

The major areas of mismatch risk include:

- notional principal;
- maturity;
- floating index;
- floating rate index reset dates and payment frequencies;
- payment dates;
- coupon.

Mismatching notional principal and maturity is identical to having excess long or short swap positions. For example, if an A$20m five year swap is matched with an A$10m five year swap the effect is simply that of an open US$10m five year position. Similarly, if an A$20m five year is matched with an A$20m 10 year swap, the result is greater price volatility on the longer position and a five year open position starting five years in the future.

A major area of mismatch relates to the index used to calculate the floating rate payments. It may be desirable for the market maker to consider mismatching the index in order to create an arbitrage between the two floating rates. A common example of this type of practice in the US$ market is to receive six month LIBOR while paying three month LIBOR, or to receive three month LIBOR while paying one month CP.

Another major mismatch area is the reset dates. Even a one day mismatch on the floating rate index dates potentially exposes the principal to large daily changes in the index. As the size of a portfolio increases though, diversification may reduce the significance of small reset date mismatches as the gains and losses may tend to offset each other out. In contrast, if the swap book has only one mismatched transaction, it may have a loss with no prospect of an offsetting gain.

Payment dates represent another important area of potential mismatch. A payment date mismatch results from either payment cycle mismatches, that is, annual to semi-annual or when the cycle is the same, semi-annual to semi-annual, but the date of payment is different.

There are two risks with payment mismatches. The first risk is that a payment will be made and there is no reciprocal receipt, thus creating a credit exposure for the payment amount. This is reduced by specifying net payments when applicable. However, netting payments is not applicable when the payment cycle is different. The semi-annual payer has credit exposure to the annual payer for the entire semi-annual payment for six months.

In addition to any credit risk there is the reinvestment risk incurred in mismatching payments. At the time of the transaction the assumption is made that the semi-annual coupon received will be reinvested at the yield to maturity of the swap, or some other specified reinvestment rate. If the coupon is reinvested at a lower reinvestment rate than assumed then the semi-annual receiver suffers a loss.

The final significant area of mismatch risk is the coupon mismatch on two swaps. One of the objectives of putting together a matched swap may be to realise the spread between the two fixed coupons. However, if the swaps do not have similar coupon structures an assumption needs to be made on reinvestment rates or funding costs. For example, the coupon mismatch after adjusting for the result of hedging gains or losses which are being amortised against the swaps, or fees paid or received in a premium or discount swap, incurs potentially significant reinvestment or funding rate risk. Where money is paid or received (be it from hedges or coupon mismatches) the assumption is made that the money received will be reinvested at an assumed but unknown rate, and money paid is borrowed at an assumed but unknown rate.

The currency risk assumed in the case of spread below or above a floating rate index in currency swaps is a special case of mismatch risk.

Each potential mismatch, in practice, must be evaluated carefully, as to the potential risk of the mismatch and the return expected. The risk analysis should incorporate the impact of cumulative portfolio mismatches. For example, a date mismatch on one transaction may be offset by the exact but opposite mismatch in another transaction. The market maker may also want to investigate possible offsetting or compounding effects of mismatches among different classes of mismatches.

SWAP PORTFOLIO RISK: AN EXAMPLE

The risks inherent in swap portfolio management are best illustrated utilising an example. *Exhibit 26.1* sets out a hypothetical series of transactions and the overall final position of this portfolio. *Exhibit 26.2* sets out the detailed portfolio cash flows.

Exhibit 26.1
Example of Swap Portfolio

Assume the following sequence of swap transactions are booked by financial institution, Bank A (A), over a period of less than three weeks. The sequence assumes that the institution is able to maintain a spread of 20bps, that is, B + 40/B + 60 (where B = Australian Commonwealth government securities of the relevant maturity).

15/2/X5—Swap 1*

Three year A$50m A$ fixed and US$ LIBOR swap off a EuroA$ bond issue commencing 12/3/X5 and maturing 12/3/X8 is booked. The specific terms are as follows:

• A pays A$ 13.00% pa (A) in arrears commencing 12/3/X6 and ending 12/3/X8.
• A receives six month US$ LIBOR—60bps (S/A) commencing 12/9/X5 and ending 12/3/X8.

Bonds = 13.00% pa (S/A) and the swap pricing incorporates all appropriate yield adjustment to the base price of 13.40% pa (S/A). Exchange rate on 12/3/X5 = US$0.7120/A$1.00.

16/2/X5—Swap 2

Three year A$20m A$ fixed and US$ LIBOR swap commencing 18/2/X5 and maturing 18/2/X8:

• A receives A$13.30% pa (S/A).
• A pays six month US$ LIBOR (S/A).

Bonds = 12.70% pa (S/A). Exchange rate on 18/2/X5 = US$0.7040/A$1.00.

24/2/X5—Swap 3

Three year A$20m interest rate swap commencing 25/2/X5 and maturing 25/2/X8:

• A receives 13.67% pa quarterly.
• A pays three month BBR quarterly.

Bonds = 13.30% pa (S/A).

27/2/X5—Swap 4

Three year A$10m interest rate swap commencing 28/2/X5 and maturing 28/2/X8:

• A receives 13.80% pa (S/A).
• A pays six month BBR (S/A).

Bonds = 13.20% pa (S/A).

5/3/X5—Swap 5

Three year A$30m A$BBR and US$ LIBOR currency swap commencing 7/3/X5 and maturing 7/3/X8:

• A pays six month US$ LIBOR (S/A).
• A receives six month BBR (S/A).

Exchange rate on 7/3/X8 = US$0.6950/A$1.00.

The overall swap portfolio is as follows:

Bank pays

A$ fixed rate

13.00% pa annually on A$50m

A$ floating rates

{ 3 month BBR quarterly on A$20m
{ 6 month BBR semi-annually on A$10m

US$ floating rate

{ 6 month LIBOR semi-annually on US$14.08m
{ 6 month LIBOR semi-annually on US$20.85m

Bank receives

{ 13.30% pa semi-annually on A$20m
{ 13.67% pa quarterly on A$20m
{ 13.80% pa semi-annually on A$10m

6 month BBR semi-annually on A$30m

6 month LIBOR minus 60bps
semi-annually on US$35.6m

Note: All swaps in this sequence are identified by a unique number which is used to identify specific cash flows in *Exhibit 26.2*.

Exhibit 26.2

Swap Portfolio Cash Flows (US$m or A$m)

Period	Bank pays[1] Principal	Bank pays[1] Interest	Bank receives[1] Principal	Bank receives[1] Interest
Year X5				
18/2/X5				
25/2/X5	(2) + US$14.08		(2) − A$20	
28/2/X5				
7/3/X5	(5) + US$20.85		(5) − A$30	
12/3/X5	(1) − US$35.6		(1) + A$50	
25/5/X5		(3) − (90 BBR × A$20 × 0.25)		(3) + (13.67% × A$20 × 0.25)
18/8/X5		(2) − (LIBOR × US$14.08 × 0.50)		(2) + (13.30% pa × A$20 × 0.50)
25/8/X5		(3) − (90 BBR × A$20 × 0.25)		(3) + (13.67% × A$20 × 0.25)
28/8/X5		(4) − (180 BBR × A$10 × 0.50)		(4) + (13.80% × A$10 × 0.50)
7/9/X5		(5) − (LIBOR × US$20.85 × 0.50)		(5) + (180 BBR × A$30 × 0.50)
12/9/X5				(1) + (LIBOR − 60bps × US$35.6 × 0.50)
25/11/X5		(3) − (90 BBR × A$20 × 0.25)		(3) + (13.67% × A$20 × 0.25)
Year X6				
18/2/X6		(2) − (LIBOR × US$14.08 × 0.50)		(2) + (13.30% × A$20 × 0.50)
25/2/X6		(3) − (90 BBR × A$20 × 0.25)		(3) + (13.67% × A$20 × 0.25)
28/2/X6		(4) − (180 BBR × A$10 × 0.50)		(4) + (13.80% × A$10 × 0.50)
7/3/X6		(5) − (LIBOR × US$20.85 × 0.50)		(5) + (180 BBR × A$30 × 0.50)
12/3/X6		(1) − (13.00% × A$50)		(1) + (LIBOR − 60bps × US$35.6 × 0.50)
25/5/X6		(3) − (90 BBR × A$20 × 0.25)		(3) + (13.67% × A$20 × 0.25)
18/8/X6		(2) − (LIBOR × US$14.08 × 0.50)		(2) + (13.30% × A$20 × 0.50)
25/8/X6		(3) − (90 BBR × A$20 × 0.25)		(3) + (13.67% × A$20 × 0.25)
28/8/X6		(4) − (180 BBR × A$10 × 0.50)		(4) + (13.80% × A$10 × 0.50)

Exhibit 26.2—continued

Date	Bank pays	Bank receives
7/9/X6	(5) − (LIBOR × US$20.85 × 0.50)	(5) + (180 BBR × A$30 × 0.50)
12/9/X6		(1) + (LIBOR − 60bps × US$35.6 × 0.50)
25/11/X6	(3) − (90 BBR × A$20 × 0.25)	(3) + (13.67% × A$20 × 0.25)
Year X7		
18/2/X7	(2) − (LIBOR × US$14.08 × 0.50)	(2) + (13.30% × A$20 × 0.50)
25/2/X7	(3) − (90 BBR × A$20 × 0.25)	(3) + (13.67% × A$20 × 0.25)
28/2/X7	(4) − (180 BBR × A$10 × 0.50)	(4) + (13.80% × A$10 × 0.50)
7/3/X7	(5) − (LIBOR × US$20.85 × 0.50)	(5) + (180 BBR × A$30 × 0.50)
12/3/X7	(1) − (13.00% of A$50)	(1) + (LIBOR − 60bps × US$35.6 × 0.50)
25/5/X7	(3) − (90 BBR × A$20 × 0.25)	(3) + (13.67% × A$20 × 0.25)
18/8/X7	(2) − (LIBOR × US$14.08 × 0.50)	(2) + (13.30% × A$20 × 0.50)
25/8/X7	(3) − (90 BBR × A$20 × 0.25)	(3) + (13.67% × A$20 × 0.25)
28/8/X7	(4) − (180 BBR × A$10 × 0.50)	(4) + (13.80% × A$10 × 0.50)
7/9/X7	(5) − (LIBOR × US$20.85 × 0.50)	(5) + (180 BBR × A$30 × 0.50)
12/9/X7		(1) + (LIBOR − 60bps × US$35.6 × 0.50)
25/11/X7	(3) − (90 BBR × A$20 × 0.25)	(3) + (13.67% × A$20 × 0.25)
Year X8		
18/2/X8	(2) − (LIBOR × US$14.08 × 0.50); (2) − US$14.08	(2) + (13.30% × A$20 × 0.50); (2) + A$20
25/2/X8	(3) − (90 BBR × A$20 × 0.25)	(3) + (13.67% × A$20 × 0.25)
28/2/X8	(4) − (180 BBR × A$10 × 0.50)	(4) + (13.80% × A$10 × 0.50)
7/3/X8	(5) − (LIBOR × US$20.85 × 0.50); (5) − US$20.85	(5) + (180 BBR × A$30 × 0.50); (5) + A$30
12/3/X8	(1) − (13.00% of A$50)	(1) + (LIBOR − 60bps × US$35.6 × 0.50); (1) + US$35.6; (1) − A$50

Note:

1. The term pay and receive is used in this Exhibit as the bank both pays and receives. The term pay and receive is used to group cash flows under each swap, for example, the fixed rate A$ flows are regarded as "bank pays" and the corresponding principal flows are linked to it. For convenience, principals' reversals at maturity are not switched from pay to receive or vice versa to avoid confusion. The bold number in brackets refers to the swap identified in *Exhibit 26.2*.

The vital A$ Eurobond swap is ultimately matched off against one currency swap, two interest rate swaps and one floating-to-floating currency swap. However, the final portfolio position is *not* exactly matched for two reasons:

- the differences in the time of entry into the various swaps create exposures which would have had to be hedged to ensure profitability was maintained;
- the residual mismatches which will remain because of the slightly different terms of each swap.

The initial swap exposes the institution to a risk of A$ interest rates falling and the US$ depreciating against the A$. This risk is initially hedged by purchasing A$ three year government bonds and borrowing US$ to fund the purchases (the hedging methodology is described in detail in Chapter 27). The A$ bonds are sold and the US$ borrowing repaid as the offsetting swaps are entered into.

The hedges set up create two problems: hedge efficiency and funding (reinvestment) of hedge losses (profits). In the example utilised, the swap market maker's hedges yield the following cash flows:

- When Swap 2 is entered into, the sale of the A$ bonds creates a profit and the repayment of the US$ borrowing results in a loss.
- The unwinding of the *interest rate* hedges when Swaps 3 and 4 are entered into result in a loss.
- When Swap 5 is entered into, the repayment of the US$ borrowing results in a further loss.

The rate at which the loss is funded and the profit reinvested, and the accompanying coupon mismatches will significantly affect the swaps profitability. This, of course, also assumes that the hedge was in the first place efficient.

The final portfolio position while matched in a general sense, upon closer examination of *Exhibit 26.2*, reveals a series of major mismatches.

The swaps all have slightly different maturities which has the effect of distorting reset dates for the floating rate indexes. For example, it is necessary to pay out the LIBOR flows before actual receipt of the offsetting LIBOR inflow. This creates a problem that, unless managed and hedged, in a declining interest rate environment the portfolio will suffer losses. In addition, the actual cash payment must be funded which, if the funding cost is higher than LIBOR itself, will result in a further loss.

The portfolio also embodies a floating index mismatch as the swap market maker receives six month BBR semi-annually and pays three month BBR quarterly. This would result in a loss to the portfolio if the yield curve was negative as the absolute cash inflows would potentially be lower than the offsetting cash inflows. This would be compounded by the need to fund the quarterly payments if six month BBR is lower than the relevant funding cost.

The differing payment frequencies on the A$ fixed rate flows create a reinvestment problem as semi-annual and quarterly payment received must be reinvested to make the offsetting annual payments. The absolute interest rate levels and the slope of the yield curve, particularly relative to that assumed when the swap was priced and entered into, will affect the portfolio's earnings.

The most striking coupon mismatch in the sample portfolio is in the US$ floating rate flows where the margin under LIBOR creates a US$ shortfall which is presumably offset by surplus A$s elsewhere in the portfolio. This exchange risk element in the portfolio must be managed throughout the life of the transaction.

The mismatches identified in the example are relatively simple. Where the portfolio is managed using more complex hedging technology, for example, using duration concepts entailing significant mismatches in amount and maturity (see Chapter 7), the risks within the portfolio would necessarily be more complex as the date and amount mismatches would be exaggerated.

It is useful in reviewing this sample portfolio to keep in mind the absolute economic impact of changes in the numerous variables. *Exhibit 26.3* summarises the A$ value effect of fluctuation in a few of the risk dimensions discussed on an A$10m swap transaction.

Exhibit 26.3

Economic Impact of Changes in A$ and US$ Swap Variables

Variable	Change measured	Profit/loss impact of change
A$/US$ spot rate	US$0.01	A$192,911
A$ swap rates		
• 3 year	5bps	A$12,093
• 5 year	5bps	A$17,951
A$ BBR		
• 90 day	5bps	A$1,163
• 180 day	5bps	A$2,197
US$ swap rates		
• 3 year	5bps	US$12,679
• 5 year	5bps	US$19,281
US$ LIBOR rate		
• 90 day	5bps	US$1,185
• 180 day	5bps	US$2,282

Notes:

The above assumes:

A$1.00 = US$0.7150
A$ swap rates = 13.00% pa (S/A)
US$ swap rates = 10.00% pa (S/A)
A$ BBR = 12.00% pa
US$ LIBOR = 8.00% pa

All profit/loss impact is calculated on an amount of A$10m or US$10m.

MARKETMAKING AND SWAP PORTFOLIO RISK

The basic objective of marketmaking and swap portfolio management is to generate profits on a risk adjusted basis. However, in practice, this objective is seen as a by-product of the institution's overall strategy within which the swap operations must necessarily reside.

Significant differences exist in individual institutions' approaches to their swap portfolios. Some institutions regard it as a servicing function supporting other areas of business such as new issues and the underwriting and sales of securities. Other institutions treat swaps as part of their overall treasury activity. In the extreme case, some institutions run their swap activities as an identifiable and separate profit centre. Consequently, swap portfolios are operated in slightly different ways and within each framework individual transactions must be reconciled with the overall operational objectives of the institution.

Additional problems in operating swap portfolios relate to problems of measurement of the profitability of these activities. The economic impact of a swap within a swap portfolio can only be determined at the maturity of the swap, usually by matching cash inflows and outflows, adjusted for hedging and carrying costs etc. However, in practice, where a number of swaps are aggregated into an overall portfolio, such transaction by transaction measurement is not feasible.

An additional problem relates to the differences in the risk and return trade-offs within individual swap portfolios and in the swap portfolios operated by different institutions. For example, some institutions utilise their swap transactions to position to take advantage of interest rate shifts while other swap market participants are only allowed to operate on a fully hedged basis.

Generally, swap portfolios, in the current market environment are operated on a partially or fully hedged basis. Some limited positioning activity is undertaken. This positioning activity tends to be confined to trading swap spreads rather than absolute rates. In considering using swaps as part of positioning strategies, it is important to note that other markets are available which provide greater liquidity in closing positioning trades and which better allow participants to more efficiently capture anticipated rate shifts.

Where portfolios are operated on a hedged basis, marketmaking entails a different type of interest rate risk, namely, hedging risk. Hedging risk arises from the fact that there is no single perfect swap hedge instrument other than a matching identical swap. Consequently, the various hedging instruments, cash bonds or financial futures, which are utilised are at best imperfect proxies for the ideal hedge instrument. In this regard, a swap portfolio is exposed to a hedging risk from imperfect correlation in the movements of the hedge as against the swap which is sought to be hedged. The lower the correlation of the hedge instrument to the benchmark pricing instrument, the greater the hedge or basis risk.

There are variations in the difficulty of hedging of different types of swaps. Interest rate swaps are considerably easier to hedge than currency swaps. In addition, the efficiency of hedges as between swap markets vary significantly. For example, the highly liquid nature of the United States Treasury bond market allows reasonably efficient hedging of US$ swaps.

In contrast, warehousing in other currency markets, including A$ and NZ$, is considerably less efficient. While the market maker can usually cover the foreign exchange risks associated with booking a currency swap, it is difficult to engineer a hedge against movements in interest rates as government bonds in the relevant currency may only prove poor surrogate cover. This largely reflects the greater variability of swap spreads relative to the government bond yield curve in currency swap markets, such as A$, £, deutschmark, yen, etc., and also the relative liquidity of the swap market in question.

In examining the hedging risks of operating swap portfolios, it is important to examine hedging practices in terms of fixed rate as against floating rate flows. While considerable attention is focused on the hedging of the fixed rate side of swap portfolios, the floating rate side of a portfolio is less adequately hedged, reflecting the belief that the value of the floating rate side of the trade will not depart from par for an extended period of time even if there is a substantial movement in rates as the floating rate resets periodically. However, the significant potential losses arising from mismatches on the floating rate side of swap portfolios has led to increasing attention being focused on this aspect of swap portfolio management.

A particularly problematic aspect of swap portfolio management is the reconciliation of economic portfolio management technology with the accounting, tax and financial reporting implications of that technology. This is because the implications of a different hedging strategy or instrument are not always obvious and the accounting, tax and reporting implications often dictate the strategy and tactics taken in managing swap portfolios.

Chapter 27

Swap Portfolio Risk Management Techniques

OVERVIEW

The preferred method of controlling exposure to market risks on a swap transaction is to match it by entering into an offsetting swap. Where swap transactions are matched in this way, if inflows match outflows, apart from spreads taken by the intermediary as income, the intermediary should, theoretically, be fully hedged against *market* risks. Mismatches and payment dates, reset periods, etc., lessen the effectiveness of the hedge created by matching out the two swaps.

Under current market conditions, very few intermediaries match each swap as it is booked. The structure and competitive pressures in the swap market now dictate that most intermediaries enter into each swap independently, that is, most intermediaries are ready to commit themselves to one leg of a swap transaction before the offsetting leg has been arranged. This activity is undertaken on the assumption that the matching swap transaction can be completed without an adverse change in the market during the interim period.

This market risk entailed in booking open swap positions can be approached in two different ways:

- It is possible to open swap positions to speculate on swap spread and interest rate movements.
- The swap position is booked and hedged against market risk pending arrangement of the matching part to the transaction.

Under current market practice, the vast majority of intermediaries utilise a variety of swap portfolio risk management techniques to, at least partially, hedge against the risk of market movements in the period between the entry into the first swap and the entry into the offsetting transaction. In essence, intermediaries do not seek to utilise their swap activities to take positions in interest rate markets or currency markets but operate their swap portfolios on a risk averse basis.

HEDGING INTEREST RATE SWAP TRANSACTIONS

Basic concept

Hedging strategies, where interest rate swap transactions are booked without a matching counterpart transaction, are based on the fact that the exposure underlying unmatched swaps is directly analogous to cash market positions. Consequently, transactions involving physical cash market instruments or financial futures on the relevant cash market instrument can be utilised to offset the market risk assumed until the swap is matched with an offsetting transaction.

473

As discussed in Chapter 26, in an interest rate swap transaction in any currency, the physical market positions corresponding to swap positions are as follows:

- receiving fixed rate and paying floating rate is equivalent to being long fixed rate bonds and short floating rate bonds;
- paying fixed rate and receiving floating rate is equivalent to being short fixed rate bonds and long floating rate bonds.

Given these cash market equivalent positions, it is possible to hedge the market risk by effectively reversing the cash market position to provide a hedge against fluctuations in the value of the swap. Utilising this technology, the hedges are structured as follows:

- Where an intermediary receives fixed rate and pays floating rate it can hedge its exposure by shorting fixed rate bonds and purchasing or going long floating rate bonds.
- Where an intermediary pays fixed rate and receives floating rate the appropriate hedge is to go long fixed rate bonds and short floating rate bonds.

This type of hedging technique is best illustrated by example.

For example, assume an intermediary commits itself to a five year swap with a corporation when the yield on five year government bonds is 14.00% pa. Under the terms of the swap, the intermediary pays bonds plus 40bps in return for receiving six month BBR. The intermediary, not having a matching counterparty, hedges the swap temporarily by buying five year government bonds. Subsequently, a few days later, the intermediary matches out its original swap exposure by entering into a matching offsetting swap.

In the pre-closeout period, between the original swap and the matching swap, the spread on swaps has remained constant at bonds plus 40bps (bid) and bonds plus 60bps (offer). However, the yield on five year government bonds has fallen to 13.50% pa. This effectively means that in *absolute rate* terms the intermediary is paying 14.40% pa and receiving 14.10% pa on the fixed rate side of the swaps. It is assumed, in this case, that the floating rate sides, that is, the payment and receipt of floating rate BBR, are matched.

In terms of the matched swap positions, the bank loses 30bps on the notional principal at every payment date. However, this periodic loss is offset by the gain on the holdings of bonds. The government bonds bought to hedge the swap position would have increased in price when government bond rates fell from 14.00% to 13.50% pa. This gain is realised when the intermediary sells the bonds at the time it enters into the matching swap transaction to close out its exposure. Once the value of the profit on the government bonds is factored into the transaction, the intermediary will approximately earn 20bps pa, representing the spread between the bid and offer rates, on the matched swap positions.

In the reverse situation, where the intermediary had received a fixed rate under the swap, it would have hedged by selling government bonds and buying back those bonds when the offsetting swap was arranged. Under this transaction, the fall in rates would have resulted in a gain on the swap offset by a loss on the short government bond position.

Examples of this type of hedge for interest rate swap portfolios are set out in *Exhibit 27.1* and *Exhibit 27.2*.

Exhibit 27.1

Example of Interest Rate Swap Hedge (1)

As at 5/1/X7, ABC bank (ABC) enters into the following swap: ABC to pay fixed rate A$ at bonds plus 65bps for three years against receipt of six month BBR.

Swap terms are as follows:

Amount:	A$50m
Maturity:	5/1/X0
Swap fixed rate:	15.00% pa (S/A) or B + 65bps where B = 14.35% pa

Assume the three year swap market is pricing off the 13.00% 11/X9 Commonwealth bonds, although the bond maturity is less than three years. Assume that the 13.00% 11/X9 is trading at 14.35% pa and that short-term overnight rates are 18.20% pa and six month BBR is 16.30% pa.

ABC hedges through purchase of 13.00% 11/X9. Hedge amount is A$51.887m reflecting weighting of the hedge due to differing price volatilities of the swap and bond arising from different maturities and coupons.[1]

The details of the hedge are as follows:

Amount:	A$51.887m
YTM:	14.35% pa
Price:	96.877 or A$50.260
Accrued interest:	A$0.942m (13.00% of A$51.88m × $\frac{51}{365}$)
Total price:	A$51.202m

The swap is closed off on 19/1/X7 with ABC receiving fixed rate A$ versus six month BBR at B + 85bps.

The closeout swap terms are:

Amount:	A$50m
Maturity:	5/1/87 (with a short first interest period)
Swap fixed rate:	14.85% pa on B + 85bps where B = 14.00% pa

As the closeout swap is entered into, ABC sells its bond position. Assume that the 13.00% 11/X9 is trading at 14.00% pa and six month BBR is 16.40% pa.

The sales proceeds are as follows:

Amount:	A$51.887m
YTM:	14.00% pa
Price:	97.683 or A$50.678m
Accrued interest:	A$1.201 (13.00% of A$51.88m × $\frac{65}{365}$)
Total price:	A$51.879m

The overall result of the swap is as follows:

Fixed rate hedge

	A$m
Cash profit on hedge:[2]	0.418
Interest income:[3]	0.259
Funding cost:[4]	0.358
Net:	0.319

Swap flows

At first settlement date (on 5/7/X7)	A$m
Fixed rate side	
Fixed rate amount received:[5]	3.397
Fixed rate amount paid:[6]	3.719
Net:	−0.322

Exhibit 27.1—continued

Floating rate side

Floating rate amount received:[7]	4.0421
Floating rate amount paid:[8]	3.7528
Net:	+0.290
Difference:	−0.032

At subsequent settlement dates

Fixed rate side

Fixed rate amount received:[9]	3.713
Fixed rate amount paid:[10]	3.750
Net:	−0.038

All floating rate flows are assumed to match after the first period as they reprice on identical dates.

The transaction overall produces the following cash flows:

* a profit on the hedge of A$0.319m;
* a net difference at first settlement of −A$0.032m;
* a net difference at each subsequent settlement date of −A$0.038m.

Assuming that the hedge profit is reinvested at the bond rate (14.00% pa), the transaction yields a present value profit of A$0.143m which is equivalent to A$0.030m every six months or 0.12% pa. This compares to a bid/offer spread of 0.20% pa and reflects hedging costs such as the negative carry on the hedge and also the shift in the short-term BBR rate.

Notes

1. Calculated as:

$$N = \frac{(A_1 - A_2) \times FV}{(B_1 - B_2) \times FV} = \frac{(97.38 - 96.22) \times \$50m}{(99.27 - 98.15) \times \$50m} = 1.037$$

where N = hedge ratio
    A_1 = price of bond 13.00% maturing 5/1/X0 at 14.10% pa = 97.38
    A_2 = price of bond 13.00% maturing 5/1/X0 at 14.60% pa = 96.22
    B_1 = price of bond 13.00% maturing 15/11/89 at 14.10% pa = 99.27
    B_2 = price of bond 13.00% maturing 15/11/89 at 14.60% pa = 98.15

Please note that numbers are subject to rounding error. Also note that the hedge structure in this case makes compensation for the higher basic coupon and therefore different price behaviour of the swap vis-à-vis the bond.

2. A$50.678 − A$50.260.
3. A$ 1.201 − A$ 0.942.
4. 18.20% pa on A$51.20m for 14 days.
5. 14.85% on A$50m for 167 days, that is, 19/1/X7 to 5/7/X7.
6. 15.00% on A$50m for 181 days, that is, 5/1/X7 to 5/7/X7.
7. 16.30% on A$50m for 181 days, that is, 5/1/X7 to 5/7/X7.
8. 16.40% on A$50m for 167 days, that is, 19/1/X7 to 5/7/X7.
9. 14.85% on A$50m for six months.
10. 15.00% on A$50m for six months.

Exhibit 27.2

Example of Interest Rate Swap Hedge (2)

As at 5/1/X7, ABC bank (ABC) enters into the following swap: ABC to receive fixed rate A$ at bonds plus 85bps for three years against payment of six month BBR.

Swap terms are as follows:

Amount:	A$50m
Maturity:	5/1/90
Swap fixed rate:	15.25% pa (S/A) or B + 85bps where B = 14.35% pa

Assume the three year swap market is pricing off the 13.00% 11/X9 Commonwealth bonds, although the bond maturity is less than three years. Assume that the 13.00% 11/X9 is trading at 14.35% pa and that short-term overnight rates are 18.20% pa and six month BBR is 16.30% pa.

ABC hedges through short sale of 13.00% 11/X9. Hedge amount is A$51.88m reflecting weighting of the hedge due to differing price volatilities of the swap and bond arising from different maturities.

The details of the hedge are as follows:

Amount:	A$51.88m
YTM:	14.35% pa
Price:	96.877 or A$50.260
Accrued interest:	A$0.942m (13.00% of A$51.88m $\times \dfrac{51}{365}$)
Total price:	A$51.202m

The swap is closed off on 19/1/X7 with ABC paying fixed rate A$ versus six month BBR at B + 65bps.

The closeout swap terms are:

Amount:	A$50m
Maturity:	5/1/87 (with a short first interest period)
Swap fixed rate:	14.65% pa on B + 65bps where B = 14.00% pa

As the closeout swap is entered into, ABC buys back its short bond position. Assume that the 13.00% 11/89 is trading at 14.00% pa and six month BBR is 16.40% pa.

The purchase price is as follows:

Amount:	A$51.88m
YTM:	14.00% pa
Price:	97.683 or A$50.678m
Accrued interest:	A$1.201 (13.00% of A$51.88m $\times \dfrac{65}{365}$)
Total price:	A$51.879m

The overall result of the swap is as follows:

Fixed rate hedge

	A$m
Cash loss on hedge:[1]	−0.418
Interest income:[2]	−0.259
Investment earnings:[3]	+0.358
Net:	−0.319

Swap flows

	A$m

At first settlement date (on 5/7/X7)

Fixed rate side	
Fixed rate amount received:[4]	3.781
Fixed rate amount paid:[5]	3.351
Net:	+0.430

Exhibit 27.2—continued

Floating rate side	
Floating rate amount received:[6]	3.752
Floating rate amount paid:[7]	4.042
Net:	−0.290
Difference:	0.140

At subsequent settlement dates

Fixed rate side	
Fixed rate amount received:[8]	3.813
Fixed rate amount paid:[9]	3.663
Net:	0.150

All floating rate flows are assumed to match after the first period as they reprice on identical dates.

The transaction overall produces the following cash flows:

- a loss on the hedge of −A$0.319m;
- a net difference at first settlement of +A$0.140m;
- a net difference at each subsequent settlement date of +A$0.150m.

On the basis the hedge loss is funded at the swap rate (14.65% pa), the transaction yields a present value profit of A$0.380 which is equivalent to A$0.080 semi-annually or 0.32% pa (amortised at the bond rate). The discrepancy from the bid/offer spread reflects the positive earnings on the reinvestment of the proceeds of the short and also the favourable movement in BBR rate.

Notes:
1. A$50.260 − A$50.678.
2. A$1.20106 − A$0.94237.
3. 18.20% pa on A$51.20m for 14 days.
4. 15.25% on A$50m for 181 days, that is, 5/1/X7 to 5/7/X7.
5. 14.65% on A$50m for 167 days, that is, 19/1/X7 to 5/7/X7.
6. 16.40% on A$50m for 167 days, that is, 19/1/X7 to 5/7/X7.
7. 16.30% on A$50m for 181 days, that is, 5/1/X7 to 5/7/X7.
8. 15.25% on A$50m for six months.
9. 14.65% on A$50m for six months.

The basic technology described forms the basis of all swap portfolio risk management. However, a number of technical aspects of the risk management process require elaboration.

Issues in hedging swaps

Risk management objectives

The unifying principle underlying swap portfolio risk management is the desire on the part of the intermediary to maximise its earnings on a risk adjusted basis, which can be restated as:

$$PV \text{ (net)} = PV \text{ (asset inflows)} - PV \text{ (liability outflows)}$$

where PV signifies the present value of the relevant cash flows

The application of this type of approach to conventional trading activities, such as trading in securities, is relatively straightforward as the market value of the securities usually implies their true economic value. However, in the case of swaps, as it is necessary to establish economic values for inflows and outflows of both fixed and floating rates of interest at dates in the future, the application of this approach is less obvious.

Fixed versus floating rate flows

It is necessary to, first, decouple the fixed rate flows under a swap transaction from the corresponding floating rate flows. This separation is predicated on the fact that these, in general, belong to different markets and must, of necessity, be managed separately.

The fixed rate flows under a swap behave in a manner analogous to a fixed rate security or bond. In contrast, the floating rate flows behave like short-dated (six months or less) securities. As such, they closely approximate the behaviour of short-term money market securities and are usually managed accordingly.

In managing the risk of a swap portfolio, the portfolio manager of necessity seeks to substitute hedging risk for the market risk of an open swap position. The basic presumption is that by buying and selling securities of the appropriate maturity or financial futures on such securities, the risk on the fixed and floating rate flows under a swap transaction can be managed.

Hedging risk arises because hedging of the swap position is difficult because there is no single perfect hedging instrument for a swap other than a directly matching but offsetting swap transaction.

Fixed rate flows are usually hedged by utilising fixed rate securities of the appropriate maturity. It is customary to use government bonds in the relevant currency. This reflects the fact that the pricing behaviour in most swap markets implies pricings as a spread relative to the fixed rate government bond yield curve.

The efficiency of the hedge is determined by the degree of correlation between price movements of the hedge instrument and the swap pricing benchmark instrument. The lower the correlation between the two, the greater the hedging or basis risk. Where a security with differential pricing characteristics to the swap pricing benchmark is utilised, this additional hedging or basis risk must be managed. There appears to be two approaches in managing this basis risk. Some intermediaries view this as the opportunity to add value to the portfolio utilising elaborate proprietary hedging techniques. In contrast, other intermediaries seek to minimise this basis risk.

Risk management on the floating rate side entails the purchase or sale of instruments, physical securities or futures, which replicate the price behaviour of the floating rate index.

Traditionally, management of the floating rate side of a swap portfolio has attracted limited attention. This is because the floating side is regarded as being less volatile because the floating rate resets periodically at the new market rate which implies relative stability at or about par value even where there are substantial movements in rates. However, increased realisation that even minor mismatches on floating rate reset dates exposes the portfolio to large potential economic losses has forced swap portfolio managers to manage these floating rate exposures.

A number of approaches currently exist for the management of the floating rate flows under a swap transaction, including:

- hedging;
- diversification;
- positioning;
- use of basis swaps.

A number of swap portfolio managers hedge floating rate mismatches either by purchasing or selling securities or alternatively through the futures market in short-term interest rates.

An alternative approach, is to aggressively run floating rate mismatches to position risk arbitrage strategies between the two floating rates. An example of this type of strategy would be to receive six month LIBOR while paying three month LIBOR or to receive three month LIBOR while paying one month CP rates. The strategy in all these cases is to profit from the difference in the receipts on the floating rate flows under the swaps. The potential profit or loss from such risk arbitrage strategies depends on the spread relationship between the two indexes, the volatility of that spread relationship, the spot cash spread and the spread implied by the swap market itself.

A further strategy is to basically diversify the floating rate swap portfolio. The basic principle in this case is that as the size of a swap portfolio increases, it is expected that diversification will reduce the significance of small reset date mismatches as, presumably, the gains and losses will tend to offset each other. Many intermediaries often apply the term *date insensitive portfolio* to such diversified floating rate swap portfolios. In practice, elaborate simulation models are utilised to sample the portfolio and to determine risk estimates associated with date mismatches with hedging transactions being undertaken at the margin to avoid excessive mismatches within such large portfolios.

One strategy for managing floating rate mismatches within a swap portfolio is to use basis swaps to match out or eliminate mismatches within the portfolio. For example, a three month against a six month mismatch in a portfolio can be eliminated by structuring a three month against a six month basis swap which effectively matches out the risk positions in the portfolio.

Hedging efficiency and pricing

As noted above, swaps risk management essentially entails substituting hedging risk for market risk. The strategy of utilising hedging techniques to immunise portfolio value from changes in market rates is never perfect. Limitations in the hedging mechanisms, imperfections and illiquidity in the relevant bond and interest rate swap markets, generally prevent this. However, the hedging methodology usually utilised allows quantification of the residual risk after hedging and permits a high degree of control over the risks incurred.

The factors that affect the efficiency of the hedging process include:

- Hedge transaction costs which represent costs suffered in establishing and then unwinding or adjusting the hedge.
- Hedge carry or investment costs: depending on the relationship between the swap yield curve and the relevant government yield curve, hedges will entail either a carry cost or generate investment income. This loss or gain on the hedge must be factored into the overall swap transaction

requiring assumptions about reinvestment rates or alternatively funding costs. In addition, there may be costs of shorting a bond; usually the cost of borrowing the bond to maintain a hedge in a short position.

- Changes in the shape of the yield curve: hedge efficiency is usually affected by non-uniform movements of the yield curve. Where such changes in the shape of the yield curve occur, equality of the price change as between the swap and the hedge cannot be assured. A number of hedging strategies exist to adjust for these risks, provided there is no basis risk, but these are usually expensive and represent a trade-off between risk and cost avoidance.

- Basis movements: additional slippages in hedge efficiency occur in situations where movements in the swap market are imperfectly correlated with movements in the government bond market. In particular, as discussed above, the swap spread itself cannot, unlike the benchmark pricing instrument, be hedged and this intrinsically precludes an efficient hedging strategy.

- Reinvestment and funding assumptions: an inherent problem in the hedging technology developed is that the hedge will usually generate a cash profit or loss at the time the hedge is unwound. This profit or loss must then be amortised over the full life of the swap reflecting either recovery of the loss or subsidy to a deficit on matched swap payments. This requires assumptions on reinvestment rates and funding rates which are inherently subjective and, in particular, as they are forward looking, may, in actuality, not be realised thereby lowering hedge efficiency.

Although swap pricing is driven by the basic arbitrage in the market and also by supply and demand factors, the change in the market from matched counterparty transactions to a market driven by swap market makers, creates the need to have greater interaction between hedging costs and the pricing on the swap.

However, within most institutions uncertainty prevails with regard to the adequacy of returns, and minimum risk return criteria are far from clear. In this regard, it is increasingly evident that swap pricing reflects some of the risks and costs of swap portfolio management. The swap market maker has no other option but to seek compensation for the costs and risks assumed from entering into transactions on an unmatched basis. The costs of swap marketmaking, being reasonably deterministic, can be more or less determined, although, the risks of swap marketmaking are less easily captured.

Risk control

The essential process of management of the hedge swap portfolio includes certain risk control measures. This usually takes the form of daily revaluations of both the swap and the hedge portfolio with the total risk being sought to be controlled by established limit systems. In this regard, the swap hedging system is part of most institutions' formal risk control and risk limit allocation and administration processes allowing the financial risk of such transactions to be estimated and managed.

Choice of hedging instrument

In choosing hedging instruments, the principal consideration is to seek a security or derivative which has a relatively high correlation as between the hedge instrument and the benchmark swap pricing instrument to eliminate, as far as possible, hedging or basis risk.

The basic choices of hedging instruments are as follows:

- cash market instruments, usually physical securities such as government bonds or floating rate securities;
- financial futures on the relevant security.

The two instruments have different characteristics, including:

- Balance sheet impact: use of cash market instruments is usually reflected directly on the balance sheet. In contrast, futures contracts are usually off-balance sheet.
- Carry cost: in the case of futures contracts, the carry cost is built into the actual futures price, with the discount or premium relative to the spot cash security price reflecting the positive or negative carry. In the case of a physical security, the carry cost will usually reflect the difference between the coupon accrual on the security and the interest cost of funding the position which will result in actual cash surpluses or deficits.
- Institutional considerations and flexibility: the greater institutional flexibility of futures markets which in particular allow short selling may be relevant.
- Liquidity considerations: the differential liquidity as between the physical and futures markets may dictate one or other would be preferred.
- Hedge structuring: in practice, a hedge involving both physical securities as well as futures would necessitate hedge structuring to match out the relative volatilities of the swap and the hedging instrument.
- Lack of earnings and accrual: the fact that there is no interest accrual or earning on a futures position, other than effective change in carry cost, can be a disadvantage relative to using actual physical securities.

In practice, the swap market tends to favour the use of physical securities vis-à-vis futures in hedging open swap position (with the exceptions outlined below). This reflects concern over the basis risk incurred in using futures to hedge swap positions as well as the rollover risk in using futures dictated by the need to closeout a futures contract if the swap is not closed out prior to the futures settlement date with its potential cash flow impact and the risk in maintaining hedge efficiency at the point of rollover. However, futures are sometimes used to hedge swap positions, particularly in circumstances where it is difficult to go short in the physical market.

There are in effect different segments of the swap market and the choice of hedging instrument differs significantly as between the segments. The swap market, in US$ and A$, for example, can be separated into two very different segments:

- short-term interest rate swaps, usually of up to two to three years in maturity;
- long-term interest rate swaps, usually in excess of two to three years in maturity.

The short-term swaps are traditionally hedged using strips of futures. This entails the purchase or sale of a series of futures contracts to hedge the swap position. The futures trades are subsequently reversed where a matching swap counterparty is located. However, in some cases, the swap position may be left open for the full maturity of the trade with the futures positions being settled to coincide with interest settlement dates on the interest rate swap. In the US$ market, the futures contract utilised is usually the Eurodollar futures contract. In the A$ market, the 90 day bank bill futures contract is the favoured contract in hedging these types of transactions.

In contrast, swaps of longer maturity are traditionally hedged utilising physical securities.

HEDGING CURRENCY SWAPS

The basic technique of hedging currency swaps is similar to that utilised with interest rate swaps. The major difference lies in the fact that two interest rates and the currency exchange rate must theoretically be hedged on open currency swap positions.

The basic hedging concepts can be illustrated by identifying a number of common swap transactions and their analogous cash market positions in the relevant currencies:

- Receiving fixed rate A$ and paying floating rate US$ is equivalent to being long $A bonds and short US$ floating rate bonds. This type of position can be hedged by reversing the cash market positions, that is, by shorting A$ fixed rate bonds and investing the proceeds in US$ floating rate bonds. The relevant amounts in each currency are determined by the total notional principal amount of the swap and the spot currency rates as between the US$ and A$.

- Paying fixed A$ rates and receiving US$ floating rate is equivalent to being short A$ bonds and long US$ floating rate bonds which is hedged by buying fixed rate A$ bonds and funding the position by selling US$ floating rate bonds.

The hedging of a cross-currency floating-to-floating swap is similar with floating rate securities in both markets being bought and sold to hedge the currency risk positions booked.

The major differences in hedging currency swaps arise from the difficulty in hedging interest rates in both currencies. While the currency fluctuations can be hedged by simply going long and short the appropriate currencies, hedging of the interest rate levels as between the two currencies can be difficult and/or expensive depending on the efficiency and liquidity of the relevant securities markets.

The high cost of hedging and the fact that the hedging instruments provide poor surrogate cover has led to some currency swap market makers covering only the currency risk by taking open positions on the interest rate differential as between the two currencies. Hedging of the floating rate flows on a cross-currency swap is also relatively approximate in practice. For example, the long or short positions in the currencies are basically taken on a short-term, usually overnight, basis with the funding and/or investment in the relevant currency being rolled each day until the position is closed out. This means that while the spot exposure on the currency is largely covered, there is still exposure in the changes in the first period floating rate interest set which must be separately managed, for example, by utilising financial futures in the relevant short-term interest rates.

The exposure to currency rate fluctuations inherently creates greater risk from mismatches than in corresponding interest rate swaps. Cash flow surpluses or deficits arising from these mismatches, for example, as a result of margins above or below the relevant index can create interest rate and/or currency exposure which can lead to significant economic losses within the swap portfolio if not properly matched.

The existence of these difficulties means that there are fewer currency swap market makers than interest rate swap market makers. It also means that the bid/offer spread in currency swap transactions is significantly greater to cover the added costs and risks of running currency swap portfolios. The absence of consistent relationships between currency swap rates and the relevant government bond rates means booking open currency swap positions requiring more complex exposure management techniques making the currency swap market more related to the LTFX market and less towards the classic arbitrage model of the interest rate swap market.

Exhibit 27.3 sets out an example of hedging a currency swap.

Exhibit 27.3
Example of Currency Swap Hedge

Assume ABC bank (ABC) enters into the swap described in *Exhibit 8.8* on 8/3/X6.

Under the terms of the swap therefore:

- At commencement (assuming a spot exchange rate of US$0.70/A$1.00), ABC will receive issue proceeds of A$49.50m from swap counterparty; in return, ABC will pay US$34.65m. ABC will also pay US$0.35m being reimbursement of fees of 1.00% or A$0.5m.

- Over the life of the swap:
  —every six months, ABC will receive six month LIBOR less 56bps upon US$35m;
  —every year on the coupon payment date, ABC will pay a payment of A$7m representing 14.00% on A$50m.

- At maturity, ABC will pay its counterparty A$50m to make the principal repayment to the bondholders; ABC will receive US$35m from the swap counterparty.

Assume that the swap is priced off the 13.00% 8/Y1 bond and ABC is quoting B+60/B+80 versus six month LIBOR. The current bond yield is 14.00% pa (S/A) and, therefore, the corresponding all-in swap rate is 14.60%/14.80% pa (S/A). The specific swap pricing reflects the adjustments described in more detail in *Exhibit 8.8*.

Also assume: A$ short-term rates are 16.00% pa; US$ interest rates are 7.00% pa for overnight; six month US$ LIBOR is 8.00% pa (S/A); and US$ five year rates are 10.00% pa (S/A).

The swap is initially hedged by buying the 13.00% 8/Y1 bond and borrowing US$ on an overnight basis.

The specific details of the hedge are as follows:

- ABC buys A$47.214m face value of the 13.00% 8/Y1[1] on the following terms:

Amount:	A$47.214m
YTM:	14.00% pa
Price:	96.255 or A$45.446m
Accrued interest:	0.754 or A$0.356m
Total price:	A$45.802m

- ABC borrows US$35m on an overnight basis.

Exhibit 27.3—continued

- In an overall cash flow basis, ABC's position is:

  A$

Receipts from swap exchange:	+A$49.500m
Payment for bond:	−A$45.802m
Net:	+A$ 3.698m

  This balance is invested in the overnight cash market.

  US$

US$ borrowing:	+US$35.0m
Payment under swap exchange:	−US$35.0m
Net:	—

As a separate matter, the sub-LIBOR margin has to be hedged. This hedge is separate from the pricing adjustment described in *Exhibit 8.8* although it follows the same logic. This hedge operates as follows:

- ABC has an A$ surplus of 68bps pa or A$0.34m annually and a corresponding US$0.098m shortfall semi-annually being 56 bps on US$35m.
- ABC therefore borrows the present value at 15.25% pa (A) of the A$ surplus that is A$1.133m.
- This A$ borrowing is exchanged in the spot market or US$0.793m (at US$0.70/A$1.00) and the US$ are invested at an average rate of 8.00% pa (S/A).
- Every six months, the US$ investment matures to produce a cash flow of US$0.098m which offsets the US$ shortfall under the swap structure.
- Every year, annually the A$ surplus is allocated to reducing the A$ borrowing incurred.

Under this structure, the A$ borrowing and the US$ investment declines over the life of the transaction. Please note in practice, precise borrowing and lending transaction may not be executed to hedge the margin exposure with the exposure being absorbed into the institution's overall treasury activities.

The open, albeit hedged, swap position is closed off on 15/3/X6 with ABC receiving fixed A$ versus six month LIBOR at the original spread of B + 80. The precise closeout terms are:

Amount:	A$50m
Maturity:	8/3/Y1 (with a short first interest period)
Swap fixed rate:	14.00% pa (S/A) or 14.49% pa (A) based on B + 80 where B = 13.20% pa.

As at 15/3/X6, the spot exchange rate has moved to US$0.6940/A$1.00 while six month LIBOR has remained unchanged at 8.00% pa.

Under the terms of the closeout swap:

- On 15/3/X6, ABC will pay A$50m and receive US$34.7m.
- Over the life of the swap:
  —every six months, ABC will pay six month LIBOR on US$34.7m.
  —every year, on 8/3/X7 through to 8/3/Y1, ABC will receive the equivalent of 14.49% pa on A$50m.
- On 8/3/Y1, the initial exchange will be reversed.

As the closeout swap is entered into, ABC will unwind its hedges as follows:

- ABC sells its A$47.214m face value of the 13.00% 8/Y1 on the following terms:

Amount:	A$47.214m
YTM:	13.20% pa
Price:	99.215 or A$46.844m
Accrued interest:	1.006 or A$0.475m
Total price:	$47.318m

- ABC repays its US$35m borrowing with interest.

Exhibit 27.3—continued

- ABC's overall cash position is:

A$

Payment under closeout swap:	−A$50.000m
Sale of bond:	+A$47.318m
Proceeds of maturing cash surplus:[2]	+A$ 3.709m
Net:	+A$ 1.027m

US$

Receipts from swap exchange:	+US$34.70 m
Repayment of US$ borrowing:[3]	−US$35.047m
Net:	−US$ 0.347m

- At current exchange rates, this creates a cash surplus of A$0.527m after offsetting the A$0.500m shortfall (US$0.347m at US$0.6940/A$1.00).

The actual swap after that will be as follows:

Fixed rate A$ side

On first settlement date (on 8/3/X7)	A$m
Fixed amount received:[4]	+7.106
Fixed amount paid:[5]	−7.000
Repayment of A$ borrowing:[7]	−0.340
Net:	−0.234

On subsequent settlement dates	
Fixed amount received:[6]	+7.245
Fixed amount paid:[5]	−7.000
Repayment of A$ borrowing:[7]	−0.340
Net:	−0.095

Floating rate US$ side

On first settlement date (on 8/9/X6)	US$m
Floating amount received:[8]	+1.412
Floating amount paid:[9]	−1.346
Maturing US$ investment:[10]	+0.098
Net:	−0.164

On subsequent settlement dates	
Floating amount received:	+(LIBOR × US$35m) − $0.098m
Floating amount paid:	−(LIBOR × US$34.7m)
Maturing US$ investment:[10]	−$0.098m
Net:	+ (LIBOR × US$0.30m)

The transaction overall produces the following cash flows:

- A hedge profit of A$0.527m.
- A net difference on the fixed A$ payments of:
  - −A$0.234m on the first settlement;
  - −A$0.095m on subsequent settlements.
- A net difference on the floating rate US$ payment of:
  - +US$0.164m on the first settlement;
  - +US$0.012m on subsequent settlements (assuming LIBOR of 8.00% pa).

The overall transaction profit can be determined as follows:

- Discount back the A$ loss at the appropriate rate, say 15.25% pa (A), giving a current value of approximately A$0.438m.

Exhibit 27.3—continued

- Discount each of the US$ profits at the appropriate rate say 8.00% pa (S/A), giving a current value of approximately US$0.244m or, at US$0.6940/A$1.00, A$0.351m.

The total profit is therefore A$0.440m which amortised (at the bond rate) yields a profit margin of approx 0.25% pa, slightly different from the original bid/offer spread.

Notes:

1. The hedge amount is calculated as:

$$N = \frac{(A_1 - A_2) \times FV}{(B_1 - B_2) \times FV} = \frac{(97.351 - 95.636) \times \$50m}{(97.923 - 96.107) \times \$50m} = 0.944$$

where N = hedge ratio
A_1 = price of 13.00% bond maturing 8/3/X1 at 13.75% pa = 97.351
A_2 = price of 13.00% bond maturing 8/3/X1 at 14.25% pa = 95.636
B_1 = price of 13.00% bond maturing 15/8/X1 at 14.10% pa = 97.923
B_2 = price of 13.00% bond maturing 15/8/X1 at 14.60% pa = 96.107

2. A$3.698m (principal) + A$0.011m (interest @ 16.00% for seven days).
3. US$35m (principal) + US$0.047m (interest @ 7.00% for seven days).
4. 14.49% on A$50m for 358 days, that is, 15/3/X6 to 8/3/X7.
5. 14.00% on A$50m for 365 days, that is, 8/3/X6 to 8/3/X7.
6. 14.49% on A$50m for 365 days.
7. Repayment of A$0.340m pa on borrowing to hedge sub-LIBOR margins.
8. 8.00% pa on US$35m for 184 days, that is, 8/3/X6 to 8/9/X6.
9. 8.00% pa on US$34.7m for 177 days, that is, 15/3/X6 to 8/9/X6.
10. Maturing US$ investment to hedge sub-LIBOR margin.

HEDGING LTFX

The risk entailed in LTFX transactions is usually managed in one of two ways:

- as fixed-to-fixed zero coupon currency swaps;
- as outright forward contracts.

As discussed previously, LTFX contracts are identical to zero coupon fixed-to-fixed currency swaps. Consequently, one approach to pricing and managing the risks inherent in booking an open LTFX position is to incorporate these transactions into the overall cross currency swap portfolio. In this regard, LTFX contracts can be incorporated very readily in swap portfolios operated on a portfolio basis as one period single cash flows.

The structuring of an LTFX hedge is complex. The currency swap structure, as it entails an exchange of principal at both the beginning and end of the swap at the current swap rate at the outset of the transaction, creates a series of cash flows in which the interest differentials between the two currencies are spread over the life of the swap as differentials in the value of the interest flows being exchanged. These interest flows can be characterised as a series of LTFX contracts with implied forward currency exchange rates. This allows the currency swap to be divided into a series of forward-to-forward contracts. By treating each settlement separately, a number of LTFX contracts can be created by fixing the foreign currency cash flows in one of the swap currencies for an equivalent amount of the other currency calculated at the current LTFX rate. This type of structure creates either a funding requirement or alternatively creates reinvestment risks for the intermediary as illustrated in *Exhibit 27.4*.

Exhibit 27.4

Currency Swap versus LTFX Trade

Assume the following market scenario:

Currency and interest rate swap market

A standard five year A$ fixed and US$ floating currency swap is quoted at 14.75/14.55% pa (A) versus six month LIBOR.

The US$ interest rate swap market is showing prices of 7.70/7.65% pa (A) versus six month LIBOR.

LTFX market

The A$ and US$ LTFX market is showing the following prices:

Spot forward	US$ per A$1.00
	0.70
1 year	0.6412
2 year	0.6018
3 year	0.5649
4 year	0.5326
5 year	0.5067

Under these circumstances, A bank (A) enters into the following two swaps:

- A$10m currency swap whereby A is to pay A$ fixed at 14.75% pa (A) versus receipt of six month LIBOR.
- US$7.0m interest rate swap whereby A is to receive US$ fixed at 7.65% pa versus payment of six month LIBOR.

The two swaps produce the following net cash flows:

Year	US$m	A$m
1	0.5355	− 1.475
2	0.5355	− 1.475
3	0.5355	− 1.475
4	0.5355	− 1.475
5	7.5355	−11.475

The six month US$ LIBOR flows net out.

The A$ flows are now covered using the LTFX market:

Year	Exchange rate	A$m purchased	US$m
1	0.6412	1.475	0.9458
2	0.6018	1.475	0.8877
3	0.5649	1.475	0.8332
4	0.5326	1.475	0.7856
5	0.5067	11.475	5.8144

This produces the following net US$ position:

Year	Swap flow	LTFX flow	Net US$ position
1	0.5355	−0.9458	−0.4103
2	0.5355	−0.8877	−0.3522
3	0.5355	−0.8332	−0.2977
4	0.5355	−0.7856	−0.2501
5	7.5355	−5.8144	+1.7211

The net cash flow position shows a surplus of US$0.4108m. Assuming a US$ cost of funding the US$ deficit of 7.50% pa, the transaction yield is net present value of US$0.0855m. As long as the funding cost is under 10.37% pa, the trade is profitable to A.

As mentioned previously, almost all currency swaps are based on a fixed rate in the currency against a floating rate in US$. The first step is, therefore, to combine a typical currency swap with an interest rate swap in US$ which results in known flows in both US$ and the relevant currency.

The difficult problem is to evaluate properly the resulting net US$ position, since its value is highly dependent on funding rates for the shortfall in the first four years, which will be offset by the surplus of US$1.2m in year five. This is a matter for the individual bank treasury.

In the example in *Exhibit 27.4*, the net US$ position implies a break-even reinvestment rate of 10.37% pa. If the intermediary expects the reinvestment rates to be lower than this level or alternatively can lock in all or part of the funding rate risk through forward interest rate agreements, it can create a profitable arbitrage by essentially creating a vector of LTFX contracts at margins away from interest rate parity.

The alternative hedging technology for LTFX entails treating the LTFX contract in a manner akin to normal foreign exchange outright forward-to-forward transactions. This approach, until recently, entailed LTFX trades beyond one year to be perfectly matched against a counterparty. The transactions were not usually executed until both counterparties were in position although the bank usually intermediated the transaction. A number of major commercial banks now routinely transact LTFX trades without having a counterparty. In these circumstances, the currency exposure is usually hedged against positions in the swap currency with the interest rate risk being left unhedged on the basis that the forward points, reflecting the interest rate differential between the two currencies, will remain relatively stable. Where LTFX trades are hedged in this way, the dealing spread is structured to protect against minor movements in interest rate differentials and consequently the forward points.

A variation on this technique is to utilise forwards mismatched as to maturity to hedge LTFX positions. Utilising this technique, the intermediary may not match the offsetting LTFX contract as to the cash flow maturities. For example, a bank may sell A$ forward for value in five years' time and purchase A$ forward for value in one year's time. The mismatch in value dates represents a gap which is managed within gap position limits until a counterparty can be found or the transaction squared in a different way. These gap mismatches in maturity are managed through futures and options contracts or through the institution's swap portfolio.

SWAP PORTFOLIO MANAGEMENT

There are basically two general approaches to swap portfolio management:

- a hedging approach, entailing individual hedges for each swap transaction undertaken;
- a portfolio approach, based on the practice of hedging entire swap portfolios using duration techniques.

Hedging approach

The hedging approach usually entails the following steps:

- When a swap position is booked, the corresponding hedge is established.
- Once a matching swap is arranged, the hedge is unwound by reversing the original hedge consisting of securities or futures to coincide with the entry into the matching swap.

The hedging approach requires the original swap to be matched relatively closely by the offsetting swap in terms of maturity, interest rate levels (adjusted for hedge profit and losses) as well as notional principal amounts. In essence, a five year swap is matched with another five year swap. The hedging approach is predicated on a par yield valuation methodology which assumes a constant stream of interest payments that creates a single discount rate that can be applied to the whole cash flow. It is most effective at matching up transactions with similar, preferably identical, yields, maturities and notional principals.

The basic advantage of this technique is that it is relatively riskless. Individual swaps can be identified and profitability can be determined for each transaction as basically the swap cash flows and the hedge flows which are capable of being determined objectively. The main disadvantage with the hedging approach is that it is relatively inflexible. For example, it is difficult to book non-generic swaps, that is, swaps with cash flow profiles significantly different from normal swaps, within the hedging framework.

The basic hedging approach is particularly relevant and useful in the context of transactions which are booked by swap market makers on an assignment basis. Under these types of transactions, the positioning intermediary would commit to one part of a swap on an assignment basis with the intention of assigning the swap to the eventual counterparty when this counterparty was located. In the interim pre-closeout period, the intermediary would maintain an individual hedge which would be unwound at the time of assignment. Consequently, the hedging approach is likely to continue to exist and find favour with institutions who prefer to operate on an assignment basis.

The examples used so far in this chapter are predicated on the hedging approach.

Portfolio approach

The portfolio approach to swaps portfolio management entails hedging the entire swap portfolio utilising duration techniques. A brief explanation of duration as it applies to swap hedging technology is set out in the Appendix to this chapter.

The portfolio approach models the existing portfolio of swaps by aggregating the individual fixed and floating rate cash flows and calculating the net present value and duration of the fixed portfolio and duration reset date and present value of the floating portfolio. Current swap market yields are then used to discount the cash flows. The net present value difference is then hedged. As new positions are added, the duration of the portfolio is recalculated with appropriate adjustments to the hedge.

An extension of this technique is to measure the swap portfolio interest rate exposure and currency exposure and offset these exposures against predetermined institutional asset or liability mismatches thereby allowing the integration of the swap portfolio into the overall asset and liability structure of the institution. There are a number of variations on this basic methodology utilised by individual organisations.

The basic impetus to implement the portfolio approach came from the increasing need for structuring flexibility as swap market makers sought to accommodate the increased demand for non-generic swap structures.

The portfolio approach, utilising duration concepts, can be based on either par or coupon yields or zero coupon interest rates.

Par yield structures implicitly assume that all coupons or intermediate cash flows are reinvested *at the relevant yield rate.* As reinvestment rates can only be verified ex post, the final maturity value of a par yield coupon bearing investment or liability is only known with certainty at maturity. In contrast, zero coupon rates as they are pure discount interest rates for securities with *no* intermediate coupons, do not incur any reinvestment risk.

Unlike the hedging approach which can only utilise par yield valuation techniques, the portfolio approach is increasingly predicated on utilising zero coupon rates to value swap cash flows. The basic concept is to regard a swap as no more than a series of forward cash flows. Each swap cash flow is treated as a zero coupon cash flow which is discounted back to present value using the interest rate appropriate for the relevant maturity. In this way, each cash flow is hedged, based on its present value, utilising an interest rate relevant to that cash flow rather than one discount rate for the whole stream of cash flows under the par yield approach.

An example of a portfolio or duration based swap hedge is set out in *Exhibit 27.5.*

The portfolio approach gives the swap market maker flexibility in taking on non-generic swap structures. This is because the portfolio approach focuses on a set of *individual* cash flows, rather than on a *stream* of cash flows which means that each new cash flow booked in the swap portfolio can be aggregated with other cash flows and the residual risk then managed. This means that the swap market maker is not concerned about matching up equal, but opposite, partners on both sides of the swap transaction thereby allowing it to incur greater mismatches.

The advantage of added flexibility must be weighed against the fact that the profitability of individual transactions under a portfolio approach is considerably more difficult to establish. Profitability can only be meaningfully calculated on the basis of overall portfolio performance rather than for individual components of the portfolio.

An important point about the portfolio approach is that it tends to show a significantly different perspective of risk and profitability relative to that measured by the normal financial accounting process for the portfolio. An advantage in this regard is that it enables the sensitivity of the portfolio to be tested to changes in pricing and portfolio structure. Another important advantage is that assumptions about reinvestment rates are not required under the portfolio approach as the discount rates used for present valuing of all cash flows are based on spot rates for single period cash flows, that is, the yield on a zero coupon bond, instead of on par yield which implicitly assumes reinvestment at the same rate over the full term.

Exhibit 27.5

Example of Duration Based Swap Hedge

The equivalent duration based hedges for the two examples set out in *Exhibit 27.1* and *Exhibit 27.2* are as follows:

Example	Interest rate (% pa)	Modified duration product	Three year equivalent (A$)
ABC pays	15.00	125,463,000	50.38
ABC receives	14.85	125,176,000	50.26
ABC receives	15.20	125,846,000	50.53
ABC pays	14.65	125,793,000	50.11
		119,818,000	46.96

The modified duration products are based on:

• The following zero swap curve.

Tenor (years)	Swap yield curve (% pa)	Zero or spot curve (% pa)	Forward rates (% pa)
0.00	—	—	15.739
0.25	15.375	16.375	15.508
0.50	16.250	16.250	15.277
0.75	16.125	16.125	15.008
1.00	16.000	15.990	14.642
1.50	15.750	15.723	14.121
2.00	15.500	15.450	14.254
2.50	15.375	15.315	13.972
3.00	15.250	15.174	14.697

• The following zero bond curve for the 13.00% 11/X9 maturity, face value A$50.00m.

Tenor (years)	Swap yield curve (% pa)	Zero or spot curve (% pa)	Forward rates (% pa)
0.00	—	—	16.085
0.25	16.750	16.750	15.624
0.50	16.500	16.500	15.161
0.75	16.250	16.250	14.624
1.00	16.000	15.980	13.893
1.50	15.500	15.448	12.857
2.00	15.000	14.904	12.723
2.50	14.675	14.549	12.004
3.00	14.350	14.185	13.859

The hedge ratios implied would be as follows:

Example	Interest rate (% pa)	Hedges
ABC pays	15.00	Buy A$53.64 of 13.00% 11/X9
ABC receives	14.85	Sell A$53.51 of 13.00% 11/X9
ABC receives	15.20	Sell A$53.80 of 13.00% 11/X9
ABC pays	14.65	Buy A$53.35 of 13.00% 11/X9

Please note that as the duration of the bonds and the swaps have been determined utilising two different sets of yields—the *bond* and *swap* yield curve respectively—the efficiency of the hedge, as reflected in the offsetting price change relative to rate movements, will be satisfactory if the relationship between the two, that is the swap spreads, do not change.

Note: The modified duration and hedge ratios have been created with the help of Citibank Limited.

Appendix to Chapter 27

Duration and Swap Hedging Technology

CONCEPT OF DURATION

Duration

While term to maturity is widely utilised as a measure of the length or maturity of securities, it is a highly deficient measure in that it only indicates when the final payment falls due ignoring the time pattern of any payment received in the intermediate time span preceding the final payment. This deficiency of the concept of term to maturity can be overcome utilising the duration measure. Duration, as proposed in 1938 by Frederick R. Macaulay, is the weighted average of the times in the future when interest and principal payments are to be received. Mathematically, duration can be measured as follows:

$$D = \frac{\sum\limits_{t=1}^{n} \dfrac{C_t(t)}{(1+r)^t}}{\sum\limits_{t=1}^{n} \dfrac{C_t}{(1+r)^t}}$$

where C_t = interest and/or principal payments at time t

t = length of time to the interest and/or principal payments

n = length of time to final maturity

r = yield to maturity

For example, assume a four year bond with an 8.00% coupon rate and yielding 10.00% pa to maturity. Assume also that interest payments are received at the end of each of the four years and that the principal payment is received at the end of the fourth year. The duration of the bond would be:[1]

$$D = \frac{\dfrac{\$80(1)}{(1.10)} + \dfrac{\$80(2)}{(1.10)^2} + \dfrac{\$80(3)}{(1.10)^3} + \dfrac{\$1,080(4)}{(1.10)^4}}{\dfrac{\$80}{(1.10)} + \dfrac{\$80}{(1.10)^2} + \dfrac{\$80}{(1.10)^3} + \dfrac{\$1,080}{(1.10)^4}} = 3.56 \text{ years}$$

---

1. The example is based on Van Horne (1984), pp. 138,139.

If the coupon rate were 4.00%, its duration would be:

$$D = \frac{\dfrac{\$40(1)}{(1.10)} + \dfrac{\$40(2)}{(1.10)^2} + \dfrac{\$40(3)}{(1.10)^3} + \dfrac{\$1,040(4)}{(1.10)^4}}{\dfrac{\$40}{(1.10)} + \dfrac{\$40}{(1.10)^2} + \dfrac{\$40}{(1.10)^3} + \dfrac{\$1,040}{(1.10)^4}} = 3.75 \text{ years}$$

If the coupon rate were zero, however, duration would be:

$$D = \frac{\dfrac{\$1,000(4)}{(1.10)^4}}{\dfrac{\$1,000}{(1.10)^4}} = 4 \text{ years}$$

If there is only a single payment, duration must equal maturity. For bonds with interim coupon payments, however, duration is always less than maturity.

The relationship between duration, maturity and coupon is set out in the following table:

Duration (in years) for bonds yielding 8.00%[2]
(S/A coupons)

Years to maturity	Coupon rate			
	2%	4%	6%	8%
1	0.995	0.990	0.985	0.981
5	4.742	5.533	4.361	4.218
10	8.762	7.986	7.454	7.067
20	14.026	11.966	10.922	10.292
50	14.832	13.466	12.987	12.743
100	13.097	13.029	13.006	12.995
Perpetual	13.000	13.000	13.000	13.000

Typically, there is an inverse relationship between coupon and duration. High coupon bonds effectively have shorter durations than lower (or zero) coupon bonds of the same maturity. As the term to maturity extends, the disparity between duration and maturity for a given coupon also increases. Generally, duration falls when market yields rise because the present value of distant future payments falls relatively more than those closer to the present. As would be expected, when interest rates fall, duration rises for exactly the opposite reason.

Modified duration

Modified duration, which was independently developed by Hicks in 1939 without any reference to Macaulay duration, provides a particularly useful

---

2. The source of the table is Lawrence Fisher and Roman L. Weil (1971).

measure of the interest rate sensitivity or volatility of a given security. Mathematically, modified duration can be expressed as:

$$D_{mod} = \frac{D}{1 + y/f}$$

where D = Macaulay duration

y   = yield to maturity (in decimal form)

f   = frequency of cash flow payments per year

y/f = periodic yield (in decimal form)

For semi-annual coupon bonds, this formula becomes:

$$D_{mod} = \frac{D}{1 + y/2}$$

Modified duration can be used to estimate the percentage price volatility of a fixed income security. The relationship follows:

$$\frac{\Delta P}{P} \times 100 = -D_{mod} \times Y$$

Percentage price change = −modified duration × yield change (in absolute percentage points).

Qualifications to duration: single versus multiple factor duration

Given that duration can be utilised to measure the interest rate risk of a particular asset or liability, it would then appear possible to immunise against that interest rate risk by assuming an offsetting liability or asset with an equivalent duration. However, there are a number of qualifications to the duration measure which must be recognised in any such immunisation practice:

• Duration assumes a flat term structure of interest rates and parallel shifts of the yield curve.

• Regardless of the properties of the particular duration measure utilised, duration is a proxy for price risk only for relatively small changes in interest rates. Therefore, as market interest rates change, the duration of the relevant security also changes requiring adjustment of any offsetting hedge.

In the situation where the first assumption of flat term structure of interest rates and parallel shifts is violated, it would not be usually possible to effect immunisation of interest rate risk by simply holding an offsetting asset or liability with equivalent duration. In response to this qualification to the duration measure, a number of multiple factor duration models have been developed to provide a more complex mapping of the stochastic processes governing interest rate movements. For example, Schaefer (1984), has proposed a multi-factor duration model where duration is a measure of two factors, namely, the long-term interest rate and the short-term interest rate. This approach implicitly seeks to model changes in the yield curve shape and the resultant effect on the duration of the relevant security.

The difference between a single factor model and a two factor model is set out below:

Single factor model—level shift only

Movement in all intermediate and short rates = A × Movement in Long Rates + Error Term

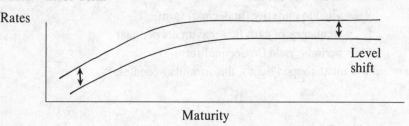

Two factor model—shift level + (yield curve change)

Movement in all intermediate and short rates = A × Movement in Long Rates + B × Movement in Spread + Error Term

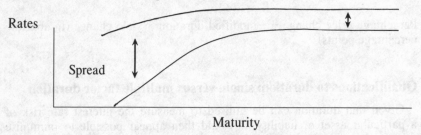

DURATION AND THE SPOT RATE YIELD CURVE

It is clearly feasible in theory to calculate duration utilising either normal conventional par or coupon yields or spot interest rates for pure discount securities. For example, the original Macaulay formulation rather than estimate interest rates for each future period and use them to discount the security payments to present value, for reasons of computational convenience, uses yield to maturity as the discount rate throughout. However, it is not reasonable to assume that yields to maturity on different assets or liabilities will always change by the same amount given that yields to maturity are complex averages of the underlying spot rates or zero coupon yields. Consequently, in general a given shift in the spot rate curve will result in the yields to maturity on different assets changing by different amounts.

To understand the interaction between duration and the spot rate yield curve, it is necessary to define the following terms:

- Spot rate which is the rate of exchange between a cash flow now and a cash flow at a *single date in the future*, that is, the yield on a pure discount bond or zero coupon security.

- Coupon or par yield to maturity which is the standard internal rate of return formula which discounts *all payments* on a *coupon* bond at the same rate.

The difference between the two interest rates lies in the fact that actual realised returns only equal the normal redemption par yield to maturity if reinvestment rates on intermediate cash flows, typically the coupon, are actually equal to the redemption yield. In practice, reinvestment rates on coupon cash flows will rarely equal the redemption yield as forward rates (see Chapter 10) are the only true measure of the reinvestment rates, and even then, the forward rates implicit in the yield curve at any point in time do not guarantee that these reinvestment rates are *actually achieved*. In contrast, determining present values using spot rates, which are implicit in normal par redemption yields, do not involve any assumptions as to the reinvestment rate as no intermediate cash flows are involved.

The actual computation of the spot rate yield curve requires some explanation. In theory, for each future payment of a coupon security, there exists a spot rate that discounts that payment to its present value. These rates constitute the "spot rate yield curve", points along which represent the yield to maturity of a zero coupon bond for the appropriate maturity rate. It is possible to estimate the spot rate curve from the existing par bond yield curve. This basically entails calculating equilibrium spot rates which value each component of the cash flow of a coupon security in an internally consistent fashion, that is, so that all par bonds would have the same value as the sum of their cash flow components.

The table below shows the simple calculation of a spot rate.[3] Given that a one year par bond has a coupon (and yield to maturity of 10.00%, by discounting each coupon and the corpus at 10.00%, a total price of $1m is derived. However, if the six month bill has a yield of 5.00% (not 10.00%) and the first coupon is discounted accordingly at 5.00%, the 12 month payments must be discounted at a rate higher than the yield to maturity (10.128% in this case) to maintain the equilibrium price of $1m. In a similar fashion, a break-even spot rate for each maturity can be calculated and a theoretical spot rate curve derived. However, in practice, estimating spot rates from actual securities is more complex.

Break-even spot rates (10.00%, 12 month Bond @ 100)

Positive Yield Curve

Years	Payment	Present Value @ 10%	Spot rate	Present value @ spot rates	Difference
0.5	$50,000	$47,619	5.000%	$48,780	$1,161
1.0	$50,000	$45,351	10.128*	$45,296	−55
1.0	$1,000,000	$907,030	10.128*	$905,924	−1,106
	$1,000,000	$1,000,000		$1,000,000	0

* 12 month break-even spot rate (10.128%).

As an alternative method, it is possible to determine the spot rate curve by using the forward rates implicit in the current yield curve and assuming compounding of intermediate cash flows at the implicit forward rates.

3. The example is taken from Klaffsky (1982).

Duration measures as currently applied to swap hedging techniques utilise the relevant spot rate yield curve to discount back the cash flows to arrive at overall portfolio duration.

DURATION AND SWAP HEDGING

The interest rate risk on the fixed rate component of the swap can be measured utilising duration. The duration of the fixed rate on a swap provides a measure of price volatility with respect to interest rate movements. It is now almost customary to hedge open interest rate or currency swap positions, at least the interest rate risk component, utilising duration as a measure of sensitivity of a position to movements in interest rates. Under this strategy, physical securities or futures contracts are held to offset potential changes in value on the swap position the level of hedge being determined by the duration factor. The basic duration hedging strategy is as follows:

Change in PV of Hedging Portfolio = −Change in PV of Swap Portfolio

Single factor model

| Book value
×
adjusted duration | Must be equal for both portfolios |

Two factor model

Book value × adjusted (long-term) duration	
and	Must be simultaneously equal for both portfolios
Book value × adjusted (short-term) duration	

The concept of duration based swap hedging assumes that cash flows generated by the swaps booked by a financial institution form a portfolio of assets and liabilities which will vary with interest rates and with maturity. The use of duration based hedging seeks to solve the problem of ensuring solvency, irrespective of interest rate movements, by matching the durations of the asset and liability cash flow streams. The underlying assumption is that irrespective of interest rate movements, and despite the fact that the cash flows are not perfectly matched, changes in values in the asset and liability portfolio would substantially offset each other.

The use of duration matching implicitly divides underlying market interest rate movements into two components:

• Systematic movements whereby rates for all maturities move in some statistically determined constant proportion to one or two index rates, such as the long and short interest rates depending on whether single or multi-factor duration measures are utilised.

• Non-systematic movements which is the residual interest rate movement, unexplained by movements in the indexes utilised, and this is assumed to be randomly or normally distributed.

Duration matching only provides a formula to hedge away systematic market movements. Inefficiencies in hedge performance may result from the non-systematic risk component which cannot be effectively hedged under this approach.

Duration matching is utilised in preference to maturity matching because it is usually felt to reduce basis risk and to overcome imperfections in the hedge market, such as unavailability of securities of the appropriate maturity, as well as reducing the actual expense of hedging as, generally, significantly lower levels of hedges will need to be maintained.

The floating rate component of the swap is also capable of being hedged on a duration basis. It is possible to calculate the duration of a floating rate security. As a swap is essentially a combination of a long and short position in a fixed rate instrument and a floating rate instrument, the volatility or interest rate risk component of the total swap can be calculated as the net value of the different price risk of each component. This volatility can then be aggregated with the volatility of the portfolio to derive the total duration of the portfolio including the new swap.

The use of duration matching techniques in swap hedging requires some practical problems to be overcome. For example, to deal with the practical difficulties of matching durations and present values within a large portfolio, it is typically necessary to concentrate all cash flows to certain maturity points within the portfolio. For example, cash flows may be concentrated at monthly intervals over the life of outstanding transactions. Duration of the net cash flow at each allocation point for the portfolio can be then netted out against the present values for the hedge portfolio as a simple additive manipulation.

Although this type of cash flow concentration or allocation to particular maturity point greatly simplifies the management of risk, it is necessary to ensure that it allows sufficient precision of duration matching to eliminate the desired quantum of interest rate risk within the portfolio.

Chapter 28
FRA Portfolio Risk Management Techniques

FRA HEDGING APPROACHES

There are two basic approaches to managing exposures under FRA transactions:

- cash market transactions involving mismatches in borrowing and lending;
- utilising futures transactions.

The risk management approaches closely reflect the pricing methodology for FRAs detailed in Chapter 10.

HEDGING BY UTILISING BORROWING AND LENDING TRANSACTIONS

FRA transactions can be hedged by the intermediary providing the FRA by creating mismatched borrowing and lending transactions on its own balance sheet. For example, an intermediary may provide an FRA to hedge a drawdown on a loan for one of its clients by borrowing for a maturity coinciding with the maturity of the FRA contract but investing for a shorter period, the maturity of the investment coinciding with the commencement date of the FRA. The mismatched investment and borrowing transaction is engineered to cover the risk under the FRA transaction created. In contrast, the intermediary could borrow for a short period and invest for a longer period to create an FRA position for an investor seeking to lock in rates on a future investment.

An example of an FRA hedge utilising borrowing and lending transactions is set out in *Exhibit 28.1*.

This type of hedging technique utilises the intermediary's balance sheet. This type of balance sheet utilisation can be justified where the intermediary would have undertaken the borrowing or lending transaction in any case as part of their general asset liability management activities but merely has restructured either the borrowing or investment decision to encompass the FRA transaction written for its client. However, where the FRA position cannot be engineered as part of its general treasury activities, it can be priced as an arbitrage to create a synthetic borrowing or investment away from implied forward rates earning the institution an arbitrage profit which compensates it for its balance sheet utilisation.

Another alternative may be to offset the risk exposure under an FRA against a mismatch in the institution's overall swap portfolio. For example, where the intermediary is matching a normal, immediate start swap against a deferred or forward swap, it might be possible to characterise the deferral period or delayed start as a string of FRA contracts to effectively match out the risk positions within the swap portfolio.

Exhibit 28.1

FRA Hedge Utilising Borrowing and Lending Transactions

Assume that a bank (B) is approached by a client to quote for and provide an FRA to hedge a loan drawdown for three months commencing in three months' time for an amount of A$10m, that is, B is selling a 3 × 6 FRA.

Current interest rates are:

Three months	11.00/11.20% pa
Six months	11.80/12.00% pa

B would price and hedge its FRA as follows:

- B borrows A$10m for six months at 12.00% pa and lends it for three months at 11.00% pa (note that it lends (borrows) at the market bid (offer) rates).

- B then sells the A$10m 3 × 6 FRA to essentially provide it with a replacement for the investment which matures in three months' time.

- B seeks to earn a spread of 0.25% pa on the FRA, that is, it must earn 12.25% pa over the six months. Therefore, B quotes an FRA rate of 13.51% pa.

After the transaction is executed, at the end of three months, B would need to re-lend the maturing A$10m for three months. The FRA would be settled and the cash payment by or to the client would have the effect of locking in the rate of 13.51% pa. The FRA could also be structured as a physical transaction whereby B actually provided funding for its client at the FRA rate.

If B had been asked to hedge an investment, by buying an FRA, B would have lent A$10m for six months at 11.80% pa and funded the loan for three months at 11.20% pa with the FRA locking in its refinancing cost. Using the same profit margin as above, the FRA rate quoted would be 11.90% pa. Notice the compounding effect of the different bid offer spreads.

HEDGING BY UTILISING FUTURES

Basic concept

FRAs can be hedged by utilising financial futures on short-term interest rates as these futures markets offer a means to hedge the risk of unexpected price changes in that they permit the future purchase or sale of an asset at a price determined today. The basic hedge structure utilising futures entails the intermediary selling futures to hedge itself against the price risk of writing an FRA designed to protect a borrower and, conversely, buying futures to hedge its risk where it books FRAs to protect investment yields.

An example of using futures to hedge FRAs is set out in *Exhibit 28.2*.

Where the structure of the FRA coincides perfectly with the specification of the futures contract and the dates, including the commencement date of the FRA and futures contract, as in the example in *Exhibit 28.2*, the futures contract can be used as a perfect substitute for the FRA and a perfect or, at least, highly efficient hedge can be created. However, in practice, the terms of the FRA will depart significantly from the specifications of the futures contract used to hedge the FRA requiring considerable structuring of the hedging process.

Exhibit 28.2

FRA Hedge Utilising Futures

Assume a borrower approaches a bank (B) seeking to purchase a FRA to hedge an A$ bank bill drawdown for 90 days only, drawing down in early December 19X8. Assume it is *now* mid September and December futures are quoted as:

Sale	Bid	Offer
88.95	88.94	88.95

B will *sell* contracts to hedge its FRA position, so it must look to the opposite party, the buyer, that is, 88.94. A price of 88.94 *plus* a margin of 0.25% pa means a quote of 11.31% to the client.

In early December, the client drawsdown its bills and settles the FRA with B at the agreed yield rate of 11.31% pa. At the same time, B closes out the futures position by buying contracts at or about the same yield that the client can sell the physical securities.

If, in the example, the client was an investor, B would need to *buy* contracts (sellers at 88.95) and *deduct* its margin. The rate would be 10.80% pa.

Structuring the hedging process

Hedging and basis risk

The objective of utilising futures to hedge an FRA position is to construct positions in the futures market which offset the intermediary's position in the FRA such that the dollar price change for a given movement in interest rates will be identical but opposite in direction on the hedge.

However, the efficiency of the hedge will be affected by the changing relationship between the value of the security being hedged and the price at which the corresponding futures contract trades and how this relationship evolves over time. The difference between the cash and futures price is referred to as the "basis". Utilising futures to hedge FRAs essentially entails substituting basis risk for absolute market risk on changes in interest rates.

Utilising futures to hedge FRA positions, therefore, requires considerable structuring of the hedge itself, including:

- adjusting and anticipating basis fluctuations;
- determining the appropriate hedge ratios;
- selecting the appropriate contract and delivery month.

Appropriate hedge management requires determination of possible gains and losses due to basis fluctuation.

The effect of basis changes on the efficiency of the hedge can be viewed as the basis either increasing in value (strengthening) or decreasing in value (weakening). This necessarily means that a short hedger who buys the basis will have a net gain as the basis strengthens (that is, the basis becomes increasingly more positive or less negative), while a long hedger will have a net gain as the basis has weakened (that is, where the basis has become increasingly more negative or less positive).

Where these basis changes occur, the net profit or loss on the futures positions will not exactly offset the gain or loss in the cash position. This will effectively create a cash flow mismatch with resulting economic gains or losses between the settlement on the FRA contract and the settlement on the futures contract. Consequently, intermediaries when they are using futures to hedge FRAs must seek to adjust the hedge for the anticipated changes in basis by slightly over or under hedging.

Hedge ratio determination

The hedge ratio, that is, the number of futures contracts required to hedge the FRA position, must be determined to ensure that the hedge performs as expected. The hedge ratio must be determined to equate the price changes of the FRA and the futures contract which often will not be of the same magnitude because of differences in the contract specifications as between the FRA and the futures contract. The hedge ratio represents the principal face value of the futures contract held relative to the principal face value of the FRA position.

There are a number of techniques for calculating the hedge ratio. These include:

- Volatility matching or the basis point model whereby the hedge is structured to match the change in the dollar value of the FRA to be hedged with the change in the dollar value of the futures contract.

- Regression model whereby a regression relationship between the FRA contract price movements and the futures contract price movements is established on the basis of historical data with the hedge being structured as the value of the futures position that reduces the variability of price changes of the hedged position to the lowest possible level.

- Duration model whereby the number of futures contracts utilised over the life of the hedge are designed to ensure changes in the value of the futures position will offset the changes in the value of the cash position by equating the duration of the FRA and the futures contract.

There are a number of other models for calculating the hedge ratio, each of which has implicit assumptions, and will be appropriate in one or other situation.

In the case of FRAs, basis point equivalency is commonly utilised to make the necessary hedge adjustments. An example of hedge ratio determination using this technique is set out in *Exhibit 28.3*.

Delivery month and contract selection

A critical decision for the intermediary utilising futures to hedge FRAs is to:

- select the contract to be utilised to effect the hedge;
- select the delivery month in which the hedge will be placed.

Selection of the contract is usually based on the correlation between movements in the prices of the relevant futures contract and the price of the FRA. For example, Eurodollar futures will be utilised to hedge LIBOR based FRAs while 90 day bank bill futures contracts will naturally be utilised to hedge A$ FRAs which settle against the 90 day BBR.

Exhibit 28.3

FRA Hedge Ratio Determination

Refer to the situation described in *Exhibit 28.2*. Assume, however, that the borrower wishes to hedge a drawdown for 60 days. Given that the instrument underlying the futures contract is 90 day A\$ BBR, the number of contracts utilised will need to be adjusted as follows:

$$N = \frac{(A_1 - A_2) \times FV_A}{(B_1 - B_2) \times FV_B}$$

where: N = hedge ratio

$\quad\quad A_1$ = the price of the underlying security to be hedged (60 day bank bill) at market yield minus 0.10% pa (11.05 − 0.10 = 10.95% pa)

$\quad\quad A_2$ = the price of the underlying security to be hedged at market yield plus 0.10% (11.15% pa)

$\quad\quad FV_A$ = face value of underlying security to be hedged (A\$10m)

$\quad\quad B_1$ = price of future contract at market yield minus 0.10% (10.95% pa)

$\quad\quad B_2$ = price of future contract at market yield plus 0.10% (11.15% pa)

$\quad\quad FV_B$ = face value of futures contract (A\$0.5m)

In this example:

$$N = \frac{(98.232 - 98.200) \times A\$10m}{(97.371 - 97.324) \times A\$0.5m} = 13.572$$

Therefore, B should utilise approximately 14 contracts to match the respective price volatilities of the two securities.

Note that as a 60 day security is less volatile than a 90 day security, less contracts are utilised than would be suggested by the respective face values (A\$10m/A\$0.5m = 20). If the underlying FRA had a run longer than the underlying future contract, then *more* future contracts than face value securities would be dictated.

The selection of contract month is more problematic. FRAs written to meet client requirements will rarely exactly match the traded futures delivery dates. The selection of the delivery month to be utilised generally depends on the following factors:

- the time horizon over which the hedge is designed to be maintained;
- the liquidity of the particular delivery month, both at the time the position is established and at the time the position must be closed;
- the relative pricing of contracts across delivery months or the basis relationship between contract dates.

A variety of hedging strategies are available in regard to delivery month selection. These range from placing the hedge in the nearest liquid contract month to the relevant FRA to utilising a basket of delivery months and contracts, appropriately weighted, to effect the hedge. Two types of special hedging techniques (stack hedging and structured arbitrage) require special mention.

Stack hedging and structured arbitrage

Stack hedging refers to front loaded hedges where most of the futures positions are concentrated in certain contract months in an attempt to improve overall hedge performance. Front loading seeks to take advantage of the higher available liquidity in the nearby futures contract months. Utilising a stack hedge, an FRA contract starting some time in the future is hedged

---

Exhibit 28.4
Example of Stack Hedge

A company decides to use a stack hedge to hedge 91 day CP issuances for two years. On 6/6/X6, it issues US$250m face value of 91 day CP and establishes a futures hedge which is fully stacked in the front month contract. The initial and subsequent transactions necessary to keep the stack hedge in place are shown below:

16/6/X6   Sell 1708 September 86 Eurodollar contracts (1708 = 7 future CP issuances to be hedged × 244 contracts per CP issuance).

15/9/X6   Close out the September 86 position and sell 1464 (6 × 244) December 86 contracts.

15/12/X6   Close out the December 86 position and sell 1220 (5 × 244) March 87 contracts.

16/3/X7   Close out the March 87 position and sell 976 (4 × 244) June 87 contracts.

15/6/X7   Close out the June 87 position and sell 732 (3 × 244) September 87 contracts.

14/9/X7   Close out the September 87 position and sell 488 (2 × 244) December 87 contracts.

14/12/X7   Close out the December 87 position and sell 244 (1 × 244) March 88 contracts.

Of course, the hedge could be stacked in other futures contract months. For example, the company could have strip hedged the first three CP issuances and stacked the remainder of the hedge in the fourth contract month.

Note: The number of contracts is based on an assumed hedge ratio of 0.9760 and a Eurodollar futures contract with face value of US$1m.

---

by entering into futures contracts which will expire prior to the commencement date of the FRA with the futures position being rolled at each settlement date until the commencement of the FRA.

An example of a stack hedge is set out in *Exhibit 28.4.*

The risk of a stack hedge is that the basis between the months could alter, that is, the yield curve could change its shape such that deferred contract months will either become more expensive or cheaper relative to nearby contracts exposing the stack hedger to altered inter-contract month price spreads when rolling the stack hedge. This can result in a marked decline in hedge efficiency. Some additional aspects of stack hedging are discussed below in the context of strip hedging.

The structured arbitrage option is an alternative to stack hedging where there is little or no trading in a particular futures month, particularly in the more distant months. In this situation, the structured arbitrage trade entails an intermediary taking both sides of the futures transactions and incorporating the side that would usually have been taken by a counterparty into its futures portfolio.

The rationale in such structured arbitrages is that it is always possible to enter into a futures trade at a price but usually, the counterparty will trade, particularly in the more distant lightly traded months, at a price designed to give the other party an arbitrage or a particularly attractive price. Accordingly, the structured arbitrage is predicated on taking that arbitrage internally and rolling out of that arbitrage by either creating a synthetic security or alternatively maintaining the position until such time as it can be liquidated.

Strip hedging

On occasions, the intermediary will be asked to hedge not a single FRA but a series of FRAs commencing at some point in the future involving the rolling of say short securities either from the perspective of a borrower or investor. For example, a borrower may wish to drawdown funding in nine months time and maintain the funding for a period of 12 months involving four rolls, each with a maturity of 90 days. In the extreme, the client could wish to enter into a series of FRAs over a period of two or three years. As will be readily apparent, this type of transaction is similar to an interest rate swap, particularly, the short-term (two years and under) interest rate swaps discussed above.

These types of transactions are hedged utilising a technique known as strip hedging whereby each roll of the FRA is hedged with a series of futures contracts whose settlement dates closely follow the relevant rollover dates of the FRAs.

The strip hedge operates in two phases:

- Initially, a series of futures contracts are bought and sold to hedge the rollovers on the FRAs. In essence, the strip is bought or sold.

- After the hedge is established, where the FRAs are not matched up against counterparties, the hedge must be rolled periodically, usually every 90 days. This involves lifting the futures leg by buying or selling the appropriate futures contract month and settling the corresponding leg of the FRA.

An example of a strip hedging operation is set out in *Exhibit 28.5*.

Exhibit 28.5

Example of Strip Hedge

An investor wants to enter into a series of FRAs, with a bank (B) to lock in investment rates for just under a year through to September X8, drawing down early October in X7. B does not need to hedge the first leg in the futures, as drawdown is today. Instead, the first leg is priced at where either the investor or B can *buy* bank bills on the spot market. The subsequent legs of the strip of FRAs are hedged in the futures market.

Assume the following rates prevail:

70 day physical bank bills, maturing early December	10.60
Buy December futures	11.05
Buy March futures	12.45
Buy June futures	13.30

B now takes a weighted average of the rates and offers the investor one rate for the complete term, that is:

$$\frac{(10.6 \times 70) + (11.05 \times 90) + (12.45 \times 90) + (13.3 \times 90)}{340} = 11.92\% \text{ pa}$$

Deduct B's profit margin (0.25% pa) = 11.67% pa.

At each rollover, fresh bank bills would be purchased by the investor and the FRA contracts closed out. B would simultaneously closeout its futures position with the gain or loss on the futures more than offsetting the FRA settlement amount to provide B with its profit.

As discussed in Chapter 27, many interest rate swaps with maturities of two years or less are hedged in this way utilising a strip of futures contracts.

As will be evident, stack hedges can be viewed as a substitute to strip hedging techniques. For example, instead of purchasing or selling a strip of futures, a stack hedge could be executed with the stack hedge being gradually rolled out as futures contracts expire with the amount of contracts maintained being adjusted as at each settlement date.

Strip hedging has a number of advantages over stack hedging including:

- fewer transactions and therefore lower commission costs;
- more certainty about the final performance of the hedge;
- lower hedge management requirements.

In contrast, a front loaded stack hedge has a number of advantages over a strip hedge including:

- The fact that a stack hedge involves trading in the more liquid contracts may minimise lower transaction costs, as reflected by the lower bid/offer spreads in the more liquid months.

- By maintaining the hedge in the liquid nearby contract months, the hedger has increased flexibility in adjusting the hedge position in response to changing market conditions and corporate objectives.

Chapter 29

Caps Portfolio Risk Management Techniques

HEDGING CAPS: THE ALTERNATIVES

Caps, collars and floors are, as detailed in Chapter 5, essentially a series of options on debt instruments. The exposures incurred in creating these instruments for clients are identical, conceptually, to exposures incurred in writing or granting debt options.

Providers of cap, collar and floor facilities, as writers of options, seek to manage the exposure on options written utilising active hedge management techniques involving cash and/or options markets.

There are basically two alternative types of strategies available in hedging debt options:

* purchasing matching options;
* creating synthetic options (utilising delta or gamma hedging).

PURCHASING DEBT OPTIONS

The only certain way to completely hedge an option is through the purchase of an equivalent option, identical with respect to all relevant terms of exercise price, face value and expiration date. The premium cost of an option purchased as a hedge is roughly equal to that received for an option written. Therefore, if options written are hedged with identical options purchased, the profit will, in principle, be limited to the bid/offer spread between the two.

The supply of options available for utilisation to hedge cap portfolios is limited to:

* exchange traded options;
* options created through capital market transactions.

Exchange traded options may be available to assist cap providers to hedge their portfolio exposures. However, the exchange traded options markets do not, generally, extend beyond two years thereby limiting their role in absorbing the risk assumed by cap providers.

Options created or engineered through capital market transactions are an increasingly important source of supply of options for intermediaries acting as providers of caps. The main source of this type of debt option has been issues of capped FRNs and CDs. The detailed structure of these options created through capital market instruments is discussed in Chapter 17.

Despite the increased supply of debt options with longer maturities, intermediaries acting as principal providers of caps frequently need to resort to synthetic option creation techniques to manage the exposures on their cap portfolios.

SYNTHETIC OPTIONS (DELTA AND GAMMA HEDGING)

One of the most common techniques for managing the risk entailed in cap portfolios is to utilise synthetic option technology to replicate the price characteristic of options on the relevant asset. A synthetic option is created from a portfolio of existing traded instruments which with proper management over time can replicate the return characteristics of an option. This is also referred to as "delta" or "gamma hedging".

A synthetic option, normally a call option, is created by using a portfolio consisting of two instruments:

- the instrument into which the option can be exercised, whether it be a cash market instrument or futures and forwards on the underlying asset; and

- a risk free asset, usually cash or high quality securities.

The key to creating a synthetic call option is to determine the proportion of cash and asset to maintain in the portfolio. This proportion is adjusted through time in a very specific way to replicate the price behaviour of a call option. In practice, such a portfolio can be created and properly managed to give approximately the same premium and outcome as a traded call option on the underlying asset.

The intuition for synthetic options derives from the fact that the price behaviour of a call option is similar to combined positions involving the underlying asset and borrowing. Although the price of a call option and the price of the underlying asset change in the same direction, the effect on the price of the call option of a given change in the asset price, depends on the current price level of the asset. This is because the number of units of the asset held in the replicating portfolio must be sufficient to equate to the slope of the call option price curve at that particular price level or the particular option delta.

Delta is a measure of the sensitivity of the option value to changes in the price of the underlying asset. For example, a call option with a delta of 0.5 will increase in value by A$5 for an A$10 increase in the underlying asset value.

The delta of an option has a value between 0 and 1. A delta of 1 means that the value of the option increases in proportion to the price of the underlying asset: one dollar for every one dollar increase in the value of the underlying asset. A deeply in-the-money option will have a delta close to or equal to 1, since the intrinsic value of the option will increase in proportion close or equal to the increase in the price of the underlying asset, while the time value will become very small. A deeply out-of-the-money option will have a delta close to 0, since it will have no intrinsic value and low time value owing to the small chance that it will become profitable.

Deltas for call options are positive and deltas for put options are negative. Put deltas are negative because put prices move in the opposite direction to the underlying asset price. The underlying asset delta is always 1 with positive 1 indicating a long asset position and negative 1 a short position.

Delta hedging basically operates on the basis that a writer of a call option can cover its price risk by purchasing an amount of the underlying asset in proportion to the delta, for any given price of the underlying instrument.

For example, a call option written on US$1m against A$ with a delta of 0.60%, an at-the-money option, will rise or fall in value by about 0.60% for each 1.00% fall or rise in the value of the US$. Therefore, the option writer can purchase US$0.6m in the forward market and in theory the value of the cash position will move in exactly offsetting fashion to the value of the option written. The US$0.6m in our example is referred to as the equivalent delta position being the delta of the option multiplied by the par value of the option. An option which is hedged by an offsetting cash position according to this approach is said to be delta hedged or delta neutral.

The replicating portfolio must be adjusted as the asset price changes. This will usually entail selling assets as the asset price falls and buying assets as the asset price rises. As the portfolio is never fully invested when the asset price increases, nor fully disinvested when the asset price falls, this process of portfolio adjustment will reduce the initial investment. Theoretically, by the expiration of the call option, the cumulative depreciation should approximately equal the initial theoretical value of the call option.

The concept of synthetic options permits option granters to replicate not only call options, but many other option positions. Using replicating portfolios the granter of options can, where it has created a risk position by writing options, cover these open positions creating synthetic options which hedge the existing exposure.

However, dèlta only holds for very small changes in the asset price. Therefore any movement in the asset price outside a small range leads to diminished hedge efficiency. This change in the asset price exposes the portfolio to what is commonly referred to as gap/jump risk or gamma risk.

Gamma is the change in delta as the underlying asset price changes. As changes in delta produce exposure in a portfolio, the level of gamma can be utilised to quantify the risk of an option portfolio. The gamma of an option is not stationary but changes as the asset price changes. Gamma is highest when the option is at-the-money and lowest when the option is deep in- or out-of-the-money.

The basic problem of delta hedging, therefore, is that while the delta of an option varies substantially through its life, the delta of the cash markets is always fixed. Consequently, in theory, continual rehedging is required to keep the portfolio perfectly delta neutral. This problem is sometimes sought to be averted by a technique known as gamma hedging whereby the intermediary seeks to match the rate at which the deltas themselves vary with changes in interest rates.

The concept of gamma neutral hedging recognises that adjusting the portfolio to delta neutrality after each market move does not give adequate protection to a portfolio. A gamma hedge is a hedge strategy that attempts to reduce the exposure of the portfolio by reducing total portfolio gamma.

A portfolio which is perfectly hedged will have both a zero delta and a zero gamma. The only means of creating a zero gamma position is to match each option with the offsetting position in that option series. Consequently, gamma is sought to be minimised, but never reduced to zero, by changing the composition of the option side of the portfolio. Changing the underlying asset side of the portfolio has no impact on gamma. For example, the gamma impact of selling at-the-money puts can be minimised by buying out-of-the-money puts.

With this background, the notions of delta and gamma neutrality can be stated more simply. A delta neutral option or book of options (at least partially hedged with offsetting positions in the underlying asset) is one whose *value* is unaffected by (small) changes in the price of that underlying asset. A gamma neutral option portfolio is one that *remains delta neutral* as the price of the underlying asset changes (by small amounts).

There are three important characteristics of gamma:

• the shorter the time to expiration the higher the gamma will be;

• at-the-money options have the highest gammas in relation to other options in the same expiration period; and

• gammas vary with volatility, but in a complex way.

Gammas tend to decrease on medium to long-term options (that is, options with 60 days or more to expiration). For short-term options (with 45 days or less to expiration), the gammas of out-of-the-money options increase as volatility increases, but decrease as volatility increases for at-the-money options. These features of the gamma are important considerations for delta hedging management as they address the need for active rehedging of option positions.

A simple example of a synthetic cap portfolio hedge is set out in *Exhibit 29.1*.

Exhibit 29.1

Synthetic Cap Portfolio Hedge

Assume a bank is asked to enter into a cap agreement with a client on 15/2/X3. The bank proposes to write or sell the cap and hedge its position using delta hedging or synthetic option technology.

The cap has the following terms:

Expiration date:	15/9/X3
Interest rate index:	90 day BBR
Cap level:	13.00% pa

The bank must first price the cap as follows:

Expiration date	Amount (A$m)	Cap rate (% pa)	Forward rate (% pa)	Volatility (% pa)	Option premium (% pa)	Option delta
15/9/X3	1.0	13.00	12.25	18	0.35	−0.33

The bank marks up the theoretical price of the cap of A$810.22 (35bps at A$23.15 per basis point at the strike yield level of 13.00% pa) per A$1m and charges the customer A$1,041.75 (or 45bps) per A$ million. The A$231.53 (A$1,041.75—A$810.22) represents profit to the bank while the A$813.13 is reserved for utilisation in hedging the position.

In this case, the customer buys an A$10m cap providing the bank with an initial premium inflow of A$10,417.10.

The bank now proceeds to hedge by selling the 90 day bank bill futures contract with a settlement date of September X3, coinciding closely with the expiration date of the cap.*

---

* The example, for reasons of simplicity, makes a number of assumptions. Futures trades are assumed to be able to be transacted at the forward price. Bid/offer spreads are also ignored. In addition, the problems associated with fractional contracts and commissions are ignored.

Exhibit 29.1—continued

The bank matches the delta of the option, −0.33, by selling futures equivalent to A$3.3m (0.33 × A$10m). This involves selling seven contracts, each with a face value of A$500,000, or a total contract value of A$3,397,380).

The hedge is then adjusted to reflect the changes in the option delta which reflects changes in the key variables affecting the value of the option. In theory, the option hedge should be adjusted continually, however, in this example the hedge is adjusted at six finite intervals as set out in the Table below.

Table

Date	2/3/X3	4/5/X3	12/7/X3	3/8/X3	26/8/X3	7/9/X3
Forward rate (% pa)	12.78	12.62	12.95	12.60	12.20	12.10
Volatility (% pa)	23	23	23	18	18	18
Option premium (% pa)	0.67	0.51	0.47	0.15	0.02	0.00
Delta	−0.46	−0.42	−0.49	−0.31	−0.10	0.00
Opening Hedge portfolio	−A$3.5m @ 12.25% pa	−A$3.5m @ 12.25% pa −A$1.0m @ 12.78% pa	−A$3.5m @ 12.25% pa −A$0.5m @ 12.78% pa	−A$3.5m @ 12.25% pa −A$0.5m @ 12.78% pa −A$1.0m @ 12.95% pa	−A$3.0m @ 12.25% pa	−A$1m @ 12.25% pa
Hedge adjustment	−A$1.0m @ 12.78% pa	+A$0.5m @ 12.62% pa	−A$1.0m @ 12.95% pa	+A$2.0m @ 12.60% pa	+A$2.0m @ 12.20% pa	+A$1m @ 12.10% pa
Closing hedge	−A$3.5m @ 12.27% pa −A$1.0m @ 12.78% pa	−A$3.5m @ 12.25% pa −A$0.5m @ 12.78%pa	−A$3.5m @ 12.25% pa −A$0.5m @ 12.78%pa −A$1.0m @ 12.95% pa	−A$3.0m @ 12.25% pa	−A$1.0m @ 12.25% pa	—
Realised gains (losses)	—	(A$185)	—	(A$614)	(A$232)	(A$349)
Cumulative gains (losses)	—	(A$185)	(A$185)	(A$799)	(A$1031)	(A$1380)

Exhibit 29.1—continued

Notes:

1. Negative (−) signs indicate sold or short futures positions.
2. Figures in brackets indicate losses on the trades.
3. A last in first out rule is used in respect of open futures positions.
4. The data used in the example is artificial.

The Table indicates that as the cap moves closer in-the-money the bank sells additional futures to hedge its position, while buying back the sold contracts as the cap moves further out-of-the-money. The hedge adjustments usually realise losses because the delta matched hedger generally buys contracts after prices rise and sells after prices fall reflecting that delta rises as the underlying price rises causing the hedger to buy futures.

In this example, the accumulated losses on the hedge portfolio total A$1,380 as against a theoretical hedge premium reserve of A$8,131. Differences between the losses on the hedge and the theoretical premium will reflect the impact of the following factors:

- Market jumps which manifest themselves in changes in the desired delta while the level of actual delta remain static. Gamma hedging seeks to correct this over and under hedging problem.

- Changes in volatility which can be hedged using vega matching techniques.

Please note that the above example does not factor in the impact of investment returns and funding costs on cash flows relating to the option and the hedge.

SPECIAL CONSIDERATIONS IN MANAGING THE RISK OF CAP PORTFOLIOS[1]

There are a number of special considerations in managing the risk of cap portfolios.

Caps, collars and floors are usually modelled as a strip of European options on the relevant floating rate index with expiration date corresponding to the settlement frequency and strike prices corresponding to the interest rate cap or floor level under the agreement. Where the cap or floor level is done at a single interest rate, then the distant periods typically are either deep in-the-money or out-of-the-money depending on the shape of the yield curve. This, in certain circumstances, allows the distant periods to be hedged at nearly a one to one hedge ratio or delta with a relatively illiquid long-term instrument, such as a bond, as the low gamma of that section of the commitment should, in theory, require infrequent rebalancing of the hedge. In these circumstances, the shorter term portion of the cap is hedged separately.

This type of approach requires complex modelling techniques which split these types of agreements into various constituent elements which are analysed and hedged separately. The separation of the various elements of these agreements is important as typically each element reflects significant differences in market conditions and/or rate expectations. Consequently, for example, once a cap is decomposed it can be hedged using portfolio hedging techniques such as a strip of delta hedges, or option gamma matching techniques.

---

1. This discussion and the later discussion on the risks of delta hedging draws on Cristobal Conde, "Risk Management Techniques for Writers of Caps and Floors" in *Interest Rate Caps, Floors and Collars* (1986).

A special problem relating to long-term caps and floors is that their long maturities extend well beyond the usual hedging tools utilised to manage delta hedge portfolios in debt options such as futures contracts which are only available for periods up to two years. In these circumstances, it is increasingly common to construct hedges which combine standard option hedging strategies with interest rate swap transactions. This can be seen from the following example.

Assume a flat yield curve at 8.00% pa. A five year cap on six month US$ LIBOR is equivalent to a position in a five year floor plus long position in a par interest rate swap with a fixed semi-annual coupon of 8.00%, when both the cap and the floor are struck at the swap rate and if the fixed rate is paid on the same basis as the floating.

For all changes in rates, it can be shown that these positions will generate equivalent cash flows. For rates above the cap level, say 10.00%, the holder of the cap will be paid the difference between LIBOR and 8.00%, which is 2.00%. The floor and the swap combination generate the same cash flow. Since rates are above 8.00%, the floor by itself generates no income, while the swap entitles the holder to the difference between the 8.00% fixed outflow and the 10.00% floating index, also a net payment of 2.00%. For rates below the cap level, say 6.00%, the cap holder receives no payment. The floor generates a positive cash flow equal to the difference between 8.00% and the index level, that is, 2.00%, which covers the shortfall on the interest rate swap between the fixed payment outflow of 8.00% and the floating payment received, 6.00%. At exactly 8.00%, none of the securities generate cash flows.

Since these two positions are equivalent, the cost of the two portfolios should be the same. Thus, the cost of the cap will be the same as the cost of the interest rate swap plus the cost of the floor. Since an at-the-market swap is a par swap, no swap fee would pass between the two parties, and the cost of the floor would equal the cost of the gap.

CAP PORTFOLIO MANAGEMENT

The approach to cap portfolio management adopted by various intermediaries varies significantly depending, primarily, on the risk attitudes of the intermediary. There would appear to be two general approaches:

• a positioning approach to cap portfolio management;
• a hedged approach to cap portfolio management.

Under the positioning approach, the exposure in the cap portfolio is managed consistent with the intermediary's view on the direction of underlying interest rates. A variation on this type of positioning strategy is to operate a cap book with a good dispersion of exercise prices and maturities as well as caps and floors on the assumption that the book would be self-hedging. The essential theory behind this latter approach is that the various combinations of purchased and written puts and calls would be shown to be synthetic forward positions in the underlying asset market. Consequently, these synthetic forward positions could be managed against existing asset liability mismatches within the intermediary's balance sheet.

However, this type of approach has often proved to be unworkable as customer demand for options tended to cluster around certain exercise prices and maturities and there are frequent imbalances which tended to create portfolio exposures.

The alternative approach has been to operate cap portfolios on a hedged basis, traditionally using delta neutral hedging approaches. Delta or gamma neutral hedging does not completely eliminate risk. The risks include:

Volatility risk

Option positions hedged by utilising synthetic option technology are susceptible to losses upon an increase in the volatility of the market. Increases in volatility will boost theoretical premiums. This volatility risk can only be eliminated by hedging options with options.

This is because the cash and futures markets, however, are not, at least theoretically, affected by changes in volatility and the increase in value in the option granted position is not offset by any gain in value of the delta hedge.

Interest rate shifts

As interest rates move, different instruments in the portfolio will be affected differently. Shifts through time are particularly problematic as they require modelling the behaviour of forward-forward rates through time based on the underlying yield curve.

Jump or "gap" risk

A major problem relates to the fact that the delta hedge requires constant rebalancing which is not practically feasible. Where periodic rebalancing is used, the portfolio is adjusted after asset prices *have moved* which means that the wrong proportion of asset is held in the portfolio. This problem is accentuated where asset prices jump or gap significantly as the change in value of the hedge position is different from that which would be achieved with an option. This problem is complicated where the position is whipsawed. As rebalancing of the hedge is undertaken after the initial move in asset prices, any immediate reversal in the asset price, after adjustment of the hedge can lead to the option grantor sustaining losses as a result of holding the wrong number of contracts.

Hedging risks

The computation of the option position requiring hedging must properly be compared against the hedge instrument being utilised. When dealing with long-term instruments having intermediate cash flows, the reinvestment rates must be correctly adjusted when modelling yield curve shifts, especially when non-parallel shifts are employed.

Yield curve shifts

Assumptions must be made in relation to the basis relationship between instruments exhibiting different yield curves as well as the shape of various yield curves.

Settlement policies

Different settlement policies as between the option granted and the hedge instruments have to be accounted for in the computation of the hedged risk position for those instruments.

Transaction costs

Trading always has positive transaction costs. In volatile markets these transaction costs can become very large, as bid/offer spreads widen and markets become thin. Even if volatility remains fairly stable, strict delta hedging can be more costly than expected if a market becomes nervous and choppy. Delta hedging also requires the writer to monitor the position to continually adjust hedge positions, an approach which can be quite costly.

Despite these deficiencies, delta hedging is widely used in practice. Recent research[2] concludes that:

- the technique generates ex post option prices that approximate the ex ante theoretical value;
- the simulation study results were not sensitive to different adjustment gap sizes;
- the key to success in this type of hedging appears to be anticipating changes in volatility.

For example, *Exhibit 29.2* compares the performance of a theoretical and a synthetic delta hedged cap. The analysis indicates that the delta hedged cap tracks the value of the theoretical cap reasonably closely over time in the period under analysis.

As the cap and debt options market grew rapidly in the early 1980s, intermediaries relied heavily on delta hedging of their option exposure, and several institutions created very sizeable books of options on this basis. However, the deficiencies of delta hedging large exposures resulted in a number of instances of large losses on cap books. The most aggressive banks have since sharply curtailed the amounts of options they were willing to write without cover in the form of an offsetting option.

The reassessment of delta hedged exposure limits by a number of major banks has apparently led to some redistribution of option positions among active option trading institutions. It is likely that, as a result, less of the total outstanding amounts of options written for customers are delta hedged, but instead have been transferred to option specialists who hedge using a variety of specialised trading strategies.

2. Asay and Edelsburg (1986), pp. 63-70.

Exhibit 29.2

Performance of Synthetic Eurodollar Cap

Eurodollar interest rate caps may be created or hedged using Drexel Burnham's modern option replication (MOR) system. MOR selects a portfolio of United States Treasury bills, options contracts on Eurodollar futures and Eurodollar futures contracts that optimally achieve the same price sensitivities of a Eurodollar cap. At expiration of the shorter term, exchange traded options (or perhaps earlier), the MOR nearby futures and options positions are rolled into the next exchange traded contract cycle. A new MOR portfolio is optimally selected at the time of the roll that also has the same price sensitivities of the longer term Eurodollar cap. Since the price sensitivities are equal at any point in time, the MOR created portfolio has the same approximate value as the longer term Eurodollar cap.

The diagram below presents the performance comparison of a theoretical and an MOR created cap for hedging a five year $100m cap on three month Eurodollar interest rates with a strike price of 9.50% from 20 May 1985 through 1 December 1987. The analysis incorporated actual prices of Eurodollar futures and options, implied volatilities, and Eurodollar yield curves over the two and a half year period. The MOR positions were rebalanced only once per quarter, and no attempt was made to hedge either shifts in volatility or changes in yield curve spreads. This methodology resulted in the MOR positions being influenced by normal hedging risks at each quarterly rollover.

Eurodollar interest rates generally declined during the two and a half year period studied (as reflected by Eurodollar futures rates shown in the diagram below) so the value of a five year 9.50% cap also decreased in value. The cumulative change in value of the theoretical five year cap is the dashed line in the exhibit. These two lines show that the value of the MOR created cap closely tracked the value of the theoretical cap over the two and a half year period despite the volatile movement in Eurodollar interest rates over this period.

FIVE YEAR CAP ON 90 DAY EURODOLLAR RATES CUMULATIVE CHANGE IN VALUES

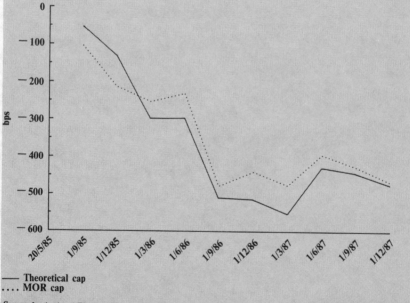

—— Theoretical cap
.... MOR cap

Source: Institutional Financial Futures Division
Drexel Burnham Lambert, Incorporated
MOR is a trademark of DBL, Inc.

Part 9

Credit Exposure in
Swap Transactions

Chapter 30

Swap Credit Exposure Measurement and Management Issues

CREDIT EXPOSURE IN SWAP TRANSACTIONS: SPECIAL FEATURES

Swap transactions like other financial transactions are subject to default risk. Default risk in any particular swap is primarily a function of:

- credit risk;
- market risk.

The overall default risk in any particular swap is a function of the counterparty's credit risk (the probability of a counterparty defaulting) and market risk (the level of swap rates at the time of default).

There are a number of features that distinguish the credit exposure associated with swap transactions:

- limited initial exposure;
- the exposure is a function of the movement of exogenous variables (interest and currency rates);
- the exposure can be negative as well as positive;
- the exposure is stochastic and cannot be determined, accurately, in advance.

A swap transaction typically does not initially result in any credit exposure to the counterparties as, by definition, the original exchange, if any, involves cash flows of equal value with no resulting net credit exposure at the time of commencement of the transaction. However, swap exposure can arise over time, reflecting changes in market conditions up to conclusion of the transaction, primarily, in exchange and interest rates, from those prevailing at the time of commencement of the transaction. These changes in exchange and interest rates affect the present value of the cash flows creating a net difference which represents the exposure of one counterparty to the other.

As the exposure under a swap is the function of exogenous variables, it is axiomatic that swap exposure can take on negative or positive values for a particular party to a transaction. Negative exposures in this context refer to situations when movements in rates are such that the counterparties would suffer a loss if the intermediary defaulted, or to put it from the perspective of the intermediary, the intermediary would gain if the counterparty defaulted.

A key point to note, is that as swap exposures are determined by the movements of exogenous variables, the exposure cannot be determined *in advance*.

These features distinguish the credit exposure associated with swap transactions from credit exposure incurred under more traditional financial transactions, such as loan transactions. The exposure under swap transactions has some similarity to exposures under a number of derivative instruments such as options and futures which also involve stochastic exposures.

The issue of credit risk in swap transactions is usually considered primarily with reference to financial intermediaries who, regularly, intermediate swaps through until maturity of the transaction. However, the issue of credit exposure is also relevant to end users of swap transactions who must assess the credit standing of financial intermediaries to control any potential loss from default *by the intermediary* under the swap.

MEASUREMENT OF CREDIT EXPOSURE: THE THEORETICAL BASIS

Basic concepts

The basic methodology used to measure credit exposure involves *matched* pairs of *identical* but mirror opposite swaps entered into by the intermediary. The credit exposure is then measured where the counterparty under one of the matched swaps defaults in the performance of its obligations under the agreement.

Credit exposure under a swap transaction arises because swap agreements between an intermediary and the two counterparties are independent agreements. Consequently, the intermediary must fulfill the terms of the contract with a remaining counterparty, even if the other counterparty defaults.

The basic concept used to measure credit exposure is "replacement cost". The replacement cost method of analysis estimates the economic impact on the intermediary from a default as a function of the original contract fixed rate and the market or replacement rate that would be used when finding a substitute counterparty. The loss or gain is effectively the difference between the original contract fixed rate and the replacement rate discounted to the termination date. This method of analysis implicitly assumes that the intermediary is unable to recover damages from a defaulting counterparty as specified in the swap agreement and closes out its exposure arising from a defaulting swap by writing a replacement swap or selling the now unmatched swap in the secondary market.

It is important to note that this approach, which focuses on the fixed rate component in swap transactions, assumes that the rate loss in replacing the floating rate side of a swap will be minimal as the swap payments are based on a market rate which readjusts periodically. Consequently, it is assumed that the replacement floating rate side will generally pay the same rate at any date, regardless of how long ago it was negotiated.

A number of swap transaction structures, depending on the pattern of cash inflows in relation to the pattern of cash outflows, result in settlement risk elements as payments to the intermediary are made in advance of receipt of payments from the counterparty. This creates a settlement risk arising from the fact that default may occur prior to the next inflow. A common structure incorporating settlement risk occurs with annual, fixed rate cash inflows offset by semi-annual floating rate outflows. An extreme case of this problem is a zero coupon swap where semi-annual floating rate payments out are made in exchange for a single lump sum interest payment at final maturity.

Swap transactions also give rise to delivery risk arising from the fact that in many foreign exchange transactions, because of the difference in the timing of currency settlement between the two jurisdictions, it is frequently impractical to verify the receipt of items or cash from the counterparty prior to paying out or delivering the item exchanged. This creates a settlement risk which can be equated to the maximum loss in such circumstances which is the total value of the cash or items to be received from the counterparty on any one day or series of days depending on when receipt can be verified.

The measurement of credit exposure in the various types of swap transactions is discussed below. However, before examining the mechanical aspects of quantifying the credit exposure in individual transactions, a number of boundary conditions, based on an overall analysis of swap transactions, should be mentioned. The essential considerations governing exposure from swaps and related transactions include:

- the exposure is stochastic in nature;
- the exposure is critically dependent on movements in the currency and interest rates in question;
- the magnitude of this exposure will normally be substantially less than 100.00% of the original par value of the swap.

Interest rate swaps

The credit risk of interest rate swaps is a function of the movement in fixed interest rates over the life of the transaction.

For example, assume a bank enters into a swap with a company which agrees to pay 11.00% pa for three years in exchange for receiving six month LIBOR. After one year has elapsed, the company has gone bankrupt. In order to cover its exposure, the bank undertakes a swap contract to receive a fixed rate for the remaining two years of the transaction. If rates have risen, for example, to 13.00% pa for two years, then the bank can crystallise a gain of 2.00% pa over the remainder of the term of the swap; conversely, if rates had fallen to 9.00% pa, the bank would have incurred a 2.00% pa loss.

This exposure under an interest rate swap is computed as the difference between the fixed rate of interest of the swap and the market fixed rate to the same maturity at the time of default or closeout, multiplied by the notional principal amount and discounted back at the prevailing rate of interest from each settlement date to the closeout date. In quantifying the exposure, the principal amounts are ignored, as the principal amounts are not exchanged in an interest rate swap. *Exhibit 30.1* sets out an example of the calculation of credit exposure in an interest rate swap.

Exhibit 30.1
Calculating Credit Exposure in Swaps

Interest rate swap

Assume the following transaction: Bank B (B) receives A$ fixed rate of 14.50% pa (S/A) from Company C (C) in exchange for paying six month BBR.

The transaction is for notional principal of A$10m for a maturity of three years.

The exposure of B from a default by C is as follows assuming forecasted rate highs and lows of 17.50% pa and 11.50% pa.

Year	Payment due to B	Payment due to B under replacement swap if C defaults if swap rates are:		Differential if swap rates are:		Exposure of B at commencement of period if swap rates are:	
		17.50%	11.50%	17.50%	11.50%	17.50%	11.50%
0.0	—	—	—	—	—	−0.6779	0.7434
0.5	0.7250	0.8750	0.5750	0.15	−0.15	−0.5873	0.6362
1.0	0.7250	0.8750	0.5750	0.15	−0.15	−0.4886	0.5228
1.5	0.7250	0.8750	0.5750	0.15	−0.15	−0.3814	0.4028
2.0	0.7250	0.8750	0.5750	0.15	−0.15	−0.2648	0.2760
2.5	0.7250	0.8750	0.5750	0.15	−0.15	−0.1379	0.1418
3.0	0.7250	0.8750	0.5750	0.15	−0.15	—	—

The negative number indicates a *gain* to the intermediary.

In percentage terms, the maximum exposure of B is 7.43% of the national principal.

Currency swap

Assume the following transaction: Bank B receives from Company C A$ fixed rate of 15.00% pa (A) in exchange for paying six month LIBOR.

The transaction is for notional principal of A$100m for three years.

In order to facilitate the risk exposure calculation, it is necessary to convert the floating rate US$ payments to a fixed rate equivalent. Utilising the current rates in the US$ interest rate swap market for three years, the six month LIBOR rate is converted into a fixed rate of 8.00% pa (A).

Assume the current spot rate is A$1.00/US$0.70 and forecast ranges for currency and swap interest rates are as follows:

Exchange rate:	US$0.60 to US$0.80 increasing to US$0.55 to US$0.85
A$ swap rates:	12.00% pa to 18.00% pa
US$ swap rates:	6.00% pa to 10.00% pa

The exposure of B from a default by C is as follows:

Year	Swap cash flows A$	US$	PV of US$ payments if rates are 10%	6% (a)	PV of A$ payments if rates are 18% (b)	12%	Assumed exchange rates High	Low (c)	Maximum A$ exposure of US$ payments $(d)=\dfrac{(a)}{(c)}$	Maximum exposure under swap (d)−(b)
0	—	—	66.5	73.7	93.5	107.2	0.80	0.60	122.8	29.3
1	15.0	5.6	67.6	72.6	95.3	105.1	0.82	0.57	127.4	32.1
2	15.0	5.6	68.7	71.3	97.5	102.7	0.85	0.55	129.6	32.1
3	115.0	75.6	—	—	—	—	—	—	—	—

The maximum exposure of B, in percentage terms ranges between 29.30 and 32.10% of notional principal.

The general impact on the intermediary of a default in an interest rate swap is determined by the direction of rate changes and by which party defaults:

Interest rate environment	If counterparty A (fixed payer) defaults	If counterparty B (fixed receiver) defaults
Rate same as contract rates	No effect	No effect
Rates higher than contract rates	Intermediary gains	Intermediary incurs loss
Rates lower than contract rates	Intermediary incurs loss	Intermediary gains

The exposure under an interest rate swap typically decreases over time. The exposure is also at a higher level, irrespective of the outstanding maturity of the transaction, at or just prior to each settlement period. Typically, the exposure of interest rate swaps represents 5.00% to 20.00% of the notional principal amount, depending on the forecast interest rates and the maturity of the swap.

Currency swaps

The quantification of exposure under currency swaps is similar to that under interest rate swaps. The major difference is that the exposure under a currency swap is affected by interest rates in the two currencies involved as well as fluctuations in the currency exchange rate as between the two currencies.

Exposure in currency swaps is quantified as the difference between the present values of the two payment streams, discounted as at default, translated into a single currency. As the principal amounts are denominated in different currencies and are repayable at maturity, they are incorporated in the exposure analysis and affect the size of the intermediary's exposure under the currency swap. *Exhibit 30.1* sets out an example of the calculation of credit exposure in a currency swap.

The general impact on the intermediary for a default in a fixed A$ to fixed US$ currency swap is summarised below:

	If counterparty A (fixed A$ payer and fixed US$ receiver) defaults	If counterparty B (fixed A$ receiver and fixed US$ payer) defaults
Interest rate environment		
Rates same as contract rate	No effect	No effect
A$ rate higher than contract rate	Intermediary gains	Intermediary loses
A$ rate lower than contract rate	Intermediary loses	Intermediary gains
US$ rate higher than contract rate	Intermediary loses	Intermediary gains
US$ rate lower than contract rate	Intermediary gains	Intermediary loses
Currency rate environment		
Rate same as contract rate	No effect	No effect
A$ appreciates against US$	Intermediary loses	Intermediary gains
A$ depreciates against US$	Intermediary gains	Intermediary loses

The quantum of exposure under a currency swap tends to depend on the types of instruments utilised. The fixed-to-fixed currency swaps are exposed as to interest rates on both currencies and the exchange rate. In contrast, fixed-to-floating currency swaps are exposed only on the fixed rate currency interest together with the exchange rate, while, the floating-to-floating currency swaps are exposed only in terms of currency amounts.

The nature of exposures on currency swaps can be summarised as follows:

- The exposure of currency swaps tends to increase with time, depending on currency fluctuations, and reaches a maximum near the maturity of the transaction.
- The exposure under a currency swap typically represents up to 50.00% to 60.00% of the principal amount, depending upon the currency and the maturity of the transactions.

LTFX

The exposure in the case of LTFX contracts is largely identical to those discussed in connection with a fixed-to-fixed currency swap as the LTFX contract pricing is based on the interest rate differential between the two currencies and will be affected by changes in the interest rates as between the two currencies and movements in the spot exchange rate.

FRAs

The exposure under a FRA contract is similar to that under an interest rate swap. The exposure represents the cost of replacement of the FRA counterparty, in the case of default, which will be determined by movements in short-term interest rates between the time of entry into the transaction and the default. As the maturity of FRAs are generally short, despite the often significant volatility of short-term interest rates, the exposure in such contracts is generally relatively small.

Caps, collars and floors

The approach to calculating exposures under cap, collar and floor agreements is similar to that utilised with interest rate swaps. However, where the intermediary writes the option in question, that is, it provides the cap or floor, it usually incurs *no* credit exposure to the counterparty. This is because as the grantor of the option, the *intermediary* has the performance obligation under the contract. Providing the option premium is paid at the time of entry into the transaction, the purchaser of the cap or floor does not have any further performance obligations and therefore the intermediary has no credit exposure to the purchaser. Where the premium is amortised and paid in instalments over the life of the transaction, it is equivalent to a loan transaction and credit exposure thereupon should be treated in a manner identical to that of a loan.

The basic exposure of an intermediary arises where it purchases an option from the counterparty. This occurs where, for example, the counterparty enters into a collar with an intermediary which entails the counterparty agreeing to make payments to the intermediary in case rates fall below the floor level of the collar.

The purchaser of an option, in all cases, assumes a credit risk in respect of the intermediary as it implicitly assumes that the intermediary will be capable of fulfilling its obligations under the contract if called upon to do so.

The exposure under such agreements can be equated to the replacement cost of substituting another intermediary should the counterparty fail to perform under the agreement. This replacement cost is equal to the cost of purchasing a substitute series of options. The cost of the substitute options will depend on the remaining time to maturity of the contract, and the changes in interest rate levels between the time of entry into the original contract and the time of default. In addition, the replacement cost of the options will be affected by changes in expectations as to the volatility of future interest rates in the relevant currency. The replacement cost can be estimated utilising option pricing methodology. Within this framework, the credit exposure in such contracts can be equated to the pricing of compound options or options on options.

MEASUREMENT OF CREDIT EXPOSURE: SOME ISSUES

A number of special issues relating to the measurement and quantification of credit exposure and swap transactions require additional comment. These issues include:

- timing considerations;
- liquidity issues;
- individual transaction versus portfolio approaches;
- option pricing approaches to swap exposures.

A major consideration in quantifying swap exposures is that credit risk under such transactions is not static over time. At the time of commencement of a transaction, its replacement value is by definition nil. However, as time elapses, if there is any deviation between the contract rates, both interest rate and currency rates (if applicable), and market rates, the replacement cost changes from zero. At the same time, as the outstanding life to maturity of the swap becomes shorter, and required contractual payments are made, the number of payments which remain exposed to any adverse movement in rates decrease. These two offsetting effects suggest the credit exposure of a swap transaction over its term may alter significantly. Importantly, the actual economic impact (the potential gain or loss) on a swap transaction held until maturity by an intermediary can only be determined definitively *at the maturity* of a swap.

In utilising the concept of replacement cost in quantifying the credit exposure in swap transactions the existence of a liquid secondary market in swaps is implicitly assumed. While it is clear that a secondary market in swaps, particularly interest rate swaps, has developed, a number of considerations relevant to utilising the secondary market must be considered.

The problems in dealing in secondary market swaps include:

- documentation;
- counterparty approval;
- payment of compensation.

In dealing in secondary market swaps, at least, on an assignment basis the documentation must often be accepted as originally entered into. In addition, counterparty approval must be obtained before an assignment can be completed. Finally, a payment (often substantial) between the parties must be effected in order to adjust the swap's fixed coupon to current market levels. Consequently, it is necessary to price swaps in the secondary market at a level attractive to conventional de novo transactions. This discount to market, to the extent that it deviates from normal pricing, has to be factored into the credit exposure assessment under swap transactions. This is because the liquidity premium will work against the party seeking to sell or buy a swap in the secondary market.

Consequently, it is necessary to make an assessment of the liquidity of the particular swap market when utilising the replacement cost concept to value the credit exposure. In markets where the relative liquidity is such that a replacement contract may not be capable of being easily arranged, the replacement cost may have to be calculated with reference to the purchase or sale of an asset to match the exposure on the swap on which default has occurred. In this case, the cost of the particular physical transaction, including carrying costs and balance sheet utilisation costs, must be included in determining the credit exposure in entering into such a transaction.

An additional problem in the case of interest rate swaps which are structured as net settlement contracts may be that because of the particular yield curve shape prevailing, it may be desirable not to closeout the defaulted position by entering into a replacement swap at all. For example, at one level, the exposure in an interest rate swap is a function of the probability that the rate being paid will average more than the rate being received over the life of the swap. For example, where an intermediary is receiving the fixed rate and paying a floating rate index, in an upward sloping or positive yield curve environment, no actual cash flow loss would be incurred until such time as short-term rates move above the fixed rate. Consequently, if the matching counterparty defaults, the intermediary may choose, given its view of interest rates, not to close up the position and to run the risk of changes in the yield curve shape.

A major issue relating to quantification of credit exposure is whether transaction exposure should be calculated on a transactional or portfolio basis. Initially, the risk associated with swap transactions was assessed independently of the intermediary's other activities. However, as intermediaries have created portfolios of swap transactions, risk measurement processes based on the marginal increase in overall risk as a new swap transaction is added to the portfolio have emerged.

Where each swap is treated individually, and the total intermediary exposure is taken to be the sum of the exposures on individual transactions, an extremely conservative assessment of risk is produced as the analysis assumes that each swap counterparty defaults at the worst possible point in time for the intermediary. It is, however, intuitively plausible that in a portfolio of swaps, diversified with respect to counterparties, the required return for the portfolio could well be less than that which would be suggested from the pricing of individual swaps, depending on the extent of portfolio diversification. This implies that the nature of swap credit exposures alters as intermediaries acquire larger portfolios of swap transactions.

For an intermediary with a significant swap portfolio the risk of a marginal swap transaction is not simply the maximum worst case loss in the context of that particular swap but rather is its marginal contribution, estimated at the expected replacement cost if a default occurs, to the overall risk of the portfolio. The approach recognises that the expected replacement cost if there is a default could equal any one of a range of values rather than a single worst case value and that the probability of each of these values occurring will vary.

Utilising this approach, the expected cost of a swap is treated as the weighted average of all possible replacement costs, using the probability of adverse rate movements as weights. Statistically, this measure gives the best estimate of actual replacement cost if a default occurs. This will almost certainly be less than the worst case measure of individual swap credit exposure.

The procedure for determining the expected replacement cost involves a specification of a probability distribution for future interest rates and is mathematically similar to the procedure for calculating the value of interest rate options or currency options (in the case of currency swaps). Increasingly, intermediaries are using an option pricing model to generate market risk estimates based upon interest rate volatility at current market rates and the remaining life of the swap. This type of model implies that the longer the maturity of the swap, or higher the volatility of interest rates, the greater the amount of risk.

It is important to note that the expected value approach to swap exposures is appropriate only in the case of intermediaries with a substantial portfolio of outstanding swaps. With smaller portfolios, a more conservative approach may be appropriate although this may place the institution in question at a competitive disadvantage since it would have to price its intermediation function for a higher assumed risk.

There is an inter-relationship between the measurement of exposure under swap transactions and the termination provisions of swaps. It is desirable that these termination provisions represent accurately the available methods of neutralising any default exposure under a swap transaction in case of default.

MEASUREMENT OF CREDIT EXPOSURE IN PRACTICE

Measurement of credit exposure under swap transactions in practice requires the operationalising of the theoretical principles outlined above. The major problem in this regard is that swap exposures cannot be determined in advance and are in this regard significantly different from other financial transactions such as loan transactions where the amount of exposure is immediately discernible.

There are basically two approaches, in practice, to the quantification of credit exposure in swap transactions on an ex ante basis:

• exposure measurement utilising statistical evaluation technology;

• exposure valuation utilising a mark-to-market technique.

The statistical methodology, commonly used by banks, bases swap exposure on assumptions of interest rate movements calculated from analyses of historical data combined with some subjective judgments. The approach requires an assessment of the potential exposure in a worst case scenario within given confidence limits over the life of the transaction. One potential approach is to evaluate actual exposure over a certain historical period and use this as a proxy for future exposure. An alternative approach is to assume that interest rate and exchange rate markets can be characterised by a predictable distribution of outcomes (for example, a normal or log normal distribution). Under the second method, the mean and standard deviations of these distributions are then evaluated and used to project swap exposure at the desired level of confidence.

In contrast, the mark-to-market technology continually evaluates current exposure by effectively revaluing each swap transaction utilising current market rates.

The advantage of the statistical technique is that it is possible to calculate an absolute number representing the *anticipated* exposure under the transaction. The disadvantage of this approach is that the exposure determined is based on historical data which may not accurately reflect the actual fluctuations in exchange and interest rates over the life of the transaction.

The mark-to-market methodology has the advantage that the exposure calculated does not overstate or understate the risk of a swap. The mark-to-market methodology does not require a complex set of assumptions for risk assessment and essentially creates a self-regulatory system with the intermediary required to expand or contract its swap exposures with market forces. However, the mark-to-market methodology does not provide an institution with a single indicia of the exposure under the swap on an ex ante basis. This means that the intermediary does not know in advance the amount of capital required to support its swap operations, the extent to which the transaction is likely to exceed the credit limits it has extended to the particular counterparty, and, most importantly, it does not allow the pricing of intermediation fees for the particular swap transaction.

These difficulties with the mark-to-market approach mean that the statistical valuation methodology is currently the most commonly utilised technique.

The approach to quantification of swap exposures is highly subjective, ultimately reflecting the objectives and risk profile of the participant. For example, it is entirely possible that regulators as against intermediaries will seek to place significantly different exposure limits on swap transactions (see Chapter 31). For example, at one extreme, an ultra-conservative approach to measurement of exposures on swap transactions would be to ignore the statistical origins of a swap transaction and value the swap as a loan requiring that the various risk ratios be computed using 100.00% of the par value of the swap.

The difficulty in practice entails specifying the worst case scenario for potential exposure for an individual transaction or for a portfolio. Initially, swap exposures were measured on the basis of conservative worst case levels for exchange and interest rates. This led to excessively conservative assessments on exposures and relatively large credit fees. However, because of the increasingly portfolio approach to credit risk adopted by intermediaries, as well as the fact that in a diversified swap portfolio interest rate and exchange rate movements can partially offset each other (that is, they are less than perfectly correlated), intermediation fees on swap transactions have declined. This decline also reflects the increased competitive nature of the swap market and the expansion of the volume of transactions which has also reduced the cost of each swap as overheads are now distributed over more transactions allowing intermediaries to realise economies of scale in the administration of these transactions.

An interesting issue in the estimation of credit exposures in swaps is the impact of interest rate cycles and the pattern and institutional structure of the market itself which may significantly influence the exposures under such transactions.

In practice, total diversification of a swap portfolio is difficult because there is a built in market bias against swap transactions being booked at the extremes in interest rate cycles. For example, when rates are very high, there are few counterparties willing to pay fixed rates, and when rates are very low, counterparties may be reluctant to receive fixed rates. Similarly, market biases may exist in currency swaps at the high and low points of currency cycles.

A further complication is the fact that counterparties traditionally most vulnerable to higher interest rate environments are most likely to be payers of the fixed rate which could, ironically, result in a gain to the intermediary if default occurs in a higher rate environment.

In practice, most intermediaries utilise a predetermined percentage of the nominal amount of a swap transaction as the relevant exposure in determining the amount to be used for credit approval purposes. Typically these percentages are as follows:

- For interest rate swaps, the percentages range from 5.00% to 50.00% depending upon maturity of the transaction. In the case of floating-to-floating interest rate or basis swaps, the relative minor risk means that either no credit risk percentage is computed or alternatively a relatively low figure such as 5.00% to 10.00% is utilised.
- For currency swaps and LTFX, percentages ranging from 20.00% to 60.00% of the notional principal of the transaction, depending upon maturity, are utilised.
- For FRAs, percentages range from 3.00% to 5.00% for transactions maturing within one year. For longer dated FRAs, percentages similar to those applicable to interest rate swaps are utilised.

Exhibit 30.2

Credit Exposure in Swap Transactions
(as percentage of notional principal)

Major Reserve Currencies[1]

	3 year swap	5 year swap	7 year swap	10 year swap
US$ interest rate swap	12.30	17.00	21.00	26.30
Fixed-to-fixed cross-currency swap				
C$	6.82	9.56	12.18	15.35
DM	16.14	21.83	23.57	23.55
FF	17.33	20.99	21.77	22.90
£	17.59	20.13	17.99	19.64
¥	17.65	21.24	22.38	23.04
SFR	20.51	27.68	32.17	32.96
Fixed-to-floating cross-currency swap				
C$	5.25	6.62	7.92	9.11
DM	15.87	20.94	22.18	20.97
FF	16.29	19.47	19.92	20.57
£	19.65	23.03	21.28	22.26
¥	17.07	20.14	20.50	19.59
SFR	20.16	26.92	30.99	30.47

A$[2]

	2 year swap	5 year swap	10 year swap
A$ interest rate swaps	3-6	8-10	12-15
Fixed-to-fixed cross-currency swap			
US$/A$	15-20	18-30	25-35

Notes:

1. Source: Bankers Trust Company, "The International Swap Market" Supplement to *Euromoney* September 1985.
2. Author's calculations based on historical data.

- For cap rate agreements, no credit exposure is recorded, while for collar transactions, percentages ranging from 10.00% to 50.00% depending upon the maturity of the agreement are utilised.

The actual percentages utilised will clearly vary as between currencies reflecting differing underlying volatilities in currency and interest rates. *Exhibit 30.2* sets out the total percentage exposure relating to swap transactions in and in between the major currencies as well as comparative figures for A$ swaps.

Credit officers in some institutions merely approve or disapprove credit extensions on swaps, charging the exposure against the institution's overall credit line to the counterparty. Others approve the swap only if the institution receives a certain number of basis points for credit risk. In some cases the swap dealer actually pays the credit officer "shadow" income for the exposure. Typically, however, the swap dealer does *not* pass this charge explicitly into the quoted price of the swap. If the swap trader cannot cover this charge at the prevailing swap price in the market, he or she does not enter into the transaction.

An estimate of the minimum spread required between two offsetting swaps for profitability can be obtained by charging such a premium on the estimated credit exposure. A shadow charge of 6bps to a particular customer might be arrived at in the following fashion. A loan to a customer would normally incorporate a spread of 0.375% pa over the bank's cost of funding the loan. For a swap where the credit exposure is calculated to be 16.00% of notional amount, the charge to cover the credit risk is 0.375% pa of the 16.00%, or 6bps (0.0006% pa). This covers the exposure to the failure of one counterparty.

In addition to setting aside credit lines for expected exposure, most swap dealers also monitor actual swap exposure as prices change. Management is periodically informed of the potential exposure if some or all counterparties were to default.

Practice differs among dealers on whether they monitor their credit exposure to a counterparty with which they have swaps in opposite directions. Some examine their exposure on a gross basis on the assumption that the counterparty could default on each swap only when interest rates have moved in the wrong direction. Others monitor exposure on a net basis, assuming that if the counterparty fails, the bank gains on some swaps and loses on others. Rights of offset provided by the swap contracts and the governing law under which the contracts are made are important factors in making this choice (see discussion in Chapter 31).

In most institutions, credit lines available for a particular customer are finite, and swap dealers must compete with other divisions of the bank for credit approval on the basis of earnings generated relative to limit utilisation.

MANAGEMENT OF CREDIT EXPOSURES

Overview

There are essentially three approaches to the management of credit exposure under swap transactions:

- acceptance and management of the credit exposure;
- passing the credit risk to another intermediary;
- enhancement of the credit exposure through various techniques.

The approach utilised by different organisations reflects their different business operations, objectives, and their respective capacities to assume and bear risk.

Management of credit exposure

The acceptance and management of credit exposure in swap transactions entails the following separate tasks:

- risk assessment;
- risk pricing.

Risk assessment entails quantification of the credit exposure under the swap transaction itself and an assessment of the counterparty's financial status and, thereby, its capacity to meet its financial obligations under the transaction. The assessment of counterparty risk in a swap transaction is not significantly different from general credit assessment involved in financial transactions. Once an overall limit for the particular counterparty has been established, the risk of the particular swap is quantified utilising the techniques discussed and, if the overall limit to the counterparty is sufficient to enable the swap transaction to be entered into, the transaction is then booked thereby reducing the available credit that the intermediary can extend to the counterparty.

The process of pricing of the risk, that is, the setting of the intermediation fees, is considerably more complex. Generally, the difference between the interest paid and the interest received on the fixed rate component of a swap, the bid/offer spread, represents income to the intermediary. This income must be sufficient to compensate for the risk incurred and to provide a sufficient level of earning relative to the capital utilised.

In practice, the intermediation fee is calculated as the earnings required to provide the intermediary with the required rate of return on the transaction for a counterparty of comparable risk based on the calculated exposure under the transaction. Elaborate models exist to accurately measure the required rate of return on such a transaction. An illustration of calculating swap intermediation fees utilising return on risk criteria is set out in *Exhibit 30.3*.

Exhibit 30.3
Calculating Swap Intermediation Fees Utilising Return on Risk Criteria

Credit intermediation fees for an interest rate swap can be determined, utilising return on risk criteria, using the following method:

- Calculate the risk asset (that is, the exposure under the swap).
- Apply to the risk asset the required rate of return to calculate the dollar income sought.

Exhibit 30.3—continued

- Calculate the equivalent annual fee in dollars which gives the same net present value as that of the dollar income.

Using the same scenario utilised in illustrating the credit exposure in interest rate swaps, the following risk asset can be generated:

Year	Maximum loss if fixed rate payer defaults (% of notional principal)	Maximum loss if floating rate payer defaults (% of notional principal)
0.0	6.25	6.78
0.5	5.48	5.87
1.0	4.60	4.89
1.5	3.63	3.81
2.0	2.55	2.65
2.5	1.35	1.35
3.0	—	—

The minimum earning rate on risk assets will vary between one institution and another and will also reflect the credit standing of the counterparty. For illustration purposes assume that:

- the payer of the floating rate in the swap is a strong credit for which a bank might provide a three year letter of credit or guarantee for a fee of the order of 0.25% pa;
- the payer of the fixed rate in a swap is a weaker credit for which a three year letter of credit or term bank guarantee might be priced at say 1.00% pa.

The letter of credit or guarantee fees are used as a proxy or benchmark of the credit risk premium to be charged because the swap is not a fully funded balance sheet obligation and therefore funding margins are not relevant.

The earning required (per A$100m) will be as follows:

Year	Fixed asset (fixed rate payer)	Required return (@ 1.00% pa)	Risk asset (floating rate payer)	Required return (@ 0.25% pa)
0.0	6.25	—	6.78	—
0.5	5.48	0.0313	5.87	0.0085
1.0	4.60	0.0274	4.89	0.0073
1.5	3.63	0.0230	3.81	0.0061
2.0	2.55	0.0182	2.65	0.0048
2.5	1.35	0.0128	1.38	0.0033
3.0	—	0.0068	—	0.0017
NPV of required return @ 14.00% pa		0.0993		0.0265
Equivalent % pa (on notional principal)		0.0417		0.0111

This requires a credit intermediation fee in this transaction of 0.0528% pa (S/A).

In the above approach, the likelihood of default as between the parties to the swap is "built-in" to the differential required return for the two counterparties. An alternative method would entail the potential risk exposure being multiplied by the probability of default (as determinable from actual default experience on, for example, securities issued by an issuer of the relevant credit standing). This would provide a projected cost of default on the swap which could be used as the risk asset level on which to base an absolute earning level on risk.

The above example focuses on interest rate swaps but the methodology of calculating swap intermediation fees for currency swaps is identical.

Swap transactions are priced to give a return on risk which is consistent with the required return for comparable off-balance sheet items, such as letters of credit and guarantees. Intermediation fees are also charged against swap income earnings according to a graduated scale which depends upon the creditworthiness of the swap counterparty resulting in a tiering of swap prices.

The essential technique in the management of the credit exposure of a swap portfolio is diversification. Diversification can be achieved at a number of different levels.

Diversification by counterparty will reduce the default risk associated with the default of any one counterparty. In addition, a portfolio can be diversified in such a manner as to maturity and levels of interest rates as to minimise the risk of economic loss upon default. A further type of diversification entails the entry into swaps with the *same* counterparty at different times and in different markets to achieve different transactional objectives. The objective is to create *parallel* swaps to the extent that the swaps are opposite but equal such that the positive and negative exposures net to zero. In practice, it is not possible to transact identical swaps but entry into similar swaps can be utilised to manage exposures on the overall portfolio. Further dimensions of diversification within a swap portfolio is to reduce risk by structuring by country, industry, maturity and floating rate index on a selective basis.

The process of management of the exposures on a swap portfolio is dynamic and may require amendments from time to time as new information becomes available.

Passing on credit exposure

An alternative means of managing credit exposure is to pass on the exposure to a third party willing to assume the default risks entailed.

The credit exposure on a swap may be passed on in a number of ways. A number of institutions seek to take on already completed swaps for an intermediation fee. The second approach, somewhat similar, entails the assignment of swaps from one counterparty to another. The basic difference between the two approaches is that the first does nothing to reduce the total amount of credit required to support the total market as an intermediating role is still being performed while the second approach reduces the credit demands on the market.

Credit enhancement

In certain circumstances, an intermediary may accept the credit exposures in booking swaps directly on the basis of enhancing the underlying credit of the counterparty utilising one of a number of available techniques, including:

- netting exposures;
- collateralisation;
- insurance.

The approach to netting of exposures between counterparties is designed to reduce the exposure recorded for individual counterparties. Netting as between counterparties active in the interbank swap market can dramatically reduce interbank credit line utilisation assuming that business is written in both directions. Netting as a technique is primarily restricted to institutions who are using the swap market not as end users (which traditionally means an inbuilt bias to be either one side of the swap or the other) but as intermediaries acting on behalf of clients with diverse needs and who may be using the interbank market to close out positions.

Collateralisation of the obligations of a party under a swap is a more recent development. Collateralisation has its origins in the participation in the swap market of such United States financial institutions as saving and loan associations and smaller regional banks. The basic rationale in collateralisation is to secure the performance of a party's obligations under a swap agreement to protect the capital gain of the counterparty should interest or exchange rates move in a direction favourable to that party.

Collateralisation usually operates in one of two ways:

- In certain swaps, weaker counterparties are required to post collateral at the inception of the swap. The exposure on the swap is constantly monitored and if the level of collateral falls below a certain level of the termination exposure, the counterparty would be required to post further collateral to maintain the cover. The failure to produce further collateral is itself an event of default and consequently exposure under the swap on termination can never exceed the value of the collateral posted.

- An alternative approach is to provide for either party to require the other to provide collateral against the exposure under a swap agreement in the event that the exposure increases dramatically and/or the credit quality of either institution changes significantly.

The types of collateral traditionally utilised include:

- a pledge of government securities;
- a pledge of other marketable assets such as loans secured by mortgages or deed of trust or mortgage backed securities;
- standby letters of credit from an acceptable financial institution;
- a guarantee from a creditworthy third party.

The basic types of collateral utilised are government securities and marketable mortgage backed securities which are types of collateral readily available to United States thrift institutions which are the primary participants in the collateralised swap market.

The amount of collateral required to be posted is a matter for negotiation between the counterparties but reflects both the default and market risk of the transaction. For example, the guidelines of the Federal Home Loan Bank Board for US$ interest rate swaps by Federal Home Loan Banks requires that member savings and loan associations specify that for a fixed-to-floating interest rate swap, collateral must be not less than 3.00% of the notional principal amount of the swap for each of the first five years remaining to maturity plus 2.50% pa for any remaining period to maturity. The Federal Home Loan Bank Board guidelines provide that for a floating-to-floating swap, the dollar amount must be sufficient to compensate for the risk of differences in the indices. The Federal Home Loan Bank Board guidelines also specify that for a standby letter of credit backing a swap, the Federal Home Loan Bank issuing the letter of credit must obtain a dollar amount of collateral not less than the present value of the letter of credit amount outstanding.

Collateralisation is primarily a feature of the US$ swap market. Additional credit support, primarily by way of bank letter of credit, is, however, utilised in other swap markets as well.

An interesting development in the credit enhancement of swaps has been the development of a swap insurance programme, implemented initially in March 1986, between the World Bank and Aetna Insurance Company providing for the insurance of direct counterparty swaps between the World Bank and A or AA rated corporations. Under the arrangement, the World Bank was able to expand the number of counterparties beyond the AAA rated corporates to which it has been restricted as well as financial institutions with a credit quality equivalent to those with whom the World Bank places its funds.

The swap insurance scheme operates as follows. The World Bank pays variable insurance fees to Aetna calculated with reference to the credit exposure under a nominated set of swaps which are marked-to-market each week. The fee scale may run from a nominal commitment fee based on no credit exposure to higher amounts based on an exposure ceiling of 30.00% to 50.00% of the par value for the swap. The insurance programme is designed to provide a backstop to the World Bank in the event of default to provide the funds needed to reconstitute the swap at the then prevailing market levels. The World Bank apparently decided to implement the swap insurance scheme to expand its universe of swap counterparties because the number of its potential counterparties was too limiting. This limitation had led to a fairly high concentration of counterparties within the World Bank portfolio. For example, approximately 40.00% of its swaps had apparently been done with only five institutions.

The swap insurance arrangement as structured provides three main benefits:

• It allows diversification of the World Bank swap portfolio.

• It is considered more cost effective than comparable bank intermediation.

• It is likely that swap insurance will provide even better credit quality than swaps with only AAA rated corporations as the probability of both a counterparty and the insurer failing is more remote than the probability of potential failure of a AAA counterparty.

The swap insurance programme effectively allows the World Bank to completely segregate the credit aspects of the swap from the trading aspects. It is understood that the World Bank is seeking to expand its swap insurance programme.

The World Bank, more recently, negotiated a facility with Deutsche Bank, a AAA rated institution, whereby in return for receiving a fee the bank insures the World Bank against counterparty default. The agreement appears to have been designed to expand the World Bank's potential counterparties in Europe and Japan where ratings from the major United States ratings agencies are not common, given that the World Bank is restricted by its board to accepting only AAA rated corporations although it can in limited circumstances accept AA rated banks. An unusual feature of the Deutsche Bank facility is that the World Bank has the choice of requiring payment of a defaulting counterparty's swap coupon and/or principal stream or of taking the up-front termination value of the swap.

A number of United States insurance companies, primarily financial insurers active in providing financial guarantees, are examining the possibility of providing financial guarantees in support of swap transactions.

Chapter 31

Swap Credit Exposure:
A Regulatory Perspective

THE IMPETUS FOR REGULATION

The swap market has developed under negligible regulatory attention. However, the increased importance of swaps and other off-balance sheet commitments has attracted regulatory attention.

The primary areas of regulatory concern include:

- credit exposure of swaps;
- market risks associated with swaps;
- the pricing of swaps.

The regulatory authorities have recognised that banks, etc. who act as principals in swaps incur credit exposures to the counterparties involved for the term of the transaction. Furthermore, where they are intermediating a swap or trading swaps, they effectively take on the credit exposure of *at least* two counterparties; that is, the risk to the banks concerned doubles. In addition, the regulatory authorities have recognised that many institutions under their supervision take on large market risks primarily interest rate and currency exposure in making markets and trading in swaps.

An associated concern has been that market prices for swaps did not accurately reflect the actual risk involved in undertaking these transactions. The concern amongst regulators, in relation to pricing of swaps, was based on a number of factors:

- banks involved did not sufficiently understand the risks of swaps;
- more importantly, competitive pressures have not allowed banks to generate returns on capital commensurate with the risk of swaps.

Typically, intermediaries make a yes or no credit decision on a counterparty. Consequently, there is usually only one price in the swap market with minimal price tiering for differential credit quality. This price reflects only the *average expected exposure of all counterparties* in the swap market and not the *specific* risk of counterparties being dealt with.

The regulators concern over the pricing of swaps and allocation of capital to cover the risks has been exacerbated by evidence of *deliberately* mispriced swaps to secure mandates for securities transactions.

BANK OF ENGLAND AND FEDERAL RESERVE PROPOSALS

In March 1987, the Bank of England and the United States Federal Reserve issued a consultative document outlining risk based capital requirements in connection with off-balance sheet items, including swaps, designed to ensure stronger capital bases for regulated banks.

540

The Central Banks' release follows the publication of the "Agreed Proposal on Primary Capital and Capital Adequacy Assessment" in early January 1987. The proposal established five risk weights (between 0 to 100%) to be applied to the principal amounts of assets and selected off-balance sheet items to calculate total weighted risk assets. The principle was that for the purposes of calculating total weighted risk assets, the notional principal amount of off-balance sheet items would first have to be converted into a balance sheet equivalent credit exposure. The resulting "credit equivalent amount" should then be assigned one of the five risk weights in the same way that weights are assigned to balance sheet assets (that is, essentially on the basis of the type of counterparty and the risk inherent in the transaction).

Under the proposed guidelines, the credit equivalent amount for each contract would be measured as the sum of the mark-to-market value (positive or negative) of the contract on the reporting date (the current exposure), and an estimate of the potential future credit exposure over the remaining life of the instrument (the potential exposure).

The sum of these two components may turn out to be negative. In this case the credit equivalent amount would be set equal to zero because the bankruptcy of a counterparty would not necessarily relieve the banking organisation of its obligation to make payments stipulated in the contract (that is, it would not necessarily realise a profit). However, under certain conditions, negative credit equivalent amounts could be netted against positive credit equivalent amounts *to the same counterparty*.

Assessing the risk involved in swap and option positions on the basis of the mark-to-market value of the contracts is already standard practice with major participants in these markets. The mark-to-market value is defined as the amount the banking organisation would have to pay to replace the net payment stream specified by the contract if the contract were to default.

Negative mark-to-market values would be taken into account in the calculation of credit equivalent amounts, not because the banking organisation could benefit from a default but because the negative mark-to-market value reduces the likelihood that credit exposure will arise over the remaining life of the contract. The market value of a contract is the loss of (theoretical) profit that would result from the counterparty's default. A contract has positive market value if default would result in loss and negative market value if default would result in a (theoretical) profit. The mark-to-market value would include the value of interest that has accrued but has not been received. United States banking organisations would measure mark-to-market values in US$ and United Kingdom banking organisations in £, regardless of the currency or currencies specified in the contract.

The proposed guidelines on calculating *potential* exposure have created controversy. Potential exposure is defined as "the additional exposure that may arise over the remaining life of the contract as a result of fluctuations in interest rates or exchange rates". A rise in the value of a contract entails a concomitant increase in the replacement cost to the banking institution were its counterparty to default. This in turn involves a commitment which "requires capital support beyond what is necessary to support the current credit exposure on the reporting date".

The potential credit exposure is proportional to the notional principal amount. In the proposed guidelines the so-called credit conversion factor for potential exposure, that is, the ratio for potential exposure, varies across contracts depending on the remaining maturity and the volatility of the foreign exchange and/or interest rates to which the contract is indexed. Under the scheme devised by the Bank of England and the United States Federal Reserve, potential exposure on a contract would be determined by multiplying the notional principal amount by the proposed conversion factor. Once the credit equivalent amounts have been calculated, they are allocated to the appropriate risk category on the basis of the type of counterparty and, in some cases, the remaining maturity of the contract or the presence of certain types of collateral or guarantees.

Potential Credit Exposure

Proposed conversion factors

Interest rate and foreign exchange contracts
(percentage of notional principal amount)

Remaining maturity	Interest rate	Exchange rate
Less than one year		
Less than 3 days	0	0
3 days to 1 month	0	1.00-2.00%
1 month to 3 months	0	2.00-4.00%
3 months to 1 year	0	4.00-8.00%
One year or longer	0.50%-1.00% per complete year	5.00-10.00% + 1.00-2.00% per complete year

Thus the deemed Credit Equivalent Value (CEV) is given by the expression:

$$CEV = MM_i + P_i \times F_i$$

where: MM_i = mark-to-market value of swap transaction i
    P_i = principal value of swap i
    F_i = "conversion" factor applied to swap i

This then implies a capital ratio of:

$$\text{Capital ratio} = \frac{K}{\sum\limits_{i=i}^{n} [(MM_i + P_i F_i) \times RW_i]}$$

where: RW_i = risk weight applied to transaction i according to type of
counterparty; maturity of transaction, etc.
 K   = capital, as defined
 n   = number of transactions

An example of the calculation of credit equivalent amounts under the joint proposal is set out in *Exhibit 31.1*.

A number of key aspects of the proposal should be noted. The approach adopted effectively creates a hierarchy of risks of off-balance sheet business, including swaps. This hierarchy is structured in terms of the conversion factor applied (Fi), and the risk weighting applied (RWi).

A swap attracting a high conversion factor and risk weighting will require a higher capital allocation than a swap attracting a low conversion factor and low risk weighting. This may create a bias among regulated banks towards swaps attracting low conversion factors and/or low risk weightings.

Exhibit 31.1

Bank of England and Federal Reserve Proposal

CALCULATION OF CREDIT EQUIVALENT AMOUNTS, INTEREST RATE AND FOREIGN EXCHANGE RATE RELATED TRANSACTIONS

Type of contract (remaining maturity)	Notional principal (US$)	Exposure conversion × Factor	Potential exposure = (US$)	Current exposure[1] + (US$)	Credit equivalent = (US$)
1. 120 day forward foreign exchange	5,000,000	0.04	200,000	100,000	300,000
2. 120 day forward foreign exchange	6,000,000	0.04	240,000	−120,000	120,000
3. 3 year single currency fixed-to-floating interest rate swap	10,000,000	0.015	150,000	500,000	650,000
4. 3 year single currency fixed-to-floating interest rate swap	10,000,000	0.015	150,000	−600,000	0
5. 7 year cross-currency floating-to-floating interest rate swap	20,000,000	0.12	2,400,000	−1,300,000	1,000,000
Total	51,000,000				2,070,000

Note:

1. These numbers are purely illustrative.

Source: Bank of England.

The credit conversion factors for long-dated and/or exchange rate contracts are considerably higher than for short-term interest rate swaps, reflecting the additional potential credit risk which is perceived in these contracts. This reflects the assessment that:

- the longer the maturity outstanding the greater the potential for credit risk to arise;

- volatility of exchange rates are greater than volatility of interest rates, that is, therefore the higher the potential exposure which may arise from swap contracts involving exchanges of currencies.

The model of potential exposure is based upon the notion of matching contracts where the bank is acting as an intermediary in a swap between two separate counterparties. As banks often act as intermediaries between end users of swap contracts resulting in a portfolio of matched or nearly matched pairs, measuring potential exposure on a matched pair basis should result in a much lower measure than if calculations are conducted on a single contract basis. However, no allowance is made for portfolio diversification and the approach taken by the Central Banks falls far short of a portfolio risk assessment procedure.

The model relies on past interest rate and exchange rate volatility as a guide to future rate volatility. While the estimates of conversion factors are based on an objective model of the probability distributions of potential replacement costs of swap contracts, the model in itself does not indicate how large potential exposure limits on these distributions should be. This is done by utilising a confidence interval for the average replacement cost (and hence conversion factor) derived from the models. Exposure thus is defined in terms of a confidence limit for average replacement cost of a matched pair of swaps. The choice of confidence limits that the estimates of potential exposure should satisfy is necessarily *subjective*.

A number of exceptions should be noted:

- Interest rate and foreign exchange contracts such as futures and options contracts, that are traded on organised exchanges and are subject to daily mark-to-market provisions and payment of variation margins, are excluded.

- Swap contracts used *solely* for hedging interest rate and exchange rate exposures would be exempted.

- No potential credit exposure will be calculated for single currency floating-to-floating interest rate swaps. The credit exposure on these contracts would be evaluated solely on the basis of their mark-to-market value.

- The existence of collateral and guarantees would *not* generally be recognised in calculating deemed credit equivalent amounts. However, some adjustment would be made by assigning a lower risk weight where the collateral held is domestic national government debt; cash on deposit in the lending or swap intermediary; and (for the United States only) debt of United States government agencies and United States government sponsored agencies.

MARKET RESPONSE TO REGULATORY PROPOSALS*

The swap market's response to the joint Bank of England and Federal Reserve proposal was predictably hostile. While acknowledging the need for some regulation, the proposal was criticised on a number of bases:

- the use of potential exposure;
- the volatility implied;
- "uneven" treatment of different participants.

The inclusion in the proposal of potential exposure on swaps as part of the deemed credit risk calculations, has been criticised on the basis that it significantly overstates the risk associated with swaps. Some comments have suggested that the approach overstates the credit risk of swaps by a factor of between two and four times.

The ISDA, for example, has argued that a mark-to-market measure produces a value that *includes* potential risk. It argued that future exposure would be of concern only for swaps at or near par value rather than those in- or out-of-the-money. The basis for ISDA's reasoning is that for par swaps the current replacement cost will be low. In these instances it would be reasonable and would not severely distort risk to add a factor for potential future exposure to a mark-to-market evaluation of current replacement cost. ISDA argued that as a swap moves away from par, the mark-to-market value will at some point exceed any reasonable measure of average future replacement costs. In these instances there is no longer a need to add a factor for potential exposure to mark-to-market values to reflect average expected replacement costs sought to be measured under the Banks' proposal.

The ISDA approach is predicated on an option pricing basis for valuing swaps. A swap that had moved substantially in one direction or another would be more likely to move in the opposite direction. An out-of-the-money swap or in-the-money swap would be more likely to move towards par value. Until such time as it reaches par value, the risk of the swap would be effectively captured in the mark-to-market value of the swap.

The volatility measures utilised have been criticised as being too conservative. For example, *Exhibit 31.2* sets out material from a Security Pacific Technical Paper to the Federal Reserve which compares the average replacement cost of the proposal vis à vis the institution's own estimates.

One of the major criticisms of the proposals has been that they did not apply to all participants in the swap market, the consequence being that the proposal was tantamount to applying a tax on swaps, restricting those institutions to which it applied in favour of those institutions to which it did not apply. In particular, the implementation of the proposal would, it was argued, enable German and Japanese banks and United States investment banks to win a substantially increased market share of swap business since they would not be formally required to hold capital against their swap business. The concern was that even if the proposal was extended to these other institutions it would not be implemented for some time, giving those institutions a competitive, albeit temporary, advantage.

---

* The material in this section draws on material prepared by W. R. Jones (1987).

Exhibit 31.2
Average Expected Replacement Cost for Par Exchange Rate Contracts

Maturity Currencies	1 year	3 years	5 years	7 years	10 years
		(% of aggregate notional amount)			
US$/DM	2.8	4.9	5.7	6.1	6.4
US$/SFR	3.1	5.3	6.3	6.7	7.0
US$/¥	2.8	4.8	5.7	6.1	6.4
US$/£	2.7	4.6	5.5	5.9	6.1
DM/SFR	1.4	2.4	3.0	3.3	3.6
DM/¥	2.1	3.7	4.4	4.9	5.3
DM/£	1.6	2.9	3.5	3.9	4.1
Joint proposal					
High	12.0	16.0	20.0	24.0	30.0
Low	6.0	8.0	10.0	12.0	15.0

Source: Security Pacific Merchant Banking Group.

Under an alternate approach proposed by ISDA, banks would still calculate credit equivalent amounts as the sum of a mark-to-market evaluation of current replacement costs (that is, current exposure) plus a factor to measure expected future replacement costs (that is, potential exposure). However, banks would have the option to calculate the factor for expected future replacement costs according to one of two formulas. The two options proposed are:

- *Option A*: a factor that takes into account differences in risk between par swaps and premium/discount swaps and, for interest rate swaps, is computed based upon remaining life to maturity; or

- *Option B*: a specified percentage of the aggregate notional amount of all swaps, with the percentage varying between different types of swaps.

The factors to be applied to the calculation of credit equivalent amounts under the ISDA approach are set out in *Exhibit 31.3*.

The ISDA approach placed a greater emphasis on mark-to-market than the Bank of England and Federal Reserve proposal. Further, the technical analysis on which the approach adopted by ISDA is based differs from the Central Banks' proposal as follows:

- It is based on expected values of replacement costs, rather than values designed to achieve specified confidence intervals.

- Measures change for calculating in future replacement costs as rates change, consistent with option valuation approaches.

- It expressly discounts expected future replacement costs to their present values.

- It is based on different volatility assumptions.

The ISDA approach would broadly tend to lower the amounts to be counted in the risk asset calculations vis à vis the Central Banks' approach. However,

Exhibit 31.3

ISDA Proposed Conversion Factors, Interest Rate and Currency Swaps

(% of notional principal amount)

INSTITUTIONS MAY CHOOSE BETWEEN OPTION A OR OPTION B

The proposed factors for each method are as follows:

Option A	Factor
Par Swaps[1]	
Interest rate swaps	0.15% of notional amount for each full year in remaining life of each swap
Currency swaps[2]	
High volatility[3]	3.00% of aggregate notional amount
Low volatility	1.50% of aggregate notional amount
Premium and discount swaps[1]	
All swaps	0%

Option B	Factor
Interest rate swaps	0.50% of aggregate notional amount
Currency swaps	
High volatility[3]	2.00% of aggregate notional amount
Low volatility[3]	1.00% of aggregate notional amount
All currency swaps	1.50% of aggregate notional amount

Notes:

1. Par swaps are swaps which have a mark-to-market value, regardless of sign, less than a given percentage of notional principal amount, and premium or discount swaps are swaps which have a mark-to-market value greater than or equal to such percentage. The percentage is 0.50% times number of years to maturity for interest rate swaps, 11.00% flat for high volatility currency swaps and 7.00% flat for low volatility currency swaps.
2. Currency refers to cross-currency swaps.
3. High volatility currency swaps are swaps between currencies with an exchange rate volatility in excess of 10.00%. Low volatility currency swaps are swaps between currencies with an exchange rate volatility of 10.00% or less.

Source: ISDA.

in some instances, the ISDA approach would result in a more conservative risk assessment (and hence a higher charge against capital) than would apply under the Banks' proposal.

BASLE COMMITTEE—PROPOSED GUIDELINES ON CAPITAL ADEQUACY

In December 1987, the Basle Committee on Banking Regulation and Supervisory Practices (the Basle Committee) released its "Proposals for International Convergence of Capital Measurement and Capital Standards" outlining guidelines to apply in each member country for the establishment of bank capital adequacy.

A key feature of the proposal was the inclusion of off-balance sheet activities, including swaps, in the measurement of capital adequacy. The approach recommended is similar to that of the joint Bank of England and Federal Reserve proposal.

The incorporation of off-balance sheet exposures uses a system of "credit conversion factors". Each type of off-balance sheet activity is assigned a credit conversion factor expressed as a percentage of notional (par) principal of the contract. The converted principal amount is then assigned to the risk category of the contract counterparty.

The major differences between the Basle Committee and the Central Banks' proposal relate to the calculation of credit conversion factors for foreign exchange and interest rate related contracts. The Basle Committee allowed a *choice* between the current exposure method and original exposure method.

Under the current exposure method, the credit conversion factor is the sum of:

- the total replacement cost (obtained by marking-to-market) of all its contracts with positive value; and

- an amount for potential future credit exposure calculated on the basis of the total notional principal amount of its book, split by residual maturity as follows:

Residual maturity	Interest rate contracts	Exchange rate contracts
Less than one year	nil	1.00%
One year and over	0.50%	5.00%

No potential credit exposure would be calculated for single currency floating-to-floating interest rate swaps; the credit exposure on these contracts would be evaluated solely on the basis of their mark-to-market value.

Under the original exposure method, the credit conversion factors are calculated as the notional principal amount multiplied by the following suggested conversion factors:

Maturity	Interest rate contracts	Exchange rate contracts
Less than one year	0.50%	2.00%
One year and less than two years	1.00%	6.00% (that is, 2.00% + 4.00%)
For each additional year	1.00%	4.00%

While the original exposure method is computationally easier, the fact that it generally results in a higher credit equivalent amount is likely to favour the current exposure method. Supervisors in countries, such as the United States and the United Kingdom, whose regulated banks have entered into large volumes of these types of contracts will also be likely to favour the current exposure method.

The Basle Committee proposal incorporates some of the comments made in respect of the original Central Banks' proposal, including:

- There is now a recognition of par and non-par instruments (that is, in-the-money, at-the-money or out-of-the-money) in the proposals. This has the effect of reducing the credit exposure recognised since risks are considered on a portfolio basis.
- A lower confidence limit has been used.
- Cash flows are now discounted (at a rate of 5.00% pa).

The recommended method of calculating the "add-ons" is significantly less complex, both in that it omits a year by year maturity breakdown and in that the potential exposure factor is not applied to each contract singly, but to the total notional principal of each bank's portfolio whether or not the contracts have a positive current exposure.

RESERVE BANK OF AUSTRALIA—PROPOSED GUIDELINES ON CAPITAL ADEQUACY

The Reserve Bank of Australia, in February 1988, released a discussion paper outlining a risk based measurement of Australian banks' capital adequacy which covered both on-balance and off-balance sheet transactions, including swaps. The proposal was largely consistent with the earlier Bank of England and Federal Reserve and Basle Committee's proposals.

In respect of exposure on swaps (classified as "interest rate and exchange rate related transactions"), the Reserve Bank of Australia adopted the Basle Committee proposal allowing Australian banks to adopt either the current exposure or original exposure method. Banks which conducted a significant volume of swap transactions were expected to adopt the current exposure or mark-to-market approval. The credit conversion factors proposed by the Reserve Bank of Australia were identical to those suggested by the Basle Committee.

In August 1988, the Reserve Bank published its final regulations on capital adequacy. The Bank's proposals were similar to its earlier proposals. The only significant change from the original discussion paper was some minor changes to the original credit conversion factors. The new factors were as follows:

> "Current Exposure Method
> (Mark-to-market approach)
>
> Credit equivalent amounts are represented by the sum of current credit exposure and potential credit exposure:
>
> (i) Current Credit Exposure
> This is the mark-to-market valuation of all contracts with a positive replacement cost.[2]
> (ii) Potential Credit Exposure[3]
> This is calculated as a percentage of the nominal principal amount of a bank's portfolio of interest rate and exchange rate related contracts split by residual maturity as follows:

Remaining Term to Maturity of Contracts	Interest Rate Contracts	Exchange Rate Contracts
Less than one year	nil	1.00%
One year or longer	0.50%	5.00%

Original Exposure Method
(Rule-of-thumb approach)

Credit equivalent amounts would be calculated by applying credit conversion factors to the principal amounts of contracts according to the nature of the instrument and its *original* maturity.

Original Maturity of Contracts	Interest Rate Contracts	Exchange Rate Contracts
Less than one year	0.50%	2.00%
One year and less than two years	1.00%	5.00% (i.e. 2% + 3%)
For each additional year	1.00%	3.00%

2. Replacement costs which are fully collateralised by cash and government securities, or backed by eligible guarantees, may be given the weight of the underlying security or guarantor.

3. No potential credit exposure is calculated for single currency floating-to-floating interest rate swaps; the credit exposure on these contracts is evaluated solely on the basis of their mark-to-market value.

The credit equivalent amounts would be risk weighted within the general framework according to the weight assigned to the counterparty. However, as an exception to the 100.00% weight applicable to non-bank counterparties generally, the weight assigned to interest rate and foreign exchange contracts for this group of organisations was 50.00%."

IMPLICATIONS OF IMPLEMENTING PROPOSED REGULATIONS

It is obvious that moves by regulatory authorities to incorporate risks associated with swaps in a measure of risk assets will have implications for banks and in turn for the swap market as a whole. While the term "bank" is utilised, to the extent that risk asset capital requirements will be extended to most financial intermediaries engaged in swaps, then the term should largely be read as synonymous for financial intermediaries in general.

While the effect of the proposed regulations will clearly vary between individual institutions, overall a number of major effects *on the swap market* are identifiable:

• the level of capital committed by banks to swap activities;

• the pricing of swap transactions;

• the level of risk undertaken, for example the type of swap business undertaken and the counterparties with whom this business is undertaken;

• liquidity and volumes in the swap market;

• changes in the institutional structure of the swaps market to modify or alleviate the impact of the proposals.

Given that capital is a scarce commodity then the risk asset ratios imposed under the proposals will ultimately force internal capital allocation to swap activities. This may, for example, result in marginal participants withdrawing from the swap market.

The deemed credit equivalent value applied will have a powerful impact on the pricing of swaps. Those swaps carrying a high capital charge, for example, a long-term currency swap, will carry a higher price. A distinct stratification in swap prices, with prices varying according to type of counterparty, maturity of swap, etc. may result.

Spreads on swaps are anticipated to widen significantly. It has been suggested that spreads on US$ interest rate swaps could widen by around 5 to 15bps pa. Spreads on currency swaps, in light of their greater capital requirements, are expected to widen even further.

In addition to an increase in price, the manner in which swaps are priced may change. There could be a shift towards banks employing a variable intermediation fee instead of the current fixed fee. This could conceptually change the pricing mechanism for swaps from the one presently used of a fixed fee (based on average cost pricing utilising some statistical valuation of expected average exposure) to a variable fee (based on marginal cost pricing using actual exposure plus some potential exposure factor).

Depending on competitive pressures in the swap market, the ability of all banks dealing in swaps to raise prices may be limited. For some banks the effect of the proposals may be to make participation in swaps generally, or in specific types of swaps, uneconomic. The capital cost and resulting changes in swap prices may, in fact, make swap arbitrage uneconomic. This could also result in a substantial drop in the volume of swap business.

The net effect then of the implementation of the Banks' proposal would be a less liquid swap market. This could be across the board or in specific types of swaps. Insofar as this takes place this will obviously reduce the attractiveness of swaps and the willingness of parties to intermediate in swaps.

By early 1989, many of these developments had already manifested themselves in the swap market. The major developments include:

- the withdrawal of some institutions from some types of swaps altogether;
- greater specialisation among banks in the types of transactions entered into; and
- some increases in swap spreads with institutions increasingly willing to turn away marginal transactions where the return does not generate the required levels of return on capital.

The impact of central bank action on the further development of the swap market is difficult to forecast. However, the regulatory action is likely to accelerate the implementation of netting arrangements between intermediaries and also the establishment of a clearing house for swap transactions.

The action by regulatory authorities is likely to accelerate the trend towards master agreements with comprehensive netting provisions as between major market participants which provide for the netting of amounts receivable from and payable to a counterparty, resulting in a single stream of payments between counterparties. The United States Federal Reserve and Bank of England and Federal Reserve guidelines as well as the Basle Committee proposal recognise that such netting arrangements may reduce credit risk and are likely to encourage their further development and implementation. If such netting arrangements and standard master agreements enjoy general, market wide application and unambiguous legal acceptance, it is conceivable that central banks may modify their guidelines to treat multiple contracts with a single counterparty within the terms of such a master agreement as a single contract.

A sizeable market (estimated at approximately US$600m) in notional mark-to-market swaps has emerged as a rudimentary form of netting. The concept, originated by a number of primarily United States money center banks, including Manufacturers Hanover, Chase Manhattan, J. P. Morgan, Bankers Trust and Citicorp, is designed to ease the capital requirements of substantial interbank swap transactions.

Under the system, all swaps are periodically marked to market with cash payment being made between counterparties to effectively "zero" the credit exposure on the contract. This process can potentially eliminate or, at least, greatly reduce the capital requirement of swaps entered into under this arrangement under the proposed capital adequacy guidelines. This is because the mark-to-market provision eliminated current exposure under the contract and the potential exposure beyond one year (irrespective of the outstanding maturity of the contract) is eliminated because the contract provides for a mark-to-market every three or six months.

The concept was originally applied to interest rate swaps and has been extended to currency swaps.

The development of a swap clearing house, currently under study by a special committee of ISDA, may also be accelerated by the action of the regulatory authorities. Such a swap clearing house would, of course, be required to have its own credit criteria and presumably would operate in a manner analogous to futures and options exchanges, requiring margin calls and deposits, etc. to be posted. Presumably, all interbank swaps would be written with the clearing house so that the exposure to the clearing house and the clearing house's exposure to the institution would be the intermediary's net exposure to the market as a whole. Thus, instead of a series of independent exposures to a range of counterparties, which may be positive or negative, there could be a single net exposure to the clearing house. The clearing house proposal is thus analogous to the netting of exposures between two counterparties described above but could operate as between a larger number of counterparties.

The clearing house proposal would have the effect of standardising credit ratings of market participants. This can be seen as greatly enhancing the liquidity of the underlying swap market and assisting in the expansion of a secondary market in swaps. However, the issue is likely to be a political and highly divisive one.

The clearing house proposal may be particularly attractive to investment banks who want swaps to become freely transferable, so that a transaction can be terminated by simple assignment to another company, through the clearing house, without the investment bank having to take a position as principal, except for a short period. This reflects the perspective of some investment banks which see swaps as another trading and arbitrage vehicle in their trading portfolios, in contrast to commercial banks who view swaps as akin to longer term commitments such as an extension of credit. However, the commercial banks also, given their generally larger balance sheets and capital bases which allow them to warehouse swaps, may see it as being potentially to their strategic advantage to limit the negotiability of swaps through such a clearing house.

Part 10

Accounting, Taxation and Legal Aspects of Swaps

Chapter 32

Accounting for Swaps, FRAs and Caps, Collars and Floors

INTRODUCTION

The proliferation of financial instruments has outpaced the accounting profession. The international accounting bodies are cognisant of the need for authoritative guidance on the accounting treatment for the latest financial instruments. The immediate future should see the promulgation by the worlds leading accounting bodies of accounting standards to assist practitioners in accounting for these financial instruments.

This chapter examines the basic components of interest rate and currency swaps, FRAs and caps, collars and floors from the accounting perspective and provides general guidance on the accounting treatment and disclosure of these financial instruments.

For each instrument the accounting principles are established at the outset. This is followed by an analysis of the accounting treatment likely to be adopted by both financial institutions and corporate sector entities in recording the instruments. The disclosure requirements and prudential supervision in relation to each instrument concludes each section.

ACCOUNTING FOR INTEREST RATE AND CURRENCY SWAPS

General accounting principles

The accounting treatment to be applied to interest rate and currency swaps must follow the economic substance of the transactions to produce a true and fair view of an organisation's activities.

When accounting for swaps, there are two constituent parts that need to be dealt with:

- the principal amounts, which may be notionally or physically exchanged; and
- the interest flows, which may be in the same or different currencies.

Principal

The principal amounts exchanged, whether they are actual or notional, are not in the legal form of loans or deposits and since a swap does not involve the provision or receipt of finance, it is not appropriate to record the amounts exchanged in the balance sheet. However, the principal amounts should be recorded in general ledger memorandum accounts. Therefore, in a cross-currency swap where there may be an actual exchange of principal, there is no grossing up of the balance sheet, the amounts merely pass through the bank or nostro accounts.

Assume company A and company B have entered an interest rate swap based on a notional principal of A$10m under which company A receives floating rate interest and pays fixed rate interest. The arrangement is depicted diagramatically in *Exhibit 32.1*.

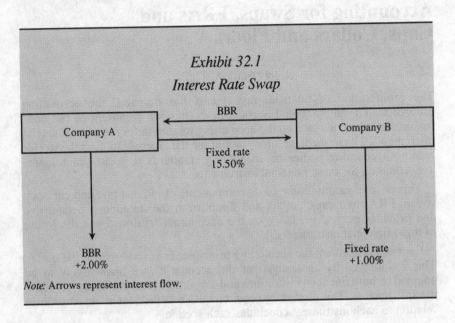

Exhibit 32.1
Interest Rate Swap

BBR

Company A

Company B

Fixed rate
15.50%

BBR
+2.00%

Fixed rate
+1.00%

Note: Arrows represent interest flow.

The accounting entries to recognise the notional principal balances in the books of company A are:

	A$	A$
At deal date		
DR floating interest rate swap receivable (memo)	xxx	
CR fixed interest rate swap payable (memo)		xxx

To record notional principal balances in memorandum accounts

At maturity date		
DR fixed interest rate swap payable (memo)	xxx	
CR floating interest rate swap receivable (memo)		xxx

To reverse the notional principal balances recorded in the memorandum accounts above

Interest flows

There are two alternative treatments for recognising the interest flows associated with a swap: accrual or revaluation.

Accrual

The accrual treatment is based on the traditional "matching" concept which seeks to apportion the income or expense associated with a transaction into the periods to which it relates. As swap payments and receipts are in the nature of interest they should also be treated in a similar manner as interest income or expense. Intuitively this treatment is most suited to swaps which are driven by the provision or receipt of finance. It is also appropriate for swaps that are used to hedge financial assets and liabilities where the revenue and expense associated with those assets and liabilities is recognised on an accruals basis.

Again with reference to *Exhibit 32.1* assume company A is receiving floating rate interest based on BBR and paying fixed rate interest.

The accounting entries to recognise the interest accruals in the books of company A are:

At balance date

	A$	$A
DR floating interest rate swap receivable (B/S)	xxx	
CR swap interest (P/L)		xxx
DR swap interest (P/L)	xxx	
CR fixed interest rate swap payable (B/S)		xxx

To record swap interest accruals

At interest settlement date

DR swap interest (P/L)	xxx	
CR floating interest rate swap receivable (B/S)		xxx
DR fixed interest rate swap payable (B/S)	xxx	
CR swap interest (P/L)		xxx

To record reversal of swap interest accrual entries above

DR nostro (B/S)	xxx	
CR swap interest (P/L)		xxx

To record floating rate swap interest received

DR swap interest (P/L)	xxx	
CR nostro (B/S)		xxx

To record fixed rate swap interest paid

Revaluation

The concept of revaluation stems from the fact that a swap is a financial instrument with a value. The value may be calculated by discounting the future swap cash flows. When the flows are actually paid or received they should be taken directly to the swap trading account in the profit and loss account. This is normally only appropriate for an entity that is trading in swaps and is discussed below. Where an entity uses a swap as a hedging instrument it would not be appropriate to revalue the deal to market interest rates unless the hedged instrument itself was recognised in the profit and loss on a revaluation basis. Financial institutions should make the distinction between swaps that are held as hedges against their own balance sheet and swaps that are trading instruments.

The accounting entry to recognise a profit on the revaluation of a trading swap is:

	A$	A$
DR revaluation suspense (B/S)	xxx	
CR swap revaluation (P/L)		xxx

The revaluation of swaps is discussed in detail below.

LTFX

The essence of applying LTFX as a currency swap substitute rests with the treatment of the forward margin implicit in the actual forward rate. As the forward margin reflects the interest rate differential existing between the two currencies, given the application of the LTFX contract to an underlying funding position the margin is considered in the nature of interest.

The forward margin should therefore be taken out of the foreign exchange position at the inception of transaction and amortised to the profit and loss account. The net effect of this process together with the interest expense associated with the underlying funding position is to reflect a true and fair profit and loss position, that is, this position will be similar to the position that would have been reflected if the organisation had arranged its funding in the other currency.

Foreign exchange implications

A currency swap in isolation does not create a foreign exchange exposure in respect of the principal amount underlying the deal. This exposure is eliminated due to the agreement of the parties to re-exchange the same amount of principal at the conclusion of the swap. The principal exchange and re-exchange of an A\$ and US\$ currency swap can be illustrated as:

	A\$	US\$
Exchange of principals at deal date	xxx	(xxx)
Re-exchange of principals at maturity	(xxx)	xxx
Foreign exchange exposure	Nil	Nil

Currency swaps, however, do create an exposure in respect of the forward cash flows representing the interest payments and receipts. For this reason, some care is required in revaluing currency swaps by reference to market exchange rates and interest rates.

Swap accounting decision model

The issue of whether a swap is a hedge or a trade is a crucial one in determining the most appropriate accounting treatment. The decision model set out in *Exhibit 32.2* will assist in determining the most appropriate accounting treatment.

Accounting treatment—financial institutions

The motive for entering the swap market is the best indication as to the most appropriate accounting treatment to be adopted with respect to that transaction, that is, either accrual or revaluation treatment.

Irrespective of the motive behind the transaction the financial institution may fulfil one of two roles. The financial institution may fulfil the role of a broker, merely arranging the transaction and receiving a fee.

Alternatively the financial institution may be one of the counterparties to a swap. In the latter case, although the financial institution may have no direct interest rate or exchange rate exposure, it has a credit risk dependent in part on these two factors.

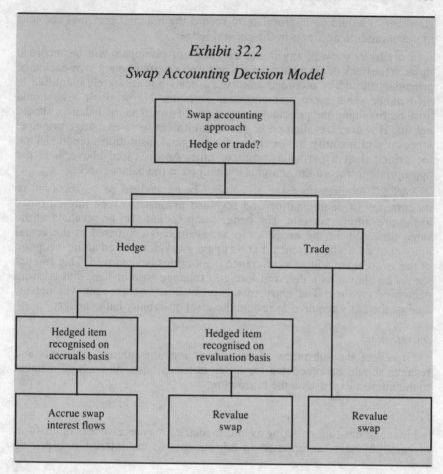

Exhibit 32.2

Swap Accounting Decision Model

Hedging with swaps

Both financial institutions and corporate sector entities may use swaps as part of an asset and liability management strategy.

Typically corporations enter hedging swaps to transfer funds received from the issue of a medium term bond or note, into another currency and/or to convert fixed rate finance into floating rate finance or vice versa. The accounting treatment for these transactions is the same whether or not that entity is a financial institution or a corporate sector entity.

Hedging swaps do not involve the provision of finance but rather involve the transfer or conversion of the original provision of finance. Assuming, therefore, that the principal amounts are not expressed in legal form as loans and deposits, the principal amounts should not be recorded in the balance sheet.

Principal

In an interest rate swap, the notional principal is *not* exchanged. The only flow of funds relates to interest on the notional principal amount.

However, it would be appropriate to record the notional principal amounts in memorandum accounts in the general ledger.

In a currency swap, any initial exchange of principals will be recorded through the bank or nostro accounts. The forward commitment to re-exchange principals should be recorded as forward deals but separately identified in off-balance sheet swap memorandum accounts. No profit or loss should arise on revaluing the principal components of swaps as the balances should net off. However, revaluation of the commitment to re-exchange principal amounts will quantify the extent of the financial institution's credit risk on the principal at a particular point in time. As discussed above, it is not appropriate to record the amounts exchanged in the balance sheet.

AAS 20 requires an asset or liability being hedged to be recorded in its currency of denomination and revalued against the reporting currency at the prevailing spot rate. The hedge swap should also be revalued at the same time. Where the hedge swap as revalued is compared to the actual amount of domestic currency that was paid away or received at the inception of the swap, there will be a difference if spot rates have moved. This amount should be shown as a deferred foreign exchange gain or loss, that is, swap debtor or creditor. The entry in the profit and loss account will net off against the entry required to restate the asset or liability being hedged.

Interest flows

To reflect the substance of the transaction, the interest payments and receipts should be accounted for on an accruals basis, as a net adjustment to the interest expense on the borrowing.

Fees

Financial institutions acting as intermediaries may receive fees in the form of cash payments as opposed to adjustments to the interest rate pricing levels.

Broker's fees should be recognised on deal date because they are remuneration for bringing the parties together.

Fees received for intermediation services need to be reviewed in the light of the overall profitability of a deal. Where a large fee is received on deal date and no return is generated, consideration should be given to amortising the fee over the life of the deal to match income with the expense of administering the deal and absorbing the credit risk. In the situation where the intermediary acts as broker as well as intermediary, the distinction between the constituent parts of the fee becomes blurred. Some of the fee could be recognised on deal date to recognise the work done in bringing the parties together, the rest being amortised over the life of the deal. In such a situation it would be preferable for the financial institution to determine a formal policy for accounting for fees, in particular the basis for calculating the amount of fee that can be recognised on deal date, and to apply this consistently.

Accounting entries

The accounting entries to recognise both interest rate and currency (unless indicated) hedging swaps are as follows:

- At deal date:
  —record notional principal balances in memorandum accounts (interest rate swap);
  —record exchange of principals in bank or nostro accounts (currency swap);
  —record commitment to re-exchange principals at maturity in memorandum accounts (currency swap).
- At balance date:
  —record swap interest accruals (pay and receive);
  —revalue the asset or liability being hedged to the current spot rate taking the difference to the profit and loss account (currency swap);
  —revalue the forward commitment to re-exchange principals at the current spot rate and take the difference to the profit and loss account. The revaluation surplus and deficit arising from the above revaluations will contra against each other in the profit and loss account (currency swap);
  —recognise the deferred foreign exchange gain or loss created as a result of a revaluation of the forward commitment as a sundry debtor or creditor in the balance sheet (currency swap).
- At interest payment date:
  —reverse swap interest accruals;
  —record swap interest payments and receipts.
- At maturity date:
  —reverse notional principal balances recorded in memorandum accounts (interest rate swap);
  —record re-exchange of principals in nostro accounts (currency swap);
  —reverse commitment to re-exchange principals recorded in memorandum accounts (currency swap);
  —reverse swap interest accruals;
  —record swap interest payments and receipts.

An example of the accounting entries in respect of hedging currency swaps is illustrated below in *Exhibit 32.3*.

Trading in swaps

For those financial institutions active in the swap market the instruments are seen as more than tools to hedge existing exposure. Swaps are financial instruments with value and as such qualify as legitimate trading instruments. The value of a swap contract is most commonly calculated by discounting the swaps cash flows. In the development years of the swap market a vast majority of swaps had cash flow characteristics similar to a bond. That is, the institution paid or received a fixed payment every six months. Hence, a revaluation methodology was developed based on a bond equivalent yield. This method assumed a constant stream of interest payments which could be invested and allowed for a single discount rate to be applied to all payments.

As the market has matured, there has been an increase in non-standard transactions such as delayed starts, zero coupons, step-ups and step-downs (in which the notional principal amount changes over time) and non-

Exhibit 32.3
Hedging—Currency Swap

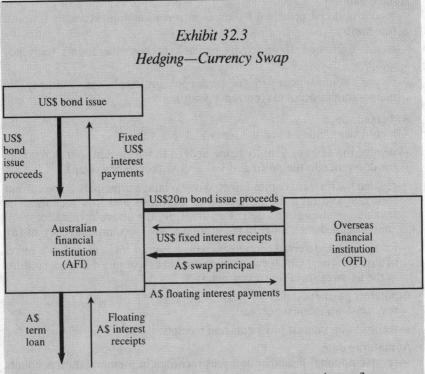

Note: Bold arrows represent principal flows whilst thin arrows represent interest flows.

ACCOUNTING ENTRIES—HEDGING WITH CROSS-CURRENCY SWAPS

Assume an Australian financial institution (AFI) has raised US$20m from a bond issue. To meet a term loan commitment in A$ AFI has entered a swap whereby the proceeds of the US$20m issue are swapped for A$. Over the term of the swap AFI will receive US$ interest on the US$20m and will pay A$ interest on the A$ balance it receives under the swap.

Additional information

Bond issue:

Term:	three years from 31 December 19X8
Coupon rate:	12.00% pa paid annually in arrears
Interest calculation:	CD basis (actual/360)
Interest paid:	31 December

Term loan:

Term:	three years from 31 December 19X8
Interest rate:	BBR + 1.00% set semi-annually in advance
Interest paid:	31 December

Currency swap:

Term:	three years from 31 December 19X8
Interest rate:	fixed rate (receive): 12.00%
	floating rate (pay): BBR + 1.00%
Swap fee:	A$200,000

Interest rates:

BBR set at:	13.00% at 31 December 19X8
	14.00% at 30 June 19X9

Exhibit 32.3—continued

Exchange rates:

31 December 19X8	A$1/US$0.625
30 June 19X9	A$1/US$0.650
31 December 19X9	A$1/US$0.725

The following accounting entries are required in the books of AFI to account for the bond issue, term loan and currency swap:

Entries at 31 December 19X8

Bond issue

1. DR US$ nostro (B/S)   US$20,000,000
   CR bond issue (B/S)   US$20,000,000

   To record Euronote issue and receipt of proceeds

Term loan

2. DR term loan (B/S)   A$32,000,000
   CR A$ nostro (B/S)   A$32,000,000

   To record term loan advance

Currency swap

3. DR prepaid swap fees (B/S)   A$200,000
   CR A$ nostro (B/S)   A$200,000

   To record payment of swap fee

4. DR A$ nostro (B/S)   A$32,000,000
   CR swap position (memo)   A$32,000,000

   DR swap position (memo)   US$20,000,000
   CR US$ nostro (B/S)   US$20,000,000

   To record initial exchange of amounts under currency swap

5. DR swap position (memo)   A$32,000,000
   CR forward swap payment (memo)   A$32,000,000

   DR forward swap receipt (memo)   US$20,000,000
   CR swap position (memo)   US$20,000,000

   To record commitment to re-exchange principal amounts under currency swap at maturity

Entries at 30 June 19X9

Bond issue

6. DR bond interest (P/L)   US$1,216,666
   CR accrued bond interest (B/S)   US$1,216,666

   To record accrued interest payable on the Euronote issue,
   that is, US$20,000,000 × 12.00% (365/2)/360 = US$1,216,666

Term loan

7. DR accrued interest receivable (B/S)   A$2,240,000
   CR term loan interest (P/L)   A$2,240,000

   To record accrued interest receivable on term loan

Currency swap

8. DR swap interest (P/L)   A$2,240,000
   CR A$ nostro (B/S)   A$2,240,000

   DR US$ nostro (B/S)   US$1,200,000
   CR swap interest (P/L)   US$1,200,000

   To record interest entitlements and obligations under currency swap,
   that is, (A$32,000,000 × 14.00% (BBR + 1.00%))/2 = A$2,240,000
           (US$20,000,000 × 12.00%)/2 = US$1,200,000

Exhibit 32.3—continued

9. DR swap fee expense (P/L)	A$33,333	
CR prepaid swap fees (B/S)		A$33,333

To record amortisation of swap fee, that is, 1/6th of A$200,000 = A$33,333

10. DR swap interest (P/L)	US$1,200,000	
CR bond interest (P/L)		US$1,216,666
DR spot position (memo)	US$16,666	
CR swap interest (P/L)		A$1,846,154
DR bond interest (P/L)	A$1,871,794	
CR spot position (memo)		A$25,640

To "deal out" US$ profit and loss account into A$ which recognises the position created by the currency swap receipt against bond interest payable

Entries at 31 December 19X9

Bond issue

11. DR bond interest (P/L)	US$1,216,667	
DR accrued interest (B/S)	US$1,216,666	
CR US$ nostro (B/S)		US$2,433,333

To record payment of bond interest

Term loan

12. DR A$ nostro (B/S)	A$4,640,000	
CR accrued interest receivable (B/S)		A$2,240,000
CR term loan interest (P/L)		A$2,400,000

To record receipt of term loan interest

Currency swap

13. DR swap interest (P/L)	A$2,400,000	
CR A$ nostro (B/S)		A$2,400,000
DR US$ nostro (B/S)	US$1,200,000	
CR swap interest (P/L)		US$1,200,000

To record interest entitlements and obligations under currency swap

14. DR swap fee expense (P/L)	A$33,333	
CR prepaid swap fees (B/S)		A$33,333

To reflect amortisation of swap fee, that is, 1/6th of A$200,000 = A$33,333

15. DR swap interest (P/L)	US$1,200,000	
CR bond interest (P/L)		US$1,216,667
DR spot position (memo)	US$16,667	
CR swap interest (P/L)		A$1,655,172
DR bond interest (P/L)	A$1,678,160	
CR spot position (memo)		A$22,988

To "deal out" US$ profit and loss account into A$ which recognises the position created by the currency swap receipt against bond interest payable

Closing entry

16. DR spot position (memo)	A$2,652	
CR FX revaluation (P/L)		A$2,652
DR forward swap payment (memo)	A$32,000,000	
CR forward swap receipt (memo)		A$27,586,206
CR swap creditor (B/S)		A$4,413,794

To close out memorandum accounts and consolidate results.

Exhibit 32.3—continued

A$	31 December 19X8	30 June 19X9	31 December 19X9	Net balance
Balance sheet				
A$ nostro	2. 32,000,000 CR 3. 200,000 CR 4. 32,000,000 DR	8. 2,240,000 CR	12. 4,640,000 DR 13. 2,240,000 CR	40,000 CR
Term loan	2. 32,000,000 DR			32,000,000 DR
Prepaid swap fee	3. 200,000 DR	9. 33,333 CR	14. 33,333 CR	133,334 DR
Accrued term loan interest receivable		7. 2,240,000 DR	12. 2,240,000 CR	Nil
Profit and loss				
Term loan interest		7. 2,240,000 CR	12. 2,400,000 CR	4,640,000 CR
Bond interest		10. 1,871,794 DR	15. 1,678,160 DR	3,549,954 DR
Swap interest		8. 2,240,000 DR 10. 1,846,154 CR	13. 2,240,000 DR 15. 1,655,172 CR	978,674 DR
Swap fee expense		9. 33,333 DR	14. 33,333 DR	66,666 DR
Memorandum accounts				
Forward swap payment	5. 32,000,000 CR			32,000,000 CR
Spot position	4. 32,000,000 CR	10. 25,640 CR	15. 22,988 CR	48,628 CR
Swap position	5. 32,000,000 DR			Nil
	Nil	Nil	Nil	Nil

Exhibit 32.3—continued

US$	31 December 19X8		30 June 19X9		31 December 19X9		Net balance
Balance sheet							
US$ nostro	1.	20,000,000 DR	8.	1,200,000 DR	11.	2,433,333 CR	33,333 CR
	4.	20,000,000 CR			13.	1,200,000 DR	
Bond issue	1.	20,000,000 CR					20,000,000 CR
Accrued Euronote interest payable		Nil	6.	1,216,666 CR	11.	1,216,666 DR	Nil
Profit and loss							
Bond interest			6.	1,216,666 DR	11.	1,216,667 DR	Nil
			10.	1,216,666 CR	15.	1,216,667 CR	
Swap interest			8.	1,200,000 CR	13.	1,200,000 CR	Nil
			10.	1,200,000 DR	15.	1,200,000 DR	
Memorandum accounts							
Forward swap receipt	5.	20,000,000 DR	10.	16,666 DR	15.	16,667 DR	20,000,000 DR
Spot position	4.	20,000,000 DR					33,333 DR
Swap position	5.	20,000,000 CR					Nil
		Nil		Nil		Nil	Nil

Exhibit 32.3—continued

Worksheet	US$	Equivalent A$ @ 0.725	A$	Total A$	Closing journal	A$ consolidated
Balance sheet						
Nostro	33,333 CR	45,976 CR	40,000 CR	85,976 CR		85,976 CR
Term loan			32,000,000 DR	32,000,000 DR		32,000,000 DR
Bond issue	20,000,000 CR	27,586,206 CR		27,586,206 CR		27,586,206 CR
Prepaid swap fee			133,334 DR	133,334 DR		133,334 DR
Swap creditor					4,413,794 CR	4,413,794 CR
Profit and loss						
Term loan interest			4,640,000 CR	4,640,000 CR		4,640,000 CR
Bond interest			3,549,954 DR	3,549,954 DR		3,549,954 DR
Swap interest			978,674 DR	978,674 DR		978,674 DR
Swap fee expense			66,666 DR	66,666 DR		66,666 DR
Foreign exchange revaluation					2,652 CR	2,652 CR
Memorandum accounts						
Forward swap payment	20,000,000 DR	27,586,206 DR			32,000,000 DR	Nil
Forward swap receipt	33,333 DR	45,976 DR	32,000,000 CR	32,000,000 CR	27,586,206 CR	Nil
Spot position			48,628 CR	27,586,206 DR	2,652 DR	Nil
				2,652 CR		
	Nil	Nil	Nil	Nil	Nil	Nil

Note: The aggregate of the swap creditor and debtor and bond issue should always equal the balance disclosed as term loan, that is, A$32m being the amount swapped in the currency swap.

coterminous payments where the fixed and floating payments are not paid at the same time.

In light of this, the larger dealers and traders have made changes regarding their valuation methodology. The estimated market value of swap agreements is now usually calculated by present valuing each individual cash flow using a zero coupon yield curve, rather than assuming a bond equivalent yield method. The rates used to derive the zero coupon curve are quoted interest rate swap market rates obtained from independent parties. The depth of the markets in the major currencies is such that the use of market quotations in revaluing these agreements better approximates the value of the agreement. The rates obtained from the interest rate swap market are constant par yield rates (since they assume the constant stream of interest payments) and are converted through a formula to obtain the zero coupon rates which are applied to each individual cash flow.

Financial institutions typically handle their swap books in one of two ways:

• Matched book where swaps are taken onto the book and the position is hedged through the use of appropriate treasury instruments. If a matching swap (a swap that offsets the exposures created by the initial swap) is undertaken then the hedge will be unwound.

• Portfolio or warehouse where hedging action is taken against the net exposure, but a match is not identified for each swap.

Financial institutions that run a sizeable swaps book generally experience problems of hedge identification, particularly where a swap book is run on the portfolio approach. For major institutions with an active and sizeable swap book the only appropriate method is to mark all positions to market.

There are currently three methods in use for the revaluation of trading swaps. These are:

• revaluing the fixed interest stream of the swap only;

• revaluing both the fixed interest and the known floating interest streams of the swap;

• revaluing both the fixed interest and floating interest streams of the swap. This method involves projecting rates for the floating interest streams using a synthetic yield curve.

Examples of the profit calculation and accounting entries in respect of the revaluation of a trading swap are illustrated below in *Exhibit 32.4*.

As stated earlier revaluing swaps involves discounting the associated cash flows. A key factor in the net present value calculations is what discount rate to use. The three options are:

• constant par yield rate, for example, semi-annualised Treasury bond redemption yield of the relevant maturity;

• zero coupon curve rate, a different rate for cash flows of different maturities. The zero coupon curve rates represent the discount rates required to give the swap a net present value of nil where the fixed side of the swap is the coupon curve rate; or

• swap mid rate, that is, market rates quoted in financial press.

Exhibit 32.4
Trading—Interest Rate Swap

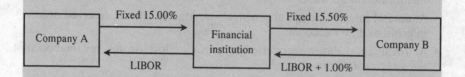

ACCOUNTING ENTRIES—TRADING IN INTEREST RATE SWAPS

Assume the financial institution has entered into a US$ interest rate swap with company A, whereby it will pay floating interest at LIBOR and received fixed interest at 15.00% pa. In order to lock itself into a profit the financial institution matches this swap with another transacted with company B except that this time the financial institution will receive floating interest at LIBOR + 1.00% and pay fixed interest at 15.50% pa. The financial institution is taking 1.00% pa on the floating rate side and paying 0.50% pa on the fixed rate side.

Additional information:

Deal date:	1 January 19X7	
Maturity date:	31 December 19X8	
Balance date:	31 December	
Interest payments:	31 December	
Fixed rate:	Pay	15.50%
	Receive	15.00%
		(0.50%)
Floating rates:	Pay	LIBOR
	Receive	LIBOR + 1.00%
		1.00%
Notional principal:	US$10m	
Zero coupon rates:	14.00%, 15.00% for Years 1, 2 respectively	

Cash flows for Years 1 and 2

	Net floating rate receivable	Net fixed rate payable	N.P.V. cash flow	US$
Year 1	100,000	(50,000)	$50,000 \times \dfrac{1}{(1 + 0.14)^1}$	= 43,860
Year 2	100,000	(50,000)	$50,000 \times \dfrac{1}{(1 + 0.15)^2}$	= 37,807
				81,667

The financial institution would therefore record a profit of US$81,667.

The following accounting entry is required in the books of company A to account for the profit on the interest rate swaps.

Entry at 1 January 19X7

DR revaluation suspense (B/S)	US$81,667	
CR swap revaluation (P/L)		US$81,667

Accounting entries

The accounting entries to recognise trading swaps are as follows:

- At deal date—record notional principal balances in memorandum accounts.
- At maturity date—reverse the notional principal balances recorded in the memorandum accounts above.
- At date of interest receipt or payment—recognise interest received or paid in profit and loss account.
- At revaluation date—recognise the profit or loss on the revaluation of the swap cash flows.

Accounting treatment—corporate sector

Corporate sector entities utilise the swap market principally to access sources of finance at interest rates more favourable than those available in the open market or as a risk management instrument.

The accounting treatment for swaps undertaken by corporate sector entities will normally be identical to the treatment advocated for financial institutions in the section "Hedging with Swaps". The accounting treatment to be adopted is not dependent upon the status of the counterparty, that is, corporate sector versus financial institution, but rather the reason for the transaction.

Corporate sector entities will generally not be involved in trading swaps.

When accounting for swaps undertaken by corporate sector entities it is important to remember the underlying purpose of the swap, that being to reduce the entities' overall funding costs. The swap transaction can be considered a secondary or ancillary transaction undertaken to mitigate the exposure generated by the core borrowing transaction. Accordingly the interest payments and receipts made under the swap should be offset against the borrowing costs of the corporate sector entity when performing a cost of borrowing calculation.

Disclosure requirements

The accounting profession is yet to specifically address many of the more complex issues relevant to the banking industry. Very little consideration has been given to interest rate and currency swaps in the existing accounting standards. However, many countries do have foreign exchange standards which have some application to currency swap contracts.

The disclosure requirements in Australia, the United States and the United Kingdom with respect to swaps are compared below.

Australia

There are currently no specific disclosure requirements with respect to interest rate and currency swaps for Australian statutory reporting purposes. The existence of swap contracts should be disclosed if their omission would impact the overall truth and fairness of the financial statements.

Many Australian financial institutions refer to the existence of swap contracts in a commitments and/or contingent liabilities note. The United States practice of quantifying the notional principal amounts and the net open risk position with respect to swaps has rarely been followed in Australia.

Limited guidance is available in relation to the following issues:

- Swap interest: Sched. 7 of the *Companies Regulations* requires the disclosure of interest both credited and debited to the profit and loss account. Technically swap receipts and payments are not interest as they do not represent a cost of funding. However, it is still considered an acceptable policy to include swap interest streams in the amount disclosed as interest.

- Foreign currency implications: AAS 20 (in two parts, that is, AAS 20 Part A and Part B) issued by Australian Accounting Bodies in December 1987 and ASRB 1012 issued by the Accounting Standards Review Board in September 1987 are the only sources of definitive guidance available in Australia on accounting for foreign exchange and, in particular, the hedging of foreign exchange exposure. It therefore should be complied with by entities using the mechanism of a currency swap to hedge foreign currency exposure. In this respect it must be remembered that the swap itself does not create or eliminate a spot position, rather the underlying cash flows must be analysed to ensure that the correct foreign currency exposure is recognised and any revaluation necessary is performed in an appropriate manner.

- Hedging swaps: ASRB 1012 has made progress in the swap accounting debate by making specific reference to the accounting for hedging swaps at para. (xxiv) of the commentary section.

The standard states that "a further manner in which a foreign currency monetary item might be hedged is by swapping or exchanging repayment schedules with another party. This will usually involve the company in an arrangement cost and will either effectively change the foreign currency in which exposure to exchange rate changes will occur or, if the swap leads to adoption of a domestic currency repayment schedule, elimination of such exposure. A contingency may exist in respect of the original repayment schedule in the event of a default. Once a swap is in place the company is to account for exchange gains and losses (if any) on the adopted monetary item (in the normal manner, as set out in paras (v) and (vii))." Referring to para. (v) we are instructed that "exchange differences on foreign currency monetary items are required to be calculated by translating the foreign currency amount of the monetary item at the spot rate current at the balance date and comparing the resulting amount with the same foreign currency amount translated at the date on which the original transaction took place".

ASRB 1012 also specifies the treatment for arrangement costs incurred in entering into hedging transactions stating that costs should be "account(ed) (for) by deferral and amortisation to the profit and loss account over the life of the adopted item".

The ASRB guidance detailed above is identical to the guidance offered in AAS 20.

- Trading swaps (or speculative swaps): under the standards the treatment of speculative foreign currency transactions differs from that of hedging (or non-speculative) transactions. "Speculative dealing" is defined in ASRB 1012 as "the taking of a position in a foreign currency, whether by entry into a foreign currency contract or otherwise, solely for the purpose of profiting from movements in the exchange rate for that currency." A hedging transaction is an ancillary transaction undertaken to mitigate existing or anticipated exposure associated with the main transaction of acquiring goods or services.

This definition needs careful analysis as any foreign exchange dealings not undertaken solely for this purpose must be accounted for under the measurement rules in the standards, not just the disclosure requirements. For example, some transactions are entered into for arbitrage reasons on the comparative interest rates between two countries and not for profit on exchange rate movements.

Whilst the standards do not propose a method of accounting for speculative foreign exchange transactions, they do require certain disclosures in respect of such transactions. Both ASRB 1012 and AAS 20 require the disclosure where material, of the methods used in translating the transactions involved (for example, whether resulting monetary balances and gains or losses have been determined by reference to movements in forward rates) and the net gain or loss on such dealing taken to the profit and loss account for the financial year.

United States

There are currently no specific United States accounting standards issued in respect of interest rate and currency swaps.

Principal commitments under interest rate swaps are not recorded on the balance sheet since the agreements relate only to the exchange of interest streams and not to the notional principal.

Generally speaking, all swaps are revalued to market unless they meet specific hedge criteria. Those swaps designated as hedge positions must meet hedge criteria similar to those for financial futures (SFAS 80).

United Kingdom

Under United Kingdom company law and accounting standards there are currently no specific disclosure requirements in respect of interest rate and currency swaps for statutory reporting purposes. Disclosure is likely to be required, however, for a set of accounts to show a true and fair view, as is required by the *Companies Act* 1985 (U.K.).

The level and type of disclosure will be different depending on whether the accounts are prepared by a bank or by a non-banking company.

• Banks: United Kingdom incorporated banks prepare their statutory accounts under Sched. 9 of the *Companies Act* 1985. There are no prescribed formats for either the balance sheet or profit and loss account and the required extent of note disclosure does not focus on off-balance sheet instruments. In general any accruals of swap payments or receipts and any revaluations are included in the balance sheet as part of "Other Accounts" but are not separately identified. No analysis of income or expenditure is provided in the profit and loss account, the disclosed details starting with "Profit before Tax".

The existence of swaps as an activity of the bank is in most cases only disclosed by a note on the accounting policy used for swaps and a note as follows: "In addition the bank had commitments in respect of interest rate and currency swaps." It is unusual for a United Kingdom bank to quantify the notional principal amounts or the open risk positions.

The format of United Kingdom bank accounts will be "standardised" and the extent of disclosure will be increased with the adoption of the EEC Bank Accounts Directive. This Directive must be brought into law by member states by 31 December 1990 and must apply to accounting periods beginning on or after 1 January 1993. A consultative paper setting out the United Kingdom government's proposals for implementing the Directive is due to be published in 1989.

- Other companies: for United Kingdom tax reasons non-banking companies have not generally been involved in swap transactions in the United Kingdom except as end users.

United Kingdom companies which are not banks are required to prepare statutory accounts in accordance with the provisions of Sched. 1 of the *Companies Act* 1985. This Schedule sets down prescribed formats for the balance sheet and the profit and loss account but makes no specific provision for the treatment of swaps.

Generally accepted practice is to reflect swaps in statutory accounts as part of the financing transaction to which they relate. Net payments or receipts in respect of swaps are treated as adjustments to interest receivable or payable but are not separately disclosed. The notes to the accounts will generally disclose the existence of the swap and possibly its financial effect.

In November 1987 the Technical Committee of the Institute of Chartered Accountants in England and Wales issued Technical Release TR 677 which stated the following in respect of interest rate swaps: "There should be full disclosure of the arrangement in the notes to the financial statements, so that the commercial effect of the whole transaction, including any possible risk of exposure in the event of the failure of the swap party, is clearly explained." This Technical Release has no statutory power but is designed to assist in the preparation of statutory accounts required to show a true and fair view.

Disclosure examples

Exhibit 32.5 sets out extracts from the financial statements of two of the four largest local banks in Australia together with the leading United States and United Kingdom banks insofar as they concern the swap activities of the bank.

Prudential supervision

Introduction

Technological and increased financial market sophistication have encouraged the development and growth of new financial instruments and techniques. Many off-balance sheet financing techniques are complicated and expose unsuspecting bankers to undue risk. For this reason central banks the world over are now paying much closer attention to monitoring the proliferation of off-balance sheet business and particularly the growth in the volume of swaps transactions.

The approach employed by the central banks to monitoring and supervising the off-balance sheet activities of the leading trading banks is gaining global

Exhibit 32.5

Note Disclosure—Examples

AUSTRALIA

Australia and New Zealand Banking Group Limited—September 1987

Note 23 off-balance sheet financial instruments

The Group is an active market participant in off-balance sheet financial instruments, principally forward exchange contracts, interest rate and currency swaps, forward rate agreements, financial futures and options traded in the financial markets throughout the world.

These instruments are used by the Group to:

- facilitate prudent and strategic management of the interest rate and currency risks inherent in the Group's banking activities;

- provide financial services as an intermediary to enable customers to modify, transfer or reduce their interest rate or foreign exchange risks; and

- enable arbitrage between the various financial markets or positions to be adopted which take advantage of profitable trading opportunities.

Management of these instruments is integrated into the Group's prudential risk management practices. In particular, assessment of any credit risk is included in the evaluation of the exposure of the Group to customers.

Adequate provision has been made for any unrealised losses and it is not envisaged that any irrecoverable liability will arise from the settlement of these types of transactions.

Westpac Banking Corporation—September 1987

Note 25 commitments and contingent liabilities

The Bank and Group have commitments in respect of forward purchases and sales of foreign currencies, interest rate and currency swap transactions, futures operations, provision of credit, underwriting facilities, purchases of assets and other engagements entered into in the normal course of business.

UNITED STATES

Citicorp—December 1987

Note 16 non-funds related financial products interest rate and foreign exchange products

Citicorp offers interest rate and foreign exchange futures, forwards, options, and swaps which enable customers to transfer, modify, or reduce their interest rate and foreign exchange risks. Futures and forward contracts are commitments to buy or sell at a future date a financial instrument or currency at a contracted price and may be settled in cash or through delivery. Swap contracts are commitments to settle in cash at a future date or dates based on differentials between specified financial indices as applied to a notional principal amount. Option contracts give the acquirer, for a fee, the right but not the obligation to buy or sell within a limited time a financial instrument or currency at a contracted price and may also settle in cash based on differentials between specified indices.

In most cases, Citicorp manages the exposures related to these products as part of its overall interest rate and foreign exchange trading activities, which include both funded asset and liability positions and non-funded positions. For example, Citicorp may hold a security in its trading portfolio and at the same time have futures contracts to sell that security. The losses on one position may substantially offset gains on the other position. These products are also utilised by Citicorp to reduce exposures outside the trading portfolios, as hedges of interest rate gaps and foreign exchange positions.

The market and credit risks inherent in traditional banking services are also present in these specialised financial products, as are the various operating risks that exist in all financial activities. Notional principal amounts are often used to express the volume of these transactions but do not represent the much smaller amounts potentially subject to risk.

Exhibit 32.5—continued

Market risk is the exposure created by fluctuations in interest and foreign exchange rates, and is a function of the type of product, the volume of the transaction, the tenor and terms of the agreement, and the volatility of the underlying interest rate or exchange rate. Market risk is affected by the mix of the aggregate portfolio and the extent to which positions have offsetting exposures. The market risk of an interest rate swap, for example, will be reduced by the presence of securities, financial futures, or other interest rate swap positions with offsetting exposures. Citicorp manages its trading activities in these specialised financial products on a market value basis that recognises in earnings the gains or losses resulting from changes in market interest or exchange rates. Trading limits and monitoring procedures are used to control the overall exposure to market risk.

A variety of monitoring procedures are used to control the overall exposure to market risk. These monitoring procedures include risk points, a system that measures the exposure to movements in market interest rates; cost to close, a concept that determines the cost of covering an open position; and earnings at risk which estimates the earnings impact of changes in market interest rates based on historical interest rate volatility.

Credit risk is the exposure to loss in the event of non-performance by the other party to a transaction, and is a function of the ability of the counterparty to honor its obligations to Citicorp. For these specialised financial products the amounts due from or due to the counterparty will change as a result of movements in market rates, and the amount subject to credit risk is limited to this fluctuating amount. Citicorp controls credit risk through credit approvals, limits, and monitoring procedures, and the recognition in earnings of unrealised gains on these transactions is dependent on management's assessment as to collectibility. Credit losses related to these interest rate and foreign exchange products have not been material.

Citicorp has significant presence in the markets for these interest rate and foreign exchange products. The notional principal amount of Citicorp's outstanding interest rate swaps was US$116 billion and US$63.4 billion at 31 December 1987 and 1986, respectively. At 31 December 1987, an estimate of the related credit risk equalled US$2.9 billion. This measure of credit risk related to interest rate swaps can be estimated by calculating the present value of the cost of replacing at market rates all outstanding agreements; this estimate of credit risk does not consider the impact that future changes in interest rates will have on such cost.

Commitments to purchase and sell money market instruments or securities and commitments to settle against financial indices under interest rate futures, forward, and option contracts were US$94.7 billion and US$78.9 billion at 31 December 1987 and 1986, respectively, and commitments to purchase and sell currencies under foreign currency spot, forward, and option transactions were US$341.8 billion and US$216.3 billion at 31 December 1987 and 1986, respectively. These amounts are gross volume indicators only and do not reflect the extent to which positions may offset one another. As discussed above, the amounts potentially subject to market and credit risk are substantially smaller than the gross volumes indicated here.

Manufacturers Hanover—December 1987

At 31 December 1987, assets with a book value of US$5,470m are pledged, as required or permitted by law to secure certain public and trust deposits, to secure repurchase agreements or for other purposes.

In the normal course of business, various commitments and contingent liabilities are outstanding that are not reflected in the consolidated financial statements. A summary of these commitments and contingent liabilities at 31 December 1987 and 1986 is presented below.

	1987 (US$m)	1986 (US$m)
Standby letters of credit and foreign guarantees[1]	7,564	9,241
Other letters of credit	1,818	1,544
Commitments to extend credit (excluding credit cards and related plans)	21,094	21,571
Commitments to purchase and sell foreign exchange	90,777	64,439
Forward and futures contracts:		
commitments to purchase	5,267	6,789
commitments to sell	9,369	3,263
Written options:		
commitments to purchase	6,290	496
commitments to sell	3,694	422

Exhibit 32.5—continued

The notional principal amount of interest rate swaps and swap related products outstanding is US$70.0 billion at 31 December 1987 and US$37.5 billion at 31 December 1986.

In the opinion of management, there are no material commitments or contingent liabilities that represent unusual risks.

Note:

1. Standby letters of credit are net of risk participations of US$858m and US$727m at 31 December 1987 and 1986, respectively.

UNITED KINGDOM
Barclays PLC—December 1987

Note 32 contingent liabilities and commitments

". . . [T]here are financial futures contracts, forward contracts for the purchase and sale of foreign currencies, option contracts and various other facilities to customers which are not reflected in the consolidated balance sheet. The majority of these facilities are offset by corresponding obligations of third parties and it is not envisaged that any material irrecoverable liability will arise from these transactions.".

Midland Bank PLC—December 1987

Note 29 contingent liabilities

". . . [T]here were outstanding financial futures contracts, contracts for the sale and purchase of foreign currencies and bullion, currency options contracts, forward rate and interest rate swap agreements and other financial instruments entered into in the normal course of business. Midland Bank plc has guaranteed the performance of a subsidiary in respect of certain of these items."

---

uniformity. This uniformity has been strengthened by the adoption by the world's major central banks of the Basle Supervisors Committee statement "International Convergence of Capital Measurement and Capital Standards".

The current prudential supervisory standards in Australia, the United States and the United Kingdom with respect to swaps are compared below. The recent adoption of the Basle guidelines on capital adequacy by each country's central bank will result in a similar system of prudential supervision being used in each country in the near future.

Australia

Swap activity undertaken by the trading banks in Australia is monitored by the Reserve Bank of Australia (RBA) through its banking supervision division.

The swap activities of the trading banks are monitored via the off-balance sheet business returns submitted quarterly by all trading banks. The return requires trading banks to disclose details of the "gross exposure" and "assessed risk" for products falling into three categories:

- contingent liabilities (including guarantees, standby letters of credit, warranties, bill indorsements);
- commitments (including outright forward purchases, commitments to provide financial facilities and underwriting facilities); and
- foreign exchange, interest rate and other foreign exchange rate related transactions (including interest rate swaps and currency swaps).

"Gross exposure" is measured as the face value of the contracts whilst the "assessed risk" represents a risk weighted gross exposure.

Many trading banks have in the past applied risk factors calculated by overseas parent companies when calculating assessed risk for RBA reporting. However, as a consequence of the adoption of the Basle Committee's guidelines for the measurement of capital adequacy by the RBA in August 1988 many trading banks are now using this basis for the calculation of assessed risk.

The RBA now effectively controls and monitors trading bank's exposures relative to swaps and other off-balance sheet instruments as a result of their adoption of the Basle guidelines and the requirement for trading banks to periodically lodge returns setting out the calculation of their ratio of capital to risk weighted assets.

Monitoring of swap activity carried on by authorised foreign exchange dealers is carried out through the open position reports lodged by authorised foreign exchange dealers. Currently, there is no formal lodgement of off-balance sheet business returns similar to trading bank returns by authorised foreign exchange dealers. With continuing improvements in RBA supervisory capacity the formal reporting of off-balance sheet business by authorised foreign exchange dealers may become mandatory.

United States

Swap activities undertaken by banks in the United States are subject to prudential supervision by the United States Federal Reserve as a consequence of its adoption of the Basle guidelines on capital adequacy in March 1989.

United Kingdom

To date swap activities undertaken by banks in the United Kingdom have not been subject to prudential supervision by the Bank of England. Swap activities will be brought within the scope of supervision once the Basle proposals on capital convergence have been implemented in the United Kingdom which will be by the end of 1989. In October 1988 the Bank of England issued a notice to institutions explaining how it intends to implement the agreement in the United Kingdom. This is to assign credit conversion factors to the principal amounts of all off-balance sheet interest rate and exchange rate agreements to calculate an on-balance sheet equivalent and to include the resulting equivalent in the overall risk calculation.

ACCOUNTING FOR FRAs

General accounting principles

Experience in accounting for FRAs is limited and as yet no country has issued accounting standards which specifically cover them. The methodology to be adopted in accounting for these instruments is dependent on the intention underlying the transaction, that is, whether they are for hedging or trading purposes.

Accounting treatment—financial institutions

Hedging with FRAs

In general, for a FRA to qualify as a hedge the following conditions would have to be met:

- the financial institution or corporate must have net assets or liabilities which are subject to interest rate risk and in determining this condition the company must first take into account commitments and anticipated transactions which offset or reduce the exposure;
- the FRA must reduce that exposure and be designated as a hedge. The FRA must be designed in such a way (with regard to maturities, etc.) that the result of the FRA will substantially offset the effect of interest rate changes on the exposed item.

Intention is important in determining whether a hedging state exists. Since it is frequently rather subjective, internal procedures should provide for the identification of hedging transactions at the outset, and for the documenting of such decisions. Mere existence of positions is not enough; the accounting should reflect the results of management decisions, and if a conscious decision was not taken, then the FRA should be treated as a trading FRA. However, as FRAs can be closely tailored it should often be easier for an FRA to qualify as a hedge than it is for a financial future.

When an FRA qualifies as a hedge in accordance with the above criteria, the amount paid or received by the company on settlement day should be deferred and appropriated to profit and loss over the fixed rate period on a straight line basis (the discount element can usually be ignored as immaterial) to match and offset the effect of the hedged item.

Accounting entries

The accounting entries to recognise a hedging FRA are as follows:
- At deal date—record the principal sum of the FRA transaction in memorandum accounts.
- At settlement date:
  —record the cash impact of the transaction, that is, the bank balance and a deferred account in the general ledger;
  —reverse memorandum account entries raised on deal date;

The gain or loss at settlement should then be amortised on a straight line basis to the profit or loss account over the period for which the hedge was obtained.

An example of the accounting entries in respect of hedging FRAs is illustrated below in *Exhibit 32.6*.

Trading in FRAs

Most FRAs will probably fall within the criteria for treatment as a hedge. However, some financial institutions will enter into FRAs as part of their trading activities. In such cases, those FRAs outstanding at the end of the reporting period should be marked-to-market. In marking the FRA portfolio to market interest rates, settlement rate quotations for the relevant period should be obtained from an independent source.

Accounting entries

The accounting entries to recognise trading FRAs are as follows:
- At deal date—record the principal sum of the FRA transaction in the memorandum accounts.

Exhibit 32.6

Accounting Entries—Hedging with FRAs

Assume that at 31 December 19X8 a financial institution has A$100m in assets yielding an average of 15.00% (with rate adjustment after one year) funded by A$100m in liabilities costing 13.00% (with rate adjustment after nine months). To eliminate its exposure to an increase in BBR when its liabilities are subject to rate adjustment on 30 September 19X9, the financial institution enters into an FRA (at 31 December 19X8) at 13.00%. The contract amount of the FRA will be A$103,312,329 since at the contract rate of 13.00% the proceeds will be A$100m, the amount being hedged. Assume that at 30 September 19X9 the three month BBR is 17.00%.

Before recording the FRA transaction, the financial institutions profit and loss account for the year to 31 December 19X9 would be as follows:

Interest income
A$100,000,000 × 15.00%   = A$15,000,000

Interest expense
$$A\$100,000,000 \times \left(\frac{13}{100} \times \frac{272}{365} + \frac{17}{100} \times \frac{93}{365} \right) = A\$14,019,178$$

Net income   A$ 980,822

On 30 September 19X9 the financial institution will receive A$976,865 from the counterparty under the FRA, calculated using the settlement sum formula as follows:

$$\frac{36,500 \times 103,312,329}{(93 \times 13) + 36,500} - \frac{36,500 \times 103,312,329}{(93 \times 17) + 36,500}$$

= 100,000,000   −   99,023,135

= A$976,865

This amount should be deferred and released to income over the period 30 September to 31 December 19X9. Including the FRA transaction, the financial institution's profit and loss account for the year to 31 December 19X9 would be as follows (assuming that the cash received in settlement of the FRA is invested to yield BBR):

	A$
Interest income	15,000,000
Interest expense	(14,019,178)
Settlement income from FRA	976,865
Interest income on FRA settlement	42,313
	2,000,000

Or, in other words, a net spread of 2.00% for the entire period of one year.

The following accounting entries are required in the books of the financial institution to account for the hedging FRA:

Entries at 31 December 19X8

	A$	A$
DR FRA hedge—borrowing (memo)	103,312,329	
CR FRA hedge—position (memo)		103,312,329

To record FRA commitment in memorandum accounts

Entries at 30 September 19X9

DR nostro (B/S)	976,865	
CR FRA—interest in advance (B/S)		976,865

To account for receipt of FRA settlement sum

DR FRA hedge—position (memo)	103,312,329	
CR FRA hedge—borrowing (memo)		103,312,329

To reverse FRA commitment following FRA settlement

Exhibit 32.6—continued

Entries required each day during the hedge period—1 October to 31 December 19X9

DR FRA—interest in advance (B/S)   10,504
CR FRA—interest received (P/L)   10,504

Being amortisation of FRA interest received in advance on straight line basis, over the 93 days

---

- At revaluation date—recognise the gain or loss in the balance sheet and profit and loss account. These entries should be reversed at the beginning of the next period.
- At settlement date
  —record the gain or loss on the transaction, that is, the cash impact on the bank account and the corresponding impact on the profit and loss account;
  —reverse memorandum account entries raised on deal date.

An example of the accounting entries in respect of trading FRAs is illustrated below in *Exhibit 32.7.*

Accounting treatment—corporate sector

The accounting treatment for FRAs undertaken by corporate sector entities will normally be identical to the treatment outlined for financial institutions in the section "Hedging with FRAs".

Corporate sector entities will generally not be involved in trading FRAs.

Disclosure requirements

To date there have been no specific accounting standards issued by any of the major international accounting bodies covering the disclosure requirements with respect to FRAs. Disclosure with respect to FRAs will be dependent on the individual circumstances of each entity's FRAs activity, pertinent legislation in each country and the application of that country's relevant accounting standards.

The disclosure requirements in Australia, the United States and the United Kingdom with respect to FRAs are compared below.

Australia

At present, there are no disclosure requirements specifically related to FRAs, and banks generally treat them in a similar way to financial futures and forward foreign exchange deals from an accounting disclosure viewpoint, that is, the existence of FRA commitments is disclosed but not quantified.

Specifically, the following points should be considered when addressing the issue of accounts disclosure:

- Where the accounting policies adopted for FRAs are significant in the context of the financial statements such policies should be disclosed in the notes to the accounts, and they should distinguish between hedge FRAs and trading FRAs.

Exhibit 32.7

Accounting Entries—Trading in FRAs

Assume that on 31 October 19X8 a financial institution enters into a three against six FRA at 15.00% on A$1m. The FRA is part of its portfolio.

At 31 December 19X8 the financial institution must estimate its probable gain or loss under the FRA and therefore must estimate three month BBR on 31 January 19X9. If the estimated three month BBR for 31 January 19X9 was 16.00% the estimated loss would be A$2,288 as follows:

$$\frac{36,500 \times 1,000,000}{(90 \times 15) + 36,500} - \frac{36,500 \times 1,000,000}{(90 \times 16) + 36,500}$$

$$= 964,333 \quad - \quad 962,045$$

$$= A\$2,288$$

This loss would be provided for in the 31 December 19X8 financial statements.

The following accounting entries are required in the books of the financial institution to account for the trading FRA:

	A$	A$
Entries at 31 October 19X8		
DR FRA trade—borrowing (memo)	1,000,000	
CR FRA trade—position (memo)		1,000,000
To record FRA commitment in memorandum accounts		
Entries at 31 December 19X8		
DR FRA trade—unrealised profit and loss (P/L)	2,288	
CR FRA trade—payable (B/S)		2,288

Being revaluation of FRA on mark-to-market basis. The revaluation entry should be reversed on first day of following month

Entries at 31 January 19X9		
DR bank (B/S)	xxx	
CR FRA trade—settlement profit (P/L)		xxx
To record FRA profit and loss on settlement		
DR FRA trade—position (memo)	1,000,000	
CR FRA trade—borrowing (memo)		1,000,000
To reverse FRA commitment recorded in memorandum accounts		

- Consideration should be given to quantifying the commitments under FRAs at year end where the amount is material.

United States

The United States has no specific disclosure requirements in respect of FRAs. Generally banks have looked to the guidance contained in SFAS 80—Accounting for Futures Contracts in determining the accounting and disclosure requirements in respect of FRAs as interest rate futures and FRAs have the same economic substance.

United Kingdom

The United Kingdom has no specific disclosure requirements in respect of FRAs. Generally accepted practice is as described above for Australia.

Prudential supervision

Introduction

FRA hedging and trading activity by trading banks is monitored by most central banks through the regular submission of supervision reports. The FRA hedging and trading activity of corporate sector entities is largely unsupervised.

The current prudential supervisory standards in Australia, the United States and the United Kingdom with respect to FRAs are compared below.

Australia

FRA activity undertaken by the trading banks in Australia is monitored by the Reserve Bank of Australia through its banking supervision division.

The FRA activities of the trading banks, as with swaps, are monitored via the off-balance sheet business returns submitted quarterly by all trading banks. The return requires trading banks to disclose details of their "Gross Exposure" to FRA contracts and the "Assessed Risk" in respect of their FRA activity.

Monitoring and control of trading bank exposures in relation to FRA activity is also effected via the capital adequacy requirements in the same manner as described for swaps previously.

FRA activity by corporate sector entities is not formally monitored by any supervisory authority.

United States and United Kingdom

As with other off-balance sheet interest rate products the system of supervision now in use in the United States and to be introduced in the United Kingdom is that set down in the Basle agreement on capital convergence.

ACCOUNTING FOR CAPS, COLLARS AND FLOORS

General accounting principles

The accounting treatment to be adopted is dependent on the nature of the transaction, that is, whether it is a cap, collar or floor and the perspective of the party to the transaction, that is:

- floating rate borrower;
- floating rate investor;
- party with matched positions; or
- party with unmatched positions.

These treatments are outlined in detail in the rest of this section. The accounting treatment is similar to that for options.

Accounting treatment—financial institutions

Hedging with caps, collars and floors

- Purchase of an interest rate cap: the risk when borrowing floating rate funds is that interest rates will escalate and force a rise in borrowing costs. The purchase of an interest rate cap protects against this escalation and effectively places a ceiling on the interest rate the borrower will pay.

Accordingly the cost of the cap premium becomes an integral part of the overall borrowing cost calculation. The cost of the cap premium should be deferred and charged to profit and loss over the term of the cap.

An example of the accounting entries in respect of an interest rate cap is illustrated below in *Exhibit 32.8.*

Exhibit 32.8

Accounting Entries—Interest Rate Cap

Assume that on 1 January 19X7 company A issued US$10m of FRNs maturing in five years' time, on 31 December 19X1. The interest rate on the FRNs is set at London LIBOR plus 10bps, which is fixed semi-annually on 30 June and 31 December.

Company A is concerned at the recent volatility in United States interest rates and decides to hedge against excessive upward movements by purchasing a strip of interest rate caps covering each rollover period. The cost of the cap is set at 0.50% for each six monthly rollover, (that is, 1.00% pa). The total cost of the cap is therefore US$500,000 which is paid on 1 January 19X7 (for purposes of the example the pricing ignores the time value impact on the premium).

At the start of the contract, US$ six month LIBOR is standing at 8.00%. The strike rate on each of the caps is 9.00%.

Average LIBOR and actual funding costs over the first two periods are as follows:

	LIBOR	Funding costs
30 June 19X7	10.00%	10.10%
31 December 19X7	7.50%	7.60%

The following accounting entries are required in the books of company A to account for the interest rate cap:

Entries for six months to 30 June 19X7

	US$	US$
Dr premium suspense	500,000	
Cr cash		500,000

Being payment of cap premium

Dr profit and loss—interest expense	505,000	
Cr cash		505,000

Being interest on US$10m at 10.10% for six months (provided on a straight line basis over the six month period)

Dr sundry debtors	55,000	
Cr profit and loss		55,000

Being the anticipated receipt under the interest rate cap

$$(10.10\% - 9.00\%) \times \$10,000,000 \times \frac{180}{360}$$

Dr cash	55,000	
Cr sundry debtors		55,000

Being receipt of the intrinsic value under the cap

Dr profit and loss	50,000	
Cr premium suspense		50,000

Being amortisation of one-tenth of the cap premium

Exhibit 32.8—continued

Entries for six months to 31 December 19X7

Dr profit and loss—interest expense	375,000	
Cr cash		375,000

Being interest on US$10m at 7.50% for six months

Dr profit and loss	50,000	
Cr premium suspense		50,000

Being amortisation of one tenth of the cap premium

In summary

	US$ FRNs issued	Premium suspense	Cash	Profit and loss
Issue of FRNs	(10,000,000)		10,000,000	
Purchase of cap		500,000	(500,000)	
6 months to 30 June 19X7				
Interest expense			505,000	505,000
Recovery under cap			55,000	55,000
Amortisation of cap premium		(50,000)		50,000
	(10,000,000)	450,000	9,050,000	500,000
6 months to 31 December 19X7				
Interest expense			(375,000)	375,000
Amortisation of cap premium		(50,000)		50,000
	Nil	(50,000)	(375,000)	425,000
	(10,000,000)	400,000	8,675,000	925,000

The accrual method of accounting results in the following effective funding costs being shown in the accounts of the company:

	Average borrowing	Total "interest" cost	Funding rate
6 months to 30 June 19X7	US$5,000,000	500,000	10.00%[1]
6 months to 31 December 19X7	US$5,000,000	425,000	8.50%[2]

Notes:

1. Since the cap rate is set at 9.00% and the annualised cost of the cap is 1.00%, the maximum total cost of borrowing is 10.00%. When the cap is in-the-money the accrual method of accounting produces the correct result.

2. When the cap is out-of-the-money, as in this case, the effective funding cost is the actual rate (7.50%) plus the cost of the premium (1.00%); again, as reflected by the accruals method of accounting. As the cap was acquired out-of-the-money, the premium represented wholly time value, which is also the position at 31 December. Although time value does not decay evenly over the life of the cap, straight line amortisation is usually a good enough approximation for accounting purposes.

- Purchase of an interest rate collar: the purchase of an interest rate collar should be accounted for similarly to the interest rate cap. However, as the collar also includes an interest rate floor this may result in the borrower having to pay amounts to the writer of the collar if the interest rates fall below the specified floor rate. If the collar is purchased to hedge floating rate borrowings then any payment to the writer should be treated in a similar way to any receipt received in the event the interest rate rises above the cap rate, that is, to include it as part of the total cost of funding.

- Purchase of an interest rate floor: the accounting treatment of the floor premium will depend on the strategy behind the underlying asset to which the floor relates, that is, whether the asset was acquired for hedging or trading purposes.

    Where the underlying asset has been acquired for hedging purposes it should be carried at cost in the balance sheet. The floor premium should be considered an integral part of the yield and therefore should be spread over the term of the floor. When the floor is in-the-money accrued receipts on the floor should be taken to income.

    Where the underlying asset is acquired for trading purposes and is carried at market value or the lower of cost and market value the coupon on the security should be accrued and the value of the floor assessed at each fixing date to determine whether there is any income receivable under the floor contract.

Writing caps, collars and floors

Investment banks are typically active in writing caps, collars and floors. Accounting for the writing of these instruments is not as straightforward as the accounting for the instrument from the purchaser's perspective. The difficulties arise due to the lack of depth in the secondary market from which to derive fair market values for the instruments and the plethora of hedging techniques.

There are three accepted alternatives to account for caps, collars and floors when writing, rather than purchasing, the instrument:

- Amortise the premium received on a straight line basis over the life of the instrument. Inappropriate in many cases due to the differing motive in most cases of writer and purchaser.

- Amortise the present value of the instrument such that it decays in accordance with the theoretical profile, and revalue the intrinsic value of the instrument. Difficult to implement in practice.

- Revalue the instrument and recognise gains and losses as they arise. Preferred method although problems may be encountered in valuing instrument.

The revaluation approach appears to be the most appropriate accounting approach. The revaluation approach also enjoys the advantage of being consistent with the mark-to-market concept currently being adopted in relation to the measurement of profits and losses on many of the new financial instruments.

Trading in caps, collars and floors—party with matched positions

A matched position, for example, a matched cap position is most likely to arise where a financial institution acts as intermediary, either merely as a conduit or as a principal to each counterparty. If one party to the deal did not fulfil its obligations the financial institution would normally have no further commitments if it was acting as a conduit. If, however, the financial institution was acting as principal to each side it would have a remaining commitment to the party that had not breached the agreement.

In the simplest case the financial institution will merely act as a conduit. Any receipts will normally be recognised as profit with deferral of an amount sufficient to cover known outgoings. Regard must nevertheless be had to the fact that an intermediary may retain a credit risk not only for the amount of an individual payment but also for the whole value of one side of the transaction, should one party fail.

Subject to these constraints, the suggested treatment which might be applied to various intermediary situations is set out in the following matrix.

	Single up-front payment	**Periodic payment**
Single up-front receipt	All to profit and loss on receipt	Defer sufficient receipt on discounted basis to cover future payments as they fall due
Periodic receipt	Discount receipts and take the net profit up-front	Discount all future payments and receipts and recognise the net profit up-front

(All profit should be recognised in the profit and loss account as fees on a net basis.)

Where the bank acts as principal, profit should be spread over the period of the cap, to compensate for the credit risk involved, and any up-front payments or receipts should therefore be deferred and released to profit and loss over the period of the cap.

Trading in caps, collars and floors—party with unmatched positions

In an unmatched position, for example, an unmatched cap position, the purchaser of the cap receives, in return for a consideration paid up-front or periodically, the right to receive interest payments when the cap rate is exceeded.

The value of the purchaser's right to receive payments when interest rates exceed the cap rate will depend on a number of factors including:

• the principal on which the deal is based;
• the remaining period to maturity of the cap;
• the relationship between the cap rate and prevailing market rates;
• market expectations as to future rate movements.

If there were an active and liquid cap market the appropriate accounting treatment would be to mark the caps to market value with any increases or decreases in market value being dealt with through the profit and loss account. As the maturity approached there would be a tendency for the value of the cap to fall to zero.

However, at present the market for caps is unlikely to be sufficiently active and liquid to enable reliable market values to be determined and consequently another approach has to be adopted. Banks may be able to develop mathematical models based on the above factors which can be demonstrated to provide a reasonable simulation of market values and it may be appropriate to adopt these valuations. In the absence of such models, however, the most appropriate accounting treatment will probably be to write off the consideration paid for the cap on a straight line basis over the period to maturity.

An exactly analogous treatment would apply to a writer of a cap. In this situation the amount received for writing the cap would comprise the intrinsic value reflecting the factors outlined above, together with a fee for writing the cap. The fee inherent in the cap price would normally be stripped out and recognised as income on signing the agreement while the revaluation over the life of the cap would recognise the remainder as income in accordance with the effect of changes in market interest rates on the intrinsic value.

Accounting treatment—corporate sector

Corporate sector entities are most likely to enter into caps or collars where they are floating rate borrowers and floors where they are floating rate investors. The accounting treatment for caps, collars and floors undertaken by corporate sector entities is identical to the treatment for financial institutions.

Corporate sector entities will generally not be involved in trading caps, collars and floors.

Disclosure requirements

Introduction

To date there have been no specific accounting standards issued by any of the major international accounting bodies covering the disclosure requirements with respect to caps, collars and floors. Disclosure with respect to caps, collars and floors will be dependent on the individual circumstances of each entity's cap, collar and floor activities, pertinent legislation in each country and the application of that country's relevant accounting standards.

The disclosure requirements in Australia, the United States and the United Kingdom with respect to caps, collars and floors are compared below.

Australia

The approach to disclosure depends on each individual circumstance. If the instrument's impact is material to the accounts then there should be a disclosure note identifying the method of accounting by the entity in addition to an attempt to quantify the commitment of the entity to cap, collar and floor contracts at year end.

United States and United Kingdom

There are no specific disclosure requirements in respect of caps, collars and floors in either the United States or the United Kingdom. Generally the disclosure of these instruments is as for Australia.

Prudential supervision

Introduction

Few prudential supervisory authorities formally monitor hedging and trading activity in caps, collars and floors. However, option hedging and trading activity (the building block of a cap, collar or floor) is monitored by most central banks through the regular submission of supervision reports. The cap, collar and floor hedging and trading activity of corporate sector entities is largely unsupervised.

The current prudential supervisory standards in Australia, the United States and the United Kingdom with respect to caps, collars and floors are compared below.

Australia

Hedging and trading in options and their derivative products is formally monitored by the RBA via the off-balance sheet business returns submitted quarterly by all trading banks. The return requires trading banks to disclose details of the "Gross Exposure" to option contracts and the "Assessed Risk" in respect of their option activity. They are also covered in the system of supervision of capital adequacy as described in relation to swaps.

Cap, collar and floor activity by corporate sector entities is not formally monitored by any supervisory authority.

United States and United Kingdom

In the United States, caps, collars and floors are now covered by the system of supervision contained in the Basle agreement on capital convergence. By the end of 1989 the same system will apply in the United Kingdom.

LIKELY DEVELOPMENTS IN ACCOUNTING AND PRUDENTIAL SUPERVISION

The immediate future will see the major international accounting bodies addressing the issues of accounting treatment and disclosure for the new financial instruments.

Following a dialogue between the accounting bodies and the interested industry parties the accounting bodies should issue authoritative accounting standards promulgating the most appropriate accounting treatment for the new financial instruments.

The leading central banks of the world are under increasing pressure to ensure that use of the new financial instruments by the financial institutions within their jurisdiction is adequately monitored. In most centres we will see a tightening of control over the activities of those institutions not previously supervised, that is, non-bank financial institutions. The implementation of the requirements of the Basle Supervisors Committee and in particular the requirement to hold set amounts of capital for each transaction will ensure closer scrutiny of the off-balance sheet activities of the leading banks by both the supervisory authorities and bank management.

Chapter 33

Taxation Aspects of Swaps, FRAs and Caps, Collars and Floors

GENERAL FRAMEWORK

This chapter provides a general overview of the taxation implications, in a number of countries, of the following financial instruments:

- interest rate swaps;
- currency swaps;
- LTFX;
- FRAs;
- caps, collars and floors.

The countries surveyed are Australia, the United States, the United Kingdom and Canada.

Generally, it can be said that the income tax legislation and the substantial body of the case law in the countries surveyed does not specifically address the tax consequences of the above-mentioned financial instruments. Accordingly, recourse must usually be made to the general statutory provisions and established taxation principles. In many cases, the income tax legislation is being interpreted and applied to financial instruments which were not specifically contemplated by the legislators.

Accordingly, the application of the income tax legislation to specific financial instruments often gives rise to areas of uncertainty and generally each case involves an analysis of the facts that are specific to the taxpayer's situation.

The major taxation issues addressed in this chapter are the characterisation of the payments and receipts arising from the above-mentioned financial instruments and the time that they are included in the computation of income subject to tax. It is also important to determine whether revaluations of the financial instruments for financial reporting purposes result in a taxable event as well as considering whether exchange gains or losses are bought into the tax computation.

Where a financial instrument involves a party in a foreign jurisdiction, international tax issues may impact the transaction and the existence of any applicable double tax treaty needs to be considered in conjunction with the domestic legislation.

TAXATION CONSIDERATIONS IN AUSTRALIA

Interest rate swaps

The characterisation of payments under interest rate swap contracts has generally been analysed by having regard to the taxation treatment of the

591

financing commitments of the underlying borrowing transaction which the interest rate swap seeks to impact, and to the purpose of entering into the relevant swap contract.

Where a party has entered into an interest rate swap it generally indicates that the party has adopted a certain position in regard to its exposure to interest rates. The swap payments are seeking to impact the party's financing commitments so that its interest rate exposure is consistent with that position.

The unavoidable relationship with the underlying borrowing transaction and the financing commitments of the party to the lender in respect of that borrowing, give considerable support for the conclusion that the characterisation of the swap payments would normally be determined by the underlying transaction test.

Thus, the netting payments under the interest rate swap to a counter party would usually be considered deductible for income tax purposes pursuant to s. 51 of the *Income Tax Assessment Act* (the ITAA) where the underlying interest obligations are deductible. Where the purpose of the underlying borrowing is to utilise the funds in connection with the production of assessable income then the netting payments under the swap should be deductible given the fact that interest obligations on the underlying borrowing should be deductible. This general proposition appears to have been accepted by the Australian Taxation Office in its Income Tax Ruling IT 2050 (*Exhibit 33.1*) dealing with interest rate swaps.

Furthermore, whilst the netting payments are referable to the underlying financing commitments, they do not represent a cost in borrowing the underlying loan principal. They are a cost in connection with the financing commitments attaching to the loan principal. Accordingly, the netting payments should not be considered borrowing expenses for the purposes of s. 67 of the ITAA as it is not expenditure incurred in borrowing the principal.

In respect of swap receipts the above reasoning should be equally applicable so that the receipts are assessable for income tax purposes pursuant to s. 25(1) of the ITAA (or possibly s. 26(j)).

Currency swaps

It is useful to view a typical currency swap as an interest rate swap augmented by an exchange of loan principal amounts with a mutual

---

Exhibit 33.1
IT 2050 "Interest Swapping" Transactions

Date of Ruling: 13 July 1983

TEXT OF RULING

Preamble

1. Consideration has recently been given to the income tax implications of a form of interest hedging arrangement known as "interest swapping".

Exhibit 33.1—continued

2. An Australian resident borrower of moneys from overseas at a floating rate of interest, say London Inter-Bank Offered Rate (LIBOR) + 1.00%, would ordinarily seek to limit its exposure to fluctuations in interest rates. As an alternative to conventional hedging arrangements involving, as they would usually do, interest rate futures contracts there have developed "interest swapping" transactions.

3. In its simplest form, a foreign banking concern would provide a "swapping" facility to the borrower by itself raising a loan, at a fixed interest rate readily available to it, of an amount equivalent to the amount of floating rate funds which were originally obtained by the borrower from other foreign sources. The Australian resident borrower and the foreign banking concern would then exchange their respective interest commitments, quite independently of the relevant loans with third parties and without affecting those contracts in any way, by undertaking to pay to each other from time to time amounts equal to the other's interest obligations before payment of fees, commissions, margins, etc. to the bank for the facility. The arrangement would usually provide for the corresponding payments to be offset against each other so that only a single net payment would be made by one party to the other.

4. There may also be situations in which one party is unwilling to accept the risk of the other party to the swap arrangement fulfilling its obligations for payment and a third party intermediary, also usually a bank or other financial institution, would be interposed between the parties and would bear the risk of default by either party. In this way performance of all commitments by the parties to each other is effectively guaranteed. This variation does not otherwise alter the swapping techniques nor the income tax consequences.

Ruling

5. An "interest swapping" arrangement is a form of interest hedging facility and is a transaction quite independent of any loan obligations of the parties to which the arrangement might be referable. It does not involve any additional loans between the parties or any disturbance of existing loans and obligations to pay interest as it falls due.

6. The payments made by the parties to each other in accordance with the terms of the agreement are not amounts of interest as the term is defined for withholding tax purposes in s. 128A(1).

7. An "interest swapping" arrangement involving an Australian resident borrower would not, in the circumstances which have been described, involve any interest withholding tax liability additional to that which might otherwise exist in respect of the borrower's existing interest obligations.

8. It is also accepted as a general principle that payments made by the parties in accordance with the interest swapping agreement are attributable to existing interest expenses and are themselves revenue in nature. As a consequence the payments would be assessable to the recipient and deductible to the payer as the case may be. The involvement of an intermediary would not alter the character of the payments.

9. It is necessary to say that the advice in the preceding paragraph operates as a general principle. As the arrangements are presently understood it would seem usual for the parties to have raised loans at rates of interest which are more or less comparable, though one is variable and the other fixed. If there were substantial differences between the two at the time that the parties enter into the interest swapping arrangement the particular circumstances would require examination to decide whether they were truly of a revenue nature.

10. Because the various incidental expenses which are associated with an interest swapping transaction relate to an existing interest expense they would ordinarily be deductible in accordance with s. 51(1) of the ITAA 1936 in the same way as the incidental costs associated with a conventional interest hedging arrangement. Any payments which might be made by the parties upon early termination of the whole of the arrangements would also be of a revenue nature in the usual case, that is, assessable or deductible to the parties as the case may be.

11. In the event that interest was to be charged on overdue swap payments, any interest which might be paid to a non-resident would be subject to withholding tax.

commitment to re-exchange principal loan amounts on the maturity of the loans. Accordingly, it is necessary to consider both the tax treatment of recurrent payments under the swap and the treatment of exchange differences on the principal loan amounts. The currency swap participants will recognise a foreign exchange gain or loss on re-exchange of the principal amounts which may well hedge an equal but opposite foreign exchange gain or loss in respect of the underlying foreign currency borrowings.

The taxation consequences for the interest netting payments or receipts in respect of currency swaps should broadly follow the analysis set out above in respect of interest rate swaps.

Where the cross-currency swap is entered into to protect the exchange risks of foreign currency receivables and payables, the underlying transaction approach is to be preferred. There should be no difference in the treatment of the regular netting payments relating to interest swaps even though the interest rate divergencies may be greater. The characterisation should arguably still follow the underlying commitments.

An additional question arises as to the taxation treatment of any payment or receipt in regard to the exchange fluctuation on the principal component under the counterparty's obligations. Prior to the introduction of legislation governing foreign currency exchange gains and losses, it was arguable that, consistent with the underlying transaction approach, such payments should be viewed as having a similar taxation treatment to an exchange gain or loss on the party's principal obligations.

Pursuant to Pt III, Div. 3B of the ITAA, the foreign currency exchange gain and loss legislation introduced with effect from 18 February 1986 has application to gains and losses realised on capital account that are attributable to currency exchange rate fluctuations (the general income and deduction provisions still apply to those on revenue account).

The legislation operates in respect of post 18 February 1986 contracts and where the contract is a hedging contract (which should encompass a currency swap) entered into after 18 February in relation to another contract which is also post 18 February, then any gain or loss should be assessable or deductible provided the other provisions of the legislation are satisfied. It should however be noted that deductibility may be denied by the Commissioner of Taxation unless certain notification requirements are satisfied.

Unfortunately, the Australian Taxation Office's own views on cross-currency swaps have yet to be made public and indeed Income Tax Ruling IT 2050 suggests that where substantial interest rate differentials occur (which may well be the case in cross-currency swaps) the assessability or deductibility of any netting receipts or payments is uncertain. This uncertainty may, however, have arisen due to the fact that Pt III, Div. 3B of the ITAA had not been enacted when IT 2050 was released and accordingly there may have been some concern that substantial netting payments under the cross-currency swap would have been deductible whilst any currency adjustment receipt may have been tax free.

Limitations of underlying transaction approach

By definition, this approach of characterising the netting payments under swap contracts is only appropriate where the payments are referrable to some underlying commitment.

It should not mean that this approach is only valid where there is a specific underlying interest bearing borrowing similar to the notional principal amount in the swap contract. Rather, where it can be seen that the swap contract has been entered into so as to adjust the party's financing commitments, whether wholly or in part, then the netting payments should be assessable or deductible where the underlying financing commitments are assessable or deductible. Moreover, the fact that the timing of the netting payments may not exactly match the timing of the underlying financing commitments should not in itself alter the characterisation of the netting payments. For example, an Australian borrower with fixed financing commitments may have a preference to pay on the basis of floating rates. However, rather than receive a fixed amount on a periodical basis the borrower may also have some preference to receive such payments on an accelerated or deferred basis.

This adds another dimension to the underlying transaction approach because presumably there are additional factors which the party considered in opting for a stream of swap payments which diverges from the stream of underlying financing commitments. In general, however, it is considered that the characterisation of the netting payments should not alter merely because of a mismatch in the cash streams. A mismatch would normally be utilised by the party in its management of its current and future financing commitments and its particular cash flow requirements. These additional factors are unlikely to change the characterisation of the payments merely because a decision was taken to receive the payment in advance or in arrears of underlying obligations.

It is, however, much more difficult to determine the appropriate taxation treatment for the netting payments where there is an absence of any underlying financing commitments or where the swap is only partly explicable by underlying financing commitments.

The absence of any underlying obligations requires the swap to be analysed at face value in order to characterise the netting payments. The substance of the transaction is that the parties to the swap are agreeing to exchange certain cash streams. However, the amounts to be paid by each party may or may not be quantifiable at inception of the swap; the timing of the payments by each party may or may not match; and the cash streams could range from lump sum to periodical.

In the absence of any underlying transaction the characterisation of the netting payments to a party requires an analysis of the business of the relevant taxpayer and the structure of the cash flows.

Thus, for an institution which as part of its ordinary business activities provides financial intermediary services or conducts swap warehousing activities, it should be appropriate to characterise the netting payments as being part of its regular receipts and outgoings from its financial operations. It should therefore be appropriate to regard the netting payments on revenue account.

However, for an entity with an absence of such business activities an analysis of the party's intentions for entering into the swap will be paramount.

In this regard the cash streams themselves could be indicative of those intentions. For example, a party to a swap transaction with one or both legs being floating is essentially a speculative transaction as to future movements in the floating rates. This may give some indication that there is a profit-making motivation in existence in which case the provisions of ss 25(1) and 25A of the ITAA should be considered in seeking to bring to account as assessable income any profit pursuant to the transaction. Indeed, it may be more appropriate to recognise the net profit or loss from such a swap rather than seeking to reflect gross receipts and payments as being income and deductions.

The appropriate taxation treatment is also uncertain where there is an identification of dual purposes for entering into the swap contract. It may be that an entity in seeking to alter its financing obligations may also wish to adopt a speculative position which can be accommodated in a single swap transaction.

The underlying transaction approach may therefore only have limited application in respect of such swap transactions and it would appear necessary to place greater emphasis on the party's business activities and the cash flows relating to the swap in seeking to characterise the netting payments under the swap.

Timing of assessability and deductibility of swap payments

Interest rate swaps

In the more conventional swaps it is considered that the timing of any deduction for the netting payment arises upon the existence of the liability to make that payment. When an enforceable obligation for payment has crystallised, that is, the netting payment is due and payable, then the expenditure should be seen to be incurred.

Similarly, it is considered that any netting income is earned at the time when the amounts become due and receivable to the recipient.

The correctness of the above assertions has been placed in some doubt following recent case law which has given greater recognition to accounting principles (in particular, the accruals concept) when seeking to determine a proper reflection of a taxpayer's income. Nevertheless, it is considered that the above conclusions are to be preferred for the taxpayer who views the interest rate swap as a form of interest hedging.

The accruals approach may, however, be more appropriate in respect of financial institutions acting as intermediaries or conducting warehousing activities. In the context of the business operations of such financial institutions there are stronger arguments to suggest that the creation of the liability to pay and receive the netting amounts is of less relevance in seeking to reflect the true income of such a business than the matching of gains against associated losses.

Currency swaps

Similar conclusions to those above apply in respect of the netting payments relating to interest. Indeed, there are probably stronger arguments to suggest that such amounts are only assessable or deductible when receivable or payable, having regard to the fact that there may be the added uncertainty as to exchange movements. Further, consistent with Australian taxation principles which require any exchange gains or losses to be brought to account on a realisation basis, any currency adjustment payments should only be assessable or deductible when the liability has crystallised. Any accrual for unrealised gains or losses should not be recognised for tax purposes.

Accelerated or deferred payment swaps

Questions arise as to whether it is appropriate to recognise accelerated swap income as having been earned when there is a requirement to make future payments, and whether it is appropriate to recognise that accelerated swap costs can be said to be fully incurred when they are referable to deferred income. This is all the more so when accounting principles would indicate that the accruals approach is to be preferred, especially as it would appear that accounting principles are becoming increasingly important in determining the timing of income and expense recognition for tax purposes.

In considering accelerated payments it is difficult to see why any part of the expenditure should be incurred other than at the time when the liability to pay arose and when payment did occur (however, refer below to comments on the prepayment legislation). In respect of accelerated income, case law has suggested that in identifying whether income has been earned, regard must be had to the nature and extent of future commitments to be made so as to make a determination whether the income can be said to have "come home" to the taxpayer. Questions of refundability and the necessity to provide services in the future have appeared to be important in looking at the question as to whether income is earned. In the context of swap contracts, it is, however, somewhat doubtful whether it can be said that the obligation to pay the agreed cash streams in the future is sufficient to conclude that the accelerated cash streams received do not represent income earned.

In respect of deferred expenditure the absence of any enforceable right for payment would suggest that an accruals approach is not appropriate. Although it is recognised that recent case law has allowed deductions on an accruals basis for deferred expenditure, it is by no means clear whether such case law has wide application.

For the financial institutions there is probably a stronger case to be argued that the accruals basis should be adopted in respect of accelerated and deferred transactions for the reasons as outlined previously concerning the inherent nature of their business.

It should be noted, however, that in May 1988 legislation was enacted which, broadly, would seek to allow a tax deduction for prepaid expenses only on an accruals basis (rather than when paid) where the prepayment was referable to a period exceeding 13 months. Accordingly certain accelerated swap payments may fall within the legislation.

Deferred interest securities

In considering the timing of the assessability and deductibility of swap payments, consideration also needs to be given to the provisions of Div. 16E of the ITAA dealing with deferred interest securities.

Broadly these provisions statutorily dictate an accruals income or expense recognition method in respect of qualifying securities.

A qualifying security is any "security" (which is defined to include any contract under which a person is liable to pay any amount) the term of which exceeds one year and has an eligible return.

In determining whether the security has an eligible return, it must be reasonably likely that at the time the security is issued, the sum of all payments (other than periodical interest payments) under the security will exceed the issue price of the security.

In many swap contracts it may not be reasonable to conclude, at the time of issue, whether an eligible return exists given the uncertainty as to future movements in interest rates and their effect on the swap payments. Consequently the exact terms of any swap contract will need to be carefully considered to determine the application or otherwise of Div. 16E of the Act.

It can be seen from the definition of "security" that the potential scope of the provisions are very wide and it is likely that certain swap contracts (particularly some accelerated or deferred payment swaps) could fall within the definitions. If so, then provided the swap payments would otherwise have been assessable or deductible, an accruals method of income or expense recognition would appear necessary (although it is doubtful as to whether the legislation intended for the provisions to apply to swap contracts).

Associated swap costs

Income Tax Ruling IT 2050 concludes that where the netting payments are on revenue account then the incidental expenses incurred in respect of the swap contract should be considered to be on revenue account and deductible pursuant to s. 51 of the ITAA. Again, such costs should be considered referable to the new financing obligations which are being undertaken rather than costs in connection with borrowing money. Thus the costs should be deductible pursuant to s. 51 rather than s. 67 of the ITAA.

Such expenses would include swap arrangement fees, documentation costs, credit risk fees and also the counterparty's borrowing costs borne by the higher credit risk party. For the higher credit risk party the bearing of the borrowing costs of the counterparty should still be characterised as a cost of altering the higher credit risk party's underlying financing commitments rather than as a borrowing cost. Again, the proposed prepaid expense legislation may impact the timing of deductions for certain swap costs.

On the other side, the recipient would normally be required to recognise the fee income at the time it was due and receivable. However, it should be noted that some of the fees may in fact constitute a receipt in advance for services rendered over the duration of the swap agreement and accordingly, it may be possible to bring such income to account on an accruals basis. Much depends on the characterisation of the fees and the relevant surrounding documentation.

Swap revaluations

The concept of marking-to-market at the end of a reporting period is generally viewed for taxation purposes as the recognition of unrealised gains and losses. Thus, such revaluations are inappropriate for taxation purposes where there is an inability to treat swap contracts as being trading stock for the purposes of the ITAA. Until the market develops to an extent to which the relevant rights and obligations pursuant to the swap contract can be actively bought and sold then no revaluation to market (or indeed to any other value) is probably available. The gains and losses only arise for taxation purposes as they are derived or incurred.

International tax issues

Generally, a non-resident recipient of a netting payment should only suffer Australian income tax where the swap gain has an Australian source; and

- If the recipient is a resident of a country with which Australia has concluded a double tax treaty, the gain can be said to be attributable to a permanent establishment in Australia.

- If the recipient is a resident of a country with which Australia has not concluded a double tax treaty, the existence of a permanent establishment will be irrelevant and Australian tax will be suffered.

- The non-resident recipient should not be specifically exempt from Australian income tax. Obviously, in these circumstances no Australian tax would be suffered.

It would generally be unlikely for a non-resident recipient to have a permanent establishment in Australia. However, with the increased activity of foreign banks in Australia there is a possibility that foreign banks may utilise their Australian operations to organise any Australian leg of a swap transaction and yet seek to book that swap overseas. The extent of any activities conducted in Australia therefore need to be carefully considered.

The source of any swap gain or loss is not only important to a non-resident recipient but also to an Australian counterparty to a cross-border swap pursuant to Australia's foreign tax credit legislation. The current foreign tax credit legislation seeks to quarantine foreign sourced losses against foreign income. Thus, Australian parties to swap transactions will also need to give careful consideration to a question of the sourcing of swap income. In general, it would appear that the source of any swap gain or loss is most appropriately referable to where the negotiation and execution of the swap contract is conducted, and the mere booking of a contract in a particular country is unlikely to be determinative in identifying the appropriate source.

Withholding taxes

In Income Tax Ruling IT 2050, the Australian Taxation Office has stated that the netting payments under an interest rate swap agreement are not amounts in the nature of interest for the purposes of the withholding tax provisions.

Accordingly, the netting payments to a non-resident recipient should not be subject to Australian interest withholding tax. The payments should not be considered as interest or amounts in the nature of interest which is a prerequisite for the application of the interest withholding tax provisions.

The question of what constitutes interest or amounts in the nature of interest has long been the subject of contention. It is, however, generally considered that to be in the nature of interest there must be some form of financial accommodation between the parties, interest being characterised as the return or price for the use of money.

It is difficult to identify in most swap contracts any financial accommodation between the parties and thus it is generally considered that there is an absence of any payment which could be characterised as being in the nature of interest. It is, however, recognised that swap contracts are extremely flexible instruments and it may be possible to structure certain swap contracts so as to achieve what in reality is a provision of finance. In such circumstances, it may be easier to characterise certain netting payments as being in the nature of interest.

Moreover, should the swap contracts fall within the definition of qualifying securities for the purposes of the deferred interest security legislation, then there also exists in the ITAA provisions which may statutorily dictate certain amounts to consist of interest for the purposes of the withholding tax provisions. These provisions could give rise to a withholding tax exposure although it is noted that there are certain limitations within these provisions which may preclude their application to swap contracts. In particular, the provisions require a *transfer* of a qualifying security and this may be absent in many swap contracts.

The views of the Australian Taxation Office concerning interest withholding taxes on currency swaps have not been made public. In practice, however, it would appear that the payment of withholding taxes on cross-currency swaps is not required.

LTFXs

The determination of the taxation treatment of an LTFX requires consideration of the nature of the transaction in the context of the taxpayer's business (that is, whether on revenue or capital account) and the application of statutory provisions as well as established taxation principles dealing with the tax consequences of gains and loss attributable to currency exchange movements.

In broad terms, gains or losses arising from LTFXs which have been entered into as a hedge against underlying revenue transactions would normally be assessable or deductible for tax purposes under the general income and deduction provisions. The recognition of any such gain or loss for tax purposes should occur at realisation.

Similar conclusions should arise for traders in LTFXs. The marking-to-market of LTFXs for traders represents the recognition of unrealised gains and losses, and given the fact that LTFXs probably do not constitute trading stock (as defined for income tax purposes), the timing of income and deductions should be at realisation.

The statutory provisions of Div. 3B of the ITAA are broadly concerned with the tax treatment of currency exchange gains and losses under contracts which are on capital account. In general, the legislation has sought to treat exchange gains and losses on capital account on a similar basis to those on revenue account. That is, gains or losses on capital account are assessable or deductible on a realisation basis.

It should also be appreciated that an LTFX may merely comprise one leg of a more complex series of events. In such circumstances it is possible that the correct reflection of a taxpayer's income may require that tax should be paid having regard to the entire transaction rather than considering each leg of the transaction in isolation.

FRAs

Characterisation of settlement sum

Typically, for taxation purposes the characterisation of any payments under a contract which may be viewed as being in the nature of forward cover or a hedge has involved an analysis of the underlying transaction being hedged.

In circumstances where the taxpayer has entered into the FRA to minimise its future interest exposure on an underlying principal amount which is being used in the production of assessable income, any settlement sum receivable or payable would normally be viewed as being on revenue account and therefore assessable or deductible.

Where the taxpayer's business activities include the taking of speculative positions in the financial futures markets then any gains or losses from FRA contracts are likely to be viewed as forming part of the taxpayer's ordinary business income. Future development of an active secondary market in FRA contracts may give rise to questions as to whether such contracts can be classified as trading stock for tax purposes. Currently, however, this would seem unlikely.

Where a taxpayer takes isolated speculative positions under FRA contracts it may be that such gains or losses would not be characterised as being of an income nature. In this case, the provisions of the taxation legislation dealing with capital gains and losses may need to be considered.

Timing of assessability and deductibility of settlement sum

Normally, at settlement date the present value of the net interest differential between the agreed and actual interest rate is paid in a lump sum to the counterparty which must be compensated under the terms of the FRA.

Prior to settlement date, any gain or loss from the FRA could not be said to have been realised for taxation purposes and accordingly, any revaluation of the FRA (for example, FRA held for trading purposes) during the period up to settlement date would not represent a taxable gain or loss.

However, at settlement date, it is likely that the settlement sum can be said to have been derived or incurred by the respective parties and accordingly, it is at settlement date that the income or deduction has crystallised. Whilst the quantum of the payment does have a direct relationship with interest rates, it is not a payment which can be said to be "interest". In these circumstances adoption of an "accruals approach" to the recognition of the settlement sum is unlikely to be acceptable (refer, however, to previous comments in connection with the income recognition methods for financial institutions).

It is noted that the deferred interest security legislation has been introduced to give legislative effect to the adoption of an accruals approach to income and expense recognition in respect of certain securities. However, notwithstanding the very broad definition's provisions in this legislation, it would normally be difficult to argue that FRAs come within the ambit of such provisions.

The prepaid expense legislation may, however, impact the timing of the deduction for a settlement payment in certain FRA contracts and may in fact dictate an accruals deduction. This legislation should not however impact the recognition of income under the FRA.

Withholding tax issues

In transacting cross-border FRAs, consideration needs to be given to the question of whether the settlement sum constitutes interest or an amount in the nature of interest for the purposes of the withholding tax provisions.

In this regard, it is noted that the terms and conditions for FRAs often characterise the counterparties as "borrower" and "lender"; the settlement sum is quantified by reference to interest differentials; and the settlement sum may be accounted for in the books of the parties as interest income or expenses.

However, notwithstanding the above, the legal relationship between the counterparties is not that of borrower and lender. There is no loan transaction between the parties nor any financial accommodation which could be said to give rise to a payment which is the return for the use of money or is in the nature of such a return. It is therefore considered that the payment of a settlement sum to a non-resident party should not give rise to a withholding tax liability, assuming of course the transaction is on an arm's length footing.

Interest rate options—caps, floors and collars

The taxation consequences of interest rate option contracts entered into as a means of hedging underlying financing commitments should follow the underlying transaction approach.

Where the underlying financing commitments being hedged are on revenue account and relate to the generation of the taxpayer's assessable income, the gains and losses arising from interest rate option contracts should be on revenue account and subject to tax pursuant to the ordinary income and deduction provisions of the ITAA.

Cap, floor and collar rate agreements are merely interest rate option contracts designed to achieve specific hedging objectives. That is, options can be written so as to give the hedger the ability to establish a maximum predetermined borrowing rate, a minimum investment yield, or a combination of both.

Characterisation of settlement sums

Profit and losses derived by taxpayers whose business includes trading in such option contracts should also have their gains or losses as being on revenue account and fully subject to taxation. In the absence of a developed market in which option contracts can be readily bought and sold, as opposed to merely being closed out, the ability to characterise option contracts as trading stock is limited. Thus option traders who seek to value options by marking-to-market are in effect recognising unrealised gains and losses, which from a taxation viewpoint are unlikely to constitute a taxable event.

For taxation purposes, it is likely that the gains or losses only become subject to taxation at the time the option contract is closed out. However, this general conclusion will be subject to the specific terms of the contract and the acceleration or deferral of any settlement sum may alter the timing of income and deductions. It would be necessary to review the particular contract to determine when the liability to make the settlement sum payment crystallises.

Timing of assessability and deductibility of fees

Fees or premiums paid in consideration for the granting of the option should similarly be on revenue or capital account having regard to the characteristics of the underlying transaction. Premiums on revenue account should be deductible at the time the obligation to make the payment arises, although the prepaid expense legislation may impact the timing of such deductions for option contracts extending over 13 months.

The option writer is also likely to be assessable at the time the premiums are due and receivable and it is doubtful whether premiums received in advance can be brought to account on an accruals basis, although again the terms of the contract and the particular features of the writer's business need to be reviewed.

Structured caps, collars, floors

A separate analysis of the taxation consequences detailed above will be required where there are option contracts without any underlying transaction, or where off-market rates are utilised. The above analysis will not necessarily apply as a matter of course to such transactions.

Such contracts need to be reviewed in the context of the taxpayer's business and intentions in entering into such contracts. For taxpayers entering into isolated and speculative contracts it may be more appropriate to bring to account a net profit or loss at the conclusion of such transactions as being the proper reflection of the taxpayer's income. Alternatively, the contract may be on capital account which may require consideration of the capital gains tax provisions of the ITAA.

Withholding tax issues

The settlement sums and premiums arising pursuant to any cross-border caps, collars and floors should generally not be subject to Australian interest withholding tax. These amounts should not be considered as interest or amounts in the nature of interest which is a prerequisite for the application of the interest withholding tax provisions.

The legal relationship between the counterparties is not that of borrower and lender. There is no loan transaction between the parties nor any financial accommodation which could be said to give rise to a payment which is a return for the use of money or in the nature of such a return.

TAXATION CONSIDERATIONS IN THE UNITED KINGDOM

Interest rate swaps

At present, the United Kingdom legislation does not specifically address the tax consequences of swaps, and the current taxation treatment is largely based on Inland Revenue practice which is not in all respects consistent.

However, the Inland Revenue issued on 14 March 1989 a press release setting out a proposed new regime for swaps. This is discussed further below.

In general the taxation treatment of swap transactions does depend on the taxation treatment of any underlying borrowing or lending transactions.

Swap payments do not constitute interest, because there is no underlying debt obligation between the parties. The tax treatment of swap payments further depends on whether or not one of the parties is a bank recognised by the Inland Revenue as carrying on a bona fide banking business in the United Kingdom, including United Kingdom branches of foreign banks, or (following an amendment to the Inland Revenue's practice with effect from 14 March 1989) is a "recognised swaps dealer". A recognised swaps dealer is a company listed by the Bank of England as an exempted person for the purposes of the *The Financial Services Act* 1986 (U.K.) or authorised as a member of the Securities Association to carry on investment business; and confirmed by the Bank of England or the Securities Association to be entering swaps as part of its regular business activity. Swap payments can generally be made to and by United Kingdom recognised banks or swap dealers acting as principals (whether as counterparty or intermediary), without deduction of United Kingdom tax at source. For the remainder of this analysis of the United Kingdom position relating to swaps, references to banks and banking business should be taken to include recognised swaps dealers and their dealing business, unless otherwise stated.

The taxation position of the counterparties where an institution other than a recognised bank or swaps dealer is involved is not certain. However, generally the payer will be required to deduct United Kingdom income tax and pay it to the Inland Revenue in order to obtain a tax deduction for the swap payment. If the paying company fails to make the deduction, and the recipient is another United Kingdom resident company, the payment may not qualify for a tax deduction and the payer may still be liable for the basic rate tax not deducted.

It should also be noted that not all swap payments involving banks are in fact entered into in the ordinary course of banking business. (For example, the bank may be operating on capital account as part of its funding strategy.) We understand that the Inland Revenue regards seven years as a significant period in determining whether a borrowing by a bank is on capital or on revenue account, there being a presumption that a borrowing for a period of seven years or more is on capital account.

Where a bank has entered into a swap agreement on capital account, the Inland Revenue might be able to argue that, unless the payment was made to another recognised United Kingdom bank, that such payment should be made after deduction of basic rate income tax. It appears in practice that the Inland Revenue may not take this point.

Currency swaps

The only difference in the taxation treatment of recurring payments and fees between currency swaps and interest rate swaps is that payments made by a trading company (not carrying on a financial trade) to a United Kingdom bank are treated as trading expenses in the case of currency swaps but as charges on income in the case of interest rate swaps. Trading expenses are computed on an accruals basis whereas charges on income are on a cash basis (refer below).

Currency swaps do not normally give rise to any exchange differences on revenue account, although when they do these will be taxable or deductible in computing trading profits.

Where a currency swap is on capital account, a capital gain or loss may arise, not so much on the swap itself but from the assets and liabilities associated with the swap. Broadly speaking, capital gains or losses arise only on *disposal* of chargeable assets. Accordingly, no chargeable gain or allowable loss occurs in respect of translation differences on a capital asset reflected in the accounts of the company prior to disposal. Some assets are not chargeable assets (for example, trade debts) and no capital gain or loss arises on a discharge of a liability. Thus although a currency swap may constitute a perfect economic hedge, the selective taxability of capital gains and losses can result in a mismatched position.

Timing of assessability and deductibility of swap payments

The timing of recognition for tax purposes of swap payments depends on whether the swap payments and receipts are categorised as annual payments and receipts or trading deductions and receipts but this distinction depends in turn on the category of the taxpayer and the counterparty.

Annual payments are, broadly, payments which are both recurrent and are "pure income profit" in the hands of the recipient. Annual payments are taxed in the hands of the recipient under Sched. D, Case III (thus on a cash basis) whilst the payers obtain relief as a charge on income. Charges on income are payments which are deducted from total profits rather than in computing profits chargeable under a particular schedule or case, thus the payer has a choice of which profits to deduct the charges from. Only payments (not accrued expenses) are deductible as charges on income.

Trading expenses and receipts are computed on an accruals basis.

Swap payments and receipts made or received by companies carrying on a banking or financial trade in the ordinary course of that trade would normally be deductible or assessable as trading expenses.

For companies not carrying on financial trade, swap payments and receipts on capital account are deductible or assessable as annual payments except for *payments* made by *trading* companies under *currency* swaps to United Kingdom *banks* which are deductible as trading expenses. Presumably this now applies to equivalent payments to United Kingdom recognised swaps dealers, following the change of practice mentioned above, although the relevant Inland Revenue press release does not make the point clear.

Accelerated or deferred payment swaps

For a bank or financial trader the position in relation to the accelerated or deferred payment swaps would be similar to a conventional swap as the payments would be spread or accrued and tax assessed on the profit recognised for accounts purposes.

For a non-bank entity there may be no recurrent element in the payments and receipts so that they would not seem to be deductible as an annual payment. A trading company might claim relief for the payment as a trading expense which, if accepted by the Inland Revenue, would probably be allowed on the same basis as for accounting purposes. An investment company would most likely obtain no relief for such a one off payment. The receipts would probably be taxable when received.

Associated swap costs

Swap arrangement fees should normally be trading receipts or expenses of banks. For non-banks the position is less clear.

The incidental costs of raising loan finance are not usually regarded as trading expenses and thus are not deductible as incurred wholly and exclusively for the purpose of trade. However, relief is often available under s. 38 of the *Finance Act* 1980 (U.K.). It should be recognised that this relief does not extend to fees and expenses incurred in arranging swaps as no new loan is created as a result of the swaps. In order to avoid losing taxation relief for swap fees and expenses altogether, where commercially possible these costs should be subsumed into the margins on recurring payments made over the period of the swap.

Swap revaluations

The concept of marking-to-market is an accepted accounting policy in the United Kingdom for a bank or financial trader with a swap book. The Inland Revenue are generally reluctant to bring unrealised gains and losses into account for tax purposes, but have agreed to accept marking-to-market in certain specific cases which have been discussed with them.

International tax issues

The general requirement described above to deduct basic rate income tax from swap payments (unless paid to a United Kingdom bank or paid by a bank or financial trader) may be reduced or eliminated on payments made to recipients not resident in the United Kingdom if permitted by the provisions of a double taxation agreement. Such relief (if any) that is available is normally given under the "other income" or "business profits" article of the relevant agreements. As the payments are not interest, the "interest" article should not be in point. If relief is available, with the prior permission, it should be possible to make payments gross or at a reduced rate, in accordance with the terms of the double taxation agreement. The gross payments will be relievable on a cash basis.

It should be noted that in order for relief to apply under a double taxation agreement, it may be necessary that, if the non-United Kingdom resident recipient trades in the United Kingdom through a permanent establishment, the swap transaction is not effectively connected with a permanent establishment. Further, the effects of foreign withholding taxes should be considered when dealing with overseas counterparties.

The booking of banking business is an area of great dispute between the Inland Revenue and taxpayers at present. In a head office to branch relationship, the Inland Revenue do not consider it possible for one office to book business generated by another.

Value added tax (VAT)

VAT is not a major issue in swap transactions. Supplies made under interest rate swap agreements are treated as exempt for VAT purposes unless the recipient of the supply belongs in a country, other than the Isle of Man, which is not a member state of the EEC. However, in such circumstances it should be zero rated in any case.

In neither case will VAT be chargeable; however, exempt (and zero rated) recipients must be taken into account in computing the restrictions on a bank's or financial trader's ability to recover its input VAT under the partial exemption rules.

Proposed legislative framework

On 14 March 1989, in addition to announcing the change of practice with respect to United Kingdom recognised swaps dealers noted above, the Inland Revenue also published a Consultative Document which proposed a new legislative framework for interest and currency swaps and invited comments. Legislation will not be introduced until 1990 at the earliest, although the Revenue's intentions seem fairly settled. The key features of the proposed framework include:

Relief for swap payments

Swap fees are broadly to be assimilated to interest, although without the requirement to deduct tax except in certain cases. Thus commercial swap fees will generally be deductible in accordance with the normal rules for interest, including the existing anti-avoidance provisions. One difference is that all swap fees payable for trading purposes will be deductible as trading expenses on an accruals basis—there will be no distinction between "short" and "annual" swap payments, as there is for interest. Swap fees payable otherwise than as a trading expense will be deductible as a charge when paid.

Deductibility of swap fees will be dependent on their being paid for bona fide commercial purposes and being no more than an arm's length amount. Charging and payment dates must occur at least annually and must be simultaneous for each party. (This latter requirement might be a practical difficulty in the case of United Kingdom and Australian swaps because of time differences.) Recurrent swap fees that do not meet these requirements will remain taxable on the recipient.

Anti-avoidance provisions are proposed for swaps related to deep discounted securities.

If anti-avoidance provisions are introduced to catch interest paid by "thinly capitalised" companies these will be extended to include swap payments.

Initial swap arrangement fees will be deductible, in the same way as loan arrangement fees. (There is no provision for terminal fees to be deductible.)

Assimilation to interest means that swap fees may be treated as a distribution when paid to a non-resident associated company. The consultative document notes that this treatment could be over-ridden by the terms of a double tax treaty. However, this could depend on the wording of the treaty concerned. A number of United Kingdom double tax treaties include a definition of interest as including "other income assimilated to income from money lent by the taxation law of the State in which the income arises", and in such cases swap fees should be treated as interest for treaty purposes following the changes in United Kingdom law. However, in other cases (for example the United Kingdom and Australian treaty) there is no definition of interest and the term will therefore have its normal meaning. In such cases it is doubtful whether the interest article extends to swap payments (see above).

Deduction of tax at source

Income tax will not generally be deducted from swap payments. However, tax will have to be deducted from payments to non-residents except where:

- the swap payments are chargeable to tax in the United Kingdom (that is, as branch profits); or
- they are paid in the ordinary course of business by a financial dealer.

The document states that the requirement to deduct tax in these cases is to avoid exploitation by international groups. This suggests that the Revenue might perhaps be willing to limit the withholding requirement to payments to related parties, although the Revenue would no doubt be concerned about back-to-back arrangements.

Taxation of swap receipts

Swap receipts will generally be taxable like interest when received. However, where they are receivable on revenue account under an agreement entered into for trading purposes, they will be taxable as trading items on an accruals basis.

Other matters

The consultative document does not address the significant tax problems that can arise on the exchanges of currency itself in currency swaps.

LTFXs

The treatment of LTFXs is in principle no different from normal foreign exchange contracts, although for non-financial companies they are more likely to be on capital account. For banks, forward foreign exchange contracts are normally marked-to-market for taxation purposes except where associated with loan and deposit transactions when the profit or loss would be amortised over the life of the contract. For long-term contracts the market value is harder to determine and there is an argument that because the market is thin, unrealised profit or losses should not be taxed. In practice a bank is unlikely to have substantial unhedged long forward positions.

FRAs

Again, in the United Kingdom the tax treatment of FRAs is an area of some uncertainty. As yet there is no case law or published guidance from the Inland Revenue on the subject.

Characterisation of settlement sum

Where the FRA is entered into by a bank or financial trader as part of their business activities any income or expense arising from the FRA should be taken into account in computing its profit as part of its existing trade (that is, on an accruals basis).

Timing of assessability and deductibility of settlement sum

The current view expressed by the Inland Revenue is that whether or not the FRA is a hedge, no part of the income or expense from the FRA can be spread forward for tax purposes into accounting periods later than that in which the value date falls.

VAT

VAT is not a major issue in FRAs. It would appear that any receipt from an FRA would be regarded as income from dealing in money. The receipt would be a supply of services for VAT purposes but would be exempt under Item 1, except where the supply is to a person who belongs in a country outside the EEC and the Isle of Man, in which case it would be zero rated.

Therefore, in neither case will VAT be chargeable on the receipt; however, where the FRA receipt is treated as an exempt supply it must be taken into account in computing the restrictions on the bank's or financial trader's ability to recover its input VAT under the partial exemption rules.

Interest rate options—caps, floors and collars

Characterisation of payments

The Inland Revenue consider that neither initial nor periodic payments to purchase a cap, floor or collar, nor payments and receipts under a cap, floor or collar constitute interest for tax purposes. The reason being that there is no underlying debt obligation between the payer and the recipient.

For a bank or financial trader, receipts or payments made under a cap, floor or collar agreement would normally be trading items taxable or allowable as trading receipts or expenses. Similarly, lump sum payments for the purchase or sale of a cap, floor or collar by a bank should fall within the computation of trading profits.

In the case of a trading company any payments made, whether for the purchase of such an instrument or in settlement, may be allowable as a trading deduction provided the payment is made wholly and exclusively for the purpose of the trade and it is not paid in relation to a sum employed as capital in the business. In these circumstances receipts would likewise be taxable as trading income.

In other circumstances (for example, for an investment company), FRAs or caps to which a person carrying on investment business in the United Kingdom is the counterparty, will be treated as assets which are dealt with under capital gains tax rules. Any payments made would thus be deductible from capital profits, although they cannot be deducted from trading profits.

Where the counterparty to the FRA or cap is not a person carrying on investment business in the United Kingdom, the tax position is less clear. It is likely to be difficult to obtain a deduction for any payments made, unless they are deductible as a trading expense.

Timing of assessability and deductibility of payments

It would seem that the Inland Revenue might argue that any settlement payments received or paid by a bank or financial trader under a cap, floor or collar should be recognised on a cash rather than accruals basis.

Where a bank or financial institution sells a cap, floor or collar to a third party the Inland Revenue's view is that for tax purposes the full amount of the fee should be brought in when received, although a provision for future payments to be made may be allowed if these can be reasonably estimated by reference to long-term interest rates or other market rates. It is, however, arguable that any receipt is a fee which has not been earned when it has been received but which should be spread over the period of the agreement. If an institution purchases a cap, floor or collar the converse arguments would apply.

For a taxpayer which is a trading company engaging in transactions in caps, floors or collars for the purposes of its trade, the timing of payments and receipts will be dealt with as for financial institutions, although it may be more difficult to defer recognition of any sums received on a sale.

Where capital gains tax rules apply, the taxable event is the disposal of the asset. In the case of the purchase of a cap there is likely to be part disposal whenever a settlement payment is received. In the case of a sale of a cap there is a particular problem in that, whilst the sale is the taxable event and the disposal proceeds are known, the deductible expenditure (that is, settlement payments made subsequently) will not be finally ascertained until the cap expires, when they will need to be related back to the original sale.

VAT

As for FRAs, dealings in caps, floors and collars are basically exempt, but are zero rated if supplied to a person belonging outside the EEC and Isle of Man.

TAXATION CONSIDERATIONS IN THE UNITED STATES

Interest rate swaps

Swap payments do not involve a sale or exchange. As a result, payments pursuant to a swap will be considered ordinary income. Although akin in many respects to interest, they are not to be treated as interest. Further, while economically similar to futures contracts, interest rate swap contracts are not classified as s. 1256 contracts which generally receive mark-to-market treatment (and are treated as 60 per cent long-term gain and 40 per cent short-term gain).

Interest rate swaps where periodical netting payments are made pursuant to the swap contract will be taxable to the payee and deductible to the payer in accordance with the taxpayer's method of accounting (that is, cash or accrual). Where the contract calls for a lump sum adjustment payment then the periodical receipt or outgoing analysis is not relevant. Where the swap hedges an investment position, deductibility may be limited by the straddle rules. Under these rules, losses are deferred to the extent of unrealised gains in offsetting positions.

Lump sum payments received and paid in connection with a swap agreement should be amortised over the swap period by the payer. The exact methodology for amortising such payments is unclear.

Currency swaps

As with interest rate swaps there will be periodical netting payments combined with a currency exchange payment at the termination of the swap.

The tax analysis applicable to the interest rate swap above will apply where throughout the period of the swap, periodical payments are made that do not contain a foreign currency element.

The *Tax Reform Act* 1986 (U.S.) codified the United States tax treatment of currency exchange gains and losses by the introduction of s. 988. Section 988 transactions include futures contracts, forward contracts, options and similar financial instruments. Under s. 988, the foreign exchange element in an s. 988 transaction is given ordinary income or loss treatment. A currency swap would generally fall under s. 988. Although the rules with respect to currency swaps are very unclear, it appears that interim payments are deductible (or taxable) and the final exchange should give rise to ordinary gain or loss.

The exception to s. 988 is where a foreign currency borrowing or loan by a United States taxpayer has been fully hedged against currency risk. In instances where a foreign currency borrowing has been fully hedged the borrower may elect to treat a US$ borrowing as a foreign currency borrowing in the reverse circumstances. The Internal Revenue Service is also empowered to compel integration of an exact hedge with an underlying transaction.

In summary, if any part of the swap payment can be characterised as containing a foreign currency element then an s. 988 analysis is necessary.

Timing of assessability and deductibility of swap payments

Swap payments will be recognised according to the ordinary accounting methods of the taxpayer. Further, the timing issues to be applied to currency swaps will generally follow those applicable to ordinary income principles.

Accelerated or deferred payment swaps

The most common variation of an interest rate swap is the zero coupon swap. Generally, a fixed rate recipient receives a lump sum payment in lieu of fixed rate payments over the life of the swap. Lump sum payments received or paid should be amortised over the life of the contract. The exact method of amortising such payments is unclear.

Associated swap costs

Such costs would normally be deductible for tax purposes and are most likely to be amortised over the duration of the swap.

Swap revaluations

A taxpayer may in respect of certain financial instruments mark-to-market that instrument. The Internal Revenue Service has ruled that currency swaps need not be market-to-market under the rules of the Internal Revenue Code, s. 1256. Interest rate swaps are also not subject to the mark-to-market rules of s. 1256. Although security dealers can generally adopt a mark-to-market valuation method for inventory, the use of such a method for swaps is highly questionable as swaps do not generally constitute property but rather agreements to exchange property in the future.

Withholding tax

The source of the interest rate swap will be directed to the residence of the recipient. Thus where an interest rate swap payment is made to a non-resident there will be no withholding tax issues for the payment will not be sourced within the United States. This rule currently only applies technically to a swap with a United States corporate counterparty, although the extension of the rule to swaps with United States branches of foreign corporations is expected.

The withholding tax issue on currency swap payments is far from settled, however, it would seem appropriate to follow the interest rate swap tax analysis.

LTFXs

LTFXs entered into through the interbank market prior to 22 October, 1988 are subject to the mark-to-market and capital gain or loss rules of s. 1256 if the underlying currency is traded in the regulated futures markets. LTFX that do not meet these criteria are subject to the rules of s. 988 and the taxpayer's method of accounting. Section 1256 contracts that are part of an identified hedge or for which a "mixed straddle" election are made are not subject to s. 1256 and are taxed in the same manner as non-s. 1256 contracts. LTFX contracts entered into after 21 October, 1988 are subject to the s. 988 ordinary characterisation and residency sourcing rules, regardless of whether marked to market under s. 1256.

FRAs

FRAs resemble interest rate swaps, except that the interest rate is set at the beginning, rather than the end of the relevant period. The tax considerations applicable to interest rate swaps should be applicable to forward rate agreements. The Internal Revenue Service has not indicated whether it would include FRA payments within the scope of its announcement regarding interest rate swaps. For this reason, there remains a withholding risk where a payment is made to a non-resident alien. Several arguments that are available against withholding are set out in the discussion below dealing with interest rate options.

Interest rate options—caps, floors and collars

As with other countries there are no definitive rules specifically on point regarding the tax treatment of caps, floors and collars. However, by analogy, the tax rules regarding loan commitment fees would most likely be applicable to up-front fees paid for a cap, floor or collar.

Characteristics of payment

For the borrower, any up-front payment paid for a cap, floor or collar would most likely for tax purposes be required to be capitalised. Alternatively, for the provider, the most likely result under general tax accounting principles would be for a taxpayer in the business of providing caps, floors or collars to recognise up-front fees as ordinary income.

Interest differential payments received by the borrower or purchaser of a cap, floor or collar most likely will be required to be treated as gross income. Payments received by the borrower will generally be considered ordinary income, not capital, since there is no sale or exchange. Although no specific authority on point exists, payments received by a purchaser of the cap, floor or collar with no specific borrowing will most likely be considered ordinary income, not capital, again, because no sale or exchange occurs. This result may be different if the cap takes the form of an option in which case payments are likely to be a sale or exchange.

For a taxpayer in the business of providing caps, floors or collars the payment of the excess interest should be considered an ordinary and necessary business expense.

Timing of assessability and deductibility of payments

Up-front payments to enter into this agreement are likely to be amortised over the life of the agreement by both the payer and the receiver.

Interest differential payments under these agreements are likely to be treated in the same manner as up-front payments.

Withholding tax on interest rate caps

The United States Internal Revenue Code imposes a 30.00% tax on amounts received from sources within the United States by non-United States corporations and non-resident aliens on income such as interest, dividends, salaries and other fixed or determinable annual or periodic gains, profits and income (FDAP income) to the extent such amounts are not effectively connected with the conduct of a trade or business.

In contrast, no withholding is imposed on gains from the sale of property, unless such gains are effectively connected with a trade or business in the United States. For instance, gains from positions in futures contracts or options would not be taxable nor subject to withholding in the absence of a trade or business in the United States.

At present, there are no rules for determining the source of income paid in connection with a cap payment. By contrast, the rules for determining the source of an interest rate swap payment, which in many respects is similar to an interest rate cap, have been determined (source is determined by the residence of the recipient). The Internal Revenue Service has indicated that it will resolve the withholding issue in the very near future.

If the provider of the cap or collar is a United States entity and the borrower is a non-United States entity, the payments from the provider might be subject to United States withholding tax. However, the payments do not appear to be interest because they are not paid for the use or forebearance of money. The cap, floor or collar payments may be considered non-interest FDAP income.

If the borrower is a United States entity and the provider is a non-United States entity, United States withholding issues relative to up-front fees paid to the provider may be considered similar to service income or otherwise fall under the definition of FDAP. As service income, an argument may be made that the source of income was the final location, thereby eliminating the United States withholding tax requirement.

Tax treaties with the United States provide that foreign corporations in a treaty country (that is, Australia, the United Kingdom) are exempt from United States withholding tax on United States source business or "industrial or commercial" profits except to the extent that they are effectively connected with a United States permanent establishment of the foreign corporation. It is not clear whether payments from cap, floor and collar agreements can be included in the category "business, industrial or commercial" profits. The argument in favour of inclusion is that the payments are not passive FDAP type income, but are instead related to an exempt business activity, specified in the business profits article of a treaty (for example, a banking business). Such payments also do not appear to be addressed in other treaty articles (for example, interest) so as to preclude consideration under a business profits article. Another provision in tax treaties with the United States specifies that income items not covered by the treaty are only taxed by the country where the recipient of the income resides. At present, only tax treaties with Hungary and the United Kingdom have such provision.

In such case, there would appear to be no possibility of withholding, as such payments do not appear to be specifically covered by provisions of the treaty (for example, interest).

TAXATION CONSIDERATIONS IN CANADA

Interest rate swaps

In determining the income tax implications of payments pursuant to swap contracts, regard must be had to the legal substance of the transactions as well as the intentions of the parties entering into the swap.

The application of Canadian tax legislation to swaps may give rise to areas of uncertainty to the parties to the swap, depending on their circumstances and motivation, the nature of the Canadian parties and the structures adopted. Canadian taxation legislation adopts or contains no specific statutory provisions that specifically address swap transactions. Accordingly, for the most part recourse must be had to the general statutory provisions and to a substantial body of case law. However, none of the case law is specifically on point but only serves to establish certain general income tax principles. Thus each case involves an analysis of the facts that are specific to the taxpayer's situation.

Generally, amounts payable and receivable under an interest rate swap agreement by a Canadian participant should be fully deductible or included in income under the general rules for computing business profits. For a business, a taxpayer's income for tax purposes is its profit therefrom for the year determined in accordance with ordinary business and accounting practices but subject to modification by various provisions contained in the *Income Tax Act* (Canada). This follows either because they typically arise from transactions undertaken in the normal course of business or as adventures in the nature of trade, or because the net profit or loss is regarded as arising from a transaction entered into to hedge what is an income or revenue item. Revenue Canada's current administration position would appear to be consistent with this interpretation.

Currency swaps

Currency swaps may be motivated by a variety of objectives. The Canadian tax implications of currency swaps are similar to those for interest rate swaps although they are complicated by the fact that currency swaps involve two currencies.

The Canadian participant will recognise a foreign exchange gain or loss on re-exchange under the currency exchange agreement which should, in almost all cases, be equal but opposite to the foreign exchange loss or gain realised on the repayment of the foreign currency borrowings. It is only where both the gain and the loss are either on capital account or on income account that no issue arises.

Financial institutions and certain other corporates entering into currency swaps against trade assets or liaiblities will normally be able to recognise both foreign exchange transactions on revenue account. However, the result is less certain where the original borrowing in the foreign currency by the corporate is on capital account as will normally be the case where the end use of the funds raised in the foreign currency is the acquisition of capital assets or the expansion of a permanent working capital base. In order to characterise a foreign exchange gain or loss on repayment of an outstanding debt, the Canadian courts have, as a rule, looked to the nature of the obligation. Where the corporate borrower's purpose in raising funds is to obtain capital, the foreign exchange gain or loss on repayment will be on capital account.

Accordingly, it will be important that the offsetting foreign exchange loss or gain on re-exchange of the currencies under the currency swap agreement is also on capital account.

Timing of assessability and deductibility of swap payments

Interest rate swaps

The deduction for income tax purposes of a netting payment arising from a conventional swap occurs when an amount becomes payable under the terms of the contract. Thus when an enforceable obligation of a payment has arisen the amount is an expense which is deductible in computing income for tax purposes. In practice, however, the amount is deducted in computing income for income tax purposes on the same accruals basis as is used in Canadian accounting practices and to date the Canadian tax authorities have not challenged this treatment.

Similarly when an amount becomes due and receivable then that amount is included in income for tax purposes although in practice the amounts are recorded on an accrual basis.

Currency swaps

Under cross-currency swaps the same conclusions can be derived with respect to the netting payments relating to interest. With respect to any gains or losses arising on the repayment of the currency under current Canadian administrative practice where the foreign exchange gains or losses are on account of income they may be accounted for on an accruals basis or a realised basis. However, where the foreign exchange gains or losses are on account of capital then the taxpayer must record for income tax purposes the foreign exchange gains or losses on a realisation basis.

Accelerated or deferred payment swaps

Questions arise as to whether it is appropriate to recognise the accelerated swap income as having been earned where there is a requirement to make future payments and whether it is appropriate to recognise that the accelerated swap costs can be said to be fully incurred when they are referable to deferred income. For the most part, recourse must be had to the general statutory provisions contained in the *Income Tax Act* (Canada) which uses accounting profit as a starting point in determining income for tax purposes. The accounting principles would indicate that the accrual method be used to include the payments in income on a basis that provides the best matching of income and expense.

In considering accelerated payments it is difficult to see how expenditure has been incurred for income tax purposes before the actual liability to pay that amount has become due under the terms of the contract. In respect of accelerated income the amount will be included in income for tax purposes pursuant to specific sections contained in the *Income Tax Act* (Canada) but a reserve may be claimed in respect of services that it is reasonably anticipated will have to be rendered after the end of the fiscal period. This raises the question as to what service is being rendered and what portion, if any, of the total payment is refundable if the services are not provided.

In respect of deferred expenditures the absence of any forcible right of payment suggests that an accrual approach is not appropriate as an outlay or expense has not been incurred until the amount becomes payable. However, since Canadian income tax law is not specific, general income tax concepts must be used in examining these issues.

Associated swap costs

Fees and other costs of the swap should also be fully deductible on the same basis as amounts payable and receivable under an interest rate swap. Although depending on the terms of the transaction there may be a debate over the proper timing of the deduction.

Withholding taxes

Where the counterparty or the arranger of the swap is a non-resident of Canada, the question of withholding tax will also arise. If the amount paid to the non-resident is found to be interest, withholding tax would be applicable. The rate of withholding tax with respect to interest is 25.00% of the amount paid or payable to a non-resident of Canada unless reduced by a double taxation agreement, in which case the rate is generally 15.00%. Swap payments themselves are not generally regarded as legally constituting interest in that there is no exchange of a principal obligation and, as such, the Canadian domestic tax legislation should not otherwise catch swap payments whether paid on a gross or on a net basis (that is, there would normally be no Canadian withholding tax concern).

Fees and other costs, to the extent that they are incurred in the normal course for services performed at arm's-length outside Canada, will similarly not be subject to withholding tax.

An issue arises where, for one reason or another, the parties have agreed to a mismatching schedule of payments and, as a result, the Canadian participant to the swap will receive payments in advance of its liability to pay. The revenue authorities take the view that a portion of the outbound payment made by the Canadian must be regarded as interest on the one or more short-term advances received by the Canadian during the course of the year against its promise to pay a future liability. The interest portion is then dissected from the swap payment made by the Canadian participant and, as no Canadian domestic withholding exemption exists for interest on short-term funds, it is chargeable to Canadian withholding tax.

LTFXs

The Canadian income tax considerations arising with respect to foreign exchange gains and losses involves an examination as to whether there is an underlying transaction which is being hedged and whether the underlying transaction is on account of income or on account of capital.

In general terms, foreign exchange gains or losses arising from foreign exchange contracts which have been entered into as a hedge against underlying transactions will take on the characterisation of the item being hedged. For instance, if the item being hedged is on account of capital then normally the gain or loss arising on the foreign exchange contract is also on account of capital. It appears that a reasonably good argument can be made to support this position. However, case law indicates that taxpayers have had difficulty in obtaining the concurrence of the Canadian taxation authorities that a particular transaction is a hedge rather than a foreign currency speculation where the transaction is not an isolated transaction.

With respect to traders of foreign exchange contracts who value their inventory at market, the gain or loss is usually recognised for income tax purposes in the same period in which they are accounted for. There may be some opportunity, using the inventory valuation provisions, to value LTFXs for income tax purposes in a manner different from the value used for accounting although this may be subject to challenge by the tax authorities.

Where a taxpayer has entered into an isolated foreign exchange contract on a speculative basis the taxpayer may choose to utilise the Canadian taxation authorities' administrative policy to consistently report these transactions either being on account of income or on account of capital.

If the foreign exchange contract is on account of income then the gain or loss is recognised on an accruals basis except where the taxpayer chooses to follow the administrative practice of the taxation authorities and include the amounts on a realised basis. Where the gain or loss is on account of capital it may be recognised for income tax purposes on a realised basis.

FRAs

Characterisation of settlement amounts

A taxpayer's income for tax purposes is the "profit" from a business determined in accordance with commercially accepted accounting practices subject to various adjustments required by the *Income Tax Act*. At the present time there are no provisions contained in the *Income Tax Act* and no cases have been litigated dealing specifically with the tax treatment of payments made or received on settlement of an FRA. For Canadian financial statement purposes an amount paid or received on settlement for an FRA would generally be treated on an accruals basis as a component of interest expense or interest income in computing financial statement income. The income tax treatment in Canada of these amounts would appear to follow the financial statement treatment and thus forward rate settlement payments should be considered to be on income account to the extent the amount is reasonable and the interest is deductible which is usually the case where the underlying borrowed funds have been borrowed for the purpose of earning income.

Since forward rate settlement amounts are considered to be part of the trading activities of a financial institution they are treated as being on account of income. For a non-financial institution the position might be taken that the transaction represents an "adventure in the nature of trade", which is included in the definition of "business" for Canadian income tax purposes. Amounts paid or received with respect to an adventure in the nature of trade are treated as being on account of income and fully deductible or included in determining income for Canadian income tax purposes.

Where the taxpayer has taken an isolated speculative position which is not related to the business he or she may take an income or a capital position with respect to any gain or loss realised.

Timing of recognition of settlement amounts

The recognition of forward rate settlement amounts for Canadian income tax purposes is based on Canadian financial statement accounting. Where the contract date and the settlement date straddle the fiscal year end of a taxpayer an amount is recorded in income for Canadian financial statement purposes to reflect the accrued gain or loss. This financial statement accrual has generally been recognised for Canadian income tax purposes although some doubt continues to exist that the amount should not be recognised for income tax purposes until the settlement date.

Canadian non-resident income tax

Where a payment on settlement of a forward rate agreement is made to a non-resident person by a resident of Canada, Canadian withholding tax is generally not exigible. This results from the fact that the amount of the payment under an FRA does not represent interest since a creditor and debtor relationship does not exist between the parties to the agreement. Accordingly, the Canadian withholding tax provisions do not have application in these circumstances.

Interest rate options—caps, floors and collars

Characterisation of settlement

Similar to FRAs, provisions do not exist in the *Income Tax Act* governing the taxation of interest rate caps, collars and floors and therefore the taxation in Canada of amounts arising from a cap, collar or floor generally follows the Canadian financial statement accounting. Amounts paid or received are accounted for on an accruals basis as a part of the interest component of the underlying hedged assets.

For financial institutions such amounts represent the trading profit of the institution which is reflected in financial statement income. A concern may exist for non-financial institutions that the payment under the transaction may be considered to be on account of capital. If the Canadian taxation authorities were to take this position, any gain or losses arising on settlement would be a capital gain or loss. Only a portion of a capital gain is included in income for tax purposes while capital losses may only be deducted against capital gains.

However, the Canadian taxation authorities may take the position that for these taxpayers, an interest rate cap, collar or floor represents an "adventure in the nature of trade" and accordingly any payments are on account of income.

Timing of recognition of settlement amounts

The recognition of an amount paid or received on the settlement of an interest rate cap, collar or floor would generally follow its recognition for Canadian financial statement purposes. The Canadian taxation authorities have accepted this treatment to date although it would appear that recognition for income tax purposes should not occur until the settlement date.

However, should the transactions be considered to be a capital amount then amounts paid or received may be recognised at the settlement date when the gain or loss is crystallised from a legal point of view.

Canadian non-resident income tax

Generally, the provisions dealing with Canadian withholding tax on interest are not applicable since the payment does not represent "interest" as a debtor and creditor relationship does not exist.

Exhibit 33.2

Taxation Aspects of Swap Transactions

SUMMARY TABLE

Interest rate swaps	Australia	United Kingdom	United States	Canada
Character of netting payments	Generally analysed by having regard to the taxation treatment of the financing commitments of the underlying borrowing transaction which the interest rate swap seeks to impact	In general, the taxation treatment does depend on taxation treatment of any underlying borrowing or lending transaction	Since swap payments typically relate to the hedge of underlying debt or assets generating investment income, they will be considered ordinary income under the hedging doctrine	Regard must be had to the legal substance of the transaction as well as the intentions of the parties entering into the swap
Timing of inclusion of netting receipts or payments in the computation of taxable income for companies and financial institutions	*Companies* In the more conventional swaps it is considered that the timing of any deduction arises upon the creation of a liability to make that payment. Similarly, it is considered that any netting income is earned at the time when the amounts become due and receivable	*Companies* Generally deductible or assessable as annual payments (that is, on a cash basis). There is a general requirement to deduct basic rate income tax from swap payments (unless paid to a United Kingdom bank or paid by a bank or financial trader)	*Companies* Swap payments will be recognised according to the ordinary accounting methods of the taxpayer	*Companies* At law, the deduction of netting payments occurs when an amount becomes payable under the terms of the contract. Similarly, it is considered that netting income is earned when an amount becomes due and receivable. In practice, payments or receipts are included in the computation of taxable income on the same basis as used in Canadian accounting practice

Exhibit 33.2—continued

Interest rate swaps	Australia	United Kingdom	United States	Canada
	Financial institutions	*Financial institutions*	*Financial institutions*	*Financial institutions*
	The accruals approach may be more appropriate in respect of the financial institutions	Payments or receipts in the ordinary course of trade would normally be deductible or assessable as trading expenses (that is, on an accruals basis)	Swap payments will be recognised according to the ordinary accounting methods of the taxpayer	In practice, payments or receipts are included in the computation of taxable income on the same basis as used in Canadian accounting practice
Currency swaps				
Netting payments	The tax consequences for the regular net payments or receipts in respect of currency swaps broadly follows the analysis set out above	Similar to interest rate swaps. The only difference in the taxation treatment of recurring payments and fees between currency swaps and interest rate swaps is that payments made by a trading company (not carrying on a financial trade) to a United Kingdom bank are treated as trading expenses in respect of a currency swap	Tax analysis applicable to interest rate swaps will apply where the periodical payments do not contain a foreign currency element	The same conclusions can be derived with respect to the netting payments or receipts as interest rate swaps
Currency Gains and Losses	Pursuant to the introduction of specific legislation most currency exchange gains would be assessable and most currency exchange losses would be deductible for income tax purposes.	Currency swaps do not normally give rise to any exchange differences on revenue account. Where a currency swap is on capital account, a capital gain or loss may arise, not so much on the swap itself but from the assets and liabilities associated with the swap	Under s. 988 the foreign exchange element in a s. 988 transaction is given ordinary income or loss treatment. The exception is where a foreign currency borrowing is fully hedged against currency risk. The timing issues to be applied to currency swaps will generally follow those applicable to ordinary income principles	Financial institutions and certain other corporates entering into currency swaps against trade assets or liabilities will normally be able to recognise both foreign exchange transactions on revenue account. The treatment on capital account is less certain. In the case of a corporate, the Canadian courts have, as a rule, looked

Exhibit 33.2—continued
Currency swaps

	Australia	United Kingdom	United States	Canada
				to the nature of the obligation. With respect to any gains or losses arising on the repayment of the currency, under current Canadian administrative practice, where the foreign exchange gains or losses are on account of income they may be accounted for on an accruals basis or a realised basis. However, where the foreign exchange gains or losses are on account of capital then the taxpayer must record the foreign exchange gains and losses on a realisation basis.
Associated swap costs	Where the netting payments are on revenue account then the incidental expenses incurred in respect of the swap contract should be considered to be on revenue account and deductible. They should be deductible when paid and the recipient would normally recognise the fee income at the time it was due and receivable	Should normally be trading receipts or expenses for banks. For non-banks the position is less clear	Would normally be deductible for tax purposes and most likely to be amortised over the duration of the swap	Should be fully deductible on the same basis as amounts payable and receivable under an interest rate swap. Although depending on the terms of the transaction there may be a debate over the proper timing of the deduction

Exhibit 33.2—continued

Currency swaps

	Australia	United Kingdom	United States	Canada
Withholding tax	In IT 2050 the Australian Taxation Office has stated that the netting payments under an interest rate swap agreement are not amounts in the nature of interest and should not be subject to Australian interest withholding tax	The general requirement to deduct basic rate income tax (noted above) may be reduced or eliminated on payments made to recipients not resident in the United Kingdom if permitted by the provisions of a double tax Agreement	The source of the interest rate swap will be directed to the residence of the recipient. Thus where an interest rate swap agreement is made to a non-resident there will be no withholding tax issues for the payment will not be sourced within the United States	Swap payments themselves are not generally regarded as legally constituting interest and should not be subject to withholding tax
VAT	Not applicable	VAT is not a major issue in swap transactions	Not applicable	Not applicable

Chapter 34

Legal and Documentation Issues in Swap Transactions

STANDARDISATION OF SWAP DOCUMENTATION

The growth in size, flexibility and sophistication of the market consisting of swaps and related currency and interest rate hedging and arbitrage instruments such as FRAs, caps, floors and collars[1] has been paralleled by corresponding developments in the area of documentation. Beginning in 1985 with the promulgation of the International Swap Dealers Association's Code of Standard Wording, Assumptions and Provisions for Swaps (the ISDA Swap Code); the British Bankers Association's Interest Rate Swap (BBAIRS), Forward Rate Agreements (FRABBA) and Foreign Currency Option (LICOM) Terms; and the Australian Financial Markets Association's General Terms and Conditions for Australian Dollar Fixed and Floating Interest Rate Swaps (AIRS Terms), there has been a general movement toward standardisation of the terms and conditions under which such transactions are documented.[2] This movement was highlighted by ISDA's publication in 1987 of two standard agreements, one for documenting US$ denominated interest rate swaps, which incorporates the ISDA Swap Code, and one for interest rate and currency exchange swaps in any currency, for which ISDA published a separate set of definitions.[3]

Standardisation of swap documentation has been an inevitable process, motivated by several factors including the following:

- Swaps typically are documented after the transaction has been agreed and commenced; standardised documentation reduces the possibility of future disagreements over the basic terms and conditions of the transaction.

- The narrowing margins and sheer volume of transactions necessitate minimisation of the time and expense involved in documenting swaps.

- Standardised documentation facilitates the development of a secondary market in swap transactions.

In particular, master agreements have become attractive to many market makers, both as a means of simplifying documentation and because they enable market makers to enter into multiple transactions with particular counterparties which, on a net basis, fall within established credit limits.[4]

---

1. For a discussion of recent variations to currency and interest rate hedging and arbitrage products, see Cooper (1989).
2. See generally Stoakes (1985) (March).
3. See generally International Swap Dealers Association Inc. (1987).
4. Chemical Bank has led an effort, joined by 11 other banks, called the FX Netting Project, to develop a clearing house scheme through which banks will contract directly with each other on a bilateral basis to net foreign exchange transactions on a continual basis under a single master agreement. Information concerning FXNET, which is now operational, is available from FXNET 180 Strand, London WC2R 1EX.

The ISDA Interest Rate and Currency Exchange Agreement (the ISDA Agreement) and accompanying Interest Rate and Currency Exchange Definitions (the Definitions) have achieved fairly wide acceptance as the market standard since their publication in 1987.[5] This chapter focuses particularly on the ISDA Agreement and Definitions in discussing legal issues related to documentation of swap transactions.

GENERAL NATURE OF SWAP CONTRACTS

A swap contract is similar in appearance to loan agreements and other contracts to provide financial accommodation, typically containing the following basic provisions:

- payment obligations and mechanics;
- yield protection;
- representations and warranties;
- covenants;
- termination events (which are comparable to events triggering a right or obligation to prepay a loan);
- events of default;
- consequences of default, indemnity and liquidated damages provisions; and
- miscellaneous provisions (contractual currency, notice, governing law, assignability, etc.).

The fundamental difference between a swap contract and a loan agreement is that a swap generally creates mutual obligations rather than a debtor-creditor relationship.[6] This distinction is significant in negotiating a swap contract, inasmuch as the provisions of the contract, in particular the covenants, representations, events of default and related provisions, will apply to both parties (unless expressly drafted to apply to one party only, as might occur in the case of a swap between two parties of disparate credit standing), whereas in a loan agreement such provisions apply only to the borrower.

5. The Bank of England supports the efforts of ISDA and the British Bankers' Association to establish uniform standards and encourages the use of the ISDA Interest Rate and Currency Exchange Agreement and, for swap transactions in the London interbank market with maturities of less than two years, the BBAIRS Terms. See "The London Code of Conduct—Part 2: The Swap Market" (1987), paras 1, 27, 40 (hereinafter London Code of Conduct).

6. Although the view generally taken is that swap contracts, since they involve reciprocal obligations, do not give rise to debts, that is, that they are not contracts to provide financial accommodation, this characterisation begins to break down in situations where payments are exchanged at different intervals, for example, swaps involving annual fixed payments and quarterly or semi-annual floating payments; zero coupon swaps in which one party makes periodic payments and the other party makes a single payment at the end of the swap; or specifically tailored swaps in which one party makes a substantial payment upon commencement of the transaction that is offset by periodic payments at a higher rate during and/or an additional payment at the end of the swap. See Cunningham and Rogers (1987), pp. 417, 438-441.

The ISDA Agreement is intended to function as a master agreement, incorporating its basic terms and conditions and all swap transactions entered into thereunder into a single contract. In contrast, many earlier master agreements prepared for use by individual market participants constitute a set of standard terms and conditions incorporated into a series of individual contracts, each covering a single swap transaction entered into between the parties, which simplifies documentation but is perhaps less beneficial in reducing credit risk.[7] The AIRS Terms, to which over 100 banks and financial institutions are signatories, operate in the latter fashion, being incorporated by reference into confirmation telexes by which A$ interest rate swaps between signatories are documented under AIRS.

The ISDA Agreement has been prepared for use under either New York or English law. It has also been employed with little change by Australian market makers under New South Wales law. Regardless of the governing law of the contract, however, certain provisions of local law, particularly the bankruptcy and insolvency laws of a party's jurisdiction of incorporation, will govern the enforceability of the agreement against such party when applied by the courts of such jurisdiction.

PAYMENT PROVISIONS

Care must be taken in documenting the payment mechanics of swaps, including the determination of floating interest rates. Where a swap is matched to a particular asset or transaction, payment dates, non-business day conventions, interest payment calculations and related terms must be carefully drafted to match the payment provisions of the swap to the underlying cash flow. Where the swap includes a floating rate calculation period that does not correspond to a period for which a rate is quoted by the reference source specified in the documentation, the documentation should specify clearly how the interest rate for such period will be calculated, for example, by obtaining quotes from reference banks, by taking a weighted average of two quoted rates, etc. In using the ISDA Agreement, the particulars of individual swaps are documented by reference to the Definitions in a confirmation letter or telex, which is deemed incorporated into and part of a single contract with the ISDA Agreement and all prior confirmations.

Interest rate swap payments generally are made on a net basis by a single party, which reduces the parties' credit exposure. In the Schedule to the ISDA Agreement, which consists in part of a menu of optional provisions that the parties may select, the parties may (and in practice generally do) choose also to net off payments due on the same date and in the same currency in respect of different transactions, which, in the limited circumstances in which it applies, also reduces risk.[8] However, to the extent that there is a mismatch in payment dates, for example, annual fixed rate payments and semi-annual floating rate payments, the party making semi-

---

7. See Stoakes (1985) (March).
8. Such a provision would be of limited utility unless there were numerous swaps between the parties. It would be of greater utility in connection with the FX Netting Project (see above, n. 4) since it is likely that foreign exchange transactions between major banks would be relatively more numerous than swaps.

annual payments necessarily assumes the additional risk in making payments at more frequent intervals that its counterparty will not default in making corresponding payments at a later date.

A similar problem arises with respect to payments due in different currencies on the same date. Because of time zone differences, one party effectively may be required to make its payment one day prior to the corresponding payment by its counterparty.[9] Various approaches to this problem (sometimes referred to as "clean credit risk") have been suggested, such as use of irrevocable payment instructions or escrow arrangements, but these have generally been regarded as too burdensome for use in swap transactions.[10]

A provision often included in swap agreements to obviate the problem of clean credit risk is one which states that a party receiving a payment from its counterparty prior to making the payment due from it on the same date, must hold the amount received by it in trust for the payor until it has made its corresponding payment. The effect of such a provision is that if a party is bankrupt or insolvent at the time it receives a payment and fails to make its corresponding payment, the payment it received, if traceable, should be recoverable in the payee's bankruptcy or insolvency proceeding by the payor, since it was held in trust for the payor and therefore does not comprise part of the payee's assets.[11]

Many swap agreements, including the ISDA Agreement, contain conditionality clauses, which make each party's payment obligations

9. In practice, this problem arises even in the absence of time zone differences whenever corresponding payments are due on the same date, since confirmation delays and the volume of payments made by a bank each day make it impractical from an operational point of view to withhold making any particular payment until receipt of the corresponding payment can be confirmed. A party's back office may set in motion a transfer of funds, such as through the New York Clearing House Interbank Payments System (CHIPS), only to learn as the transfer is occurring that a receiver has been appointed for or bankruptcy proceeding commenced by its counterparty, the failure of Bankhaus Herstatt in 1974 being the most notorious example. See *Delbrueck & Co. v. Manufacturers Hanover Trust Co.* 464 F. Supp. 989 (S.D.N.Y.); affd, 609 F. 2d 1047 (2d Cir. 1979).
10. In situations involving parties of disparate credit standing, particularly transactions between a bank and a corporate counterparty, the documentation may provide simply that the party of lower credit standing must always pay first.
11. Such provisions appear infrequently in swap documentation prepared in Australia (although they are common in documentation of cross-border swaps prepared elsewhere but with an Australian party) because of a concern that their inclusion would result in swap agreements being subject to stamp duty as "declarations of trust". A reasonable argument can be made that such provisions are merely incidental to the purpose of swap agreements and hence not separately dutiable. See generally Tolhurst, Wallace and Zipfinger (1979), ss 1.42-1.46 ("leading and principal object" rule versus "several distinct matters" rule). However, even if swap agreements containing such provisions would be separately dutiable as declarations of trust, since the funds which are the subject of the trust are not vested at the time the swap agreement is executed, duty would not be chargeable at ad valorem rates. Morever, should an Australian party to a swap with an off-shore counterparty be required to participate in the bankruptcy proceeding in such party's jurisdiction of incorporation to recoup the payment subject to trust, the payment or non-payment of duty should not arise as an issue in the context of such proceeding. The potential that a payment in trust provision might enable an Australian party to recover a substantial payment to an insolvent counterparty suggests that Australian market makers and their solicitors should consider carefully whether the stamp duty implications of such provisions outweigh their utility.

conditional upon the other party having performed its obligations under the agreement. While such a provision would allow a party to withhold payments to a defaulting counterparty or one that was unable or unlikely to make its corresponding payment on the relevant date, it would not be helpful in enabling a payor to recoup a payment made to an insolvent counterparty that failed to make its corresponding payment to the payor, since such a provision generally would not result in a trust being imposed on the payment in question. Rather, non-payment would constitute a breach of contract giving rise to a claim for damages and a right to treat the contract as repudiated, which in a bankruptcy proceeding would leave the payor in the position merely of a competing creditor.

TAX INDEMNITIES

Swap agreements generally require parties to make payments free of deduction or withholding in respect of taxes, but allow an "affected party" (one that is required to "gross up" swap payments subject to withholding) to terminate affected transactions on a "no fault" basis. The ISDA Agreement contains particularly broad and complex provisions in this regard.

Under the ISDA Agreement, a party is only required to gross up if a tax imposed is an "indemnifiable tax" which is any tax other than a tax imposed as a result of "a present or former connection" between the jurisdiction imposing the tax and the recipient of the payment being taxed. Moreover, a party is not required to gross up in respect of an indemnifiable tax that would not have been imposed had the "payee tax representations" of the recipient of the payment been true, unless the imposition has been made as a result of a "change in tax law". The payee tax representations consist of a menu of optional provisions in the Schedule to the ISDA Agreement, principal of which are that a party is eligible for the "business profits" and "interest" provisions of the relevant, specified tax treaty and is not carrying on business through a permanent establishment in the jurisdiction in which its counterparty is located. A change in tax law is broadly defined to include a change in any treaty, law or regulation or in its interpretation or application.[12]

It is by no means clear that use of the payee tax representations is necessary or desirable in all cases. Consider, for example, the operation of the ISDA Agreement tax provisions from the perspective of an Australian party in the context of an A$ Eurobond-driven swap with a German counterparty. The relevant treaty would be the Australian-German tax treaty. The "business profits" payee tax representation of the German counterparty adds nothing to the ISDA Agreement, since the tax treaty excepts business profits of the German counterparty derived from Australia from Australian tax so long as it does not do business through a permanent establishment in Australia. However, if the German counterparty is deemed to be doing business through a permanent establishment in Australia, the Australian party would not be obligated to gross up even absent the "business profits" representation, since Australian taxes imposed as a result of "a present or former connection"

12. See generally Bates (1988).

of the German counterparty with Australia would not be an "indemnifiable tax".

Although the position is yet to be clarified in most jurisdictions, swap payments generally are regarded as constituting "business profits" rather than "interest". If, however, at some future date a relevant authority characterised such payments as interest, the payee tax representation respecting the "interest" provision of any Australian tax treaty would not be relevant to an Australian counterparty to a swap, since no Australian treaty reduces the rate of withholding on interest payments below the statutory rate of 10.00%. (By way of comparison, the statutory rate of withholding on interest payments under the United States Internal Revenue Code is 30.00%, but certain United States and European country treaties reduce the rate of withholding on interest payments to zero.) In other words, the Australian party in our example would be required to gross up since such withholding was required whether or not its counterparty's representation was true. Moreover, given the widely held view that swap payments do not constitute interest and the absence of any significant effort to date by the tax authorities in any material jurisdiction to assert otherwise, a characterisation of swap payments as interest arguably would constitute a "change in tax law", in which case there would be an obligation to gross up regardless of the payee tax representations.

In the view of a working group within ISDA of German banks that are major swap market participants, the ISDA approach represents a major departure from the traditional gross up clause, "which burdens each party with the information risk for tax developments in its own country, which risks it can access and influence better than the foreign counterparty".[13] However, they single out the definition of indemnifiable tax as the problem.

Generally, this author is in accord with the thrust of the position of the German ISDA members. However, the problem is not with the definition of indemnifiable tax, which, in referring to taxes imposed as a result of a "present or former connection" with the taxing jurisdiction, essentially is a variation on the typical exclusion from taxes subject to gross up obligations of taxes on net income. Rather, the problem is with the payee tax representation, which may, if they prove to be false, compel a party to accept payments net of withholding or deductions for the duration of a swap. Given the complexity and uncertainty of legal issues relating to taxation of swap payments and taking the view that the parties to a swap are generally sophisticated and have contracted on the basis that swap payments can be made free of withholding, it seems more in keeping with commercial expectations that a swap will be terminable on a no-fault basis should a tax be imposed on payments than that a party in certain cases should be relieved of an obligation to gross up and its counterparty be left to accept payments in such circumstances net of withholding.

In any event, it should be clear that the drafters have embodied certain basic assumptions about allocation of risk in the ISDA Agreement with which any party using the document should be certain that it is in agreement. It should also be clear that completion of Pt 2 of the Schedule to the ISDA

---

13. German ISDA Members, Memorandum for ISDA, (23 February 1988), s. 1(c).

Agreement, which contains the tax representations of the parties, should not be regarded simply as a mechanical process of filling in and checking off any provision that fits.

The drafters of the ISDA Agreement and Definitions have scrupulously avoided using the word interest in connection with swap payments. While swap agreements still in use by some market participants often use the word interest in describing fixed and floating rates, fixed and floating rate payments, payment dates and calculation periods, it is unlikely that the form of agreement would affect a determination of whether, in substance, swap payments constitute interest, should a tax authority assert this position.

REPRESENTATIONS AND COVENANTS

The ISDA Agreement incorporates several basic representations, including due organisation; power to execute and perform the agreement; no conflict with law or other documents; existence of all necessary consents; and that the agreement is legal, valid, binding and enforceable; as well as absence of any event of default or termination event; absence of any material litigation (this representation is often deleted in the Schedule by parties using the Agreement); and the accuracy of any written information provided by a party and any tax representation of a party specified in the Schedule. The ISDA Agreement also provides that each party agrees to provide documents specified in the Schedule or any confirmation by the date specified therein; to maintain and obtain in the future all necessary consents and to comply with all applicable material laws; to give notice upon becoming aware that any payee tax representation is untrue; and to pay any stamp tax imposed by the jurisdiction in which it is located.

RIGHT TO TERMINATE

Events that give rise to a right to terminate swap agreements generally fall into two categories—events of default and termination events. Under the ISDA Agreement, events of default include:

- failure to pay any amount due within three business days after notice of such failure is given to a party;
- failure to perform any other obligation under the agreement within 30 days of notice;
- a representation (other than a tax representation), which only relieves the non-defaulting party in certain circumstances of its obligation to gross up proving to be untrue;
- default under and termination of any specified swap (as such term is defined by the parties in the Schedule) of a party;
- bankruptcy, insolvency, dissolution or liquidation of a party; and
- merger of a party without its successor entity assuming the obligations of the party under the agreement.

The agreement contains an optional cross-default provision and credit support default provisions if a party's obligations are supported by a credit support document specified in the Schedule. Any of the specified swap, cross-default and bankruptcy provisions can be extended to affiliates of a party by identifying affiliates in the Schedule as specified entities of such party in respect of each such provision.

Termination events under the ISDA Agreement include:

- an illegality, which is the occurrence of an event that makes it illegal for a party (or a specified entity of such party) to make any payment due or to perform any other material obligation under the agreement (or, with respect to a specified entity, under a credit support document);
- a tax event, which is the imposition of an indemnifiable tax on payments under the agreement or a substantial likelihood that such an imposition will be made on the next payment due;
- a tax event upon merger, which is the imposition of an indemnifiable tax as a result of the merger of a party; and,
- if so specified in the Schedule, a credit event upon merger, which is the merger of a party if the creditworthiness of its successor entity is materially weaker than that of such party prior to merger.

The agreement provides that an event which would constitute both an illegality and an event of default shall be treated as an illegality.

Under the ISDA Agreement, upon the occurrence of an event of default the non-defaulting party may by notice specify an early termination date within 20 days of such notice for all (but not less than all) outstanding swaps, except that an early termination date will be deemed to have occurred as of the time immediately preceding the bankruptcy or insolvency of a party. Upon the occurrence of a termination event, the affected party (which is the party that cannot perform because of an illegality, the party that must gross up because of a tax event, or the surviving entity of a party in the case of a tax event upon merger or a credit event upon merger) must give notice to the other party of such event and the transactions affected thereby. In the case of an illegality or a tax event, if there is one affected party that party as a condition to designating an early termination date must use reasonable efforts to transfer its obligations within 30 days to a branch, office or affiliate in another jurisdiction that would eliminate such event without causing such party to incur a material loss; if there are two affected parties, each party must use reasonable efforts to eliminate such event. Failing the foregoing, either party in the case of an illegality, any affected party in the case of a tax event, the party required to gross up or to receive a payment net of withholding in the case of a tax event upon merger or the non-affected party in the case of a credit event upon merger, may give notice setting an early termination date within 20 days of such notice for all swaps affected by such termination event (which may be less than all outstanding swaps).

The foregoing provisions often are modified or supplemented by parties using the ISDA Agreement. Among the typical variations to the agreement are:

- including a change in majority ownership of a party as an event of default;
- reducing the 30 day period within which a party must use reasonable efforts to transfer its obligations upon the occurrence of a termination event if a payment date for an affected swap falls within such period;

- the elimination of insolvency (but not the initiation of any action or proceeding relating to insolvency, bankruptcy, dissolution or liquidation) as an event of default (on the grounds that it is often unclear when a party may be deemed as a matter of law to have become insolvent); and
- the elimination as a tax event of a "substantial likelihcod" of imposition of an indemnificable tax (also because of the uncertainty of such provision).

COMPENSATION ON TERMINATION

In the early years of the development of the swap market, damage provisions typically followed either the general indemnification approach or the formula approach. Under the indemnification approach, the agreement provides that the defaulting party shall indemnify the non-defaulting party for its costs and losses resulting from termination of the swap without specifying how such costs and losses are to be calculated. Under the formula approach, compensation is based on the amounts that must be borrowed or invested in certain specified government securities to simulate a fixed rate cash flow or the present value of a floating rate cash flow. However, with the emergence of market makers maintaining swaps warehouses and the shift by such market makers in hedging their portfolios from matching swaps with reciprocal cash flows to general cash flow analysis and mark-to-market techniques, replacement value has become the predominant approach in swaps documentation.[14]

Under the ISDA Agreement, in the event of an early termination the non-defaulting party (or the non-affected party in a one affected party situation) must attempt to obtain quotations from four leading market makers in the relevant swap market for each outstanding swap to replace the remaining payments due under such swap from the defaulting (or affected) party. If four quotations are obtained, the market quotation for the swap is the average of such quotations disregarding the highest and lowest; if three quotations are obtained, the market quotation is the middle quote. If less than three quotations are obtained, the general indemnity method is used to calculate the non-defaulting (or non-affected) party's gain or loss.

In the case of an event of default, the amount due to the non-defaulting party is the absolute value of the net amount of all market quotations on swaps that would result in a payment to the non-defaulting party plus such party's gains on swaps for which market quotations could not be obtained plus all unpaid amounts owing to the defaulting party, set off against all market quotations that would require a payment by the non-defaulting party plus such party's losses on swaps for which market quotations could not be obtained plus all unpaid amounts owing to the non-defaulting party, although no payment is required to the defaulting party if such amount results in a net gain to the non-defaulting party. Alternatively, the agreement provides that the parties may specify that an amount may be payable to the defaulting party, in which case a net figure favourable to the non-defaulting party on all market quotations and gains and losses on swaps, before unpaid amounts are set off, is not taken into account.

14. See generally Gooch and Klein (1984); Henderson (1986).

As noted previously, compensation is calculated for swaps terminated in affected party situations on a no-default basis. In one affected party situations, the amount due is determined by the non-affected party as above, except that the non-affected party is required to pay a net gain on all terminated swaps to the affected party.[15] In two affected party situations, each party calculates its gains and losses on the terminated swaps and the difference is halved in calculating the final net payment due. (In effect it is assumed that one party's gain on a particular swap may not be equal to the other party's loss.) As many market participants take the view that neither party should bear a disproportionate burden or receive a windfall, however small, for the occurrence of an illegality or a tax event in the jurisdiction in which either of them is located, it is not unusual for such parties to specify that in affected party situations compensation will always be calculated as if there were two affected parties.

The default interest rate under the ISDA Agreement for late payments is 1.00% over the payee's cost of funds. Interest is due on the amount payable above from the early termination date to the date such payment is due (which is the date that notice of the amount due is given in the case of an event of default and two business days following such date in the case of a termination event) at the default rate, in the case of an event of default, and at the default rate less 1.00%, that is, the payee's cost of funds, in the case of a termination event.

The ISDA Agreement states that compensation determined as above constitutes a reasonable pre-estimate of loss and not a penalty. Generally, liquidated damages clauses, which are contractual formulae for calculating damages regardless of a party's actual loss, are not enforceable unless they satisfy the foregoing test, but the mere statement in a contract that a liquidated damages formula meets this standard will not be conclusive of the issue. There is some concern that taking the average or middle market quotation provided by leading market makers, rather than the lowest quotation, could be challenged as an unreasonable formula for calculating damages.[16]

IMPACT OF BANKRUPTCY

Regardless of the governing law of the contract, the bankruptcy law of the jurisdiction in which a bankrupt party to a swap is organised will dictate the rights of the other party to the transaction. Generally, however, in any bankruptcy situation such other party will necessarily be confronted by delay

---

15. A formulation often found in non-ISDA documentation for one affected party situations is generally as follows:
    - if the non-affected party will incur losses, the affected party shall pay to the non-affected party the amount of such losses;
    - if the non-affected party will make profits, it will pay to the affected party the smaller of its profits and the affected party's losses;
    - if neither party will incur losses, no payment shall be made.
    The foregoing formulation and, to a lesser extent, the ISDA Agreement, favour the non-affected party in a one affected party situation.
16. See *Drexel Burnham Lambert Products Corp. v. M Corp* (unreported, Del. Sup. Ct., 17 February 1989) (enforcing swap termination on summary judgment; replacement value clause used lowest quote obtained); Klein (1989).

and uncertainty in terms of hedging decisions, avoidance powers, realisation on security (if any), and a host of considerations relating to priority, preferences and subordination[17] which are dependant in part on whether such party is regarded as providing financial accommodation under the swap contract.[18]

Widespread acceptance of the ISDA Agreement was given added impetus by the joint United States/United Kingdom and Cooke Committee proposals on bank capital adequacy.[19] These proposals, which attached risk-weighted capital requirements to off-balance sheet items, did not permit banks to engage in netting when risk-weighing their swap portfolios. The proposals did suggest, however, that netting might be permitted if market participants developed standardised master agreements which achieved widespread market acceptance and if there were unambiguous legal opinions that the netting provisions of such agreements would be enforceable.[20]

Of particular concern is the risk, with respect to United States incorporated companies subject to the United States *Bankruptcy Code*, that such companies or their trustee-in-bankruptcy would be entitled in a bankruptcy proceeding to "cherry pick" among multiple swap transactions with particular counterparties, that is, to enforce contracts favourable to the bankrupt but to reject unfavourable ones.[21] By treating all swap transactions together with the master agreement as comprising a single contract, the ISDA Agreement is intended to eliminate the possibility of "cherry-picking" among transactions.

Following the announcement of the United States and the United Kingdom bank capital adequacy proposal, under the auspices of ISDA, a leading English law firm and a group of prominent New York law firms prepared memoranda

---

17. See Taylor (1987), pp. 65, 132-136.
18. See above, n. 6. ISDA has lobbied the United States Congress to amend the *Bankruptcy Code* to require that swap contracts continue to be honoured in bankruptcy. See Pollard (1988). Such special treatment presently is accorded to commodities, forward and securities contracts.
19. See Agreed Proposal of the United States Federal Banking Supervisory Authorities and the Bank of England on Primary Capital and Capital Adequacy Assessment (January 1987); Agreed Proposal; Credit Equivalent Amounts for Interest Rate and Foreign Exchange Rate Related Instruments (March 1987) (hereinafter Agreed Proposal; Credit Equivalent Amounts); Basle Committee on Banking Regulations and Supervisory Practices, Bank for International Settlements, Consultative Paper, Proposals for International Convergence of Capital Measurement and Capital Standards (December 1987) (hereinafter BIS Proposal); see also Reserve Bank of Australia, Discussion Paper, Supervision of Capital Adequacy of Banks (29 January 1988); Reserve Bank of Australia, Capital Adequacy of Banks, Prudential Statement No. 16 and Explanatory Memorandum (Nos 88-21 and 88-22, 23 August 1988) (hereinafter Reserve Bank Prudential Statement).
20. Agreed Proposal; Credit Equivalent Amounts, s. IV(c); BIS Proposal, Annex 3, p. 3.
21. The company or its trustee-in-bankruptcy are able to selectively assume and reject executory contracts regardless of whether bankruptcy constitutes an event of default under such contracts, because the United States *Bankruptcy Code* invalidates all bankruptcy default clauses in executory contracts, as well as all contractual restrictions on assignability of such contracts. However, domestic and foreign banks are not subject to the United States *Bankruptcy Code*. United States laws relating to bank receivership presently do not contain express provisions invalidating bankruptcy default and restriction on assignment clauses, although it is problematic whether the relevant authorities would view such clauses as enforceable. See Cunningham and Rogers (1987), pp. 460-467.

for submission to the Bank of England and the Board of Governors of the Federal Reserve System on the enforceability in bankruptcy of the ISDA Agreement termination provisions.[22] While both memoranda reach the reasoned conclusion that such provisions would be given effect under English and United States law, respectively, they acknowledge the absence of legal precedent directly on point and the existence of unfavourable precedent on somewhat analogous facts.[23] The Cooke Committee apparently was unpersuaded by these submissions as, in its final report, it concluded that banks may net contracts subject to novation but may not net contracts subject to closeout or payment netting "since the effectiveness of such agreements in an insolvency has not yet been tested in the courts, nor has it been possible to obtain satisfactory legal opinion that liquidators would not be able to overturn them".[24] In a netting by novation agreement, each new transaction when entered into would immediately result in the discharge of all existing obligations and the creation of a single new net obligation. The ISDA Agreement is not a netting by novation agreement but a closeout and payment netting agreement.[25]

OTHER PROVISIONS

Assignment

The ISDA Agreement provides that a party may not transfer any interest in the agreement without the other party's prior written consent, and that any purported transfer without such consent will be void. However, at least under New York law there is authority that if a clause restricting assignment of rights under a contract does not eliminate the power as well as the right to assign, then an assignment in violation of such a restriction will be effective, giving rise only to a right to damages for breach of the clause.[26] Since the ISDA Agreement is not by its terms non-assignable, it is unclear whether, if New York law is chosen as the governing law, the provision that purports to render an assignment without prior consent void would be effective.

22. Linklaters and Paines, Memorandum for International Swaps Dealers Association, Inc., Interest Rate and Currency Exchange Agreements (14 May 1987); Cravath, Swaine and Moore, Davis Polk and Wardwell, Milbank, Tweed, Hadley and McCloy, Simpson Thatcher and Bartlett, Sullivan and Cromwell, Wachtell, Lipton, Rosen and Katz, White and Case, Memorandum for the Bank of England and the Board of Governors of the Federal Reserve System, The Status of Swap Agreements under Section 365 of the United States Bankruptcy Code (1 June 1987); see also Houghton (1987); Kerr (1987) at 20-21. Linklaters and Cravath (1986) have addressed similar issues with respect to foreign exchange transactions in connection with the FX Netting Project. See above, n. 4.
23. See also Cunningham and Rogers (1987) at 451-457. In a recent response to an inquiry by ISDA, the General Counsel of the United States Federal Deposit Insurance Corporation indicated that he thought that a United States court would not permit cherry-picking of swaps under a master agreement by a bank of which the Federal Deposit Insurance Corporation is appointed as receiver. See "FDIC Tells Swap Dealers Failed Banks' Swaps Would Likely be Honoured" (1989).
24. Committee on Banking Regulations and Supervisory Practices, "International Convergence of Capital Measurement and Capital Standards", Annex 3, (July 1988), p. 5.
25. The FX Netting project was designed as a "netting by novation agreement". See above nn. 4 and 22.
26. *University Mews Assoc. v. Jeanmarie* 122 Misc. 2d 434; 471 N.Y.S. 2d 457 (1983).

Contractual currency

The ISDA Agreement provides that the obligation to make payments in the currency specified in the agreement shall not be discharged by a payment or by execution of a judgment in another currency, to the extent that such payment or execution of such judgment upon conversion does not yield the amount due in the specified currency, and that a shortfall in the amount due to the payee upon conversion shall give rise to a separate and enforceable obligation of the payer to indemnify the payee for such shortfall. There is some question whether such indemnity obligations are enforceable, particularly in the case of a court judgment that has been satisfied.

Multibranch parties

The ISDA Agreement permits the parties to specify that swap payments may be made and received through any branch specified in the Schedule. For multibranch parties, the confirmation must specify the particular branch for payment with respect to each swap, which may not be changed without the prior written consent of the other party. Each multibranch party also represents that, notwithstanding the designated place of payment, the obligations of each branch are for all purposes the obligations of the multibranch party.

Notices

The ISDA Agreement provides that notices may be given by hand, overnight courier, telex, or certified or registered mail (airmail if overseas). Many parties using the agreement include in the Schedule a provision that notices also may be given by facsimile, requiring that parties first attempt to give notice by telex or facsimile before reverting to courier or mail.

Jurisdiction

The ISDA Agreement provides that each party submits to the non-exclusive jurisdiction of the English courts, if the agreement is expressed to be governed by English law, or the courts of the State of New York and the United States District Court located in the Borough of Manhattan in New York City, if the agreement is expressed to be governed by the laws of the State of New York. However, while New York law permits non-residents to contract to submit to the jurisdiction of New York courts (provided that the amount at stake is above a minimum threshold), United States federal courts may not have subject matter jurisdiction over a dispute between two foreign parties.

Waiver of immunities

The ISDA Agreement provides that each party waives to the fullest extent possible all immunity on grounds of sovereignty or other similar grounds. Under the *Foreign Sovereign Immunities Act* 1976 (U.S.), a federal court may have jurisdiction over a suit by a foreign plaintiff against a foreign defendant if the defendant raises sovereign immunity as a defence.[27]

27. *Verlinden B.V. v. Central Bank of Nigeria* 461 U.S. 480 (1983).

SCHEDULE

Various optional provisions contained in the Schedule to the ISDA Agreement have been discussed above. In addition, parties often add to the Schedule amendments to the agreement of their own design.

Included in the Schedule is a section where the parties may specify tax forms, documents and certificates to be delivered in connection with the agreement, the date by which such documents are to be delivered and whether each such document is covered by the party's representation that such document is true and accurate. Such documents generally include evidence of due authorisation and signature authority at a minimum, and may also include periodic and annual financial statements, legal opinions and, in the case of United States parties, IRS Form 1001, which relates to the eligibility of a foreign party to receive interest payments without withholding.

Many market participants regard ongoing requirements to deliver financial statements and other information as unnecessarily burdensome and, particularly in interbank transactions, parties that routinely specify that such information is required in their standard documentation often will drop such provisions if pressed. Similarly, most parties regard exchanging legal opinions as an unwarranted burden and expense in connection with swap documentation, particularly if they must obtain an opinion from outside counsel. A requirement that legal opinions be exchanged may be troublesome when the form of opinion is appended to the Schedule by the party requiring it, since such forms of opinion typically are broadly worded and largely unqualified. For inhouse counsel, giving such an opinion may not be a problem, but a party that agrees to deliver such an opinion and then must obtain it from outside counsel likely will find that outside counsel insists on adding extensive qualifications to the required form.

With regard to IRS Form 1001, as the position being taken in the market is that swap payments do not constitute interest, this form is not strictly necessary. Since the ISDA Agreement requires that parties deliver tax forms that may be required from time to time to avoid withholding, the author believes that non-United States parties should resist providing Form 1001 to their United States counterparties. In the event that it is asserted at some future date by the Internal Revenue Service that swap payments constitute interest,[28] the requirement that Form 1001 be delivered prior to such assertion will merely provide support for the characterisation by the Internal Revenue Service of such payments as interest. Such a requirement is certainly at odds with the care taken by the drafters of the ISDA Agreement in avoiding the use of the word "interest" in the agreement and the Definitions in describing swap payments.

FORMATION AND SECONDARY TRADING OF SWAPS CONTRACTS

A form of confirmation for use with the ISDA Agreement is exhibited to the Definitions, which contemplates that it may be exchanged by the parties

---

28. The Internal Revenue Service has ruled that cross-border US$ denominated interest rate swap payments do not constitute interest (see Kleinbard, Duncan and Greenberg (1987)) but has not ruled specifically on cross-currency swaps.

either by telex or letter.[29] In practice, parties typically enter into transactions orally by phone, then exchange confirmation telexes, then document the transaction under the ISDA Agreement by a confirmation in letter form. Not infrequently, parties supplement the ISDA Agreement by an amendment in the Schedule that spells out the foregoing procedure and provides that a binding obligation comes into existence when a swap transaction is agreed orally. The BBAIRS Terms specifically provide that under BBAIRS a legally binding contract is established at the point that the parties agree to terms, which will usually be by phone, and that confirmations only evidence the particulars of an already established contract and not the contract itself.[30]

Nevertheless, questions may arise as to when a legally binding contract comes into existence between the parties. Statements that a binding contract exists when the parties agree to terms beg the question with regard both to people's subjective understanding and to the factors that the law has defined over the years as indicia of agreement and intention to be bound.

In jurisdictions that have an English-style *Statute of Frauds*, which requires that contracts not to be performed within one year be in writing, a swap contract may not be enforceable until at least confirmation telexes have been exchanged. However, if the oral agreement has been recorded (in many dealing rooms all calls are recorded), the recording may satisfy the writing requirement.[31]

A confirmation sent or agreed by the party to be bound setting forth even the barest terms of a swap transaction should suffice as a writing evidencing a binding contract, although this position could be undermined by language in the confirmation such as "subject to documentation".[32] In *Homestead Savings v. Life Savings of America*[33] one of the few cases to be litigated involving swaps, a jury rejected Life Savings' attempt to avoid two swaps that had become unprofitable on the ground that formal documentation had not been executed and awarded $6.2m to Homestead.[34] However, any non-standard terms should be included in the confirmation since definitive documentation generally is concluded after the swap commences and parties have little incentive to agree to such terms.[35]

Another problem arising in reaching a binding agreement on swaps related to bonds is that both the issuer of the bonds and the intermediary bank

29. The Bank of England recommends that confirmations conform to the ISDA or BBAIRS forms, see London Code of Conduct (1987), para. 42.
30. Compare London Code of Conduct (1987), para. 40. ("The Bank believes that institutions should treat themselves as bound to a swap contract at the point where the commercial terms of the transactions are agreed.").
31. See, for example, *London v. City of Gainesville* 768 F. 2d 1223, 1227-8, n. 4 (11th Cir. 1985).
32. Compare London Code of Conduct (1987), para. 40. ("The practice by some institutions of making the transaction subject to agreement on legal documentation can increase the possibility of disagreement over the terms of the deal and be followed by lengthy delays before the long-form documentation is agreed and executed. In order to minimise the likelihood of disputes concerning documentation, listed institutions should agree with their counterparties all material points during the negotiation of commercial terms.").
33. Unreported, N.D. Cal., 20 January 1987, No. 85-1690.
34. See Taylor (1987), pp. 156-158.
35. See above, n.32.

that will be entering into offsetting swaps with the issuer and a third party want the other to commit to the issue or the swap first, as relevant.[36] There is no satisfactory solution to this difficulty, other than one party bearing the ultimate risk of entering into its leg of the transactions and being left without a matching hedge.

The Definitions are expressly incorporated by return reference in the ISDA form of confirmation, and specify certain substantive terms that will apply unless expressly varied in the confirmation. These terms include the definitions of business day for relevant dates relating to 14 different currencies, for example, a business day is a day on which commercial banks and foreign exchange markets settle payments in Sydney if the currency is A$; period end dates, which are defined as payment dates unless separately specified; and floating rate day count fraction, which is the basis upon which floating rate interest is calculated, for example, the floating rate day count fraction for most floating rate calculations is actual number of days divided by 360 unless otherwise specified. The Definitions also contain detailed provisions of an operative nature, such as the method for calculating fixed and floating payments, rounding, and correcting erroneous information displayed by screen quotation services, which are not, strictly speaking, definitions at all. For this reason, it is preferable that the ISDA Agreement be used with the Definitions, rather than with specially drafted definitions included in the Schedule or confirmation.

The largest section of the Definitions is devoted to a menu of options for determining floating interest rates for 15 different currencies. Unfortunately for Australian parties using the ISDA Agreement, the Definitions do not include the Reuters Screen BBSW page as a floating rate option for A$, although this is the source generally used in the domestic market.

There are three basic categories of secondary trades in swaps:

- the swap reversal, in which a party to a swap enters into a mirror swap at the prevailing rates, which enables the party to lock in a profit or loss on the original swap over time;

- the swap sale, in which a party assigns a swap to another party in consideration of payment or receipt of a negotiated amount; and

- the swap closeout, in which a party terminates a swap in consideration of payment to or receipt from its counterparty of a negotiated amount.[37]

Proposals for a swaps clearing house have been afoot for several years,[38] but thus far have not made much headway.[39]

OTHER EXCHANGE AND INTEREST RATE HEDGING CONTRACTS

In terms of legal issues and documentation, there is little substantive distinction between swap contracts and FRA's, LTFX's, collars, swaptions and

---

36. See Taylor (1987), p. 158.
37. See Rogers (1987).
38. Shirreff (1985) at 248-251.
39. See generally Note, *Legal Doctrines Restricting the Secondary Market in Interest Rate Swaps* (1988) 25 *Columbia Journal of Transnational Law* 313.

comparable hybrid instruments that provide a hedging mechanism involving two parties that assume mutual obligations to each other to be settled at a future date. Swaps are, however, distinguishable in many respects from caps, floors and comparable instruments involving payment of an up-front premium in order to receive protection against future movements in exchange or interest rates, since in such instances one party has discharged its obligations at the outset by paying the premium.

Swaps are, however, in a category distinct from back-to-back and parallel loans. Swap contracts give rise to reciprocal contractual obligations rather than debts, which takes on particular significance in the bankruptcy context. For example, the provision of the United States *Bankruptcy Code* that entitles a bankrupt or its trustee-in-bankruptcy to assume or assign executory contracts does not extend to contracts to provide financial accommodation, such as loan agreements. On the other hand, swap contracts, by effectively embodying back-to-back and parallel loans in a single agreement, avoid the difficult problems inherent in such dual transaction structures, such as accounting complexities and inadequate set-off rights.

CONCLUSION

Swaps occupy a middle ground between standardised, freely tradeable money market instruments and complex, carefully documented capital market facilities such as Eurosecurities and cross-border loans.[40] While much progress has been made in standardising sophisticated documentation for swaps, a number of problems remain unresolved. First, such documentation embodies certain assumptions that have not been tested by litigation and for which there has existed no precisely analogous legal precedent to guide practitioners.[41] Second, many end users of the ISDA Agreement are confused about the operation and effect of some of its provisions, which may be attributable to the fact that the agreement was drafted not by the user's own lawyers but by a remote committee of experts, and the fact that the agreement is quite complex and yet was quickly accepted for use as the market standard by many parties without careful study and analysis. Finally, many institutions have been inattentive to documentation once swap transactions are confirmed, which may be attributable to the fact that responsibility for swaps is generally consigned to the treasury rather than capital markets sector of banks and to dealers who ordinarily do not have to be concerned about formal documentation.[42]

40. See London Code of Conduct (1987), para. 16. ("The long-term and reciprocal nature of the liabilities which swaps generate necessitates the adoption of market practices which are different to the ones that exist in the foreign exchange and money markets.")
41. Shirreff (1985) at 247-249.
42. The Bank of England has taken the hardly unreasonable position that:
    "It is vital that the long-form documentation governing a swap is agreed and executed as soon as possible. Listed institutions must make every effort to progress the finalisation of documentation. The Bank would like to see this accomplished within *two months* of the deal being struck whenever possible, and will be concerned should the process exceed *three months.*"
    London Code of Conduct, (1987), para. 40 (emphasis added). In fact, most market makers have numerous transactions that remain undocumented for periods longer than three months and some that are never documented at all.

To date, participants in the swap market have experienced a remarkably successful and uneventful run. The most explosive growth in the market occurred during a period of worldwide economic expansion and stabilising interest rates. There have been very few defaults.[43] It is inevitable, however, that at some point the strength of the market will be tested, whether by recession, the insolvency of a major market maker or end user of swaps, the reimposition of exchange controls for a heavily swapped currency or some other event. At that time, many of the unanswered questions concerning the legal status of swaps and swap documentation may finally be answered, with substantial sums riding on the outcome.[44]

43. See "Survey Shows Losses Are Low in Swap Market" (1988) at 2 (ISDA study prepared by Arthur Andersen found that outstandings in swap market have surpassed US$1 trillion while losses have totalled only US$33m, with only one loss from a currency swap).
44. See Shirreff (1985). While ISDA and major market participants heretofore generally have taken the position that the joint United States, United Kingdom and Cooke Committee risk-weighting formulae overstate the credit risk associated with swaps, increased concern about credit risk is now being expressed within the swaps market as well. See "Swap Credit Risk" (1989); Henderson (1989).

Part 11

Summary and Conclusion

Chapter 35

The Swap Market: Current "State of Play" and Future Developments

CURRENT "STATE OF PLAY"

The swap market, at least in its modern configuration, has existed since the early 1980s. During this period, the market has shown dramatic growth. This growth largely reflects the capacity of swaps to be utilised in a variety of roles and to the broad cross-section of end users who have embraced the technique. The capacity of swaps to encompass structural variations and spawn a variety of related instruments has also assisted in the growth of the market as a whole.

However, the growth in the swap market also has a fundamental economic basis. Swaps have acted as an instrument of market integration linking various national and international money and foreign exchange markets. The growth of swaps has, not coincidentally, parallelled a period of profound change in financial markets in general, highlighted by deregulation in many national markets. In addition, swap transactions have allowed the economics of comparative advantage to be extended from commodity and service markets to the capital markets. This fundamental economic basis of the swap market necessarily means that its potential for future development and growth is sound.

However, there are a number of factors that continue to impede the swap market's continuing growth and development:

- regulations;
- liquidity;
- accounting and tax treatment of swap transactions;
- back office procedures and systems for recording swap transactions.

Regulatory pressures exist on two levels: internal and external. Internal pressures relate to the need for a standardisation of conventions in documentation, quoting, yield mathematics and trading. The emergence of the International Swap Dealers Association (ISDA) and parallel bodies in the United Kingdom and Australia has gone some way towards addressing these matters (see discussion below).

External regulatory pressure has come for the most part from bank regulators concerned with the credit risk aspects of off-balance sheet swap transactions. The recent proposals by various bank regulators (see Chapter 31) represent a response to the perceived need for external regulation in the swap market.

Liquidity is essential to the development of any trading market, including the swaps market. While a secondary market in swaps has developed in recent years, primarily in interest rate swaps, a number of fundamental problems remain.

645

The attempts at standardisation of documentation and language conventions in swaps have assisted in the development of the secondary market. However, outside the US$ interest rate swap market, the attempt to create a traded secondary market particularly in the currency swap markets, has been less successful.

The other major factor in improved liquidity is credit risk. The term nature of swap obligations dictates that availability of credit limits between major participants in the swap market restricts the growth of a truly liquid secondary market. As discussed in Chapter 31 the development of a swap clearing house, netting arrangements between financial institutions, as well as improvements in swap assignment technology are essential to the further development of the secondary market. The development of the secondary market is particularly important as it is the key to improving the potential application of swaps as a generalised financial management instrument.

Different and often inconsistent accounting and tax treatments of swap transactions in different jurisdictions continues to be a problem for the growth of the market. The fact that swap transactions must usually be accommodated within existing accounting and tax frameworks dictates that sometimes anomalous balance sheet and earnings or expense results occur. The need for a relatively uniform, global accounting and tax treatment of these types of transactions is desirable, although unlikely to be achievable in the foreseeable future.

As the sophistication of swap instruments and markets has grown, the systems, procedures and controls for recording and providing management information have increasingly lagged further and further behind. It is only in recent years, that attention has been focused on the systems aspects of swap transactions. Increasingly, "off-the-shelf" swaps software is available, with a number of small boutique firms also available to design custom made software to suit a particular user's specifications. With the significant advances in micro-personal computer technology, software for both analysis of swaps portfolios as well as general systems for recording of swap transactions and consolidating these into an accounting and reporting structure have become available.

However, despite these advances, the problems of reconciliation of the underlying economics of a transaction with its accounting and tax treatment continue. In particular, disagreements about the actual earnings of a particular transaction are evident as no one answer is particularly meaningful. The adoption of complex portfolio systems greatly complicates such profit and loss computations.

ISDA: ORIGINS, OBJECTIVES AND ROLE

The primary impetus to the development of ISDA came from the need to establish standard market conventions and common terminology and to standardise documentation to both lower transaction costs and to assist in the further development of the secondary market in swaps.

Against this background, ten major swap dealers first met on 30 May 1984 to find ways for developing market conventions and a standard vocabulary for swaps. This group ultimately evolved into ISDA which by early 1988 had approximately 87 members from a wide variety of countries.

ISDA has essentially four main purposes:

- It acts as a forum for the discussion of issues relevant to swap market participants.
- It seeks to advance public understanding of the swap market.
- It acts as an industry group representing the common interest of members before regulatory authorities.
- It seeks through the development of standard documentation and market terminology to ensure the development and maintenance of an efficient and productive market facilitating trading activity and enhancing market liquidity.

The primary achievement of ISDA has been the development of the ISDA Swap Code. Originally published in June 1985, after 13 months of work, the Code sought to establish a basis on which participants may communicate more effectively without eliminating either freedom of choice or the flexibility to structure swaps in any way that best suits the parties. The Code was also designed to reduce documentation costs and increase the speed of documenting transactions. The original ISDA Code has been subsequently developed and in March 1987 the ISDA released two so-called Master Swap Agreements which aim at simplifying and standardising swap documentation. These Master Swap Agreements continue to be updated regularly and ISDA is currently spearheading an effort to create standard documentation to cover interest rate caps.

The Master Swap Agreements aim is to simplify and standardise swap documentation. The two forms, an Interest Rate Swap Agreement and an Interest Rate and Currency Exchange Agreement, can be used, by any market participant to document interest rate swaps, currency swaps and cross-currency swaps. The forms are complete contracts, reflecting "a fair basis for transactions".

The two Codes were originally planned as a single one but were made distinct in order to make life simpler for the huge US$ interest rate swap market, though the one including currencies can serve for United States market purposes as well. They represent the latest extension of ISDA's Code, of which two earlier editions were published and which now is incorporated into the interest rate Master Swap Agreement.

The two new contracts are master form agreements which can govern multiple swap transactions. The particular economic terms of each transaction will be documented in a separate confirmation that will constitute a supplement to the agreement. This set up is expected to substantially reduce the considerable waste of back office resources currently involved in the swap business and which are only compounded by the market's growth. Use of the master agreements is expected to save about US$10,000 per contract in legal fees. A major encouragement to ISDA was the decision by Gaz de France, a major swap user, to adopt the interest rate and currency master agreement.

Despite its considerable achievements, ISDA continues to be very much a United States bank dominated organisation although the balance is gradually changing. The impact of ISDA is most evident in US$ interest rate swaps and in currency swaps in the major reserve currencies.

As the swap market has become increasingly global, a number of other industry bodies have formed usually as a subset of established finance industry bodies. The two main bodies, other than ISDA, are:

- the British Bankers Association (BBA);
- the Australian Swap Dealers Association (ASDA), which operates as a part of the Australian Financial Markets Association.

The objectives of both the BBA and ASDA are similar to ISDA and both bodies have close relationships with ISDA.

The BBA have published the British Bankers Association Interest Rate Swap (BBAIRS) Terms which recommend terms and conditions for London interbank interest rate swaps, single currency fixed floating swaps, cross-currency swaps and cross-currency floating rate swaps.

The BBAIRS terms:

- cover interbank transaction with maturity up to and including two years;
- are applicable to all transactions unless otherwise specified;
- affect transactions in US$, £, deutschmarks, Swiss francs and Japanese yen.

Intermediaries can also adopt BBAIRS terms for longer dated swaps, provided both parties agree.

ASDA has developed a standard interest rate swap document known as the Australian Interest Rate Swap (AIRS) document. The AIRS document covers interbank trading only in swaps, it covers certain credit items and also only governs A$ swap transactions. It is likely that the AIRS document will remain, for the moment, as the most appropriate means of documenting domestic A$ swaps. This reflects the fact that it has been developed under Australian law and structured to suit the Australian financial environment.

Other forms of documentation also exist including French and German language documents which are utilised in the relevant domestic markets.

The relationship between the ISDA Code, the ASDA AIRS Code and the BBAIRS terms are at the moment under consideration by the three bodies.

OCTOBER 1987: THE IMPACT ON SWAPS

In October 1987, the collapse in the prices of equities on major stock exchanges throughout the world forced a major reassessment of the swaps market. In the immediate aftermath of the stock market collapse, there was widespread pessimism about the future of all derivative products, including swaps. However, in the immediate period after the stock market collapse, the swap markets continued to operate albeit with significant changes from its pre-crash operations.

The major changes in the operation of the market included:

- a marked decrease in liquidity and volumes transacted;
- parallelling the decline in liquidity, bid/offer spreads increased by up to 0.15% pa;

- swaps spreads as a whole increased significantly.

The changes in the swap market were largely predictable, reflecting logical responses to altered market conditions. The decrease in liquidity was primarily prompted by increased counterparty risk concerns exacerbated by the precipitous decline in equity values around the world. This reassessment of credit limits between counterparties naturally reduced the volume of swap transactions undertaken.

The decreased liquidity contributed to the widening bid/offer spreads. The lack of liquidity significantly increased the risk of market makers. In addition, the increased credit risk perceived was sought to be compensated for by higher spreads.

The overall change in spread levels in swap markets was part of the wider reassessment of credit risk and price relationships in capital markets. During the period following the stock market collapse, corporate bond spreads increased dramatically ultimately flowing through into higher swap spreads. In addition, the extreme volatility in money, bond and foreign exchange markets contributed to an increasing spread which reflected a premium for uncertainty particularly for market makers.

The capacity of the swap market to actually adjust quickly to the changed market environment arguably augers well for the long-term viability of these types of transactions. Ironically, the changes in the market will probably open new opportunities for growth:

- In the aftermath of the equity market collapse, reassessment of credit risks will most likely create a more marked credit risk differential structure. This will inevitably mean wider credit differentials for lower rated borrowers which ultimately will allow greater levels of new issue arbitrage between fixed and floating interest rate markets in the same currency. Increased credit differentials between markets may ultimately also create greater currency swap arbitrage opportunities.

- The focus on the credit risk of swap counterparties and the move to charge realistic intermediation costs will allow participants to generate profits more in keeping with the risks of swap transactions. This will, in the longer term, be healthy for the market. Close scrutiny of the credit ratings of swap counterparties will ultimately limit the number of market makers, thereby reducing some of the competitive pressures within the swap market, allowing a return to economic levels of profitability.

- The aftermath of the crash and the reinforcement of basic business fundamentals will eliminate the worst excesses of the swap market creating a better environment for healthy future growth.

Importantly, the swap markets adjusted, over the 1987/1988 period, with spreads, in fact, falling sharply while liquidity and volumes quickly returned to pre-crash levels and continue to grow strongly.

THE FUTURE OF THE SWAP MARKET

The swap market, as a whole, is entering a consolidation phase. However, the basic rationale of swap transactions continue to remain the same as before:

- the trading of economic advantages in capital markets;
- the creation of surrogate or synthetic transaction structures by linking swaps to an underlying borrowing or investment decision.

While the basic rationale remains the same, the consolidation of the swap market will prompt some changes in the way that the market operates. These changes will be in the area of the applications of swaps, swap structures, swap currencies, participants, etc.

To date, swaps have been used as a mechanism for new issue arbitrage funding as well as for asset liability management.

More recently, swaps have been used for speculative or positioning purposes. Financial institutions and, to a lesser extent, corporations have utilised swaps as an off-balance sheet speculative instrument. While the use of swaps for such positioning purposes is likely to continue amongst financial institutions, the worst excesses of corporate speculation utilising swaps are likely to be substantially reduced in the aftermath of October 1987.

Innovations in swap structure are likely to continue. The pressure to develop new products or new variations to existing products will be driven as much by client requirements as by attempts by intermediaries to move away from low profit to high profit transactions, predicated on changing market opportunities. However, to a large extent the newer products are likely to be more precise, better tailored versions of existing structures.

In particular, swap structures will evolve increasingly into a process of cash flow manipulation whereby one set of cash flows are adjusted to better meet the requirements of a particular investor or borrower. An added feature will be the increased integration of the various swap products. The *product* focus will to some extent be superseded by a client-driven or application focus: swaps will come to be seen as a generic risk management tool as well as an arbitrage tool for creating new assets and liabilities.

The range of swap currencies will continue to widen. The depth of markets in existing swap currencies will increase.

The penetration of the end user market for swaps will also increase as the already wide base of market participants will be broadened. In particular, as swap structures are refined and newer applications develop, both existing participants and newer entrants will look to swaps as an increasingly important asset and liability management instrument.

The presence of market makers in swaps will continue to be important. However, the number of market makers may well shrink as a number of institutions, in the light of the new capital adequacy requirements, reassess returns on their swap activities. As part of this reassessment, it is likely that a number of institutions will withdraw from the swap business as precious capital resources are reallocated to more profitable uses reflecting the competitive advantages of the particular institution. Newer participants will also be attracted for precisely the same reasons. The relatively small group of swap market makers will evolve rapidly into a two-tier structure:

- a very limited number of truly global swap institutions acting in a wide range of swap markets;
- more narrowly focused swap market makers usually specialising in swaps in one or two (usually related) currencies.

The approach to swap marketmaking may also undergo significant change. Some market makers will tend to view their swap businesses as part of their new issue and secondary market securities businesses. Others may operate their swap businesses on a stand alone basis leveraging off their strengths in other areas such as foreign exchange and money markets. Increased specialisation among swap houses may also become apparent.

The factors identified will contribute to continuing growth in the swap market. However, the *rate of growth* may in fact decrease as the market approaches maturity. The secondary market in swaps, including the secondary market for currency swaps will continue to develop.

The changes predicted in the structure and operation of the global swap markets in no way detract from their continuing bright future. As the market enters a period of consolidation after a number of years of dramatic growth, increased attention will be focused on the fuller exploitation of the potential of the swap technique.

Fundamentally, swaps represent perhaps the most significant financial innovation in capital markets in the latter half of the 20th century. In its role as the catalyst for integration of various markets, swaps are a major factor in developing more efficient global intermediation processes. Swaps serve to foster more rapid growth in international trade and capital flows allowing the channelling of excess savings in one market to another. These are all fundamental changes which will ensure the continuing and ever increasing role of swaps in global markets in the future.

Index